strada lex

How to activate a book online

Identification code

If you have a subscription to our database Strada lex **www.stradalex.com**, Strada lex Luxembourg **www.stradalex.lu**, or Strada lex Europe **www.stradalex.eu** you can activate the digital version of this book* for free by entering the identification code mentioned above.

If a problem occurs during the activation, you can contact our helpdesk: tel. : **+32(0)2 548 07 20** • fax : **+32(0)2 548 07 22** • **info@stradalex.com**. You will be asked for a proof of purchase.

The identification code can only be used once by one Strada lex subscriber. Once activated, the book can only be consulted on the Strada lex platform in accordance with the terms of the subscription.

If you have not yet subscribed to our databases and would like some more information or a presentation by one of our representatives, please contact us at the following e-mail address: info@stradalex.com.

** If the book is included in one of the mentioned databases. Please visit www.larcier.com to check in which database(s) this monograph is available.*

DEFINITION OF INSOLVENCY

DEFINITION OF INSOLVENCY

Proposals for Harmonisation in the European Union

Reinhard Bork
Michael Veder
Ben Schuijling

with the assistance of an international working group of national reporters:

Christian Koller and Kevin Labner (Austria), Frederik De Leo (Belgium), Hristina Kirilova (Bulgaria), Jasnica Garašić (Croatia), Andrie Kypridemou (Cyprus), Tomáš Richter (Czech Republic), Line Langkjaer and Lasse Lindekilde (Denmark), Anto Kasak (Estonia), Tuomas Hupli (Finland), Reinhard Dammann (France), Reinhard Bork (Germany), Stathis Potamitis (Greece), Zoltan Fabok (Hungary), Simon Murphy (Ireland), Renato Mangano (Italy), Madara Sturite (Latvia), Frank Heemann (Lithuania), Pier Mario Lupinu (Luxembourg), Arthur Galea Salomone (Malta), Ben Schuijling and Michael Veder (The Netherlands), Marek Porzycki and Anna Rachwał (Poland), Catarina Serra (Portugal), Flavius-Iancu Moţu and Andreea Deli-Diaconescu (Romania), Dávid Oršula (Slovakia), Miodrag Dordevic (Slovenia), Nuria Bermejo (Spain), Hans Renman (Sweden), and Sarah Paterson (United Kingdom)

INTERSENTIA
Cambridge – Antwerp – Chicago

Intersentia Ltd
8 Wellington Mews
Wellington Street | Cambridge
CB1 1HW | United Kingdom
Tel: +44 1223 736 170
Email: contact@larcier-intersentia.com
www.larcier-intersentia.com

Distribution for the UK and
Rest of the World (incl. Eastern Europe)
NBN International
1 Deltic Avenue, Rooksley
Milton Keynes MK13 8LD
United Kingdom
Tel: +44 1752 202 301 | Fax: +44 1752 202 331
Email: orders@nbninternational.com

Distribution for Europe
Lefebvre Sarrut Belgium NV
Hoogstraat 139/6
1000 Brussels
Belgium
Tel: +32 (0)2 548 07 13
Email: contact@larcier-intersentia.com

Distribution for the USA and Canada
Independent Publishers Group
Order Department
814 North Franklin Street
Chicago, IL 60610
USA
Tel: +1 800 888 4741 (toll free) | Fax: +1 312 337 5985
Email: orders@ipgbook.com

Definition of Insolvency. Proposals for Harmonisation in the European Union

ISBN 978-1-83970-557-1
D/2024/7849/117
NUR 826

British Library Cataloguing in Publication Data. A catalogue record for this book is available from the British Library.

CONTENTS

LIST OF CONTRIBUTORS

Nuria Bermejo

Professor of Commercial Law, Universidad Autónoma de Madrid, Spain

Reinhard Bork

Faculty of Law, University of Hamburg, Germany; Senior Research Fellow, Commercial Law Centre, Harris Manchester College, Oxford, UK; Visiting Professor, Radboud University, Nijmegen, the Netherlands

Reinhard Dammann

Professeur affilié, École de droit de Sciences Po, Paris, France

Frederik De Leo

Attorney, NautaDutilh; Visiting Professor, KU Leuven, Belgium

Andreea Deli-Diaconescu

PhD, Lawyer, member of the Bucharest Bar Association, Romania

Miodrag Dordevic

PhD, Chief Justice, President of the Supreme Court, Slovenia

Zoltán Fabók

Counsel, DLA Piper Budapest; Visiting Lecturer, ELTE University, Budapest; Fellow of INSOL International

Arthur Galea Salomone

Galea Salomone Advocates, Malta

Jasnica Garašić

PhD, Full-time Professor of Civil Procedural Law, Faculty of Law, University of Zagreb, Croatia

Frank Heemann

Partner, bnt attorneys in CEE

Tuomas Hupli

Professor of Procedural Law, Faculty of Law, University of Turku, Finland

Anto Kasak

Lecturer of Insolvency Law, University of Tartu, Estonia; Partner, Law Firm Kasak & Lepikson

Hristina Kirilova

Partner, Kambourov and Partners Attorneys at Law, Bulgaria

Andrie Kypridemou

Head of EK Insolvency, Partner, EK Insolvency Ltd, Nicosia, Cyprus

Kevin Labner

Postdoctoral research and teaching assistant, Department of Civil Procedure Law, University of Vienna, Austria

Pier Mario Lupinu

Research Fellow, University of Florence, Italy; PhD in Banking and Finance Law, University of Luxembourg and Roma Tre University, Italy

Renato Mangano

PhD, Full Professor of Commercial Law and Insolvency Law, University of Palermo, Italy

Flavius-Iancu Moțu

PhD, Judge, Specialized Court of Cluj, Romania

Simon Murphy

Partner, Beauchamps LLP, Dublin, Ireland

Mgr. Ing. Dávid Oršula

Partner, bnt attorneys in CEE

Prof. Sarah Paterson

London School of Economics and Political Science, UK

Dr Marek Porzycki

Chair for Business Regulation and Economic Policy, Faculty of Law and Administration, Jagiellonian University, Krakow, Poland

Stathis Potamitis

Senior Partner, POTAMITISVEKRIS, Athens, Greece

Dr Anna Rachwał

Chair for Civil Law, Faculty of Law and Administration, Jagiellonian University, Krakow, Poland

Hans Renman

Partner, Schjødt law firm, Stockholm, Sweden

Tomáš Richter

Advocate, JŠK, advokátní kancelář, Prague, Czech Republic

Catarina Serra

Professor of Law, University of Minho, Braga, Portugal; Justice, Portuguese Supreme Court

Ben Schuijling

Director and Professor of Business Law, Radboud Business Law Institute, Nijmegen, the Netherlands; Adviser, Clifford Chance LLP, Amsterdam

Mag.iur. Madara Stūrīte

Attorney at Law, Senior Associate, bnt attorneys in CEE

Michael Veder

Professor of Insolvency Law, Radboud Business Law Institute, Nijmegen, the Netherlands; Attorney/adviser, RESOR N.V.

PART I

REPORT ON THE DEFINITION OF INSOLVENCY

CHAPTER 1
THE PROJECT

I. SETTING THE SCENE

This research project, triggered by the European Commission's Proposal for a Directive harmonising certain aspects of insolvency law,[1] deals with the term *insolvency* and its subspecies *inability to pay debts* (*cash flow insolvency*), *cessation of payments*, *likely* or *imminent inability to pay debts*, and *overindebtedness* (*balance sheet insolvency*[2]). These terms have in common that they address a stage of the financial crisis of a debtor where his or her estate and/or earning capacities are not (or not likely to be) sufficient for satisfying all creditors' claims in a timely manner. As will be explained in more detail below, they mark the moment from which it is justified to switch from individual enforcement to collective enforcement through liquidation proceedings[3] and to place the creditors' interests above those of the debtor and – in the case of a company – its shareholders. 1.1

---

1 Proposal for a Directive of the European Parliament and of the Council harmonising certain aspects of insolvency law, 2022/0408 (COD) of 7 December 2022, text available at https://eur-lex.europa.eu/legal-content/EN/TXT/?uri=CELEX%3A52022PC0702&qid=1673856579802 (last visited 16 January 2023) – hereafter "Harmonisation Proposal".

2 As regards terminology, see *infra* Chapter 8, at para. 8.77.

3 For restructuring, regardless of whether it is addressed in the context of a distinct set of proceedings or as an alternative to liquidation in proceedings which comprise both outcomes, see *infra* at para. 1.18.

1. RELEVANCE OF THE LEGAL TERM *INSOLVENCY*

1.2 While insolvency is a common practical phenomenon in all jurisdictions, the terminology used is not, even not within the English-speaking world.[4] In the United States, for example, the term "bankruptcy" is preferred and used for legal entities (corporate insolvency) as well as for individuals (personal insolvency), both entrepreneurs and consumers. In contrast to that, in England "bankruptcy" is reserved for individuals (section 264(1) Insolvency Act 1986) whilst "insolvency" is the legal term used for legal entities.[5] In this book, we will follow the English example and use "insolvency" for corporate insolvency proceedings and "bankruptcy" for insolvency proceedings concerning natural persons (both consumers and entrepreneurs).

1.3 "Bankruptcy" is a very old expression which has its origins in the Italian term *banca rotta* (the trading bench of an insolvent merchant was broken by his colleagues, signifying that he was no longer worthy of participating as a member of the mercantile community[6]) while the word "insolvency" is even older: it goes back to the Latin word *insolventia* (impossibility to pay). Other languages have this Latin root too (cf. the French *insolvabilité*, the German *Insolvenz*, the Dutch *insolventie*, or the Spanish *insolvencia*), whereas a further group builds upon the Latin *fallere* (to fail or to break a promise) by using *fallimento* (Italian), *faillite* (French), or *faillissement* (Dutch).

1.4 "Insolvency" in this sense is used here as a term of substantive insolvency law. It is not a synonym for "insolvency proceedings", which is a *topos* of procedural law, describing the proceedings conducted with respect to the insolvent's estate. "Insolvency" – as examined here – is understood as substantive insolvency, referring to the state of the debtor's financial affairs. This state may give rise to liquidation, but also to restructuring proceedings and must be thoroughly distinguished from them. However, when speaking of "insolvency proceedings" in this book, we understand this term in the broad sense used in Article 1 of the European Insolvency Regulation (EIR).[7]

1.5 The variants of insolvency as enumerated *supra*[8] can be found – individually or together – in all national insolvency laws.[9] Legislators use these terms in a

---

4 For the following, see *Bork*, Corporate Insolvency Law, 2nd ed., Intersentia, Cambridge/Antwerp/Chicago 2023, para. 1.15.

5 This was quite clear in the original version of the Insolvency Act 1986 which in the Heading of Part I used the phrase "Company Insolvency".

6 See *van Zwieten*, Goode on Principles of Corporate Insolvency Law, 5th ed., Sweet & Maxwell, London 2018, paras. 1–10, fn. 41.

7 See fn. 22 *infra*. As regards restructuring proceedings, see *infra* at para. 1.18.

8 At para. 1.1.

9 For a first overview, see *Bork*, Corporate Insolvency Law (fn. 4), para. 1.15 et seq. and the national reports in *Faber/Vermunt/Kilborn/Richter*, Commencement of Insolvency Proceedings, Oxford University Press, Oxford 2012, each at para. 5.1.

wide variety of contexts. They are used (*inter alia*) to describe the circumstances under which insolvency proceedings (whether aimed at liquidation of the debtor's estate or restructuring of the debtor's capital structure) can be commenced,[10] they are elements of norms-regulating transactions avoidance laws,[11] they identify the point in time where the beneficiaries of directors' duties shift from shareholders to creditors, and they are used to define the point in time when directors may be obliged to commence insolvency proceedings.[12] Moreover, these expressions are found even in criminal law, tax law, and other legal norms.

2. THE NEED FOR HARMONISATION

However, when it comes to the details, considerable differences can be observed in national laws. For example, not all insolvency laws of the Member States of the European Union are familiar with the concept of "overindebtedness" as a triggering event.[13] The terms "likely" or "imminent inability to pay debts"[14] are not used in all insolvency statutes, or are used in laws regulating the restructuring of a debtor rather than the liquidation of its assets.[15] Further, "inability to pay debts" is not uniformly understood in a particular sense.[16] 1.6

Surprisingly, the same holds true at the level of European law. The terms "inability to pay debts", "insolvent", "insolvency", or "insolvency proceedings" are used in many legal instruments of the European Union, often without any further definition. Examples are (among others) Article 2(j) Settlement Finality Directive,[17] Article 8 Financial Collateral Directive,[18] Article 43(1) Solvency II Directive,[19] Article 36(2) MiCAR,[20] and Article 1(1)(b) Restructuring and 1.7

---

10 For substantive insolvency as a prerequisite see the national reports in *Faber/Vermunt/Kilborn/Richter* (fn. 9), each at para. 5.2. See also *infra* fn. 49.

11 See Art. 6(1)(a) Harmonisation Proposal (*supra* fn. 1).

12 For the latter, see Arts. 36, 37 Harmonisation Proposal (*supra* fn. 1).

13 See *infra* Chapter 7.

14 On them, details *infra* in Chapter 6.

15 As defined *infra* at para. 1.18.

16 More *infra* in Chapter 4.

17 Directive 98/26/EC of the European Parliament and of the Council of 19 May 1998 on settlement finality in payment and securities settlement systems, OJ of 11 June 1998, L 166/45.

18 Directive 2002/47/EC of the European Parliament and of the Council of 6 June 2002 on financial collateral arrangements, OJ of 27 June 2002, L 168/43.

19 Directive 2009/138/EC of the European Parliament and of the Council of 25 November 2009 on the taking-up and pursuit of the business of Insurance and Reinsurance (Solvency II) (recast), OJ of 17 December 2009, L 335/1.

20 Regulation (EU) 2023/1114 of the European Parliament and of the Council of 31 May 2023 on markets in crypto-assets, and amending Regulations (EU) No. 1093/2010 and (EU) No. 1095/2010 and Directives 2013/36/EU and (EU) 2019/1937, OJ of 9 June 2023, L 150/40.

Insolvency Directive,[21] the latter expressly leaving the definition to national laws in its Article 2(2)(a)/(b). Even the EIR,[22] which refers to "insolvency" in Article 1(1), offers no further explanation. The same holds true for the Harmonisation Proposal,[23] which displays the term "insolvent" *inter alia* in Article 23 and also refers to the relevant national law. At least, a first attempt is available in Article 38(2) Harmonisation Proposal, which defines "insolvency" as the "general inability to pay debts as they mature", albeit again leaving the details to national laws.[24] As a final example we point to Recital 57 of the Single Resolution Mechanism Regulation (Regulation (EU) 806/2014),[25] which refers to a financial entity being "balance sheet insolvent". The Regulation explains in Article 18(4)(b) that "the assets of the entity are, or there are objective elements to support a determination that the assets of the entity will, in the near future, be less than its liabilities", and equates this in Article 18(4)(c) with the situation that the debtor, "in the near future, [will] be unable to pay its debts or other liabilities as they fall due". The same wording is available in Article 32(4)(b)/(c) of the Banking Recovery and Resolution Directive (Directive 2014/59/EU).[26]

1.8 This matches more or less the UNCITRAL Legislative Guide.[27] While nothing is available in the UNCITRAL Model Law on Cross-Border Insolvency,[28] the Legislative Guide, at paragraph 12(s), provides the following definition for the

---

21 Directive 2019/1023/EU of the European Parliament and of the Council of 20 June 2019 on preventive restructuring frameworks, on discharge of debt and disqualifications, and on measures to increase the efficiency of procedures concerning restructuring, insolvency and discharge of debt, and amending Directive (EU) 2017/1132 (Directive on restructuring and insolvency), OJ of 26 June 2019, L 172/18.

22 Regulation (EU) 2015/848 of the European Parliament and of the Council of 20 May 2015 on insolvency proceedings, OJ of 5 June 2015, L 141/19.

23 *Supra* fn. 1.

24 Art. 38(2) Harmonisation Proposal reads: "A microenterprise shall be deemed insolvent for the purposes of simplified winding-up proceedings when it is generally unable to pay its debts as they mature. Member States shall set out the conditions under which a microenterprise is deemed to be generally unable to pay its debts as they mature and ensure that these conditions are clear, simple and easily ascertainable by the microenterprise concerned."

25 Regulation (EU) 806/2014 of the European Parliament and of the Council of 15 July 2014 establishing uniform rules and a uniform procedure for the resolution of credit institutions and certain investment firms in the framework of a Single Resolution Mechanism and a Single Resolution Fund and amending Regulation (EU) No. 1093/2010, OJ of 30 July 2014, L 225/1.

26 Directive 2014/59/EU of the European Parliament and of the Council of 15 May 2014 establishing a framework for the recovery and resolution of credit institutions and investment firms and amending Council Directive 82/891/EEC, and Directives 2001/24/EC, 2002/47/EC, 2004/25/EC, 2005/56/EC, 2007/36/EC, 2011/35/EU, 2012/30/EU and 2013/36/EU, and Regulations (EU) No. 1093/2010 and (EU) No. 648/2012, of the European Parliament and of the Council, OJ of 12 June 2014, L 173/190.

27 *United Nations Commission on International Trade Law*, Legislative Guide on Insolvency Law, Parts 1 and 2, United Nations Publications, New York 2005.

28 *United Nations Commission on International Trade Law*, UNCITRAL Model Law on Cross-Border Insolvency Law with Guide to Enactment and Interpretation, United Nations Publications, New York 2014. The term "insolvency" is used throughout the Model Law yet is not defined in Art. 2.

term "insolvency": "when a debtor is generally unable to pay its debts as they mature or when its liabilities exceed the value of its assets". This refers to both inability to pay debts and to overindebtedness, but leaves out the details.

In our view, this finding demonstrates the clear need to take a closer look at these terms and to think about the options for harmonising the definition of substantive insolvency on a European level. The Harmonisation Proposal uses the terms "insolvent", "insolvency", or "inability to pay debts" in the context of harmonising transactions avoidance laws,[29] "pre-pack" proceedings,[30] directors' duties,[31] and insolvency proceedings for microenterprises,[32] but without providing a uniform definition of these terms. It seems to us that this gives rise to significant legal uncertainty and thwarts all harmonisation efforts if these terms are not defined in the European legal instrument itself. 1.9

This view is shared by practitioners, particularly (yet not exclusively) when advising multi-national groups of companies. For example, where a group with companies in Austria, Czech Republic, Germany, and Poland is in financial turmoil and the group asks for advice on how to avoid the directors' duty to file for insolvency proceedings, triggered by substantive insolvency,[33] it would be most helpful to have a uniform understanding of the relevant terms (e.g. inability to pay debts, overindebtedness). Otherwise, the avoidance of substantive insolvency in Austria would require quite different means compared to Poland and avoidance in Germany could require financial means which trigger the substantive insolvency in the Czech Republic all the more. Restructuring groups would be significantly assisted by harmonising the relevant terms of substantive insolvency. 1.10

More generally speaking, the attempt by the European Commission to harmonise certain aspects of insolvency law must be seen as a step towards completing the set of rules for the players in the internal market of the EU. With various instruments on company law, the EU has regulated (elements of) market entry. A multitude of norms (e.g. concerning capital markets laws) address market behaviour. What is missing so far is legislation that addresses the market exit of ordinary companies, which brings (*inter alia*) insolvency law to the table. Hence, it is consistent with the legislative efforts undertaken so far and desirable that the EU completes its set of rules with substantive insolvency law. However, this requires first and foremost a definition of what insolvency actually is. 1.11

---

29 See Art. 6(1)(a), (2)(b) Harmonisation Proposal: "the debtor was unable to pay its mature debts".

30 See Art. 23 Harmonisation Proposal: "where the debtor is in a situation of likelihood of insolvency or is insolvent".

31 Art. 36 Harmonisation Proposal: "where a legal entity becomes insolvent".

32 Art. 38(1) Harmonisation Proposal: "microenterprises, when insolvent"; see also *supra* fn. 24.

33 For details, see *infra* Chapter 3, at para. 3.11.

II. OUTLINE OF THE RESEARCH PROJECT

1.12 Against this background, we have initiated the present research project.

1. TOPICS

1.13 Its aim is to formulate a proposal for a definition of the term "insolvency" as used in, for example, the Harmonisation Proposal.[34] This includes definitions of the subspecies mentioned *supra* in paragraph 1.1. These definitions will be presented in the form of Model Rules. As an independent research group, we decided to elaborate Model Rules as an academic undertaking rather than drafting articles of a Directive. In principle, the latter can better be done by the official bodies of the European Union. However, since definitions are part of all statutory instruments of the EU (mostly in Article 2 of these instruments), we decided to draft the Model Rules in such a way that they could be inserted directly into these catalogues of definitions.[35]

1.14 Against this background, our proposal primarily contains recommendations as to how the subspecies of the term insolvency addressed in Regulations and Directives of the EU should be defined. In this respect, we preferred a "minimum approach" by restricting the scope of our project to terms used in the European legislative texts in order to avoid unnecessary sideshows. Further, we decided to aim at a proposal for Model Rules which contributes to a harmonised application of the rules of European law which have "insolvency" or one of its subspecies as part of their prerequisites and which tie their legal consequences in the event of such insolvency.

1.15 Initially, we did not set out to develop a proposal for harmonisation of the term insolvency in national laws. In particular, we did not intend to make suggestions on how Member States should shape their reasons[36] for opening insolvency or restructuring proceedings. Instead, our endeavour was restricted to suggesting a common understanding of such terms as they are used in the European instruments, in particular the EIR, the Directive on restructuring and insolvency and the Harmonisation Proposal. We were aware that, when adopted, our proposal might indirectly influence the understanding of equivalent norms in national laws or might even encourage national legislators to amend their laws. In any case, this is not what this study was aiming at.

---

34 *Supra* fn. 1.

35 More details *infra* Chapter 8, at para. 8.7.

36 In this project, "reason" is used as an equivalent to "triggering events" or "grounds" to open proceedings.

However, during the course of the project, we realised that such a restriction could not be consistently adhered to. The reason lies in Article 36 Harmonisation Proposal, which provides for a duty for directors to file for insolvency proceedings "where a legal entity becomes insolvent". It would certainly be possible to define the term "insolvent" autonomously in this context. However, if this definition in the Harmonisation Proposal does not match the definition of insolvency as a reason to open insolvency proceedings under the respective national law, the result would be that European law would require the directors to file for insolvency proceedings whereas national law would not provide for the possibility of actually opening the requested proceedings. The directors' duty to file for insolvency proceedings comes to nothing where the debtor company is insolvent under European law but not under the respective national law. We therefore had to recognise that our study would possibly affect a wider area of application than originally planned. 1.16

As regards the personal scope, our research project covers all debtors which are subject to the EIR. This covers entrepreneurs[37] and consumers or – seen from a slightly different perspective – natural persons (bankruptcies), as well as legal entities (insolvencies). Unlike Article 1(2)(h) Harmonisation Proposal, we have extended it to all debtors that may be within the scope of the EIR. This does not mean that we necessarily suggest including debtors that are currently exempted, in the Harmonisation Proposal, let alone encouraging national legislators to amend their respective national laws. It only means that we have examined the term "insolvency" for all possible debtors, no matter whether they will be included in the Harmonisation Proposal or not. 1.17

The main target of our research project is insolvency law. In our understanding, this covers rules on both liquidation and restructuring proceedings. In many jurisdictions, restructuring may take place in liquidation proceedings (then sometimes labelled "reorganisation proceedings"). Where this is the case, the definition of insolvency may be the same for both kinds of proceedings. However, national laws may also refer to different stages of a debtor's financial distress, depending on the type of proceedings in relation to which the term is used, i.e. liquidation or restructuring (with the latter including proceedings that may be regarded as pre-insolvency rather than actual insolvency proceedings). With respect to the term "pre-insolvency", we note that Article 4(1) Directive on restructuring and insolvency[38] refers to the "likelihood of insolvency" and 1.18

[37] In line with the exclusion in Art. 1(2) EIR, this research project does not address banks, insurers, investment firms, etc. (see Art. 1(2) Harmonisation Proposal). They are subject to special legal regimes and are not within the scope of our study. However, this would not prevent the European legislator from using our definitions if they were thought fit in this context as well.

[38] *Supra* fn. 21.

this term has been discussed more closely in all Member States during the transformation process. This has given further input to our research material.[39]

2. WORKING GROUP

1.19 Our project has been conducted in six steps. The first step was to assemble a working group of insolvency law experts who were willing to deal with our topic – based on their respective national laws – and to participate in our project. This was not difficult insofar as we were able to convince most of the members of an earlier expert group that had dealt with the harmonisation of transactions avoidance law[40] to participate in the present study too. In our working group, all Member States of the EU and the UK were represented by 33 proven experts (10 female, 23 male; 14 academics, 4 judges, 15 practitioners).[41]

3. QUESTIONNAIRE

1.20 The second step was initiated with a questionnaire. This project could not be carried out without taking national laws into account. The (ordinary[42]) existing rules of the jurisdictions involved are of special importance. They do not only provide necessary and valuable information about the definition of insolvency (and its subspecies), the legal culture in this field of law in general and the details of the use and understanding of this term in particular. They also reveal commonalities shared by all jurisdictions as well as possible obstacles to a Europe-wide harmonisation, which have to be considered when drafting a proposal for Model Rules. Hence, stocktaking of national laws was due.

---

39 See *infra* in Chapter 6.

40 The final report of this expert group has been published by *Bork/Veder*, Harmonisation of Transactions Avoidance Laws, Intersentia, Cambridge/Antwerp/Chicago 2022.

41 In alphabetical order of the Member States, members of the working group were Christian Koller and Kevin Labner for Austria; Frederik De Leo for Belgium; Hristina Kirilova for Bulgaria; Jasnica Garašić for Croatia; Andrie Kypridemou for Cyprus; Tomáš Richter for the Czech Republic; Line Langkjaer and Lasse Lindekilde for Denmark; Anto Kasak for Estonia; Tuomas Hupli for Finland; Reinhard Dammann for France; Reinhard Bork for Germany; Stathis Potamitis for Greece; Zoltan Fabok for Hungary; Simon Murphy for Ireland; Renato Mangano for Italy; Madara Sturite for Latvia; Frank Heemann for Lithuania; Pier Mario Lupinu for Luxembourg; Arthur Galea Salomone for Malta; Ben Schuijling and Michael Veder for the Netherlands; Marek Porzycki and Anna Rachwał for Poland; Catarina Serra for Portugal; Flavius-Iancu Moţu and Andreea Deli-Diaconescu for Romania; Dávid Oršula for Slovakia; Miodrag Dordevic for Slovenia; Nuria Bermejo for Spain; Hans Renman for Sweden; and Sarah Paterson for the United Kingdom.

42 We have left all crisis-related amendments and exceptions, e.g. in the context of the COVID-19 pandemic, aside.

For this purpose, all members of the working group were requested to complete a questionnaire,[43] with the aim of collecting relevant information from a national perspective. It was meant to provide the authors of this book with the input necessary to develop a common understanding, particularly regarding the existing rules and their underlying principles.

The aim of the questionnaire was primarily to collect necessary information about the legal situation and its analysis in the jurisdictions involved. However, it did not yet present proposals for a wording of concrete rules and it also did not request the ideas of the national reporters on what would be a proper common understanding of the terms examined here. This was left for a subsequent phase of the project, since it could not be done without evaluating the information collected by the questionnaire, preferably by discussing the results among the members of the working group. 1.21

The text of the questionnaire is divided into six sections. It starts with collecting general information on the term "insolvency" in the national laws (Section I.) and continues with detailed questions on the use, meaning, and establishment of the terms "inability to pay debts" (Section II.), "cessation of payments" (Section III.), "likely" or "imminent inability to pay debts" (Section IV.), and "overindebtedness" (Section V.). A space for additional information concludes the questionnaire (Section VI.). 1.22

The response rate was more than satisfying. All 28 national reporters returned the questionnaire in due time. Hence, all EU jurisdictions and the UK are covered by this study. The national reports are included in this book[44] and are also accessible to the public online. The national reporters provided the authors of this book with very detailed and helpful information and enabled them in turn to draft their report on the characteristics of the relevant rules in the EU Member States and the UK. 1.23

4. FURTHER STEPS

As a third step, we evaluated the answers and drafted a report. The fourth step consisted of discussing the first seven chapters of the draft report with the working group at a conference held in Amsterdam on 10 November 2023. The complete report was the topic of a second (online) conference on 25 April 2024. Collecting impact assessments was the fifth step, which resulted in a set of 1.24

43 The questionnaire is included at the beginning of Part III.

44 An exception is Denmark, since the Danish members of the working group were unable to finalise their national questionnaire for personal reasons and felt therefore uncomfortable to include it in this book. However, they have not objected to the references to Denmark in this report.

26 impact assessments.[45] Finally, step six was the finalisation of this report to be sent to the European Commission.

III. METHODOLOGY

1.25 As regards methodology, we have had good experiences with a principle-based approach.[46] This means, in a nutshell,[47] that we have aligned our project with the principles of insolvency law[48] and, where necessary, balanced conflicting principles. Hence, the research approach chosen here was to create a proposal on a principle-oriented basis whereby "principles" are to be understood as basic values. Such principles can be used to assess existing regulations as well as to develop rules *de lege ferenda*, thereby applying a principle-oriented approach to harmonisation which works for all legal cultures, even if their legislative process normally uses a different method.

1.26 However, this methodological approach was less self-evident than in our previous project on the harmonisation of transactions avoidance laws. The reason is that, basically, the definition, application, and balancing of principles of insolvency law presupposes the insolvency of the debtor. The definition of insolvency precedes the operation of these principles. In other words, if the debtor is not insolvent, the principles of insolvency law cannot be applied. Having said that, two restrictions should be emphasised. First, it may very well become necessary to take the pre-impact of the principles of insolvency law into account. Second, and more importantly, the impact of the definition of insolvency brings the principles of insolvency law into play. Generally, at least the opening of traditional liquidation proceedings, i.e. collective enforcement proceedings divesting the debtor of the control over its assets,[49] is – particularly where applied for by a creditor – one of the most invasive actions a debtor may have to endure. This raises the question as to when such invasive action is justifiable. This brings us

45 We received 26 impact assessments, including all jurisdictions involved except for Denmark and the UK. These impact assessments are printed below as Part II to this book.

46 For details, see *Bork/Veder* (fn. 40), para. 1.6 et seq.

47 For detailed information, see *infra* Chapter 2.

48 On them, see *Bork/Veder* (fn. 40), Chapter 2, para. 2.11 et seq.

49 As we will see in more detail *infra* (Chapter 3, at para. 3.6), the opening of most insolvency proceedings is connected to the debtor's insolvency. We therefore assume in the following that insolvency is a typical prerequisite for the opening of insolvency proceedings. In doing so, we leave aside for the moment that there are also – primarily restructuring-oriented – proceedings that are not linked to the debtor's insolvency. For example, in the USA, substantive insolvency is only required if the application for insolvency proceedings comes from a creditor (involuntary cases) whereas insolvency is irrelevant in voluntary cases (§301 Bankruptcy Code).

to the core of the matter: from what point in time does the financial situation of the debtor justify the opening of an insolvency (liquidation or restructuring) proceeding and the application of insolvency law instead of ordinary civil law, in particular contract law. Here, principles such as the creditors' autonomy, debtor protection, and collectivity will, in any event, compete.[50]

[50] More on the principles of insolvency law *infra* Chapter 2, at para. 2.5 et seq.

CHAPTER 2

THE MEANING OF PRINCIPLES OF INSOLVENCY LAW

As explained above, this research project makes use of the principle-based approach to develop a common understanding of the term "insolvency" used in the European instruments.[51] 2.1

[51] This approach has been elaborated extensively for *Cross-Border* Insolvency Law in *Bork*, Principles of Cross-Border Insolvency Law, Intersentia, Cambridge/Antwerp/Portland 2017; see further *Bork*, Corporate Insolvency Law (Chapter 1, fn. 4), para. 1.9 et seq.; *Bork*, Cross-Border Insolvency Law, Edward Elgar, Cheltenham/Northampton 2023, p. 10 et seq.; *Bork/Veder* (Chapter 1, fn. 40), chapter 2.

I. THE METHOD

2.2 Legal rules are seldom of a purely technical, valueless nature. They instead link back to basic principles, here defined as core values and not, like in the Anglo-American linguistic tradition, as meaningful regulatory objects. These principles have a systemising function, as well as a legitimising one. They can help to understand, to apply, and to further develop the law, be it through courts, be it through the legislator, or be it through academic discussion.

2.3 The benefits of a principle-based approach are manifold. Principles have systematising force: they can be used as criteria to explain the structure of the law and describe correlations between different rules. We can call such principles "structural principles". In insolvency law, examples are the principles of equal treatment of creditors on the one hand and of protection of trust on the other hand as systematising factors in, for example, transactions avoidance law. Principles can also have normative force: they can be used for justifying rules, legitimising the legal consequences of those rules as well as supporting the decisions of both legislators and courts, and they can also support the substantive coherence of rules. We can call such principles "substantive principles". Examples are the principle of equal treatment of creditors, the principle of creditors' autonomy, and the principle of social protection. Principles in this context can serve as unwritten sources of law. Courts can base their decisions on principles where the written law does not (or does not satisfactorily) address the issue in question, and principles can help judges to fill lacunae or to construe unclear or overly generalised statutes. Furthermore, principles are supportive in optimising the law, through a demand for principle-oriented decisions from legislators.

2.4 Against this background, a principle-based approach can also support harmonisation. This is shown by our project on the harmonisation of transactions avoidance laws. The proposals that we developed in this respect[52] did not start from the existing national laws. Instead, we established the principles of insolvency law in general and of transactions avoidance law in particular, selected the principles relevant for the issues at hand, and pondered the importance of each principle in relationship to others. By "taking off the national glasses" and employing a neutral academic approach, we avoided unhelpful discussions on the advantages and disadvantages of national laws. In the end, this resulted in a proposal for a Model Law on transactions avoidance law[53] which obtained the consent not only of the members of the working group we had assembled

[52] See *supra* Chapter 1, fn. 16.
[53] Available in *Bork/Veder* (Chapter 1, fn. 40), pp. 3–9.

for that project but also of the European Commission's expert group,[54] which recommended the adoption of our Model Law. The European Commission followed this advice and the Model Law is now part of the Harmonisation Proposal.[55] This demonstrates that the principle-based approach can be a helpful tool in the process of harmonising national laws in general and insolvency laws in particular.

II. THE PRINCIPLES

The principles of insolvency law were intensively developed and illustrated in our previous project. Hence, reference can be made to our report on the harmonisation of transactions avoidance laws.[56] For the purposes of this study, a short overview may suffice, starting with the statement that the principles of insolvency law can be summarised into two groups: procedural principles and substantive principles. In the following, these groups will be introduced primarily with respect to regular liquidation proceedings (sections 1./2.). However, since restructuring is also in the focus of this study,[57] the relevance of the principles for restructuring proceedings deserves a closer look, too (section 3.). 2.5

1. PROCEDURAL PRINCIPLES

Since insolvency proceedings are procedures, they are shaped by procedural principles which are partly general principles of law and not only principles specifically underlying insolvency law. The first principle to be mentioned in this context is the principle of *collectivity*. It refers to the distinction between individual enforcement and collective insolvency proceedings, and emphasises that insolvency proceedings are conducted in respect of the debtor's estate in the common interest of all (or at least a group of) creditors. A second procedural tenet is the principle of *efficiency* – according to which the proceedings must provide the required protection of rights as comprehensively as possible – which means that, in liquidation proceedings, creditors should receive their share of the proceeds as quickly and as comprehensively as possible, and in restructuring proceedings efficiency is also of the essence. The third is the principle of *creditors' autonomy*: insolvency proceedings are conducted in the interests of the creditors 2.6

54 Group of experts on restructuring and insolvency law (E03362); details at https://ec.europa.eu/transparency/expert-groups-register/screen/expert-groups/consult?groupID=3362&lang=en (last accessed 28 July 2023).
55 See Arts. 2(q), 3–12 Harmonisation Proposal.
56 See *Bork/Veder* (Chapter 1, fn. 40), chapter 2.
57 See *supra* Chapter 1, at para. 1.18.

who should be entitled to influence the administration of the proceedings. In addition, there is the principle of *transparency*: proceedings must be conducted transparently, so that those affected by them can take part and can bring their legal positions into the discussion. Of particular relevance is the principle of *predictability* (*legal certainty*), which means that creditors must be able to foresee (or be reliably advised on) not only their legal position but also how they can exercise their rights against an insolvent debtor and how they are expected to contribute to the proceedings (e.g. by providing necessary information within certain deadlines). This is closely connected to the principle of *procedural justice*. Insolvency proceedings, like all procedures, have to be organised and administered in a fair and just way and the procedural rights of all affected parties must be respected. Finally, the principle of *priority* must be taken into account, according to which a first set of insolvency proceedings precludes the opening of a second set.

2. SUBSTANTIVE PRINCIPLES

2.7 Alongside the procedural principles, a second set of principles shapes insolvency law: the group of substantive principles. Substantive principles reflect the impact of insolvency proceedings on substantive legal positions. The most important example of a substantive principle of insolvency law is the principle of *equal treatment of creditors* (the *pari passu* rule), according to which creditors of the same rank are to be treated identically, regarding not only their procedural rights but also their substantive rights. Another substantive insolvency principle is the principle of *best possible realisation of the debtor's assets* (also known as the principle of *optimisation*), according to which insolvency law and insolvency proceedings must be shaped in a way that guarantees the best possible realisation or restructuring of the debtor's estate with which the debtor is liable to his or her creditors. To some extent, this principle mirrors the principle of *best possible satisfaction of the creditors' claims* (also known as the principle of *satisfaction*), which has regard to the fact that the main purpose of insolvency proceedings is to satisfy the creditors' claims to the greatest possible extent in accordance with the creditors' out-of-insolvency entitlements and priorities. On the other hand, the principle of *protection of the debtor's rights* requires that the debtor's legitimate interests be taken into – procedural and substantive – account. Of significant importance is the principle of *protection of trust*, according to which the legitimate expectations of (for example) secured creditors or contractual partners must be observed. Further, the principle of *social protection*, e.g. for employees or tenants, is of special relevance. Also, the *fixation* principle has been elaborated, which supports the distinction between assets, creditors, and creditors' rights that are subject to the insolvency proceedings from those that are not. Finally, the principle of *proportionality* – according to which all legal measures must pursue a legitimate objective, must be suitable to attain this goal, and must not go beyond what is necessary to achieve this goal – has a massive impact.

3. RELEVANCE FOR RESTRUCTURING PROCEEDINGS

Following this, we will now briefly consider which of the principles listed above are relevant to restructuring proceedings. As regards the group of procedural principles, nearly all of them are meaningful, since restructuring proceedings are also procedures the regulation of which is based on certain tenets of law. This certainly holds true for the principles of *efficiency*,[58] *transparency*, *predictability* (*legal certainty*), *procedural justice* and *priority*. Only the applicability of the principles of collectivity and creditors' autonomy deserves some explanation. As regards *collectivity*, it is important that restructuring mostly affects a plurality of creditors. Of course, reorganisation negotiations can take place with individual important creditors and then it is a matter of individual, not collective, relationships. However, as soon as judicial assistance is sought, it is – not only, but primarily – about an enforcement ban (stay) against one or more groups of creditors[59] and usually about the confirmation of a restructuring plan.[60] As a rule, this will affect one or more groups of creditors, and is therefore already a collective procedure,[61] meaning that the principle of collectivity also has its significance. Further, since the restructuring plan needs the consent of the affected creditors,[62] the principle of *creditors' autonomy* has its relevance. Notwithstanding rules on "cross-class cram-down",[63] it is for the (majority of the) creditors to decide whether or not they want to support the debtor's restructuring plan, which is a typical example of creditor autonomy. 2.8

The relevance of the substantive principles of insolvency for restructuring proceedings is less clear. *Equal treatment of creditors* is also necessary in judicial 2.9

---

58 This includes efficient access to restructuring tools and judicial assistance; see Arts. 1(1)(c), 10(4), 16(2), 25(b) Directive on restructuring and insolvency (*supra* Chapter 1, fn. 21).

59 See Art. 6 Directive on restructuring and insolvency (*supra* Chapter 1, fn. 21).

60 See Art. 10 Directive on restructuring and insolvency (*supra* Chapter 1, fn. 21).

61 This is broadly discussed for Art. 2(a) UNCITRAL Model Law on Cross-Border Insolvency, which requires "collective" proceedings. It is prevailing opinion that restructuring proceedings that affect not all but only a group of creditors are collective within the meaning of this rule. See *Re Smile Telecoms Holdings Ltd.* [2022] EWHC 740 (Ch) at [60]; *Mevorach/Walters*, The Characterization of Pre-insolvency Proceedings in Private International Law, 21 (2020) EBOR 855 at 871. See also, albeit for Art. 1 EIR, *Re gategroup Guarantee Limited* [2021] EWHC 304 (Ch) at [110]. Differently, *Eidenmüller*, What Is An Insolvency Proceeding?, 92 (2018) American Bankruptcy Law Journal 53 et seq.

62 For example, according to Art. 9 Directive on restructuring and insolvency (*supra* Chapter 1, fn. 21).

63 See Art. 11 Directive on restructuring and insolvency (*supra*, Chapter 1, fn. 21).

restructuring proceedings (unless otherwise accepted by the unequally treated creditors), not only in procedural, but also in substantive terms (e.g. within a class of creditors affected by a restructuring plan[64]). Obviously, the principles of *optimisation* and *satisfaction* are also relevant, since restructuring proceedings aim at the preservation and restoration of the value of the debtor's business (estate) to the benefit of the creditors on the one hand and the debtor (or its shareholders respectively) on the other. As restructuring proceedings are typically debtor-in-possession proceedings,[65] so that the debtor keeps control over its assets and business operations, the principle of *protection of the debtor's rights* is also of significant importance. Further, the principle of *protection of trust* comes into play *inter alia* where a restructuring law provides for the termination of, or amendments to, executory contracts.[66] Tenants and employees may also be affected by restructuring proceedings, which brings the principle of *social protection* into play.[67] Finally, the principle of *proportionality* is also of special relevance, e.g. when norms of restructuring law require the debtor to be likely unable to pay debts[68] as a justification for providing for interference in the creditors' rights by an enforcement stay or a majority decision on a restructuring plan.[69] Only the *fixation* principle arguably does not influence pre-insolvency restructuring law, since it is connected to the opening of insolvency proceedings (regardless of whether they ultimately result in liquidation or reorganisation[70]).

III. PRINCIPLES RELEVANT TO THE DEFINITION OF INSOLVENCY

2.10 If one wants to determine which principles influence the definition of insolvency, it is best to first turn to the function of this term. In a first approach, insolvency has occurred if the debtor's estate is not sufficient to pay all the creditors. As soon as this state of the debtor's financial crisis has arrived, the legal regime

---

64 This is correctly expressed in Art. 10(2)(b) Directive on restructuring and insolvency (*supra* Chapter 1, fn. 21), according to which Member States must ensure that "creditors with sufficient commonality of interest in the same class are treated equally".

65 See Art. 5 Directive on restructuring and insolvency (*supra* Chapter 1, fn. 21).

66 See Art. 7(4)/(5) Directive on restructuring and insolvency (*supra* Chapter 1, fn. 21).

67 This is taken account of in Art. 13 Directive on restructuring and insolvency (*supra* Chapter 1, fn. 21).

68 E.g. Art. 4(1) Directive on restructuring and insolvency (*supra* Chapter 1, fn. 21).

69 In other words, the principle of proportionality requires that restructuring law is available in a timely manner: early enough to support the rescue of the business but not too early, so that interferences in creditor rights (e.g. by a stay or a restructuring plan) are justified.

70 See *infra* Chapter 3, at para. 3.12. However, it may very well be that under some national laws the start of the restructuring proceedings can also trigger some fixating rules, such as a division between an old debt that can be affected by the plan and a new debt that arises during the proceedings and will have to be paid in full.

applicable to the debtor's affairs – particularly with regard to his or her creditors, contractual partners, and other stakeholders – changes. Subject to respective rules of national law, to avoid personal liability, at least from that moment on, the debtor and its management have to give priority to the interests of the creditors instead of the interests of the debtor and its shareholders and must consider applying for the opening of either restructuring or insolvency proceedings. As regards enforcement of the creditors' claims, collective proceedings replace individual proceedings. Debtors are generally divested of control over their assets, and special rules of insolvency law (e.g. for executory contracts, set-off or transactions avoidance) interfere with ordinary civil law, particularly in contract law. As to the legal consequences, it is important to determine the exact point in time at which the shift takes place from the applicability of rules of general civil law to insolvency law. It is the task of the term "insolvency" to concretise this point in time, since legislators in all jurisdictions – following an "if-then" pattern (*if* the debtor is insolvent, *then* special legal consequences arise) – have linked the occurrence of certain legal consequences to the substantive insolvency of the debtor.[71] To put it simply, the application of insolvency law requires the debtor's insolvency and it is the function of this term to determine the demarcation line between application of general civil law and of insolvency law. Against this background, taking a closer look at the legal consequences typically connected to the term "insolvency" reveals the principles relevant for the present task.[72]

1. PROCEDURAL PRINCIPLES

To begin with the procedural principles referred to above,[73] the principles of collectivity, creditors' autonomy, predictability, and efficiency must be taken into account. 2.11

a) Collectivity

The first principle to be dealt with in some detail is the principle of collectivity.[74] It emphasises that insolvency proceedings are collective proceedings conducted in respect of the debtor's estate in the common interest of all creditors and it is a coining and indispensable tenet of insolvency law. Hence, when defining the term "insolvency" as the admission ticket to insolvency law, particular emphasis must be placed on whether the financial condition of the debtor's estate requires switching from general contract law to insolvency law and whether collective 2.12

71 For details, see *infra* Chapter 3.
72 See also the answers to Questionnaire Q. 2.
73 At para. 2.6.
74 Details by *Bork/Veder* (Chapter 1, fn. 40), para. 2.16 et seq.

enforcement proceedings are now preferable to individual enforcement proceedings. The principle of collectivity requires the determination, as exactly as possible, of the point in time where the common interests of the general body of creditors trump the individual interests of the debtor and of each individual creditor. Insolvency law must not be applied too early, since as long as the debtor is able to pay its creditors, general contract law should prevail. And it must not be applied too late, since this would cause damage to the estate and thus to the general body of creditors because the protective effects of insolvency law would not intervene in time.

b) *Creditors' Autonomy*

2.13 Equally relevant is the procedural principle of creditors' autonomy.[75] It refers to the fact that the creditors, as main economic stakeholders in insolvency proceedings, are entitled not only to articulate, pursue, and coordinate their (common) interests, but also to influence – if not, in some cases, render – the key decisions in the proceedings. If the debtor is substantively insolvent, insolvency proceedings must be opened, which, at least in ordinary liquidation proceedings,[76] shift the focus from the debtor to the creditors and other stakeholders. Unless debtor-in-possession proceedings are provided for, it is no longer up to the debtor to manage and dispose of the estate. This is the task of the Insolvency Practitioner, who acts under the supervision and in the common interests of the creditors, and the proceedings are no longer debtor-centred but creditor-oriented. It is therefore of significant importance to define as precisely as possible the prerequisites and the point in time when this shift takes place and the creditors take over control. This includes first and foremost the definition of the term "insolvency".

c) *Predictability (Legal Certainty)*

2.14 Further, the principle of predictability (or legal certainty)[77] merits a closer look. It means that all stakeholders must be able to predict (or be reliably advised on) not only their legal position but also how they can exercise their rights and how they are expected to contribute to the proceedings (e.g. by providing necessary information within certain deadlines). In the present context, a clear, precise, and reliable definition of the term "insolvency" is important not only for the debtor and his or her creditors but also for other parties involved. This includes contractual partners who need to know whether their contractual relationships

[75] More on this principle at *Bork/Veder* (Chapter 1, fn. 40), para. 2.24 et seq.
[76] See *supra* Chapter 1, at para. 1.25.
[77] More on this principle at *Bork/Veder* (Chapter 1, fn. 40), para. 2.29 et seq.

continue unaffected by the special insolvency regime (e.g. if payments from the substantively insolvent debtor are at risk of being challenged in any anticipated insolvency proceedings under the applicable transactions avoidance law). It also includes the directors of an insolvent company who need to be sure whether they now have to orientate themselves more towards the interests of creditors than towards the interests of the shareholders and whether they may even be obliged to file for insolvency or at least to initiate restructuring measures. Since this shift of duties is connected to the debtor's substantive insolvency, legal certainty regarding this term is of utmost importance.

d) *Efficiency*

Finally, the principle of efficiency comes into play.[78] All laws should be shaped 2.15
in a way that they can be efficiently enforced. It should be as easy as possible for all stakeholders to establish whether a debtor is insolvent or not. This overlaps broadly with the principle of legal certainty. Norms which are clear and easy to apply avoid unnecessary, costly, and time-consuming disputes and thus contribute to efficient insolvency proceedings. Hence, all rules which connect their legal consequences to the debtor's substantive insolvency are useless if the term "insolvency" is defined in such a complicated and burdensome way that it is, in practice, difficult, if not impossible, to find out whether the relevant rule is applicable or not. For example, a norm that obliges the directors of an insolvent company to file for insolvency proceedings is ineffective if it is – even for the directors – difficult to find out whether the company is insolvent within the meaning of the respective norm.[79] Similarly, a norm of transactions avoidance law which requires the debtor's substantive insolvency at the time when the transaction was performed is not efficient if the definition of insolvency is too difficult to handle. On the other hand, efficient norms should be flexible enough to allow the relevant circumstances of the individual case to be taken into account. Rules that are too rigid may be easier to apply, but can lead to unfair results in individual cases, which should be avoided as far as possible when formulating the rules, in the interests of efficiency.

2. SUBSTANTIVE PRINCIPLES

Alongside the procedural principles, nearly all substantive principles as set 2.16
out above[80] are relevant. This particularly holds true for the principles of

[78] Details at *Bork/Veder* (Chapter 1, fn. 40), para. 2.19 et seq.

[79] That is precisely the issue with Art. 36 Harmonisation Proposal; see *supra* Chapter 1, at para. 1.7.

[80] At para. 2.7.

optimisation, satisfaction, protection of the debtor's rights, equal treatment of creditors, protection of trust, fixation, and proportionality.

a) Best Possible Realisation of the Debtor's Assets ("Optimisation")

2.17 The first substantive principle to be mentioned here is the principle of best possible realisation of the debtor's assets.[81] It takes into account that the most prominent interest of creditors, at least in liquidation proceedings, is to receive satisfaction of their claims out of the proceedings as quickly and as comprehensively as possible. As regards the opening of insolvency proceedings, this should take place as early as possible. Experience shows that the later the proceedings are opened, the less value is retained in the estate, since the value of assets decreases every day and the debtor typically dissipates assets and creates new debts with every day that one delays in open proceedings, so that the benefit for the creditors becomes smaller and smaller. It is therefore generally in the best interest of creditors to open the proceedings when the assets are still available and still of reasonable value, which amounts to: as early as possible. This depends – among other things – on the definition of insolvency as a prerequisite for the opening of the proceedings.

b) Best Possible Satisfaction of the Creditors' Claims ("Satisfaction")

2.18 The principle of best possible realisation of the debtor's assets goes hand-in-hand with the principle of best possible satisfaction of the creditors' claims.[82] Both principles – optimisation and satisfaction – are closely related, since the best possible realisation of the debtor's assets contributes decisively to the best possible satisfaction of the creditors' claims. Hence, a definition of the term "insolvency" which enables proceedings to be opened as early as possible contributes to an estate that is as valuable as possible and thus to the best possible satisfaction of the creditors' claims.

c) Protection of the Debtor's Rights

2.19 On the other hand, the principle of protection of the debtor's rights[83] requires attention. Although insolvency law is primarily designed to protect the legitimate interests of creditors, the procedural and substantive rights of the debtor must also be taken into account. This also has an impact on the definition of the term "insolvency". Admittedly, an insolvent debtor must accept that he

---

81 More on this principle at *Bork/Veder* (Chapter 1, fn. 40), para. 2.43 et seq.

82 For details, see *Bork/Veder* (Chapter 1, fn. 40), para. 2.47 et seq.

83 More on this principle at *Bork/Veder* (Chapter 1, fn. 40), para. 2.51 et seq.

or she is deprived of the power of administration and disposal of the estate, unless debtor-in-possession proceedings are provided for. However, this only holds true if he or she *is* insolvent, which depends decisively on the definition of this term. Even from the perspective of an honest debtor, it should at least be designed in a way that prevents insolvency proceedings from being opened too early or too easily, i.e. at a point in time where it is not yet necessary or justified to switch from individual to collective proceedings and to apply insolvency law instead of general contract law. The principle of protection of the debtor's rights is therefore an important counterweight to the principles which support the opening of the proceedings as early as possible.

d) *Equal Treatment of Creditors*

Further, the principle of equal treatment of creditors[84] must be included in the analysis. In the present context, this is closely related to the principle of collectivity. Where a debtor is insolvent, collective enforcement proceedings are conducted in the best interest of all creditors, among whom "the pain is to be shared".[85] This not only culminates in a distribution of the proceeds in which all creditors must be treated equally through a strict application of the *pari passu* rule; it also entails the requirement that creditors shall be given the same procedural rights, which includes their being subjected to a common and collective procedure. While creditors may be treated individually and differently outside the debtor's insolvency, they must, in principle, be treated uniformly and jointly within the insolvency. Therefore, under the principle of equal treatment of creditors too, it is of great importance *when* the debtor is substantively insolvent and thus when the time has come for a change from individual (and possibly different) to collective (and thus equal) treatment of creditors. 2.20

e) *Protection of Trust*

Another substantive principle to be considered is the principle of protection of trust.[86] It refers to the legitimate expectations of (for example) creditors or contractual partners. People need to be sure about their legal rights and positions. Once they have acquired these rights, they trust in their stability and continuity and expect, with good reason, to be protected against unjustified changes or deprivation. However, they do so in the context of a wider regime of the applicable law, which can include rules weakening their legal position under certain conditions. In particular, this holds true in the context of insolvencies 2.21

84 More on this principle at *Bork/Veder* (Chapter 1, fn. 40), para. 2.38 et seq.
85 *Re Nortel Networks Corporation* [2015] ONSC 2987 at [226].
86 More on this principle at *Bork/Veder* (Chapter 1, fn. 40), para. 2.54 et seq.

where the creditor's individual relationship with the debtor is influenced by the collective interests of the general body of creditors. When people trust in the stability of their legal position, they must take into consideration that insolvency law is part of the legal regime governing their relationship with the debtor. Hence, the principle of protection of trust requires the term "insolvency" to be defined in such a way that it can justify the reduced protection of legitimate expectations and so that it is recognisable to anyone dealing with the debtor that reliance on the stability of one's legal position is henceforth less protected than before the occurrence of insolvency.

f) Fixation

2.22 The fixation principle[87] also plays a role. It is the underlying tenet of all norms demarcating the personal and substantive scope of insolvency proceedings and supports the distinction between assets, creditors, and creditors' rights that are subject to the insolvency proceedings and those that are not. This is typically connected to the opening of insolvency proceedings and thus to the occurence of the debtor's insolvency.[88] From this point of view, too, it is therefore important to define the term insolvency in such a way that it justifies subjecting certain assets of the debtor and certain parties to the insolvency law regime.

g) Proportionality

2.23 Finally, the principle of proportionality[89] must be taken into account, according to which all legal measures must pursue a legitimate objective, must be suitable to attain this goal, and must not go beyond what is necessary to achieve this goal. The latter, in particular, can be of relevance for the definition of the term "insolvency". As we will explain in more detail below,[90] a typical problem in this context is the treatment of only temporary (or transient) insolvency. Even if all the requirements of the definition are fulfilled on a certain day, it may nevertheless be disproportionate to allow all the legal consequences to occur that are linked to this constituent element if it is reliably foreseeable that the debtor will very soon be able again to fully satisfy his or her creditors. For example, this may be the case because a tax refund is due that has already been determined

---

87 More on this principle at *Bork/Veder* (Chapter 1, fn. 40), para. 2.84 et seq.

88 Interestingly, under the French Code de Commerce of 1807, which was applicable also in Belgium and the Netherlands from 1810 until 1838, the opening of insolvency proceedings had retroactive effect to the point in time when the debtor first ceased payments. As a result, the fixation effects were connected to the occurrence of the debtor's substantive insolvency. Nowadays, they are triggered by the decision to open proceedings, effective *ex nunc* (see Arts. L 641-9(1), 641-3(1) read with 622-21(2) Code de Commerce).

89 More on this principle at *Bork/Veder* (Chapter 1, fn. 40), paras. 2.89 et seq.

90 At Chapter 4, at para. 4.11.

by the tax authorities or a purchase price payment by a reliable buyer is to be expected with a sufficient degree of certainty. The principle of proportionality requires consideration of such typical circumstances and shaping the definition of insolvency accordingly.

IV. INTERIM RESULTS

In summarising our conclusions so far, at least two results can be noted. First, 2.24
under a principle-based approach, the definition of the term "insolvency" must be as clear, precise, and easy to apply as possible. This is supported by the principles of creditors' autonomy, predictability, efficiency, protection of trust, and fixation. Since the law connects severe legal consequences to the debtor's insolvency – most notably the shift from general civil law to insolvency law (and its generally invasive effects) – it must be clear for all stakeholders whether this prerequisite is met. Second, it is important to find a definition that determines the correct point in time when the shift from the applicability of general civil law to insolvency law is justified. The intervention of insolvency law must come neither too early nor too late. This is primarily supported by the principles of collectivity, optimisation, satisfaction, equal treatment of creditors, protection of the debtor's rights, and protection of trust. Finally, the principle of proportionality serves as a corrective.

CHAPTER 3

"INSOLVENCY" IN THE NATIONAL LAWS

I. "INSOLVENCY" AS A PREREQUISITE

3.1 In the Harmonisation Proposal,[91] the European Commission has used the terms "insolvency", "inability to pay debts", and "likelihood of insolvency" as a precondition for certain legal consequences.[92] However, the meaning of these expressions is far from clear. In most norms, the Harmonisation Proposal abstains from giving any definition at all.[93] In others, it refers to the applicable national law.[94] The only rule which comes close to an autonomous definition is Article 38(2) Harmonisation Proposal (referenced in Article 41(2)(b) Harmonisation Proposal). It refers to inability to pay debts,[95] but even here, the European Commission leaves the details to the national laws of the Member States.

3.2 In contrast to that, the UNCITRAL Legislative Guide[96] provides, at paragraph 12(s), the following definition for the term "insolvency": "when a debtor is generally unable to pay its debts as they mature or when its liabilities exceed the value of its assets". This leaves many detailed questions unanswered, but at least it can be said that the Legislative Guide understands the term "insolvency" to mean both "inability to pay debts" and "overindebtedness".

3.3 Against this background, the analysis of the national reports, contained in the questionnaires completed by the members of our working group, starts with a general overview of the definitions and uses of the term "insolvency" and its

---

91 *Supra* Chapter 1, fn. 1.
92 See, among others, Recitals 8, 33, 37 and Arts. 6, 23, 36, 38, 41 Harmonisation Proposal.
93 See, for example, Arts. 36, 41 Harmonisation Proposal.
94 Cf. Art. 23 Harmonisation Proposal ("insolvent in accordance with national law").
95 For the wording, see *supra* Chapter 1, fn. 24.
96 *Supra* Chapter 1, fn. 27.

subspecies as a prerequisite for concrete legal consequences in the national insolvency laws of the EU Member States and the UK. This was done regardless of whether these terms are used with an identical definition or meaning and it was generally focused on traditional liquidation proceedings.[97]

3.4 Interestingly, the term "insolvency" (or "bankruptcy" respectively), although used in combinations such as "insolvency debtor" or "insolvency proceedings", is in some jurisdictions not defined in statute.[98] An example is Germany, where the law requires a reason for the opening of insolvency proceedings (§16 Insolvenzordnung) and lists inability to pay debts (§17 Insolvenzordnung), imminent inability to pay debts (§18 Insolvenzordnung), and overindebtedness (§19 Insolvenzordnung) as such reasons. Hence, only the relevant subspecies of insolvency are defined. As opposed to that, other national laws do offer a definition of the term "insolvency".[99] For example, in Cyprus, §202N Company Law provides – albeit for restructuring proceedings only – that "insolvency" means "the case in which a company is unable to pay its debts". In Italy, according to Article 2.1.b Codice della crisi d'impresa e dell'insolvenza, "insolvency" is "the debtor's state that is displayed either by the debtor's non-fulfilment of obligations or by other symptoms proving that the debtor is no longer able to satisfy his or her obligations regularly".

3.5 As regards the various subspecies of insolvency,[100] nearly all national laws are familiar with the term "inability to pay debts".[101] Exceptions are Belgium, Luxembourg, and the Netherlands, which refer to "cessation of payments" only,[102] a term which is also used in many other[103] but by no means in all states.[104] A special case is France which, in Article L 631-1 Code de Commerce, refers exclusively to "cessation of payments" but defines this in exactly the same way that "inability to pay debts" is defined in other jurisdictions,[105] which is

---

97 For restructuring see *infra* at para. 3.12.

98 Croatia, Germany, UK.

99 Belgium, Cyprus, Czech Republic, Denmark, Estonia, Finland, France, Italy, Lithuania, Luxembourg, Poland, Portugal, Romania, Slovakia, Spain, Sweden.

100 Questionnaire Q. 3.

101 Austria, Bulgaria, Croatia, Cyprus, Czech Republic, Denmark, Estonia, Finland, Germany, Greece, Hungary, Ireland, Italy, Latvia, Lithuania, Malta, Poland, Portugal, Romania, Slovakia, Slovenia, Spain, Sweden, UK; in Belgium in company law only. – For details, see *infra* at Chapter 4, at para. 4.1 et seq.

102 Art. XX.99 Belgian Code de droit économique (insolvency law only), Art. 437(1) Luxembourgian Code de Commerce (which requires in addition that the debtor's credit is undermined); Art. 1(1) Dutch Faillisementswet (here and in Belgium, "inability to pay debts" is equated to an apparent "cessation of payments").

103 Austria, Bulgaria, Croatia, Czech Republic, Denmark, Finland, Germany, Greece, Hungary, Poland, Portugal, Romania, Spain, Sweden. – Cf. *infra* Chapter 5, at para. 5.1 et seq.

104 Not in Cyprus, Estonia, Ireland, Italy, Latvia, Lithuania, Malta, Slovakia, Slovenia, UK.

105 Art. 631-1(1) Code de Commerce: "A debtor who is unable to meet its current liabilities with its available assets is in suspension of payments"; similarly Greece.

why, from now on, we will include the French "cessation of payments" among "inability to pay debts". "Overindebtedness" is also a subspecies of insolvency known in many national insolvency laws.[106] As far as future developments of the debtor's financial situation are concerned, many national laws operate – with slightly varying wording – on the basis of "likely inability to pay debts",[107] others upon "imminent inability to pay debts".[108] Still others abstain from using this expression for the opening of liquidation proceedings[109] and reserve it for the commencement of restructuring proceedings.[110] We will deal with this in more detail below.[111]

It is a not very surprising result of our survey that the term "insolvency" and its subspecies are first and foremost used as reasons to commence or open insolvency proceedings.[112] This particularly holds true for inability to pay debts, on which applications for, or the commencement of, insolvency proceedings can be based in nearly all jurisdictions[113] (with the exception of Belgium, Luxembourg, and the Netherlands, which require cessation of payments[114]). Some national laws also accept overindebtedness as an autonomous reason[115] (whereas others treat this as an indication or subspecies of inability to pay 3.6

106 Austria, Bulgaria, Croatia, Czech Republic, Denmark, Estonia, Finland, Germany, Hungary, Italy, Lithuania, Poland, Portugal, Slovakia, Slovenia; in Belgium in company law only; for individual insolvencies also in France and Luxembourg. In the UK, the definition of inability to pay debts in sec. 123(2) Insolvency Act 1986 comes close to what is understood as "overindebtedness" or the "balance sheet insolvency/test" in other jurisdictions; the same holds true for Latvia. – More *infra* Chapter 4, at para. 4.5 et seq.

107 Czech Republic, Estonia, Hungary, Lithuania, Slovenia, Spain (but only for "pre-packs"), the Netherlands; in Malta, the expression "imminently likely to become unable to pay debts" is used and in the UK the expression "likely to become unable to pay its debts". See *infra* Chapter 6, at para. 6.4 et seq.

108 Croatia, Germany, Greece, Hungary, Portugal, Slovakia, Spain. In Belgian and Polish law, the expression "threatening insolvency" is used. We understand that this is equivalent to "imminent" insolvency (which includes "imminent overindebtedness"). However, while Czech law also uses a concept named "threatening insolvency" in its literal translation, the substance of the rule is much closer to that of the "likely inability to pay debts" as that concept is used in this report. More *infra* Chapter 6, at para. 6.10.

109 Cyprus, Ireland.

110 See *infra* at para. 3.12.

111 Chapter 6.

112 Questionnaire Q. 6.

113 Austria, Bulgaria, Croatia, Cyprus, Czech Republic, Denmark, Estonia, Finland, Germany, Greece, Hungary, Ireland, Italy, Latvia, Lithuania, Poland, Portugal, Romania, Slovakia, Slovenia, Spain, Sweden, UK.

114 Cf. *supra* fn. 102. – Note that "cessation of payments" is an autonomous reason to open insolvency proceedings not only in Belgium, Luxembourg (albeit only with the debtor's inability to gain credit as an additional requirement), and in the Netherlands but also (alongside other reasons) in Greece.

115 Austria, Bulgaria, Croatia, Czech Republic, Estonia, Germany, Hungary, Italy, Lithuania, Poland, Portugal, Slovakia, Slovenia.

debts only[116]). Occasionally, imminent inability to pay debts is recognised as a reason to open liquidation proceedings[117] whereas likely inability to pay debts plays no significant role in this context.[118]

3.7 Inability to pay debts[119] or cessation of payments[120] is also relevant for the opening of bankruptcy proceedings (regarding natural persons, particularly consumers). The majority of those national laws that accept overindebtedness as a reason for corporate insolvencies do not use this term for personal bankruptcies.[121]

3.8 Interim measures during the application stage[122] are typically not dependent on substantive insolvency of the debtor[123] because, during this phase of the proceedings, the substantive insolvency is to be examined first as a prerequisite for opening the proceedings. However, where national laws refer to the debtor's substantive insolvency (e.g. as a requirement for appointing a provisional Insolvency Practitioner), the respective terms are used in the same way as for the opening of proceedings.[124]

3.9 Alongside these "classical" reasons for the opening of insolvency proceedings, additional triggering circumstances[125] (e.g. unsuccessful statutory demands for payment of a debt exceeding a certain amount, unsuccessful individual enforcement of a judgment) exist in some jurisdictions,[126] occasionally as autonomous reasons for the opening of proceedings, mostly as rebuttable or irrebuttable presumptions of cessation of payments or inability to pay debts. However, they must be distinguished from other, not necessarily insolvency-related but company-law-based reasons for liquidating a company (e.g. the resolution of a shareholders' meeting, cessation of the last remaining shareholder, omission to commence or continue business for a certain time period after the

116 Cyprus, Ireland, Malta, UK. More *infra* Chapter 4, at para. 4.5.

117 Croatia, Germany, Greece, Portugal, Spain; for the debtor's petition only also Hungary, Romania.

118 In contrast in Estonia and the Czech Republic, the likely inability to pay a substantial part of debts allows the debtor (but not a creditor) to open insolvency proceedings. In the UK, likelihood of inability to pay debts suffices for opening administration proceedings, which are considered insolvency proceedings, but not liquidation proceedings.

119 Austria, Croatia, Cyprus, Denmark, Germany, Greece, Estonia, Finland, Italy, Latvia, Lithuania, Poland, Portugal, Romania, Slovakia, Slovenia, Spain, UK. In contrast: Hungary, Ireland.

120 Austria, Belgium, Denmark, Greece, Malta, the Netherlands, Portugal, Spain.

121 Austria, Croatia, Czech Republic, Germany, Lithuania, Poland. – This does not hold true for Hungary, Italy, Portugal, Slovenia. See further *supra* fn. 106.

122 Questionnaire Q. 4.

123 Examples are Cyprus, Estonia, Germany, Poland. No interim measures are available in Finland, Italy, the Netherlands, Sweden.

124 Austria, Belgium, Bulgaria, Czech Republic, Greece, Hungary, Ireland, Latvia, Lithuania, Luxembourg, Malta, Portugal, Romania, Slovakia, Slovenia, Spain.

125 Questionnaire Q. 8.

126 Details *infra* Chapter 4, at para. 4.14.

incorporation), including reasons pursuing public interests and the liquidation being "fair and equitable".[127] We will deal with this in detail below.[128]

Variants of insolvency are also used as prerequisites in norms on transactions avoidance.[129] In many Member States, inability to pay debts is a prerequisite for challenging certain transactions which are detrimental to the general body of creditors.[130] In particular, this holds true for the avoidance of preferences.[131] Other states also refer – additionally or exclusively – to "cessation of payments",[132] "overindebtedness",[133] "likely insolvency",[134] or even "imminent inability to pay debts"[135] in their transactions avoidance law. However, there are also Member States which do not require substantive insolvency of the debtor in the context of transactions avoidance.[136] 3.10

Further, in some jurisdictions, insolvency influences the duties of a company's directors. First, where the company's inability to pay debts is at least likely[137] or imminent,[138] some national laws provide for a shift of directors' duties towards the interests of creditors rather than the interests of the shareholders[139] or at least emphasise that the directors shall have regard to the interests of all creditors, members, and other stakeholders. Second, some national laws impose a duty on the directors[140] to file for insolvency proceedings[141] if the company is substantively 3.11

---

127 The latter is particularly available in the common law tradition, cf. Cyprus, Ireland.

128 Chapter 4, at para. 4.16 et seq.

129 Questionnaire Q. 9.

130 Austria, Bulgaria, Croatia, Cyprus, Czech Republic, Denmark, Finland, France (see *supra* at para. 3.5), Germany, Ireland, Italy, Lithuania, Poland, Portugal, Sweden, UK; similarly, Romania. For clarification: in some jurisdictions, the *actio pauliana* is regulated in civil law rather than in insolvency law and does therefore not require any detriment to the general body of creditors.

131 See also *Bork/Veder* (Chapter 1, fn. 40), para. 4.84.

132 Belgium, Denmark, Greece, Luxembourg.

133 Austria, Bulgaria, Czech Republic, Estonia, Finland, Portugal, Slovenia. In Denmark and Sweden, lack of overindebtedness is a defence against avoidance of gratuitous transactions, wage payments, etc.

134 Malta, Sweden.

135 Portugal, Sweden.

136 Hungary, Latvia, the Netherlands, Slovakia, Spain (although avoidance actions can only be brought within insolvency proceedings).

137 See, following the lead of Art. 19 Directive on restructuring and insolvency (*supra* fn. 21), the laws of Croatia, Cyprus, Ireland, Lithuania, Malta, Slovenia, Sweden. Similarly in the UK not the insolvency but the opening of insolvency proceedings must be "probable".

138 Hungary, Slovakia, Sweden.

139 Italy attaches this legal consequence to the debtor's overindebtedness (here defined as "insufficiency of the company's assets for the satisfaction of the creditors' claims").

140 Spanish law provides for a duty of *all* debtors to file for insolvency proceedings; in Luxembourg, it is a duty of the debtor, the creditors, and the court to commence insolvency proceedings. In Greece, all debtors that are in a state of cessation of payments must file for insolvency/bankruptcy. Directors are personally liable for the failure to do so.

141 In Belgium, Bulgaria, and Malta, the directors are obliged to convene a shareholders' meeting which is to decide on the company's termination; in Hungary, that decision is a last resort; in Ireland they have to start voluntary liquidation.

insolvent, which includes inability to pay debts,[142] cessation of payments,[143] imminent inability to pay debts,[144] and – where available[145] – overindebtedness.[146] Other national laws provide for a duty to take steps to avoid insolvency,[147] connect an obligation to pay damages to certain unpaid creditors in case of directors' wrongful trading,[148] or to inform certain public creditors (e.g. tax authorities).[149]

3.12 Similar observations can be made regarding restructuring or reorganisation proceedings.[150] In some Member States, restructuring is a possible outcome of uniform insolvency proceedings (where the decision between liquidation and restructuring is made after the opening of the proceedings).[151] Hence, the triggering circumstances are the same if restructuring is strived for in such insolvency proceedings. However, Member States always had[152] or – having transposed the Directive on restructuring and insolvency[153] into national laws – now have pre-insolvency restructuring proceedings which are available outside regular insolvency proceedings. Admittedly, the triggering events for such proceedings differ between national laws. For preventive restructuring proceedings, most states require some sort of likelihood of insolvency.[154] Alternatively or in parallel, imminent inability to pay debts is also used,[155] as is actual inability to pay debts,[156] cessation of payments,[157] or even

142 Austria, Bulgaria, Croatia, Czech Republic, Estonia, France (see *supra* at para. 3.5), Germany, Latvia, Lithuania, Poland, Portugal, Romania, Slovakia, Slovenia, Spain.

143 Belgium, Greece, Spain.

144 Croatia.

145 See *supra* at para. 3.6.

146 Austria, Bulgaria, Croatia, Czech Republic, Estonia, Germany, Lithuania, Poland, Slovakia, Slovenia.

147 Austria, Bulgaria, Croatia, Estonia, Germany, Ireland, Lithuania, Malta, the Netherlands, Romania; indirectly also in Greece.

148 Belgium, Denmark, Hungary, Malta, the Netherlands, Romania, UK.

149 The Netherlands.

150 Questionnaire Qs. 5, 6, 7.

151 Austria, Bulgaria, Croatia, Czech Republic, Estonia, Finland, Germany, Portugal, Romania, Spain.

152 Examples are *inter alia* France, Poland, UK.

153 *Supra* Chapter 1, fn. 21.

154 Cyprus, Czech Republic (but the definition of "likelihood of insolvency" used here differs from that under regular insolvency law), Denmark, Estonia, Hungary, Ireland, Italy, Lithuania, the Netherlands, Romania, Spain (for pre-insolvency restructuring proceedings only), Sweden; further Greece ("probable insolvency"), Malta ("imminently likely to become unable to pay its debts"), Slovenia ("great probability").

155 Austria, Belgium, Bulgaria, Croatia, Finland, Germany, Greece, Poland, Portugal, Slovakia, Slovenia, Spain, Sweden.

156 Cyprus, Croatia, Denmark, Greece, Finland, Ireland, Italy, Latvia, Lithuania, Poland, Slovakia, Spain, Sweden. – As opposed to this, in some jurisdictions, inability to pay debts serves as a bar to preventive restructuring proceedings, Austria, Czech Republic, France (see para. 3.3), Germany, Hungary, the Netherlands.

157 Denmark, Greece, Luxembourg, Spain.

overindebtedness.[158] Occasionally, a difficult economic situation for the debtor suffices.[159]

Finally, there are other fields of law where the term "insolvency" and its subspecies are available.[160] Examples are separate discharge laws on debt relief orders or payment plans for consumers[161] (which, in other jurisdictions, might be included in ordinary insolvency statutes) or rules in penal (or criminal) codes criminalising fraudulent bankruptcy or certain forms of preferential treatment of creditors.[162] Another example is tax law.[163] 3.13

II. SUBSPECIES OF INSOLVENCY

It follows from what has been observed so far[164] that all forms of insolvency listed above[165] occur in the national insolvency laws examined in this study. This certainly holds true for traditional liquidation proceedings[166] but can also be stated for restructuring laws.[167] However, it should be emphasised from the outset that the common use of a term in national insolvency laws does not mean that this term is understood, interpreted, and applied in the same way in all jurisdictions. We will therefore deal with these terms in greater detail in the further course of this study. At this point, it may suffice to highlight the common use of the expressions. 3.14

To begin with "inability to pay debts", this is the most common appearance of insolvency in national insolvency laws. Nearly all Member States have this expression in the vocabulary of their insolvency statutes. It is not only frequently used to characterise a reason to commence or open insolvency proceedings[168] (albeit only rarely for restructuring proceedings[169]) and as a prerequisite for challenging preferences[170] but also for demarcating the point in time where 3.15

---

158 Croatia, Italy, Luxembourg (for natural persons only), Poland, Slovakia, Slovenia. – Further Cyprus (at least as a subspecies of inability to pay debts (except for personal bankruptcies)). Basically, the same holds true for Austria. Italy accepts the likelihood of inability to pay debts (*crisi probabile*) as a reason to commence restructuring proceedings too.

159 France, Portugal, Romania, Sweden, UK; see also Austria.

160 Questionnaire Q. 11.

161 Cyprus, the Netherlands.

162 Austria, Belgium, Bulgaria, Croatia, Estonia, Finland, France, Germany, Hungary, Lithuania, Luxembourg, Poland, Portugal, Romania, Spain, the Netherlands.

163 E.g. Bulgaria, Finland, Romania.

164 In particular, *supra* at paras. 3.5 and 3.12.

165 Chapter 1 at para. 1.1.

166 Questionnaire Q. 3.

167 On them, see *supra* at para. 3.12.

168 See *supra* fn. 113.

169 References *supra* fn. 156.

170 See para. 3.10.

the directors' duties are changed.[171] It is the central and most widespread appearance of insolvency and deserves special attention, which will be paid below in Chapter 4.

3.16 Only a few countries operate with the term "cessation of payments". In Luxembourg and the Netherlands, it is a reason to open liquidation proceedings; in other jurisdictions, for bankruptcy proceedings (personal insolvencies).[172] In yet other jurisdictions, it is used as the basis of a presumption for inability to pay debts.[173] As regards restructuring, no national law refers to cessation of payments. Details on this appearance of insolvency will be explained below in Chapter 5. Apart from this, the term does not play a significant role in European insolvency law.

3.17 This is slightly different for "overindebtedness". This appearance of insolvency is – at least for legal persons – a reason to open liquidation proceedings[174] (or at least an indication of, or subspecies of, inability to pay debts[175]) and restructuring proceedings.[176] It is also used to legitimise the shift of directors' duties from shareholders to creditors.[177] In transactions avoidance law, however, overindebtedness is not a relevant prerequisite. Overall, this manifestation of insolvency plays a significantly smaller role than inability to pay debts. We will deal with it below in Chapter 7.

3.18 Likely inability to pay debts only has a limited role in liquidation proceedings. It is not used as a reason to open such insolvency proceedings[178] or as a prerequisite for transactions avoidance.[179] However, in some jurisdictions, it leads to a shift (or at least amendment) of the directors' duties.[180] Its main playing-field is restructuring law.[181] We will come back to this below in Chapter 6.

3.19 In some jurisdictions, imminent inability to pay debts is a reason to open liquidation[182] or restructuring[183] proceedings. However, apart from that, imminent inability to pay debts is rarely used in European insolvency law. Details will also be explained in Chapter 6.

---

171 See para. 3.11.
172 Details at para. 3.6.
173 See Chapter 4, at para. 4.17.
174 See fn. 115.
175 Cf. fn. 116.
176 References in fn. 158.
177 See at para. 3.11.
178 *Supra* at para. 3.6.
179 See para. 3.10.
180 Cf. para. 3.11.
181 More *supra* fn. 155.
182 Examples are available *supra* fn. 117.
183 See fn. 156.

As illustrated above,[184] some jurisdictions use additional circumstances as triggers for insolvency proceedings. However, the meaning of these rules is unclear for now and needs further exploration, which will be offered below in Chapter 4.[185] 3.20

In the foregoing paragraphs, we have shown that, in many jurisdictions, the term "insolvency" and its appearances are used in various rules of the same national law. For example, in Germany, the expression "inability to pay debts" is found both in the description of the reasons for opening insolvency proceedings and in the demarcation between insolvency proceedings and pre-insolvency restructuring proceedings, as well as in criminal law. However, in all these statutes, the term is defined in the same way and has an identical meaning. The same holds true for other jurisdictions.[186] It can generally be said that national laws define the same expression for insolvency, wherever used, identically rather than in different ways, depending on the statute the expression is contained in.[187] 3.21

III. INTERIM RESULTS

In summary, an overview of the use of the term insolvency and its subspecies already supports the need for clarification and definition of these terms. If such terms are used without a definition in European instruments, they cannot be expected to be construed and applied in a homogenous manner by national legislators and judges. Although nearly all national laws are familiar with nearly all of these expressions, the existing understandings of them from a national perspective are too different to assume that the terms are or will be used consistently in all Member States. This will be reasoned in more detail in the following chapters. Hence, detailed exploration and a proposal for a definition of the meaning of these terms when used in European law are necessary. 3.22

184 At para. 3.9.

185 Chapter 4, at para. 4.16 et seq.

186 Austria, Belgium, Bulgaria, Croatia, Czech Republic, Estonia, France, Greece, Ireland, Italy, Latvia, Lithuania, Luxembourg, the Netherlands, Portugal, Romania, Slovakia, Slovenia, Spain; in contrast, see Finland, Poland, Sweden.

187 Questionnaire Q. 12.

CHAPTER 4

INABILITY TO PAY DEBTS

I. INTRODUCTION

When dealing in more detail with the subspecies of insolvency, it is advisable to start with inability to pay debts. As has been amply documented above,[188] nearly all national insolvency laws – to some extent, Belgium, Luxembourg, and the Netherlands are exceptions[189] – are familiar with this appearance of insolvency[190] and use it at least as a reason to open regular liquidation proceedings.[191] It is accepted as a qualified, advanced stadium of the debtor's financial crisis and it is not identical to the more general term "financial difficulties"[192] (although this term is also used in many laws, albeit in the context of restructuring proceedings rather than liquidation proceedings).[193] In many jurisdictions covered by this study,[194] the term "inability to pay debts" is defined in statute,[195] albeit sometimes subject to further interpretation in case law,[196] whereas other 4.1

188 At Chapter 3, at paras. 3.5 and 3.6.
189 See Chapter 3, fn. 102; for France, see para. 3.5.
190 References *supra* in Chapter 3, fn. 102.
191 See Chapter 3, fn. 113.
192 Austria, Belgium, Bulgaria, Croatia, Cyprus, Czech Republic, Estonia, Finland, France, Germany, Greece, Hungary, Ireland, Italy, Lithuania, Luxembourg, Malta, the Netherlands, Poland, Portugal, Romania, Spain, Sweden, UK.
193 Questionnaire Q. 21.
194 Questionnaire Q. 13.
195 Bulgaria, Croatia, Cyprus, Czech Republic, Denmark, Estonia, Finland, France (see *supra* Chapter 3, at para. 3.5), Germany, Greece, Hungary, Ireland, Lithuania (for individuals), Romania, Slovakia, Slovenia, Sweden, UK.
196 Germany, Sweden.

national laws use this expression but only offer "signs of insolvency",[197] instead of a definition or leave the details to be clarified by the courts.[198] However, when comparing the details in the following paragraphs, we will not distinguish between characteristics laid down in statute and those elaborated in case law.

4.2 In EU law, the term "inability to pay debts" is used, but rarely defined. An exception is Article 38(2) Harmonisation Proposal[199] which, for the first time in European insolvency law, endeavours to define the term "insolvency" as a general inability to pay debts as they mature, albeit restricted to the context of winding-up insolvent microenterprises. In this respect, it mirrors the approach of the UNCITRAL Legislative Guide[200] which, at paragraph 12(2), defines insolvency with "when a debtor is generally unable to pay its debts as they mature". This gives first hints on how to understand "inability to pay debts", but, as will become clear in the following, it by no means answers all questions.

4.3 For the purposes of developing a common interpretation of the term "insolvency" in the European instruments,[201] it seems promising to build on this commonality, assuming that it might be the basis for a proposal for a definition that is generally acceptable to the Member States. However, this commonality appears less clear when one looks at the details. In the Member States that *do* use the concept of inability to pay debts, some typical issues are relevant, because it depends on them in detail to determine whether the debtor is insolvent or not. If, for example, certain liabilities are not taken into account when assessing the occurrence of inability to pay debts, this may lead to the conclusion that the available liquid assets are sufficient to pay the outstanding claims. As we will see below, some differences exist with respect to those issues. In the following, we will therefore examine them in more detail and clarify which liabilities (2.) and which assets (3.) are taken into account in the assessment of insolvency, which requirements are placed on the extent of the liquidity gap (4.) and on its duration (5.). Furthermore, questions of evidence must be taken into account (6.).

II. RELEVANT DEBTS

4.4 The first question to be answered concerns the liabilities that must be taken account of when assessing whether inability to pay debts exists.[202] Most national

---

197 On them, see *infra* at para. 4.16.

198 Austria, Lithuania (for legal persons), Portugal, Spain.

199 See further Art. 18(4)(c) Regulation (EU) 806/2014 (*supra* Chapter 1, fn. 25) and Art. 32(4)(c) Directive 2014/59/EU (*supra* at Chapter 1, fn. 26).

200 *Supra* Chapter 1, fn. 27.

201 See *supra* at para. 1.15.

202 Questionnaire Q. 14.

laws restrict the scope of the assessment to mature[203] debts.[204] This is an important criterion for distinguishing current insolvency from impending insolvency[205] and overindebtedness.[206] Whether a debt is mature is a matter of the applicable contract law (or law of obligations generally). We think it justified not to deal with this aspect in more detail, since this study is about the common understanding of the term "insolvency" in the European instruments and not about the harmonisation of contract law or the law of obligations in general.

However, some national laws require contingent and future liabilities to be taken into account when assessing the existence of inability to pay debts.[207] This may simply mean that a prognosis is required on how the debtor's liquidity will develop in the future.[208] However, where these legal systems simultaneously compare this broad coverage of the relevant liabilities with the value of all existing or even future assets (i.e. not only those available in the short term[209]), it is a matter of overindebtedness rather than of inability to pay debts in the sense defined here. In these countries, there is therefore a broad concept of inability to pay debts, which on the one hand includes the narrower concept used here and on the other hand that of overindebtedness. In other words, in some countries overindebtedness is either a subcategory of inability to pay debts in the broader sense[210] or the basis for a presumption that the debtor is unable to pay its due debts.[211] In the following paragraphs, we will only use the narrower definition and deal with overindebtedness separately later.[212] 4.5

In some national laws the scope of the liabilities that may be taken into account is restricted to private or public debts stemming from commercial 4.6

[203] Some national laws distinguish mature from due debts and from payable debts. We neglect these differences and understand "due", "mature", and "payable" to cover all claims that the debtor is now (i.e. at the relevant point in time) obliged to pay and the creditor could now successfully sue for.

[204] Austria, Belgium, Bulgaria, Croatia, Cyprus, Czech Republic, Denmark, Estonia, France (see *supra* Chapter 3, at para. 3.3), Germany, Greece, Hungary, Ireland, Latvia, Lithuania, Poland, Portugal, Romania, Slovakia ("overdue"), Slovenia, Spain, UK; in a different context (see *supra* Chapter 3, fn. 102) also Luxembourg. An exception is Italy.

[205] See *infra* Chapter 6, at paras. 6.8, 6.14.

[206] Details *infra* Chapter 7, at para. 7.5. – Where national laws include contingent and prospective or future liabilities in their definition of inability to pay debts, we understand this as overindebtedness being a "sign of insolvency" (see *supra* Chapter 3, fn. 116 and *infra* at para. 4.5).

[207] Cyprus, Denmark, Ireland, Malta, Sweden, UK.

[208] Denmark.

[209] See *infra* at para. 4.9.

[210] Cyprus, Ireland.

[211] Malta, UK.

[212] *Infra* Chapter 7.

or business activities.[213] This results from the general scope of the respective insolvency law, since in these jurisdictions insolvency law is part of commercial or company law and its scope covers merchants and businesses only (regardless of whether they are natural persons or legal entities/companies).

4.7 Another feature that reduces the stock of relevant liabilities is the undisputed nature of the claim. In some jurisdictions, the only claims taken into account are those which are undisputed or not seriously disputed, i.e. where it is obvious that the debtor has no viable defence and is only disputing the claim in order to avoid insolvency proceedings and to gain a reprieve.[214]

4.8 Occasionally, other restrictive characteristics can be found in the national laws. For example, such characteristics can be the exclusion of certain debts,[215] the duration of the maturity[216] (e.g. "more than 30 days overdue"[217]), the number of liabilities or creditors involved,[218] the debtor's inability to obtain credit,[219] or that the creditor has "seriously demanded" payment of the debt.[220]

III. RELEVANT ASSETS

4.9 When assessing whether a situation of inability to pay debts exists, the second step is to ascertain the relevant assets that must be taken into account.[221] Nearly all national laws which operate with the term "inability to pay debts" refer to the "acute", "available", "liquid", "present", or "quick" means or assets.[222] This means that one has to examine what financial means are available to meet

---

213 Bulgaria.
214 Cyprus, Romania, Spain.
215 E.g. fraudulent loans in France.
216 Czech Republic, Slovakia, Poland (for applying the presumption of inability to pay). For the duration of the liquidity gap, see *infra* at para. 4.9.
217 Czech Republic.
218 Czech Republic and the Netherlands (at least two creditors), Poland (at least two creditors, not applicable for consumer bankruptcy), Slovakia (at least two monetary obligations to more than one creditor).
219 Luxembourg.
220 Germany, Lithuania. In Germany, the requirements for this element are not too high. In principle, a single serious demand for payment would be sufficient since the requirement of a "serious demand" only aims to exclude such claims that have been deferred purely in fact – i.e. without an intention to be legally bound or a recognisable declaration. All that has to be presented is conduct from which the creditor's intention to demand performance from the debtor can be inferred. For such conduct, the sending of an invoice is itself sufficient.
221 Questionnaire Q. 15.
222 Austria, Belgium, Bulgaria, Cyprus, Denmark, France (see *supra* Chapter 3, at para. 3.5), Germany, Lithuania, Poland, Slovakia, Slovenia, Sweden, UK; on a case-by-case basis also Estonia. The issue is not addressed (neither in statute nor in case law) in Croatia, Greece, Hungary, Ireland.

the due debts in the short term. This includes cash at hand and in bank accounts, available committed credit lines, publicly listed shares, and other assets that can be monetised quickly.[223] In some jurisdictions, assets that will be acquired soon (e.g. future receivables for goods or services that have already been ordered) are also taken into account,[224] whereas other jurisdictions only look at assets available on the specific day for which the insolvency is determined[225] and/or take future assets into consideration when determining the liquidity gap.[226] Only a minority of the laws included in this study take all (i.e. present and future) assets into account.[227]

IV. EXTENT OF THE LIQUIDITY GAP

If the sum of the relevant mature liabilities exceeds the value of the pool of relevant assets, there is a liquidity gap and thus an inability to pay debts.[228] However, some jurisdictions, either in statute or in case law, require the liquidity gap to exceed a certain threshold.[229] The policy behind this might be that minor liquidity problems cannot justify the (sometimes immense) costs and impact of insolvency proceedings. Further, minor gaps can often be expected to be closed in the near future, which connects this feature to the topic of duration of the inability to pay debts.[230] Hence, if debtors can manage to meet the predominant part of their due debts lying beyond the threshold, they are not considered insolvent. Depending on the relevant national laws, the range extends from concrete percentages[231] (which are guidance levels rather than exact thresholds) to general terms.[232] It should be mentioned, though, that the majority of national laws do not address this question by providing for such a restriction, but instead insist on any liquidity gap to be relevant, without prejudice to an overall assessment of all circumstances of the specific individual case within the scope of the discretion granted to the courts.[233] 4.10

223 In Romania, only cash resources are taken into account; Slovakian law refers to "financial/monetary assets" and enumerates them in statute.
224 Bulgaria, Lithuania, Portugal.
225 Cyprus and the jurisdictions listed in the following footnote.
226 Austria, Estonia, Germany, Poland – see *infra* at para. 4.11.
227 Finland, Italy, Latvia, Malta, Spain.
228 Questionnaire Q. 16.
229 Austria, Belgium, Czech Republic, Germany, Lithuania, Malta, Slovakia, Sweden.
230 On the latter, see *infra* at para. 4.11.
231 5% (Austria, according to case law), 10% (Czech Republic, Germany, Slovakia).
232 "Minor gaps" (Belgium, Lithuania, Malta, Sweden).
233 Bulgaria, Denmark, Estonia, Finland, France (see *supra* at para. 3.5), Greece, Ireland, Italy, Latvia, Poland, Portugal, Romania, Spain, UK.

V. DURATION OF THE LIQUIDITY GAP

4.11 This leads us to another important characteristic of inability to pay debts: the required duration of this inability.[234] In many jurisdictions, the law – be it in statute or in case law – only accepts liquidity gaps that exceed a certain, significant time-span.[235] The policy behind this requirement might be that the opening of expensive, complex, and time-consuming insolvency proceedings is pointless if these proceedings have to be terminated after a short time because the debtor is solvent again having managed to close the liquidity gap. It may then be reasonable for creditors instead to wait for the foreseeable restoration of solvency. However, there are significant differences regarding the required length of this time-span.[236] The range extends – looking forward from the point in time for which inability to pay debts must be established – from three weeks[237] to eight weeks[238] to 60 days[239] to three or five months,[240] adjustments mostly being subject to the circumstances of the case at hand. Other jurisdictions are content with a more general approach, for example by requiring the illiquidity to be "permanent" or "persistent" (or "not being temporary", or "short-term", respectively).[241] However, a significant number of national laws have no such prerequisite[242] or leave this to the discretion of the court.[243]

4.12 It seems advisable to add a few remarks on the difference from "likely inability to pay debts" at this point.[244] Where national laws require the debtor's inability to pay debts to persist for a certain period of time, this appearance of insolvency cannot be established where the debtor is (or is likely to be) able to close the liquidity gap within this time-span. The result is therefore that there is no actual inability to pay debts and the debtor is not considered insolvent at the present time. Nevertheless, the debtor may be regarded as likely or imminently unable to pay its debts[245] when they fall due if a liquidity gap has not yet arisen but is

234 Questionnaire Q. 17.

235 Austria, Czech Republic, Denmark, Estonia, Finland, Germany, Lithuania, Slovakia, Slovenia, Spain.

236 In the following, we disregard time-span elements which are part of "signs of insolvency" (on these, see *infra* at para. 4.16), e.g. payment delay for more than 60 days (Romania) or three months (Poland), neglecting to pay a statutory demand for more than three weeks (Cyprus) or an execution for more than 24 weeks (Malta).

237 Germany.

238 Czech Republic.

239 Slovakia, Slovenia.

240 Austria.

241 Belgium, Bulgaria, Croatia, Denmark, Estonia, Finland, Greece, Lithuania, Luxembourg, Poland (according to generally accepted interpretation), Spain, Sweden.

242 Cyprus, France (see *supra* Chapter 3, at para. 3.5), Hungary, Italy, Latvia, Poland, Romania.

243 Ireland, Malta, Portugal, UK.

244 Questionnaire Q. 18. This aspect is irrelevant for those laws that rely entirely on the "signs of insolvency" (see fn. 236), e.g. Latvia, Malta.

245 For details of this appearance of insolvency, see *infra* Chapter 6.

likely to occur.[246] In just a few jurisdictions the debtor can – depending on the concrete circumstances of the case at hand – be considered presently illiquid if it is foreseeable that the liquidity gap will soon occur.[247] Against this background, it is safe to say that most jurisdictions[248] reserve this term (i.e. inability to pay debts) to the debtor's current, and not its future, situation.[249] On the other hand, the question of whether the current illiquidity is reversible or irreversible plays a role at best in the required duration of the liquidity gap.[250] Apart from that, a reversible illiquidity is also a current illiquidity,[251] which admittedly gives the debtor reason to think about preventive restructuring measures.

VI. ESTABLISHING INABILITY TO PAY DEBTS

Where the opening of insolvency proceedings requires a court decision (or a decision by any other authority) and this decision shall be based on inability to pay debts, this reason for the opening of insolvency proceedings needs to be established. In most jurisdictions, the court must assess this *ex officio*[252] (which does not exclude the assistance of an interim Insolvency Practitioner, if appointed, or of an expert witness commissioned by the court). Whether a situation of inability to pay debts exists, in most jurisdictions, is not subject to party autonomy, meaning that it is for the judge to decide whether inability to pay has occurred, and parties cannot bind the judge by agreeing upon it.[253] Regardless of whether an application (filed by the debtor or a creditor) is required and whether it is the task of the procedural parties or the court to obtain the 4.13

246 This is the legal situation in Austria, Croatia, Estonia, Germany, Hungary, Italy, Lithuania, Poland, Portugal, Romania, Slovakia, Slovenia, Spain, and the UK, presumably also in the Czech Republic and Greece. Naturally, this holds not true for those jurisdictions that are not familiar with the concept of likely or imminent inability to pay debts in insolvency (liquidation) proceedings (Bulgaria, Cyprus, Ireland).

247 Denmark, Finland, Sweden.

248 Questionnaire Q. 22.

249 Austria, Belgium, Bulgaria, Croatia, Czech Republic, Finland, Germany, Greece, Hungary, Italy, Latvia, Lithuania, the Netherlands, Poland, Portugal, Romania, Slovenia, Spain. Note, however, that in some jurisdictions contingent and future liabilities are taken into account, which refers to "overindebtedness" rather than "inability to pay debts". See *supra* at para. 4.5.

250 See *supra* at para. 4.9. In Belgium and Luxembourg, the debtor's credit may not be impaired (see *supra* Chapter 3, fn. 102).

251 Austria, Czech Republic, Germany, Hungary, Italy, Latvia, Lithuania, Portugal, Romania, Slovenia, Spain, Sweden. In contrast, some countries take the view that reversible insolvency is only temporary (Bulgaria, Greece, Poland) or likely (Finland) or relevant within the discretion of the court (Ireland, Malta, UK).

252 Questionnaire Q. 20.

253 Austria, Belgium, Bulgaria, Croatia, Cyprus, Czech Republic, Denmark, Estonia, Finland, France (see *supra* Chapter 3, at para. 3.3), Germany, Greece, Italy, Luxembourg, Malta, Poland, Portugal, Romania, Slovakia, Slovenia; differently Sweden.

information necessary for reaching a decision, the court must in any case be convinced that there is inability to pay debts. The mere assertion by a petitioning creditor or debtor is generally not sufficient. Only a few national laws have opted for a certain degree of party autonomy,[254] for placing the burden of proof on the debtor,[255] or for providing that the court may assume the debtor's insolvency without further examination if the debtor him- or herself files for insolvency proceedings or the directors of the company make a corresponding declaration because there is then a presumption of insolvency.[256]

4.14 Things are different, however, where "inability to pay debts" is a prerequisite for an individual claim contested in court between two opposing parties. For example, where a payment to a creditor is challenged by the Insolvency Practitioner after the opening of insolvency proceedings, under transactions avoidance law, and the relevant norm requires the debtor to be substantively insolvent at the relevant point in time, the court will not examine this prerequisite *ex officio*. Instead, it is the task of the party bearing the burden of proof to convince the court of the debtor's inability to pay debts through the general means of evidence under the applicable procedural law.[257]

4.15 It follows from what has been explained above that establishing inability to pay debts can be a burdensome task.[258] In particular, for creditors who want to file an insolvency petition and need to show that the debtor is insolvent (in the sense of unable to pay its mature debts), it can be difficult, if not impossible, to obtain the necessary information on mature liabilities on the one hand and on the existence and value of liquid assets on the other hand. Hence, a formal liquidity status ("liquidity balance sheet", to be distinguished from the ordinary annual balance sheet) in many jurisdictions, is a possible and ideal piece of evidence in the hands of the debtor or the Insolvency Practitioner, but it is not invariably required.[259] In some jurisdictions, the same holds true for proof by a sample of daily liquidity data which do not amount to a proper liquidity status but show insufficient available funds on different days within a certain period of time.[260]

---

[254] Ireland, Latvia, UK.

[255] Hungary (for the debtor's petition), Lithuania, Slovakia.

[256] Estonia, Finland. In Spain, this is only the case if a creditor's application for insolvency proceedings is not opposed by the debtor.

[257] For details, see *Bork/Veder* (Chapter 1, fn. 40), para. 4.286 et seq.

[258] Questionnaire Q. 19.

[259] This applies to Austria, Belgium, Bulgaria, Croatia, Cyprus, Czech Republic, Estonia, Finland, France, Germany, Greece, Ireland, Italy, Latvia, Lithuania, Malta, Poland, Portugal, Slovakia, Sweden, UK. In contrast are applications by the debtor to open insolvency proceedings Bulgaria, Estonia, Hungary, Romania.

[260] Possible, but not necessary in Austria, Croatia, Finland, France, Germany, Portugal, Sweden. Not sufficient in Bulgaria, Cyprus, Czech Republic, Estonia, Hungary, Ireland, Italy, Latvia, Lithuania, Luxembourg, Malta, Poland, Romania, Slovakia, Spain, UK.

Instead, most jurisdictions operate with presumptions.[261] These can be statutory or may have been developed in case law, and they can be either rebuttable or irrebuttable.[262] In liquidation or restructuring proceedings, typical circumstances that trigger such presumptions – also labelled "signs" or "features of insolvency" – are: 4.16

- the debtor's acknowledgement of insolvency or filing for insolvency proceedings;[263]
- lack of payment within a certain time-span after the creditor's claim becoming mature;[264]
- lack of payment to a petitioning creditor within a certain period of time after a reminder or payment notice[265] or statutory[266] demand;[267]
- lack of payment within a certain time-span after the commencement of individual enforcement;[268]
- non-compliance with a final judgment;[269]
- lack of payment to employees;[270]
- lack of payment to public creditors;[271]
- lack of payment to credit institutions;[272]
- lack of payment to creditor secured by mortgage;[273]
- enforcement of claims by public creditors;[274]

---

261 Austria, Bulgaria, Croatia, Cyprus, Czech Republic, Estonia, Finland, Germany, Greece, Ireland, Italy, Latvia, Malta, Poland, Portugal, Romania, Slovakia, Slovenia, Spain, UK. In Hungary, these circumstances serve as stand-alone reasons to open insolvency proceedings rather than as the bases of presumptions of inability to pay debts.

262 All or some presumptions are irrebuttable in Cyprus, Hungary, Latvia, and Spain.

263 Denmark, Estonia, Finland, Romania, Spain, Sweden; see also Austria.

264 Croatia (more than €2,656 and 90 days, albeit for consumers only), Czech Republic (three months), Latvia (two months), Poland (three months), Romania (60/90 days and €10,000), Slovenia (two months, 20% of all liabilities). Similarly Portugal (no concrete time-span but reference to the circumstances of the case at hand).

265 Sweden (one week and creditor applies for insolvency proceedings within three week).

266 A "statutory demand" is a term of art in common law countries where the insolvency statutes impose certain formal requirements for the demand, for example the use of a specific form or service by an official person or at a more closely defined address of the debtor.

267 Cyprus (three weeks and more than €5,000); Finland (one week); Hungary (20 days and €530), Ireland (21 days and more than €10,000/20,000), Latvia (three weeks and more than €2,134/4,268), UK (three weeks and more than £750). This, by the way, is heavily criticised in Hungary (Questionnaire Q. 56).

268 Croatia (60 days for execution on bank accounts), Denmark and Estonia (three months), Bulgaria, Finland, and Sweden (six months), Malta (24 weeks).

269 Hungary, UK.

270 Croatia (three consecutive months' salaries), Latvia, Portugal (more than six months), Spain (more than three months).

271 Greece (at least 40% of all due debts, these exceeding €30,000, for more than six months); Portugal (more than six months), Spain (more than three months).

272 Greece (at least 40% of all due debts, these exceeding €30,000, for more than six months).

273 Portugal (more than six months).

274 Austria (although strictly speaking only applicable on restructuring proceedings).

- lack of complete satisfaction by way of individual enforcement;[275]
- non-performance of a payment or restructuring plan adopted in previous proceedings;[276]
- existence of previous failed insolvency or bankruptcy proceedings;[277]
- lack of necessary announcements in the commercial or company register;[278]
- failure to submit the audited financial statements;[279]
- lack of unencumbered assets;[280]
- dissipation, abandonment, hasty or ruinous liquidation of assets;[281]
- fictitious creation of assets;[282]
- the debtor's hiding from creditors;[283]
- the debtor's suicide.[284]

These "signs of insolvency" are mostly evidence of inability to pay debts rather than autonomous reasons to commence insolvency proceedings (i.e. they are not stand-alone appearances of insolvency).[285] In other words, they are of a procedural rather than a substantive nature.

4.17 An important basis of a presumption of inability to pay debts, available in many jurisdictions,[286] is cessation of payments (although, in Belgium and the Netherlands, it is just the other way around: inability to pay debts is just an appearance of cessation of payments[287]). We will deal with this in more detail below.[288]

4.18 Alongside these presumptions, a long list of circumstantial evidence of inability to pay debts (or, alternatively, of cessation of payments), developed in case law and literature, is available in some jurisdictions.[289] These circumstances are indirect evidence of inability to pay debts rather than statutory presumptions. For

---

275 Czech Republic, Hungary, Portugal, Romania, Slovenia (60 days); also for enforcement of judgments Cyprus, Ireland, UK.
276 Denmark, Hungary, Portugal, Slovenia.
277 Hungary, Spain.
278 Bulgaria (within the last three years).
279 Portugal (more than nine months). A similar mechanism is available in Hungary.
280 Portugal, Spain.
281 Portugal; Spain.
282 Portugal.
283 Italy, Portugal.
284 Italy.
285 Only Hungary differs in this respect; see *supra* fn. 261.
286 Austria, Bulgaria, Croatia, Czech Republic, Denmark, Finland, Germany, Poland, Portugal, Spain, Sweden. In Lithuania and Romania, cessation of payments is recognised as circumstantial evidence.
287 See *supra* fn. 102.
288 In Chapter 5.
289 Austria, Belgium, Finland, Germany, Lithuania, Romania.

example, in Germany, the Federal Supreme Court – and in other jurisdictions, similar circumstances are referred to – resorts to the following:

- the debtor's confession to having ceased payments or to being unable to pay debts;
- pressure by creditors through massive reminders and/or enforcement;
- sluggish payments to existentially important creditors (i.e. creditors on whose continued supply the continuation of the debtor's business operations crucially depends);
- non-payment of a substantial part of due liabilities (even if it is just one single but substantial claim);
- (several months of) non-payment of social security contributions;
- putting off payment of a substantial amount of arrears for as long as possible (not merely delaying payments);
- not responding to invoices and reminders;
- informing a major creditor of the liquidity issues;
- closing the business premises;
- escaping from creditors (e.g. by fleeing the country);
- recovery by suppliers of goods subject to retention of title;
- bounced cheques;
- a failed attempt at a direct debit (because the debtor has insufficient funds available);
- strategic partial payments (to the most pressing creditors only);
- slow payment of wages and salaries;
- a debtor's request for payment in instalments subsequent to the conclusion of the original contract agreements, that are not customary for the business;
- non-compliance with instalment payment agreements (as referred to under the previous bullet point).

VII. INTERIM RESULTS

It follows from the above that "inability to pay debts" is the most common appearance of insolvency. It denotes a qualified form of the debtor's financial crisis, refers to the present situation, and is therefore to be distinguished from future – currently only likely – inability to pay debts. 4.19

CHAPTER 5

CESSATION OF PAYMENTS

I. INTRODUCTION

Closely related to inability to pay debts (as discussed above in Chapter 4) is another appearance of insolvency: cessation of payments (occasionally also labelled "suspension of payments"). We have already seen[290] that this term is used in many – but by no means all[291] – jurisdictions, albeit with different functions. In Belgium, Luxembourg, and in the Netherlands,[292] this is the only autonomous reason to commence liquidation proceedings. In Greece it is one reason among others.[293] Other national laws[294] use it as the basis of a presumption of inability to pay debts[295] or at least as circumstantial evidence,[296] whereas in Belgium and the Netherlands it is just the other way around (inability to pay debts as an appearance of cessation of payments[297]). Against this background, we have to deal with the definition (Section II.) and the establishment (Section III.) of cessation of payments. 5.1

---

290 Further to Questionnaire Q. 24.

291 The term is unknown in the laws of in Cyprus, Estonia, Ireland, Italy, Latvia, Lithuania, Malta, Slovakia, Slovenia, UK; see *supra* Chapter 3, fn. 104.

292 References *supra* in fn. 102; for France, see *supra* Chapter 3, at para. 3.5.

293 Questionnaire Q. 25.

294 Questionnaire Q. 26.

295 Austria, Bulgaria, Croatia, Czech Republic, Denmark, Finland, Germany, Poland, Portugal, Spain, Sweden. See also *supra* Chapter 4, at para. 4.17.

296 Lithuania, Romania; cf. *supra* Chapter 4, fn. 286.

297 See *supra* Chapter 3, fn. 102. In the Netherlands, mere non-payment without good reason suffices. This means that a debtor can be declared insolvent if he or she is able to pay but does not.

II. DEFINITION

5.2 When evaluating the national reports,[298] a remarkable conceptual blurring can be observed. Some national laws define "cessation of payments" as "inability to pay debts",[299] i.e. no differences between the two terms are visible. This also seems to be the approach taken in the Harmonisation Proposal, which, in its Recital 37, reads: "The cessation of payments test and the balance sheet test are the two usual triggers among Member States for opening of standard insolvency proceedings." This appears to be either wrong (since most Member States accept "inability to pay debts" rather than "cessation of payments" as a reason to open standard liquidation proceedings[300]) or conceptually fuzzy (since "cessation of payments" is not the same as "inability to pay debts").

5.3 However, things become a little clearer when looking at the UNCITRAL Legislative Guide.[301] Here, at paragraph 23, the text deals with the "liquidity, cash flow or general cessation of payments test". At first glance, cessation of payments is also equated here with inability to pay debts. However, if one reads more closely, one realises that the test under discussion is essentially about how a creditor, who – unlike the debtor – has no insight into the debtor's factual stock of due liabilities and immediately available liquid assets, should be able to prove the debtor's insolvency. The Legislative Guide lists "indicators of a debtor's general cessation of payments [which] may include its failure to pay rent, taxes, salaries, employee benefits, trade accounts payable and other essential business costs", and continues: "As such, this test puts the defining factors within the reach of creditors." This proves that "cessation of payments" is a more factual approach to the debtor's insolvency.

5.4 When analysing the answers to our questionnaire, it turns out that only a few national laws present an entirely independent definition, albeit in case law rather than in statute. Under Czech case law, for example, cessation of payments is defined as

> the debtor's intentional action, its decision, to no longer pay its monetary obligations, usually accompanied by a declaration that the debtor will not pay. It shall suffice if the debtor does this with at least a substantial part of its obligations.[302]

In Finland, it is emphasised that the suspension of payments should be "general" (i.e. not only regarding payments to one creditor or a couple of them) and not include disputed claims (provided, of course, that the reason for the dispute

[298] Questionnaire Q. 27.
[299] France, Greece.
[300] Details *supra* at paras. 3.6 and 5.1.
[301] *Supra* fn. 27.
[302] Czech Supreme Court, *In re Oleo Chemical*, case no. 29 NSČR 24/2013, of 30 April 2015.

is not manifestly inadequate). Similarly, in Belgium, Luxembourg, and Spain, the cessation of payments must be definitive, general, irreversible, persistent, or present, and sometimes related to due and undisputed claims. In Germany, cessation of payments is defined in case law as

> the external behaviour of the debtor in which an inability to pay is typically expressed. The relevant public must have the justified impression that the debtor is not in a position to fulfil his or her due payment obligations. Whether this is the case, depends on a comprehensive evaluation of all relevant circumstances.[303]

In all, it should be noted that none of the insolvency laws included in this study offers a clear and precise definition of "cessation of payments". It is probably fair to say that this term either is equated with "inability to pay debts" or is based on comparable characteristics (particularly the non-payment of the predominant part of all due and undisputed debts). Ultimately, this amounts to the insight that, by using the term "cessation of payments" as a prerequisite, legislators are linking factually to the debtor's actual behaviour (namely the non-payment of due liabilities), whereas with "inability to pay debts" it is linking normatively to an advanced phase of the debtor's financial crisis.[304] The former means that the debtor is (or is presumed to be) insolvent because he or she *does not* pay (regardless of whether he or she is unable or only unwilling to pay), the latter means that the debtor is insolvent because he or she *cannot* pay even if some creditors are still satisfied by certain payments. In other words, the former is fact-related, the latter feature-related. 5.5

III. ESTABLISHING CESSATION OF PAYMENTS

The unclear definition corresponds to the fundamental lack of procedural facilitation of proof. In most jurisdictions, cessation of payments can only be established by applying the regular rules of evidence according to the law of civil procedure.[305] However, circumstantial evidence is generally possible; often, the same circumstances are relevant as for establishing inability to pay debts.[306] It is only in the Netherlands (where the burden of proof is eased to the extent that cessation of payments must only be summarily established by means of a brief, simple examination) and in Poland (where cessation of payments is presumed if the delay in meeting monetary obligations exceeds three months) that special rules apply. 5.6

303 German Federal Supreme Court (BGH), 6.5.2021 – IX ZR 72/20, BGHZ 230, 28 para. 15.
304 See also *infra* Chapter 8, at para. 8.39.
305 Austria, Belgium, Bulgaria, Czech Republic, Finland, France, Germany, Greece, Hungary, Luxembourg, Portugal, Romania, Spain, Sweden.
306 See *supra* Chapter 4, at para. 4.18.

IV. INTERIM RESULTS

5.7 In summing up then, for many jurisdictions, the concrete demarcation between cessation of payments and inability to pay debts remains unclear. Both deal with the same topic, namely the non-payment of (the predominant part of) the due (mature) debts, yet they approach this topic from different sides. "Cessation of payments" starts with the facts perceivable not only by the debtor but also by creditors and third parties; "inability to pay debts" starts with an analysis of the positive and negative components of the debtor's estate and its financial data.

CHAPTER 6

LIKELY AND IMMINENT INABILITY TO PAY DEBTS

I. INTRODUCTION

The present chapter deals with two other appearances of insolvency: likely (or probable or possible or foreseeable) and imminent (or threatening) inability to pay debts. Both terms refer to the debtor's future financial situation and imply that the debtor is currently still able to pay its mature debts but will probably become unable to do so within a foreseeable period. As we have already seen above,[307] one or both terms are available in many, albeit not all,[308] Member States of the EU,[309] sometimes in the context of liquidation proceedings, sometimes in the context of restructuring proceedings. To be more precise, 10 legislators have decided to use "likely inability to pay debts",[310] eight of them to use "imminent inability to pay debts",[311] and five national laws are familiar with both terms.[312] 6.1

307 Chapter 3, at para. 3.18.

308 Not in France, Latvia, Luxembourg.

309 Questionnaire Q. 31.

310 Cyprus, the Czech Republic (see Chapter 3, fn. 108), Denmark, Estonia, Ireland, Italy, the Netherlands, Slovenia; further Malta ("imminently likely to become unable to pay its debts"); UK ("likely to become unable to pay its debts").

311 Austria, Belgium, Bulgaria, Croatia, Finland, Germany, Poland (see Chapter 3, fn. 108), Portugal.

312 Greece, Hungary, Romania, Spain, Sweden.

6.2 "Likelihood of insolvency" is also available in EU law[313] and mentioned in the UNCITRAL Legislative Guide.[314] Both legal frameworks do not offer a definition of this term, though. Instead, they refer to national laws[315] or are completely silent on this matter. In the end, the meaning of these terms is far from clear, and it is necessary to look more closely at the definition of both terms (Section II.) and at the establishment of this prerequisite (Section III.).

II. DEFINITION

6.3 In many jurisdictions, "likely inability to pay debts" or "imminent inability to pay debts" is – if at all – defined in case law and literature rather than in statute.[316] However, in Bulgaria, Croatia, the Czech Republic, Estonia, Finland, Germany, Hungary, Italy, Lithuania, Poland, Slovakia, Slovenia, and Spain, a statutory definition is available. As regards the content of these definitions, one would guess, as a first approach, that "likely" and "imminent" inability to pay are not the same. Instead, one would assume that "likely" is a term of probability whereas "imminent" is a term of urgency, the latter being characterised by a significantly shorter time perspective than the former. However, this is not – or at least not consistently – the case. When analysing national laws, it turns out that some national laws equate "likely" with "imminent" (or *vice versa*).[317] A good example is Austria, where §6(2) Restrukturierungsordnung reads: "Likely insolvency exists if the existence of the debtor's company would be endangered without restructuring, in particular in the case of imminent inability to pay debts." In other jurisdictions, there is no awareness of the distinction between likely and imminent inability to pay debts. For example, Germany transposed Article 4(1) of the Directive on restructuring and insolvency[318] ("Member States shall ensure that, where there is a likelihood of insolvency, debtors have access to a preventive restructuring framework …") with the wording "For the sustainable elimination of an imminent insolvency within the meaning of section 18(2) of the Insolvency Code, the procedural aids of the stabilisation and restructuring framework (instruments) referred to in paragraph 2 may be used".[319] However, regarding the possible occurrence of inability to pay debts within the foreseeable

313 Examples are Arts. 1(1)(a), 3(1), 4(1), 19 Directive on restructuring and insolvency (*supra* Chapter 1, fn. 21); Art. 23 Harmonisation Proposal (*supra* Chapter 1, fn. 1).

314 *Supra* Chapter 1, fn. 27, p. 244, Recommendation 160 in the context of restructuring proceedings only.

315 See Art. 2(2)(b) Directive on restructuring and insolvency (*supra* Chapter 1, fn. 21).

316 Questionnaire Q. 34.

317 Austria, Finland, Lithuania, Ireland.

318 *Supra* fn. 21.

319 §29(1) Act on the Stabilisation and Restructuring Framework for Enterprises, StaRUG.

future, §18(2) sentence 2 Insolvency Code (InsO) provides for a prognosis period of two years. This is clear evidence that the German legislator does not distinguish between "likely" and "imminent" inability to pay debts and defines "imminent" as a term of probability, not of urgency. Against this background, it seems advisable to distinguish between both terms as follows.

1. LIKELY INABILITY TO PAY DEBTS

Before going into the details of likely inability to pay debts, a possible misunderstanding of this term should be avoided. As explained above,[320] some national laws provide for "signs of insolvency", i.e. standardised circumstances upon which a rebuttable or irrebuttable presumption is founded that the debtor is unable to pay his or her debts. For example, where, as in Latvia, the debtor's insolvency is irrebuttably presumed if he or she has neither paid nor disputed a due sum of more than €4,268, demanded by the creditor in the prescribed way,[321] one might argue that, under these circumstances, it is most likely that the debtor is unable to pay its debts. However, this assumption refers to the *present* financial state of the debtor (which is likely to exist) and not to the *future* inability to pay debts (which is likely to occur). In the context of this study, the legal term "likely inability to pay debts" characterises the future deterioration of the financial resources of a debtor that is currently not in a state of inability to pay, and hence refers to a situation that is likely to occur in the future. 6.4

a) *Prognosis*

If the term, or a similar term to, "likely inability to pay debts" deals with the future development of the debtor's financial affairs, then a forecast must necessarily be made as to how the debtor's ability to pay will develop.[322] The term "likely" as such already implies that a prognosis is required and most jurisdictions that have this term in their laws require such a forecast.[323] This does not mean that a formal prognostic calculation is necessary; it only means that the near future, i.e. the coming months or years, is taken into account and that it must be assessed whether the debtor is likely to become unable to pay its due debts within this period of time. 6.5

---

320 Chapter 4, at para. 4.16.

321 Art. 57(1), No. 2 Latvian Insolvency Act.

322 Questionnaire Q. 35.

323 Cyprus, the Czech Republic, Estonia, Greece, Ireland, Italy, Lithuania, the Netherlands, Romania, Slovenia, Spain, Sweden.

6.6 As regards the length of the prognosis period,[324] the national insolvency laws show a colourful picture. Insofar as specific time periods are mentioned at all, they range from two years[325] to one year[326] to three months.[327] The latter is rather short and would justify allocating this to "imminent" rather than to "likely" inability to pay debts. Other jurisdictions have abstained from fleshing out the prognosis period by providing for any specific intervals. Instead, they either stipulate that the time-span should be "short"[328] or leave it entirely undefined.[329]

6.7 Since nobody is able to predict the future, a prognosis is necessarily subject to some uncertainty.[330] However, most jurisdictions leave this to the discretion of the court,[331] whereas others require a specific degree of certainty, be it by using the phrase "more likely than not",[332] or be it by requiring a "predominant probability", i.e. a probability of more than 50%.[333] Less precisely, some national laws refer to a "substantial likelihood"[334] or require a "sufficient" degree of certainty.[335]

b) Relevant Factors

6.8 For the arithmetic side, the question arises as to which liabilities and which assets are to be taken into account.[336] It is in the very nature of things that not only the existing debts that are and will be left unpaid but also the future debts must be taken into account, at least if it is to be expected with the necessary degree of certainty that such future debts will come into existence and mature before the end of the prognosis period. Thus, not surprisingly, this is reflected in nearly all national laws which use the term "likely inability to pay debts".[337]

6.9 The same holds true for the asset side of the liquidity plan, since present and future debts (coming into existence and falling due during the prognosis period)

324 Questionnaire Q. 35.
325 Romania (albeit for preventive restructuring proceedings only), Spain.
326 Cyprus, Italy, Slovenia.
327 Lithuania.
328 Sweden.
329 The Czech Republic, Denmark, Estonia, Greece, Hungary, Ireland, the Netherlands, UK.
330 Questionnaire Q. 36.
331 Cyprus, the Czech Republic, Estonia, Greece, Hungary, Ireland, Italy, the Netherlands, Slovenia.
332 UK (albeit in case law, not in statute).
333 Romania, Spain.
334 Lithuania.
335 Sweden.
336 Questionnaire Qs. 37–39.
337 Cyprus, the Czech Republic, Estonia, Greece, Hungary, Italy, Lithuania, Malta, the Netherlands, Romania, Spain, Sweden, UK; in contrast see Slovenia.

are harmless as long as they are covered by assets available when the debts mature. Consequently, national laws consider all those assets which presently exist (and will still be available) and those which, with the necessary grade of certainty, will come into existence during the prognosis period.[338]

2. IMMINENT INABILITY TO PAY DEBTS

Similar observations can be made for the term "imminent inability to pay debts". 6.10

a) *Prognosis*

As regards the necessity of a prognosis,[339] most jurisdictions which refer to this term require such a forecast,[340] even if it is not always clear whether this is a legal requirement or whether this necessity follows more from the nature of the matter. Only in Hungary, in the context of wrongful trading litigation, is imminent inability to pay debts assessed retrospectively from the perspective of the insolvency that eventually occurred, which renders the requirement of a prognosis superfluous.[341] 6.11

The duration of the prognosis period[342] varies considerably. Whilst the time-span is entirely undefined in some jurisdictions,[343] other national laws provide for concretisations ranging from "a short time"[344] to three months[345] to one year[346] up to two years.[347] At least the latter proves that there is no clear distinction in those jurisdictions between likely and imminent inability to pay debts.[348] 6.12

Concerning the necessary degree of certainty as to whether inability to pay debts will occur during the prognosis period,[349] the picture is colourful again. Some national laws are quite specific in requiring a predominant probability, i.e. that the occurrence is more likely than not, which amounts to a degree of certainty of 6.13

---

338 The Czech Republic, Estonia, Greece, Hungary, Italy, Lithuania, the Netherlands, Romania, Spain, Sweden; differently Slovenia. Interestingly, in the UK, future liabilities (see *supra* fn. 337) but not future assets are taken into account.

339 Questionnaire Q. 35.

340 Austria, Bulgaria, Finland, Germany, Greece, Poland, Portugal, Romania, Slovakia, Spain, Sweden; differently in Belgium, Croatia.

341 Hungary.

342 Questionnaire Q. 35.

343 Finland, Greece, Portugal, Romania.

344 Poland (which is interpreted with "up to six months"), Sweden.

345 Spain.

346 Austria, Bulgaria, Hungary, Slovakia.

347 Germany.

348 See already *supra* at para. 6.3.

349 Questionnaire Q. 36.

at least 50.1%.[350] However, other jurisdictions are rather vague in demanding that there is a "danger" or "threat" of inability to pay debts[351] or that the occurrence is "sufficiently"[352] probable or with a higher degree of probability than required for likely inability to pay debts.[353] Not surprisingly, most jurisdictions refrain from making a concrete determination and leave this to the discretion of the court in the individual case to be decided.[354]

b) *Relevant Factors*

6.14 When determining the relevant debts and assets,[355] the approaches are very similar to those regarding the establishment of likely inability to pay debts.[356] On the liability side, nearly all jurisdictions that refer to imminent inability to pay debts include all debts that presently are and still will be due and those coming into existence and falling due with the necessary probability during the prognosis period.[357] This is mirrored on the asset side, since typically all assets are included that will be available (i.e. present or to be acquired with the necessary probability) during the prognosis period.[358]

6.15 Interestingly, and in contrast to the results obtained for likely inability to pay debts (where this topic is not addressed in the national reports), there are sometimes variations in the necessary liquidity gap. As elaborated above,[359] some jurisdictions require the liquidity gap to exceed a certain threshold. However, two of these national laws decide differently in respect to future liquidity gaps relevant in the context of imminent inability to pay debts.[360]

III. ESTABLISHING LIKELY/IMMINENT INABILITY TO PAY DEBTS

6.16 The last topic to be addressed in this chapter is the requirements for establishing likely or imminent inability to pay debts.[361] The situation is special in that

---

350 Austria, Germany, Slovakia.
351 Finland (danger); Poland (threat); for Hungary see *supra* fn. 341.
352 Sweden.
353 Romania.
354 Bulgaria, Croatia, Greece, Portugal, Spain.
355 Questionnaire Qs. 37–39.
356 On the latter, see *supra* at para. 6.8 et seq.
357 Austria, Bulgaria, Croatia, Finland, Germany, Greece, Poland, Portugal, Slovakia, Spain, Sweden. In Romania, currently not due debts are considered, but not non-existing debts.
358 Austria, Finland, Germany, Greece, Poland, Portugal, Romania, Slovakia, Spain, Sweden. The issue is not addressed in Bulgaria.
359 Chapter 4, at para. 4.10.
360 Austria.
361 Questionnaire Q. 40.

these subtypes of insolvency are often used by legislators in connection with restructuring proceedings. In this context, national restructuring laws may provide that these proceedings are only available upon application of the debtor, who must then explain the restructuring prospects and submit extensive documentation on his or her current and future financial situation, which can be done by delivering a concrete liquidity plan.[362] In Croatia, imminent inability to pay debts can be derived from certain irrebuttable presumptions. Apart from that, no special means are provided for. Instead, the ordinary rules of evidence (including the commissioning of an expert witness or auditor and also circumstantial evidence) apply according to the law of civil procedure.[363] It is only in rare cases that a summary decision of the court[364] or a low threshold[365] is provided for.

IV. INTERIM RESULTS

In all, the definition of likely and imminent inability to pay debts in Europe is far from clear. The overview given above illustrates that the dividing line between the two terms is not, or at least not sufficiently, clearly drawn. It is at least fair to say that a certain terminological confusion prevails. On the other hand, many commonalities are visible. In the vast majority of national laws, a prognosis is required for both appearances of insolvency, although the length of the prognosis period and the required degree of certainty that inability to pay will occur vary significantly for both terms. However, there is always widespread agreement that not only the current but also the future liabilities and assets must be taken into account in the calculation to be prepared for the forecast period. This concerns, on the one hand, debts that come into existence and that mature during the relevant time-span and, on the other hand, assets that the debtor is likely to acquire during the prognosis period with the necessary degree of certainty. 6.17

362 Austria, Belgium, Denmark, Germany, Poland, Romania, Slovakia.
363 Cyprus, the Czech Republic, Estonia, Finland, Germany, Greece, Hungary, Ireland, Italy, Lithuania, Portugal, Slovenia, Spain.
364 Hungary (for likely inability to pay debts).
365 Sweden.

CHAPTER 7

OVERINDEBTEDNESS

I. INTRODUCTION

7.1 The last subspecies of insolvency to be included in this survey is overindebtedness (sometimes also labelled as "balance sheet insolvency"[366]). We have already seen[367] that this category is available (but sometimes subject to opposition as to its necessity[368] or efficiency[369]) in many[370] but by no means all[371] jurisdictions covered by this study. It is sometimes expressly mentioned,[372] sometimes indirectly referred to, e.g. by including non-mature, contingent, and future liabilities within the scope of the assessment whether inability to pay debts exists.[373] It serves mostly as an autonomous reason to open liquidation (or, less frequently, restructuring[374]) proceedings[375] but occasionally as the

---

366 On this, see Chapter 8 *infra*, at para. 8.77.

367 Chapter 3 *supra*, at para. 3.5.

368 Abolishment is discussed in Austria, and Germany, not least because it is seen as an obstacle to restructuring.

369 Criticised in Bulgaria, Cyprus, Estonia, Poland.

370 Austria, Bulgaria, Croatia, Cyprus, Czech Republic, Denmark, Estonia, Finland, Germany, Hungary, Ireland, Italy, Lithuania, Malta, Poland, Portugal, Slovakia, Slovenia, Sweden, UK (see Chapter 3, fn. 106); for individual insolvencies also in France and Luxembourg.

371 Not available in Greece, Latvia, the Netherlands, Romania, Spain; in company law only in Belgium.

372 Austria, Bulgaria, Croatia, Czech Republic, Estonia, Finland, France, Germany, Hungary, Italy, Lithuania, Luxembourg, Poland, Portugal, Slovakia, Slovenia, Sweden.

373 Cyprus, Ireland, Malta, Sweden, UK; see Chapter 4 *supra*, at para. 4.5.

374 See Chapter 3 *supra*, at para. 3.12.

375 Austria, Croatia, the Czech Republic, Estonia, Finland, Germany, Hungary (for debtor applications only), Italy, Lithuania, Poland, Portugal, Slovakia, Slovenia; for insolvency proceedings (which include liquidation and restructuring proceedings) also Bulgaria, for individual insolvencies also in France and Luxembourg.

basis of a presumption of, circumstantial evidence of, or a "sign of" insolvency only.[376, 377]

7.2 In a first approach, overindebtedness means (at least in a commercial sense) that the value of all the debtor's assets is less than the amount of all the debtor's liabilities. This corresponds to the wording in the UNCITRAL Legislative Guide on Insolvency Law.[378] As distinguished from inability to pay debts, not only the due debts and not only the liquid assets are taken into account. The test is rather whether the debtor's total pool of assets, in the event of a liquidation of those assets, would be sufficient to pay all the debts to which those assets are liable, including those that have not yet fallen due, are still subject to conditions precedent, or have not yet been (fully) incurred. However, one may assume that most enterprises would not stand up to this test because the liquidation value of the assets is in most cases not sufficient to meet all liabilities. Hence, two questions arise. First, is it correct to assess the assets through their liquidation value (or should it rather be the book value or the going concern value)? Second, should this "value of the estate" test be accompanied by a prognosis serving as a corrective (since it does not seem appropriate to put a company into insolvency proceedings if it has a positive viability prognosis, even if it is arithmetically overindebted); if so, how should this prognosis be shaped and what would be the difference to the prognosis necessary when establishing *likely* inability to pay debts?

II. SCOPE

7.3 When we look at the national laws referring to overindebtedness, the picture is quite colourful. This starts with the scope of this subspecies of insolvency.[379] In most jurisdictions familiar with this term, the scope is restricted to certain legal persons, in particular to publicly listed companies, limited liability companies, and similar organisations.[380] Only in rare cases is it applicable to individuals,[381] or it is used in quite a different context such as transactions avoidance.[382]

376 Cyprus, Denmark, Ireland, Malta, UK.

377 For the relevance for directors' duties, see Chapter 3 *supra*, at para. 3.11, fn. 146.

378 See Chapter 1 *supra*, at paras. 1.8, 3.2.

379 Questionnaire Q. 44.

380 Austria, Bulgaria, Croatia, Cyprus, the Czech Republic, Estonia, Finland, Germany, Lithuania, Poland, Portugal, Slovakia; for companies in general in Ireland, UK, for all debtors in Denmark, Hungary, Italy, Slovenia.

381 The Czech Republic for individual businesspersons; France, Luxembourg for consumers; for all debtors in Denmark, Hungary, Italy, Slovenia.

382 Denmark, Finland, Slovenia, Sweden.

III. DEFINITION

As regards the definition of overindebtedness,[383] some jurisdictions provide for a statutory definition.[384] Others rely on the interpretation in case law and academic literature.[385] Either way, many definitions provide for two elements: arithmetical overindebtedness and a viability prognosis. However, there are many differences concerning the details. 7.4

First, on the liability side of the balance sheet,[386] typically all debts are considered, i.e. not only the mature debts but all existing debts, no matter whether they are mature or not and whether they are contingent or even not fully incurred[387] (provided, of course, they come into existence and fall due during a relevant prognosis period[388]). However, there are occasional exceptions,[389] particularly for certain subordinated claims (e.g. shareholder claims), regardless of whether the subordination is ordered by statute or based on a subordination agreement.[390] 7.5

Second, on the asset side of the balance sheet,[391] normally all assets are considered, no matter whether they are liquid or otherwise available within a short time.[392] Regarding the valuation of these assets,[393] most national laws have decided on the liquidation value,[394] not for the book value[395] or the "going concern" value.[396] This means that every single asset gets a price tag which mirrors the price realisable in a sale of this particular asset on the market when liquidating 7.6

---

383 Questionnaire Q. 45.
384 Bulgaria, Croatia, Cyprus, the Czech Republic, Estonia, Finland, Germany, Hungary, Italy, Lithuania, Luxembourg, Poland, Slovakia, Slovenia.
385 Austria, Denmark, Ireland, Malta, UK.
386 Questionnaire Q. 46.
387 Austria, Bulgaria, Croatia, Cyprus, the Czech Republic, Estonia, Finland, Germany, Hungary, Ireland, Italy, Lithuania, Luxembourg (but for non-commercial debts only), Malta, Poland, Portugal, Slovakia, Slovenia, Sweden, UK.
388 On this, see *infra* at para. 7.7.
389 Questionnaire Q. 47.
390 Austria, Germany, Poland, Slovakia; probably also on a case-by-case basis in Finland and Lithuania.
391 Questionnaire Q. 48.
392 Austria, Bulgaria, Croatia, Cyprus, the Czech Republic, Estonia, Finland, Germany, Hungary, Ireland, Italy, Lithuania, Luxembourg, Malta, Poland, Portugal, Slovakia, Slovenia, Sweden; differently UK for contingent assets, see *supra* fn. 338.
393 Questionnaire Q. 49.
394 Austria, Estonia, Germany, Ireland, Poland.
395 As in Bulgaria, Cyprus, Hungary, Portugal, Slovenia; on a case-by-case basis in Lithuania, Slovakia, UK.
396 By contrast, in Croatia and the Czech Republic: the going concern value applies if the prognosis is positive, liquidation value applies if the prognosis is negative. Undecided in Finland.

the estate. However, where there is the possibility to sell the enterprise (or parts of it) as a whole, the liquidation value assigned to every single part of the entity that is sold may be positively influenced.

7.7 Third, since the valuation of the assets against their liquidation value frequently leads to arithmetical overindebtedness, many jurisdictions provide for a prognosis requirement[397] as a corrective.[398] The prognosis concerns the viability of the company, i.e. the prospects for the company to continue the business over a certain period of time[399] or the prospects of avoiding the occurrence of inability to pay.[400] This prognosis period ranges from one year[401] to the ongoing and the next accounting or financial year,[402, 403] yet is sometimes undefined and therefore left to the discretion of the court.[404] The prognosis is positive if it can be established that the company will be able to pay all its debts falling due during this time-span as measured against the available assets at liquidation value.[405] This either leads to the denial of overindebtedness[406] or to a different valuation standard, meaning that the assets are now valued at their going concern value and then it is checked again whether there is arithmetical overindebtedness.[407]

7.8 It should be clarified that this prognosis is of a similar kind to the prognosis necessary in the context of likely or imminent inability to pay debts.[408] Both types concern the debtor's ability to meet his or her due debts when they fall due over a certain period of time. The difference is mostly in the length of the forecast period. In Germany, for example, the prognosis covers the next 12 months in the context of overindebtedness and the next 24 months in the context of likely inability to pay debts. Such an approach facilitates access to legally regulated restructuring procedures that presuppose a likely inability to pay debts but are no longer available in the event of overindebtedness, provided that the inability to pay debts is only to be expected for the time after the expiry of the 12-month period for the overindebtedness test.

---

397 Questionnaire Qs. 50–52.

398 Austria, Croatia, the Czech Republic, Finland, Germany, Italy, Lithuania, Poland, Portugal, Slovakia; on a case-by-case basis in Estonia, UK; no prognosis in Bulgaria, Cyprus, Hungary, Ireland, Luxembourg, Malta, Slovenia.

399 Austria, Croatia, Germany, Italy, Lithuania; probably also in the Czech Republic.

400 Poland.

401 Germany.

402 Austria.

403 In Poland, there is a two-year period, but this is part of the definition of insolvency itself rather than a prognosis period; see *infra* at para. 7.9.

404 Croatia, the Czech Republic, Finland, Italy, Lithuania, Poland, Portugal, UK.

405 Austria, Germany, Poland.

406 As in Austria, Germany, Poland.

407 As in Croatia.

408 On them, see Chapter 6 *supra*, at paras. 6.5, 6.11.

Fourth, a further limitation, different from a prognosis requirement, exists in Poland.[409] Here, the law requires that the situation defined as arithmetical overindebtedness persists for at least two years before it can be considered to establish a state of insolvency that justifies the opening of insolvency proceedings. Such requirement differs from a prognosis in the fact that the debtor is only considered insolvent once arithmetical overindebtedness has already persisted for the defined period. This means that even a negative prognosis at the beginning of this period does not lead to insolvency if other conditions (e.g. inability to pay) are not met. As such a requirement leads to including only cases of persistent overindebtedness, i.e. that continue to exist a considerable time after arithmetical overindebtedness has arisen, it is intended to limit the application of this criterion. In all, Polish law assigns greater importance to the inability to pay debts as a principal form of insolvency. 7.9

IV. ESTABLISHING OVERINDEBTEDNESS

In most jurisdictions, overindebtedness is to be established[410] by a formal balance sheet, which can start from the regular commercial balance sheet but must include the undisclosed reserves and display all assets with their relevant value.[411] Further, a liquidity status is necessary which shows that the debtor will not be able to meet all debts falling due during the prognosis period.[412] The debtor can submit the necessary documents him- or herself but the court can also commission an expert witness to prepare them. Only in a few jurisdictions is a presumption for overindebtedness available,[413] whereas others have no special rules,[414] which leaves establishing overindebtedness to general norms of the law of civil procedure. 7.10

V. INTERIM RESULTS

In all, it turns out that overindebtedness plays a certain role in many jurisdictions. It has its essential meaning as a corrective to the limited liability of companies without unlimited personal liability of shareholders. However, 7.11

---

409 Poland (which also has a prognosis requirement, see *supra* at para. 7.7).

410 Questionnaire Q. 53.

411 Austria, Estonia, Germany, Hungary, Ireland, Poland, Slovakia; possible, but not necessary in Croatia, Finland, Lithuania, Luxembourg.

412 Austria, Germany, Poland.

413 Italy (debtor's escape or suicide), Poland (if liabilities exceed the book value of assets), Slovenia (same as for inability to pay debts).

414 Czech Republic, Denmark, Finland, Lithuania, Malta, Portugal, Slovenia.

it is mostly subordinate to inability to pay debts rather than an equal partner to this appearance of insolvency. While nearly all national laws referring to overindebtedness agree that all (not only mature) debts and all (not only liquid) assets are to be considered, many details are divergent or unclear, in particular the correct means of valuation of the assets and the necessity for, and specifics of, a prognosis.

CHAPTER 8

ELABORATING A PROPOSAL FOR A MODEL LAW

I. INTRODUCTION

8.1 The purpose of this study is to elaborate a proposal for a definition of the term "insolvency" and its subspecies which can be used in European statutory instruments, in particular the European Insolvency Regulation (EIR), the Directive on restructuring and insolvency, and the Harmonisation Proposal. We are aiming at a Model Law that offers definitions suitable for European law. We suggest that wherever terms such as "insolvency", "inability to pay debts", etc. are used in EU law, they should be defined autonomously and understood consistently in the same sense. This holds true not only within a certain Regulation or Directive but also for the entirety of all statutory instruments of EU law in which the respective expressions are used. It is therefore a question of a generally applicable definitions.

8.2 Based on the principle of legal certainty, we also suggest that the European legislator should be very precise and very specific about how certain terms should be understood. In both national and European law, the expressions dealt with in this project are used as prerequisites that trigger specific legal consequences. A good example is Article 36 Harmonisation Proposal, which provides

> that, where a legal entity becomes insolvent, its directors are obliged to submit a request for the opening of insolvency proceedings with the court no later than 3 months after the directors became aware or can reasonably be expected to have been aware that the legal entity is insolvent.

From what we have seen so far, the word "insolvent" is not precise enough in this context. It is understood quite diversely in the Member States, covering inability to pay debts in most jurisdictions[415] but also overindebtedness[416]

[415] Details *supra* Chapter 3 and 4, at paras. 3.5 and 4.1.

[416] See *supra* Chapters 3 and 7, at paras. 3.5 and 7.1.

or even cessation of payments[417] in others. Still others refrain from linking insolvency to these subspecies and instead consider a debtor insolvent if he or she fulfils certain criteria, such as failing to pay a debt despite it being due.[418] One could leave the definition of the term "insolvent" to the national legislators. However, with regard to Article 36 Harmonisation Proposal, this would have the effect that directors are obliged to file for insolvency proceedings in some jurisdictions but not in others, which is particularly difficult in the context of an insolvent group of companies.[419] It would also not lead to the "level playing-field" that the European Commission seeks to promote in its efforts to establish a Capital Markets Union. However, if one decides to define the term "insolvent" independently for European law, one must also clearly state which manifestations of insolvency are meant and how these manifestations are to be understood in more detail. Beyond doubt, the European legislator is free to use the word "insolvent" in a broader sense, e.g. comprising inability to pay debts as well as overindebtedness.[420] However, if that is what is meant, then it should be explicitly stated and the terms "inability to pay debts" and "overindebtedness" should be defined as precisely as possible.

What has been said in the previous paragraph influences the scope of our study 8.3 significantly. Initially, we were planning to restrict the scope of this project to those expressions that are already used in European law. This comprises the terms "insolvent", "inability to pay debts", and "likelihood of insolvency" understood as "likelihood of inability to pay debts". It would leave out "overindebtedness", "cessation of payments", and "imminent inability to pay debts". However, it turned out that such a restriction is not advisable. As explained above, "insolvent" is understood diversely in the Member States, and the European legislator is called upon to take a clear position and define which forms of insolvency are meant. This does not mean that the EU legislator are obliged to link certain legal consequences to certain subtypes, e.g. to link the duty of directors to file for insolvency proceedings to overindebtedness. We are not proposing this here, just as we have generally refrained from analysing or commenting on certain rules or legal consequences of the Harmonisation Proposal. However, if the European legislator decides to make certain subtypes of insolvency a prerequisite for specific legal consequences, then it must make clear what is meant by the terms used. This implies that those subspecies that are not to be used must be clearly

417 More *supra* Chapter 3 and 5, at paras. 3.5 and 5.1.

418 This holds true for Hungary, see *supra* Chapter 4, at para. 4.16, fn. 261.

419 See *supra* Chapter 1, at para. 1.10.

420 To be clear, we are not suggesting that the directors' duty to file for insolvency proceedings should be connected to overindebtedness in Art. 36 Harmonisation Proposal. We leave this to the European legislator. However, *if* this legislator understands "insolvent" as meaning not only "unable to pay debts" but also "overindebted", then this should be made clear.

defined as well. If, for example, the term "likely inability to pay debts" is used in a rule, then it must be clear that a decision has been made against the use of "imminent inability to pay debts". Under the principle of legal certainty, it is therefore necessary to include all legal appearances of insolvency in the scope of our project.

8.4 In national insolvency laws, the term "insolvency" and its subspecies are primarily used to describe reasons for opening insolvency proceedings (here understood as ordinary liquidation proceedings). To put it simply, insolvency proceedings require the debtor's insolvency. So far, the European Union does not intend to harmonise the prerequisites for the opening of such proceedings. This topic is not included in the Harmonisation Proposal, and we are not suggesting doing this. However, as already explained earlier,[421] this approach cannot be strictly adhered to. The reason is not only that the directors' duty to file for insolvency proceedings is meaningless if such proceedings cannot be opened under national law because the debtor is insolvent under European, but not under national law;[422] the reason is also that the definition of insolvency law in European law has at least indirect effect on national laws insofar that national legislators will probably (and should) avoid having two different meanings for the same term. If (e.g.) the term "inability to pay debts" is defined and used in a rule on transactions avoidance law in the Harmonisation Proposal and therefore has to be transposed into national law with the same meaning, it would be more than unfortunate to define the same term as used in a rule on the commencement of proceedings in national insolvency law in a different way. Consequently, the definition given to the term "insolvency" and the subspecies thereof will influence the way in which those terms are to be understood in the national laws of the Member States.

8.5 These findings therefore also influence our endeavour to restrict our proposals to a "minimum approach". In principle, we would not object if national laws had a different understanding when using (e.g.) "inability to pay debts" in contexts not addressed by European law or if they decided to legislate for additional reasons to open insolvency proceedings. However, in view of the de facto obligation to understand the terms defined and used in national law in the same way as in European law, little remains of this approach. Under no circumstances would we recommend giving the Member States a choice between different definitions, as it would thwart all efforts at harmonisation if, for example, the term "inability to pay debts" were to be defined differently in some Member States than in others.

---

421 *Supra* Chapter 1, at para. 1.15.

422 See again *supra* Chapter 1, at para. 1.16.

When elaborating our Model Law, we will try to base our findings on the principles of insolvency law. It is therefore advisable to remind oneself of the fundamental decisions. As explained in detail above,[423] the principles of creditors' autonomy, predictability (legal certainty), efficiency, protection of trust, and fixation require the definition of the term "insolvency" to be as clear, precise, and easy to apply as possible. The law connects severe legal consequences to the debtor's insolvency – most notably the shift from the application of general civil law to insolvency law (and its generally invasive effects) – and it must therefore be clear for all stakeholders (and not only experts in the field of insolvency law) whether this prerequisite is met. This is correctly expressed in Article 38(2) sentence 2 of the Harmonisation Proposal when it states that the Member States shall "ensure that these conditions are clear, simple and easily ascertainable". Further, the principles of collectivity, optimisation, satisfaction, equal treatment of creditors, protection of debtor's rights, and protection of trust require finding a definition that determines the correct point in time when the shift from the application of general civil law to insolvency law is called for. The interference of insolvency law must come neither too early nor too late. As a corrective, the principle of proportionality must be taken into consideration. 8.6

Our findings will be summarised in a proposal for a Model Law.[424] We suggest formulating definitions that can be included in the catalogue of definitions typically found in the EU's statutory instruments, for example in Article 2 EIR, Article 2 Directive on restructuring and insolvency, and Article 2 Harmonisation Proposal. However, as already explained above,[425] the definitions should be the same for all statutory instruments. This suggests the following wording: 8.7

Article 2

Definitions

For the purposes of this [statutory instrument], the following definitions apply:

...

- "insolvency" means
- "inability to pay debts" means
- "cessation of payments" means
- "likelihood of insolvency" means
- "imminent insolvency" means
- "overindebtedness" means

....

[423] Chapter 2, at para. 2.10 et seq.

[424] See *supra* Chapter 1, at para. 1.13.

[425] At para. 8.1.

II. INABILITY TO PAY DEBTS

8.8 With this in mind, we can turn first to inability to pay debts. We do not start with the term "insolvency", since this expression most likely comprises various subspecies that should be defined first. We will deal with "insolvency" in more detail below.[426]

8.9 As regards inability to pay debts, it is common ground that this appearance of insolvency addresses the liquidity problems of a debtor who does not have the necessary financial means to pay what he or she is obliged to pay. The wording of Article 38(2) sentence 1 Harmonisation Proposal ("A microenterprise shall be deemed insolvent for the purposes of simplified winding-up proceedings when it is generally unable to pay its debts as they mature") is a step in the right direction. Hence, we can start formulating our Model Law as follows:

Article 2
Definitions

For the purposes of this [statutory instrument], the following definitions apply:

...

- "inability to pay debts" means the debtor's inability to pay its debts;

....

8.10 However, this text as such is meaningless, since it "defines" an expression by only using the words contained in the expression itself. It is no more than a framework for further concretisation. More importantly, it leaves many questions unanswered and does not suffice for the present purposes. Under the principles mentioned above,[427] in particular under the principle of predictability (legal certainty), it is necessary to be more precise and to define in more detail the conditions under which the shift from the application of general civil law to insolvency law takes place.

1. RELEVANT POINT IN TIME

8.11 A first and decisive decision to be made concerns the point in time at which inability to pay debts is determined. Since this subspecies of insolvency is not an end in itself but serves as a prerequisite for specific legal consequences

---

426 At para. 8.81.
427 At para. 8.6.

(as required by national law after transposition of a Directive or by a European Regulation), we propose that it be determined at the specific point in time that is relevant for the legal consequences. This can be illustrated by some examples. First, where the question arises whether a director was obliged to file for insolvency proceedings on 23 November 2023, inability to pay debts must be determined for this specific day. Second, if a judge is to decide on 5 May 2023 whether to grant an application for the opening of insolvency proceedings based on inability to pay debts, this subspecies of insolvency must exist on this date. Finally, if a payment made by the debtor on 6 September 2022 is challenged by the Insolvency Practitioner under transactions avoidance law, the debtor's inability to pay debts, if required by the relevant rule of transactions avoidance law, must be established for this very day, since the debtor must be insolvent at the point in time the contested payment is made.[428]

Against this background, we prefer working with "point-in-time" illiquidity over "time period" illiquidity. This not only strengthens the clarity of the rule and promotes legal certainty but also makes it easier to distinguish inability to pay debts from imminent or likely inability to pay debts and overindebtedness. The existence of inability to pay debts is assessed for a very specific point in time; developments in the past or future are generally irrelevant. As opposed to this, the determination of imminent and likely inability to pay debts is forward-looking[429] and the same applies – as will be shown below[430] – to overindebtedness. In a slightly exaggerated formulation, this means that a debtor who is still able to pay its debts today but not tomorrow is not unable to pay its debts today, but only likely or imminently unable to pay its debts. It is true that, under the principles of optimisation[431] and satisfaction,[432] opening proceedings as early as possible may be in the interest of the general body of creditors and facilitates restructuring. However, this does not mean that a debtor who will only become unable to pay its debts in the future should be confronted with insolvency proceedings now. If the legislator so wishes, it can define imminent or likely inability to pay debts as a trigger for the opening of insolvency proceedings. An expansive interpretation of the concept of (actual) inability to pay debts is not necessary for this. 8.12

We therefore suggest implementing a reference to the relevant point in time in the Model Law. This would lead to the following wording: 8.13

428 For details, see *Bork/Veder* (Chapter 1, fn. 40), paras. 4.34, 4.84, 4.89.
429 See para. 8.57 et seq., 8.63.
430 See para. 8.71 et seq.
431 See *supra* at para. 2.17.
432 See *supra* at para. 2.18.

Article 2
Definitions

For the purposes of this [statutory instrument], the following definitions apply:

...

- "inability to pay debts" means the debtor's inability *at the relevant point in time* to pay its debts;

....

2. RELEVANT DEBTS

8.14 This perspective also influences the definition of the relevant debts that must be taken into account. Under the concept of point-in-time illiquidity, it is in the nature of things that only those liabilities that the debtor is obliged to pay at the relevant point in time can be considered relevant. Debts which do not exist, are contingent, not due, or to which legal defences apply do not have to be paid. This is met with widespread approval in the Member States[433] and deserves support, as it reinforces the principles of legal certainty and efficiency. The wording of a respective rule should mirror this accordingly. It is therefore not recommended to use the drafting of Article 38(2) Harmonisation Proposal ("as they mature") because this could be interpreted as pointing towards the future and comprising debts which are not yet payable at the relevant point in time. In accordance with Article 6(1) lit. (a), (2) lit. (b), (3) sentence 2 Harmonisation Proposal, we suggest referring to "mature debts" instead, understanding "mature" in a broader sense: non-mature describes all debts which do not have to be paid because they do not yet exist, are contingent, have not reached the day of maturity, or are rightfully faced with other defences (e.g. based on prescription periods or a right to suspend performance); mature debts are debts that would be enforced in court today. It would also be possible to use the word "payable" or "due" instead of "mature". However, we decided in favour of the conventional term "mature".

8.15 In some jurisdictions, only undisputed (or not seriously disputed) claims are taken into account when establishing inability to pay debts.[434] We do not suggest following this lead, since it mixes up the substantive prerequisites of inability to pay debts with the proof thereof. If a debtor disputes a claim, he or she asserts that the claim does not exist, is still subject to a condition, is

433 Details *supra* Chapter 4, at para. 4.4.
434 See *supra* Chapter 4, at para. 4.7.

not due, or is not payable for other reasons, for example because it is opposed by defences. It goes without saying that including the word "undisputed" in the definition of inability to pay debts would facilitate establishing this appearance of insolvency significantly, because all disputed claims would be automatically disregarded. While this may be supported by the principles of efficiency and protection of debtors' rights (the debtor has a legitimate interest not to be declared insolvent due to alleged but in fact not payable claims), it is not compatible with most other principles, in particular the principles of legal certainty, collectivity, and equal treatment of creditors, because it would enable a clever debtor to conceal its inability to pay and the fact that the shift from the application of general civil law to insolvency law is justified, by skilfully disputing claims. It would also ignore the fact that such a facilitation is not justified in all procedural situations. The required level of judicial certainty may be different for establishing inability to pay debts as a reason to open insolvency proceedings as compared to inability to pay debts as a substantive prerequisite for transactions avoidance laws or directors' liability. The desire for judicial certainty is not proportional to excluding all disputed claims from the scope of inability to pay debts. It is a question of burden of proof, which has nothing to do with the definition of the term "inability to pay debts" and which we must leave to the respective national procedural law as applicable in the procedural situation at hand.

In some jurisdictions, further restrictions on the debts to be included in the 8.16
assessment of a debtor's inability to pay are available.[435] We do not recommend following this example. If certain debts (e.g. claims based on fraudulent loans, claims due for no longer than 30 days, etc.) are excluded, this will not provide an accurate picture of the debtor's ability to pay. This is because it may very well be the case that when the excluded claims are left out of the equation, the debtor is able to service the remaining, non-excluded claims and is therefore not considered insolvent, even though he actually is, because he cannot cover the sum of all mature claims, including the excluded claims. If the latter exist and are mature, then they must be included in the assessment of a debtor's (in)ability to pay debts. If this assessment results in the conclusion that the debtor is unable to pay (all) its debts, the principles of collectivity, equal treatment of creditors, and fixation require and justify the conclusion that the debtor is illiquid in a legal sense. It would severely infringe the creditors' rights if one were content with the debtor being able to fulfil only part of his or her mature claims although the shift from the application of general civil law to insolvency law is called for.

---

[435] Details *supra* Chapter 4, at para. 4.8.

8.17 In sum, we suggest adding only the word "mature" to the definition of inability to pay debts, which amounts to:

Article 2
Definitions

For the purposes of this [statutory instrument], the following definitions apply:

...

- "inability to pay debts" means the debtor's inability at the relevant point in time to pay its *mature* debts;

....

3. RELEVANT ASSETS

8.18 Similar deliberations are necessary for the assets available for paying the mature debts. The decision for point-in-time illiquidity entails that only those assets that are available at the relevant point in time can be considered. This is widely acknowledged in the national laws[436] and also supported in our proposal. In practice, this means that only those assets that can be used at the relevant point in time to pay the mature debts may be taken into account. This includes mainly financial means, in particular cash at hand and in bank accounts, available committed credit lines, but also assets that can be turned into cash on that day, such as publicly listed shares. Not included are receivables,[437] assets which cannot be monetised on the relevant day but only days or weeks later, and assets that will be acquired soon (such as receivables for goods or services that have already been ordered). One might argue that this quite restrictive view leads to unnecessary insolvencies, since it assesses debtors as being unable to pay their debts which will recover (i.e. close the liquidity gap) fairly shortly. This is a valid point. However, we suggest that this should be taken into account in the context of the assessment of the liquidity gap,[438] rather than the determination of the relevant assets.

8.19 Against this background, we propose to add a phrase to the definition that clarifies that only those assets which are available to satisfy the mature claims on the same day shall be taken into account. Among the choice of expressions – "acute", "available", "liquid", "present", or "quick" – we decided on the term

436 See *supra* Chapter 4, at para 4.9.

437 However, if they are paid the same day, cash or bank account facilities resulting from this payment can be taken into consideration.

438 See *infra* at para. 8.24.

"liquid" because it best expresses the connection with (il)liquidity. In sum, we suggest the following wording:

Article 2
Definitions

For the purposes of this [statutory instrument], the following definitions apply:

...

- "inability to pay debts" means the debtor's inability at the relevant point in time to pay its mature debts *from its liquid assets*;

....

4. LIQUIDITY GAP

In principle, a debtor is unable to pay its debts if the sum of all mature debts exceeds the value of all liquid assets. However, two further details must be addressed. 8.20

a) *Extent of the Liquidity Gap*

The first detail concerns the required extent of the liquidity gap. Is it desirable to implement a caveat in the definition of inability to pay debts that the difference between mature debts and liquid assets should exceed a certain threshold? We have seen before[439] that only a few national laws contain such a condition, but most laws do not. In finding a principle-based solution, one could argue that the principles of collectivity, equal treatment of creditors, and fixation speak against such an exception: if the debtor is not able to pay all its mature debts, the collective interests of the creditors come to the fore and the shift from the application of general civil law to insolvency law is called for. However, this might be a vicious circle, since this shift is called for if the debtor is substantively insolvent and whether he or she is substantively insolvent or not depends on the definition of insolvency, here: on the definition of inability to pay debts. At any rate, the principles of efficiency and proportionality speak in favour of requiring a sufficiently serious liquidity gap. If a debtor has mature debts in the amount of €100,000 and liquid assets in the amount of €99,990, it does not make sense to open insolvency proceedings or to apply the strict rules of insolvency law. The costs – including transaction costs – are far too high to be considered an appropriate response to such a small liquidity gap. Hence, in this case, the principle of proportionality takes precedence. 8.21

439 *Supra* Chapter 4, at para. 4.10.

8.22 However, this does not solve the problem of how to draft such an exception. In national laws, two options are available: first, to require the value of the liquid assets to amount to a specific percentage of the mature debts; or, second, to be content with a rather generalised restriction.[440] Although the requirement of a certain percentage would be supported by the principle of predictability (legal certainty), a more general expression, based on the principle of efficiency,[441] allows the individual circumstances of each case to be taken into account and to give debtors, advisors, judges, and other stakeholders a little bit of necessary flexibility. As regards terminology, we would neither plead for leaving the determination of the liquidity gap entirely to the discretion of the courts – since this hampers the idea of predictability and legal certainty – nor would we suggest adopting the wording of Article 38(2) sentence 1 Harmonisation Proposal, because the word "generally" gives the impression that any exception is permissible. Instead, one could carve out "minor gaps" or require an "essential", "predominant", "significant", or "relevant" gap. We suggest using the term "insignificant", since this leaves a little room for discretion but is not too vague and does not render the norm inapplicable. For example, where the liquidity gap is less than 1%, we would generally consider this to be insignificant. This means that the term "insignificant" should be interpreted relative to the total amount of all mature claims.

8.23 This is reflected in the following formulation:

Article 2
Definitions

For the purposes of this [statutory instrument], the following definitions apply:

...

- "inability to pay debts" means the debtor's inability at the relevant point in time to pay *all but an insignificant part* of its mature debts from its liquid assets;

....

b) Duration of the Liquidity Gap

8.24 Similar deliberations are necessary for the duration of the liquidity gap. As elaborated above,[442] a significant number of Member States require the liquidity gap to persist for a certain time-span. This prerequisite becomes relevant if the debtor is illiquid at the relevant point in time, but at the same time, it is foreseeable that the liquidity gap will be closed again in the short term. The reason for this prognosis may be that some of the debtor's assets can be

440 For references, see *supra* Chapter 4, fns. 231, 232.
441 See *supra* Chapter 2, at para. 2.15.
442 At Chapter 4, para. 4.11.

converted into cash (not today but) at short notice or that payments from third parties (e.g. customers or tax authorities) are to be expected. If this increase of liquidity is sufficiently certain, it might be useless to open expensive, time-consuming, and invasive insolvency proceedings that will have to be terminated again after a few days. Instead, it seems preferable to make creditors wait for a short period of time. Hence, under the principle of proportionality, it seems advisable to insert an exception for merely temporary illiquidity.

However, here again, the difficult task is to find an appropriate rule. Under the principle of predictability (legal certainty), it seems advisable to put an exact figure on the time-span,[443] e.g. one month. This would set the debtor a specific deadline within which he or she must remedy the illiquidity. On the other hand, such a legal "grace period" would only create a sham certainty. It would not exempt those applying the rule from making a prognosis at the relevant point in time as to whether the liquidity gap can be closed within this period. Furthermore, a rigid deadline cannot take sufficient account of the concrete circumstances of the individual case. Against this background, we prioritise the principle of efficiency by deciding in favour of a more general clause. Learning from the examples in national laws,[444] this can be done by requiring the liquidity gap to be "permanent" or "persistent" or not to be "temporary" or "short-term". When choosing from this basket, one should have in mind that flexibility must not turn into arbitrariness, that discretion is always an obstacle to legal certainty, and that the "grace period" must not be too long. The longer the period of time, the more difficult it is to make a forecast, the greater the undermining of legal certainty, and the fewer creditors can reasonably be expected to wait. In light of these considerations, we suggest restricting the exception to short-term illiquidity only, i.e. where it is reasonable to expect that the liquidity gap can be cured in the short term (meaning: a high probability that the relevant liquidity gap will be closed). For example, we would generally consider a time-span of less than three weeks irrelevant. 8.25

This supports the following wording: 8.26

Article 2

Definitions

For the purposes of this [statutory instrument], the following definitions apply:

...

- "inability to pay debts" means the debtor's inability at the relevant point in time to pay all but an insignificant part of its mature debts from its liquid assets, *unless it is to be reasonably expected that this inability can be cured in the short term*;

....

---

[443] This is the case in some national laws, see for references *supra* Chapter 4, fn. 237 et seq.

[444] References *supra* Chapter 4, fn. 241.

5. PRESUMPTIONS AND CIRCUMSTANTIAL EVIDENCE

8.27 A major problem in the present context is the establishment of inability to pay debts. For a debtor (e.g. when applying for insolvency proceedings or defending him- or herself against a creditor application), it will be feasible to list the mature debts and the liquid assets existing at the relevant point in time. The same holds true for the Insolvency Practitioner (e.g. when challenging a payment under transactions avoidance law), since he or she has access to the information and documents related to the debtor's estate. However, a creditor (e.g. when filing for insolvency proceedings) or a third party (e.g. when suing a director for breach of the duty to file for insolvency proceedings) will generally not have access to such information and means of evidence. It is for this reason that many national laws provide for "signs of insolvency", i.e. for (rebuttable or irrebuttable[445]) presumptions of insolvency or at least for a catalogue of substantial evidence showing inability to pay.[446]

8.28 As pointed out above, we do not think it is advisable to leave the detailed definition of inability to pay debts to the national legislators. The same holds true for leaving the "signs of insolvency" to the national legislators. It is not clear whether Article 38(2) sentence 2 Harmonisation Proposal may be understood that way. If this was intended by the European Commission, we would not support it. Given the diversity of "signs of insolvency" in the national laws of the Member States,[447] this would hamper the harmonisation effect of the Directive significantly. Member States would most certainly adhere to the existing (evidentiary) rules with the effect that inability to pay debts will be assessed very differently in State A than in State B.

8.29 When applying a principle-based approach, it seems well founded to provide the court and the parties with some facilitation of evidence. This is primarily supported by the principles of efficiency[448] and predictability (legal certainty)[449] but also by the principle of protection of trust,[450] which all require that it be easily ascertainable whether the debtor is insolvent or not. As already referred to above,[451] this is correctly expressed in Article 38(2) sentence 2 of the Harmonisation Proposal, where it is stated that the Member States shall "ensure that these conditions are clear, simple and easily ascertainable", which not only holds true for the national legislators but also for the European Union itself.

---

445 References *supra* Chapter 4, fn. 262.
446 Details *supra* Chapter 4, at para. 4.13 et seq.
447 Ibid.
448 See *supra* Chapter 2, at para. 2.15.
449 See *supra* Chapter 2, at para. 2.14.
450 For details, see *supra* Chapter 2, at para. 2.21.
451 At para. 8.6.

However, deciding concretely in what way evidence should be facilitated is not an easy task, precisely because national laws differ so much on this point. Against this background, we submit the following deliberations.

a) *Irrebuttable Presumptions*

First, irrebuttable presumptions, as some Member States provide for, must be approached with scepticism. They are too rigid and inflexible and do not allow the relevant circumstances of the individual case to be taken into account. In the present context, although they could be based on the principles of efficiency[452] and predictability (legal certainty),[453] irrebuttable presumptions are not compatible with the principle of protection of the debtor's rights[454] in the first place, since the debtor must have the chance to prove that the prerequisites of inability to pay debts are not met. The same holds true for other stakeholders whose legal position – for example in transactions avoidance cases – depends on the establishment of the debtor's inability to pay its debts. Further, irrebuttable presumptions are often misused as debt collection instruments by creditors who threaten the debtor with the commencement of insolvency proceedings based on such a presumption, even though they know (or at least suspect) that the debtor is not actually unable to pay its debts. This is against the principles of collectivity,[455] equal treatment of creditors,[456] and fixation,[457] which refer to the specific point in time at which the shift from the application of general civil law to insolvency law is called for and do not accept that the triggering prerequisite for this shift is presumed rather than established. 8.30

b) *Circumstantial Evidence*

Whilst irrebuttable presumptions are the strongest statutory facilitation of proof, circumstantial evidence is the weakest. It can be no more than a collection of typical circumstances pointing to the inability to pay, as exemplified above.[458] However, it is neither necessary nor advisable to implement into European law a list of such typical circumstances showing inability to pay. Irrespective of our research project being about the harmonisation of a certain topic of insolvency law and not about the harmonisation of the law of civil procedure, circumstantial evidence is a fundamental feature of forming judicial persuasion, which cannot 8.31

---

452 Details *supra* Chapter 2, at para. 2.15.
453 On this, see *supra* Chapter 2, at para. 2.14.
454 *Supra* Chapter 2, at para. 2.19.
455 Cf. *supra* Chapter 2, at para. 2.12.
456 See *supra* Chapter 2, at para. 2.20.
457 More Chapter 2, at para. 2.22.
458 Chapter 4, at para. 4.18.

be prescribed by law. Where inability to pay debts is a prerequisite for specific legal consequences, judges must be convinced that this prerequisite is met. They will form their opinion by evaluating direct evidence (such as documents, witness statements, or expert opinions) or by weighing and balancing the relevant individual circumstances of the case at hand. Which circumstances are available depends on the case, and how they are interpreted depends on the judge. Typical relevant circumstances might be (without offering an exhaustive list):

- the debtor's admission of having liquidity issues;
- multiple creditors issuing default notices or commencing individual enforcement;
- delayed or non-payments to creditors upon whose continued supply the continuation of the debtor's business operations crucially depends;
- non-payment of a significant part of the debtor's mature liabilities (even if it is only one single but significant claim);[459]
- non-payment of liabilities where this is a criminal offence;
- not responding to invoices and reminders;
- the debtor's whereabouts being unknown;
- removal of collateral from the control of the debtor;
- selective payments of certain mature debts only (e.g. debts of personal interest to the debtor);
- delayed or non-payment of wages and salaries;
- non-compliance with a payment scheme for previously matured debts.

However, legislators should not interfere in this process of judicial opinion-building by providing for a list of relevant circumstantial evidence in the statute.

c) *Rebuttable Presumptions*

8.32 This leaves us with the question whether our proposal should include rebuttable presumptions of the existence of inability to pay. If we review the presumptions available in the individual national laws,[460] we can see that there are some circumstances for which it is easy to agree that they indicate presumed inability to pay debts. A first and very important example is cessation of payments,[461] which is recognised as the basis of a presumption of inability to pay in many countries.[462] We suggest following this example. The mere fact that the debtor

---

459 Note that it is only necessary to use this as circumstantial evidence where Member States do not follow the proposal to use cessation of payments (as defined *infra* at para. 8.46) as the basis of a rebuttable presumption.

460 For an overview, see above Chapter 4, at para. 4.16.

461 As defined *infra* at para. 8.38 et seq.

462 References *supra* Chapter 4, at para. 4.17.

no longer regularly pays as usual in the ordinary course of business gives strong grounds for presuming (albeit rebuttably only) that he or she cannot pay the mature debts. Using cessation of payments as the foundation of a presumption of inability to pay debts makes it easier for a creditor and other external third parties to provide evidence, not by relying on the debtor's accounting figures, which are only available internally, but on external circumstances ascertainable to third parties.

A second group of cases in which inability to pay debts can be inferred is characterised by the fact that the debtor has been in default for several months or with several payments vis-à-vis essential creditors, i.e. creditors on whose continued supply the continuation of the debtor's business operations crucially depends.[463] If the debtor does not even pay these creditors (let alone all others) for a relevant period of time (which we propose to be set at three months[464]), then it can be assumed that he or she is unable to pay. This is in line with the UNCITRAL Legislative Guide on Insolvency Law[465] which, at paragraph 23, lists "indicators of a debtor's general cessation of payments [which] may include its failure to pay rent, taxes, salaries, employee benefits, trade accounts payable and other essential business costs" and continues: "As such, this test puts the defining factors within the reach of creditors." Admittedly, the Legislative Guide does use the non-payment of essential business costs as circumstantial evidence for cessation of payments rather than as the foundation of a presumption of the existence/occurrence of inability to pay debts. However, we suggest at least permitting the national legislators to decide in favour of relevant presumptions, since, in our view, the non-payment of essential creditors is such a strong indicator that it is very well founded to conclude from this circumstance that the debtor is unable to pay its debts. With this in mind, one could tie the presumption to the non-payment of all essential (business) costs or one could restrict it to non-payment of certain essential creditors, such as employees or public creditors. The former choice could lead to discussions as to which costs are essential and which are not, which is cause for concern under the principle of predictability (legal certainty), but might deserve support from the principle of efficiency, since it gives the courts some flexibility in referring to the individual circumstances of the case at hand. The latter choice is more concrete but would probably raise the question of the admissibility of an analogy and relegate the reference to other essential creditors to the realm of circumstantial evidence. In weighing and balancing the principles involved, we have decided in favour of the slightly broader version and to include all essential creditors. However, we would not 8.33

[463] Similarly for executory contracts, Art. 27(1) Harmonisation Proposal.

[464] If the default does not exceed three months, we would still consider it circumstantial evidence of inability to pay; see *supra* at para. 8.31.

[465] *Supra* Chapter 1, fn. 27.

recommend referring to "business" creditors, since this would not be suitable for individual insolvencies, where debtors not only have business creditors but also private creditors (and the former only if they are entrepreneurs).

8.34 However, there are other presumptions in national laws that do not necessarily indicate an inability to pay mature debts. These include, for example, default on claims of a certain amount or for a certain time-span,[466] enforcement attempts by creditors[467] or non-compliance with a final judgment.[468] In particular, the mere passage of time after a receivable falls due[469] says little or nothing about the inability to pay debts and is likely to be (ab)used as a debt-enforcement instrument rather than as a means to establish inability to pay debts.

8.35 Against this background, and having in mind that the law of civil procedure in general and of evidence in particular is not the focus of our research project, we restrict our proposal to a few significant rebuttable presumptions. In our view, following this proposal should mean two things. Firstly, it should be clear that Member States are limited to the proposed bases for the presumption and may not provide for further bases in their national laws, since otherwise the harmonisation would be endangered significantly. Secondly, it goes without saying that the courts are free to consider all the bases for the presumption that are currently available in national laws but not incorporated in this Model Law as circumstantial evidence.[470]

8.36 These considerations are reflected in the following formulation:

Article 2

Definitions

For the purposes of this [statutory instrument], the following definitions apply:

...

- "inability to pay debts" means the debtor's inability at the relevant point in time to pay all but an insignificant part of its mature debts from its liquid assets, unless it is to be reasonably expected that this inability can be cured in the short term; *Member States may provide that inability to pay debts is rebuttably presumed, but only if the debtor has ceased payments or is in default to an essential creditor with at least two payments or one payment for at least three months;*

....

466 Details *supra* at Chapter 4, fns. 265–267.

467 More *supra* at Chapter 4, fns. 268, 275.

468 See at Chapter 4, fn. 269.

469 Examples *supra* at Chapter 4, fn. 264.

470 Cf. *supra* at para. 8.31.

6. PROPOSAL

In all, our findings regarding inability to pay debts can be summarised as follows: 8.37

Article 2
Definitions

For the purposes of this [statutory instrument], the following definitions apply:

...

- "inability to pay debts" means the debtor's inability at the relevant point in time to pay all but an insignificant part of its mature debts from its liquid assets, unless it is to be reasonably expected that this inability can be cured in the short term; Member States may provide that inability to pay debts is rebuttably presumed, but only if the debtor has ceased payments or is in default to an essential creditor with at least two payments or one payment for at least three months;

....

III. CESSATION OF PAYMENTS

As explained in more detail above,[471] cessation of payments plays an important role in many jurisdictions, be it as an autonomous reason to open insolvency proceedings, be it as the basis of a presumption or as circumstantial evidence of inability to pay debts. Following our intention to clarify all terms that are used in European legislative instruments[472] and assuming that the European legislator will take on our proposal, a definition of this term is called for as well, since we have also decided to include cessation of payments as the basis of a rebuttable presumption of the existence of inability to pay debts.[473] However, it should be stressed from the beginning that we do not recommend using "cessation of payments" as an autonomous trigger for insolvency proceedings or in any other context than as the basis of a rebuttable presumption of inability to pay debts. Hence, the development of our definition below is entirely restricted to this rebuttable presumption. 8.38

1. ACTUAL BEHAVIOUR

Such a definition should take the special features of cessation of payments into account. As already elaborated above,[474] "cessation of payments" is a description 8.39

471 Chapter 5, at para. 5.1 with references in fn. 291 et seq.
472 Cf. *supra* at para. 8.1.
473 *Supra* at para. 8.32.
474 Chapter 5, at para. 5.5.

of the debtor's actual behaviour: he or she does not pay. It is not a description of a certain phase of the debtor's financial crisis that could be calculated with certain figures and it is not a normative term. In order to facilitate the task of proving the debtor's inability to pay debts, a presumption is grounded on the debtor's external behaviour as ascertainable by third parties.[475] It simply refers to the provable fact that the debtor no longer regularly makes payments as usual in the ordinary course of business.

8.40 Against this background, we suggest starting the definition of this term as follows:

Article 2

Definitions

For the purposes of this [statutory instrument], the following definitions apply:

...

– *"cessation of payments" means that the debtor does not pay its debts;*

....

2. RELEVANT DEBTS

8.41 However, this is not yet a satisfactory and complete definition. On the one hand, given that there is no significant difference between "cessation" and "stop", it is not very meaningful, since it more or less uses what is to be defined for the definition. On the other hand, this wording is not precise enough, since it gives rise to the impression that a complete stop of payment is necessary, which is not the case. Having in mind that, in our proposal, "cessation of payments" is primarily used as the basis of a rebuttable presumption of "inability to pay debts", two specifications of the relevant debts are necessary. First, only those debts which are germane to the establishment of inability to pay debts are relevant. As further explained above,[476] this refers to mature debts[477] only. Second, it is by no means necessary that the debtor has stopped paying *all* (or *all but an irrelevant part*) of its mature debts, as it is for inability to pay debts.[478] If one has to prove, in order to invoke the rebuttable presumption, that the debtor has completely stopped making all payments, one can also prove that the debtor is unable to pay. The presumption would therefore be pointless. It should suffice that the

---

475 Cf. *supra* at para. 8.32.

476 At section II.2.

477 As defined *supra* at para. 8.14.

478 Cf. *supra* at para. 8.21.

debtor actually does not pay a relevant part of its mature debts. However, we do not suggest including this aspect in the wording of our proposal by the phrasing "'cessation of payments' means that the debtor has stopped paying a substantial part of its mature debts". Referring to a "substantial part" would raise the question as to whether the unpaid part of the mature debts is substantial or not. This would depend on the circumstances of the case at hand,[479] which are not visible to the public and not ascertainable for creditors and courts without further inside information from the debtor. This would render the presumption useless, since creditors and courts would have severe difficulties in establishing the prerequisites of the presumption. Instead, we suggest being content with the debtor being in default vis-à-vis at least two creditors. This requires a qualified state of non-payment, i.e. default, as it is understood under the applicable national law of obligations. Further, it refrains from considering as relevant creditors only significant creditors, i.e. those who have receivables of a certain absolute or (in relation to the total receivables portfolio) relative size. A creditor within the meaning of our definitions is anyone who has a claim against the debtor, regardless of its amount or significance. This is supported by the principle of predictability (legal certainty), as it is easy to handle and facilitates access to the proceedings for creditors and decision-making for judges. It is also supported by the principle of collectivity, as it requires non-payment to more than one creditor, which prevents cessation of payments from being abused as a debt-enforcement instrument. On the other hand, it seems to us that default vis-à-vis two (and not three or more) creditors suffices. One might argue that this should be viewed sceptically under the principle of protection of the debtor's rights. However, it must be highlighted that we are only dealing with a rebuttable presumption which Member States may include in the interest of creditors.[480] The debtor is free – and in fact obliged in order to avoid the opening of insolvency proceedings – to prove that these two claims (or one of them) do not exist, are contingent, not due, or not payable for other reasons, are insignificant compared to the total amount of all his or her liabilities, or that he or she is not in default. On the other hand, we would not suggest including further features of the necessary mature debts. This particularly holds true for a reference to "undisputed debts". If it is irrelevant for the establishment of inability to pay debts whether the debtor has disputed certain debts,[481] it should also be irrelevant for cessation of payments. This does not exclude the debtor's right to rebut the presumption by proving that at least one of the debts does not

479 For example, where a debtor has mature debts (to either one or more creditors) in the amount of 10,000, a sum of 1,000 would be substantial, whereas 1,000 is more or less irrelevant where the total amount is 1,000,000.

480 See *supra* at para. 8.32.

481 Reasoning *supra* at para. 8.15.

exist, is contingent, not due, or not payable for other reasons, is insignificant compared to the total amount of all his or her liabilities, or that he or she is not in default with this payment.[482]

8.42 If one follows these suggestions, the relationship between the two bases of the presumption of insolvency developed above[483] presents itself as follows: if the debtor is in default with payments to at least two creditors, he or she has ceased payments and inability to pay debts can be presumed.[484] It can also be presumed if the debtor is in default with at least two payments or one payment for at least three months to only one creditor and this creditor is essential for the continuation of the business.[485] Hence, the fact that the single creditor is essential justifies the presumption in the same way as cessation of payments, i.e. default vis-à-vis two creditors.

8.43 In sum, we propose to amend the wording of the definition of "cessation of payments" as follows:

Article 2

Definitions

For the purposes of this [statutory instrument], the following definitions apply:

...

- "cessation of payments" means that the debtor *is in default with payments to at least two creditors*;

....

3. FURTHER RESTRICTIONS

8.44 In our view, further restrictive requirements are not indicated. In contrast to the definition of inability to pay debts, nothing needs to be said here about the assets available, because the cessation of payments is only about the fact that the debtor does not actually pay, but not about whether he or she *can* pay at all and why he or she does not pay. As a result, any reference to intentions or declarations on the part of the debtor are not called for. Where available, they can serve as circumstantial evidence for establishing cessation of payments,[486]

482 See again at para. 8.15.

483 At para. 8.32 et seq.

484 *Supra* at para. 8.32.

485 *Supra* at para. 8.33.

486 Experience shows that debtors often turn to major creditors, tell them that they are unable to make payments on time and that they need a standstill. Such declarations regularly lead to the conclusion that payments have been ceased.

but they are not indispensable requirements. Further, a liquidity gap does not need to be established, which entails the irrelevance of the size and the duration of the liquidity gap. Whether the payment stop is irreversible or persistent is also of no importance. That a certain duration is required is readily apparent from the words "cessation" and "stopped". Hence, we do not think that it is necessary to include this aspect explicitly in the definition. It may suffice that an objective bystander, assessing the available circumstances of the case at hand in general and the debtor's actual payment behaviour in particular, has no doubt that the debtor has ceased payments.

4. ESTABLISHING CESSATION OF PAYMENTS

Although cessation of payments serves as the basis of a rebuttable presumption 8.45
of the existence of inability to pay debts and is therefore an important means for establishing inability to pay debts, it may need to be established by the court itself. Since we are not intending to harmonise the law of civil procedure, we will not make any proposals regarding this topic. It may suffice to point out that cessation of payments will presumably be established by means of circumstantial evidence. However, under the principle of efficiency, which requires some flexibility for the courts in order to be able to do justice to the individual particularities of the specific case,[487] we recommend abstaining from further specification in the definition of cessation of payments.

5. PROPOSAL

Overall, this amounts to the following proposal: 8.46

Article 2

Definitions

For the purposes of this [statutory instrument], the following definitions apply:

...

- "cessation of payments" means that the debtor is in default with payments to at least two creditors;

....

[487] Cf. *supra* at para. 2.15.

IV. LIKELY AND IMMINENT INABILITY TO PAY DEBTS

8.47 In European instruments, the term "likelihood of insolvency" is used repeatedly. This particularly holds true for Article 23 Harmonisation Proposal[488] and for Articles 1(1)(a), 3(1), 4(1), 19 Directive on restructuring and insolvency,[489] the latter leaving the definition in its Article 2(2)(b) to the national legislators. However, as explained in more detail above,[490] national laws differ significantly in this respect. Hence, a common understanding of this term is not available and harmonisation cannot succeed if the European legislator sticks to this approach. Against this background, we suggest avoiding the term "likelihood of insolvency" and use instead "likelihood of inability to pay debts" (IV.1.) and – for demarcation purposes – "imminent inability to pay debts" (IV.2.) more precisely. This is not only required in the interest of successful harmonisation but also clearly supported by the principle of predictability (legal certainty)[491] as well as by the other principles of insolvency mentioned above.[492] We also stress that "likelihood" automatically includes that the debtor is not yet unable to pay debts.[493]

1. LIKELY INABILITY TO PAY DEBTS

8.48 To begin with "likelihood of insolvency", we will start with some clarifying remarks on terminology (*a*) before we consider more closely the terms "inability to pay debts" (*b*) and "likely" (*c*).

a) Terminology

8.49 As regards terminology, it is striking that the term "likelihood of insolvency" as used in European law is translated to "likely inability to pay debts" in most jurisdictions.[494] This is done either by using this term directly or by defining "likely/imminent/threatening insolvency" as "likely/imminent/threatening inability to pay debts".[495] It is apparently the general view that "likely insolvency" always refers only to "likely inability to pay debts" and not to "likely

---

488 *Supra* Chapter 1, fn. 1.
489 *Supra* Chapter 1, fn. 21.
490 Chapter 6, at para. 6.4 et seq.
491 See *supra* Chapter 2, at para. 2.14.
492 At para. 8.6.
493 See *supra* at para. 8.12.
494 See Questionnaire Q. 31 et seq.
495 For the latter, see Belgium, Cyprus, Czech Republic, Denmark, Finland, Greece, Hungary, Malta, Portugal, Romania, Slovakia, Spain, Sweden.

overindebtedness".[496] We would support this view and encourage the European legislator to adapt the terminology used in the European statutory instruments accordingly. Under the principle of predictability (legal certainty), it seems to us to be necessary to formulate terms very precisely here and to state clearly what is meant. In view of the fact that the term "likely overindebtedness" is hardly ever used in national legislation, we assume that "likelihood of insolvency" actually means "likelihood of inability to pay debts", which should then be clearly formulated as such. With this in mind, the following text will refer to "likelihood of insolvency" as "likelihood of inability to pay debts", or use the expression "likely inability to pay debts" respectively. However, since the European instruments currently use the expression "likelihood of insolvency" (which we strongly recommend be changed[497]), we will define this term.

Hence, we start our definition as follows: 8.50

Article 2
Definitions

For the purposes of this [statutory instrument], the following definitions apply:

...

- *"likelihood of insolvency" means that the debtor will become unable to pay debts;*

....

b) *Inability to Pay Debts*

If one agrees with this, little needs to be said about the financial situation the likelihood of which is to be assessed. The term "likelihood of inability to pay debts" refers to the question of whether a debtor who is currently not yet unable to pay its mature debts will become so at a certain point in time in the foreseeable future. There is no reason to define the term "inability to pay debts" differently here than as already defined above.[498] In both cases, inability to pay debts must be established, except that the point in time for which this form of insolvency is determined is different. In the case of *current* inability to pay debts, the question is whether it exists at the point in time relevant under substantive law. In the case of *likely* inability to pay debts, on the other hand, the question is whether it will occur in the future. In both cases, the relevant financial status of the debtor is the same, and so too is the definition. 8.51

496 In Belgium, Czech Republic, Lithuania, and Poland, "likely insolvency" includes "likely overindebtedness"; see also *supra* in Chapter 3, fn. 108.

497 If this recommendation is followed, the word "insolvency" must be replaced by "inability to pay debts" without any further amendments to the definition being necessary.

498 At para. 8.8 et seq.

8.52 Under this premise, nothing needs to be said about the relevant debts, the relevant assets, or the extent or duration of the liquidity gap. Here, the same applies as to the definition of inability to pay debts.[499] By using the term "inability to pay debts" as part of "likely inability to pay debts" or "likelihood of inability to pay debts" in the catalogue of definitions in a European legislative instrument, implied reference is made to the definition of "inability to pay debts" in the same catalogue as suggested here.[500] Hence, what must be likely is that the debtor will, at a future point in time, become unable to pay all but an insignificant part of its mature debts[501] from its liquid assets, unless it is to be reasonably expected that this inability can be cured in the short term.

8.53 This gives reason to keep the definition as follows:

Article 2
Definitions

For the purposes of this [statutory instrument], the following definitions apply:

...

- "likelihood of insolvency" means that the debtor will become unable to pay debts;

....

c) Likelihood

8.54 It follows from the above that only the term "likelihood", or "likely" respectively, needs further clarification. Without question, the term "likely" refers to the future. If a norm requires that a fact is likely, then it must be examined whether it can be expected with a sufficient degree of certainty that this fact will occur in the future. It is therefore a matter of a prognosis regarding future circumstances. The prognostic element is an indispensable part of every likelihood test. Likelihood as a legal term cannot be determined without a prognosis. This raises two questions: Firstly, what degree of certainty is required, i.e. *how* likely must it be that the circumstance will occur in the future? Secondly, over what period of time does this forecast extend?

aa) Degree of Certainty

8.55 As regards the necessary degree of certainty, legislators are free to define the degree of probability in more detail, for example to require that the occurrence

499 For details, see *supra* at para. 8.8 et seq.

500 *Supra* at para. 8.37.

501 This includes not only debts that are due at the point in time *when* the prognosis is made but also debts that will have come into existence or will have become mature at the future point in time *for which* the prognosis is made.

of the relevant circumstance is to be expected with a probability of at least 75%. However, not only the European, but also all national legislators have refrained from doing so.[502] They have contented themselves with the general concept of likelihood. This suggests that a predominant or preponderant probability (expressed in figures: more than 50%) is sufficient. The Supreme Court of the United Kingdom – albeit in different contexts – has aptly described this with the phrase "more likely than not".[503] We will follow this approach, having in mind that probability cannot be measured or calculated precisely and its determination is in any case associated with a large margin of discretion.

Hence, we propose to supplement our definition of "likelihood of inability to pay debts" as follows: 8.56

Article 2

Definitions

For the purposes of this [statutory instrument], the following definitions apply:

...

- "likelihood of insolvency" means that it is *more likely than not* that the debtor will become unable to pay debts;

....

bb) Prognosis Period

This leaves the question of whether a prognosis period needs to be defined and, if so, how long it should be. The answer depends to some extent on the function of the term "likely inability to pay debts". In European law, this expression is predominantly used in norms that entitle the debtor to apply for judicial support for restructuring proceedings,[504] yet also in norms that impose certain duties on directors.[505] At least the latter brings the principle of predictability (legal certainty) into play, which supports a precise determination of the prognosis period. 8.57

What this means exactly can be explained using the following example. Let us assume that the prognosis period is set at one year. This means that the directors, 8.58

502 See the answers to Questionnaire Q. 36.

503 *BTI 2014 LLC v. Sequana SA and others* [2022] UKSC 25 at [116], [200], [216], [238], [428], [430], [435].

504 Art. 23 Harmonisation Proposal: enforcement stay; Art. 4(1) Directive on restructuring and insolvency: access to a preventive restructuring framework.

505 Art. 19 Directive on restructuring and insolvency: duty to have due regard to the interests of creditors, equity-holders, and other stakeholders; the need to take steps to avoid insolvency; and the need to avoid deliberate or grossly negligent conduct that threatens the viability of the business.

if they wish to fulfil their duties conscientiously, must continuously prepare a cash-flow forecast for the next 12 months in order to assess whether the debtor company is more likely than not to be able to fulfil its payment obligations during this period. If the debtor wishes to apply for court support for restructuring, it must demonstrate that inability to pay debts is more likely than not to occur in the next 12 months. If it is not expected to occur before 13 months or even later, judicial assistance in restructuring efforts cannot be utilised. If, due to the debtor's particular circumstances, it is not possible to prepare a cash-flow forecast for the next 12 months (but perhaps only for the next six), this is relevant for judicial assistance. In that case, judicial assistance can only be utilised if the inability to pay debts is likely to occur in the next six months, but not if it might occur in the second half of the prognosis period. The directors cannot be accused of breaches of duty, as a breach of duty requires proof of predominant probability, which cannot be provided if a corresponding forecast is objectively impossible.

8.59 This example leads to the question as to whether it is necessary to implement a concrete prognosis period in the definition of likelihood of insolvency. Although at first glance, this seems to be supported by the principle of predictability (legal certainty), we do not suggest including such a fixed period. The first reason for this is that it would limit the debtor's access to judicial assistance for its restructuring efforts. For example, if the prognosis period is one year and it is more likely than not that the debtor will be unable to pay its mature debts in 13 months, the debtor has to wait one month before he or she can apply to the court for judicial support. This is clearly a wasted month and is hardly compatible with the principles of optimisation,[506] satisfaction,[507] and protection of the debtor's rights,[508] since it is desirable in the interest of all stakeholders to start restructuring efforts – if necessary, with the help of the court – as early as possible, which could be hampered by a restrained prognosis period. Hence, where the debtor can show that the company will become unable to pay its debts in more than one year, they should have access to the judicial restructuring instruments now. There is no need to provide for a fixed time-span that limits these possibilities. Further, this is also compatible with the directors' interests. On the one hand, they are interested in a fixed and very short prognosis period, since this would limit their duties in connection with likely inability to pay debts.[509] However, it is hardly justifiable that they would not have to take the interests of other stakeholders into account *if* it were more likely than not that inability to pay debts would occur not in the near but in the foreseeable future. At any rate, the directors can live with a longer time-span because they

506 Details *supra* Chapter 2, at para. 2.17.

507 More *supra* Chapter 2, at para. 2.18.

508 See *supra* Chapter 2, at para. 2.19.

509 See *supra* fn. 505.

cannot be accused of a breach of duty if the solvency forecast is not possible after a certain point in time. Hence, the only limitation for the prognosis period should be the foreseeability of the future, depending on the circumstances of the individual case, which does not need express mentioning in the wording of the definition, since it is an implied element of any prognosis. We therefore do not suggest a fixed prognosis period (but would not object if the European legislator implemented such a period in the interest of legal certainty).

This sums up to the following formulation: 8.60

Article 2
Definitions

For the purposes of this [statutory instrument], the following definitions apply:

...

- "likelihood of insolvency" means that it is more likely than not that the debtor will become unable to pay debts;

....

d) *Proposal*

Overall, we suggest the following definition of likely inability to pay debts: 8.61

Article 2
Definitions

For the purposes of this [statutory instrument], the following definitions apply:

...

- "likelihood of insolvency" means that it is more likely than not that the debtor will become unable to pay debts;

....

2. IMMINENT INABILITY TO PAY DEBTS

Imminent inability to pay debts is currently not used in European statutory instruments. Hence, this point can be kept short. However, given the findings of our survey among the Member States,[510] we recommend agreeing on a definition for this term as well, primarily in order to clarify the relationship between likely and imminent inability to pay debts (independent of which 8.62

510 See *supra* at para. 6.10 et seq.

legal consequences national legislators decide to connect to "imminent" but not to "likely" inability to pay debts[511]).

8.63 As regards the details, reference can first be made to the remarks on likely inability to pay debts. As already elaborated above,[512] the difference between likely and imminent inability to pay debts is that the former is a term of probability whereas the latter is a term of urgency. When a debtor is imminently insolvent, inability to pay debts is just around the corner; it is certain that it will occur and that it will occur very soon.[513] We suggest taking this into account by avoiding any reference to probability or likelihood. However, in the interest of legal certainty we recommend limiting the use of this term to a certain period, so that it is clear for the debtor or the directors whether rights are restricted or duties are imposed. We therefore suggest a term of three months.

8.64 If one agrees with that, the following wording can be suggested:

Article 2
Definitions

For the purposes of this [statutory instrument], the following definitions apply:

...

- *"imminent insolvency" means that in the next three months the debtor will become unable to pay debts;*

....

3. PROPOSAL

8.65 To sum up, then, we suggest the following definitions for the debtor's future inability to pay debts:

Article 2
Definitions

For the purposes of this [statutory instrument], the following definitions apply:

...

511 Typically, the debtor's right to apply for insolvency proceedings is connected to likely inability to pay debts, whereas imminent inability to pay debts comes with restrictions of rights or additional duties.

512 At para. 6.3.

513 However, we do not suggest making this higher degree of probability a prerequisite for imminent inability to pay debts. "Predominant likelihood" should suffice here as well. Although the degree of certainty will normally increase the shorter the forecast period, it is not necessary to elevate this typically existing circumstance to the status of a prerequisite.

- "likelihood of insolvency" means that it is more likely than not that the debtor will become unable to pay debts;
- "imminent insolvency" means that in the next three months the debtor will become unable to pay debts;

....

V. OVERINDEBTEDNESS

The last subspecies of insolvency to be dealt with is overindebtedness. This appearance of insolvency is only rarely mentioned in the European instruments so far.[514] Here again, we do not utter any opinion as to whether and for which situations the European Union should introduce it into European law.[515] This particularly holds true for a duty to file for insolvency proceedings attached to the occurrence of overindebtedness (as available in many national laws[516]). This is a policy choice for the European and the national legislators to make and we do not express any opinion thereon. However, since the expression is used in many national laws, we think the following to be necessary in the interest of clarity. 8.66

1. FUNCTION OF OVERINDEBTEDNESS

It should be made clear right from the outset what the function of overindebtedness is, in particular, whether it has an independent role in relation to inability to pay debts and likely[517] inability to pay debts. To begin with, the reference to overindebtedness responds to a situation where the debtor would not withstand a hypothetical liquidation test: if the debtor's estate (i.e. the entirety of all assets that have been used as a basis for obtaining credit and are liable for the debtor's debts) would be realised at a relevant point in time, would the proceeds be sufficient to cover all the debtor's liabilities? If the answer is "yes", then the debtor is not overindebted. However, if the answer is "no", then taking a closer look is indicated. As already explained above,[518] mere arithmetical overindebtedness is a 8.67

---

514 The only appearances of overindebtedness (albeit without using this term) are in Art. 18(4)(b) Regulation EU) 806/2014 (*supra* Chapter 1, fn. 25) and Art. 32(4)(b) Directive 2014/59/EU (*supra* Chapter 1, fn. 26). The term is also used for entrepreneuers in Art. 19 et seq. Directive (EU) 2019/1023, but incorrectly defined in Art. 2 No. 13, which equals overindebtedness with inability to pay debts.

515 It is for this reason that we do not deal with the personal scope of overindebtedness (on this, see *supra* Chapter 7, at para. 7.3). Whether it should be used for all debtors or only for legal persons, is left at the discretion of the European legislator.

516 Cf. *supra* Chapter 3, fn. 146.

517 The distinction between likely and imminent inability to pay debts is ignored in this section of the study.

518 Chapter 7, at para. 7.2.

reason to be worried but does not automatically mean that the debtor is insolvent in a legal sense. The reason for this is that the assessment of overindebtedness not only includes the liabilities that are currently mature but *all* liabilities, including those that have not yet been fully incurred, those that are subject to conditions precedent, those that are not yet due, or those to which legal defences apply. However, the fact that the asset pool is not sufficient to fulfil all these liabilities is initially no cause for insolvency proceedings, as many of them *are* currently not due for payment. Further, under the principle of protecting the debtor's rights, it is not appropriate to put a company into insolvency proceedings only because it is arithmetically overindebted if it nevertheless has a positive viability prognosis. Hence, arithmetical overindebtedness is only an (albeit important) early warning sign; it is nothing more, but also nothing less than a reason to be careful and take a closer look.[519] "Taking a closer look" means asking whether the company's financial strength is sufficient in the medium term to fulfil the liabilities due for payment within the forecast period. If this is the case, the company is not insolvent in a legal sense and there is no reason to open insolvency proceedings and to apply insolvency law now. Hence, a liquidity-related viability test supplements the asset-related liquidation test. However, combining the liquidation test with the liquidity/viability test raises the question of the distinction between overindebtedness, inability to pay debts, and likely inability to pay debts.

8.68 The answer is easy regarding the relationship between overindebtedness and (actual) inability to pay debts. The latter relates to the present and takes only currently mature debts (and currently liquid assets) into account. The former relates to the future insofar as all debts are taken into account. This includes not only currently mature debts but also not fully incurred, contingent, and not yet due debts. It also includes liabilities that a reasonable debtor would expect to incur in the ordinary course of business within the prognosis period (e.g. wages or taxes and debts stemming from new contracts). Hence, it covers all liabilities, whereas inability to pay debts covers only a subset of these liabilities. The result may be that a debtor is unable to pay its debts but not overindebted (e.g. because valuable assets belonging to the estate would suffice to pay all debts but cannot be taken into account when assessing inability to pay debts as they are not convertible into cash at short notice and therefore are not "liquid"). The result of the assessment may also be that a debtor is overindebted but not unable to pay its mature debts (e.g. because the current credit facilities suffice for paying the currently mature debts, but the liquidity would not suffice in a medium-term

---

519 This explains why some jurisdictions use overindebtedness as a "sign" of inability to pay debts (references *supra* in Chapter 7, fn. 376). If arithmetical overindebtedness is an early warning sign, it justifies assigning the burden of proof for being solvent (i.e. being able to pay the mature debts) to the debtor.

perspective). In this case, the occurrence of substantive insolvency (measured by overindebtedness) is brought forward compared to inability to pay debts, since overindebtedness occurs earlier than inability to pay debts.

The latter example in particular leads us to the distinction between overindebtedness and likely inability to pay debts. Both have in common that they require a liquidity test for the foreseeable future. If this test is positive, the debtor is neither likely to be unable to pay its debts nor overindebted, the latter regardless of the result of the liquidation test. If the liquidity test is negative, the debtor is likely to be unable to pay its debts and it can also be overindebted, provided the liquidation test is also negative. This proves a significant overlap between overindebtedness and likely inability to pay debts, which raises the question of the need for overindebtedness as a subspecies of likely inability to pay debts. The answer follows from the legal consequences that legislators may attach to these terms rather than from the definition itself. As the evaluation of national laws has shown, many legislators link overindebtedness to duties, while likely inability to pay debts is linked to rights. For example, where inability to pay debts is only likely or imminent, the debtor, under many national laws, is entitled but not obliged to file for liquidation or restructuring proceedings,[520] whereas overindebtedness is frequently linked to the directors' duty to file for insolvency proceedings.[521] In our view, overindebtedness is a more severe phase of the debtor's financial crisis, since the negative liquidity/viability test is amplified by a negative liquidation test. In the context of directors' duties, overindebtedness means prompting the directors to review the liquidity of their company continuously. If the liquidity test is negative (which amounts to likely inability to pay debts), then (and only then) the liquidation test must be carried out. This should encourage the directors to take countermeasures in good time if overindebtedness is established. It is a means of further protecting the general body of creditors by forcing the directors to intervene and eliminate the overindebtedness before it is too late. At the same time, following our definition of overindebtedness creates an excellent "early warning tool" as required by Article 3 Directive on restructuring and insolvency. 8.69

Hence, from a principle-based point of view, overindebtedness also marks the point in time where the shift from the application of general civil law to insolvency law may take place, and the principles of insolvency law require a precise and appropriate definition of this prerequisite. As elaborated in more detail above,[522] this is supported by nearly all principles of insolvency law, in 8.70

520 Details *supra* Chapter 3, at paras. 3.6, 3.12.
521 Cf. *supra* Chapter 3, at para. 3.11, fn. 146.
522 Chapter 2, at para. 2.10 et seq., summarising at para. 2.24.

particular by the principles of collectivity, creditors' autonomy, predictability (legal certainty), efficiency, optimisation, satisfaction, protection of the debtor's rights, equal treatment of creditors, protection of trust, and fixation.

8.71 Having this in mind, we suggest starting the definition of overindebtedness in accordance with the UNCITRAL Legislative Guide on Insolvency Law,[523] as follows:

Article 2
Definitions

For the purposes of this [statutory instrument], the following definitions apply:

...

- *"overindebtedness" means that the liabilities of the debtor exceed the value of its assets;*

....

2. RELEVANT POINT IN TIME

8.72 Among the details, the first aspect to be clarified is the relevant point in time. In this respect, the two elements of overindebtedness – the liquidation test and the liquidity/viability test – must be distinguished. The liquidity or viability test is related to the future. A negative liquidation test gives cause to examine the company's viability understood as its future liquidity. This requires a liquidity prognosis for a certain period of time. We will deal with the details, and in particular with the question of how long this period should be, below.[524]

8.73 In contrast to that, the liquidation test (arithmetical overindebtedness) as triggered by a negative liquidity test must be established for the point in time for which the legal consequences shall apply. Here, the same applies as for inability to pay debts.[525] For example, if one wishes to know whether the debtor is overindebted today, the liquidation test must be carried out for today. If the legal consequences are dependent on whether the debtor was overindebted on 12 December 2023, the liquidation test must be related to that day.

---

523 See *supra* at Chapter 1, at para. 1.8, Chapter 3, at para. 3.2; similarly Art. 18(4)(b) Regulation EU) 806/2014 (*supra* Chapter 1, fn. 25) and Art. 32(4)(b) Directive 2014/59/EU (*supra* Chapter 1, fn. 26); see *supra* Chapter 1, at para. 1.7.

524 At para. 8.65.

525 See *supra* at para. 8.11 et seq.

This results in the following amendment of our proposal for a definition of overindebtedness: 8.74

Article 2
Definitions

For the purposes of this [statutory instrument], the following definitions apply:

...

- "overindebtedness" means that, *at the relevant point in time*, the liabilities of the debtor exceed the value of its assets;

....

3. LIQUIDITY/VIABILITY TEST

As explained above, the liquidity or viability test concerns the expected liquidity of the debtor. It may show that the debtor will more likely than not become unable to meet all debts that are or become mature in the foreseeable future from its then liquid assets. In principle, reference can be made to the explanations regarding likely inability to pay debts.[526] What must be determined is the relationship between overindebtedness and likely inability to pay debts.[527] In our view, overindebtedness is an amplified form of likely inability to pay debts. Both require a cash-flow test, but additionally, overindebtedness requires a negative liquidation test (which may justify a legislator's decisions to impose more severe legal consequences compared to those attached to mere likely inability to pay debts). As a consequence, as explained in more detail above in relation to likelihood of inability to pay debts, we suggest refraining from implementing a fixed prognosis period within the definition of overindebtedness. 8.75

This leads to the following wording: 8.76

Article 2
Definitions

For the purposes of this [statutory instrument], the following definitions apply:

...

- "overindebtedness" means that, at the relevant point in time, the liabilities of the debtor exceed the value of its assets and *the occurrence of the debtor's inability to pay debts is more likely than not*;

....

---

526 *Supra* at para. 8.51 et seq. This includes the necessary degree of certainty (more likely than not) regarding future developments, see *supra* at para. 8.55.

527 Details *supra* at para. 8.69.

4. LIQUIDATION TEST

8.77 As regards the liquidation test, the first challenge to take up is the valuation of the debtor's current assets. While it is relatively easy to list the liabilities and assets and to assess the liabilities at their nominal value,[528] the valuation of the assets is difficult. In this respect, we suggest that the values recognised in the annual balance sheet (so-called "book value") should not be used in any circumstances. They are frequently influenced by special tax and accounting provisions, particularly by depreciation rules, and do not mirror the real value of the assets listed in the balance sheet. It is for this reason, that – in order to avoid any misunderstandings – we do not use the term "balance sheet insolvency".

8.78 If one accepts this premise, the liquidation value and the going concern value come into consideration. As the context is a liquidation test, it is the logical consequence to start with the liquidation value as a basis. This is supported by our view that overindebtedness is an amplified form of likelihood of insolvency in which state a liquidation is to be reckoned with. The question is therefore what price can be realised for each individual asset in the context of a piecemeal liquidation. However, it must be taken into account that liquidation may lead to the sale of the entire estate (or essential parts of it), which in the case of corporate insolvencies can mean the sale of the business or larger parts of the business. If it is more likely than not, based on the circumstances of the case, that the debtor's business will be sold as a going concern, then this value must be used as the comparator.[529]

8.79 With this in mind, we suggest amending our proposal for a definition as follows:

Article 2

Definitions

For the purposes of this [statutory instrument], the following definitions apply:

...

- "overindebtedness" means that, at the relevant point in time, the liabilities of the debtor exceed the *liquidation* value of its assets and the occurrence of the debtor's inability to pay debts is more likely than not;

....

---

528 This means that a creditor's claim of €100,000 is assessed as a liability of the debtor of €100,000.

529 However, it should be stressed that we suggest reference to the liquidation value at the relevant point in time irrespective of whether the applicable accounting rules, standards, and practices limit this approach to a later stage of the debtor's financial crisis.

5. PROPOSAL

In all, we suggest defining the term "overindebtedness" as follows: 8.80

Article 2
Definitions

For the purposes of this [statutory instrument], the following definitions apply:

...

- "overindebtedness" means that, at the relevant point in time, the liabilities of the debtor exceed the liquidation value of its assets and the occurrence of the debtor's inability to pay debts is more likely than not;

....

VI. INSOLVENCY

Finally, we return to the definition of the term "insolvency". As argued above,[530] we find it difficult to use this expression not as a description of a factual phenomenon but as a legally defined prerequisite for concrete legal consequences, since the meaning of this word is ambiguous. Although this would be a rather radical step, we would recommend avoiding this word as far as possible and using "inability to pay debts" instead (if this is what is actually meant[531]). If the European legislator were to follow this step, no definition of the term "insolvency" would be necessary. However, we take into account that the European legislator shies away from such a radical move, will stick to the present wording of the existing instruments, and will at best avoid this term in future instruments. In this case, the word "insolvency" needs a proper definition. Two options are available here. 8.81

On the one hand, it is possible to define insolvency in a more technical sense and understand it as a generic term for the manifestations of the financial difficulties addressed in this study. This would cover inability to pay debts and all subspecies of likely inability to pay debts (i.e. including imminent inability to pay debts and overindebtedness), since these terms address future circumstances rather than 8.82

530 E.g. at para. 8.49.
531 This is expressly clarified in Recital 37 Harmonisation Proposal, which states that between inability to pay debts and overindebtedness as the usual triggers for insolvency proceedings, only the former is suitable for winding-up microenterprises; see *supra* Chapter 5 at para. 5.2.

the existence of actual inability to pay debts. In this case, a proper definition would read as follows:

Article 2
Definitions

For the purposes of this [statutory instrument], the following definitions apply:

...

- *"insolvency" means inability to pay debts, overindebtedness, likely and imminent inability to pay debts;*

....

8.83 On the other hand, it is possible to react to the fact that the European legislator has used "insolvency" predominantly in the sense of "inability to pay debts" so far, unless the definition is left to the national laws of the Member States. If one wants to pay tribute to this fact, then the following definition is appropriate:

Article 2
Definitions

For the purposes of this [statutory instrument], the following definitions apply:

...

- *"insolvency" means inability to pay debts;*

....

8.84 Which of the variants offered above is chosen depends crucially on how the European legislator wants the word "insolvency" to be understood. We cannot take this decision away from them. However, in the interests of clarity and certainty, we stick to our proposal[532] to equate insolvency with inability to pay debts. For all other terms, it is for the European legislator to decide whether they are also meant to be referred to or not.

8.85 This leads to the following proposal:

Article 2
Definitions

For the purposes of this [statutory instrument], the following definitions apply:

...

- "insolvency" means inability to pay debts;

....

---

532 See *supra* at para. 8.81.

VII. FINAL PROPOSAL

Over all, we suggest the following wording: 8.86

Article 2
Definitions

For the purposes of this [statutory instrument], the following definitions apply:

...

- "insolvency" means inability to pay debts;
- "inability to pay debts" means the debtor's inability at the relevant point in time to pay all but an insignificant part of its mature debts from its liquid assets, unless it is to be reasonably expected that this inability can be cured in the short term; Member States may provide that inability to pay debts is rebuttably presumed, but only if the debtor has ceased payments or is in default to an essential creditor with at least two payments or one payment for at least three months;
- "cessation of payments" means that the debtor is in default with payments to at least two creditors;
- "likelihood of insolvency" means that it is more likely than not that the debtor will become unable to pay debts;
- "imminent insolvency" means that in the next three months the debtor will become unable to pay debts;
- "overindebtedness" means that, at the relevant point in time, the liabilities of the debtor exceed the liquidation value of its assets and the occurrence of the debtor's inability to pay debts is more likely than not;

....

VIII. FINAL INSPECTION

At the end of our study, we now verify whether we have achieved our aims. 8.87 This mainly involves three points. Firstly, are our proposed definitions fit for the European instruments? Secondly, are they applicable equally to legal and natural persons, to entrepreneurs and consumers? Thirdly, have we done justice to our aim of providing definitions that are clear, precise, and easy to apply?

1. COMPATIBILITY WITH EUROPEAN LAW

As regards suitability for the already existing European instruments, we have 8.88 no doubt that our proposals are compatible with the Regulations and Directives dealing with insolvency law.

a) *Harmonisation Proposal*

8.89 To begin with, the Harmonisation Proposal[533] uses the term "likelihood of insolvency" in its Article 23, leaving the definition to the national laws. Under the principle of predictability (legal certainty), we suggest being more precise and replacing "likelihood of insolvency" with "likelihood of inability to pay debts" (if this is what is meant), thus following the common understanding in nearly all Member States.[534] We do not think that this – and the adoption of our more detailed definition of this term – would change the essential meaning of this expression, understood as a concept of European law.

8.90 Further, Article 23 Harmonisation Proposal deals with an "insolvent" debtor. We also propose to either avoid this expression or to be more specific (e.g. by replacing "insolvent" with "unable to pay its debts") and insert respective definitions in the catalogue in Article 2.[535] In this respect, Article 38 can serve as a model, as paragraph 1 also refers to "insolvent", but then defines this in paragraph 2 as "inability to pay debts", albeit in a too general and in the end insufficient way. The same can be said for the reference to a debtor who "was unable to pay its mature debts" in Article 6(1)(a), (2)(b), and (3) sentence 2 Harmonisation Proposal. The fact that our proposal defines "inability to pay debts" in a more detailed way would clarify rather than change the meaning of this expression understood as a term of European law.

b) *Other Instruments*

8.91 The same holds true for other European instruments. For example, the Directive on restructuring and insolvency[536] uses the term "likelihood of insolvency" in its Articles 1(1)(a), 3(1), 4(1), and 19, and leaves the definition expressly to the national laws in its Article 2(2)(b). In this respect, reference can be made to paragraph 8.89 above.

8.92 Other instruments restrict themselves to using the rather general words "insolvent", "insolvency", or "insolvency proceedings" and either refer to national laws[537] or are not specific at all.[538] We would not advise sticking to this approach but rather to replace the word "insolvency" etc. by the expression that is actually meant, most likely "inability to pay debts".[539] In our opinion,

533 *Supra* fn. 1.
534 Details *supra* at para. 8.49.
535 See *supra* at para. 8.81.
536 *Supra* fn. 21.
537 See Art. 2(2)(a) Directive 2019/1023/EU (*supra* fn. 21).
538 Examples *supra* Chapter 1 at para. 1.7.
539 See also *supra* at para. 8.83.

this is at least necessary if these terms are prerequisites for concrete legal consequences. Otherwise a proper harmonisation cannot be reached, because the understanding in the Member States is – as shown in Chapters 3 to 7 above – too diverse.

As pointed out above,[540] the term "overindebtedness" is only indirectly referred to in Recital 57 read with Article 18(4)(b) Regulation (EU) 806/2014[541] and Article 32(4)(b) Directive 2014/59/EU.[542] These rules explain "balance sheet insolvency" with the phrase that "the assets of the entity are, or there are objective elements to support a determination that the assets of the entity will, in the near future, be less than its liabilities".[543] The norms do not contain a forecasting element insofar as they are based on current arithmetical overindebtedness. This can be explained by the fact that arithmetical overindebtedness is more important in the case of bank insolvencies with regard to deposit protection and the systemic importance of banks than for other companies. However, it must be said that this deviates from the definition proposed here, so that it is not advisable to speak of overindebtedness (in the sense defined here) in these legal acts. 8.93

2. PERSONAL SCOPE

The second question to be answered is whether our definitions are suitable for consumers as well as for entrepreneurs, or for natural persons as well as for legal entities respectively.[544] This question can be answered positively as far as (likely/imminent or actual) inability to pay debts is concerned. The comparison of mature debts and liquid assets makes sense for all debtors, regardless of their legal status, since all subgroups have mature liabilities and liquid assets. 8.94

The only term the suitability of which could be doubted is "overindebtedness". As explained above,[545] many jurisdictions restrict the applicability of this subspecies of insolvency to certain legal entities, mostly companies with limited liability. The main reason for this might be that it is impossible to capitalise the most important "assets" of a natural person (its honesty, reliability, creativity, perseverance, assertiveness, etc.) in a balance sheet. Hence, a liquidation test limited to assets that can be realised in a liquidation would paint a false picture. However, this does not exclude applying our definition to natural persons from 8.95

540 At para. 8.66.
541 *Supra* Chapter 1, fn. 25.
542 *Supra* Chapter 1, fn. 26.
543 See *supra* Chapter 1, at para. 1.7.
544 See *supra* Chapter 1, at para. 1.17.
545 Chapter 7, at para. 7.3.

the outset. Even if this application would lead to nearly all natural persons being arithmetically overindebted, this would be compensated for by the liquidity test for the foreseeable future, which makes sense for both natural and legal persons. In other words, it is for the legislator to decide on the scope of "overindebtedness" and to connect concrete legal consequences to the overindebtedness of natural persons.

3. EASE OF APPLICATION

8.96 The last and certainly important topic to address is whether the definitions are sufficiently easy to apply. As explained earlier,[546] Article 38(2) sentence 2 Harmonisation Proposal is right in demanding that Member States shall "ensure that these conditions are clear, simple and easily ascertainable". It follows from various principles that this demand applies to all legislators, not only the national but also the European. It is therefore advisable to check whether our proposals meet these requirements. Three points are relevant in this respect.

8.97 A first possible objection might be that our definitions are not simple enough. At least the definitions of "inability to pay debts" and "overindebtedness" contain many requirements and are not limited to two or three elements. Indeed, this renders the application of these definitions more burdensome. However, as has been explained repeatedly, a very short definition may also be difficult to apply, since it leaves many questions unanswered and does not provide the person dealing with this definition with the necessary guidance. "Simplicity" in a rule is not an end in itself but must be balanced against the necessary degree of legal certainty. We believe that our proposals offer an appropriate and balanced equilibrium between simplicity and reliability. Both are necessary if a norm is to fulfil its purpose.

8.98 In contrast to this, a second objection could be that our proposals are too rigid and do not leave enough room for judicial discretion. Admittedly, detailed definitions restrict the scope of discretion of the court. We have pointed out above[547] that the principle of efficiency calls for flexible solutions that allow the relevant circumstances of the individual case to be taken into account. With this in mind, we have refrained from being even more specific at various points in this study.[548] However, the principle of efficiency must always be balanced against the principle of predictability (legal certainty), which argues against leaving the determination of insolvency entirely to the discretion of the courts (quite apart

---

546 *Supra* Chapter 2, at para. 2.15, and para. 8.6.

547 Chapter 2, at para. 2.15.

548 For examples, see *supra* at paras. 8.22, 8.25, 8.45.

from the fact that this would seriously jeopardise harmonisation). Against this background, we have tried to find an appropriate wording that provides for legal certainty without excluding necessary flexibility when applying the rules to the individual case at hand.

Finally, one might argue that our definitions contain too many prognostic elements. It is true that the definitions of inability to pay debts ("in the short term"), likelihood of insolvency ("more likely than not"), imminent insolvency ("in the next three months"), and overindebtedness ("more likely than not") are coined by prognostic prerequisites. However, it seems to us that these prognoses are unavoidable. This certainly holds true for likely and imminent inability to pay debts, since both terms refer to the future by their very nature. Whether insolvency is imminent or likely cannot be assessed without a prognosis.[549] Further, the prognostic element in the definition of inability to pay debts is required by the principle of proportionality.[550] Since the prognosis period is a rather short one, it should not be too difficult to handle this prerequisite. Finally, the liquidity prognosis in the definition of overindebtedness is a necessary counterweight to the insufficiently informative liquidation test. The burden resulting from this prerequisite should not be too severe and should be manageable for the parties involved. 8.99

These findings are confirmed by an evaluation of the impact assessments.[551] 8.100
Notably, no country indicated that the model definitions would cause substantial disruption to their legal systems. A large majority of Member States found the proposed model definitions in insolvency law to be compatible and feasible, requiring only minimal or manageable changes to their existing legislation. Some countries foresee more substantial changes, although these changes would generally be compatible, feasible, and seen as a positive development.

549 See *supra* at para. 8.54.
550 See *supra* at para. 8.24.
551 They are printed *infra* as Part III.

CHAPTER 9
CONCLUSION

In all, the cornerstones of our study can be summarised as follows: 9.1

- Since the European Union strives for harmonisation of substantive insolvency law, it is necessary to define at a European level what substantive insolvency law is. Without that, harmonisation will fail, because the understanding of the relevant terms in the Member States is too diverse to trust that national legislators and courts will arrive at the same interpretations on their own.
- A proposal for these definitions can be based on certain principles of insolvency law, most prominently (but not exclusively) on the principle of legal certainty and the principle of efficiency. They require definitions that mark the point in time when the shift from general civil law to insolvency law takes place as clear, precise, and easy to apply as possible, and whereby the demand for legal certainty does not mean that the specific circumstances of the individual case can no longer be taken into account.
- Against this background, one cannot be content with rather general definitions as provided for in Article 38(2) Harmonisation Proposal, since they leave too many questions open and jeopardise both legal certainty and the goal of harmonisation.
- We are confident that with our proposals, we have found a reasonable and manageable balance that the European legislator can fall back on if it decides to define the term "insolvency" and its subspecies.

SYNOPSIS

Text	Explanation at para.
"insolvency"	**8.85**
means *inability to pay debts*;	8.81–8.85
"inability to pay debts"	**8.37**
means the debtor's inability *at the relevant point in time*	8.11–8.13
to pay *all but an insignificant part*	8.20–8.23
of its mature debts	8.14–8.17
from its liquid assets,	8.18–8.19
unless it is to be reasonably expected that this inability can be cured in the short term;	8.24–8.28
Member States may provide that inability to pay debts is *rebuttably presumed*,	8.27–8.31
but only	8.34–8.36
if the debtor has *ceased payments*	8.32, 8.36
or *is in default to an essential creditor with at least two payments or one payment for at least three months*;	8.33, 8.36
"cessation of payments"	**8.46**
means *that the debtor is in default with payments to at least two creditors*;	8.38–8.45
"likelihood of insolvency"	**8.61, 8.65**
means that it is *more likely than not*	8.54–8.61
that the *debtor will become unable to pay debts*;	8.48–8.53
"imminent insolvency"	**8.64, 8.65**
means that *in the next three months the debtor will become unable to pay debts*;	8.62–8.64

(continued)

(continued)

Text	Explanation at para.
"overindebtedness"	**8.80**
means that, *at the relevant point in time,*	8.72–8.74
the liabilities of the debtor exceed the liquidation value of its assets	8.66–8.71, 8.77–8.79
and the *occurrence of the debtor's inability to pay debts is more likely than not*;	8.75–8.76

PART II

IMPACT ASSESSMENTS

AUSTRIA

Kevin LABNER

Please identify to what extent the proposed Model Definitions in the proposal align with or differ from the definitions currently used in your national law and whether they would be compatible with and operable in your jurisdiction.

I. INDIVIDUAL ASSESSMENT OF THE MODEL DEFINITIONS

A comparison of the Model Definitions with the definitions in Austrian law reveals the following (please note that references to Austrian law can be found in more detail in the National Report for Austria; the following considerations therefore do not repeat references to case law and/or scholarly contributions already included in the National Report):

1. INSOLVENCY

Austrian statutory law does not provide for a uniform definition of "insolvency". "Insolvency" comprises both the terms "inability to pay debts" (*Zahlungsunfähigkeit*, §66 IO) and "overindebtedness" (*Überschuldung*, §67 IO) – the latter being only applicable to certain debtors (mainly legal persons with limited liability, see for details *infra* section 5). If a debtor is either unable to pay debts and/or overindebted (again: where applicable), the debtor (its directors) and/or its creditors are obliged (debtor) or entitled (creditors) to file for insolvency proceedings (see §69 IO).

2. INABILITY TO PAY DEBTS

The Model Definition of inability to pay debts strongly resembles the definition enshrined in §66 IO (Insolvenzordnung).

a) *Prerequisites*

The statute (Insolvenzordnung) does not define the prerequisites for inability to pay debts (*Zahlungsunfähigkeit*). As outlined in the National Report, inability to pay debts is generally defined as a situation where the debtor cannot pay *mature* debts because he or she lacks the liquid financial means and is also unable to procure the necessary means (e.g. by way of raising a credit) as soon as possible.[1] Grace periods and liquidity gaps are accepted for up to 5% (thus calling into question whether this would still reflect a mere "insignificant" part of the mature debts as set out in the Model Definition) of due debts and up to six months respectively (again, it would be questionable, whether this would still be a "short term" as proposed in the Model Definition).

In summary, it can be expected that the implementation of the Model Definition would lead to a somewhat stricter approach to the assessment of inability to pay debts. It needs to be said, however, that these *beneficia juris* (regarding the grace period and the volume of uncovered mature debts) are not enshrined in statute but have rather evolved in the jurisprudence of the Austrian Supreme Court. An implementation of the Model Definition would therefore not trigger the need for an amendment of the Insolvency Act in this regard.

b) *Presumptions*

The Model Definition of inability to pay debts presumes a status of inability to pay debts if two conditions are met, namely (i) cessation of payments (being in default with payments vis-à-vis at least two creditors) and (ii) being in default to an essential creditor with at least two payments or one payment for at least three months. All in all, this rather precise definition (presumption) goes beyond what Austrian insolvency law (explicitly) provides for.

Pursuant to §66(2) IO, inability to pay debts is to be presumed if the debtor ceases to pay ("*wenn der Schuldner seine Zahlungen einstellt.*"). This circumstance is, however, not self-evident and is open to interpretation. According to the prevailing view, the presumption may be triggered by certain behaviour, although it is not entirely clear which circumstances suffice to presume the debtor's inability to pay debts.[2]

The Model Definition's presumption (default vis-à-vis essential creditors with at least two payments or at least one payment for at least three months) might suffice to presume the debtor's inability to pay debts under current insolvency law. As often mentioned in scholarly literature, non-payment vis-à-vis public

---

1 See National Report answer to Question 13 with further references.

2 See, for relevant cases, National Report Question 19(d).

creditors (tax authorities or social security agencies) indicates inability to pay debts (albeit one could ask whether these debts relate to "essential creditors", which we would answer in the affirmative because Chapter 8, paragraph 8.33 of the Main Report explicitly mentions *public creditors*). With regard to the presumption based on default with payments to at least two creditors, one could refer to the remarks already made: If debts due to these two creditors do not amount to at least 5% of the overall debt burden and/or are not under default for more than three months, then (according to current Austrian practice) there would be no reason to open insolvency proceedings. Conversely, it may also be sufficient to be unable to pay one single creditor if his or her claim is significant (i.e. exceeding 5% of the total debt volume).

The implementation of the Model Definition would, on the one hand, probably add legal clarity and foreseeability while, on the other hand, trigger insolvency at an earlier stage than under current Austrian practice.

c) *Consequences*

As "cessation of payment" is not statutorily defined at all, the Model Definition would merely affect the current application practice of either "inability to pay debts" and/or "cessation of payments" (the latter being a presumed indicator of the former). The other presumption (regarding essential creditors) laid out by the Model Definition might therefore serve as an additional – and most probably helpful – means to determine the debtor's inability to pay debts. To be clear, in many cases, a creditor may not be aware of whether the debtor is in default vis-à-vis essential creditors. However, if there are additional circumstances suggesting the cessation of payments, after the filing for bankruptcy, the court seised would be obliged to establish whether essential creditors (as per the presumption) are affected or not and to confront the debtor with these facts, since the Insolvency Code requires the court seised to establish the relevant facts on its own motion (the inquisitorial principle). This, in turn, could certainly contribute to a swift examination of the debtor's liquidity status.

3. CESSATION OF PAYMENTS

See for details *supra* section 2(b).

4. LIKELIHOOD OF INSOLVENCY AND IMMINENT INSOLVENCY

As regards likely and imminent inability to pay debts, the following can be said.

a) *Likelihood of Insolvency*

"Likelihood of insolvency" as such only relates to a voluntary ground for the opening of restructuring proceedings (under the regime of the Restrukturierungsordnung, ReO – being, broadly speaking, the implementation act for the Restructuring Directive). Apart from that, Austrian law provides for the term "imminent inability to pay debts" (see §167(2) IO), which serves as a voluntary ground for the opening of reorganisation proceedings (*Sanierungsverfahren*). It seems to be noteworthy that "imminent inability to pay debts" is one example given by the legislator to define "likelihood of insolvency" under §6 ReO and thus reflects Article 4(1) of the Restructuring Directive.

"Imminent inability to pay debts" is not statutorily defined but – *inter alia* – serves as a means for delineation of "inability to pay debts" under §66 IO (this, in turn, is perfectly in line with the Model Definition's approach to opt for "point-in-time illiquidity" rather than "time period illiquidity").

Imminent inability to pay debts is to be assumed if debts are not yet due but it is predictable that – assuming those debts become due in the foreseeable future – the debtor will be unable to pay them at the time they fall due. Neither statute (IO/ReO) defines the relevant prognosis period, but it is assumed to be a period of no more than 12 months. The term "imminent" is therefore somewhat inappropriate and should rather be termed "likely" as it does not express urgency (as Chapter 6, paragraph 6.3 of the Main Report rightly points out). The Austrian notion of "imminent inability to pay debts" is certainly comparable and compatible with the Model Definition's notion of "likelihood of insolvency".

It appears that these concepts would be perfectly reconcilable so that Austrian law would need no amendments in this regard. This is all the more true as Austrian law also refrains from defining a fixed prognosis period.

b) *Imminent Insolvency*

As set out above (*supra* section 4(a)), Austrian law is familiar with the concept of "likely inability to pay debts" but terms it (rather inappropriately) "*imminent* inability to pay debts". The notion of Austrian law regarding "imminent inability to pay debts" – and, given that "inability to pay debts" is a subset of "insolvency", one could say that "imminent inability to pay debts" relates to "imminent insolvency" – therefore differs from the Model Definition's.

5. OVERINDEBTEDNESS

Pursuant to §67 IO, overindebtedness represents a (mandatory) ground for the opening of insolvency proceedings, applicable to certain types of debtors (in particular legal persons with limited liability such as stock companies

(*Aktiengesellschaften*, AG) or limited liability companies (*Gesellschaften mit beschränkter Haftung*, GmbH)). It is not defined by statute, but it is generally accepted that a two-tier test applies. First, the debtor must show "arithmetical" overindebtedness, meaning that the debts exceed the assets (see Model Definition: hypothetical liquidation test; in general, the liquidation valuation applies). Second, the debtor must show a negative prognosis for continuing as a going concern (a "viability test", also corresponding to the Model Definition). If the debtor can avoid the status of inability to pay debts for a period that encompasses the current as well as the subsequent business year, then the debtor is not deemed overindebted (and vice versa). Said prognosis period is not laid down in statute but has been developed in case law and the academic literature and is generally accepted.

Compared to the Model Definition, there is little or no difference. Although the Model Definition sets out a liquidity test rather than a viability test there is basically no difference in the understanding of §67 IO (as already mentioned above); the reason being that the determinant is whether the debtor is more likely than not to reach the *status of inability to pay debts* within said prognosis period. This, in essence, is rather akin to a "liquidity test". Finally, the lack of a statutory prognosis period is something that the Austrian law and the Model Definition have in common.

It seems likely that implementing the Model Definition would not result in any significant differences from current practice.

II. OVERALL ASSESSMENT

In my opinion, there would be no apparent reason to believe that the implementation of the Model Definition would be infeasible or disruptive to the current state of affairs.

To some extent, the Model Definition would probably increase the degree of certainty, particularly where grace periods or liquidity gaps are clearly defined, whereas the current Austrian practice applies some "rules of thumb" (providing a greater extent of flexibility). However, this stricter approach could lead to a somewhat lower degree of flexibility (if any or at least) in some outlier cases.

As mentioned above (*supra* I.2(b)), adding another presumption for the establishment of "inability to pay debts" could prove to be a useful tool for *creditors* filing for insolvency.

All in all, it seems rather unlikely that there would be much change from current practice.

BELGIUM

Frederik De Leo

Please identify to what extent the proposed Model Definitions in the proposal align with or differ from the definitions currently used in your national law and whether they would be compatible with and operable in your jurisdiction.

I. INDIVIDUAL ASSESSMENT OF THE MODEL DEFINITIONS

A comparison of the Model Definitions with the definitions in Belgian law reveals the following:

1. INSOLVENCY

Belgian law does not provide for a relevant definition of the term insolvency. It is instead often used as a general term to refer to cessation of payments and impairment of credit, which give grounds for the opening of bankruptcy proceedings (*faillissement/faillite*).

2. INABILITY TO PAY DEBTS

a) *Prerequisites*

Inability to pay debts is not a term defined under Belgian law. However, case law does interpret the cumulative bankruptcy criteria of "cessation of payment" and "impairment of credit" as inability to pay debts.

Under Belgian law, inability to pay debts is a means to establish that the debtor has ceased to pay debts and that the debtor's credit is impaired. The Model Definitions turn this around. Inability to pay is the central definition and cessation of payments is the basis of a circumstance which raises a presumption of such inability. However, we can compare the central definition of the Model

Definitions (inability to pay debts) with the central definitions under Belgian law (cessation of payments and impairment of credit).

Belgian law, like the Model Definitions, looks at the relevant point in time and only considers mature debts. Under Belgian law, the inability to pay debts must also be persistent (see the Model Definitions: "unless it is to be reasonably expected that this inability can be cured in the short term"). Less firmly established under Belgian law is that the inability to pay only an insignificant part of mature debts does *not* lead to cessation of payments (although in practice this follows from the requirement that the cessation of payments should be persistent). The addition about the duration of the liquidity gap in the Model Definitions ensures that a debtor who has no liquid assets but can obtain credit at short notice (what we would refer to in Belgium as "the debtor's credit is not impaired" and "the inability to pay debts is not persistent") is not considered unable to pay its debts. Hence, it can be said that the Belgian definition, as shaped by case law, largely corresponds to the Model Definitions. The practical results are therefore most likely to remain substantially the same.

b) Presumptions

The Model Definition of inability to pay debts provides for a rebuttable presumption on two alternative bases: (i) cessation of payments (defined as being in default with payments to at least two creditors) and (ii) being in default to an essential creditor with at least two payments or one payment for at least three months.

Cessation of payments is dealt with *infra* under section 3.

Regarding the presumption in case of default to an essential creditor with at least two payments or one payment for at least three months, Belgian law currently does not have such a presumption based on the non-payment of an essential creditor. The circumstance could, however, be relevant as circumstantial evidence when establishing the debtor's cessation of payments and impairment of credit. The adoption of this rebuttable presumption proposed within the Model Definitions would appear to be achievable. However, questions may arise as to what constitutes an "essential creditor".

3. CESSATION OF PAYMENTS

Both the function and definition of "cessation of payments" in the Model Definitions differ from Belgian law.

Under Belgian law, a debtor meets the bankruptcy conditions if (i) it is in cessation of payments, and (cumulatively) (ii) its credit is impaired. Cessation of payments does not ground a presumption of the debtor's inability to pay. It is rather the other way around: if the debtor cannot pay, it is considered that the debtor has ceased payments and that its credit is impaired. Cessation of payments can be demonstrated summarily, so as not to create high barriers for unpaid creditors who want to initiate bankruptcy proceedings against their debtor.

In the Model Definitions, the term "cessation of payments" (defined as being in default with payments to at least two creditors) differs significantly from the meaning under Belgian law. Under the current Belgian "cessation of payments", a default with payments to *two* creditors is neither necessary nor sufficient. This difference is readily understandable, as the current Belgian "cessation of payment" essentially corresponds to "inability to pay debts" under the Model Definitions, and "cessation of payment" under the Model Definitions is the basis only of a *rebuttable* presumption. Overall, the rebuttable presumption of inability to pay debts based on cessation of payments as defined under the Model Definitions could be compatible and operable with Belgian law.

4. LIKELIHOOD OF INSOLVENCY AND IMMINENT INSOLVENCY

As regards likely and imminent inability to pay debts, the following can be said.

a) *Likelihood of Insolvency*

Belgian law uses "likelihood of insolvency" (in the French version of the Belgian Insolvency Code, *probabilité d'insolvabilité*) and "imminent insolvency" (in the Dutch version of the Belgian Insolvency Code, *dreigende insolventie*) interchangeably as triggers for restructuring proceedings and for one type of liquidation proceedings (i.e. the transfer under judicial authority, the reason being that this used to be a restructuring proceeding). Likelihood of insolvency/ imminent insolvency is defined as the continuity of the debtor's activities being threatened either immediately or over time. Courts have only marginal discretion; it is sufficient that this condition appears to be met.

The Model Definitions define "likelihood of insolvency" as "more likely than not that the debtor will become unable to pay debts" and "imminent insolvency" as "in the next three months the debtor will become unable to pay debts". The more open standard of "likelihood of insolvency" is closer to the current Belgian criterion for opening the above-mentioned proceedings. This would probably prompt the Belgian legislator to use the term "likelihood of insolvency" (*probabilité d'insolvabilité/waarschijnlijkheid van insolventie*) in both language versions of the Belgian Insolvency Code.

b) *Imminent Insolvency*

It follows from the above that Belgian insolvency law is familiar with the term "imminent insolvency" but does not distinguish it from "likelihood of insolvency". Hence, Belgian law does not use imminent inability to pay debts in the same way as the Model Definitions. As regards the consequences in the event of transposition of the Model Definitions, reference can be made to section 4(a). above.

5. OVERINDEBTEDNESS

Overindebtedness is not a basis upon which insolvency proceedings can be initiated in Belgium. The Model Definitions would therefore not affect the Belgian Insolvency Code.

However, it may be interesting to see how this definition could *indirectly* affect the alarm bell procedure in Belgian company law. For instance, in the Belgian corporate forms of SRL/BV or SC/CV, the alarm bell procedure must be activated when (i) the net assets are likely to become or have become negative (balance sheet test), or (ii) it is no longer certain that the company will be able to pay its debts as they fall due for at least the next 12 months (liquidity test) (Articles 5:153 and 6:119 of the Belgian Code of Companies and Associations).

II. OVERALL ASSESSMENT

The introduction of the term "inability to pay", the changed function for the term "cessation of payments", and the new meaning of the term "likelihood of insolvency" would lead to several important changes to the Belgian Insolvency Code. In addition, much that can now be found in case law would be codified. Although practitioners would have to get used to the new terms, the practical results would most likely remain largely the same. I therefore consider the Model Definitions to be compatible with Belgian law and operable in Belgium.

BULGARIA

Hristina Kirilova

Please identify to what extent the Model Definitions in the proposal align with or differ from the definitions currently used in your national law and whether they would be compatible with and operable in your jurisdiction.

I. INDIVIDUAL ASSESSMENT OF THE MODEL DEFINITIONS

A comparison of the Model Definitions with the relevant definitions in Bulgarian law reveals the following:

1. INSOLVENCY

Bulgarian law does not provide for a definition of the term insolvency. Insolvency proceedings in Bulgaria are initiated for a merchant/trader or an entrepreneur, who is unable to pay debts, or a limited liability company, a joint stock company or a partnership limited by shares, that is unable to pay debts and/or is overindebted. In this sense, "insolvency" differs from the proposal in the Model Law, as it covers both the inability to pay debts (a ground applicable to a trader/merchant and/or an entrepreneur) and overindebtedness (a ground applicable only to a limited liability company, a joint stock company or a partnership limited by shares).

2. INABILITY TO PAY DEBTS

Bulgarian law currently has no legal definition of "inability to pay debts" in the sense of the proposed Model Definition. The Bulgarian legislator defines the concept of "inability to pay debts" by reference to the entities against whom the opening of insolvency proceedings can be requested (a trader/merchant and/or an entrepreneur) and to the type of obligations the non-payment of which legitimises the respective creditors to request the opening of insolvency proceedings.

a) Prerequisites

Thus, in accordance with Article 608, paragraph 1 CA,[1] a merchant is considered insolvent if he/she is unable to meet any due

- monetary obligation arising out of, or related to a commercial transaction, including its validity, performance, non-performance, termination, invalidation or cancellation, or the consequences from its termination, or
- public-law obligation to the state or municipalities related to the merchant's business, or
- obligation under a private state receivable, or
- obligation for wages to at least one-third of the workers and employees, which has not been discharged for more than two months.

With the amendments and additions to the CA (SG 66/2023), the legislator introduced insolvency for entrepreneurs. Pursuant to Article 760d, paragraph 1 CA, in addition to the grounds under Article 608, paragraph 1 CA, an entrepreneur is insolvent if he/she is unable to meet any due monetary obligation arising from or relating to his/her business/economic activities, craft or freelance operation.

Nevertheless, judicial practice has a similar understanding of "inability to pay debts" to that proposed in the Model Definition. In particular, "unable to meet debts" is generally recognised as an objective financial status of the debtor at the relevant point in time. It compares the debtor's ability to pay his/her short-term liabilities (both mature debts and debts which will become due within one year) with his/her short-term assets on the balance sheet. It should be clarified that when assessing the financial status of the debtor, his/her obligations to all creditors are taken into consideration, not just obligations to the creditors who may request the opening of the insolvency proceedings.[2]

In accordance with Bulgarian law, the inability to pay an insignificant part of the debts will not typically lead to the opening of insolvency proceedings. The request for the opening of insolvency proceedings will be also rejected if the court finds that the difficulties are temporary (expected to be overcome within a short period of time) or the debtor has sufficient assets to cover his/her debts without endangering the interests of his/her creditors.[3]

In view of the above, although "inability to pay debts" is not legally established in national law, the Bulgarian case law is broadly in line with the proposal

1 The Commerce Act, State Gazette (SG) 48/1991, amended and supplemented (CA).
2 Art. 608, para. 1 CA.
3 Art. 631 CA.

given in the Model Law. Therefore, the proposal is compatible with Bulgarian insolvency law. At the same time, the proposed definition is more precise insofar as it refers to the inability to pay mature debts, but not debts that are not payable at the relevant point in time.

b) *Presumptions*

The Model Definition of "inability to pay debts" provides for two bases for a rebuttable presumption of inability to pay: (i) cessation of payments (defined as defaulting on payments to at least two creditors) and (ii) default to an essential creditor with at least two payments or one payment missed for at least three months.

In Bulgarian law, inability to pay debts is rebuttably presumed if: (i) the debtor has ceased payments,[4] or (ii) if, under an enforcement proceeding (initiated by a creditor, who filed the application for the opening of the insolvency proceedings, for enforcement of his/her final and effective claim), the claim remained partially or fully unpaid within six months after the debtor was served with a voluntary payment notice.[5] In addition, it is assumed that the debtor is unable to fulfil an obligation under Article 608, paragraph 1 CA if, prior to the submission of the request for the opening of the insolvency proceedings, he/she has not applied for an announcement in the commercial register of his/her annual financial statements (balance sheets) for the last three years.

The approach of the Bulgarian legislator in defining "cessation of payments" differs from the approach adopted in the proposal. In particular, "cessation of payments" is not explicitly defined, but it is indicated that such a situation is present regardless of whether the debtor makes any payment or payments to any of his/her creditors. Pursuant to Article 608, paragraph 3 CA, "inability to pay debts" is rebuttably presumed when the debtor has ceased payments. This inability is also considered present when the debtor has fully or partially paid claims to certain creditors. The difference is that the Model Law defines "cessation of payments" as defaulting on payments to at least two creditors, while the understanding under Bulgarian law for this presumption is "defaulting on most of the payments to most of the creditors". Therefore, the first presumption of the Model Law would meet the requirements of Bulgarian law only if the two debts represented a significant part of the outstanding liabilities. In most cases, however, mere default vis-à-vis two creditors would not be sufficient. On the other hand, defaulting on a payment to only one creditor *would* suffice under Bulgarian law if the respective debt represented a substantial part of all debts.

---

4 Art. 608, para. 3.

5 Art. 608, para. 4 CA.

Bulgarian insolvency law is also familiar with the second presumption of the proposal, although it is not exactly the same, and the purpose of the Bulgarian legislator differs from the reasons given in the proposal. Bulgarian law provides that the non-payment of wages to at least one-third of the debtor's workers and employees for more than two months authorises the Executive Agency "General Labour Inspectorate" to claim inability to pay debts and to request the opening of insolvency proceedings for the debtor. This provision is not introduced as a presumption to facilitate the establishment of inability to pay debts, nor does it address the idea of non-payment to an essential creditor. Instead, it was added in 2017 to ensure payments to employees and protect their interests.

Hence, if necessary, there will be no difficulties in incorporating the second presumption of the proposal into Bulgarian law.

3. CESSATION OF PAYMENTS

The differences between the Model Definition and the Bulgarian definition of cessation of payments have already been explained. Hence, reference can be made to section 2(b) above.

4. LIKELIHOOD OF INSOLVENCY AND IMMINENT INSOLVENCY

As regards likely and imminent inability to pay debts, the following can be said.

a) *Likelihood of Insolvency*

Bulgarian law does not recognise the terms "likelihood of insolvency" or "likely inability to pay debts". Instead, the term "imminent inability to pay debts" is used.[6] Imminent inability to pay debts is an autonomous ground for requesting the opening of stabilisation proceedings (merchant restructuring proceedings). It is not a ground on which to commence insolvency proceedings. According to Bulgarian law, an immediate risk of insolvency (inability to pay debts) is present when the merchant – in view of the upcoming maturities of his/her monetary obligations in the 12 months following the submission of the application for stabilisation – will find himself/herself unable to fulfil these due monetary obligations or will cease payments.[7]

---

6 Art. 762, para. 1 CA.

7 Art. 762, para. 2 CA.

Compared to the Model Definitions, Bulgarian law uses "imminent inability to pay debts" but defines this more closely to the Model Definition of "likelihood of insolvency". As regards the prognosis period, Article 762, paragraph 2 CA provides for a time-span of 12 months, whereas the Model Definition does not mention any fixed prognosis period.

b) Imminent Insolvency

It follows from the above that Bulgarian insolvency law is familiar with the term "imminent inability to pay debts" but does not distinguish it from "likely inability to pay debts" and defines the former in the sense of the latter. Hence, Bulgarian law does not use imminent inability to pay debts in the same way as the Model Definitions.

5. OVERINDEBTEDNESS

Bulgarian law provides for the possibility of initiating insolvency proceedings due to overindebtedness only against legal entities with registered capital – a limited liability company, a joint stock company, or a partnership limited by shares. It is stated that a company is overindebted if its assets are not sufficient to cover its liabilities.

This current regulation suffers from certain shortcomings, namely, it does not address the method to be used to evaluate the debtor's assets and the formal approach adopted by the Bulgarian legislator (excess of liabilities over assets) does not take into consideration the potential viability of the company.

The definition proposed in the Model Law, on the other hand, differs clearly from the definition in Bulgarian law. Because of this, the adoption of the proposal would require substantial changes to the current legislation. However, it is difficult to predict whether such adoption in the national legislation would result in a change for the better or not.

II. OVERALL ASSESSMENT

The Model Definitions would likely be compatible with and operable in Bulgaria. The adoption of the Model Definitions into Bulgarian law would require some changes, but the practical results are most likely to remain the same.

CROATIA

Jasnica GARAŠIĆ

Please identify to what extent the proposed Model Definitions in the proposal align with or differ from the definitions currently used in your national law and whether they would be compatible with and operable in your jurisdiction.

I. INDIVIDUAL ASSESSMENT OF THE MODEL DEFINITIONS

A comparison of the Model Definitions with the definitions in Croatian law reveals the following:

1. INSOLVENCY

According to the Model Definitions "insolvency" means inability to pay debts.

Croatian law does not contain a definition of the term "insolvency" (*nesolventnost* or *insolventnost*). In the main legal source of Croatian bankruptcy/insolvency law, namely in the Bankruptcy Act (Stečajni zakon, hereafter SZ), this legal term began to be used only recently, in the context of the implementation of the rules of the Directive on Restructuring and Insolvency (hereafter DRI),[1] and in the context of delimiting the application of the European Insolvency Regulation and Chapter XI of the Bankruptcy Code which contains rules on autonomous Croatian international bankruptcy/insolvency law.[2]

The *debtor and its creditors* are entitled to apply for bankruptcy proceedings in the case of the debtor's inability to pay its debts and its overindebtedness (Article 109(1) SZ together with Article 5(2) SZ). Aside from that, the *debtor*

1 See Article 1a SZ – rules of the EU, Article 20b SZ in connection with Article 29 DRI – data collection, and Article 387(4) SZ together with Article 22(1) DRI – disqualification period.

2 See Article 394 SZ.

may apply for bankruptcy proceedings in the case of its imminent inability to pay its debts (Article 5(3) SZ). The *directors' duty* to apply for bankruptcy proceedings exists only in the case of the debtor's inability to pay its debts and its overindebtedness (Article 110(2) together with Article 5(3) SZ).

2. INABILITY TO PAY DEBTS

The definition of "inability to pay debts" contained in Model Definitions only partially corresponds to the definition of this legal term in Article 6 of the Croatian SZ.

a) Prerequisites

According to the Model Definitions, "inability to pay debts" means the debtor's inability at the relevant point in time to pay all but an insignificant part of its mature debts from its liquid assets, unless it is to be reasonably expected that this inability can be cured in the short term.

According to Article 6(1) sentence 1 SZ, inability to pay debts exists if a debtor is not able to pay its mature monetary obligations on a more permanent basis. Article 6(1) sentence 2 explicitly emphasises the fact that the debtor has paid or can satisfy the claims of some creditors, fully or partly, does not in itself mean that the debtor is solvent (Article 6(1) sentence 2 SZ). Namely, the debtor has to be able to satisfy the claims of *all* its creditors as these claims become due.

The definition of "inability to pay debts" in the Model Definitions is less strict. Namely, according to this definition, the inability to pay debts will not exist if the debtor is unable to pay only "an insignificant part of its mature debts". However, it is not defined what is considered "an insignificant part of the debtor's mature debts". As a kind of legal standard, it will require interpretation in judicial practice.

Both according to the Model Definitions and according to SZ, a short-term stagnation of payments is not sufficient to establish the debtor's inability to pay its debts. In both cases, the duration of the liquidity gap – the debtor's "inability can be cured in the short time" (the Model Definition) and the debtor's "inability to pay its mature monetary obligations on a more permanent basis" (SZ) – requires interpretation in judicial practice.

Unlike the Model Definitions, SZ does not mention liquid assets in its definition of inability to pay debts. However, it can be concluded that the debtor's inability to pay debts can be quickly (in a short time) remedied usually by paying from its liquid assets.

b) *Presumptions*

According to the Model Definitions the Member States may provide that inability to pay debts is rebuttably presumed, but only if the debtor has ceased payments or is in default to an essential creditor with at least two payments or with one payment for at least three months.

This presumption of inability to pay debts, which is provided for in the Model Definitions in its three forms, differs from the presumption which is provided for in the Croatian SZ in its two forms. According to Article 6(2) SZ, the debtor shall be considered unable to pay: (1) if in the Registry of the order of grounds for payment kept by the Financial Agency, the debtor has one or more registered non-executed grounds for payment in the period exceeding 60 days, which payment should have been collected from any of the debtor's accounts, based on valid grounds for payment, without any further consent of the debtor; or (2) if the debtor failed to pay three consecutive months' salary that the employee is entitled to according to a contract of employment, the ordinance on employment, a collective bargaining contract, or a special regulation or according to any other act regulating the obligations of the employer towards the employee.[3] This presumption in two forms should be interpreted as a rebuttable presumption.

Unlike the Model Definitions, the cessation of payments itself doesn't mean in Croatian bankruptcy law that the debtor is unable to pay its debts. However, the circumstances under which the debtor ceased payments may help to establish the debtor's inability to pay its debts. If the court can establish the debtor's inability to pay debts beyond doubt from the circumstances in which the debtor ceased payments, the court will not appoint an expert to examine the debtor's economic and financial condition i.e. its inability to pay its debts (Article 126(1) SZ). There is no statutory definition of cessation of payments. Most bankruptcy proceedings in Croatia are opened using the legal presumption contained in Article 6(1) no. 1 or no. 2 SZ, the content of which is connected to the cessation of payment(s) to one or more creditors.

The Model Definitions requires "default to an essential creditor with at least two payments" in the second form of its legal presumption of the debtor's inability to pay debts. In Croatian bankruptcy law, it suffices that one creditor had one claim which, despite the existence of a valid enforcement title could not be settled in the execution proceedings conducted by the court or in the proceedings of

---

3 For the special presumption of inability to pay debts in the case of the opening and closing of so-called summary bankruptcy proceedings, see National Report for Croatia, answer to Question 13.

the so-called direct collection of claims conducted by Financial Agency without involvement of the court, on the debtor's funds in bank accounts for more than 60 days due to the lack of the debtor's funds (Article 6(2) no. 1 SZ). In Croatian law there is no distinction between essential and non-essential creditors, except that Croatian law provides for a special form of legal presumption of the debtor's inability to pay debts concerning employees' claims.

The Model Definitions requires "default to an essential creditor with one payment for at least three months" in the third form of its legal presumption of the debtor's inability to pay debts. In Croatian bankruptcy law, the debtor's inability to pay debts also exists if the debtor failed to pay three consecutive months' salary to an employee (Article 6(2) no. 2 SZ). The aforementioned presumption foreseen in the Model Definitions is broader because it encompasses not only employees, but also other potential "essential creditors". However, the term "essential creditors" is not defined.

c) Consequences

The definition of the term "inability to pay debts" in the Model Definitions is less strict than in Croatian bankruptcy law because the model definition does not take into account an insignificant part of the debtor's mature debts. In the case of the acceptance of the Model Definitions on the EU level, it would require the amendment of Article 6(1) of Croatian SZ.

It must be emphasised that the application of the legal presumption of the debtor's inability to pay debts contained in Article 6(2) no. 1 and no. 2 SZ has functioned in judicial practice in Croatia very well for many years and that its application reduces the costs of bankruptcy proceedings. In the event of the acceptance of the Model Definitions at the EU level, it would require the amendment of Article 6(2) nos. 1–2 SZ. There is no doubt that this will be a challenge not only for domestic debtors and creditors, but also for the judges who conduct bankruptcy proceedings. The need to use circumstantial evidence will increase.

3. CESSATION OF PAYMENTS

The Model Definitions contains the term "cessation of payments" and provides that it means that the debtor is in default with payments to at least two creditors.

The Croatian SZ does not contain a statutory definition of cessation of payment. However, elements of the legal presumption of the debtor's inability to pay debts are connected with cessation of payment. The differences between the Model Definitions and the Croatian SZ concerning legal presumptions and consequences in the event of the acceptance of the Model Definitions at the EU level have been already mentioned above, see section 2(b)–(c).

4. LIKELIHOOD OF INSOLVENCY AND IMMINENT INSOLVENCY

As regards likely and imminent inability to pay debts, the following can be said.

a) *Likelihood of Insolvency*

In the Model Definitions it is provided that "likelihood of insolvency" means that it is more likely than not that the debtor will become unable to pay debts.

Croatian law does not use the term "likelihood of insolvency". It uses the term "likelihood of inability to pay debts", however not as a ground for the opening of bankruptcy proceedings, but only in the context of directors' duties (Article 20.a SZ).[4] It does not determine the content of the "likelihood of inability to pay debts".

b) *Imminent Insolvency*

In the Model Definitions it is provided that "imminent insolvency" means that in the next three months the debtor will become unable to pay debts.

Croatian law does not use the term "imminent insolvency", but the term "imminent [threatening] inability to pay debts" as a ground for the opening of bankruptcy proceedings (Article 5(3) SZ) as well as for the opening of pre-bankruptcy proceedings (Article 4(1) SZ). The imminent inability to pay debts exists if the submitter of the proposal to open proceedings shows that it is likely that the debtor will not be able to fulfil its existing obligations when they become due (Article 4(1) sentence 2 SZ for pre-bankruptcy proceedings and Article 5(4) SZ for bankruptcy proceedings). The definition of this ground is valid also for the procedure of extraordinary management in companies of systemic importance for the Republic of Croatia. The imminent inability to pay debts is not a ground for the opening of consumer bankruptcy proceedings.[5]

The definition of "imminent inability to pay debts" in the Croatian SZ corresponds to the definition of "likelihood of insolvency" in the Model Definitions.

Additionally, the Croatian SZ contains the legal presumption of imminent inability to pay debts in three forms. According to Article 4(2) SZ, it shall be considered that the imminent inability to pay debts exists if, at the time of submission of the proposal to open proceedings, circumstances have not arisen due to which the debtor is considered to have become permanently unable to pay and if: (i) in the Registry of order of grounds for payment kept by the Financial Agency,

4 See National Report for Croatia, answer to Question 10(a)–(c).

5 See National Report for Croatia, answer to Question 34.

the debtor has one or more registered non-executed grounds for payment, on the basis of which payment should have been collected from any of the debtor's accounts, based on valid grounds for payment, without any further consent of the debtor (Article 4(2) no. 1 SZ); or (ii) if the debtor is more than 30 days overdue with the payment of salary that an employee is entitled to according to a contract of employment, the ordinance on employment, a collective bargaining contract or a special regulation, or according to any other act regulating the obligations of the employer towards the employee (Article 4(2) no. 2 SZ); or (iii) if the debtor has not paid the contributions and taxes related to the salary referred to in Article 4(2) no. 2 SZ within 30 days from the day the debtor was due to pay the salary to the employee (Article 4(2) no. 3 SZ).

c) *Consequences*

In the event of the acceptance of the Model Definitions at the EU level, the terminology in the Croatian SZ will have to be adapted and some important changes adopted.

The Croatian legislator will have to introduce the term "likelihood of insolvency" and its definition into Croatian bankruptcy law.

The content of the Croatian legal presumption of imminent inability to pay debts differs considerably from the definition of "imminent insolvency" in the Model Definitions. It will mean the need for a significant change in the way that imminent inability to pay debts is regulated in the current Croatian SZ and how it has been established in judicial practice. The abolishment of the Croatian legal presumption of imminent inability to pay debts will increase the need to use circumstantial evidence in order to prove and establish the debtor's imminent inability to pay debts and, therefore, it will be harder to establish this ground for the opening of pre-bankruptcy and bankruptcy proceedings. This result will not follow the modern tendency of the European legislator to promote and support restructuring proceedings.

5. OVERINDEBTEDNESS

a) *Overindebtedness*

According to the Model Definitions, "overindebtedness" means that, at the relevant point in time, the liabilities of the debtor exceed the liquidation value of its assets and the occurrence of the debtor's inability to pay debts is more likely than not.

According to Croatian bankruptcy law, "overindebtedness" exists if the assets of the debtor legal entity does not cover its existing obligations (Article 7(1) SZ). However, Article 7(1) SZ must not be applied: (i) if, according to the circumstances of a case (development programme, available sources of funds, type of assets, obtained insurance, etc.) it may be reasonably presumed that by continuing its business the debtor legal entity will properly fulfil its obligations when they become due; (ii) if the company is a company of persons (*eine Personengesellschaft*) for whose obligations there is joint and several liability on the part of a shareholder of that company who is a natural person and whose assets are not subject to instituted or opened bankruptcy proceedings (Article 7(2) SZ).

Although different words are used in the definition of overindebtedness in the Model Definitions and the Croatian SZ, the essence of this ground for the opening of bankruptcy/insolvency proceedings is the same in both texts.

The liquidation test matters in both texts and it is a starting point. Do the liabilities of the debtor (i.e. all its existing obligations) exceed the liquidation value of all its assets (i.e. are not covered by all its assets)?

And additionally, the prognostic element is contained in both texts: the occurrence of the debtor's inability to pay debts is more likely than not, i.e. according to the circumstances of a case it may not be reasonably presumed that by continuing its business the debtor will properly fulfil its obligations when they become due.

However, there are important differences.

The definition of "overindebtedness" in the Model Definitions does not distinguish between legal and natural persons and therefore refers to both kinds of debtors. The Croatian SZ defines "overindebtedness" as a ground for the opening of bankruptcy proceedings only in relation to a legal person, where it also contains a special provision in the case of a company of persons.

b) Consequence

In the event of the acceptance of the Model Definitions at the level of the EU, the transposition of the definition of "overindebtedness" into Croatian law will not represent a fundamental change in the concept of "overindebtedness" that exists in the current Croatian bankruptcy law. However, in that event, the Croatian legislator will have to provide for "overindebtedness" as a ground for the opening of bankruptcy proceedings not only concerning legal persons but also concerning natural persons.

II. OVERALL ASSESSMENT

Bearing in mind the importance of the principle of legal predictability and legal certainty, the principle of transparency, the principle of procedural justice, the principle of equal treatment of creditors, the principle of protection of the debtor's rights, the principle of social protection, as well as the principle of efficiency, it would be very desirable if the European legislator gave definitions of the following legal terms in insolvency law, which would be uniformly used in EU law and the laws of Member States: "insolvency", "inability to pay debts", "cessation of payments", "likelihood of insolvency", "imminent insolvency" and "overindebtedness". The uniform definitions of these terms should be distinguished from the legal presumption on the existence of inability to pay debts, the legal presumption on the existence of imminent insolvency and the legal presumption on the existence of overindebtedness, which presumptions could be regulated by national law of the Member States. These presumptions are closely connected with the national procedural laws of Member States, including their evidence law, and the application of some of these presumptions has a very long procedural tradition in the Member States. If the definitions given by the European legislator were to abolish all national legal presumptions on the existence of ground(s) for the opening of insolvency and pre-insolvency proceedings, then the use of circumstantial evidence in order to prove or establish the insolvency ground(s) would increase, which would in turn result in higher costs of insolvency proceedings. Aside from that, the opening of insolvency and pre-insolvency proceedings would be harder. Especially in relation to restructuring proceedings, this result will not follow the goals of the EU Directive on Restructuring and Insolvency. The Member States should be bound by the definitions of the above-mentioned legal terms given by the European legislator. The European legislator may provide legal presumptions on the existence of the ground(s) for opening insolvency and pre-insolvency proceedings, but at least Member States should have the freedom to add their own national legal presumptions on the existence of the ground(s) for the opening of their national insolvency and pre-insolvency proceedings.

CYPRUS

Andrie Kypridemou

Please identify to what extent the proposed Model Definitions in the proposal align with or differ from the definitions currently used in your national law and whether they would be compatible with and operable in your jurisdiction.

I. INDIVIDUAL ASSESSMENT OF THE MODEL DEFINITIONS

The Model Definitions compared to the respective definitions in Cypriot insolvency law, where applicable that is, differ as follows:

1. INSOLVENCY

Company Law, Cap. 113 of the Laws of Cyprus,[1] §202N defines insolvency, in relation to companies petitioning for the appointment of an Examiner in order to restructure, as "inability to pay debts", as this is defined within the same part of this legislation. This definition, which is in fact the only definition of insolvency in insolvency legislation in Cyprus, is actually the same as the Model Law definition.

2. INABILITY TO PAY DEBTS

There are two definitions in CoLaw of "inability to pay debts"; one relating to the commencement of company liquidation (CoLaw §212) and the other to the appointment of an Examiner (CoLaw §202A(3)) in the company to commence its formal restructuring. Section 202A(3) CoLaw is compatible with §212 in that it includes cash-flow insolvency and balance sheet insolvency, as well as direct

1 Company Law, Cap. 113, hereinafter referred to as "CoLaw".

reference to the prerequisites set forth in §212 of CoLaw. The only difference between them is that CoLaw §212 specifies that a court should consider a company's "contingent and future liabilities" in assessing cash-flow insolvency – that is "inability to pay debts as they fall due" – while §202A(3) does not require so directly, yet it could be so interpreted through its reference to the prerequisites set out in CoLaw §212. In this respect, the definitions of "inability to pay debts" provided in CoLaw both include cash-flow insolvency, as one of the presumptions establishing "inability to pay debts",[2] which largely corresponds to the Model Law definition.

a) Prerequisites

Nevertheless, some adjustments will be required for full harmonisation of "inability to pay debts" in CoLaw with the definition provided in the Model Law, as currently (i) it considers also "contingent and future liabilities" rather than just "mature debts" and (ii) there is no exception to the rule for cases where "is to be reasonably expected that this inability can be cured in the short term".

b) Presumptions

At the same time another presumption of "inability to pay debts" set out in CoLaw §212 is when one creditor is owed an amount of over €5,000 for a period of over three weeks from the time that this payment was formally demanded by the creditor, or is owed any judgment debt and could not enforce its payment. These presumptions correspond to some extent to the last presumption provided by the Model Law for default of "one payment for at least three months", with the main difference being, quite importantly, the relevant point in time.

The other rebuttable presumption set out in the Model Definition of inability to pay debts is cessation of payments (defined as default with payments to at least two creditors). In Cypriot insolvency law there is no such presumption or requirement to establish cessation of payments to more than one creditor in order to prove inability to pay debts, even though it does not explicitly exclude such petitions by more than one creditor, each of which complies separately with one or more of the presumptions of "inability to pay debts" in CoLaw §212.

---

2 As stated in *GIP Constructions Ltd v. Director of the Social Insurances Department* (1991) 1 AAΔ 14, "The specificity of the circumstances in section 212 does not limit the generality of section 211 in relation to a company's inability to pay its debts. That is, the special reasons constitute certain circumstances that raise a statutory presumption of the existence of the inability to pay debts but do not exhaust the scope for admitting any other testimony that could tend to the same result".

c) *Consequences*

As concerns the consequences of these differences in the CoLaw definition of "inability to pay debts" compared to the Model Definition, it is important to note that the Model Definition does not permit the introduction of additional or different presumptions from those provided. Now, considering that in Cypriot insolvency law there is no obligation for the directors of a company to file for its liquidation once they identify that it's insolvent and, thus, in most cases a company will be liquidated following a petition by one of its creditors, it will be essential for Cyprus to transpose the presumptions set out in the Model Definition, as it would be nearly impossible for a creditor to prove a company's inability to pay debts otherwise, due to lack of evidence relating to all of the company's "mature debts" and "liquid assets". In this respect, perhaps the presumptions of the Model Definition of "inability to pay debts" should have been obligatory for all Member States, to ensure that petitions by creditors have a chance to succeed, especially if "cessation of payments" is not included either, as a separate prerequisite to insolvency in a Member State's insolvency law, which is the case for Cyprus in fact.

3. CESSATION OF PAYMENTS

As stated above, cessation of payments is not mentioned in Cypriot insolvency law, either for companies' liquidation or restructuring, or for personal insolvency.

4. LIKELIHOOD OF INSOLVENCY AND IMMINENT INSOLVENCY

"Likelihood of insolvency" was recently introduced in CoLaw[3] as one of the requirements for a company to commence formal restructuring proceedings through the appointment of an Examiner. "Imminent insolvency" is not to be found at all in Cypriot insolvency law.

a) *Likelihood of Insolvency*

CoLaw defines "likelihood of insolvency" as "the case where, in the opinion of the company's directors or the Court, it is reasonably likely that the company will become insolvent within twelve (12) months". This definition may seem at a glance more subjective compared to the Model Definition, which, although

[3] Companies (Amendment) Law No. 213(I)/2022, in force from December 2022.

quite vague as to the relevant point in time and the test that may be used to prove it, does not rely entirely on the opinion of a director or the court. However, the suspect period of 12 months used in the CoLaw definition of "likelihood of insolvency" can be quite precisely presented to a court through a projected cash-flow statement for such period of time. Nevertheless, it is still quite restrictive in that, once again, only the directors can provide such a cash-flow statement, as they are the only ones that have access to all the required information in the company's books.

It is important to note at this point that this definition of "likelihood of insolvency" has not been interpreted yet by the courts in Cyprus; hence one can only assume how it may be established.

At the same time, the same issues of access to the information required to establish "likelihood of insolvency" may hold true for the Model Definition of this term, due to the fact that it is quite vague and can have very wide interpretation. To this extent it might have been useful to have some rebuttable presumptions in relation to this definition as well.

b) Imminent Insolvency

As mentioned above, "imminent insolvency" is not to be found at all in Cypriot insolvency law.

5. OVERINDEBTEDNESS

Although the term "overindebtedness" is not found at all in Cypriot insolvency law, the Model Definition that the "liabilities of the debtor exceed the liquidation value of its assets" is provided in CoLaw §212 as one of bases of the presumption of inability to pay debts. Nevertheless, as "overindebtedness" as a term on its own is not present in Cypriot insolvency law, this Model Definition may not have, as such, any impact for Cyprus.

II. OVERALL ASSESSMENT

It is important to note that of all the terms of the Model Definition, only inability to pay debts is somehow mentioned in Bankruptcy Law[4] relating to the commencement of bankruptcy proceedings for an insolvent individual; and even then, it is included as just one of the presumptions that may be used by the debtor for voluntary bankruptcy proceedings. Hence it is highly unlikely that these Model Definitions will have any impact on personal insolvencies.

---

4 Bankruptcy Law, Cap. 5 of the Laws of Cyprus.

Now, as concerns their use in the liquidation of companies as provided in CoLaw, one is quite right to conclude that some major changes may emerge, mainly because the current presumptions for commencement of liquidation proceedings for a company that is unable to pay its debts would be eliminated and may or may not be replaced with the presumptions set out in the Model Definitions.

At the time that this publication is in its final stages, the Insolvency Department of Cyprus has commenced a monumental project of revising the personal insolvency law framework of Cyprus in its entirety, yet this may still be in progress for more than a year, in which case some of the provisions of the Model Law will likely be published and may be considered within this revision of Cypriot personal insolvency law.

CZECH REPUBLIC

Tomáš RICHTER

Please identify to what extent the proposed Model Definitions in the proposal align with or differ from the definitions currently used in your national law and whether they would be compatible with and operable in your jurisdiction.

I. INDIVIDUAL ASSESSMENT OF THE MODEL DEFINITIONS

A comparison of the Model Definitions[1] with the definitions in Czech law reveals the following:

1. INSOLVENCY

It seems to me that the Model Definitions, in what they define as "insolvency", really define cash-flow insolvency only. This strikes me as curious because the Model Definitions seem to be doing the very same thing in the next definition where they define the inability to pay debts as they fall due.

By contrast, Czech law, when using the term insolvency (known as *úpadek* in Czech) refers to insolvency within its broader meaning, i.e. insolvency on the basis of the cash-flow test as well as the balance sheet test.

The definition of "insolvency" proposed in the Model Definitions is therefore not consistent with current Czech law, and it does not seem to me that changing Czech law in order to comply with the Model Definition on this point would bring about any real improvement to Czech law.

---

1 This refers to the wording contained in paragraph 8.86 of the draft report dated 29 February 2024.

2. INABILITY TO PAY DEBTS

a) *Prerequisites*

The definition of the "inability to pay debts" as given in the Model Law is broadly in line with how that term is used in Czech law (referred to as *platební neschopnost* in Czech). But it seems less precise than current Czech law. Implementation of the Model Definitions on this point would therefore probably have retrograde effects on Czech insolvency law.

Section 3 of the Czech Insolvency Act defines the inability to pay debts as follows:

> (1) The debtor is insolvent if it (a) has multiple creditors, (b) has due and payable monetary debts more than 30 days overdue, and (c) is not able to pay those debts (hereafter referred to as "inability to pay debts").
>
> (2) The debtor shall be presumed to be unable to pay its monetary debts if (a) it has ceased to pay a substantial part of its monetary debts, or (b) it has been more than 3 months overdue with the payment of its monetary debts, or (c) it has not been possible to collect any of its due and payable monetary debts via execution proceedings, or (d) it has not performed a court-imposed obligation to submit the lists referred to in Section 104(1). [These are lists of assets, liabilities, and employees.]
>
> (3) A business debtor who keeps financial accounts shall be presumed to be able to pay its monetary debts if the difference between the amount of its due and payable monetary debts and the amount of its available liquidity means [hereafter the "liquidity gap"] evidenced in a liquidity statement drawn up in accordance with the relevant sub-statutory regulations, amounts to less than one-tenth of its due and payable monetary debts, or if a future liquidity model drawn up in accordance with the relevant sub-statutory regulations evidences that the liquidity gap will fall below one-tenth of its due and payable monetary debts within the period for which the future liquidity model is drawn up. The liquidity statement or the future liquidity model must be drawn up in accordance with the relevant sub-statutory regulations by an auditor, a court-sworn expert or a party specialising in economic advice in the fields of insolvency and re-structuring, who meets the criteria set in the relevant sub-statutory regulations.
>
> …
>
> (6) Sub-statutory regulations shall set out the contents, extent and the methods of drawing up liquidity statements and future liquidity models, as well as the lay-out, naming and contents of individual items of assets, liabilities, costs, earnings, incomes and expenses to be reported in liquidity statements and future liquidity models, the length of the periods for which the future liquidity models shall be drawn up, and the requirements to be met by persons authorised to draw up liquidity statements and future liquidity models.

b) *Presumptions*

Please refer to the presumptions in Sections 3(2) and (3) of the Czech Insolvency Act as translated and recited in section 2(a) *supra*.

These seem to me to be more precise than those proposed in the Model Definitions. Implementation of the Model Definitions on this point would probably not lead to an improvement of current Czech law and might have retrograde effects on Czech insolvency law.

3. CESSATION OF PAYMENTS

Czech statutory law does not define "cessation of payments". Case law has defined the concept as

> the debtor's intentional action, its decision, to no longer pay its monetary obligations, usually accompanied by a declaration that the debtor will not pay. It shall suffice if the debtor does this with at least a substantial part of its obligations. (*In re Oleo Chemical*, case no. 29 NSČR 24/2013 of 30 April 2015).

The definition as proposed in the Model Definitions is clearly much narrower. Given that the concept of cessation of payments is presently used as one of the presumptions of the inability to pay debts (see Section 3(2)(a) of the Czech Insolvency Act as translated and reproduced in section 2(a) *supra*), it is not clear to me that the definition proposed in the Model Definition would fit well into current Czech law. Implementing it would actually lead to a significant tightening of Czech insolvency law as against its current status quo, so much so that the results would probably not be deemed appropriate in, and acceptable to, the jurisdiction.

This is because in Czech insolvency law, the inability to pay debts triggers the debtor's duty to file (extending personally to the debtor's directors), and also creditors' ability to succeed with an involuntary petition. Also, it is used to determine the point of the debtor's insolvency for the purposes of avoidance of antecedent transactions.

4. LIKELIHOOD OF INSOLVENCY AND IMMINENT INSOLVENCY

As regards likely and imminent inability to pay debts, the following can be said.

a) *Likelihood of Insolvency*

Czech law does not define likelihood of insolvency in the sense in which that definition is proposed in the Model Definitions. Implementing this definition would therefore lead to a change in Czech insolvency law.

However, without knowing what operative provision(s) the new definition might serve, it seems impossible to assess the effects of such change.

b) *Imminent Insolvency*

Section 3(5) of the Czech Insolvency Act defines "threatening insolvency" (in Czech, *hrozící úpadek*) as follows:

> (5) Insolvency is threatening if, upon consideration of all relevant circumstances, the debtor may be reasonably expected not to be able to pay a substantial part of its monetary debts as and when they fall due.

This seems similar to, if not exactly the same as, the Model Definitions' definition of "imminent insolvency", though it clearly does not provide for a clear time horizon for the prediction.

In current Czech insolvency law, the concept of "threatening insolvency" allows (but does not obligate) the debtor to file, and it does not give creditors the right to file.

Any impact of implementating the proposed definition would therefore not be very significant, especially given that EU Directive 2019/1023 has been implemented by way of introducing stand-alone restructuring proceedings, conducted entirely independently of insolvency proceedings proper, and using autonomous triggering definitions.

5. OVERINDEBTEDNESS

Section 3(4) of the Czech Insolvency Act defines "overindebtedness" (in Czech *předlužení*) as follows:

> (4) A debtor who is a legal entity or an individual business person is also insolvent if it is overindebted. Overindebtedness obtains if the debtor has multiple creditors and the sum of its liabilities exceeds the value of its assets. When determining the value of the debtor's assets, the further management thereof or the further operation of the debtor's business shall be taken into account if it can be reasonably assumed, upon the consideration of all the relevant circumstances, that the debtor will be able to continue with the management of its assets or the operation of its business.

In current Czech law, the procedural effects of the definition are the same as those of the inability to pay debts – overindebtendess triggers the debtor's duty to file (extending personally to the debtor's directors), and also creditors' ability to succeed with an involuntary petition. Also, it is used to determine the point in time of the debtor's insolvency for the purposes of avoidance of antecedent transactions.

The definition is clearly different from the definition proposed in the Model Definitions, and it is not immediately clear to me whether adopting it would result in a change for better in Czech insolvency law. The Model Definitions are clearly tougher because they only look to the liquidation value of the debtor's assets. In this sense, implementation would tighten Czech insolvency law.

II. OVERALL ASSESSMENT

Overall, implementation of the Model Definitions into Czech law would lead to changes that may make Czech insolvency law stricter on debtors than it currently is. The overall impact of this is hard to gauge in a simplified exercise of this sort, but may be limited given the general availability of preventive restructuring proceedings pursuant to the national implementation of EU Directive 2019/1023.

At the same time, some of the changes resulting from an implementation of the Model Definitions may make Czech law less clear than it currently is, which would be a retrograde step.

ESTONIA

Anto Kasak

Please identify to what extent the proposed Model Definitions in the proposal align with or differ from the definitions currently used in your national law and whether they would be compatible with and operable in your jurisdiction.

I. INDIVIDUAL ASSESSMENT OF THE MODEL DEFINITIONS

A comparison of the Model Definitions with the definitions in Estonian law reveals the following:

1. INSOLVENCY

Estonian Bankruptcy Act §1(2) stipulates that the debtor is insolvent if the debtor is unable to satisfy the claim of a creditor that has fallen due and such inability, due to the debtor's financial situation, is not temporary. This is a major rule for identification of the insolvency of the debtor including individual and corporate debtors. Therefore, Estonian law corresponds to the Model Definitions.

2. INABILITY TO PAY DEBTS

The Model Definition of inability to pay debts largely corresponds to the definition of insolvency set out in the Estonian Bankruptcy Act §1(2). Nevertheless, the Estonian Bankruptcy Act is rather general and does not have any particular rule for any kind of specific presumptions, including but not limited to, restoration of the liquidity gap or ceased payments or default with payments for an essential creditor within specific time.

3. CESSATION OF PAYMENTS

The Estonian Bankruptcy Act does not recognise the concept of the cessation of payments. Furthermore, this concept has not been mentioned even once in Supreme Court practice.

4. LIKELIHOOD OF INSOLVENCY AND IMMINENT INSOLVENCY

As regards likely and imminent inability to pay debts, the following can be said.

a) *Likelihood of Insolvency*

Estonian Bankruptcy law enacts a likelihood of insolvency as a presumption of permanent insolvency if the bankruptcy is applied for by the debtor who is a legal person. Otherwise, the Estonian Bankruptcy Act is not familiar with the term of likelihood of insolvency. Nevertheless, likelihood of insolvency is a trigger to open restructuring proceedings under the Reorganisation Act for the legal person debtor and, similarly, to open the individual person debt arrangement proceedings under the Natural Person Insolvency Act.

b) *Imminent Insolvency*

Estonian law is not familiar with the explicit term "imminent insolvency". However, both statutory law and case law in Estonia acknowledge the concept of imminent insolvency. While the term itself may not be explicitly stated in the legislation, the assessment of future insolvency inherently encompasses the notion of imminent insolvency. Imminent insolvency is a trigger to declare bankruptcy of the debtor, who is a legal person, when the debtor itself applies for bankruptcy or to start its reorganisation proceeding.

5. OVERINDEBTEDNESS

According to the Estonian Bankruptcy Act §1(3), a debtor who is a legal person is insolvent also if the assets of the debtor are insufficient for covering the obligations thereof and, due to the debtor's financial situation, such insufficiency is not temporary. Claims that have not yet fallen due are also regarded as obligations. Therefore, overindebtedness is only applicable for legal person bankruptcy. Unfortunately, none of the Estonian insolvency laws give any further explanation of the term "overindebtedness".

II. OVERALL ASSESSMENT

Generally, the Model Definitions does not influence Estonian insolvency laws' substance, but the Model Definitions forces Estonian insolvency law to be more exact about the definition of insolvency. Cessation of payments and imminent insolvency are new terms for Estonian law. Therefore, the Estonian Bankruptcy Act should be amended accordingly.

FINLAND

Tuomas Hupli

Please identify to what extent the proposed Model Definitions in the proposal align with or differ from the definitions currently used in your national law and whether they would be compatible with and operable in your jurisdiction.

I. INDIVIDUAL ASSESSMENT OF THE MODEL DEFINITIONS

A comparison of the Model Definitions[1] with the definitions in Finnish law reveals the following:

1. INSOLVENCY

The statutory definition of insolvency is established in the Bankruptcy Act (120/2004, hereinafter BA), the Restructuring of Enterprises Act (47/1993, hereinafter ResEntAct), the Act on the Adjustment of the Debts of a Private Individual (57/1993) and the Act on the Recovery of Assets to Bankruptcy Estates (758/1991). In these statutes, the content of the definition is identical, with only minor divergences in the wordings. The substantive core is the same: insolvency means that the debtor is

- "unable, other than temporarily, to pay his or her debts when they fall due" (Section 4 of the Act on the Recovery of Assets to Bankruptcy Estates)
- "otherwise than temporarily unable to repay his or her debts as they fall due" (Chapter 2 Section 1(2) BA).

According to the wording of Section 3(1)(3) ResEntAct, insolvency means "the other than temporary inability of the debtor to repay its debts when they become due".

1 This refers to the wording contained in paragraph 8.86 of the draft report dated 29 February 2024.

As mentioned above, the differences in wordings are substantively meaningless. The decisive "message" of the Finnish legislator is that the definition of insolvency refers to cash-flow insolvency and, thus, not to the mere analysis of the debtor's balance sheet, or in any other way to the financial state of the debtor at certain point in time, or within a specific time-frame. In short, assessing the insolvency/solvency of the debtor requires a kind of prediction with, of course, the focus on the future. Nevertheless, there's also a retrospective element since the presumptions of insolvency are based on the circumstances that have evolved in the past.

Saying that the resolution – such as the court decision approving or dismissing the petition to open insolvency proceedings, or any other statement concerning insolvency/solvency – is always based on a prognosis (prediction) holds true, but only when the law requires a look into the future. Regarding transactions avoidance law, distribution of assets of a limited liability company, and certain criminal charges, the case concerns the past, not the future. In these contexts, there is no element of prognosis but instead an element of evaluating the circumstances afterwards and, subject to the provisions applied in a particular case, the conditions and measures occurring within a certain period of time in the past.

2. INABILITY TO PAY DEBTS

a) Prerequisites

Under the law of Finland, inability to pay debts is equated, in all relevant terms, with the concept of insolvency, as described *supra*. When comparing the Finnish law with the Model Definitions, the most significant difference is that Finnish law does not prescribe a certain number of due payments for the assessment of whether the debtor is able or unable to pay its debts.

b) Presumptions

Chapter 2, Section 3(2)(1)–(3) BA establishes the following presumptions/assumptions of insolvency:

> (2) Unless it is otherwise proven, the debtor shall also be deemed insolvent especially if:
>
> (1) the debtor has discontinued payments;
> (2) it has been determined in enforcement proceedings during the six months preceding the filing of the petition for bankruptcy that the debtor cannot repay the claim in full; or
> (3) a debtor, who is, or who during the year preceding the filing of the petition for bankruptcy has been, under the obligation to keep accounts, has not repaid the clear and due claim of the creditor within a week of the receipt of a reminder.

It is further stipulated in Chapter 2, Section 3(3) BA that:

> The debtor may be declared bankrupt under paragraph (2)(3) only if the creditor files the relevant petition within three months of the time limit referred to in that provision and the claim still remains unpaid.

The free evaluation of evidence prevails at the very core of the Finnish law of procedure. In light of that principle, it might be a difficult "project" for Finnish insolvency lawyers to accept a precise number of due claims that would trigger the presumption of insolvency. It should also be kept in mind that the assumptions, as they stand in the current Finnish law, are only applied when the debtor voluntarily files or has had traditional bankruptcy proceedings filed against it. Business restructuring, as well as debt adjustment proceedings for private individuals, falls outside the direct scope of the assumptions, although they may be considered circumstantial evidence.

In addition to the presumptions explained above, the debtor shall be deemed insolvent (unable to pay the due debts), if the debtor declares that he or she is insolvent and there are no special reasons for not accepting that declaration (Chapter 2, Section 3(1) BA). The declaration of the debtor is considered a "confession" with binding effect in relation to the court, but the binding effect can be rebutted provided that "special reasons" so require. Those reasons might take the form of the different views among the directors of a debtor company concerning its financial situation.

The Model Definitions allows the presumptions to be rebuttable. Again, the required number of defaults is incompatible (or problematic at least) with the free evaluation of evidence and, thus, might cause some doubts in the context of the prevailing regime of Finland.

As the most severe concern, it must be noted that the rebuttable presumptions based on (i) the failed enforcement effort, and (ii) the receipt of the reminder on a clear and due claim, are widely used in Finnish insolvency practice. There are strong reasons to expect that any proposal to repeal those presumptions would not be praised by Finnish lawyers, even though the harmonisation of the EU insolvency law would be increased and even though the current presumptions would still be available as circumstantial evidence.

3. CESSATION OF PAYMENTS

By adopting the BA in 2004, cessation of payments was added to the Finnish law as a presumption of insolvency. Just as was noted *supra* in the context of insolvency (inability to pay debts), no particular number of creditors/payments is required by Finnish law in order to presume that the cessation of payments is – or is not – a sufficient "signal" revealing the insolvency of the debtor. Instead, free evaluation of evidence prevails. It is stated in the preambles to the BA that the cessation ("discontinuation") of payments must be general and it must reflect the lack of financial *ability* to meet the claims as they fall due. Mere unwillingness to pay, let alone a dispute over a certain claim or some of the claims, is not a sufficient ground for this presumption to be applied.

Since the Model Definitions is based on the minimum number of creditors to which the debtor is in default, it (the Model Definitions) would require a fundamental change of thinking among the Finnish insolvency lawyers.

4. LIKELIHOOD OF INSOLVENCY AND IMMINENT INSOLVENCY

As regards likely and imminent inability to pay debts under Finnish law, the following observations are noteworthy.

a) Likelihood of Insolvency

In the Finnish law of evidence and of insolvency, the different expressions, such as "likelihood of insolvency", "imminent insolvency", "risk of insolvency" and being in the "vicinity of insolvency" are not precisely separated from each other. In this respect, the current Finnish regime is remarkably different from the Model Definitions, as the latter defines the "likelihood of insolvency" and "imminent insolvency" as separate phenomena based on the "urgency" of the debtor's financial crisis.

Regarding corporate restructuring, the Finnish law allows restructuring proceedings to be opened on the basis that "the debtor faces imminent insolvency" (Section 6(1)(2) ResEntAct). This was the content of Finnish law even before Directive (EU) 2019/1023 on preventive restructuring. According to the statutory definition (Section 3(1)(4) ResEntAct), imminent insolvency (in Finnish: *uhkaava maksukyvyttömyys*; in the Swedish version of the ResEntAct: *hotande insolvens*) simply means "that the debtor is at risk of insolvency".

The Model Definitions requires that it must be more likely than not that the debtor will become unable to pay debts. This is compatible with the classic standard of proof of "the preponderance of evidence", widely applied in Finnish courts (although not always expressly written in judgments and other resolutions). Taking into account that the general standard of evidence in civil and commercial matters is established in Chapter 17, Section 2(2) Code of Judicial Procedure (4/1734 with the latest reform in 2015) as "credible evidence", it seems likely that the Model Definitions can be implemented into the ResEntAct with no significant problems. In the preparatory works for the recent reform of Chapter 17 of the Code of Judicial Procedure, the standard of "credible evidence" is considered to require a preponderance of the evidence.

b) *Imminent Insolvency*

The cut-off period of three months, proposed in the Model Definitions, would represent a new way of thinking in Finnish insolvency law and, once again, in the general law of evidence. In Finland, the attitude towards specific time-frames has been reluctant, due to the importance of free evaluation of evidence. Of course, specific cut-off periods and time-frames are common in criminal law and in the law of transactions avoidance, but in those fields of law, the principle of precision, as a synonym for the principle of exact (even strict) legality, serves different purposes. The basic character of the time-limits prescribed in current Chapter 2, Section 3(2)(2)–(3) and Section 3(3) BA is more procedural than substantive: those time-limits urge the creditor to proceed actively, not to rely on the presumption for an undetermined period of time.

It should also be taken into account that "imminent insolvency", as it is currently considered in Finnish insolvency law, might exist even though the triggering element lies more than three months in the future; nevertheless, the triggering element may be obvious, or absolutely certain. In those cases, imminent insolvency should be applicable as a precondition for the opening of preventive restructuring proceedings without the duty to wait for the period of time required by the law.

For the reasons just explained, the implementation of the Model Definitions of imminent insolvency might raise doubts, or even face some problems, among Finnish lawyers.

5. OVERINDEBTEDNESS

To start the impact assessment concerning the Model Definition of overindebtedness, it is important to note that under Finnish law, no "going concern" entity can be declared bankrupt merely on the basis of the fact that the liabilities of the debtor exceed the value of its assets. Overindebtedness, as a prerequisite for the commencement of bankruptcy, is only available for the debtor in liquidation (usually a limited liability company), an inheritance estate and a bankruptcy estate, i.e. entities with no purpose for continuing activities but rather of terminating the entity in question. This also explains why, under Finnish law, overindebtedness is not connected to insolvency. Insolvency (and solvency) are predictions – expectations – of the debtor's financial performance in the future. For this reason, the connection created in the Model Definitions between overindebtedness and the inability to pay debts might raise doubts, or even face some problems, among Finnish lawyers.

II. OVERALL ASSESSMENT

As an overall assessment, implementing the Model Definitions into Finnish law would not be an easy task, although not impossible. Some of the Model Definitions deal closely with the free evaluation of evidence, a principle of great importance in the thinking and practices of Finnish lawyers. Many of the Model Definitions having the effect of limiting the free evaluation of evidence would, undoubtedly, make the concepts in question clearer and easier to apply in a concrete case; they would also strengthen the harmonisation of the laws of the Member States. Whether or not the price of the increased clearness and harmonisation is too high for Finnish lawyers (law drafters and various interest groups included), remains to be seen.

The most severe problem is easy to predict: Finnish lawyers would not easily accept the proposal of repealing – or turning into the circumstantial evidence only – the rebuttable presumptions based on the failed enforcement effort and on the reminder of a clear and due claim.

It must be noted, however, that none of the Model Definitions violate the fundamental public policy of the Finnish legal system. From this it follows that they might be *made* compatible with, and might be *made* operable in, the jurisdiction of Finland.

FRANCE

Reinhard DAMMANN

Please identify to what extent the proposed Model Definitions in the proposal align with or differ from the definitions currently used in your national law and whether they would be compatible with and operable in your jurisdiction.

I. INDIVIDUAL ASSESSMENT OF THE MODEL DEFINITIONS

A comparison of the Model Definitions with the definitions in French law reveals the following:

1. INSOLVENCY

French law does not provide for a definition of the term "insolvency". Article L. 631-1(1) of the French commercial code (C. com.)[1] exclusively refers to the concept of cash-flow insolvency, i.e. cessation of payments (*cessation des paiements*). The definition of cessation of payment is set forth in Article L. 631-1(1) C. com.: A debtor is considered to be insolvent when it is unable to meet its due and payable debts with its immediately available assets.

The fact that the payment of the debt has been formally requested by one or by several creditors is irrelevant.

The concept of "overindebtedness" (the "balance sheet insolvency" test) is also disregarded in French law as a mandatory triggering event for the opening of insolvency proceedings.

1 French Commercial Code, hereafter C. com.

2. INABILITY TO PAY DEBTS

The Model Definition of "inability to pay debts" differs from the definition in Article L. 631-1(1) C. com. The conceptual starting point is the same: the inability to pay mature debts. But the implementation of the French cash-flow insolvency test is quite different from the approach taken in the Model Definition.

a) *Prerequisites*

According to Article L. 631-1(1) C. com., a debtor is insolvent when it is unable to meet its due and payable debts with its immediately available assets. In addition, moratoriums that have been granted by creditors as well as credit reserves (i.e. undrawn lines of credits) are taken into consideration. It is also well established in French doctrine that debts that are benefitting from a grace period (*periode de grâce*) which has been granted by a tribunal must be disregarded in the cash-flow insolvency test.

The Model Definition refers to the concept of "at the relevant point in time", which is unknown in French law, under which the liquidity test must be made at *any* point in time. Also, French law does not apply the concept of the inability to pay an "insignificant part" of the overall debts.

Indeed, French law is very strict. The inability to pay *any* mature debt is sufficient to trigger the state of insolvency. The fact that a liquidity gap may be closed within a short period of time is irrelevant in French law.

The Model Definition also refers to the concept of "reasonable expectations" for a debtor to be able to cure its liquidity gap within a short period of time. Once again, this element is irrelevant in French law.

Hence, the French definition of cash-low insolvency is much stricter than the Model Definition.

b) *Presumptions*

The Model Definition of inability to pay debts provides for rebuttable presumptions on two bases: (i) cessation of payments (defined as default with payments to at least two creditors) and (ii) default to an essential creditor with at least two payments, or one payment for at least three months.

Again, this approach differs from French law, which requires an objective liquidity test. The amount of due and payable liabilities is determined by reference to *all* undisputed (contractual) payment obligations of the debtor. Only contingent debts are not taken into consideration.

Unlike the Model Definition, French law does not refer to any (rebuttable) presumption (like the default of two payments to an essential creditor, or late payment for at least three months) to establish a situation of cessation of payment.

On the asset side, French law is also rather strict. Only liquid assets, like available cash deposits with a bank and immediately available assets – like publicly-traded stock and securities – are taken into consideration, but not trade receivables that are due and payable.

Cash that is generated through fire sales[2] and undue financial support by banks, financial institutions, funds and group companies to finance structurally money-losing businesses, are also disregarded in the cash-flow liquidity test under French law.

c) *Consequences*

Overall, the transposition of the Model Definition would materially change the definition of cessation of payments under Article L. 631-1(1) C. com.

Such changes would be even more important if the French legislator decided to transpose the presumptions of the Model Definition.

3. CESSATION OF PAYMENTS

The differences between the Model Definition and the French definition of cessation of payments have already been explained above.

4. LIKELIHOOD OF INSOLVENCY AND IMMINENT INSOLVENCY

As regards likely and imminent inability to pay debts, the following can be said.

a) *Likelihood of Insolvency*

The Model Definition defines the term "likelihood of insolvency" as a situation where it is more likely than not that the debtor will become unable to pay debts. This concept seems to refer to the likely inability of the debtor to pay its debts in the future when they will become due and payable.

French law does not use the terms "likelihood of insolvency" or "likely inability to pay debts". Nor does not use the concept of "imminent inability to pay debts".

Pursuant to Article L. 620-1 C. com., pre-insolvency restructuring proceedings – i.e. safeguard proceedings – are available to debtors which are not in a situation of cessation of payments, but face difficulties that they are

[2] A sale of goods or assets, at significantly discounted prices, by a seller in financial distress.

unable to overcome. Initially, the law of 26 July 2005, introducing safeguard proceedings, provided for an additional test. The debtor had to demonstrate that the difficulties were of such nature that they would lead to cessation of payments. This condition of "threatening insolvency" war abrogated by the ordonnance of 18 December 2008. This provision seems to refer to the concept of "imminent inability to pay debts".

b) Imminent Insolvency

According to the Model Definition, the term "imminent inability to pay debts" refers to the situation where the debtor *will* become unable to pay its debts in the next three months. As explained *supra*, since the reform of December 2008 the condition of "imminent inability to pay debts" was abrogated in order to facilitate the opening of safeguard proceedings. The three-month period is unknown in French law.

c) Consequences

The transposition of "likelihood of insolvency" or "imminent insolvency" would render the opening of preventive restructuring (safeguard) proceedings by French courts much more restrictive.

5. OVERINDEBTEDNESS

As stated above, French law does not define the concept of overindebtedness as a triggering event for the opening of ordinary insolvency proceedings.

As regards likely and imminent inability to pay debts, the following can be said.

a) The Concept of Overindebtedness in the Model Definition

According to the Model Definition the "overindebtedness" of a debtor must meet two conditions: (i) the occurrence of the debtor's inability to pay debts is more likely than not, and (ii) the liabilities of debtor exceed the assets' liquidation value. These two conditions must occur "at the relevant point in time".

b) Consequences

The transposition of "overindebtedness" into French law would render pre-insolvency restructuring proceedings more complex and costly.

In practice, in order to avoid the opening of ordinary insolvency proceedings, it would be necessary to avoid the occurrence of a likely cessation of payments by the debtor.

In most restructuring cases, the liquidation value of the assets of the debtor is quite low by comparison to a going concern valuation. Hence, it would appear necessary not only to avoid the actual cessation of payments but also the mere likelihood of cash-flow insolvency. This would require the debtor to retain the services of independent accounting experts in order to give an opinion not only on the possible occurrence of likely cash-flow insolvency but also with respect to the liquidation value of the balance sheet.

In addition, a debtor having a negative net asset going concern value could only be restructured provided that such negative net asset value would thereby be cured. In practice this would mean increasing equity (capital increase, lease-back transactions etc.).

II. OVERALL ASSESSMENT

In all, there is every reason to conclude that incorporating the Model Definitions into French law would trigger material changes. Indeed, the Model Definitions would appear incompatible with French law and would lead to legal uncertainty. Article L. 631-1 C. com. would have to be amended to reflect to new concept of cessation of payments. In this respect, the more flexible approach of the Model Definition would lead to legal uncertainty.

It would also be necessary to introduce the overindebtedness "balance sheet test" together with the concept of likelihood of cash-flow insolvency. The consequential changes would appear rather important. A company with a negative net asset value on a going concern basis would be required to file for the opening of ordinary insolvency proceedings, or to be recapitalised.

Pre-insolvency restructuring of the debtor would become more complex and cumbersome.

Finally, it would appear necessary to introduce the triggering event of "imminent insolvency" into Article L. 620-1 C. com. as a condition of opening safeguard proceedings, thus unwinding the reform of December 2008.

GERMANY

Reinhard Bork

Please identify to what extent the proposed Model Definitions in the proposal align with or differ from the definitions currently used in your national law and whether they would be compatible with and operable in your jurisdiction.

I. INDIVIDUAL ASSESSMENT OF THE MODEL DEFINITIONS

A comparison of the Model Definitions with the definitions in German law reveals the following:

1. INSOLVENCY

German law does not provide for a definition of the term insolvency. However, it is common ground that (substantive and actual, i.e. not imminent or likely) "insolvency" covers both inability to pay debts and overindebtedness. This can be derived from the rules on directors' liability in §§15a and 15b Insolvenzordnung (InsO)[1] as well as from §§17 and 19 InsO, which entitle creditors to apply for insolvency proceedings if the debtor is unable to pay its debts or is overindebted.

2. INABILITY TO PAY DEBTS

The Model Definition of inability to pay debts largely corresponds to the definition in §17 InsO.

---

1 German Insolvency Code.

a) *Prerequisites*

According to §17(2) sentence 1 InsO, a debtor is illiquid if he or she is not able to pay their mature debts. However, it is generally recognised and has been stated several times by the German Federal Court of Justice that (i) the requirements must be established for the relevant point in time, (ii) the inability to pay an insignificant part of the debt (less than 10%) is not taken into account, and (iii) inability to pay debts does not exist if the liquidity gap can be closed again within a short period of time (three weeks). Although the Model Definition is less specific regarding the necessary size ("insignificant part") and the duration of the liquidity gap ("in the short term"), and although it is unclear how the CJEU will one day concretise this definition, it can be said for the time being that the German definition largely corresponds to the Model Definition.

b) *Presumptions*

The Model Definition of inability to pay debts provides for a rebuttable presumption on two alternative bases: (i) cessation of payments (defined as default with payments to at least two creditors) and (ii) default to an essential creditor with at least two payments or one payment for at least three months. This differs from German law.

Under §17(2) sentence 2 InsO, inability to pay debts is rebuttably presumed if the debtor has ceased payments. At first glance, this corresponds to the Model Definition. However, the German definition of cessation of payments differs from the Model Definition of this term in two respects: first, there is no statutory definition of cessation of payments; and second, the German Federal Court of Justice understands this term in a very broad way. The Court requires that the external behaviour of the debtor (in which inability to pay debts is typically expressed) can be established; the relevant public must have the justified impression that the debtor is not in a position to fulfil his or her payment obligations. In this respect, the second basis of the presumption mentioned in the Model Definition (default with payments to an essential creditor with at least two payments or one payment for at least three months) would most likely also constitute a case of (circumstantial evidence of[2]) cessation of payments under German law. The first presumption (default with payments to at least two creditors), however, would only meet the requirements of German law if the two debts were significant and their non-payment indicated an inability to pay in light of all other circumstances of the specific case. In most cases, however, mere default vis-à-vis two creditors would not be sufficient. On the other hand, default with payment to only one creditor would suffice under German

2 Cf. Main Report at para. 4.18.

law if the relevant debt were a substantial part of all debts. Hence, the Model Definition is both broader (two minor debts are sufficient) and narrower (one single debt is never sufficient) than the German understanding of cessation of payments.

c) Consequences

Regarding the consequences of these differences, it must be stressed that the Model Definition, on the one hand, does not oblige the Member States to transpose the presumptions into their national law and, on the other hand, does not permit them to introduce different presumptions. For German law, this would mean that the current presumption (cessation of payments) could only be kept if it were defined according to the Model Definition of this term. However, all other individual circumstances of the case could still be used as circumstantial evidence, albeit for inability to pay debts only, not for cessation of payments. Overall, little or nothing would effectively change under German law if the Model Definitions were transposed into German law.

3. CESSATION OF PAYMENTS

The differences between the Model Definition and the German definition of cessation of payments have already been explained. Hence, reference can be made to section 2(b)/(c) above.

4. LIKELIHOOD OF INSOLVENCY AND IMMINENT INSOLVENCY

As regards likely and imminent inability to pay debts, the following can be said.

a) Likelihood of Insolvency

German law does not know the terms "likelihood of insolvency" or "likely inability to pay debts". Instead, the term "imminent inability to pay debts" is used. However, this is defined in §18(2) sentence 1 InsO as follows: "A debtor is deemed to be faced with imminent inability to pay debts if it is likely that the debtor will be unable to meet existing obligations to pay on the date of their maturity". Compared to the Model Definitions, German law uses "imminent inability to pay debts" but defines this very similarly to the Model Definition of "likelihood of insolvency". This includes the understanding of "likelihood" as predominant likelihood ("more likely than not"). This results in German law referring to likely inability to pay debts, albeit under an incorrect label.

As regards the prognosis period, §18(2) sentence 2 InsO provides for a time-span of 24 months whereas the Model Definition does not mention any fixed prognosis period. Therefore, if the Model Definitions had to be transposed into German law, terminology would have to be adapted and the rule concerning the prognosis period would have to be cancelled.

However, this would not entail significantly different results, since a forecast of more than two years is normally not possible. Hence, an adapted definition would provide courts and debtors with more flexibility but would not noticeably change the system.

b) Imminent Insolvency

It follows from the above, that German insolvency law is familiar with the term "imminent inability to pay debts" but does not distinguish it from "likely inability to pay debts" and defines the former in the sense of the latter. Hence, German law does not use imminent inability to pay debts in the same way as the Model Definitions. As regards the consequences in the event of transposition of the Model Definitions, reference can be made to section 3(a) above.

5. OVERINDEBTEDNESS

According to §19(2) sentence 1 InsO, overindebtedness exists if the debtor's assets no longer cover its existing obligations to pay, unless it is predominantly likely, considering the circumstances, that the enterprise will continue to exist for the next 12 months. Compared to the Model Definition, the following can be said.

First, German law also provides for a liquidation test, comparing all liabilities of the debtor to its assets at the relevant point in time, the latter being assessed with their liquidation value.

Second, although German law refers to a "viability test" rather than a liquidity test, the former is understood in the sense of the latter, since the question as to whether the enterprise is predominantly likely ("more likely than not") to continue to exist is answered by reference to the company's ability to meet its debts maturing in the foreseeable future.

Third, the only difference is that German law provides for a fixed prognosis period of 12 months, whereas the Model Definition has no such limitation. Hence, if the Model Definition had to be transposed into German law, the reference to the 12-month period would have to be deleted. However, this would probably make little difference to the results, as in most cases the overindebtedness occurs within the one-year period anyway.

II. OVERALL ASSESSMENT

In all, there is every reason to conclude that incorporating the Model Definitions into German law would change little. The Insolvency Code would have to be amended in some respects and practitioners would have to get used to the fact that some cases would have to be resolved using circumstantial evidence rather than presumptions. The elimination of the fixed prognosis periods for likely inability to pay debts and overindebtedness would lead to more legal uncertainty, but also to more flexibility. However, the practical results are most likely to remain largely the same. In the end, the Model Definitions would be compatible with and operable in Germany.

GREECE

Stathis Potamitis

Please identify to what extent the proposed Model Definitions in the proposal align with or differ from the definitions currently used in your national law and whether they would be compatible with and operable in your jurisdiction.

I. INDIVIDUAL ASSESSMENT OF THE MODEL DEFINITIONS

A comparison of the Model Definitions with the definitions in Greek law reveals the following:

1. INSOLVENCY

Greek law does not provide for a relevant definition of the term "insolvency". However, it is common ground that it refers to inability to pay mature debts (i.e. those that are due and payable), which gives grounds for the initiation of insolvency or restructuring proceedings.

2. INABILITY TO PAY DEBTS

a) Prerequisites

Greek law does not have a definition of inability to pay debts. Inability to pay debts is part of the definition of "cessation of payments", which is the main insolvency characteristic and the triggering event for the initiation of insolvency proceedings. In particular, "cessation of payments" is defined as "inability to satisfy its due and payable monetary obligations generally and permanently" (Article 77 Insolvency Law). Therefore, inability of the debtor to pay its debts is a means to establish that the debtor has ceased to pay its debts.

The Model Definitions turn this around. Inability to pay is the central definition and cessation of payments is the basis of a presumption to establish such inability.

Compared to the definition of cessation of payments under Greek law, the Model Definition of inability to pay debts is more detailed and specific. Greek law has a broader definition and the determination that the debtor is in cessation of payments is left to the court with a wide margin of appreciation. However, under Greek law, it is clear that cessation of payments means general and permanent inability to pay due and payable debts. We will refer *infra* to the rebuttable presumption of cessation of payments under Greek law. There is no specific provision under Greek law regarding which assets are taken into account when assessing the inability to pay debts (e.g. all (financial) assets or only those that are liquid), possibly because cessation of payments is a finding of actual non-payment over a period of time (see *infra* in relation to the rebuttable presumption). As to whether that inability is permanent, assets that are hard to monetarise would probably not be considered. Also, in relation to the liquidity gap, Greek law does not provide for a liquidity test, other than the concept of cessation of payments. In addition, under Greek law it is not relevant whether the liquidity gap can be closed again in the short term. However, if the debtor presents before the court a secured way out of the cessation of payments (e.g. through an already initiated share capital increase or financing), in practice the court may reject the bankruptcy application.

In order to establish cessation of payments, Greek courts must assess all relevant circumstances which can serve as circumstantial evidence of the debtor's cessation of payments. According to case law, typical circumstances include:

- non-payment of a substantial part of due liabilities (even if it is only one single but substantial claim),
- (several months of) non-payment of taxes and/or social security contributions,
- non-honouring of cheques,
- failure to pay or slow payment of wages and salaries.

Also, the Model Definition would require an assessment of all of the debtor's mature debts and liquid assets. That is currently not necessary under Greek law; therefore the Model Definition would lift the threshold for initiation of insolvency proceedings.

The introduction of the Model Definition of "inability to pay" into Greek law would have a significant impact as it provides more clarity over the precise financial situation of the debtor that is required to initiate insolvency proceedings. It would provide increased legal certainty and would facilitate the filing of insolvency applications.

b) *Presumptions*

The Model Definition of inability to pay debts provides for rebuttable presumptions on two bases: (i) cessation of payments (defined as being in default with payments to at least two creditors) and (ii) being in default to an essential creditor with at least two payments or one payment for at least three months. This differs from Greek law.

Article 77 paragraph 2 of Law 4738/2020 (the Insolvency Law) introduces the following rebuttable presumption of cessation of payments:

> [the non-payment of] due and payable obligations to the State, Social Security Institutions or credit and financing institutions in an amount that is at least 40%[1] of the debtor's total due and payable obligations for a period of at least 6 months, provided that the debtor's unpaid liabilities exceed the amount of 30,000 EUR.

Greek law expressly provides that the selective satisfaction of due and payable monetary obligations does not lift the debtor's cessation of payments, which may consist in the inability to satisfy even just one material/significant monetary liability.

3. CESSATION OF PAYMENTS

Both the function and definition of "cessation of payments" in the Model Definitions differ from Greek law. The differences between the Model Definition and the Greek definition of cessation of payments have already been explained. Hence, reference can be made to section 2 *supra*.

Overall, the presumption of cessation of payments could be compatible with and operable in Greek law.

4. LIKELIHOOD OF INSOLVENCY AND IMMINENT INSOLVENCY

As regards likely and imminent inability to pay debts, the following can be said.

a) *Likelihood of Insolvency*

Greek law uses the term "likelihood of insolvency" as the third ground for initiation of restructuring proceedings, but only when the debtor files the restructuring application. Under the previous Greek Bankruptcy Code, which

1 This increases to 60% in case of small-scale bankruptcies (Article 176 Insolvency Law).

was repealed in early 2021 by the new Insolvency Law, the "likelihood of insolvency" was the third ground for initiation of insolvency proceedings (but again only when the debtor was the applicant party). However, as far as we are concerned, the use of this ground in insolvency applications was extremely limited.

The Model Definition states that to establish a likelihood of insolvency it is required that it is more likely than not that the debtor will become unable to pay its debts. This is more or less similar to current Greek law for restructuring proceedings and similar to the repealed Bankruptcy Code.

b) Imminent Insolvency

Greek law is familiar with the term "imminent inability to pay debts". The Model Definition would have no impact at this point (apart from the three-month period that it introduces), given that imminent insolvency/inability to pay debts is already the second ground for initiation of insolvency and restructuring proceedings, but only when the debtor requests it (Articles 32 and 77 Insolvency Law respectively). This means that creditors may initiate insolvency or restructuring proceedings, only if the debtor is in cessation of payments.

Finally, as already mentioned, Greek law does not specify a period of time for the prognosis regarding the point in time when actual inability to pay debts will occur. Further, Greek law does not specify how the test is satisfied. Depending on the circumstances, a finding that one or more significant debts will soon become due and that there is no expectation to refinance or pay such debts from projected cash flow should be sufficient.

5. OVERINDEBTEDNESS

Greek insolvency law does not operate with "overindebtedness" as a ground for the opening of insolvency or restructuring proceedings and is not familiar with such term.

II. OVERALL ASSESSMENT

As a general conclusion and assessment, the incorporation of the Model Definitions into Greek law would change the current application of the Insolvency Law in Greece. A number of amendments to the Insolvency Law would be necessary. The introduction of the term "inability to pay" would have the biggest impact, as would the changed function for the term "cessation of payments". Of course, these changes will lead to increased legal certainty as to which debtor should file for insolvency and would leave less room for the courts' discretion to rule on such circumstances. The new Insolvency Law has already made a significant step towards this by introducing the rebuttable presumption for cessation of payments. The introduction of the term "overindebtedness" will be something new for the Greek insolvency system.

Considering the above, the Model Definitions would be compatible with and operable in Greece.

HUNGARY

Zoltan Fabok

Please identify to what extent the proposed Model Definitions in the proposal align with or differ from the definitions currently used in your national law and whether they would be compatible with and operable in your jurisdiction.

I. INDIVIDUAL ASSESSMENT OF THE MODEL DEFINITIONS

A comparison of the Model Definitions with the definitions in Hungarian law reveals the following:

1. INSOLVENCY

Hungarian general insolvency law (unlike some sectoral laws) does not provide for a definition of the term insolvency. The concept of substantive insolvency arguably covers both inability to pay debts and overindebtedness but it plays a limited role in the opening of proceedings since the stand-alone opening grounds do not include the criterion of substantive insolvency (§27(2)(a)–(e) Insolvency Act).

By contrast, both inability to pay debts and overindebtedness can qualify as grounds for opening liquidation proceedings initiated by the debtor. Inability to pay debts is also a ground for opening corporate bankruptcy proceedings (which can only be initiated by the debtor). In the latter case, however, the threshold of proof is low, given the non-adversarial nature of the debtor-initiated insolvency proceedings. Furthermore, the debtor-initiated insolvency proceedings can also be opened due to imminent insolvency, so that the debtor does not need to rely on actual (substantive) insolvency.

Therefore, I do not expect the Model Definition of insolvency to have a significant impact on existing Hungarian (general) insolvency law, in the context of opening insolvency proceedings.

The "legal meaning" of insolvency in Hungary is closely linked to the grounds for opening liquidation proceedings listed in §27(2) Insolvency Act.

2. INABILITY TO PAY DEBTS

a) *Prerequisites*

§3(1)(b) and §27(2)(f) Insolvency Act state that the debtor is insolvent if it is unable to settle its debt (debts) on the date when they are due. That definition includes (explicitly) the criterion that the debts must be mature, and (implicitly) the criterion that the inability to pay must exist at the relevant point in time.

Apparently, the Model Definition of "inability to pay debts" is far more detailed, as it includes the additional criteria of the liquidity gap, relevant (liquid) assets and the duration of the liquidity gap.

b) *Presumptions*

The Model Definition of inability to pay debts provides for a rebuttable presumption on two bases: (i) cessation of payments (defined as being in default with payments to at least two creditors) and (ii) being in default to an essential creditor with at least two payments or one payment for at least three months.

Hungarian insolvency law does not recognise such presumptions. Given that the threshold for proving inability to pay debts in debtor-initiated proceedings (where inability to pay debts is an opening ground) is rather low, presumptions do not play a significant role.

c) *Consequences*

Under Hungarian insolvency law, inability to pay debts is a ground for opening insolvency proceedings only at the debtor's request (for creditor-initiated liquidation petitions the Insolvency Act provides for a list of stand-alone liquidation grounds, §27(2)(a)–(e) Insolvency Act). In the case of debtor-initiated proceedings, in practice, the courts tend not to examine the existence of inability to pay on the merits but instead to rely on the debtor's own declaration and the necessary documentation (e.g. balance sheet). Therefore, I would not expect the implementation of the Model Definitions into Hungarian law to have a significant impact.

However, the reform of Hungarian insolvency law is underway. This offers an opportunity to align the principles of Hungarian insolvency law with international best practice.

3. CESSATION OF PAYMENTS

Hungarian law uses but does not define the concept of cessation of payments. The term is used by the Civil Code (§§3:189, 3:270 Civil Code). It is neither an autonomous ground for opening proceedings nor the basis of a presumption that the debtor is unable to pay its debts. Cessation of payments is relevant in the context of directors' duties to convene a shareholders' meeting.

In view of the Model Definition of inability to pay debts, including the rebuttable presumption based on cessation of payments, the Model Definition of the latter appears to be practical.

4. LIKELIHOOD OF INSOLVENCY AND IMMINENT INSOLVENCY

As regards likely and imminent inability to pay debts, the following can be said.

a) *Likelihood of Insolvency*

Hungarian law defines the likelihood of insolvency (literally: likelihood of becoming insolvent) as a situation in which there are reasonable grounds for assuming that the debtor will be unable to meet his outstanding payment obligations when they fall due unless further measures are taken (§3(1) point 8 Restructuring Act). The Hungarian definition does not refer to the degree of certainty. The criterion of "more likely than not" seems to set a higher threshold as compared to the current situation.

Nevertheless, I expect that the definition could be transposed into Hungarian law without any major difficulties. In fact, the more specific guidance provided by the Model Definition (inability to pay debts is "more likely than not") may prove more helpful than the current very broad definition.

b) *Imminent Insolvency*

§33/A(3) Insolvency Act defines the concept of imminent insolvency as follows: "The occurrence of imminent insolvency [literally: a situation constituting a threat of insolvency] is on the date from which the directors of the entity foresaw, or ought reasonably (as is expected from persons in such positions) to have foreseen, that the entity would be unable to meet its debts as they fall due." Originally and primarily, imminent insolvency has been relevant in the context of directors' liability for wrongful trading: directors may be held liable for the diminution of the debtor's assets that occurred during the period of imminent insolvency.

Later, imminent insolvency also appeared as the ground for opening reorganisation proceedings (as part of the COVID-related emergency legislation) (§49 Transitional Act). The special legislation is expected to expire at the end of 2024.

Imminent insolvency can also be a ground for opening debtor-initiated bankruptcy and liquidation proceedings (§3(1)(b) and §27(2)(f) Insolvency Act).

In the last two decades Hungarian courts have dealt with hundreds of wrongful trading cases and thus the concept of imminent insolvency has been more or less clarified (in several cases, Hungarian courts have applied the "current ratio test" or the "quick ratio test"). Therefore, the Model Definition introducing a prognosis period of three months is expected to have a significant impact in Hungary, but this impact would primarily affect wrongful trading cases rather than the opening of proceedings, where the evidentiary threshold is already low.

5. OVERINDEBTEDNESS

Overindebtedness in the Insolvency Act means that the debtor's liabilities exceed the debtor's assets (§27(2)(f) Insolvency Act). Arguably, a reference to the relevant point in time is implicitly included.

However, the additional requirements in the Model Definition, namely the reference to the debtor's inability to pay debts and the application of the liquidation value of the assets (rather than the book value) would be new features.

The concept of overindebtedness is of little significance under the current (general) insolvency legislation, since it applies as a ground of application only in debtor-initiated liquidation proceedings. Here the courts do not usually require detailed evidence. Therefore, the impact of the Model Definition seems to be limited.

II. OVERALL ASSESSMENT

Given that in the current Hungarian insolvency legislation, inability to pay debts and overindebtedness are only grounds for opening debtor-initiated proceedings (and NOT for creditor-initiated proceedings) the refined Model Definitions seem to have limited impact.

The Model Definition of likelihood of insolvency would bring some changes but seems to be relatively easily implementable in the Restructuring Act.

The implementation of the Model Definition of imminent insolvency would significantly change the current concept of imminent insolvency but not primarily in the context of the opening of insolvency proceedings but rather in the context of liability for wrongful trading.

Hungary is in the process of reforming its insolvency law. This would be a good opportunity to incorporate the Model Definitions into Hungarian insolvency law. However, as discussed *supra*, implementing the new concepts is not enough. It would also be important to consider revising the grounds for opening creditor-initiated proceedings, which currently do not include any form of "substantive" insolvency (be it inability to pay or overindebtedness) but rather stand-alone grounds for opening liquidation proceedings (§27(2)(a)–(e) Insolvency Act).

IRELAND

Simon MURPHY

Please identify to what extent the proposed Model Definitions in the proposal align with or differ from the definitions currently used in your national law and whether they would be compatible with and operable in your jurisdiction.

I. INDIVIDUAL ASSESSMENT OF THE MODEL DEFINITIONS

A comparison of the Model Definitions with the definitions in Irish law reveals the following:

1. INSOLVENCY

The term insolvency is not defined in Irish law. It is instead referred to in the context of the grounds upon which a company would be considered insolvent, such as the inability of a company to pay its debts or the inability of a company to continue where it cannot by reason of its liabilities continue its business.

2. INABILITY TO PAY DEBTS

a) Prerequisites

The law in Ireland deems a company unable to pay its debts pursuant to the Companies Act, Section 570(a) wherein it is noted that

> a company shall be deemed to be unable to pay its debts ... if a creditor ... indebted in a sum exceeding €10,000 then due, has served on the company ... a demand in writing requiring the company to pay the sum so due, and ... the company has, for 21 days after the date of the service ... neglected to pay the sum ....

The Model Definitions provide a more comprehensive definition of the inability to pay debts. The Model Definitions also provide a temporal limit on the court's consideration of the inability to pay debts, but the reference to the "relevant point in time" would appear to be far preferable to the definition in Irish law – not least because the circumstances giving rise to the inability to pay debts under Irish law are rebuttable before the Irish courts.

The law in Ireland does not engage in the consideration of "mature debts" and "liquid assets". The inclusion of this level of detail in the definition of an inability to pay debts would provide additional layers to the factors currently considered under Irish law in relation to the ability to pay debts.

The Model Definitions go on to provide even greater detail with respect to a "rebuttable presumption", a concept understood and interpreted under Irish law; however, the basis for consideration of that rebuttable presumption is more sophisticated under the Model Definitions than under Irish law.

The terms for rebutting the presumption of an inability to pay debts under Irish law are not defined and are open to interpretation. Similarly, there is no definition of an "essential creditor" under Irish law or any consideration of default of payments by the debtor without action from a creditor to demand payment.

The Model Definitions would provide greater certainty in Irish law and remove some of the ambiguity as to whether there is an inability to pay debts. However, some of the proposed terms within the definition of inability to pay debts are not in use in Ireland, such as "mature debts" and "liquid assets". It would also be necessary to adopt a more comprehensive approach to an inability to pay debts if the Model Definitions were to be adopted.

b) *Presumptions*

The Model Definition of inability to pay debts provides for a rebuttable presumption on two alternative bases: (i) cessation of payments (defined as default with payments to at least two creditors), and (ii) default to an essential creditor with at least two payments or one payment for at least three months.

The cessation of payments, of itself, is not a consideration in assessing an inability to pay debts in Irish law. As this is not a consideration as a stand-alone factor, the breakdown of that cessation of payments into two separate bases for the rebuttable presumption of inability to pay would also be a new feature for Irish law.

Irish law currently has the failure to satisfy a demand for payment from a creditor as the basis for determination of an inability to pay debts. This test in practice is applied as a rebuttable presumption and so the adoption of the two bases for the rebuttable presumption proposed within the Model Definitions would appear to be achievable. However, any adoption of these rebuttable presumptions within the Model Law definitions would also require the adoption of the other definitions not utilised in Irish law, including "essential creditor".

3. CESSATION OF PAYMENTS

The concept of cessation of payments is not established in Irish law. The introduction of the concept of cessation of payments with respect to the two bases for the rebuttable presumption of an inability to pay debts and reflective of the actions of the debtor would be a new concept for Irish law.

In Ireland it is incumbent upon the creditor to demand payment of a debt from the debtor for a rebuttable presumption of an inability to pay debts to arise.

The concept of cessation of payments is not currently compatible with Irish law.

4. LIKELIHOOD OF INSOLVENCY AND IMMINENT INSOLVENCY

a) *Likelihood of Insolvency*

In Ireland Section 509 of the Companies Act 2014 states that one of the grounds for initiating an insolvency process is that "a company is, or is likely to be, unable to pay its debts".

The proposed Model Definition expands upon the position under Irish law. It would be useful to adopt the Model Definition and adopt the test that it is more likely than not that the debtor will become unable to pay debts.

This would provide for a more comprehensive consideration of the likely ability of the debtor to pay its debts.

b) *Imminent Insolvency*

Imminent insolvency is not a term used under Irish law and an imminent inability to pay debts is not a familiar concept. The Model Definition would be a new introduction in Ireland.

5. OVERINDEBTEDNESS

Overindebtedness as a stand-alone concept is not a basis upon which insolvency proceedings can be initiated in Ireland. The Model Definitions would not affect the current process in Ireland.

II. OVERALL ASSESSMENT

The Model Definitions provide a far greater level of detail and provide a more comprehensive consideration of the terms relevant to insolvency. Some of the Model Definitions are not present in Irish law currently and adoption of new concepts, including the cessation of payments, would be required to implement the Model Definitions.

ITALY

Renato MANGANO

Please identify to what extent the proposed Model Definitions in the proposal align with or differ from the definitions currently used in your national law and whether they would be compatible with and operable in your jurisdiction.

I. INDIVIDUAL ASSESSMENT OF THE MODEL DEFINITIONS

A comparison of the Model Definitions with the definitions in Italian law yields the following:

1. INSOLVENCY

At first glance, the Model Definition of "insolvency" sounds somewhat different from the Italian definition. The Italian definition of insolvency reads: "Insolvency is the debtor's state that is displayed either by the debtor's non-fulfilment of obligations or by other symptoms proving that the debtor is no longer able to satisfy his or her obligations regularly" (Article 2.1.(b) Code of Business Crisis and Insolvency (Codice della crisi d'impresa e dell'insolvenza, CCII)). Nevertheless, this difference must not be overstated. First, it is commonly accepted that the Italian definition of insolvency pivots around the "debtor's non-fulfilment" clause; secondly, and more importantly, this clause is traditionally interpreted as referring not to a situation where the debtor has ceased to pay but to an overall condition of the debtor that, through the "non-fulfilment" – albeit partial – of his or her obligations reveals his or her general condition of "inability to pay debts".

2. INABILITY TO PAY DEBTS

Italian law in the statute book contains no concept explicitly corresponding to the Model Definition of "inability to pay debts". But, as previously said (section 1 *supra*), there is something similar in Italian law in action. Moreover, compared to the Italian concept of "inability to pay debts", the Model Definition seems slightly different. First, the Model Definition refers to a specific point in time, while the Italian concept is mainly forward-looking. Secondly, the Model Definition is more detailed, while the Italian concept is more open-textured.

Nevertheless, these observations must not be overstated. First, it is true that there is no concept in Italian statute law corresponding to the Model Definition of "inability to pay debts", but it is also true that the "inability to pay debts" plays a role in insolvency law *practice* quite as significant as some key concepts in Italian insolvency statute law. Secondly, it is true that the Italian concept of "inability to pay debts" has traditionally been interpreted as forward-looking, but it is also true that, after the enactment of EU Directive 2019/1043 on preventive restructuring, it has become debatable whether the concept of insolvency, including that of "inability to pay debts", must still be interpreted as forward-looking, or whether this must mainly be linked to a specific point in time. Thirdly, it is true that the Italian concept of "inability to pay debts" is more open-textured, but it is also true that courts have always strived to standardise this by means of their rulings, the contents of which functionally coincide with the contents of the Model Definition.

3. CESSATION OF PAYMENTS

In itself, the concept of "cessation of payments" does not exist in Italian insolvency law. Nevertheless, the fact that a debtor has ceased to pay a significant part of his or her debts is usually considered to be a sign that proves that the debtor is unable to pay. As a result, the suggestion in the Model Definitions (Chapter 8, paragraph 8.38) according to which law-makers should refrain from "using 'cessation of payments' as an autonomous trigger for insolvency proceedings" fits in perfectly with the Italian legal framework.

4. LIKELIHOOD OF INSOLVENCY AND IMMINENT INSOLVENCY

As regards likely and imminent inability to pay debts, the following observations can be made.

a) Likelihood of Insolvency

The Model Definition of "likelihood of insolvency" is comparable with the Italian law definition of "crisis" (*crisi*), understood as a legal term – one must bear in mind that in non-legal terms the Italian word *crisi* simply means "crisis" or "distress". The insolvency law concept of "crisis" is defined as follows:

"crisis is a financial state that can evolve into insolvency and that occurs when the prospective cash flows are not capable of covering the firm's debts in the subsequent twelve months" (Article 2.1.(a) CCII).

The difference between the Model Definition of "likelihood of insolvency" and the Italian insolvency law definition of "crisis" is not just a question of terminology. The former reads: "likelihood of insolvency means that it is more likely than not that the debtor will become unable to pay debts", while the latter reads "crisis is a financial state that can evolve into insolvency and that occurs when the prospective cash flows are not capable of covering the firm's debts in the subsequent twelve months."

Nevertheless, the adoption of the Model Definition of "likelihood of insolvency" instead of that of "crisis" should not have any a significant impact on the Italian legal framework. Both concepts are forward-looking; both concepts aim at defining the debtor's present situation by comparing his or her present condition with his or her future condition; and both concepts adopt, as a term of comparison, the risk that the debtor might become insolvent within a reasonable period of time.

Arguably, the adoption of the Model Definition of "likelihood of insolvency" (instead of that of "crisis") should improve the Italian legal framework as regards both terminology and content.

As regards the terminology, the use of an expression such as *insolvenza probabile* (which seems a reasonable translation to Italian of the expression "likelihood of insolvency") seems more technical than that of *crisi*. As a result, this change might avoid confusion with the non-legal concept of "distress" and also facilitate communication between people from different countries. As regards the content, ascertaining the likelihood of insolvency by using non-technical standards, which, as such, do not depend on the firm's accountancy, might in some cases paradoxically prove to be more accurate. In the case of small and medium-sized debtors the determination of the cash flow may prove difficult for two reasons: first, the relevant debtors are exempted from the obligation to prepare a "management report" (Article 19(3) and (4) of EU Directive 2013/34) – even though a cash-flow statement may always be inferred from a revised classification of the profit and loss (P&L) statement; secondly, and more importantly, in the case of sole traders and partnerships, the firm's accounts are not totally reliable, since the assets and liabilities of the firm are intermingled with the assets and liabilities of those people who run the firms themselves.

b) Imminent Insolvency

There is no category in Italian insolvency law that corresponds to the Model Definition of "imminent insolvency". Nevertheless, the introduction of the definition of "imminent insolvency" into the Italian legal framework, including the specification of a fixed time reference of three months, should not have a significant impact. In Italy, a situation where a debtor is expected to become unable to pay his or her debts in the forthcoming three months is already regarded as a situation of insolvency.

5. OVERINDEBTEDNESS

The Model Definition of "overindebtedness" would certainly have a significant impact on Italian law. In fact, under Italian law the term "overindebtedness" refers to neither a specific form of distress nor a specific method for ascertaining it, but rather is an umbrella term including both "likely inability to pay debts" and "insolvency" – the latter including "inability to pay debts". As said in the National Report for Italy (answer to Question 45), this policy has been chosen in order to adopt collective law measures typical of insolvency law to deal with the *crisi* of all persons and entities that are not included in the definition of "non-small traders" without removing – at least formally – the traditional dogma according to which, in Italy, insolvency law refers to "non-small traders" only.

Nevertheless, the statement that the introduction of the Model Definition of "overindebtedness" would have a significant impact does not necessarily mean that this impact would also be undesirable. Eventually, the introduction of the Model Definition of "overindebtedness" might encourage the Italian law-maker to remove – explicitly too – the traditional dogma according to which, in Italy, insolvency law refers to non-small traders only.

II. OVERALL ASSESSMENT

To sum up, although the Model Definitions are different from the Italian definitions, and although some of them do not even exist in Italy, the introduction into Italy of the Model Definitions of "insolvency", "inability to pay debts", "likelihood of insolvency" and "imminent insolvency" should not have a significant impact.

The situation is certainly different as regards the introduction of the definition of "overindebtedness", which in Italy refers to neither a specific form of distress nor a specific method for ascertaining it, but rather an umbrella term including both "likely inability to pay debts" and "insolvency", including "inability to pay debts". Nevertheless, the fact that the introduction of the Model Definition of "overindebtedness" would have a significant impact does not necessarily mean that this impact would also be undesirable. Eventually, the introduction of the Model Definition of "overindebtedness" might encourage the Italian law-maker to remove – also explicitly – the traditional dogma according to which, in Italy, insolvency law refers to non-small traders only.

LATVIA

Madara STURITE

Please identify to what extent the proposed Model Definitions in the proposal align with or differ from the definitions currently used in your national law and whether they would be compatible with and operable in your jurisdiction.

I. INDIVIDUAL ASSESSMENT OF THE MODEL DEFINITIONS

A comparison of the Model Definitions with the definitions in Latvian law reveals the following:

1. INSOLVENCY

Latvian law does not provide for a relevant definition of the term "insolvency". Article 1 of the Latvian Insolvency Law contains a reference to a person's financial difficulties that give grounds for opening insolvency or restructuring proceedings. The term "financial difficulties" is not explained more widely. In practice this term may include various types of inability to pay debts, meaning both actual inability and potential (possible) inability. It should be noted that the Latvian Insolvency Law does not provide for a so-called "balance sheet test", which means that a court can declare insolvency even in circumstances where a person's (legal or private) assets exceed its liabilities. The law sets out specific signs of insolvency according to the Insolvency Law Article 57.

2. INABILITY TO PAY DEBTS

The Latvian Insolvency Law does not provide a legal definition for "inability to pay debts," but it is regarded as one of the signs of insolvency. For example, according to the Article 57, paragraph 1 insolvency proceedings can be initiated if, according to the initial financial report of liquidation, the debtor has insufficient assets to satisfy all the justified claims of creditors, or this condition is discovered during the course of liquidation.

3. CESSATION OF PAYMENTS

The Latvian Insolvency Law does not provide a legal definition for "cessation of payments", but it is considered one of the signs of insolvency. For example, according to Article 57, paragraph 1, if the debtor has not honoured its obligations which are overdue for more than two months, insolvency proceedings can be applied for.

4. LIKELIHOOD OF INSOLVENCY AND IMMINENT INSOLVENCY

As regards likely and imminent inability to pay debts, the following can be said.

a) *Likelihood of Insolvency*

The Latvian Insolvency Law does not provide a legal definition for "likelihood of insolvency", but when interpreted in a cross-referenced framework, it is clear that the Insolvency Law provides for both situations, where the debtor is unable to pay his debts and where the debtor is likely ("potentially" in my interpretation) unable to pay. The signs of insolvency mentioned in Article 57 of the Insolvency Law do not presume that the debtor is unable to pay debts; it is presumed that there is a possibility that the debtor will likely be unable to pay. After the insolvency proceedings have been opened, it may be possible that the sale of the debtor's assets will cover all debts, so that the debtor has in fact never been unable to pay his debts, but by establishing the sign of insolvency, it was suggested that he would likely be unable to pay.

b) *Imminent Insolvency*

Latvian law does not operate with "imminent insolvency" as a ground for the opening of insolvency proceedings. The Model Definitions would have no impact at this point.

5. OVERINDEBTEDNESS

Latvian Law does not operate with "overindebtedness" as a ground for the opening of insolvency proceedings. The Model Definitions would therefore have no impact.

II. OVERALL ASSESSMENT

Generally, the Model Definitions does not influence the Latvian Insolvency Law's substance, but implementation of the Model Definitions into Latvian law would require a substantial rewording of the definition of "insolvency" and corresponding provisions. "Imminent insolvency" and "overindebtedness" would be completely new terms in Latvian law; therefore, the Latvian Insolvency Law would have to be amended accordingly.

LITHUANIA

Frank HEEMANN

Please identify to what extent the proposed Model Definitions in the proposal align with or differ from the definitions currently used in your national law and whether they would be compatible with and operable in your jurisdiction.

I. INDIVIDUAL ASSESSMENT OF THE MODEL DEFINITIONS

A comparison of the Model Definitions with the definitions in Lithuanian law reveals the following:

1. INSOLVENCY

Insolvency is regulated in two Lithuanian statutes, the Law on Insolvency of Legal Entities (JANI), which governs restructuring and bankruptcy proceedings of legal persons,[1] and the Law on Bankruptcy of Natural Persons (FABI),[2] which regulates bankruptcy proceedings for individuals.

JANI defines insolvency as "the state of a legal person when the legal person is unable to discharge its property obligations in due time or when liabilities of the legal person exceed the value of its assets" (Article 2(7) JANI).

FABI defines insolvency of a natural person as "the condition of a natural person, where he is unable to discharge his liabilities, as they mature, exceeding

1 Law on Insolvency of Legal Entities of the Republic of Lithuania (*Lietuvos Respublikos juridinių asmenų nemokumo įstatymas*) 13 June 2019, No. XIII-2221. JANI entered into effect on 1 January 2020 and replaced two separate statutes which had previously regulated bankruptcy and restructuring proceedings for legal entities: the Enterprise Bankruptcy Law (EBL) and the Enterprise Restructuring Law (ERL). Enterprise Bankruptcy Law of Republic of Lithuania (*Lietuvos Respublikos įmonių bankroto įstatymas*) 20 March 2001, No. IX-216; Enterprise Restructuring Law of Republic of Lithuania (*Lietuvos Respublikos įmonių restruktūrizavimo įstatymas*) 20 March 2001, No. IX-218.

2 Law on Bankruptcy of Natural Persons of the Republic of Lithuania (*Lietuvos Respublikos fizinių asmenų bankroto įstatymas*) 22 December 2015, No. XII-2235.

25 minimum monthly wages approved by the Government of the Republic of Lithuania" (Article 2(2) FABI).

Hence, in the context of legal entities, insolvency covers both inability to pay debts and overindebtedness, whereas in the context of natural persons, insolvency means inability to discharge debt.

2. INABILITY TO PAY DEBTS

The Model Definition of inability to pay debts largely corresponds to the definitions of insolvency in FABI and JANI (to the extent that the definitions relate to the inability to discharge debt).

a) Prerequisites

See *supra* in section 1 the legal definitions. Court practice looks at the circumstances of each case to determine whether an inability to pay debt is of temporary nature or if a liquidity gap is immaterial for some other reason, stressing that feasible priority should be given to the restructuring of viable entities rather than putting them into bankruptcy proceedings.

b) Presumptions

The Model Definition of inability to pay debts provides for a rebuttable presumption on two bases: (i) cessation of payments (defined as being in default with payments to at least two creditors) and (ii) being in default to an essential creditor with at least two payments or one payment for at least three months. This differs from Lithuanian law.

Lithuanian statutory law does not recognise rebuttable presumptions. In the context of natural persons' insolvencies, FABI establishes a minimum threshold of debt that needs to exist for a natural person to be regarded as insolvent due to the person's inability to discharge debts. However, strictly speaking this is a condition for insolvency rather than a rebuttable presumption. Still, taking into account the aforementioned court practice, it is likely that courts might come to the conclusion that the natural person is not insolvent despite meeting the statutory illiquidity threshold if the court is satisfied that this illiquidity is of a fairly temporary nature or if other reasons exist that would lead the court to the conclusion that the natural person will be able to resume discharging his debt.

c) Consequences

The Model Definition does not oblige the Member States to transpose the presumptions into their national law, neither does it permit them to introduce different presumptions.

For Lithuanian law, this means that the legislator could choose to introduce rebuttable presumptions as proposed in the Model Definition or to refrain from doing so and instead rely on court practice to further develop the use of circumstantial evidence, including circumstantial evidence similar to the proposed rebuttable presumptions.

Overall, the Model Definitions in the context of inability to pay seem compatible with Lithuanian law.

3. CESSATION OF PAYMENTS

Lithuanian court practice looks at cessation of payments as one of the circumstances which, depending on the case at hand and its other circumstances, might lead the court to the conclusion that a debtor is insolvent due to its inability discharge its obligations. Using the Model Definition of cessation of payments, requiring default with payments to at least two creditors might add some clarity but seems to make sense only if the legislator were to choose to enact the rebuttable presumptions in the Model Definition of "inability to pay debts". Otherwise, it seems preferable to allow jurisprudence to rely on circumstantial evidence and perhaps to develop a reliable practice and definition of cessation of payment.

4. LIKELIHOOD OF INSOLVENCY AND IMMINENT INSOLVENCY

As regards likely and imminent inability to pay debts, the following can be said.

a) Likelihood of Insolvency

Likelihood of insolvency is not used in the context of natural persons' insolvencies.

In the context of legal entities, JANI defines "Likelihood of a legal person's insolvency" as "a situation in which there is a substantial likelihood of the legal person's becoming insolvent within the next three months" (Article 2(7^1) JANI). This definition was enacted in 2021 when the Restructuring and

Insolvency Directive[3] was transposed into Lithuanian law. Hence, the definition is rather new and specific court practice is still scant. However, looking at past court practice developed in the context of restructuring proceedings, as well as the general court practice which, as explained before, takes a case-by-case approach relying on circumstantial evidence, it seems likely that Lithuanian law and practice would accommodate the proposed Model Definition without difficulties.

b) *Imminent Insolvency*

Lithuanian law does not use the term "imminent insolvency". However, the definition of "likelihood of insolvency" is very similar to the proposed Model Definition for "imminent insolvency". As explained, Lithuanian court practice uses a case-by-case approach relying on circumstantial evidence. It does not make a precise distinction between "imminent insolvency" and "likelihood of insolvency". However, taking into consideration that the current definition of "likelihood of insolvency" in Article 2(7^1) JANI contains elements of both, the difference does not really seem to matter in practice. Therefore, there are no noteworthy obstacles in Lithuanian law and practice to use the proposed Model Definition.

5. OVERINDEBTEDNESS

Overindebtedness is used as an insolvency ground for legal entities. It is not used for natural persons.

There is no stand-alone statutory definition of overindebtedness. It is defined as part of the definition of insolvency (see *supra* section 1). Overindebtedness as a stand-alone insolvency ground is rather new in Lithuania, enacted as part of the new insolvency law JANI which came into effect on 1 January 2000. Specific court practice is still rare and in general if compared to the inability to discharge obligations (pay debts) overindebtnedness appears to play a less pronounced role as an insolvency ground.

JANI's statutory definition of overindebtedness differs from the Model Definition in that it does not embed a "likelihood" test, neither does it give precise guidance as to the type of valuation that should be used when assessing the debtor's assets. However, Lithuanian law as it stands does not seem to be

3 Directive 2019/1023/EU of the European Parliament and of the Council of 20 June 2019 on preventive restructuring frameworks, on discharge of debt and disqualifications, and on measures to increase the efficiency of procedures concerning restructuring, insolvency and discharge of debt, and amending Directive (EU) 2017/1132 (Directive on restructuring and insolvency), OJ of 26 June 2019, L 172/18.

incompatible with the Model Definition. As mentioned, court practice takes a flexible, circumstances-based approach and could in future adjust and flesh out its practice taking into account the Model Definition. Already today, courts assess circumstantial evidence of the case at hand to determine if a state of formal overindebtedness is in fact of a merely unsystematic and temporary nature, which is somewhat comparable to "likelihood" test in the Model Definition. In any case, there are no obstacles for the legislator to amend the statutory definition to reflect the Model Definition. Either way, the Model Definition is to be welcomed, as it adds clarity to the definition of overindebtness, which, when the current law was enacted, prompted discussions and concerns in the context of "overindebtness", as the term was new and perceived to be too blurry and broad.

II. OVERALL ASSESSMENT

In all, there is every reason to conclude that incorporating the Model Definitions into Lithuania law would change little. JANI and possibly FABI would have to be amended in some respects. Rebuttable presumptions might be used but the legislator could choose not to enact them, and rather continue relying on court practice and its use of circumstantial evidence. Adding some clarity to the definition of "overindebtedness" by implementing the Model Definition would address some concerns that were levelled at this term when the current definition in JANI was enacted. In any case, the practical results are most likely to remain largely the same. In the end, the Model Definitions would be compatible with and operable in Lithuania.

LUXEMBOURG

Pier Mario Lupinu

Please identify to what extent the proposed Model Definitions in the proposal align with or differ from the definitions currently used in your national law and whether they would be compatible with and operable in your jurisdiction.

I. INDIVIDUAL ASSESSMENT OF THE MODEL DEFINITIONS

A comparison of the Model Definitions with the definitions in Luxembourg law reveals the following:

1. INSOLVENCY

Like many other European Union (EU) Member States, Luxembourg also does not explicitly define "insolvency" in its Commercial Code. Moreover, Luxembourg law uses the term *faillite* to define bankruptcy proceedings, instead of the literal translation of insolvency which, in French, is *insolvabilité*. Luxembourg law correctly uses the term "cessation of payments" (*cessation des paiements*), but such concept is not sufficient to declare the debtor insolvent. Article 437 of the Commercial Code stipulates that a debtor is in a "state of insolvency" (*état de faillite*) when the debtor is unable to meet his commitments, while also having no access to credit, therefore experiencing a credit crunch. The two elements are connected, meaning that one is the consequence of the other. This is regardless of the solvency of the debtor or the causes that led the creditor to file for insolvency.

Concerning the Model Definitions, the proposed definition of insolvency aligns closely with Luxembourg's concept of cessation of payments. However, Luxembourg law does not explicitly define insolvency as inability to pay debts. Nevertheless, the practical application is similar, if we exclude the notions of the likelihood of insolvency or imminent insolvency, as the Luxembourg court would have to verify that the conditions explained in the previous paragraph are both present at the same time. With this in mind, should Luxembourg be allowed not to specifically include references to the notions of the likelihood of insolvency or imminent insolvency, implementing the Model Definition in Luxembourg would require minimal adjustments in terminology rather than substantive legal changes.

2. INABILITY TO PAY DEBTS

a) *Prerequisites*

The Model Definitions prescribe that a debtor is unable to pay debts when it cannot meet obligations as they mature. If referred to as cash-flow insolvency, Luxembourg law concentrates on the inability to raise credit, while the law defines cessation of payments as the inability to meet due debts with available assets. In this sense, Luxembourg's framework largely aligns with the Model Definitions' prerequisites for inability to pay debts. Both emphasise the debtor's incapacity to meet obligations as they fall due, ensuring compatibility with only minimal adjustments.

b) *Presumptions*

Presumptions are the most important part of this assessment, as the Model Definitions foresee a presumption of inability to pay debts on certain bases, such as, for example, the failure to pay significant debts. Luxembourg does not explicitly state such presumptions in its legislation but follows a similar practical approach. This means that while the introduction of explicit presumptions would probably clarify Luxembourg's insolvency procedures, in reality it would create a significant burden for the legislator to specify those presumptions in its statutory law. At the same time, apart from enhancing transparency and alignment with the Model Definitions, the introduction of specific presumptions could facilitate the work of the court but reduce its degree of discretion.

c) *Consequences*

The Model Definitions stipulate that inability to pay debts triggers insolvency proceedings. Similar consequences are present in Luxembourg law, in which the cessation of payments initiates insolvency procedures if the debtor is also unable to raise credit. The concept in the Model Definitions, which aim at clarity and minimum harmonisation, seems compatible with Luxembourg's current practices, requiring no significant changes.

3. CESSATION OF PAYMENTS

Cessation of payments is regarded as a state where the debtor has stopped meeting debt obligations. This is the primary criterion for a debtor to be considered insolvent under Luxembourg law, as stipulated in Article 437 of the Commercial Code. The proximity of the definitions in the Model Definitions and in Luxembourg law implies that the two concepts of cessation of payments are fully compatible, ensuring seamless integration.

4. LIKELIHOOD OF INSOLVENCY AND IMMINENT INSOLVENCY

a) *Likelihood of Insolvency*

The Model Definitions include provisions for the likelihood of insolvency, defined as a foreseeable inability to pay debts. As mentioned in section 1 *supra*, Luxembourg law does not specifically address the likelihood of insolvency, although the recent transposition of Directive (EU) 2019/1023 on preventive restructuring frameworks[1] by the Law of 7 August 2023 on the reorganisation of businesses[2] has opened the way for recognising situations in which the financial situation of the debtor might be deteriorating fast in such a way as to compromise the viability of a business, which require swift intervention. As the Model Definitions have a more generalised approach, with the objective to harmonise the understanding of certain key components of insolvency regimes at the EU level, the innovations introduced by the Law of 7 August 2023 seem

[1] Directive (EU) 2019/1023 of the European Parliament and of the Council of 20 June 2019 on preventive restructuring frameworks, on discharge of debt and disqualifications, and on measures to increase the efficiency of procedures concerning restructuring, insolvency and discharge of debt, and amending Directive (EU) 2017/1132 (Directive on restructuring and insolvency), OJ of 26 June 2019, L 172/18.

[2] Loi du 7 août 2023 relative à la préservation des entreprises et portant modernisation du droit de la faillite, modifiant : 1° le livre III du Code de commerce ; 2° le livre II, titre IX, chapitre II, section I du Code pénal ; 3° les articles 257 et 555 du Nouveau Code de Procédure civile ; 4° la loi modifiée du 10 août 1915 concernant les sociétés commerciales ; 5° la loi uniforme modifiée sur les lettres de change et billets à ordre, telle qu'elle a été introduite dans la législation nationale par la loi du 8 janvier 1962 ; 6° la loi modifiée du 7 juillet 1971 portant, en matière répressive et administrative, institution d'experts, de traducteurs et d'interprètes, de conciliateurs d'entreprise et mandataires de justice assermentés et complétant les dispositions légales relatives à l'assermentation des experts, traducteurs et interprètes ; 7° la loi modifiée du 23 juillet 1991 ayant pour objet de réglementer les activités de sous-traitance ; 8° la loi modifiée du 8 juin 1999 sur le budget, la comptabilité et la trésorerie de l'État ; 9° la loi modifiée du 19 décembre 2002 concernant le registre de commerce et des sociétés ainsi que la comptabilité et les comptes annuels des entreprises ; 10° la loi modifiée du 5 août 2005 sur les contrats de garantie financière. Dossier n° 6539A.

(temporarily) out of scope. Nevertheless, it must be highlighted that, even though not encompassing the element of the "likelihood" in statutory law, Luxembourg law does recognise financial distress as a precursor to cessation of payments. However, this will not be sufficient to declare a debtor insolvent inasmuch as the judge will need to verify that the debtor no longer has access to credit. Therefore, introducing the concept of the likelihood of insolvency into Luxembourg law would require legal updates to include foreseeability criteria, which do not seem immediately compatible with current Luxembourg legislation. The presence of the "barrier" of the two-fold criterion for the status of insolvent conflicts with situations in which a debtor might be declared insolvent in the absence of one of the criteria.

b) Imminent Insolvency

The Model Definitions also consider imminent insolvency as an urgent risk of the inability of the debtor to pay debts. Similarly to the likelihood of insolvency, imminent insolvency is not explicitly defined in Luxembourg law, even though it should only be understood within the broader context of the financial distress experienced by the debtor. In a similar fashion to the previous element of the likelihood of insolvency, incorporating imminent insolvency might probably enhance Luxembourg's legal precision, as it would clarify all those situations in which a debtor is in peculiar and imminent difficult financial situations. However, such alignment with the Model Definitions would jeopardise the current insolvency regime, as it would impact its core (minimal) requirements for defining a debtor as insolvent. Apart from the considerations over the new regime on the reorganisation of businesses mentioned in the previous section, the debtor could always find some credit *in extremis*, which would allow the judge to reject the creditors' demand.

c) Consequences

In the light of the above analysis, both concepts under the Model Definitions would allow for early intervention through insolvency proceedings. According to the currently applicable Luxembourg legislation, early intervention is possible, in particular under the new framework for the reorganisation of businesses, but is less explicitly structured if we consider exclusively the current insolvency regime. On the one hand, it could seem that Luxembourg's framework would benefit from adopting the concepts proposed under the Model Definitions, as it would promote proactive insolvency management. On the other hand, leaving aside the recent reform, this would entail a deep reform of the Luxembourg insolvency regime, in which context the alternative to bankruptcy proceedings has not been that popular, which in turn could imply a less favourable openness towards the introduction of new presumptions. Nevertheless, as the Luxembourg insolvency regime has long been considered more creditor-friendly, should the implementation of these presumptions tend to facilitate the creditors in their demands, one could assume that the legislator might consider those presumptions favourably despite the burden caused by the overhaul needed in order to implement them.

5. OVERINDEBTEDNESS

In the Model Definitions, overindebtedness, a subspecies of insolvency not generally defined in law, is defined as a situation where a debtor's liabilities exceed the value of their assets in addition to a "more likely" inability to pay debts. In Luxembourg law, the concept of overindebtedness as such is recognised as a financial state that may trigger insolvency but is not explicitly defined as foreseen in the Model Definitions. This derives also from the fact that the regime of overindebtedness (*surendettement*), as in other jurisdictions of the region, targets private individuals. In fact, overindebtedness under Luxembourg law should be considered to be the manifest impossibility for individuals to meet all their non-professional debts due or falling due. The Law on overindebtedness (*Loi du 8 janvier 2013 concernant le surendettement*) foresees a special regime for the collective settlement of debts. While the Model Definitions, in principle, should be considered applicable both to "merchants" and natural persons, the presence of an ad hoc regime for individuals would certainly cause problems for the implementation by the Luxembourg legislator that go beyond the sphere of terminology. Overindebtedness as envisaged in the Model Definitions could be located within the "early warning" group of presumptions as in section 4 *supra*, meaning that it would create the same problems for the Luxembourg legislator as in a potential implementation of the likelihood or imminent insolvency ground. However, in practice, a situation of overindebtedness as described in the Model Definitions would be considered very close to a situation of insolvency under Luxembourg law if the debtor failed to prove its ability to raise credit. This means that the liquidity test assumes a more prominent role.

II. OVERALL ASSESSMENT

The overall assessment shall be divided into two parts. On the one hand, the Model Definitions are largely compatible with Luxembourg's current insolvency laws regarding the concept of cessation of payments. However, on the other hand, the formal inclusion of the likelihood of insolvency and imminent insolvency as explicit bases of the presumptions of inability to pay debts are the main areas requiring a substantive reform of Luxembourg law. While these updates could enhance legal clarity and procedural efficiency, ensuring better alignment with international standards, they would require significant changes to the current statutory law which foresees few elements and a greater discretion of the judge. The peculiarity of Luxembourg insolvency law is linked to its unique financial sector landscape in Europe. In this context, companies are generally less interested in the continuity of businesses and, thus, privilege pursuing liquidation proceedings in which they can enforce their rights. Luxembourg is also well known for frequent out-of-court proceedings for the enforcement of rights against debtors and guarantors.

Over the years, the legislator built a creditor-friendly jurisdiction. This means that some of the proposed definitions could alter the current state of the art. Nevertheless, a comprehensive and clear definition of insolvency is desired and much of the impact will depend on the degree and depth of the transposition of a future Directive containing the Model Definitions.

A separate consideration shall be made for the proposed definitions concerning overindebtedness. As widely explained in the questionnaire, Luxembourg law encompasses a specific overindebtedness regime for individuals. A potential reform to include the proposed wording would cause some incompatibilities with the existing regime. Those incompatibilities are not limited to terminology but also include the need to modify the circumstances triggering insolvency under the Commercial Code.

MALTA

Arthur Galea Salomone

Please identify to what extent the proposed Model Definitions in the proposal align with or differ from the definitions currently used in your national law and whether they would be compatible with and operable in your jurisdiction.

I. INDIVIDUAL ASSESSMENT OF THE MODEL DEFINITIONS

1. INSOLVENCY

The term insolvency is not defined in Maltese law. Though not defined, its utilisation in a number of sections of the Companies Act would suggest that it is loosely used interchangeably with "inability to pay one's debts" (e.g. Section 303 dealing with Fraudulent Preferences and Section 316 dealing with Wrongful Trading), which is a defined term. Accordingly, the proposed Model Definition of insolvency as "inability to pay one's debts" is compatible with Maltese law.

It is also noteworthy to point out that although insolvency is currently not defined in Maltese law, any winding up in respect of which a "declaration of solvency" has not been filed in accordance with Section 268 is presumed to be an insolvent liquidation. In filing a declaration of solvency, the directors are required to confirm that

> they have made a full inquiry into the affairs of the company, and that, having so done, they have formed the opinion that the company will be able to pay its debts in full within such period not exceeding twelve months from the date of dissolution as may be specified in the declaration.

2. INABILITY TO PAY DEBTS

Inability to pay debts is defined in terms of Section 214(5) of the Companies Act, which specifies that a

> company shall be deemed to be unable to pay its debts:
>
> (a) if a debt due by the company has remained unsatisfied in whole or in part after twenty-four weeks from the enforcement of an executive title against the company by any of the executive acts specified in article 273 of the Code of Organisation and Civil Procedure; or
>
> (b) if it is proved to the satisfaction of the court that the company is unable to pay its debts, account being taken also of contingent and prospective liabilities of the company.

As is evident from the above, the test for inability to pay one's debts is alternative. The alternative tests have been applied in a number of cases, although in the Maltese judicial system we do not have case law in the strict sense of the term. Accordingly, principles, though judicially enunciated, do not "make law". Having said that, judgments have authoritative value for the purposes of interpretation and application of law.

It is also relevant to point out that inability to pay one's debts is one of the causes of dissolution in respect of which the court has a discretion. In fact, Section 214(2) of the Companies Act provides that

> a company *may* be dissolved and wound up by the court in the following cases –
>
> (i) if the business of the company is suspended for an uninterrupted period of twenty-four months;
>
> (ii) the company is unable to pay its debts.

It appears *prima facie* that there are fundamental differences between the current definition applicable under Maltese law and the proposed Model Definition of

> inability at the relevant point in time to pay all but an insignificant part of its mature debts from its liquid assets, unless it is to be reasonably expected that this inability can be cured in the short term.

Compatibility with the Model Definition of inability to pay one's debts would require substantial amendments to the current concepts and definitions.

First, even a superficial reading of the Maltese definition versus the Model Definition would suggest that insolvency may be precipated at an earlier stage than is currently the position under Maltese law. This would appear to mark a shift from what is currently a pro-debtor regime to more of a pro-creditor regime. Having said that, the current state of the law makes insolvency proceedings unnecessariy cumbersome. Some of the wording utilised in the Model Definition such as "[all but an] *insignificant* part of its *mature* debts" and "*liquid* assets" are currently undefined terms under Maltese law and would need further clarification.

Though the proposal in the Model Definition allowing Member States to provide that inability to pay debts is rebuttably presumed is salutary, restricting it only to instances where debtor has ceased payments or has been in default to an essential creditor with at least two payments or one payment for at least three months would currently be problematic, since "cessation of payments" is not a term used under Maltese law. Additionally, the term "essential creditor" is alien to Maltese law.

3. CESSATION OF PAYMENTS

Cessation of payments is not a legal term ordinarily used in Maltese statute or case law. *Prima facie*, the proposed Model term of cessation of payments to the effect that "the debtor is in default with payments to at least two creditors" ignores differentiation of creditors by size and/or debtor days, and appears to be an unduly rigid definition. Its impact in Maltese law cannot be ascertained given that in the current context it is not a term used, nor does it trigger any particular duty or proceedings.

4. LIKELIHOOD OF INSOLVENCY AND IMMINENT INSOLVENCY

a) *Likelihood of Insolvency*

Likelihood of insolvency is a term which was recently introduced in the Pre-Insolvency Act within the context of duties of officials of the debtor to monitor early warning signs of insolvency, as well as preventive restructuring applications. Under the Pre-Insolvency Act,

> directors shall, by reference to early warning tools and any other information reasonable available to them, continuously monitor developments that may expose the debtor to a likelihood of insolvency and, where such developments are identified, take appropriate counter measures with a view to preventing insolvency and ensuring business viability.

In practice this obligation may lead to filing for restructuring, but it need not necessarily do so.

There is currently no definition of "likelihood of insolvency". However, the suggested definition of likelihood of insolvency as "that it is more likely than not that the debtor will become unable to pay debts" is not incompatible with what would be expected of a court in ascertaining whether there is a likelihood of insolvency.

b) *Imminent Insolvency*

The terminology "*imminently* likely to become unable to pay its debts" is used within the context of company recovery procedures.

The same term (imminently likely to become unable to pay its debts) is also used within the context of Section 329A of the Companies Act (see Question 10(c) of the National Report for Malta), triggering a duty of the directors to convene a general meeting of the (private) company for the purpose of reviewing the company's position and of determining what steps should be taken to deal with the situation, including consideration of whether the company should be dissolved or, where applicable, whether the company should make a company recovery application.

There is no clearly defined test for "imminent inability to pay debts". The term "imminent" imports a sense of urgency or quasi-immediacy.

The proposed test of imminence "that in the next three months the debtor will become unable to pay debts" appears to assume that the ascertainment of inability to pay one's debts is a purely mathematical exercise which is ordinarily unequivocal, so much so that the run-up period to the state of inability to pay one's debts can be accurately calculated in advance in terms of days and months. It seems that this puts debtors and judges in too much of an artifical straitjacket. Consideration should be given to a defintion which gives more leeway to take cognisance of real-life situations where directors of companies in financial difficulties are in effect not able to predict with such precision when the state of insolvency will manifest itself.

5. OVERINDEBTEDNESS

Overindebtedness is not a term which is currently used under Maltese law.

II. OVERALL ASSESSMENT

The Model Definitions provide far greater definitional detail than is currently the case in terms of applicable Maltese law. Though this approach provides for more legal certainty, it may put debtors in far tighter a straitjacket than is currently the case. Adopting the Model Definitions would require substantive amendments to Maltese law.

THE NETHERLANDS

Ben Schuijling and Michael Veder

Please identify to what extent the proposed Model Definitions in the proposal align with or differ from the definitions currently used in your national law and whether they would be compatible with and operable in your jurisdiction.

I. INDIVIDUAL ASSESSMENT OF THE MODEL DEFINITIONS

A comparison of the Model Definitions with the definitions in Dutch law reveals the following:

1. INSOLVENCY

Dutch law does not provide for a relevant definition of the term insolvency. Rather, it is an overarching term to refer to financial difficulties that give grounds for opening one the available types of liquidation or restructuring proceedings.

2. INABILITY TO PAY DEBTS

a) *Prerequisites*

Dutch law currently has no definition of inability to pay debts. Inability to pay debts is considered a subcategory of "cessation of payments", which is the central insolvency definition and the trigger for the opening of liquidation proceedings (*faillissement*). Inability of the debtor to pay its debts is a means to establish that the debtor has ceased to pay its debts.

The Model Definitions turn this around. Inability to pay is the central definition and cessation of payments is the basis of a presumption to establish such inability. However, we can compare the central definitions of the Model Definition (inability to pay) with the central definition under Dutch law (cessation of payments).

The Model Definitions are more specific in defining what constitutes an inability to pay, even when it is considered a subspecies of a cessation of payments. Dutch law currently requires as a minimum that the debtor has at least two creditors, one of which has a claim that is mature. The determination that the debtor has ceased to pay its debts is left to the court with a broad margin of appreciation. It does not necessarily follow from the existence of debts and the failure to pay them that the debtor is in the condition of having ceased to pay its debts. Also, it is not required that the debtor's (liquid) assets fall short to cover its (mature) debts.

Also, the Model Definition would require an assessment of all of the debtor's mature debts and liquid assets. That is currently not necessary under Dutch law. In this sense the Model Definition would raise the threshold for opening liquidation proceedings.

The introduction of the term "inability to pay" into Dutch law would have quite an impact as it provides more clarity over the precise financial situation of the debtor that is required to open liquidation proceedings and will raise the bar for establishing the existence of that financial state. However, this consequence can be considered welcome, as it would provide increased legal certainty and would counteract the use of insolvency petitions as a preferred debt-collection tool by individual creditors. Taking this impact into account, the definition would be operable under Dutch law.

b) Presumptions

The Model Definition of inability to pay debts provides for a rebuttable presumption on two alternative bases: (i) cessation of payments (defined as being in default with payments to at least two creditors) and (ii) being in default to an essential creditor with at least two payments or one payment for at least three months.

Cessation of payments is dealt with below under section 3 *infra*. Regarding the presumption in case of default to an essential creditor with at least two payments or one payment for at least three months, Dutch law currently does not have such a presumption based on the non-payment of an essential creditor. The circumstance could, however, be relevant as circumstantial evidence when establishing the debtor's cessation of payments.

3. CESSATION OF PAYMENTS

Both the function and definition of "cessation of payments" in the Model Definitions differ from Dutch law.

Under Dutch law, cessation of payments currently is the only ground for opening liquidation proceedings. It is not the basis for a presumption of the debtor's inability to pay. It is rather the other way around: if the debtor cannot pay, that is considered a reason to accept that he has stopped paying his creditors. Cessation of payments can be demonstrated summarily, so as not to create high barriers for unpaid creditors who want to initiate liquidation proceedings against their debtor.

In the Model Definitions the term "cessation of payments" is quite like the meaning under Dutch law. The similarity is that both the Model Definitions and Dutch law require that the debtor has at least two creditors. The difference is that the Model Definitions require that the debtor is in default with payment to at least two creditors. Under current Dutch law the threshold is lower: it suffices that one of the creditors has a mature claim.

The mere existence of two unpaid creditors is required but not necessarily sufficient proof of the debtor's cessation of payments under Dutch law. The same can be said of the Model Definitions, since cessation of payments is the basis of a rebuttable presumption only. In both systems the definition accommodates, in particular, petitioning creditors without being decisive in respect of the debtor's state of insolvency.

Overall, the presumption based on cessation of payments could be compatible and operable with Dutch law.

4. LIKELIHOOD OF INSOLVENCY AND IMMINENT INSOLVENCY

As regards likely and imminent inability to pay debts, the following can be said.

a) Likelihood of Insolvency

Dutch law uses variations of the terms "likelihood of insolvency" or "likely inability to pay debts" for access to restructuring proceedings and natural persons' debt relief schemes.

The Model Definitions state that to establish a likelihood of insolvency it is required that it is more likely than not that the debtor will become unable to pay its debts. This is more or less similar to current Dutch law, which requires that it is reasonably likely/foreseeable that the debtor will not be able to continue to pay its debts. These differences would probably not produce different outcomes in practice.

b) Imminent Insolvency

Dutch law is not familiar with the term "imminent inability to pay debts". The Model Definitions would have no impact at this point.

5. OVERINDEBTEDNESS

Dutch insolvency law does not operate with "overindebtedness" as a ground for the opening of insolvency proceedings. The Model Definitions would therefore have no impact.

II. OVERALL ASSESSMENT

Overall, if the Model Definitions were transposed into Dutch law the introduction of the term "inability to pay" would have the biggest impact, as would the changed function for the term "cessation of payments". However, this impact can be considered welcome as it would provide increased legal certainty and would counteract the use of insolvency petitions as a preferred debt-collection tool by individual creditors. Considering this impact, the Model Definitions would be compatible with and operable in the Netherlands.

POLAND

Marek Porzycki and Anna Rachwał

Please identify to what extent the proposed Model Definitions in the proposal align with or differ from the definitions currently used in your national law and whether they would be compatible with and operable in your jurisdiction.

I. INDIVIDUAL ASSESSMENT OF THE MODEL DEFINITIONS

A comparison of the Model Definitions with the definitions in Polish law reveals the following:

1. INSOLVENCY

Polish law provides for a definition of the term insolvency, defining it in Article 11(1) and (3) BL[1] as both inability to pay mature monetary debts and (for legal persons and partnerships only) overindebtedness persisting for more than 24 months.

2. INABILITY TO PAY DEBTS

a) *Prerequisites*

According to Article 11(1), BL does not include a definition of inability to pay debts, and specifies only that insolvency is understood as the situation when the debtor has lost his or her ability to pay mature monetary debts. It is generally understood that the inability to pay debts must result from economic causes, and should be lasting and definitive.[2] The Model Definition of inability to pay

1 Polish Bankruptcy Law (Prawo upadłościowe), hereinafter BL.

2 See National Report for Poland, answer to Question 13.

is more detailed than the wording in the Polish law but broadly corresponds to it. The main difference concerns non-monetary obligations, as the Polish definition takes into account only monetary debts for establishing bankruptcy. This difference is unlikely to cause practical difficulties, as situations where the debtor has lost the ability to fulfil non-monetary obligations while continuing to pay monetary debts are very uncommon. Even if the structure of obligations of a debtor consists mostly of non-monetary obligations, at an advanced stage of economic difficulties it is likely that many such obligations have already been transformed into monetary ones.

A further difference results from the fact that Polish law does not distinguish between a significant and insignificant part of the debts, as inability to pay refers to mature monetary debts in general. This difference can also be considered of minor practical importance, especially in view of the presumption under Article 11(1a) BL referring to the cessation of payments, as continued payment of minor debts excludes neither the application of the presumption nor the general assumption that the debtor is unable to pay. Furthermore, Polish law does not refer to payment "from liquid assets" in order to assess inability to pay, giving the courts more flexibility in examining cases where assets are not readily available. When deciding such cases, the ease of accessing necessary funds should be assessed from the perspective of the general interpretation that inability to pay should be lasting and definitive.

Finally, no exception is explicitly provided for cases where the inability can be cured in the short term. However, the general understanding that inability to pay should be lasting and definitive leads to the same effect.

b) Presumptions

The Model Definition of inability to pay debts provides for a rebuttable presumption on two alternative bases: (i) cessation of payments (defined as being in default with payments to at least two creditors) and (ii) being in default to an essential creditor with at least two payments or one payment for at least three months. This is similar to the Polish law in principle but differs significantly in the detail.

Under Article 11(1a) BL, it is presumed that the debtor has lost the ability to pay mature monetary debts if the delay in payment of such debts exceeds three months. This presumption is rebuttable and is understood as referring to claims of at least two creditors (resulting from the use of the plural in the wording of Article 11(1a) BL). No differentiation is made as regards debts to plural creditors and/or plural debts to one creditor. The use of the plural for "debts" is universally understood as referring also to at least two creditors (with an exception for consumer bankruptcy where cases with one creditor are expressly allowed, Article $491^2(2)$ BL).

No differentiation is made between debts to essential creditors and other creditors for the purposes of applying the presumption. Non-payment of an *essential* creditor could, however, bear more significance when examining whether the presumption can be rebutted.

A more important difference concerns the length of the delay in payment required to trigger the presumption of inability to pay, as the Model Definition applies this presumption in principle from the moment the debtor has been in default to at least two creditors, while Polish law requires a delay of at least three months.

c) Consequences

The above differences are likely to cause some practical difficulties in the event of future alignment of the Polish law with the Model Definition.

First, the formalistic culture in the judiciary, combined with the tendency to apply literal interpretation makes it likely that even minor delays in payment of relatively insignificant debts might lead to the presumption of insolvency being applied and thus being abused for the purpose of lodging unjustified insolvency requests. Such practice led to the introduction of the current presumption with its three-months requirement in 2015.[3] The Model Definition may reverse the advantage of the 2015 reform in this respect.

Second (but less importantly), the different treatment of debts owed to essential creditors for the purposes of applying the presumption might lead to some legal uncertainty, as it might be not immediately obvious to creditors requesting the opening of insolvency proceedings which creditors are to be considered "essential".

3. CESSATION OF PAYMENTS

The differences between the Model Definition and the Polish concept of cessation of payments as used for the presumption of inability to pay have already been explained. Hence, reference can be made to section 2(b)/(c) *supra*.

4. LIKELIHOOD OF INSOLVENCY AND IMMINENT INSOLVENCY

As regards likely and imminent inability to pay debts, the following can be said.

---

[3] See Questionnaire for Poland, answer to Question 13.

a) *Likelihood of Insolvency*

Polish law uses a variation of the term "likelihood of insolvency" (literally: "threat of insolvency") for access to restructuring proceedings.

The Model Definitions state that to establish a likelihood of insolvency it is required that it is more likely than not that the debtor will become unable to pay its debts. This is broadly similar to current Polish law, which specifies that the debtor is threatened by insolvency if its economic situation indicates that it may become insolvent within a short time (Article 6(3) of the RL[4]). There is no specified probability threshold, leading some commentators to assume that even low probability can be considered probative, which differs from the Model Definition threshold of 50%.[5] As no specific percentage of probability is indicated anyway in decisions to open restructuring proceedings, this difference would probably have very little or no practical effect.

Polish law does not set any specific prognosis period, which is in line with the Model Definitions.

b) *Imminent Insolvency*

Polish law is not familiar with the term "imminent inability to pay debts". The Model Definitions would have no impact at this point.

5. OVERINDEBTEDNESS

The Model Definitions treat overindebtedness as related to likely inability to pay debts, adding a requirement that the occurrence of the debtor's inability to pay debts is "more likely than not" to the more typical wording providing that the liabilities of the debtor exceed the liquidation value of its assets at the relevant point in time.

This approach broadly corresponds to the spirit but not to the exact wording of Polish law in this regard. According to Article 11(2) BL, overindebtedness needs to persist for more than 24 months to be considered insolvency for debtors which are legal persons or organisations/entities without full legal personality, which includes mostly partnerships.[6] Article 11(6) BL introduces a prognostic element, as even in such cases the court may still dismiss the request for the opening of bankruptcy proceedings if the debtor is not under threat of losing the ability to pay within a short time. The requirement of overindebtedness

4 Polish Restructuring Law (Prawo restrukturyzacyjne), hereinafter RL.
5 See Questionnaire for Poland, answer to Question 36.
6 See Questionnaire for Poland, answers to Questions 43, 44.

persisting for at least 24 months is also quite clearly intended to filter out cases with a positive prognosis.[7] No clear reference to the liquidation value of assets is given, although commentators indicate that it should be applied in cases with a negative prognosis. However, book value is applied for an initial presumption of overindebtedness under Article 11(5) BL, based on the balance sheet of the debtor.[8]

Altogether, bringing Polish law into line with the Model Definitions as regards overindebtendess would require significant changes in the wording of the BL, including dropping the 24-months requirement and the presumption based on the debtor's balance sheet. The practical effect of those changes would probably be limited, as the Model Definitions' limitation of overindebtedness to cases including likely inability to pay would have a similar effect in excluding debtors with a positive prognosis.

II. OVERALL ASSESSMENT

Overall, no fundamental changes would be required to transpose the Model Definitions into Polish law. The changes in the presumption of inability to pay would have the biggest impact, in particular the removal of the three-month period of delay in payments which currently triggers the presumption. This impact might lead to reversal of some of the positive effects of the 2015 insolvency law reform. Other changes would be relatively minor and would not have major practical effect. Altogether, the Model Definitions would be compatible with the Polish system and operable in Poland.

7 See Questionnaire for Poland, answer to Question 50.

8 See Questionnaire for Poland, answer to Question 49.

PORTUGAL

Catarina SERRA

Please identify to what extent the proposed Model Definitions in the proposal align with or differ from the definitions currently used in your national law and whether they would be compatible with and operable in your jurisdiction.

I. INDIVIDUAL ASSESSMENT OF THE MODEL DEFINITIONS

A comparison of the Model Definitions with the definitions in Portuguese law reveals the following:

1. INSOLVENCY

The Model Definition of "insolvency" is inability to pay debts.

Portuguese law provides for a similar definition of the term insolvency. Pursuant to Article 3(1) of the Portuguese Insolvency Act (IA), insolvency means the inability to pay mature debts.

Under Article 3(2) IA, entities (legal persons and patrimonies) for whose debts no person is personally and unlimitedly liable (publicly listed companies, limited liability companies, autonomous patrimonies and similar entities) shall also be considered insolvent when the value of their liabilities significantly exceeds the value of their assets.

It follows that the term "insolvency" in Portugal covers both situations but only these two situations.

Under Article 3(4) IA, however, imminent insolvency is legally equivalent to insolvency if it is the debtor who files for insolvency.

2. INABILITY TO PAY DEBTS

The Model Definition of "insolvency" is inability to pay debts.

Portuguese law provides no legal definition of inability to pay debts. As indicated above, inability to pay (mature) debts is the definition of insolvency.

a) Prerequisites

The Model Definition of inability to pay debts requires the debtor to be unable (i) at the relevant point in time (ii) to pay all but an insignificant part (iii) of its mature debts (iv) from its liquid assets, (v) unless it is to be reasonably expected that this inability can be cured in the short term.

Although Portuguese law does not provide a definition of inability to pay debts, it is common understanding that it should be established for (i) the relevant point in time and (ii) should be general (i.e. not only in relation to all but an insignificant part (iii) of the mature debts.

It can be said that the Model Definition is more specific than (the understanding of) inability to pay debts in Portugal.

On the other hand, following classic legal literature, it is commonly emphasised that insolvency/inability to pay debts is due to lack of the debtor's own means (liquidity gap) and lack of external means (unavailability of credit).

b) Presumptions

The Model Definition of inability to pay debts provides for a rebuttable presumption which Member States may accommodate in their respective jurisdictions, based on (i) cessation of payments (defined as being in default with payments to at least two creditors) and (ii) being in default to an essential creditor with at least two payments or one payment for at least three months. This differs from Portuguese law.

Under Article 20(1) IA, it may be (rebuttably) presumed that the debtor is insolvent/ unable to pay its debts in eight circumstances. The person filing for insolvency (in all cases except when this is the debtor) has to claim and prove, at least, one of them for the insolvency petition to be formally admitted.

The circumstances which give rise to the presumption are the following:

- Paragraph (a): the general suspension of payment of mature debts.
- Paragraph (b): the default of one or more payments which, due to their amount or to the circumstances of the default, shows the inability on the part of the debtor to punctually meet most of its obligations.
- Paragraph (c): the escape of the owner of the company or of the debtor's managers/directors or the abandonment of the place where the company has its headquarters or carries out its main activity, related to the debtor's lack of solvency and without appointment of a suitable substitute.
- Paragraph (d): the dissipation, abandonment, hasty or ruinous liquidation of assets and fictitious creation of credits.

- Paragraph (e): the insufficiency of seizable assets to pay the creditor's credit verified in an enforcement proceeding against the debtor.
- Paragraph (f): the default of payments provided for in the insolvency plan or in the payments plan, under the conditions set out in Article 218(1), subparagraph (a), and 218(2) IA.
- Paragraph (g): the general default in the last six months of debts of any of the following types:
  - tax debts;
  - social security contributions;
  - debts arising from an employment contract, or from the breach or termination of this contract;
  - rent from any type of lease, including finance, installments of the purchase price or loan secured by the respective mortgage concerning the property where the debtor carries on its activity or has its statutory seat or its residence.
- Paragraph (h): if the debtor is one of the entities referred to in Article 3(2) IA, that is, a legal person or an autonomous patrimony for whose debts no natural person is personally and unlimitedly liable, the situation where the debtor's liabilities significantly exceed the value of his assets according to the last approved balance sheet, or a delay of more than nine months in approving and depositing the accounts, whenever there is such a duty.

At first glance, paragraphs (a) (referring to the general suspension of payment of mature debts) and (b) (referring to the default of one or more payments in given circumstances), either on their own or combined, globally correspond to the two presumptions of "cessation of payments" proposed in the Model Definition.

However, whilst the first presumption of the Model Definition refers to "cessation of payments" and defines it as the default with payments to "at least two creditors", paragraph (a) refers to "suspension of payments" and does not define it, requiring that it involves the "majority" of "mature" debts; whilst the second presumption refers to being in default to an "essential creditor" with at least "two payments" or "one payment for at least three months", paragraph (b) requires default of "one or more payments" which, "due to their amount or to the circumstances of the default, shows the inability" on the part of the debtor to punctually meet most of its obligations.

It is possible to say that Portuguese law uses less quantification and tends to favour open-ended concepts, which extends the scope of discretion of the court. This does not necessarily mean a lesser requirement. The first presumption (being in default with payments to at least two creditors) would only meet the requirements of Portuguese law if the two creditors are representative of the majority of creditors holding mature claims. The second presumption (being in default to an essential creditor with at least two payments or one payment for at least three months) would suffice under Portuguese law if, in light of all other circumstances of the specific case, the default indicates an inability to pay; on the other hand, default on only one payment would suffice under Portuguese law independently of the nature of the creditor and any time span, provided the other requirements are met.

In sum, for both the Model Definition and the Portuguese law, cessation of payments or similar situations are satisfied by default vis-à-vis only one creditor but the requirements concerning the circumstances of the default differ.

c) *Consequences*

Regarding the consequences of these differences, it must be stressed that the Model Definition on the one hand does not oblige the Member States to transpose the presumptions into their national law and on the other hand does not permit the introduction of different presumptions. For Portuguese law, this would mean that the term "cessation of payments" would have to be expressly mentioned and defined according to the Model Definition; the presumptions provided for in paragraphs (a) and (b) of Article 20(1) IA could be kept after due adaptation as presumptions of "cessation of payments"; and the circumstances grounding the presumption, enshrined in the remaining paragraphs of Article 20(1) IA, would continue to be used for inability to pay debts only.

3. CESSATION OF PAYMENTS

The differences between the Model Definition and the Portuguese definition of cessation of payments have already been explained. Hence, reference can be made to section 2(a)/(b) above.

4. LIKELIHOOD OF INSOLVENCY AND IMMINENT INSOLVENCY

As regards likely and imminent inability to pay debts, the following can be said.

a) *Likelihood of Insolvency*

The Model Definition defines "likelihood of insolvency" as the situation where it is more likely than not that the debtor will become unable to pay debts.

Portuguese law does not use the term "likelihood of insolvency". The term "imminent insolvency" is used instead, though not legally defined.

Hence, the Model Definition would have to be transposed into Portuguese law from scratch. In any case, the term is familiar to Portuguese scholars

(due to the Directive on Restructuring and Insolvency) and understood as a situation where there is a lower probability of insolvency than in "imminent insolvency". So, the transposition would not cause significant disturbance.

b) *Imminent Insolvency*

The Model Definition defines "imminent insolvency" as the situation where in the next three months the debtor will become unable to pay debts.

The term "imminent insolvency" is used in Portuguese law (e.g. Article 3(4) IA), but not defined. However, it is commonly understood in legal literature and case law as "the debtor's inability to pay debts when they become due".

Considering the time-span, the transposition of the Model Definition would mean a decrease of the scope of discretion of the court but an increase of legal certainty.

5. OVERINDEBTEDNESS

The Model Definition defines "overindebtedness" as the situation where, at the relevant point in time, the liabilities of the debtor exceed the liquidation value of its assets and the occurrence of the debtor's inability to pay debts is more likely than not.

Pursuant to Article 3(2) IA,

> [l]egal persons and autonomous patrimonies for whose debts no natural person is personally and unlimitedly liable, either directly or indirectly, are also deemed insolvent when their liabilities significantly exceed the value of their assets, assessed in accordance with the applicable accounting standards.

This is generally understood as a special kind of insolvency, reserved for the entities referred and commonly known as overindebtedness.

And, pursuant to Article 3(3) IA,

> [t]he provisions of the previous paragraph shall cease to apply when assets exceed liabilities, valued in accordance with the following rules:
>
> a) Assets and liabilities are deemed to include identifiable items, even if they are not included in the balance sheet, at their fair value;
> b) When the debtor is the owner of a company, the valuation is based on the prospect of continuity or liquidation, whichever is more likely, but in any case excluding the goodwill item;
> c) Liabilities do not include debts that will only be paid out of distributable funds or remaining assets once the rights of the debtor's other creditors have been satisfied or safeguarded.

The transposition of the Model Definition in this part of the legislation would represent a significant change in the way overindebtedness is envisaged and works under Portuguese law. Currently, overindebtedness is relevant as an autonomous ground (i.e. alongside inability to pay debts) for the opening of insolvency proceedings. As noted before, it is relevant only in the event that the debtor is a legal person or an autonomous patrimony for whose debts no natural person is personally and unlimitedly liable. The rule stems from previous insolvency legislation and is based on the belief that when the debtor is a person/patrimony of the kind indicated above, its overindebtedness necessarily means it is unable to pay its debts (since there are no other patrimonies liable). Put in other words, a negative result on a balance sheet test works as an irrebuttable presumption of insolvency/inability to pay debts. The transposition of the Model Definition, comprising the application of a liquidity/viability test, would imply a profound change in the function of overindebtedness in Portuguese law: from a situation which plays an independent role in relation to inability to pay debts (a solution which is, it must be said, increasingly criticised by scholars) to a situation with relevance only if it means future insolvency/inability to pay debts.

II. OVERALL ASSESSMENT

To conclude, the incorporation of the Model Definition into Portuguese law would entail a few significant changes. However, the task would be feasible. The introduction of time-spans and other quantifications as requirements for certain purposes (references to the number of creditors/payments in default) would lead to more legal certainty but also to the loss of some discretion on the part of the court.

ROMANIA

Flavius-Iancu Moțu and Andreea Deli-Diaconescu

Please identify to what extent the proposed Model Definitions in the proposal align with or differ from the definitions currently used in your national law[1] *and whether they would be compatible with and operable in your jurisdiction.*

I. INDIVIDUAL ASSESSMENT OF THE MODEL DEFINITIONS

1. INSOLVENCY

The definition of insolvency in the proposed Model Law falls back on two elements: the debtor's inability to pay his/her/its debts and the relevant point (moment) in time when the debtor becomes unable to pay his/her/its debts.

Romanian law provides for a definition of insolvency that relies on the debtor's inability to pay his/her/its debts, too; thus the proposed Model Law would bring no variation in this respect.

The relevant point (moment) in time when the debtor becomes unable to pay his/her/its debts in the Model Law seems to be a notion of substantive law, to be judicially determined by hearing evidence.

The definition of insolvency in Romanian law does not point to such a moment in time explicitly; still, the insolvency judge would examine whether the debtor is unable to pay his/her/its debts at the time the debtor's petition/the application of one creditor/the applications brought by several creditors is/are lodged with the court.

In the event that one creditor/several creditors rely on the legal (rebuttable) presumption of insolvency under Romanian insolvency law, triggered by the debtor not paying that one creditor's debt/those creditors' respective debts within 60 days (commercial insolvencies)/90 days (consumer insolvencies) after it was/they were due, the insolvency judge would consider this 60-day/90-day period as counted back from the day the application was lodged with the court.

[1] As of the reference date 22 April 2024.

Nevertheless, this moment would not be regarded as the moment when the debtor became substantively insolvent; it would merely represent a procedural time limit relevant for the opening of the insolvency proceedings.

If it is the debtor that brings his/her/its petition to open insolvency proceedings to the court, the petition itself is deemed to be an admission of insolvency according to the Romanian insolvency legislation, so the debtor would not need to prove that his/her/its debts have been due for more than 60 days /90 days before his/her/its petition is lodged with the court.

Thus, the definition of insolvency in the proposed Model Law would only have a significant impact on the Romanian legislation only if it imposed an obligation on the insolvency judge to determine the exact moment in the past (before the opening of the insolvency proceedings) the debtor became insolvent. The 19th-century Romanian insolvency legislation laid down such an obligation on the insolvency judges and they had to resort to legal presumptions to establish the said moment in time, as it was often impossible to accurately determine it by hearing other evidence.

2. INABILITY TO PAY DEBTS

a) *Prerequisites*

Romanian law does not define the debtor's inability to pay his/her/its debts, but lays down a rebuttable presumption of insolvency when the debtor is unable to pay the debt alleged in the application brought by one creditor/the specific debts in several creditors' applications at least 60 days (for commercial insolvencies)/ 90 days (for consumer insolvencies) after it was/they were due.

Unlike the legislation in other EU Member States, the Romanian insolvency legislation does not require proof of the debtor being unable to pay *all his/her/its debts (towards all his/her/its creditors)* in order to have the insolvency proceedings opened. To be more specific: when the application is brought by one creditor only, the insolvency judge will analyse just whether *that specific debt alleged by that specific creditor* is ascertained,[2] liquidated,[3] due for more than 60 days and exceeding RON 50,000 (approximately EUR 10,000) and whether the debtor is able to pay *that specific debt alleged by that specific creditor*, but not all the debtor's liabilities due at the time that creditor's application is lodged with the court.

2 In Romanian *certă*. According to the Romanian Code of Civil Procedure, Art. 663 para. 2, a debt (in Romanian *creanță*) is *certă* if its existence is beyond doubt.

3 In Romanian *lichidă*. According to the Romanian Code of Civil Procedure, Art. 663 para. 3, a debt is *lichidă* when the amount owed by the debtor is determined (e.g. EUR 100) or determinable (e.g. 0.5% of the main debt/day, running from the date the main debt is due and counting until the day the main debt is paid in full).

In cases where several creditors bring a joint claim or several claims, the situation stays the same; the judge will consider only those creditors' alleged debts, but not all the debtor's liabilities due at the time those creditors' joint application/several applications is/are lodged with the court.

The only situation where the insolvency judge will actually examine all the debtor's liabilities and his/her/its inability to pay them (all) is when the debtor petitions for the opening of his/her/its own insolvency proceedings. In this last situation, the debtor's inability to pay his/her/its debts is a particular situation of "cessation of payments".

Since the definition of the debtor's inability to pay in the proposed Model Law takes into account (almost) all the debtor's liabilities due at the relevant point in time, it would have a notable impact on the Romanian legislation, since a significant number of applications to open insolvency proceedings are brought to the Romanian courts by creditors. If a specific creditor were to bear the burden of proof that the debtor is generally unable to pay all his/her/its debts, that creditor would either need access to the debtor's books or have to rely on a presumption of a general cessation of payments on the part of the debtor.

Moreover, the second part of the definition "inability … to pay all but an insignificant part of its mature debts from its liquid assets, unless it is to be reasonably expected that this inability can be cured in the short term" would definitely entail a judicial examination of all the debtor's mature liquid liabilities, of the debtor's liquid assets and of the debtor's ability to obtain liquidities[4] in the short term.

We assume that such an examination would only be necessary when the application to open insolvency proceedings is brought by one or more creditors. The debtor should have easy access to the opening of his/her/its insolvency proceedings. In our opinion, the debtor's petition to have his/her/its insolvency proceedings opened should be construed as proof of insolvency (admission of insolvency).

Such a judicial examination seems to be rather complex and would definitely require extensive training both for the Romanian judiciary and for Romanian insolvency practitioners. The presumptions *infra* could come in useful, but in case they are not applicable, the insolvency judge would need to carefully balance the interests of the creditors and the debtor, hearing, most probably, a significant amount of specialised evidence.[5]

---

4 By way of comparison, in Romania, at present, the debtor can rebut the presumption of insolvency by simply proving that he/she/it has enough cash resources to pay the creditor/creditors that have brought the application to open the insolvency proceedings. A statement of account is usually sufficient evidence in this respect.

5 Likewise, at present, in Romania, the insolvency test relies on a rebuttable presumption; however, the said presumption infers insolvency from a closely related, easily verifiable fact (the debtor who has not paid a debt that is ascertained (uncontested), liquidated and due for more than 60 days (commercial insolvencies)/90 days (consumer insolvencies) is presumed to be insolvent).

To conclude, the debtor's inability to pay being defined as the

> debtor's inability at the relevant point in time to pay all but an insignificant part of its mature debts from its liquid assets, unless it is to be reasonably expected that this inability can be cured in the short term

brings a rather new perspective that would entail a significant change in the Romanian's judicial approach to insolvency.

b) Presumptions

The proposed Model Law provides for a rebuttable presumption on two alternative bases. The debtor is rebuttably presumed unable to pay its debts if the debtor:

(i) has ceased payments (inferred from the debtor being in default with payments to at least two creditors)
(ii) has been in default to an essential creditor with at least two payments, or one payment for at least three months.

The presumption laid down under (i) would require a novel approach in the Romanian insolvency legislation; a significant number of the applications brought to the Romanian courts are initiated by one creditor, and the debtor usually does not enter an appearance. The said creditor would never be able to rely on this presumption, as he/she/it would not have access to the debtor's books so as to identify at least one more unpaid creditor.

The presumption laid down under (ii) is somewhat similar to the present rebuttable presumption of insolvency in force under Romanian insolvency legislation; the main difference resides in the fact that the creditor needs to be an essential one (a creditor on whose continued supply the continuation of the debtor's business operations crucially depends). Going into specifics, the Romanian tax authority, which is the most active creditor seeking the opening of the insolvency proceedings of companies in default with the tax payments, could hardly qualify as an "essential" creditor. In like manner, at present, in Romania, employees could qualify as "essential creditors" only indirectly; employees may only bring an application for the opening of insolvency proceedings regarding their employer insofar as each of them is owed by the employer at least six months' national gross average salary (approx. EUR 9,500).

Therefore, presumption (ii) in the proposed Model Law would have a significant impact on the Romanian insolvency legislation, too.

3. CESSATION OF PAYMENTS

The function of the "cessation of payments" in the proposed Model Law is virtually identical to the function of the "cessation of payments" in the Romanian insolvency legislation: it is the ostensible factual element that allows for the inference of the debtor's inability to pay, within the presumption of the debtor's inability to pay.

The notion of "cessation of payment" serves other purposes, too, in the insolvency proceedings under Romanian law (for holding the insolvent company's directors liable for its debts, as the relevant provisions on the directors' liability point to this notion, too).

Yet, the legal definition of the "cessation of payments" in the proposed Model Law is significantly different: under Romanian law, the "cessation of payments" necessarily encompasses *all the creditors*, while under the proposed Model Law, it merely requires two creditors.

Should the proposed Model Law use the "debtor being in default with payments to at least two creditors" only as the basis of a legal presumption, it would be perfectly compatible with the Romanian insolvency legislation, requiring an amendment only.

Should the proposed Model Law use the "debtor being in default with payments to at least two creditors" to actually define "cessation of payments", irrespective of the number of unpaid creditors (holding mature claims), the impact on the Romanian insolvency legislation would be of some consequence.

4. LIKELIHOOD OF INSOLVENCY AND IMMINENT INSOLVENCY

As mentioned in our National Report, the term "likelihood of insolvency" is used in the Romanian legislation when regulating the prevention of insolvency proceedings. In order to have such proceedings opened, the debtor must prove his/her/its future insolvency, likely to occur in the future, which may be prevented by making changes (e.g. in the business model, in the corporate structure, etc.).

The definition of the "likelihood of insolvency" in the proposed Model Law is perfectly compatible with the Romanian legislation. Its further details (future but reversible/future but irreversible) do not adversely affect it.

As mentioned in our National Report, "imminent insolvency" has a very limited scope (the debtor only may petition for the opening of his/her/its insolvency proceedings when the insolvency is imminent, i.e. the insolvency will occur in the near future and is irreversible). Its definition in the proposed Model Law is perfectly compatible with the Romanian legislation and it would bring a much welcomed time limit (the insolvency will occur in the next three months).

5. OVERINDEBTEDNESS

As the Romanian insolvency legislation does not use "overindebtedness" as grounds for opening the insolvency proceedings, the definition in the proposed Model Law would have no impact.

II. OVERALL ASSESSMENT

The definitions in the proposed Model Law would have a significant impact on Romanian insolvency legislation: although, *prima facie*, the inability to pay would continue to be the core element in the legal definition of insolvency, the presumptions it relies on for its proof are built upon a different approach. The same goes for the definition of the "cessation of payments" and its correspondent presumption.

We venture to assert that the adoption of the definitions in the Model Law by the Romanian legislator would result in the national insolvency proceedings coming closer to their true collective nature. A significant number of insolvency proceedings are opened in Romania to allow one creditor[6] only to attempt to recover its debt.

Moreover, the present presumption of insolvency in Romanian law allows any creditor to easily try to "twist his/her/its debtor's arm" to obtain the payment of an apparently uncontested debt by bringing an application for the opening of insolvency proceedings.

All matters considered, the definitions in the proposed Model Law would be compatible with the Romanian insolvency legislation and welcome in Romania.

---

6 The Romanian Tax Authority.

SLOVAKIA

Dávid Oršula

Please identify to what extent the proposed Model Definitions in the proposal align with or differ from the definitions currently used in your national law and whether they would be compatible with and operable in your jurisdiction.

I. INDIVIDUAL ASSESSMENT OF THE MODEL DEFINITIONS

A comparison of the Model Definitions with the definitions in Slovak law reveals the following:

1. INSOLVENCY

The Slovak Act on Insolvency and Restructuring §2(1) stipulates that the debtor is insolvent if the debtor is unable to pay debts or is overindebted. For definitions of inability to pay debts and overindebtedness, see *infra*.

Therefore, Slovak law does not correspond to the Model Definitions.

2. INABILITY TO PAY DEBTS

The Model Definition of inability to pay debts partly corresponds to the definition of inability to pay debts set out in the Slovak Act on Insolvency and Restructuring §2(2). In the case of natural persons and their inability to pay debt, the Model Definition is incompatible. Further, compared to the Model Definition, the Slovak law provides for a "reversed" rebuttable presumption of *ability* to pay debts for legal persons in connection with a defined liquidity gap calculation.

3. CESSATION OF PAYMENTS

Slovak law does not recognise the concept of the cessation of payments.

4. LIKELIHOOD OF INSOLVENCY AND IMMINENT INSOLVENCY

As regards likely and imminent inability to pay debts, the following can be said.

a) *Likelihood of Insolvency*

Under Slovak law the likelihood of insolvency occurs primarily if the debtor's ratio of net equity to overall debts is less than 8%. Further, under preventive restructuring proceedings laws, a likelihood of insolvency is found if, taking into account all the circumstances, it can reasonably be assumed that inability to pay debts will occur within 12 calendar months. Likelihood of insolvency is a trigger for opening a preventive restructuring proceeding under the Preventive Restructuring Act where the debtor is a legal person.

b) *Imminent Insolvency*

Slovak law is not familiar with the term "imminent insolvency".

5. OVERINDEBTEDNESS

According to the Slovak Bankruptcy Act §2(3) a debtor who is a legal person and is obliged to keep accounts (bookkeeping), has more than one creditor, and the value of his liabilities exceeds the value of his assets, is overindebted. All debt, regardless of maturity, counts. Liabilities to affiliated creditors or subordinated liabilities are excluded from the calculation of total debt. Consequently, overindebtedness applies to legal persons only.

II. OVERALL ASSESSMENT

Implementation of the Model Definitions into the Slovak bankruptcy laws would require a substantial rewording of the corresponding provisions of the current Slovak laws.

SLOVENIA

Miodrag DORDEVIC

Please identify to what extent the proposed Model Definitions in the proposal align with or differ from the definitions currently used in your national law and whether they would be compatible with and operable in your jurisdiction.

I. INDIVIDUAL ASSESSMENT OF THE MODEL DEFINITIONS

A comparison of the Model Definitions with the definitions in Slovenian law reveals the following:

1. INSOLVENCY

According to §14(1) sentence 1 of the Financial Operations, Insolvency Proceedings, and Compulsory Dissolution Act[1] insolvency occurs:

(i) if a debtor is unable at the relevant point in time to pay his mature debts (hereinafter: "continuous illiquidity") *or*
(ii) if a debtor becomes long-term unable to pay its debts.

It is noticeable that the definition of insolvency in ZFPPIPP is broader than the definition of insolvency within Model Definitions, since it also includes the debtor's long-term inability to pay its debts. More on this particular condition will be explained in sections 4 and 5 *infra*.

2. INABILITY TO PAY DEBTS

The Model Definition of the debtor's inability to pay debts generally corresponds with the definition in §14(1), sentence 1 ZFPPIPP.

1 Slovenian Insolvency Code, hereinafter ZFPPIPP.

a) *Prerequisites*

According to §14(1) sentence 1 ZFPPIPP, a debtor is continuously illiquid if at a certain point in time it is not able to pay its mature debts. ZFPPIPP differs from the Model Definition in that it does not explicitly mention the proportion of the obligations that the debtor is unable to pay, although the legal theorists do state that the debtor has to be unable to pay a significant share of his debts. It also does not explicitly stipulate that the debtor's inability to pay pertains solely to their liquid assets. Finally, it also does not include an assessment of whether it is reasonable to expect that this inability can be cured in the short term.

The proportion of the obligations that the debtor is unable to pay is a circumstance that is taken into consideration within the rebuttable presumption that the debtor is continuously illiquid if it is not able to pay one or more debts that exceed 20% of its total debts.

The debtor's inability to pay according to the state of its liquid assets and the assessment whether it is reasonable to expect that the debtor's inability can be cured in the short term are both parts of the second condition, on which insolvency can be determined – debtor's long-term inability to pay its debts. More on that in sections 4 and 5 *infra*.

b) *Presumptions*

The Model Definition of inability to pay debts provides for a rebuttable presumption on two alternative bases: (i) cessation of payments (defined as being in default with payments to at least two creditors) and (ii) being in default to an essential creditor with at least two payments or one payment for at least three months. This differs from Slovenian law.

ZFPPIPP first regulates two different types of debtors: the first is a debtor who has not yet undergone insolvency proceedings. For such a debtor, according to §14(2) sentence 1 ZFPPIPP, continuous illiquidity is presumed if the debtor is more than two months late in paying one or more obligations that together exceed 20% of its obligations; the second sentence states that continuous illiquidity is presumed if the funds in its account are insufficient to execute an enforcement order and this situation has persisted continuously for the last 60 days or intermittently for more than 60 days in the last 90 days, and this situation persisted on the day before the filing of the insolvency petition. Continuous illiquidity is also presumed under this provision if the debtor does not possess an open bank account in Slovenia and has not settled an obligation arising from an enforcement order after 60 days.

Furthermore, there are special presumptions for a debtor who has undergone a compulsory settlement procedure. In such a case, the presumption of continuous illiquidity is established if the debtor is more than two months late in paying its obligations based on the confirmed compulsory settlement, in paying its obligations to secured creditors that arose before the commencement of the compulsory settlement procedure, or in implementing other financial restructuring measures specified in the financial restructuring plan.

Based on the above, it is evident that the scope of rebuttable presumptions in ZFPPIPP is significantly broader, since they also include a debtor that has undergone the compulsory settlement procedure.

ZFPPIPP also regulates two irrebuttable presumptions of continuous illiquidity in §14(4) ZFPPIPP: the first is that the debtor is more than two months late in paying its workers' wages up to the amount of the minimum wage, stipulated in other statutes; the second is if the debtor is more than two months late in paying the taxes and social security contributions that it is obliged to pay as part of the workers' wages.

The inclusion of irrebuttable presumptions, which is based on the principle of protection of workers' rights, also makes ZFPPIPP significantly broader than the Model Definitions.

c) Consequences

The presented differences between the rules in ZFPPIPP and the Model Definitions lead to a firm conclusion that the provisions in ZFPPIPP are significantly broader. Since the Model Definitions present only two rebuttable presumptions, this would require a broad revision of ZFPPIPP in order to assure the compliance of ZFPPIPP with the Model Definitions, wherein the specific aforementioned circumstances, which under ZFPPIPP rebuttably presume the debtor's inability to pay its debt, could only be considered by the courts in each individual case as potential proof of the debtor's inability to pay its debt, placing the burden of proof firmly on the creditor. As part of the revision, ZFPPIPP would also have to do away with the irrebuttable presumptions, which seems unlikely on a national scale due to continuous issues of a significant number of debtors not paying workers' social security contributions and later, during insolvency proceedings, there not being enough funds to fulfil these obligations, leaving the workers in a particularly vulnerable position.

Another difference between ZFPPIPP and the Model Definitions stems from the fact that ZFPPIPP does not contain a provision that would presume the debtor's inability to pay its debt, based on its being in default to an essential creditor. To align ZFPPIPP with the Model Definitions in this aspect, the ZFPPIPP would also need to be slightly amended with the addition of such specific provision.

3. CESSATION OF PAYMENTS

The difference between the Model Definition and the Slovenian definition of cessation of payments has already been explained. Hence, reference can be made to section 2(b)/(c) *supra*.

4. LIKELIHOOD OF INSOLVENCY AND IMMINENT INSOLVENCY

As regards likely and imminent inability to pay debts, the following can be said.

a) *Likelihood of Insolvency*

ZFPPIPP does not directly use the term "likelihood of insolvency". However, the circumstances covered by this term are already denoted in ZFPPIPP by the term "long-term inability to pay", which however, according to §14(1) sentence 2 ZFPPIPP, already means the (actual) insolvency of the debtor. Thus, the circumstances underlining the term "likelihood of insolvency", as presented in the Model Definitions, basically already equate to the occurrence of insolvency in ZFPPIPP, which presents a confusing situation, since the term "likelihood of insolvency" should not be equated with the term "insolvency" itself. The resolution of this confusion would require a revision of the ZFPPIPP, by which the term "insolvency" would mean only the debtor's inability to pay in the sense of "continuous illiquidity" and the independent term "likelihood of insolvency" would include the current position of "long-term inability to pay".

b) *Imminent Insolvency*

§13a ZFPPIPP uses the term "imminent insolvency", which is meant to describe a situation where there exists a likelihood of insolvency within one year. But this provision would fall naturally under the term "likelihood of insolvency", as defined in the Model Definitions, outside of the fact, that the position of insolvency also applies in the situation where there exists a long-term inability of the debtor to pay its debt, which in ZFPPIPP basically contains the position of "likelihood of insolvency". The inconsistencies in these terms, as currently regulated in ZFPPIPP, would require a revision, by which the terms insolvency, likelihood of insolvency and imminent insolvency would have to be precisely formulated to ensure the distinction of their usage.

5. OVERINDEBTEDNESS

According to §14(3) sentence 1 ZFPPIPP, overindebtedness is one of the two circumstances in which the debtor's long-term inability to pay is (rebuttably) presumed, which in ZFPPIPP means "likelihood of insolvency", as defined by the Model Definitions. Unlike the definition of overindebtedness in the Model Definitions, ZFPPIPP does not explicitly state that the value of assets is to be assessed based on their liquidation value. Since the occurrence of overindebtedness under ZFPPIPP presumes the existence of long-term inability to pay, which is defined as "likelihood of insolvency", the assessment of the likelihood of the debtor's ability to repay obligations is thus, even if not by definition, part of determining overindebtedness.

II. OVERALL ASSESSMENT

When comparing ZFPPIPP with the Model Definitions, the provisions in ZFPPIPP show notable differences. The first significant difference is that ZFPPIPP encompasses a considerably broader range of situations where the debtor's inability to pay is presumed, whether these presumptions are rebuttable or irrebuttable. In contrast, the Model Definitions include only two such presumptions. To align with the Model Definitions, ZFPPIPP would need to be amended to reduce the number of situations in which the inability of the debtor to pay its debt is presumed, in accordance with the Model Definitions. However, regarding irrebuttable presumptions, it is unlikely that such revisions would be accepted, as they are included to protect workers' rights.

The second significant difference lies in the definition of insolvency. According to the Model Definitions, insolvency is defined in terms of the inability of the debtor to pay its debt, while under ZFPPIPP, insolvency is also established in the case of long-term inability to pay, which, by its definition in ZFPPIPP, corresponds to the term "likelihood of insolvency" in the Model Definitions. To ensure consistency with the Model Definitions, an amendment to ZFPPIPP would be needed in this area as well.

SPAIN

Nuria BERMEJO*

Please identify to what extent the proposed Model Definitions in the proposal align with or differ from the definitions currently used in your national law and whether they would be compatible with and operable in your jurisdiction.

I. INDIVIDUAL ASSESSMENT OF THE MODEL DEFINITIONS

A comparison of the Model Definitions with the definitions in Spanish law reveals the following:

1. INSOLVENCY

Article 2(3) of the Spanish Insolvency Act ("Texto Refundido de la Ley Concursal", hereinafter TRLC) provides for a definition of insolvency that is consistent with the Model Definition. Although it distinguishes between current (or actual) insolvency and imminent insolvency, both terms refer to the inability to pay debts. Current insolvency is defined as the inability to regularly pay the due debts and imminent insolvency corresponds to a forecast that the debtor will not be able to pay its debts in a timely and regular manner in the three following months. Both are grounds for opening insolvency proceedings or for access to restructuring proceedings (Article 584(1) TRLC). Likewise, both entitle the debtor to apply to the court to appoint an expert with a view to inviting bids for the acquisition of one or more productive units (pre-pack sale *ex* Article 224 *ter* TRLC).

* This contribution has been produced as part of the research project PID2022-138664NB-C22, funded by the Spanish Ministry of Science and Innovation (MCIN/AEI/10.13039/501100011033/FEDER, UE).

2. INABILITY TO PAY DEBTS

a) Prerequisites

According to Article 2(3) of the Spanish Insolvency Act, a debtor is currently insolvent if it is unable to regularly pay its due debts. As is generally recognised, momentary arrears in the payment of debts do not make the debtor unable to pay. The Model Definition is more specific with regard to the relevant assets ("liquid assets"), the extent of the liquidity gap ("all but an insignificant part"), and its duration ("in the short term"). Moreover, the Model Definition makes no reference to the regularity of payments. Nevertheless, it can be said that the Spanish definition of inability to pay debts is broadly in line with the Model Definition.

b) Presumptions

The Model Definition of inability to pay debts provides for a rebuttable presumption on two alternative bases: (i) cessation of payments (defined as being in default with payments to at least two creditors) and (ii) being in default to an essential creditor with at least two payments or one payment for at least three months.

Cessation of payments is dealt with *infra* under section 3. Regarding the presumption in case of being in default to an essential creditor with at least two payments or one payment for at least three months, Spanish law currently contains a provision that regards the general cessation of payment of tax, social security, or labour-related claims for the three months preceding the filing as an external indication of insolvency (Article 2(4)(5°) of the Spanish Insolvency Act). The presumption established by the Model Definition is both broader and narrower than the external indication of insolvency under the Spanish law. On the one hand, the Model Definition is linked to the concept of an "essential creditor", which may include creditors other than those mentioned in Spanish law. On the other hand, the default refers to at least two payments, or one payment for at least three months. This would probably not be sufficient for Spanish insolvency law to consider that the debtor has generally failed to pay tax, social security or labour-related claims.

In addition, the Spanish Insolvency Act provides for other external facts indicating insolvency that are not included in the Model Definition. According to Article 2(4) of the Spanish Insolvency Act, these are: (i) the existence of a previous administrative or judicial final decision declaring the debtor's insolvency; (ii) the lack of unencumbered assets in debtor's estate against which to attach a lien and obtain payment; (iii) the existence of liens that generally encumber the debtor's estate; and (iv) asset stripping or hasty or ruinous liquidation of the debtor's assets.

Since the Model Definition does not allow other presumptions to be introduced into national law, the external indication relating to the general cessation of payments of tax, social security, or labour-related claims can only be retained in Spanish law if it is adapted to the presumption. As for the rest of the external facts, they could not be used as the bases of presumptions, but they could still be used by the courts as circumstantial evidence to establish the debtor's inability to pay debts, especially considering that they all relate to particularly serious situations of crisis. Although the new presumption will anticipate the opening of insolvency proceedings for creditors, all of this would not represent a major change in Spanish insolvency law, which could be adapted without much difficulty.

3. CESSATION OF PAYMENTS

The definition of "cessation of payments" in the Model Definitions differs from Spanish law.

According to Article 2(4)(4°) of the Spanish Insolvency Act, cessation of payments is one of the external facts indicating insolvency upon which creditors and other legitimate persons must rely to request the opening of insolvency proceedings. In both systems the definition accommodates, in particular, petitioning creditors, without being decisive in respect of the debtor's state of insolvency since the debtor can object that it is not insolvent or unable to pay its debts. However, there are important differences between them. While the Model Definition requires that the debtor is in default with payment to at least two creditors, under current Spanish law the threshold is higher. According to a general view and case law, cessation of payments must show an absolute inability to pay debts, which implies that the debtor has failed to pay the generality of its claims and not just an important one. In addition, the default must be present and definitive. Thus, the mere existence of two unpaid creditors would probably not be sufficient to establish the debtor's cessation of payments under Spanish law.

Since the Model Definition does not allow other presumptions to be introduced into national law, the external indication relating to the general cessation of payments can only be retained in Spanish law if it is adapted to the presumption. The adaptation would make it easier for creditors and other legitimate persons to open insolvency proceedings. As the presumption is rebuttable, it is unlikely to raise many concerns about unjustified requests to open insolvency proceedings.

4. LIKELIHOOD OF INSOLVENCY AND IMMINENT INSOLVENCY

As regards likely and imminent inability to pay debts, the following can be said.

a) Likelihood of Insolvency

The Spanish Insolvency Act uses the term "likelihood of insolvency" for access to restructuring proceedings (Article 584(1) TRLC) and to entitle the debtor to apply to the court to appoint an expert with a view to inviting bids for the acquisition of one or more productive units (pre-pack sale *ex* Article 224 *ter* TRLC).

According to the Model Definition, the likelihood of insolvency requires that it is more likely than not that the debtor will become unable to pay its debts. This is very similar to current Spanish law, which requires that it is reasonably likely or foreseeable that the debtor will not be able to continue to pay its debts in the following two years unless a restructuring plan is adopted. Therefore, if the Model Definitions had to be transposed into Spanish law, the provision on the prognosis period should be removed in order to ensure the necessary flexibility.

This does not seem to represent a significant change in practice since, on the one hand, the distinction between likelihood of insolvency and imminent insolvency – limited to three months – is still possible, and on the other hand, it should not lead to abuses on the part of the debtor if it corresponds to a real risk of insolvency that will occur within a relatively short period of time. These circumstances should be closely scrutinised by the affected creditors and the courts.

b) Imminent Insolvency

Spanish law is familiar with the term "imminent insolvency", which is equivalent to "imminent inability to pay debts". It is used for access to restructuring proceedings and to open insolvency proceedings. According to Article 2(3) of the Spanish Insolvency Act, a debtor is imminently insolvent when it foresees that in the three following months it will not be able to pay its debts in a timely and regular manner. The Model Definition is almost identical to the definition in the Spanish Insolvency Act. Therefore, its transposition into Spanish law would have no impact.

5. OVERINDEBTEDNESS

Spanish insolvency law does not operate with "overindebtedness" as a ground for the opening of insolvency proceedings. The Model Definitions would therefore have no impact.

II. OVERALL ASSESSMENT

In all, the incorporation of the Model Definitions into Spanish law would not entail major changes. The Spanish Insolvency Act would have to be amended to align the external facts indicating insolvency with the two bases of the rebuttable presumption of inability to pay debts contained in the proposal, and to remove the provision on the prognosis period for the likelihood of insolvency. This will (i) reduce the requirements for creditors and other legitimate persons to open insolvency proceedings or to have access to preventive restructuring frameworks, (ii) contribute to the anticipation of the opening of insolvency proceedings for the creditors, and (iii) increase the flexibility in the understanding of the likelihood of insolvency. In view of this impact, Model Definitions would be compatible with Spanish law and operable in Spain.

SWEDEN

Hans Renman

Please identify to what extent the proposed Model Definitions in the proposal align with or differ from the definitions currently used in your national law and whether they would be compatible with and operable in your jurisdiction.

I. INDIVIDUAL ASSESSMENT OF THE MODEL DEFINITIONS

A comparison of the Model Definitions with the definition in Swedish law reveals the following:

1. INSOLVENCY

There is only one statutory definition of insolvency in Swedish law. This definition can be found in Chapter 1 section 2 sub-section 2 of the Bankruptcy Act, which provides as follows: "Insolvency means that the debtor is unable to duly pay his debts and this inability is not merely temporary". This is the only statutory definition of insolvency.

The scope of the term of "insolvency" is, according to Swedish case law and legal literature, very broad and encompasses "likelihood of insolvency" and "imminent insolvency" as these terms are defined in the Model Definitions.

2. INABILITY TO PAY DEBTS

Inability to pay debts *that is not merely temporary* is the Swedish statutory definition of insolvency, see section 1 *supra*.

a) *Prerequisites*

If the Swedish definition of "insolvency" according to section 1 *supra* is compared with the Model Definition of "inability to pay", the following comments can be made:

(i) The Model Definition of "insolvency" refers to actual inability to pay at a relevant point in time. However, according to the Swedish definition of "insolvency", the relevant question is whether there is an actual inability to pay that is not merely temporary at the time of the assessment or whether it is sufficiently probable at that time that such actual inability to pay will occur in the future.
(ii) The Model Definition of "inability to pay" is more specific compared to the Swedish definition of "insolvency". The Model Definition refers to an inability to pay all but not an insignificant part of the debtor's mature debt. The Swedish definition does not specify a critical relationship between amounts of debt that can be paid at the time of the assessment and those that cannot be paid, and also includes debts that are not mature at the time of the assessment.
(iii) There is a similarity in that the Model Definition of inability to pay does not include incapacity that can be cured, but the requirement that this can be done "in the short term" is probably stricter than current Swedish law, where such vague expressions as "within an acceptable time" have been used.

b) *Presumptions*

In Swedish law, there are several presumptions, but none fully correspond to the two bases for the presumption in the Model Definition, namely that the debtor has ceased payments or has been in default to an essential creditor with at least two payments or one payment for the last three months.

This is a description of the presumptions in Swedish law that apply where a creditor makes a petition for bankruptcy (liquidation) regarding a debtor. The debtor shall be presumed insolvent if:

(i) at the time of enforcement pursuant to chapter 4 of the Enforcement Code, it has been shown that within the six months immediately preceding the bankruptcy petition, the debtor lacked assets sufficient to pay the attachment claim in full,
(ii) the debtor has declared that the debtor is suspending his/her/its payments, or
(iii) the debtor, who not later than one year prior to the bankruptcy petition has been subject to an accounting obligation, has been reminded to pay an

uncontested due and payable debt but has failed to do so within one week, and the creditor has petitioned, within three weeks after the reminder, for the debtor to be declared bankrupt, and the debt remains unpaid when the court assesses the petition.

The court can also presume that the debtor is insolvent if the debtor files for bankruptcy or consents to a creditor's application for bankruptcy (Chapter 2 section 7 of the Bankruptcy Act).

3. CESSATION OF PAYMENTS

Cessation of payments is the basis of a rebuttable presumption in Swedish law (see (ii) in section 2(b) *supra*), but that presumption is narrower than the Model Definition of "cessation of payments".

4. LIKELIHOOD OF INSOLVENCY AND IMMINENT INSOLVENCY

As mentioned under section 1 *supra* the scope of the term "insolvency" is, according to Swedish case law and legal literature, very broad and encompasses "likelihood of insolvency" and "imminent insolvency" as these terms are defined in the Model Definitions.

5. OVERINDEPTEDNESS

Swedish law refers to "overindeptedness" only under certain provisions on transaction avoidance (gifts, division of marital estate, payments of wages, fees, or pension; and transfers to pension foundations), where proof that the debtor after the transaction retained executable property which clearly corresponded to the debts is a ground for dismissal of the claim for avoidance. The Model Definition of the term "overindeptedness" will have an impact in that context of transaction avoidance but otherwise not.

II. OVERALL ASSESSMENT

The presumptions (i) and (iii) described in section I.2(b) *supra* are very effective in that they are rarely rebuttable. A removal of these presumptions is therefore likely to meet with resistance.

However, apart from in bankruptcy filing situations, it can be assumed that The Model Definitions will improve predictability compared to the current vague Swedish definitions of the same terms, and that insolvency assessments therefore will be easier to carry out, which is positive. With this impact, the Model Definitions would be compatible with Swedish law and operable in Sweden.

PART III

NATIONAL REPORTS

QUESTIONNAIRE

INTRODUCTION

1 The present research project, triggered by the European Commission's Proposal for a Directive harmonising certain aspects of insolvency law,[1] deals with the term ***insolvency*** and its subspecies *inability to pay debts* (*cash flow insolvency*), *cessation of payments*, *likely* or *imminent inability to pay debts*, and *overindebtedness* (*balance sheet insolvency*). These terms have in common that they address a stadium of the financial crisis of a debtor where his or her estate and/or earning capacities are not (or not likely to be) sufficient for satisfying all creditors' claims.

2 "Insolvency" in this sense is used here as a term of substantive insolvency law. It is not a synonym for "insolvency proceedings" which is a topos of procedural law, describing the proceedings conducted with respect to the insolvent's estate. "Insolvency" – as examined here – is understood as ***substantive insolvency***, referring to the state of the debtor's financial affairs. This state may give rise to insolvency proceedings but must be thoroughly distinguished from them. However, when speaking of "insolvency proceedings" in this paper, we understand this term in the broad sense used in Article 1 EIR.[2]

3 The variants of insolvency as enumerated above can be found – individually or together – in all national insolvency laws.[3] Legislators use these terms in a wide variety of **contexts**. They are used (*inter alia*) to describe the circumstances under which insolvency proceedings (whether aimed at liquidation of the debtor's assets or restructuring of the debtor's capital structure) can be commenced;

1 Proposal for a Directive of the European Parliament and of the Council harmonising certain aspects of insolvency law, 2022/0408 (COD) of 7 December 2022, text available at https://eur-lex.europa.eu/legal-content/EN/TXT/?uri=CELEX%3A52022PC0702&qid=1673856579802 (last visited 16 January 2023) – hereafter "Harmonisation Proposal". The proposed Directive will be abbreviated to "Harmonisation Directive".

2 Regulation (EU) 2015/848 of the European Parliament and of the Council of 20 May 2015 on insolvency proceedings (recast), OJ of 5 June 2015, L 141/19. As regards restructuring proceedings, see *infra* at para. 8.

3 For a first overview, see *Bork*, Corporate Insolvency Law, Intersentia, 2020, para. 1.15 et seq., and the national reports in *Faber/Vermunt/Kilborn/Richter*, Commencement of Insolvency Proceedings, Oxford University Press, 2012, each at para. 5.1.

they are elements of norms regulating transactions avoidance laws;[4] they tag the point in time where the beneficiaries of directors' duties shift from shareholders to creditors; and they are used to define the point in time where directors may be obliged to commence insolvency proceedings.[5]

4 However, when it comes to the details, considerable **differences** can be observed in national laws. For example, not all insolvency laws of the Member States operate with the term "overindebtedness". The terms "likely" or "imminent inability to pay debts" are not used in all insolvency statutes, or are used in laws regulating the restructuring of a debtor rather than the liquidation of its assets.[6] Further, "inability to pay debts" is not understood uniformly in a particular sense.

5 Surprisingly, the same holds true at a **European level**. The terms "inability to pay debts", "insolvent" or "insolvency" are used in many legal instruments of the European Union, albeit without any further definition. Examples are (among others) Article 43(1) Directive 2009/138/EC,[7] Recital 41 Directive 2014/59/EU,[8] and Article 1(1)(b) Directive (EU) 2019/1023,[9] the latter expressly leaving the definition to national law in its Article 2(2)(a)/(b). Even the European Insolvency Regulation,[10] which mentions "insolvency" in its Article 1(1), offers no further explanation. The same holds true for the UNCITRAL Model Law on Cross-Border Insolvency[11] and for the Harmonisation Proposal[12] which displays the term "insolvent" *inter alia* in Article 23 and also refers to the relevant

4 See Art. 6(1)(a) of the Harmonisation Proposal (*supra* fn. 1).

5 For the latter, see Arts. 36, 37 of the Harmonisation Proposal.

6 As defined *infra* at para. 8.

7 Directive 2009/138/EC of the European Parliament and of the Council of 25 November 2009 on the taking-up and pursuit of the business of Insurance and Reinsurance (Solvency II) (recast), OJ of 17 December 2009, L 335/1.

8 Directive 2014/59/EU of the European Parliament and of the Council of 15 May 2014 establishing a framework for the recovery and resolution of credit institutions and investment firms and amending Council Directive 82/891/EEC, and Directives 2001/24/EC, 2002/47/EC, 2004/25/EC, 2005/56/EC, 2007/36/EC, 2011/35/EU, 2012/30/EU and 2013/36/EU, and Regulations (EU) No 1093/2010 and (EU) No 648/2012, of the European Parliament and of the Council, OJ of 12 June 2014, L 173/190.

9 Directive 2014/59/EU of the European Parliament and of the Council of 20 June 2019 on preventive restructuring frameworks, on discharge of debt and disqualifications, and on measures to increase the efficiency of procedures concerning restructuring, insolvency and discharge of debt, and amending Directive (EU) 2017/1132 (Directive on restructuring and insolvency), OJ of 26 June 2019, L 172/18.

10 *Supra* fn. 2.

11 *United Nations Commission on International Trade Law*, UNCITRAL Model Law on Cross-Border Insolvency Law with Guide to Enactment and Interpretation, United Nations Publications, New York, 2014. The term "insolvency" is used throughout the Model Law yet is not defined in Art. 2.

12 *Supra* fn. 1.

national law. At least, a first attempt is available in Article 38(2) Harmonisation Proposal, which defines "insolvency" as "general inability to pay debts as they mature", albeit leaving the details again to national laws.[13] This matches more or less the UNCITRAL Legislative Guide,[14] which provides, at paragraph 12(s), the following definition for the term "insolvency": "when a debtor is generally unable to pay its debts as they mature or when its liabilities exceed the value of its assets".

In our view, this finding demonstrates the clear need to take a closer look at this term and to think about the options for **harmonising the definition of substantive insolvency** at a European level. It seems to us that the use of the terms "insolvent", "insolvency", or "inability to pay debts" in the context of harmonising transactions avoidance laws,[15] pre-pack proceedings,[16] directors' duties,[17] and insolvency proceedings for microenterprises[18] gives rise to significant legal uncertainty and thwarts all harmonisation efforts if these terms are not defined in the European legal instrument itself. 6

Against this background, we have initiated this research project. Its **aim** is to elaborate, where possible, a proposal for a definition of the term "insolvency" in a Directive on harmonising (certain aspects of) insolvency law. This will include the subspecies mentioned above in paragraph 1. Our proposal will also deal with a recommendation as to which subspecies should be mentioned in a Harmonisation Directive and how they should be defined if they are implemented in a respective Directive. 7

Although the main target of our research project is insolvency law, we will also take **restructuring law** into account, albeit only peripherally. In many jurisdictions, restructuring may take place within insolvency proceedings (then sometimes labelled "reorganisation proceedings"). Where this is the case, the definition of insolvency may be the same for both kinds of proceedings. However, national laws may also refer to different stages of a debtor's financial 8

---

13 Art. 38(2) Harmonisation Proposal reads: "A microenterprise shall be deemed insolvent for the purposes of simplified winding-up proceedings when it is generally unable to pay its debts as they mature. Member States shall set out the conditions under which a microenterprise is deemed to be generally unable to pay its debts as they mature and ensure that these conditions are clear, simple and easily ascertainable by the microenterprise concerned."

14 *United Nations Commission on International Trade Law*, Legislative Guide on Insolvency Law, Parts 1 and 2, United Nations Publications, New York, 2005.

15 See Art. 6(1)(a)/(2)(b) Harmonisation Proposal: "the debtor was unable to pay its mature debts".

16 See Art. 23 Harmonisation Proposal: "where the debtor is in a situation of likelihood of insolvency or is insolvent in accordance with national law".

17 Art. 36 Harmonisation Proposal: "where a legal entity becomes insolvent".

18 Art. 38(1) Harmonisation Proposal: "microenterprises, when insolvent"; see also *supra* fn. 13.

distress, depending on the type of proceeding in respect of which the term is used, i.e. liquidation or restructuring (with the latter including proceedings that may be regarded as pre-insolvency rather than actual insolvency proceedings). With respect to the term "pre-insolvency", we note that Article 4(1) Directive on restructuring and insolvency[19] refers to the "likelihood of insolvency" and we suppose that this term has been discussed more closely in all Member States during the transformation process. This might give further input to our research material.

9 We will conduct our project in five **steps**. The first step is initiated with this Questionnaire: we are aiming to collect as much information as possible on the understanding of the terms in question in the (regular[20]) laws of all Member States (and the UK). As a second step, we would then evaluate the answers and draft a report on our topic. The third step consists of discussing this proposal with the working group. As with the previous project, collecting impact assessments will be the fourth step. Finally, step five will then be the finalisation of the report to be sent to the European Commission.

10 As regards **methodology**, we have had good experiences with a principle-based approach.[21] This means, in a nutshell, that we will align our project with the principles of insolvency law[22] and, where necessary, balance conflicting principles. However, this methodological approach will presumably be less important than in our previous project on the harmonisation of transaction avoidance laws. The reason is that, basically, the definition, application, and balancing of principles of insolvency law presupposes the insolvency of the debtor, so the definition of insolvency precedes the work with these principles. In other words, if the debtor is not insolvent, the principles of insolvency law cannot be applied. Having said that, two restrictions should be emphasised. First, it may very well become necessary to take the prior impact of the principles of insolvency law into account. Second, and more importantly, the impact of the definition of insolvency brings the principles of insolvency law into play. Generally, at least the opening of traditional liquidation proceedings, i.e. collective enforcement proceedings divesting the debtor of its control over its assets, is – particularly where applied for by a creditor – one of the most invasive actions a debtor may have to endure. This raises the question as to how such an invasive action is justifiable. This brings us to the core of the matter: from what point does the

---

19 *Supra* fn. 9.

20 We suggest leaving all crisis-related amendments and exceptions (e.g. in the context of the COVID-19 pandemic) aside.

21 For details, see *Bork/Veder*, Harmonisation of Transactions Avoidance Laws, Intersentia, 2022, para. 1.6 et seq.

22 On them, see *Bork/Veder* (fn. 21), para. 2.11 et seq.

financial situation of the debtor justify the opening of an insolvency procedure. Here, at least, principles such as the creditor's autonomy, debtor protection, and collectivity will compete.

Against this background, and in order to guarantee comparability, you are kindly asked to insert your answers and thoughts **directly into the present document** – please don't write an essay on your national insolvency law! Where cross-references are necessary, please refer to the concrete question where the topic in question has been mentioned and avoid a general "see above". Where a question is not relevant for your jurisdiction (e.g. because there are no rules on directors' duties), please insert "n.a.". 11

We also intend to **publish** the national reports together with the proposal for a harmonised definition of the term "insolvency". Hence, we would very much appreciate your being as elaborate in your answers as possible – there is no word limit for the answers! While for some questions a simple "yes" or "no" might suffice, others require a more verbose answer in order to help us in understanding your national law and in ensuring a valuable publication. You might also add literature and case law where necessary to allow us and the prospective readers of your national report to better understand and access your national law. 12

In addition, please provide us with an English **translation** of your national rules on our topic, which makes comprehension and comparison easier for us. 13

The **timeline** for this project is as follows: 14

January 2023	Establishing the working group	✓
February 2023	Draft Questionnaire to be sent for comments to the national reporters	✓
March 2023	Draft Questionnaire back from national reporters	✓
May 2023	Final version of the Questionnaire to be sent to national reporters	✓
August 2023	Questionnaire back from national reporters	
October 2023	Draft report by *Bork/Schuijling/Veder*	
November 2023	Conference on the report	
December 2023	Final version of the report to be sent to the European Commission	

Hence, please send this questionnaire with your comments back to us **by 31 August 2023**.

QUESTIONS

In the following part of this Questionnaire, we will present a catalogue of 55 questions which are grouped under the three subspecies of the term insolvency.

I. GENERAL

In the first part of this Questionnaire, we kindly ask you to provide us with some general information on the term "insolvency" in your national law.

Question 1: How is insolvency (both in the context of liquidation and restructuring/reorganisation) regulated in your jurisdiction? Please give a brief overview, at least enumerating the relevant statutes.

Insert text here

Question 2: Related to paragraph 10 above of the Introduction: seen from a principle-based perspective, what justifies the opening of insolvency proceedings in your jurisdiction?

Insert text here

Question 3: Does your national law in the context of liquidation proceedings use one or more of the following terms (be it as a noun, be it as an adjective or adjunct) in whatever context:

a) inability to pay debts
Insert text here

b) cessation of payments
Insert text here

c) likely inability to pay debts
Insert text here

d) imminent inability to pay debts
Insert text here

e) overindebtedness?
Insert text here

Question 4: Are the same terms (and with the same meaning) used in the rules on preliminary/interim insolvency proceedings (e.g. concerning the application stage of the proceedings)?

Insert text here

Question 5: Does your national law in the context of restructuring proceedings (as referred to above at paragraph 8 of the Introduction, i.e. both pre-insolvency and within formal insolvency proceedings) use one or more of the following terms (be it as a noun, be it as an adjective or adjunct) in whatever context:

a) inability to pay debts
Insert text here

b) cessation of payments
Insert text here

c) likely inability to pay debts
Insert text here

d) imminent inability to pay debts
Insert text here

e) overindebtedness?
Insert text here

Question 6: Which of the terms mentioned in Questions 3 and 5 are used for defining grounds to commence proceedings (triggering circumstances)?

a) insolvency proceedings
Insert text here

b) restructuring proceedings
Insert text here

Question 7: Does the answer to Question 6 include personal bankruptcies of natural persons or only corporate insolvencies of legal entities?

Insert text here

Question 8: In your law, are there any other circumstances which trigger insolvency or restructuring proceedings?

Insert text here

Question 9: Which of the terms mentioned in Questions 3, 5, and 8 are used in the context of transactions avoidance law?

Insert text here

Question 10: Which of the terms addressed in Questions 3, 5, and 8 are used in the context of directors' duties?

a) shift of duties (from shareholders to creditors)
Insert text here

b) duties to commence insolvency proceedings
Insert text here

c) other duties (please describe)
Insert text here

Question 11: Are there any other rules in the context of which the terms addressed in Questions 3, 5, and 8 are used?

Insert text here

Question 12: Is the definition of (the subspecies of) insolvency identical in all legal fields or are there different definitions (e.g. different in insolvency law than in criminal law)?

Insert text here

II. INABILITY TO PAY DEBTS

To our knowledge, nearly all jurisdictions are familiar with the term "inability to pay debts".

Question 13: In your jurisdiction, is the term "inability to pay debts" defined in statute? If so, please give the wording in English translation. Is this definition (if any) specified in case law? If so, how?

Insert text here

Question 14: Does your law refer to all debts or only to mature debts?

Insert text here

Question 15: Which assets are taken into account when assessing the inability to pay debts: all (financial) assets or only those that are liquid, i.e. available on short notice?

Insert text here

Question 16: Is any liquidity gap (deficit between relevant financial means and relevant debts) relevant or does your law neglect minor gaps? If the latter, how is "minor" defined?

Insert text here

Question 17: As far as the time aspect is concerned, does it matter whether the liquidity gap can be closed again in the short term? If so, how long is the grace period?

Insert text here

Question 18: As far as the time aspect is concerned, is a debtor considered insolvent if the liquidity gap is not yet present but will occur soon? If so, how long is the prognosis period? (Note: this may also concern the difference between actual and likely/imminent inability to pay debts; cf. below Question 34).

Insert text here

Question 19: How is inability to pay debts established? Please communicate if there is a difference between a creditor and a debtor application or between different legal contexts.

a) Is a formal liquidity status (liquidity balance sheet) required?
Insert text here

b) Is a sample of daily liquidity data (which do not amount to a proper liquidity status but show insufficient funds on different days within a certain period of time) sufficient?
Insert text here

c) Does the law provide for a rebuttable presumption? If so, under which conditions?
Insert text here

d) Does the law provide for any technical circumstances (e.g. undisputed statutory demand, non-compliance with monetary judgments, unsuccessful enforcement proceedings, non-performance of a previous composition agreement in insolvency proceedings) the occurrence of which suffices to establish the debtor's insolvency?
Insert text here

e) Other means?
Insert text here

Question 20: Is insolvency (inability to pay debts, overindebtedness, etc.) subject to party autonomy in the proceedings or must the court clarify them *ex officio*?

Insert text here

Question 21: In an overall view, does your law distinguish "inability to pay debts" from "financial difficulties"? If so, how?

Insert text here

Question 22: In an overall view, does it matter under your law whether the debtor's inability to pay debts is present or future and reversible or irreversible?

Insert text here

Question 23: Would you like to add any further aspects not covered by the above questions?

Insert text here

III. CESSATION OF PAYMENTS

In some jurisdictions, cessation of payments is a term of art, albeit with different relevance.

Question 24: In your jurisdiction, is "cessation of payments" a legal term used either in statute or in case law? (If the answer is "no", please continue with Question 31.)

Insert text here

Question 25: Is "cessation of payments" an autonomous ground to commence proceedings (triggering circumstance)? You may refer to Questions 6/7 or add additional information here.

Insert text here

Question 26: Is "cessation of payments" a means to establish inability to pay debts? If so, by which mechanism (e.g. rebuttable presumption for inability to pay debts, cf. above Question 19(c))?

Insert text here

Question 27: How is "cessation of payments" defined? If it is defined in statute, please provide us here with an English translation of the relevant rule. Is this definition (if any) specified in case law? If so, how?

Insert text here

Question 28: How is "cessation of payments" established?

Insert text here

Question 29: Are there typical circumstances which provide circumstantial evidence that the debtor has ceased payments? If so, please list as many as possible.

Insert text here

Question 30: Would you like to add any further aspects not covered by the above questions?

Insert text here

IV. LIKELY /IMMINENT INABILITY TO PAY DEBTS

Member States' insolvency laws also refer to upcoming inability to pay debts, sometimes distinguishing likely from imminent inability to pay debts. In our preliminary understanding, "likely" is a term of probability, "imminent" is a term of urgency, yet we are eager to learn from your jurisdiction.

Question 31: Are the following terms available in your jurisdiction, either in statute or in case law? (If the answer is "no", please continue with Question 42.)

a) likely inability to pay debts
Insert text here

b) imminent inability to pay debts
Insert text here

c) other (similar) terms
Insert text here

Question 32: Is "likely/imminent inability to pay debts" an autonomous ground to commence proceedings (triggering circumstance)? You may refer to Questions 6/7 or add additional information here.

Insert text here

Question 33: If the answer to the previous Question is "yes", who may base filing for insolvency proceedings on it: only the debtor or also creditors?

Insert text here

Question 34: How are these terms defined? If they are defined in statute, please provide us here with an English translation of the relevant rules. Is this definition (if any) specified in case law? If so, how?

a) likely inability to pay debts
Insert text here

b) imminent inability to pay debts
Insert text here

Question 35: Do the terms "likely" and "imminent" require a prognosis regarding the point in time when actual inability to pay debts will occur? If so, how long is the time period for this prognosis?

Insert text here

Question 36: Does your law require a specific grade of certainty that inability to pay debts will eventually occur? If so, is 50.1% ("more likely than not") enough or are there alleviated or aggravated prerequisites?

Insert text here

Question 37: Regarding "debts" and "financial means", are they defined in the same way as in the context of inability to pay debts (cf. above Questions 14/15)? If not, what are the differences?

Insert text here

Question 38: Further to Question 37: Are "debts" considered which do currently not exist or are not yet due but will foreseeably come into existence and become due during the prognosis period?

Insert text here

Question 39: Also further to Question 37: Are "financial means" considered which do currently not exist but will foreseeably become available during the prognosis period?

Insert text here

Question 40: How are the terms "likely/imminent inability to pay debts" established?

Insert text here

Question 41: Would you like to add any further aspects not covered by the above questions?

Insert text here

V. OVERINDEBTEDNESS

Finally, some – but by no means all – national insolvency laws refer to the debtor's overindebtedness or – which will be used synonymously hereafter – balance sheet insolvency.

Question 42: In your jurisdiction, is "overindebtedness", or "balance sheet insolvency" respectively, a legal term used either in statute or in case law? (If the answer is "no", please continue with Question 56.)

Insert text here

Question 43: Is "overindebtedness" an autonomous ground to commence proceedings (triggering circumstance)? You may refer to Questions 6/7 or add additional information here.

Insert text here

Question 44: If the answer to the previous Question is "yes", is this applicable to corporate insolvencies of legal persons only or also to personal bankruptcies of natural persons?

Insert text here

Question 45: Is the term "overindebtedness" defined in statute? If so, please give the wording in English translation. Is this definition (if any) specified in case law? If so, how?

Insert text here

Question 46: Does your law refer to all existing debts or only to mature debts?

Insert text here

Question 47: Does the rank of certain debts play a role when establishing overindebtedness? In particular, is there any possibility to conclude agreements according to which certain debts shall not be taken into account (e.g. agreements on subsidiarity)?

Insert text here

Question 48: Which assets are taken into account when overindebtedness is established: the complete set of assets or only a selection of them?

Insert text here

Question 49: How are the debtor's assets valued: by referring to the liquidation value, the book value, the going concern value, or in another way?

Insert text here

Question 50: Is there any prognostic element, e.g. regarding the debtor's chances to continue the business?

Insert text here

Question 51: If the answer to the previous Question is "yes", what exactly is the topic of the prognosis and how is it established?

Insert text here

Question 52: If the answer to Question 50 is "yes", how long is the prognosis period?

Insert text here

Question 53: How is overindebtedness established?

a) Is a formal balance sheet required?
Insert text here

b) Does the yearly regular commercial balance sheet have any meaning (given that it is normally based on technical values and does not display undisclosed reserves)?
Insert text here

c) Does the law provide for a presumption? If so, under which conditions?
Insert text here

d) Other means?
Insert text here

Question 54: Is the legal link to overindebtedness undisputed in literature or are there efforts to abolish it?

Insert text here

Question 55: Would you like to add any further aspects not covered by the above questions?

Insert text here

VI. REMAINDERS

Question 56: Is there anything else you would like to share in the present context and that we should take into account?

Insert text here

AUSTRIA

Kevin LABNER

I. GENERAL

Question 1: How is insolvency (both in the context of liquidation and restructuring/reorganisation) regulated in your jurisdiction? Please give a brief overview, at least enumerating the relevant statutes.

Insolvency law in Austria is primarily regulated by the Insolvenzordnung (hereinafter referred to as "IO" (Insolvency Code/Regulation)).[1] By its major revision in 2010 (Insolvenzrechtsänderungsgesetz, IRÄG[2]) it has become the sole comprehensive statute on insolvency law (*stricto sensu*). It aims at the preservation of enterprises to the widest possible extent by means of restructuring/reorganisation (*Sanierung*) and (alongside this goal, if possible) at the best possible satisfaction of creditors. Both purposes are not necessarily contradictory of each other.[3]

In Austria, both natural persons and legal entities are eligible for insolvency proceedings.[4] For individuals, particular regulations for natural and/or non-business debtors apply (see §§181 et seq. IO).

There are basically two statutory definitions of (substantive) "insolvency" under Austrian law, namely *Zahlungsunfähigkeit* (illiquidity/inability to pay debts, §66 IO) and *Überschuldung* (overindebtedness, §67 IO). The latter, however, only applies to certain types of debtors, as defined by §67 IO (in principle, this refers to legal entities such as private limited companies/GmbH or stock companies/AG or an estate). Thus, illiquidity is considered the primary (or: general) ground for the opening of insolvency proceedings against a debtor.[5]

Moreover, §167(2) IO establishes "imminent illiquidity" (*drohende Zahlungsunfähigkeit*) as an additional ground for opening (only) "reorganisation" (or: rehabilitation) proceedings (*Sanierungsverfahren* as

---

1 An unofficial translation is available at https://www.rautner.com/wp-content/uploads/2016/05/3645187_Austrian_Insolvency-Code_ENG.pdf (last accessed: 04.09.2023).

2 BGBl I 2010/29; prior to this revision, the bankruptcy code (Konkursordnung, KO) co-existed with the "conciliation code" (Ausgleichsordnung, AO).

3 See *Dellinger/Oberhammer/Koller*, Insolvenzrecht, 5th ed. Manz, 2023, para. 16.

4 *Dellinger/Oberhammer/Koller*, Insolvenzrecht, 5th ed. Manz, 2023, para. 224.

5 *Dellinger* in *Konecny/Schubert*, Insolvenzgesetze, 01.09.1999, §66 KO para. 2.

opposed to *Konkursverfahren* – bankruptcy proceedings) under the regime of the IO. Only entrepreneurs (including legal entities respectively) are eligible for these proceedings.[6] It is, however, worth mentioning that restructuring/reorganisation itself is not limited to the commencement of reorganisation proceedings under the IO. On the contrary, a debtor may apply for the approval of a reorganisation/restructuring plan (*Sanierungsplan*, see §§140 et seq. IO) in ordinary bankruptcy proceedings as well.[7]

In 2021, the Austrian parliament adopted the Restrukturierungsordnung (ReO, Code on the Restructuring of Enterprises[8]) that established a pre-insolvency proceeding and implemented the EU Directive on restructuring and insolvency. It resembles formal insolvency proceedings. Its proceeding (*Restrukturierungsverfahren*) is available to entrepreneurs that are likely to become insolvent (see §§1 et seq. ReO); however, the commencement of the proceeding is impermissible if the debtor is already in a state of illiquidity (inability to pay debts/*Zahlungsunfähigkeit*).[9] The ReO comes with tailor-made solutions at the debtor's disposal, such as a moratorium (see §§19 et seq. ReO) and ultimately aims at the approval of a restructuring plan (on this, see §§27 et seq. ReO). Reference to ReO will be given where appropriate; however, it must be stated that, to date, the practical significance of said statute is low.[10]

Insolvency proceedings are primarily administered by an Insolvency Practitioner (IP), but debtor in possession (DIP) procedures are available in the case of reorganisation proceedings (*Sanierungsverfahren mit Eigenverwaltung*: §§169 et seq. IO) as well as for insolvency proceedings for non-entrepreneurial natural persons (see §§186 et seq. IO on this principle as well as relevant exceptions to the rule).

The prerequisites for the opening of insolvency proceedings are in general:[11]

- the debtor's legal capacity (equal to "insolvency capacity" – any person of legal capacity may file for insolvency proceedings under Austrian law, e.g. partnerships as well as natural persons, regardless of their conduct of business activity);
- the debtor is currently in the state of substantive insolvency (or: will imminently be unable to pay debts as mentioned in the section above on the reorganisation procedure);

6 *Dellinger/Oberhammer/Koller*, Insolvenzrecht, 5th ed., Manz 2023, para. 429; see §166 IO for the scope *ratione personae*.

7 *Dellinger/Oberhammer/Koller*, Insolvenzrecht, 5th ed., Manz 2023, para. 426.

8 BGBl I 2021/147.

9 See §7(3) ReO; *Mohr*, Das Restrukturierungsverfahren nach der ReO, ZIK 2021, p. 83.

10 *Schumacher* in *Koller/Lovrek/Spitzer*, IO – Insolvenzordnung, 2nd ed., 2023, §67 IO para. 1 with reference to *Konecny*, Unterschiedliche praktische Bewährung von RIRUG und GREx, ZIK, 2022, p. 81.

11 See *Dellinger/Oberhammer/Koller*, Insolvenzrecht, 5th ed., Manz 2023, paras. 224 et seq.; *Dellinger* in *Konecny/Schubert*, Insolvenzgesetze, 01.09.1999, §66 KO para. 1.

- the expenses of the proceedings can be covered by the estate (exceptions do apply);
- an application for the opening of proceedings, by either the debtor or a creditor, with the competent court.

Question 2: Related to paragraph 10 above of the Introduction: seen from a principle-based perspective, what justifies the opening of insolvency proceedings in your jurisdiction?

The opening of insolvency proceedings primarily aims at the equal treatment of creditors having the same rank (*par conditio creditorum*).[12] If a debtor is (currently or in the foreseeable future) unable to serve the entirety of his or her debts, then the insolvency proceedings shall ensure that no creditor will be favoured. In the course of the last decades, the focus has shifted from a creditor-centred to a more debtor-centred approach.[13] Therefore, the purpose of insolvency proceedings has significantly shifted from the best satisfaction of creditors, mainly by way of liquidation of assets towards the continuation of the debtor's enterprise.[14] As mentioned in the answer to Question 1 *supra*, the goal of this continuation does not mean that the creditor's claims do not play any role anymore. On the contrary, only the required majority vote of the creditors on the suggested restructuring plan will ensure that the debts will be paid on a pro rata basis (see §147 IO) while at the same time (often) the enterprise shall be enabled to thrive in the future.

Avoidance law (§§27 et seq. IO) also reflects the principle of *par conditio creditorum*, i.e. where the equal treatment rule effectively is extended to cover the pre-insolvency period. Affected transactions that meet the requirements for avoidance can be declared null and void vis-à-vis the other creditors (the insolvency estate, as appropriate).

Procedural safeguards, such as the prohibition on initiating new civil cases against the debtor (*Prozesssperre*) while already pending cases must be halted, also accompany the principle. Finally, the prohibition on enforcing debts (*Exekutionssperre*) serves the very same purpose.[15]

Question 3: Does your national law in the context of liquidation proceedings use one or more of the following terms (be it as a noun, be it as an adjective or adjunct) in whatever context:

a) inability to pay debts
Yes (*Zahlungsunfähigkeit*, §66(1) IO).

[12] See on this, e.g., *Dellinger/Oberhammer/Koller*, Insolvenzrecht, 5th ed., Manz 2023, para. 9.
[13] See *Dellinger/Oberhammer/Koller*, Insolvenzrecht, 5th ed., Manz 2023, paras. 11 et seq.
[14] See *Dellinger/Oberhammer/Koller*, Insolvenzrecht, 5th ed., Manz 2023, para. 12.
[15] See *Dellinger/Oberhammer/Koller*, Insolvenzrecht, 5th ed., Manz 2023, paras. 6 et seq.

b) cessation of payments
Yes ("*Zahlungsunfähigkeit ist insbesondere anzunehmen, wenn der Schuldner seine Zahlungen einstellt*" – §66(2) IO).

c) likely inability to pay debts
No.

d) imminent inability to pay debts
Yes (*drohende Zahlungsunfähigkeit*, §167(2) IO). However, this term is only relevant to reorganisation proceedings (*Sanierungsverfahren*) and therefore, strictly speaking, not used in the scope of "liquidation proceedings".

e) overindebtedness?
Yes (*Überschuldung*, §67 IO).

Question 4: Are the same terms (and with the same meaning) used in the rules on preliminary/interim insolvency proceedings (e.g. concerning the application stage of the proceedings)?

Yes. The law does not provide for any distinction for the "mere" application phase. The court has to examine whether the prerequisites as set out in the answer to Question 1 are met and may order preliminary measures in order to, e.g., protect the estate from the debtor's dispositions (see §73 IO).

Question 5: Does your national law in the context of restructuring proceedings (as referred to above at paragraph 8 of the Introduction, i.e. both pre-insolvency and within formal insolvency proceedings) use one or more of the following terms (be it as a noun, be it as an adjective or adjunct) in whatever context:

a) inability to pay debts
Yes.

b) cessation of payments
Yes (§66(2) IO; the ReO does not mention this term).

c) likely inability to pay debts
No.

d) imminent inability to pay debts
Yes (see §6(2) ReO alongside (practically more relevant) §167(2) IO).

e) overindebtedness?
Yes.

Question 6: Which of the terms mentioned in Questions 3 and 5 are used for defining grounds to commence proceedings (triggering circumstances)?

a) insolvency proceedings

- inability to pay debts (illiquidity, *Zahlungsunfähigkeit*); this term is exemplarily ("notably"/*insbesondere*) defined by the debtor's "cessation of payments" (§66(2) IO) – see Questions 24–29 *infra*);
- imminent ability to pay debts (note that this term/ground only constitutes an optional (not a mandatory) triggering circumstance – if the debtor merely faces imminent instead of "acute" inability to pay debts, then it is up to the debtor to decide whether to commence proceedings);
- overindebtedness (§67 IO, limited to particular debtors).

b) restructuring proceedings

- under the regime of the IO (reorganisation proceedings or bankruptcy proceedings aiming at the reorganisation of debts via a reorganisation plan, see Question 1 *supra*): inability to pay debts (§66(1) IO), overindebtedness (§67 IO, limited to certain debtors, see for more details answer to Question 44 *infra*), imminent inability to pay debts (§167 IO);
- under the regime of the ReO: imminent inability to pay debts §7(3) in conjunction with §6(2) ReO.

Question 7: Does the answer to Question 6 include personal bankruptcies of natural persons or only corporate insolvencies of legal entities?

The answer to Question 6 includes personal bankruptcies as well as corporate insolvencies except for the insolvency ground of overindebtedness. The latter does not apply to any natural person (be it an entrepreneur or consumer).

As to restructuring proceedings, both the IO as well as the ReO only apply to corporations and entrepreneurs and are therefore not applicable to consumer bankruptcies.

Question 8: In your law, are there any other circumstances which trigger insolvency or restructuring proceedings?

No. However, for the sake of completeness, it should be mentioned that under the Unternehmensreorganisationsgesetz (URG), there is the option[16] (sic!) to file for "reorganisation proceedings" if certain key figures are met (see on this Question 10(c) *infra* and Question 21, second bullet point). Strictly speaking,

---

[16] See, e.g., *Lentsch* in *Koller/Lovrek/Spitzer*, IO – Insolvenzordnung, 2nd ed. Verlag Österreich, 2023, §167 IO para. 13.

however, this does not trigger *insolvency* or restructuring proceedings and the URG has no practical significance whatsoever.[17]

Question 9: Which of the terms mentioned in Questions 3, 5, and 8 are used in the context of transactions avoidance law?

With regard to the wording, it is "inability to pay debts" (§§30, 31, 33, 36a, 36b IO); however, referring to inability to pay debts does not exclude the relevancy of overindebtedness, as §67(2) IO states that any such provisions *referring to inability to pay debts also apply to overindebtedness.*

Question 10: Which of the terms addressed in Questions 3, 5, and 8 are used in the context of directors' duties?

a) shift of duties (from shareholders to creditors)
There is no express provision on a formal shift of duties in Austrian law. However, violation of the duty to file for insolvency may lead to liability.[18] Implicitly, this might be understood as a shift of duties.[19]

It is worth mentioning that the directors/officers are called to take steps necessary to avoid substantive insolvency if the debtor is likely to become insolvent (in the sense of §6(1) and (2) ReO/Article 4(1), Article 2(2)(a) Directive on Restructuring and Insolvency – 2019/1023). Directors/officers must thereby take adequately into account the interests of creditors, shareholders, and other stakeholders accordingly.[20]

b) duties to commence insolvency proceedings
Pursuant to §69(2) IO, both overindebtedness and inability to pay debts trigger a director's/officer's duty to file for insolvency proceedings.[21]

c) other duties (please describe)
Pursuant to company law, directors or officers may face liability if they pay ignoring the inability to pay debts (in the sense of §66 IO) or overindebtedness (in the sense of §67 IO) – see §25(3)(2) GmbHG (mentioning the mandatory triggering circumstances to file for insolvency, hence §§66 and 67 IO), §84(3)(6)

---

17 See, e.g., *Dellinger/Oberhammer/Koller*, Insolvenzrecht, 5th ed., Manz, 2023, para. 582.
18 For further details see *Schumacher* in *Koller/Lovrek/Spitzer*, IO – Insolvenzordnung, 2nd ed. Verlag Österreich, 2023, §69 IO paras. 72 et seq.
19 See, on the purpose of this provision, *Schumacher* in *Koller/Lovrek/Spitzer*, IO – Insolvenzordnung, 2nd ed. Verlag Österreich, 2023, §69 IO para. 34.
20 *Mock* in *Mock/Zoppel*, ReO – Restrukturierungsordnung Kommentar, 2022, §1 ReO paras. 53 et seq.
21 See, more extensively, on this *Schumacher* in *Koller/Lovrek/Spitzer*, IO – Insolvenzordnung, 2nd ed. Verlag Österreich, 2023, §69 IO para. 34.

AktG (Stock Company Act[22]) (explicitly mentioning inability to pay debts and overindebtedness).

While the URG (Unternehmensreorganisationsgesetz[23]) does not provide for a duty to file for "reorganisation proceedings" (*Reorganisationsverfahren* – the proceeding which this statute establishes), directors/officers may face liability if they ignore the need for reorganisation, i.e. if certain key figures as laid down by §§23 et seqq. URG are met. Please note that the proceeding provided for in the URG (*Reorganisationsverfahren*) has no practical significance whatsoever.[24]

Question 11: Are there any other rules in the context of which the terms addressed in Questions 3, 5, and 8 are used?

- §159 StGB[25] (Criminal Code, Strafgesetzbuch) provides for a criminal offence on the impairment of creditors' interests where the debtor is unable to pay debts (§159 StGB: *Grob fahrlässige Schädigung von Gläubigerinteressen* – grossly negligent impairment of creditors' interests).[26]
- §19(2)(3) and §19(4) ReO: *Vollstreckungssperre* (moratorium) – no moratorium is to be granted if the debtor is unable to pay its debts – assessment by the court seised to conduct restructuring proceedings (in that case, the law provides for a rebuttable presumption[27]).[28]
- As set out in the answer to Question 10 *supra*: corporate law regarding the liability of directors/officers.
- As set out in the answer to Question 9 *supra*: avoidance law under §§27 et seq. IO.

Question 12: Is the definition of (the subspecies of) insolvency identical in all legal fields or are there different definitions (e.g. different in insolvency law than in criminal law)?

There is no particular definition in those other statutes that link their provisions to the terms rooted in insolvency as laid down above. Therefore, a uniform understanding of these terms is to be assumed.[29]

---

22 BGBl 1965/65 as last amended by BGBl I 2023/78.

23 BGBl I 1997/114 as last amended by BGBl I 2016/43.

24 See, e.g., *Dellinger/Oberhammer/Koller*, Insolvenzrecht, 5th ed. Manz, 2023, para. 582.

25 BGBl I 1974/60 as last amended by BGBl I 2023/100.

26 OGH 1 Ob 134/07y; see RIS-Justiz RS0064528 [T 9].

27 *Labner* in *Mock/Zoppel*, ReO – Restrukturierungsordnung Kommentar, 2022, §19 ReO paras. 50 et seq.

28 See on this provision *Labner* in *Mock/Zoppel*, ReO – Restrukturierungsordnung Kommentar, 2022, §19 ReO paras. 48 et seq.

29 With respect to (what is now) §66 IO and §159 StGB OGH 1 Ob 134/07y.

II. INABILITY TO PAY DEBTS

Question 13: In your jurisdiction, is the term "inability to pay debts" defined in statute? If so, please give the wording in English translation. Is this definition (if any) specified in case law? If so, how?

The term "inability to pay debts" is not (comprehensively) defined by any statutory provision. The only express hint provided by law is §66(2) IO which states: "*Zahlungsunfähigkeit ist insbesondere anzunehmen, wenn der Schuldner seine Zahlungen einstellt*", literally: "Inability to pay debts is notably to be assumed where the debtor ceases to pay debts."

In order to assess whether a debtor has already reached the status of inability to pay debts, one needs to take account of the wealth of jurisprudence issued by the Supreme Court. In essence, the Supreme Court clarified that a debtor is unable to pay debts when:[30]

- he cannot pay mature debts
- due to lack of liquid financial means, and
- is also unable to procure the necessary means, e.g. by way of raising a credit, as soon as possible.

Question 14: Does your law refer to all debts or only to mature debts?

Inability to pay debts only refers to mature debts.[31] This is important to delineate actual inability to pay debts from imminent inability to pay debts (see §167(2) IO).[32]

Question 15: Which assets are taken into account when assessing the inability to pay debts: all (financial) assets or only those that are liquid, i.e. available on short notice?

When it comes to assessing "acute" inability to pay debts, only liquid assets ought to be taken into account. It must be highlighted that regardless of currently available funds, case law of the Supreme Court allows for a certain "grace period" within which the debtor needs to show that he or she can procure the necessary financial means to cover mature debts (see Question 17 *infra*). Therefore, it may

---

30 OGH 7 Ob 526/89; RIS-Justiz RS0064528; RS0052198; see also *Schumacher* in *Koller/Lovrek/Spitzer*, IO – Insolvenzordnung, 2nd ed. Verlag Österreich, 2023, §66 paras. 3 et seq. with further references.

31 OGH 8 Ob 624/88.

32 *Schumacher* in *Koller/Lovrek/Spitzer*, IO – Insolvenzordnung, 2nd ed. Verlag Österreich, 2023, §66 para. 3.

suffice to order a lien on real estate in order to take out a loan (and therefore preserve liquidity).[33]

Question 16: Is any liquidity gap (deficit between relevant financial means and relevant debts) relevant or does your law neglect minor gaps? If the latter, how is "minor" defined?

As a rule of thumb, the case law of the Supreme Court grants a minor gap of up to 5%;[34] however, this does not necessarily mean that inability to pay debts can always be prevented below this threshold because the debtor might lack any opportunity to overcome this shortage of financial means within the time-frame as set out in Question 17 *infra*.[35]

Question 17: As far as the time aspect is concerned, does it matter whether the liquidity gap can be closed again in the short term? If so, how long is the grace period?

The statute does not provide for any grace period whatsoever. However, case law by the Supreme Court basically grants such a grace period: If the debtor is able to meet the debts within a period no longer than *three months* (in exceptional cases up to *five months* – in that case it needs to be established with a probability bordering on certainty that illiquidity can be eliminated[36]), he or she shall not be considered unable to pay the debts (§66 IO). The debtor needs to show that he or she is able to procure the financial means needed to repay overdue debts.[37]

Question 18: As far as the time aspect is concerned, is a debtor considered insolvent if the liquidity gap is not yet present but will occur soon? If so, how long is the prognosis period? (Note: this may also concern the difference between actual and likely/imminent inability to pay debts; cf. below Question 34).

If the gap is not yet present (but rather will be occurring soon, i.e. in the foreseeable future), then the debtor currently is *not* unable to pay debts (within the meaning of §66 IO) but rather faces *imminent inability to pay debts*.[38]

---

33 OGH 3 Ob 99/10w; *Schumacher* in *Koller/Lovrek/Spitzer*, IO – Insolvenzordnung, 2nd ed. Verlag Österreich, 2023, §66 paras. 31 et seq. with further references to relevant jurisprudence.

34 OGH 3 Ob 99/10w – dealing with (and rejecting it in view of the Austrian legal situation) German case law that considers a gap amounting to 10% as equally justified.

35 *Schumacher* in *Koller/Lovrek/Spitzer*, IO – Insolvenzordnung, 2nd ed. Verlag Österreich, 2023, §66 IO para. 7.

36 OGH 3 Ob 99/10w – dealing with German case law that strictly assumed a significantly shorter period of a maximum of three weeks.

37 OGH 3 Ob 99/10w.

38 *Lentsch* in *Koller/Lovrek/Spitzer*, IO – Insolvenzordnung, 2nd ed. Verlag Österreich, 2023, §167 IO para. 14. See, on the delineation of "acute" inability to pay debts (§66 IO) as opposed

The latter represents only an optional ground for the commencement of insolvency proceedings under §167(2) IO if the debtor is an entrepreneur (or legal entity that falls under the provisions of reorganisation proceedings under §§166 et seq. IO). In this case, it is the debtor's choice to decide whether insolvency proceedings are to be filed or not. Alternatively, imminent inability to pay debts acts as a voluntary triggering circumstance for the commencement of restructuring proceedings under the ReO (see §6(2) ReO).[39]

Question 19: How is inability to pay debts established? Please communicate if there is a difference between a creditor and a debtor application or between different legal contexts.

a) Is a formal liquidity status (liquidity balance sheet) required?
Under Austrian law, no formal liquidity status is required (unlike in the case of overindebtedness, see answer to Question 53(a) *infra*). However, as to the "grace period", the debtor may be required to provide an overview of the financial status within said period in order to demonstrate the ability to pay debts within the grace period (e.g. where a creditor has filed for bankruptcy and the debtor wishes to demonstrate that he or she is not in a state of inability to pay debts).[40]

b) Is a sample of daily liquidity data (which do not amount to a proper liquidity status but show insufficient funds on different days within a certain period of time) sufficient?
With respect to said grace period (see answer to Question 17 *supra*), the debtor may need to show that he or she is able to meet mature debts by raising funds (e.g. by loans).[41]

c) Does the law provide for a rebuttable presumption? If so, under which conditions?
Yes. Pursuant to §66(2) IO, inability to pay debts is to be assumed if the debtor ceases to pay debts (see answers to Questions 24 et seq. *infra*).[42] Moreover, if the debtor gives notice (vis-à-vis the court) of his or her cessation of payments, this is thought to be a clue as to the inability to pay debts and is itself considered an application for the commencement of insolvency proceedings (§69(1) second sentence IO).[43]

---

to imminent inability to pay debts (§167(2) IO) *Schumacher* in *Koller/Lovrek/Spitzer*, IO – Insolvenzordnung, 2nd ed. Verlag Österreich, 2023, §66 IO paras. 33 et seq.

39 See, e.g., *Schumacher* in *Koller/Lovrek/Spitzer*, IO – Insolvenzordnung, 2nd ed. Verlag Österreich, 2023, §66 IO para. 34a.

40 *Dellinger* in *Konecny/Schubert*, Insolvenzgesetze, 01.09.1999, §66 KO para. 52.

41 *Dellinger* in *Konecny/Schubert*, Insolvenzgesetze, 01.09.1999, §66 KO paras. 52 et seq. (*Liquiditätsplanung*).

42 *Dellinger* in *Konecny/Schubert*, Insolvenzgesetze, 01.09.1999, §66 KO para. 72.

43 *Schumacher* in *Koller/Lovrek/Spitzer*, IO – Insolvenzordnung, 2nd ed. Verlag Österreich, 2023, §69 IO para. 16.

It is worth mentioning, though, that §19(4) ReO second sentence introduced a rebuttable presumption to determine whether the debtor is unable to pay debts. NB, however, the context of said provision: §19(4) ReO is applicable if the debtor applies for a moratorium in restructuring proceedings under the ReO (see §§19 et seq. ReO). This moratorium shall support the bargaining process between the debtor and the creditors in order to reach an agreement (restructuring plan, §§27 et seq. ReO). While entering the status of being unable to pay debts (in the sense of §66 IO) excludes the opening of restructuring proceedings (see §7(3) ReO), this circumstance is only examined roughly at the opening stage.[44] If the debtor applies for a moratorium (*Vollstreckungssperre*), the court needs to examine the financial status more closely. §19(4) second sentence ReO presumes inability to pay debts if public creditors (namely social security and fiscal agencies) are currently enforcing debts against the debtor. From a methodological point of view, it seems questionable whether this provision is applicable outside the context of a moratorium in restructuring proceedings under the regime of the ReO.[45] It seems to be the prevailing opinion that said provision only acts as another clue (meaning: no formal presumption) to establish inability to pay debts.[46]

d) Does the law provide for any technical circumstances (e.g. undisputed statutory demand, non-compliance with monetary judgments, unsuccessful enforcement proceedings, non-performance of a previous composition agreement in insolvency proceedings) the occurrence of which suffices to establish the debtor's insolvency?

Doctrine and jurisprudence have developed certain clues ("circumstantial evidence") that point to the possible inability to pay debts.

Literature and case law provide examples such as:[47]

- a multitude of enforcement proceedings instigated against the debtor,
- multiple default judgments against the debtor,
- failure to pay particular debts such as vis-à-vis public creditors (taxes, social security contributions),
- attempt to initiate out-of-court settlements due to failure to pay all mature debts,

---

44 *Zoppel* in *Mock/Zoppel*, ReO – Restrukturierungsordnung Kommentar, 2022, §7 ReO para. 11.

45 See *Schumacher* in *Koller/Lovrek/Spitzer*, IO – Insolvenzordnung, 2nd ed. Verlag Österreich, 2023, §66 IO para. 41a; *Labner* in *Mock/Zoppel*, ReO – Restrukturierungsordnung Kommentar, 2022, §19 ReO para. 53 with further deliberations.

46 See *Schumacher* in *Koller/Lovrek/Spitzer*, IO – Insolvenzordnung, 2nd ed., Verlag Österreich, 2023, §66 IO paras. 43, 41a.

47 Examples taken from *Schumacher* in *Koller/Lovrek/Spitzer*, IO – Insolvenzordnung, 2nd ed. Verlag Österreich, 2023, §66 IO paras. 35–53 ("Indizien der Zahlungsunfähigkeit") with an extensive body of references.

- failure to comply with the payment of instalments,
- closure of operations.

Moreover, the Enforcement Code (Exekutionsordnung, EO) provides for a circumstance of "manifest inability to pay debts" (*Offenkundige Zahlungsunfähigkeit*, see §49a EO). This status is first and foremost relevant for the continuation of pending *enforcement* proceedings (under the EO[48]); however, the ReO refers to a similar state to shape a ground to refuse the opening of restructuring proceedings (§7(3) ReO). The circumstance of manifest inability to pay debts may act as a clue in terms of formal insolvency proceedings but does not act as a presumption or similar.[49]

e) Other means?
n.a.

Question 20: Is insolvency (inability to pay debts, overindebtedness, etc.) subject to party autonomy in the proceedings or must the court clarify them *ex officio*?

In principle, there is no scope for party autonomy regarding the opening of insolvency proceedings when the debtor has reached substantive insolvency. An important barrier to party autonomy is §70(4) IO, which provides that retracting a creditor's application does not lead to the termination of the proceedings. The court seised has therefore to examine whether the debtor is insolvent (examination *ex officio* – see on this principle on the establishment of facts §254(5) IO[50]). With regard to overindebtedness, it is possible to eliminate overindebtedness by way of a resignation of rank (§69(3) IO). This means that the respective claim does not have to be taken into account when examining a state of overindebtedness. It is subject to discussion whether the same holds true for inability to pay debts.[51]

---

48 RGBl 1896/79 as last amended by BGBl I2023/77; §49a EO was meant to facilitate a smooth transition from enforcement proceedings to insolvency proceedings if the debtor's assets turn out to be insufficient to cover all debts (in the course of enforcement proceedings); see *Deixler-Hübner* in *Deixler-Hübner*, EO, 33rd ed. 2021, §49a paras. 1 et seq.

49 See *Schumacher* in *Koller/Lovrek/Spitzer*, IO – Insolvenzordnung, 2nd ed. Verlag Österreich, 2023, §66 IO para. 41a.

50 See *Schumacher* in *Koller/Lovrek/Spitzer*, IO – Insolvenzordnung, 2nd ed. Verlag Österreich, 2023, §66 IO para. 20; more generally, *Pesendorfer* in *Koller/Lovrek/Spitzer*, IO – Insolvenzordnung, 2nd ed. Verlag Österreich, 2023, §254 IO para. 16.

51 *Schumacher* in *Koller/Lovrek/Spitzer*, IO – Insolvenzordnung, 2nd ed. Verlag Österreich, 2023, §66 IO para. 13 with further references to literature that answers the question in the affirmative.

Question 21: In an overall view, does your law distinguish "inability to pay debts" from "financial difficulties"? If so, how?

Austrian law recognises "financial difficulties" other than inability to pay debts (or overindebtedness, respectively).[52]

- Synonymously with "financial difficulties", §1(3) ReO provides for "likelihood of insolvency" (a term adopted from the Directive on Restructuring and Insolvency).
- §1 URG links reorganisation proceedings to the "need for restructuring" which is defined by §§22 et seq. URG. This status is exemplarily defined by certain figures, namely equity quota (*Eigenmittelquote*) and the (fictitious) debt repayment period (*fiktive Schuldentilgungsdauer*).
- Other relevant provisions are §36(2) GmbHG (Limited Liability Corporation Act[53]) and §83 AktG about the directors'/officers' duty to inform shareholders about the loss of half the amount of the registered capital.[54] Both duties also apply where the figures under §§23–24 URG are met (see bullet point above).
- Moreover, the Act on "equity-substituting" (EKEG, Eigenkapitalersatzgesetz[55]) defines the term "crisis". A shareholder's credit is considered equity (as opposed to debt capital).
- The annual commercial balance sheet might display negative equity (see §225(1) UGB) and give rise to concerns as to whether the entrepreneur (legal entity) might have entered the state of overindebtedness.[56]
- Finally, the auditor is obliged to point out possible financial difficulties that may be related to a current or imminent insolvency (*Redepflicht des Abschlussprüfers*, §273(2) UGB).[57]

Question 22: In an overall view, does it matter under your law whether the debtor's inability to pay debts is present or future and reversible or irreversible?

As set out above (answer to Question 14 *supra*), the inability to pay debts needs to be present, whereas a future (foreseeable) inability to pay debts represents an imminent inability to pay debts and may act as a triggering factor to initiate (voluntary) restructuring/reorganisation proceedings under the IO (or the ReO).

---

52 See *Dellinger/Oberhammer/Koller*, Insolvenzrecht, 5th ed. Manz, 2023, paras. 47 et seq.
53 RGBl 1906/58 as last amended by BGBl I 2022/186.
54 On this term and obligation see, e.g., *Dellinger* in *Konecny/Schubert*, Insolvenzgesetze, 01.09.1999, §67 KO paras. 15 et seq.
55 BGBl I 2003/92 as last amended by BGBl I 2010/58.
56 Thus OGH 6 Ob 110/00w.
57 See on the definition of "likely insolvency" under §6(1) and (2) ReO Government Bill 950 BlgNR 27. GP p. 6.

With respect to prevailing opinion, inability to pay debts is not to be assumed when the debtor can, e.g., raise credit or procure the financial means needed within a reasonable time in sufficient quantity (more on this see answer to Question 17).

Whether current inability to pay debts is reversible or not may affect the procedural outcome of insolvency proceedings. The debtor may enter into insolvency proceedings in order to restore solvency by way of a reorganisation plan (cf. *supra* Question 1).

Question 23: Would you like to add any further aspects not covered by the above questions?

No.

III. CESSATION OF PAYMENTS

Question 24: In your jurisdiction, is "cessation of payments" a legal term used either in statute or in case law? (If the answer is "no", please continue with Question 31.)

Yes, §66(2) IO.

Question 25: Is "cessation of payments" an autonomous ground to commence proceedings (triggering circumstance)? You may refer to Questions 6/7 or add additional information here.

No.

Question 26: Is "cessation of payments" a means to establish inability to pay debts? If so, by which mechanism (e.g. rebuttable presumption for inability to pay debts, cf. above Question 19(c))?

Yes, §66(2) IO provides for a (rebuttable) presumption to assess inability to pay debts (see *supra* answer to Question 19(c)).[58]

Question 27: How is "cessation of payments" defined? If it is defined in statute, please provide us here with an English translation of the relevant rule. Is this definition (if any) specified in case law? If so, how?

The cessation of payments is not defined by any statute.[59]

---

58 *Dellinger* in *Konecny/Schubert*, Insolvenzgesetze, 01.09.1999, §66 KO paras. 68 et seq., notably para. 72 (rebuttable presumption).

59 See for more details on the difficulties to define this term *Dellinger* in *Konecny/Schubert*, Insolvenzgesetze, 01.09.1999, §66 KO paras. 68 et seq.

Question 28: How is "cessation of payments" established?

There are no specific presumptions on the cessation of payments, so that the court seised with an application to open insolvency proceedings usually needs to examine *ex officio* any circumstance that indicates the cessation of payments (or the inability to pay debts, as appropriate; for some examples, see answer to Question 29 *infra*).

Question 29: Are there typical circumstances which provide circumstantial evidence that the debtor has ceased payments? If so, please list as many as possible.

There are no typical circumstances that provide circumstantial evidence for the cessation of payments. However, if the debtor has announced that he or she has ceased to pay debts, this would usually suffice to open proceedings on grounds of inability to pay debts.[60]

Question 30: Would you like to add any further aspects not covered by the above questions?

No.

IV. LIKELY/IMMINENT INABILITY TO PAY DEBTS

Question 31: Are the following terms available in your jurisdiction, either in statute or in case law? (If the answer is "no", please continue with Question 42.)

a) likely inability to pay debts
No.

b) imminent inability to pay debts
Yes (§167(2) IO; §6(2) ReO).

c) other (similar) terms
See, on similar terms, answer to Question 19(d) *supra*.

Question 32: Is "likely/imminent inability to pay debts" an autonomous ground to commence proceedings (triggering circumstance)? You may refer to Questions 6/7 or add additional information here.

Under §167(2) IO, imminent inability to pay debts is a ground to initiate insolvency proceedings. It is, however, a "voluntary" ground and insolvency

60 *Schumacher* in *Koller/Lovrek/Spitzer*, IO – Insolvenzordnung, 2nd ed. Verlag Österreich, 2023, §66 IO para. 51.

proceedings (or: restructuring proceedings under the ReO) may only be opened if the debtor chooses to file for them.[61]

Question 33: If the answer to the previous Question is "yes", who may base filing for insolvency proceedings on it: only the debtor or also creditors?

Only the debtor (§167 IO).

Question 34: How are these terms defined? If they are defined in statute, please provide us here with an English translation of the relevant rules. Is this definition (if any) specified in case law? If so, how?

a) likely inability to pay debts
n.a.

b) imminent inability to pay debts
Imminent inability to pay debts is not defined by statute. However, this is to be assumed if the debtor will prospectively not be able to pay debts that will fall due within a certain prognosis period, due to the lack of financial means at that future point in time (see for more details on the prognosis/period and the required thresholds for the establishment answers to Questions 35 et seq.).[62]

Question 35: Do the terms "likely" and "imminent" require a prognosis regarding the point in time when actual inability to pay debts will occur? If so, how long is the time period for this prognosis?

There is no statutory prognosis time period. However, according to prevailing view, the debtor will be imminently unable to pay debts if he or she will more likely than not fail to pay debts that fall due within the following 12 months.[63]

Question 36: Does your law require a specific grade of certainty that inability to pay debts will eventually occur? If so, is 50.1% ("more likely than not") enough or are there alleviated or aggravated prerequisites?

According to published opinions, the required degree of certainty (of the fact that inability to pay debts will eventually occur) is "more likely than not".[64]

---

[61] See, e.g., *Schumacher* in *Koller/Lovrek/Spitzer*, IO – Insolvenzordnung, 2nd ed. Verlag Österreich, 2023, §66 IO para. 33; *Lentsch* in *Koller/Lovrek/Spitzer*, IO – Insolvenzordnung, 2nd ed. Verlag Österreich, 2023, §167 IO para. 13.

[62] *Lentsch* in *Koller/Lovrek/Spitzer*, IO – Insolvenzordnung, 2nd ed. Verlag Österreich, 2023, §167 IO para. 14.

[63] *Lentsch* in *Koller/Lovrek/Spitzer*, IO – Insolvenzordnung, 2nd ed. Verlag Österreich, 2023, §167 IO para. 15; *Piringer*, Wahrscheinliche Insolvenz als Zugangsvoraussetzung zur ReO, SWK 2022, p. 70.

[64] *Lentsch* in *Koller/Lovrek/Spitzer*, IO – Insolvenzordnung, 2nd ed. Verlag Österreich, 2023, §167 IO para. 14.

Question 37: Regarding "debts" and "financial means", are they defined in the same way as in the context of inability to pay debts (cf. above Questions 14/15)? If not, what are the differences?

As to imminent inability to pay debts, debts and assets are also to be taken into account that fall due or will be acquired respectively during the prognosis time period.[65] Unlike with ("acute") inability to pay debts, debts that are currently not mature but will predictably fall due are to be taken into account. It is worth mentioning that minor gaps (as described in Question 16 *supra*) and grace periods (as set out in Question 17 *supra*) are not applicable to imminent inability to pay debts. This is because the prognosis time period already appropriately addresses just such developments as these.[66]

Question 38: Further to Question 37, are "debts" considered which do currently not exist or are not yet due but will foreseeably come into existence and become due during the prognosis period?

Yes. That makes for a significant difference between "imminent inability to pay debts" and "('acute') inability to pay debts".[67]

Question 39: Also further to Question 37, are "financial means" considered which do currently not exist but will foreseeably become available during the prognosis period?

Yes. A liquidity plan/analysis needs to be established in order to address the financial status of the debtor; this shall take into account financial means that will be available for the duration of the prognosis time period.[68]

Question 40: How are the terms "likely/imminent inability to pay debts" established?

The debtor needs to establish that his or her inability to pay debts will more likely than not occur within the period set out in answer to Question 35 *supra*. He or she will need to set out a financial overview that shows these financial difficulties (see Question 39 *supra*).[69]

---

65 See *Lentsch* in *Koller/Lovrek/Spitzer*, IO – Insolvenzordnung, 2nd ed. Verlag Österreich, 2023, §167 IO para. 15.

66 *Lentsch* in *Koller/Lovrek/Spitzer*, IO – Insolvenzordnung, 2nd ed. Verlag Österreich, 2023, §167 IO para. 15.

67 See *Schumacher* in *Koller/Lovrek/Spitzer*, IO – Insolvenzordnung, 2nd ed. Verlag Österreich, 2023, §66 IO para. 1.

68 *Lentsch* in *Koller/Lovrek/Spitzer*, IO – Insolvenzordnung, 2nd ed. Verlag Österreich, 2023, §167 IO para. 15.

69 *Lentsch* in *Koller/Lovrek/Spitzer*, IO – Insolvenzordnung, 2nd ed. Verlag Österreich, 2023, §167 IO para. 15 (*Liquiditätsplanung*).

Question 41: Would you like to add any further aspects not covered by the above questions?

No.

V. OVERINDEBTEDNESS

Question 42: In your jurisdiction, is "overindebtedness", or "balance sheet insolvency" respectively, a legal term used either in statute or in case law? (If the answer is "no", please continue with Question 56.)

Yes (see §67 IO).

Question 43: Is "overindebtedness" an autonomous ground to commence proceedings (triggering circumstance)? You may refer to Questions 6/7 or add additional information here.

Yes (again, see §67 IO).

Question 44: If the answer to the previous Question is "yes", is this applicable to corporate insolvencies of legal persons only or also to personal bankruptcies of natural persons?

Pursuant to §67 IO, it applies to certain legal persons (as enumerated in the wording) only. This comprises stock companies (*Aktiengesellschaften*), limited liability companies (*Gesellschaften mit beschränkter Haftung*), inheritance estates (*Verlassenschaft*) as well as partnerships with no natural person being unlimitedly liable (mostly so-called GmbH & Co KG).

Question 45: Is the term "overindebtedness" defined in statute? If so, please give the wording in English translation. Is this definition (if any) specified in case law? If so, how?

The term "overindebtedness" is not statutorily defined. It is (in essence) to be assumed if (1) the debts exceed the assets.[70] Additionally, (2) a prognosis on the prospects of "viability" needs to be negative (if the debtor is conducting business, *negative Fortbestehensprognose*; see Questions 50–52 *infra*).[71]

---

70 *Rechnerische Überschuldung* – "computational (arithmetic) overindebtedness", see *Dellinger/Oberhammer/Koller*, Insolvenzrecht, 5th ed. Manz, 2023, paras. 74, 76 et seqq.

71 The landmark case is OGH 1 Ob 655/86.

Question 46: Does your law refer to all existing debts or only to mature debts?

Unlike inability to pay debts, overindebtedness covers all existing debts (regardless of whether they are mature or not).[72] Only "real" debts (on the liabilities side of the commercial balance sheet) are to be taken into account.[73]

Question 47: Does the rank of certain debts play a role when establishing overindebtedness? In particular, is there any possibility to conclude agreements according to which certain debts shall not be taken into account (e.g. agreements on subsidiarity)?

Yes. Pursuant to §67(3) IO, certain lower-ranked debts shall not be taken into account when assessing overindebtedness: in particular, it is possible to agree on the rank after debts have accrued.[74]

Moreover, shareholder loans are considered equity for the sake of determining substantive insolvency under certain circumstances (*eigenkapitalersetzende Kredite*), notably when the credit was granted by large shareholders in times of "crisis" (as set out by §2(1) EKEG). *However*, if this shareholder did not declare his or her claim to be subordinate to other debts, it needs to be taken into account when establishing overindebtedness (!).[75]

Question 48: Which assets are taken into account when overindebtedness is established: the complete set of assets or only a selection of them?

The complete set of assets.[76]

Question 49: How are the debtor's assets valued: by referring to the liquidation value, the book value, the going concern value or in another way?

Basically, it is the liquidation value. However, it might be the case that the enterprise or parts of it may be sold as a whole rather than referring to the

---

72 *Schumacher* in *Koller/Lovrek/Spitzer*, IO – Insolvenzordnung, 2nd ed. Verlag Österreich 2023, §67 IO para. 42.

73 Thus, equity is (it goes without saying) not to be taken into account: *Dellinger* in *Konecny/Schubert*, Insolvenzgesetze, 01.09.1999, §67 KO para. 60; a more differentiating approach is necessary as to accrued liabilities: *Dellinger* in *Konecny/Schubert*, Insolvenzgesetze, 01.09.1999, §67 KO para. 62.

74 "Rangrücktrittserklärung", *Schumacher* in *Koller/Lovrek/Spitzer*, IO – Insolvenzordnung, 2nd ed. Verlag Österreich 2023, §67 IO paras. 50 et seq.

75 *Schumacher* in *Koller/Lovrek/Spitzer*, IO – Insolvenzordnung, 2nd ed. Verlag Österreich, 2023, §67 IO para. 49; OGH 9 Ob 58/11m.

76 *Schumacher* in *Koller/Lovrek/Spitzer*, IO – Insolvenzordnung, 2nd ed. Verlag Österreich, 2023, §67 IO para. 34.

isolated value of assets/items. This might alter the overall value compared to the sale of individual assets.[77]

Question 50: Is there any prognostic element, e.g. regarding the debtor's chances to continue the business?

Yes, additionally to "arithmetic" overindebtedness (as defined in answer to Question 45 *supra*), the debtor's chances to continue doing business need to be negative (*negative Fortbestehensprognose*). The prognosis is not statutorily provided but is broadly accepted[78] and can be based on the landmark case of the Supreme Court, OGH 1 Ob 655/86. Said prognosis (in accordance with its underlying rationale, see Question 51 *infra*) only applies to debtors who are doing business.[79]

Question 51: If the answer to the previous Question is "yes", what exactly is the topic of the prognosis and how is it established?

In essence, the topic of the prognosis is the debtor's ability to pay debts (or, put differently, ability to avoid inability to pay debts within the meaning of §66 IO).[80] The landmark case is OGH 1 Ob 655/86: overindebtedness not only requires the excess of debts over assets but also a negative prognosis on the ability to pay debts during the period of prognosis. The reason for this is that enterprises might generate earnings in the future in order to cover existing debts. Viable enterprises shall therefore not enter bankruptcy proceedings when they have a possible market exit.

It is to be assessed whether the debtor is financially able to continue his or her business during the ongoing as well as the ensuing financial year (see on this *infra* answer to Question 52).[81] When determining the debtor's overindebtedness, out-of-court restructuring measures can be taken into account with respect to the prognosis.[82]

---

77 *Schumacher* in *Koller/Lovrek/Spitzer*, IO – Insolvenzordnung, 2nd ed. Verlag Österreich, 2023, §67 IO para. 35.

78 See extensively *Schumacher* in *Koller/Lovrek/Spitzer*, IO – Insolvenzordnung, 2nd ed. Verlag Österreich, 2023, §67 IO paras. 4 et seq.

79 *Schumacher* in *Koller/Lovrek/Spitzer*, IO – Insolvenzordnung, 2nd ed. Verlag Österreich, 2023, §67 IO para. 4.

80 OGH 7 Ob 84/07i; 8 Ob 221/01k.

81 It is a matter of controversy whether the debtor also needs to show his or her ability to manage a (sustainable) "turn-around" or similar: *Dellinger/Oberhammer/Koller*, Insolvenzrecht, 5th ed., Manz 2023, para. 81; *Schumacher* in *Koller/Lovrek/Spitzer*, IO – Insolvenzordnung, 2nd ed., Verlag Österreich 2023, §67 IO paras. 12 et seq.

82 OGH 8 Ob 221/01k; *Schumacher* in *Koller/Lovrek/Spitzer*, IO – Insolvenzordnung, 2nd ed., Verlag Österreich, 2023, §67 IO para. 9.

Question 52: If the answer to the Question 50 is "yes", how long is the prognosis period?

Contrary to other jurisdictions, the prognosis period is not defined by statute but has evolved in case law and doctrine (see *supra* answer to Question 50 on the legal basis for the prognosis).[83] According to prevailing view,[84] the debtor needs to show the ability to avoid inability to pay debts (see §66 IO, Question 51 *supra*) for the ongoing as well as the following accounting/financial year.[85]

Question 53: How is overindebtedness established?

a) Is a formal balance sheet required?
If a debtor reckons that he or she might be in a state of overindebtedness[86] (according to jurisprudence this might be in case of negative equity displayed in the regular commercial balance sheet (see *supra* Question 21)[87]), the debtor is required to set up a formal liquidity status (*Überschuldungsstatus*; see in more detail *infra* answer to Question 53(b)).

b) Does the yearly regular commercial balance sheet have any meaning (given that it is normally based on technical values and does not display undisclosed reserves)?
It has a meaning in the first place, namely to assess whether there is imminent danger of being overindebted. It is merely a clue as to whether or not the debtor has reached formal overindebtedness. If the debts exceed the debtor's assets under regular commercial balance sheet conditions, the debtor is asked to substantiate why there is no overindebtedness within the meaning of §67 IO (§225(1) Business Code/Unternehmensgesetzbuch, UGB). This might be the case due to a positive prognosis on continuing the business or due to undisclosed reserves. However, in order to identify overindebtedness, the

83 RIS-Justiz RS0064962.

84 Although there are some controversies as to the exact duration of the prognosis period in *Schumacher* in *Koller/Lovrek/Spitzer*, IO – Insolvenzordnung, 2nd ed. Verlag Österreich, 2023, §67 IO paras. 7 et seq. in some particular cases (such as long-term loans). As *Schumacher* (ibid, paras. 11 et seq.) rightly points out, it becomes more and more difficult to realistically forecast the debtor's financial status the longer the period.

85 *Schumacher* in *Koller/Lovrek/Spitzer*, IO – Insolvenzordnung, 2nd ed. Verlag Österreich, 2023, §67 IO para. 29.

86 This may differ at the individual level, see *Dellinger* in *Konecny/Schubert*, Insolvenzgesetze, 01.09.1999, §67 KO para. 41; *Schumacher* in *Koller/Lovrek/Spitzer*, IO – Insolvenzordnung, 2nd ed. Verlag Österreich, 2023, §67 IO paras. 19 et seq. on when a debtor might be obliged to set up a financial status.

87 OGH 6 Ob 110/00w.

regular commercial balance sheet is not sufficient as the assets need to be valued according to their liquidation values as opposed to their going concern value.[88]

c) Does the law provide for a presumption? If so, under which conditions?

No, there is no statutory presumption *stricto sensu* for establishing overindebtedness (other than said clues/circumstantial evidence, see answer to Question 53(b) *supra*).

d) Other means?

No.

Question 54: Is the legal link to overindebtedness undisputed in literature or are there efforts to abolish it?

Pursuant to a minority opinion in Austria, overindebtedness should *de lege ferenda* be abolished.[89] To my knowledge, no political steps are currently being taken to turn this claim into reality. However, it is worth mentioning that during the COVID-19 pandemic (more precisely: from 1 March 2020 until 30 June 2021), overindebtedness was suspended as a mandatory ground for the opening of insolvency proceedings due to the unpredictability during acute times of crisis (see §9 2. COVID-JuBG[90]).[91] It has to be admitted that according to the figures publicly available, the significance of overindebtedness (without meeting the prerequisites for inability to pay debts under §66 IO at the same time) is very low in practical terms.[92] Moreover, critics of overindebtedness have a point when they maintain that it is difficult to assess, be it with a view to necessary opening of insolvency proceedings, or be it with respect to avoidance actions (whereby the exact point in time when the debtor became overindebted is to be established).[93]

---

88 *Dellinger* in *Konecny/Schubert*, Insolvenzgesetze, 01.09.1999, §67 KO paras. 26 et seq.

89 *Schumacher*, Das Regime der IO und die außergerichtliche Sanierung, in *Grininger/Jaufer/Schumacher*, Deutsch-österreichischer Rechts- und Praxisvergleich im Insolvenzrecht, Verlag Österreich, 2018, pp. 6 et seq., 12 et seq.

90 BGBl I 2020/24 as last amended by BGBl I 2022/224.

91 Parliamentary Bill IA 403/A 37. GP p. 47; see *Koller*, Krise als Motor der Rechtsentwicklung im Zivilprozess- und Insolvenzrecht, JBl, 2020, pp. 548 et seq.

92 *Schumacher* in *Koller/Lovrek/Spitzer*, IO – Insolvenzordnung, 2nd ed. Verlag Österreich 2023, §67 IO para. 1 with reference to *St. Mayr/Mitter/Baschinger*, Langfristiges Überleben und nachhaltige Sanierung nach Einführung des IRÄG 2010 – eine empirische Analyse gerichtlicher Sanierungen, ZIK, 2020, p. 225.

93 See, briefly, *Koller*, Krise als Motor der Rechtsentwicklung im Zivilprozess- und Insolvenzrecht, JBl, 2020, p. 548 (without, however, taking sides on the question).

Question 55: Would you like to add any further aspects not covered by the above questions?

No (but see the considerations regarding COVID legislation on overindebtedness *supra* answer to Question 54).

VI. REMAINING ISSUES

Question 56: Is there anything else you would like to share in the present context and that we should take into account?

No.

BELGIUM

Frederik De Leo

I. GENERAL

Question 1: How is insolvency (both in the context of liquidation and restructuring/reorganisation) regulated in your jurisdiction? Please give a brief overview, at least enumerating the relevant statutes.

Belgian insolvency law can be found in Book XX of the Code of Economic Law (CEL), which has been thoroughly reformed since 1 September 2023 with the implementation of the European Restructuring Directive. Belgian insolvency law is characterised by a large toolbox.

There are three main pillars: (i) detection, warning, and guidance of companies in financial difficulties, (ii) restructuring, and (iii) liquidation.

(i) Detection, warning and guidance of companies in financial difficulties

The chambers for enterprises in difficulties, i.e. specific chambers set up within the Belgian company courts, have three main roles. First, based on indicators suggesting financial difficulties (e.g. attachment notices, frequent change of the company's registered office and unpaid social security and tax debts), the chamber can summon and hear the company and, if appropriate, e.g. send the file to the public prosecutor with a view to summoning the company in bankruptcy. The company itself has access to the information collected by the chamber for the purpose of self-reflection and remediation. Second, the company itself can approach the chamber and ask the chamber to summon certain creditors in order to obtain an amicable agreement. Third, the chamber can appoint a restructuring expert to facilitate the company's recovery.

In addition, provisional measures exist. For example, at the request of any interested party or *ex officio*, the president of the company court may appoint a provisional administrator (who takes over all or part of the management of the company) when there are serious, certain, and concurring indications that the conditions for bankruptcy are met. The provisional administrator checks whether the conditions for bankruptcy are effectively met and, if appropriate, can summon the company in bankruptcy.

(ii) Restructuring

Figure 1. Out-of-court and in-court restructuring pathways

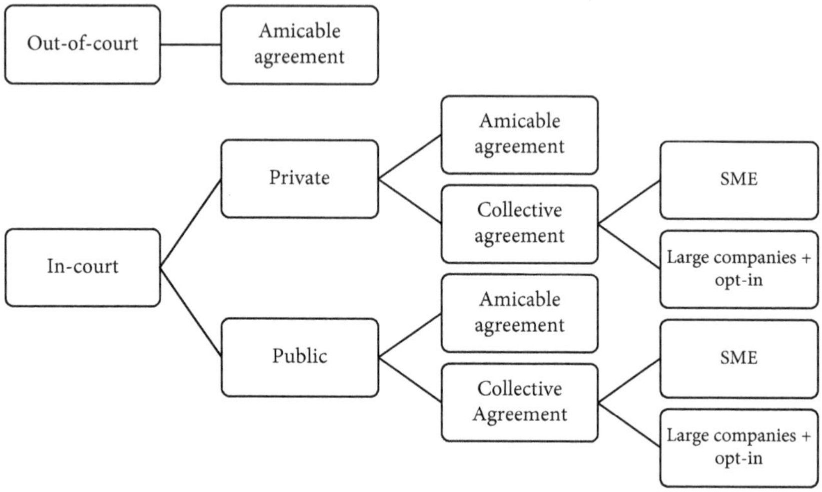

Source: Produced by the author.

First, we have the out-of-court reorganisation proceedings: a debtor can reach an amicable agreement (which may include e.g. debt reductions and/or payment deferrals) with one or more of its creditors (each creditor has to agree to the agreement to be bound by it). In principle, these proceedings are entirely out-of-court. However, any interested party can request the company court to approve the agreement with a view to obtaining an enforceable title and protection in the event of a subsequent bankruptcy procedure (the approval by the court will make it more difficult for the agreement to be challenged by a bankruptcy trustee).

Second, we have the in-court reorganisation proceedings, consisting of public variants (i.e. with publicity) and private variants (i.e. without any publicity). The public variants involve an automatic general stay of enforcement measures. The private variants involve an automatic appointment of a restructuring expert and have no automatic general stay (but the restructuring expert can request a temporary stay with regard to certain creditors).

Both the public and private variants consist of an amicable and collective agreement (which may include e.g. debt reductions and/or payment deferrals). An amicable agreement is an agreement between the debtor and one or more of its creditors (each creditor has to agree to the agreement to be bound by it). A collective agreement is an agreement between the debtor and its creditors and possibly equity holders, in which a majority binds the minority. In the public variant of the collective agreement, all creditors are involved in the proceedings (which does not mean that all creditors have to undergo e.g. debt reductions or payment deferrals). The private variant of the collective agreement may involve a limited number of creditors in the proceedings.

The collective agreement further consists of an SME scheme and a large company scheme (SMEs can voluntarily opt for the large company scheme). The large company scheme is the European Restructuring Directive regime with, for example, a best interest test, class voting and APR.[1] The SME scheme is a more simplified system where there is no voting in classes and also no need for the expensive valuations required by the best interest test and APR.

In all these restructuring proceedings, the debtor remains in possession (unless a provisional administrator is appointed to replace the board, which is only possible if the board has committed a manifest gross error, Article XX.49/1 CEL).

(iii) Liquidation

Liquidation proceedings can be divided into four proceedings: (i) transfer under judicial authority, (ii) pre-pack bankruptcy, (iii) (ordinary) bankruptcy, and (iv) dissolution and liquidation.

A transfer under judicial authority is a public auction procedure (with an automatic general stay of enforcement measures) in which a liquidation expert is appointed who solicits bids and seeks to maximise the sale proceeds (generally via a sale as a "going concern"). During these proceedings, the debtor (board/management) remains responsible for the day-to-day management (debtor-in-possession). After the sale, the transferor (often left as an empty shell) will end up in liquidation or bankruptcy. Specific to these proceedings is that the transferee can choose which employees to take over based on reasons of an economic, technical or organisational nature.

The aforementioned procedure is conceptually very similar to pre-pack bankruptcy, where a prospective receiver and prospective bankruptcy judge are appointed to prepare a bankruptcy in private (while the debtor remains in possession). When the public bankruptcy is opened (and the prospective receiver and prospective bankruptcy judge are formally appointed as receiver and bankruptcy judge), the transaction is quickly finalised.

Finally, we have normal (public) bankruptcy and liquidation proceedings, where both piecemeal liquidation and a sale as a going concern are possible (although piecemeal liquidation is more common).

---

1 The "absolute priority rule" (APR), essentially requires that a dissenting class of creditors is paid in full before any value can be distributed to a lower ranking class. The rule as adopted in the Directive allows for exceptions in specified circumstances.

Question 2: Related to paragraph 10 above of the Introduction: seen from a principle-based perspective, what justifies the opening of insolvency proceedings in your jurisdiction?

Insolvency proceedings prevent value destruction and should benefit creditors. They do so by solving common pool and anti-commons problems. Common pool problems are countered by the secrecy of private restructuring proceedings and pre-pack bankruptcy (so that not every creditor is immediately aware of the opening of the proceedings), the stay (in restructuring proceedings) and the *concursus creditorum* (in liquidation proceedings). All these techniques prevent creditors from exercising their individual enforcement rights (which individually is the most rational thing to do, but is disastrous for the collectivity of creditors), so that the company can still be sold or restructured as a going concern (so that creditors are ultimately better off than without insolvency proceedings). The anti-commons problem, for example, is countered in restructuring proceedings by allowing a consenting majority of creditors to bind a dissenting minority of creditors through the collective agreement (thereby also countering any hold-out behaviour).

Restructuring can also be seen as a sale to creditors: sometimes market conditions are so poor that creditors consider the company to be worth more than a sale to outsiders would yield and are therefore willing to undergo a debt reduction (which could be seen as a sale to creditors). In addition, restructuring is often beneficial to other stakeholders, such as employees keen to keep their jobs.

Question 3: Does your national law in the context of liquidation proceedings use one or more of the following terms (be it as a noun, be it as an adjective or adjunct) in whatever context:

a) inability to pay debts
No (but see answer to Question 8).

b) cessation of payments
Yes.

c) likely inability to pay debts
No (but see answer to Question 1 about the provisional administrator and answer to Question 8).

d) imminent inability to pay debts
No (but see answer to Question 8).

e) overindebtedness?
No.

Question 4: Are the same terms (and with the same meaning) used in the rules on preliminary/interim insolvency proceedings (e.g. concerning the application stage of the proceedings)?

Yes.

Question 5: Does your national law in the context of restructuring proceedings (as referred to above at paragraph 8 of the Introduction, i.e. both pre-insolvency and within formal insolvency proceedings) use one or more of the following terms (be it as a noun, be it as an adjective or adjunct) in whatever context:

a) inability to pay debts
No. If this criterion is met, it would probably mean that the bankruptcy conditions are met. However, this does not preclude the company from opening or continuing restructuring proceedings.

b) cessation of payments
No. If this criterion is met, it would probably mean that the bankruptcy conditions are met. However, this does not preclude the company from opening or continuing restructuring proceedings.

c) likely inability to pay debts
No (but see answer to Question 8).

d) imminent inability to pay debts
No (but see answer to Question 8).

e) overindebtedness?
No.

Question 6: Which of the terms mentioned in Questions 3 and 5 are used for defining grounds to commence proceedings (triggering circumstances)?

a) insolvency proceedings
Cessation of payments (Article XX.99 CEL).

b) restructuring proceedings
n.a. (but see answer to Question 8)

Question 7: Does the answer to Question 6 include personal bankruptcies of natural persons or only corporate insolvencies of legal entities?

Both, as long as the natural person is an enterprise. For natural persons who are not enterprises, there are separate proceedings.

Question 8: In your law, are there any other circumstances which trigger insolvency or restructuring proceedings?

Liquidation proceedings:

- A debtor meets the bankruptcy conditions if *both* (i) it is in cessation of payments in a persistent manner (reference is made to sections B (Inability to Pay Debts) and C (Cessation of Payments) of this report) *and* (ii) its credit is impaired (Article XX.99 CEL). These criteria are not defined in statute.

  If creditors are no longer willing to wait for payment and thus refuse to extend further "credit", or the company no longer obtains credit from financial institutions (or other parties), credit is said to be impaired.

  Case law has emphasised that impaired credit is very closely related to cessation of payments, as cessation of payments is a consequence of impaired credit (e.g. Cass. 2 December 1963, Pas. 1984, 346). Non-payment of debts can also impair credit due to the debtor's failure to pay creditors what is owed to them (e.g. Cass. 7 September 1992, Arr.Cass. 1991–1992, 1073). In fact, the elements that may point to impaired credit are the same as those that point to cessation of payments. For instance, the non-payment of social security contributions can be classified as a cessation of payments, but also as artificially granting oneself credit that the debtor could not obtain on the market (because its credit is impaired).

  The criterion of impaired credit is therefore regularly criticised as being redundant. The (only) situation where this criterion is still relevant today is in a voluntary liquidation: although the company may be in cessation of payments, the liquidator may still enjoy the confidence of the creditors, so that there is no impaired credit, and the bankruptcy conditions are thus not met.
- The transfer under judicial authority can be opened if "the continuity of the debtor's activities is threatened either immediately or over time", which could be considered a functional equivalent of "imminent inability to pay debts" (Article XX.45, §1 CEL and Article I.23, 29° CEL).

  Please note that the Dutch-language version of Article I.23, 29° CEL uses the term *dreigende insolventie* (which can be translated as "imminent insolvency") while the French-language version uses the term *probabilité d'insolvabilité* (which can be translated as "likelihood of insolvency"). Both terms, however, are defined the same (i.e. a situation in which the continuity of the debtor's activities is threatened either immediately or over time). Given this definition, the Dutch-language version is the better one.

Restructuring proceedings:

- Restructuring proceedings can be opened if "the continuity of the debtor's activities is threatened either immediately or over time", which could be considered a functional equivalent of "imminent inability to pay debts" (Article XX.45, §1 CEL). On the discrepancy between the Dutch- and French-language versions of the statutory text, see above.

Question 9: Which of the terms mentioned in Questions 3, 5, and 8 are used in the context of transactions avoidance law?

Cessation of payments (Articles XX.111–XX.113).

Question 10: Which of the terms addressed in Questions 3, 5, and 8 are used in the context of directors' duties?

a) shift of duties (from shareholders to creditors)
In Belgium, the shift of duties is neither regulated nor defined in case law. It is controversially discussed in literature, but no clear picture can be drawn.

b) duties to commence insolvency proceedings
The debtor is obliged to file for bankruptcy within one month of the "cessation of payments" (Article XX.102 CEL). The obligation to file for bankruptcy is suspended as soon as a restructuring procedure is opened. Intentionally late filing for bankruptcy is also criminally sanctioned (Article 489*bis*, 2° Criminal Law Code).

c) other duties (please describe)
The Belgian Code of Companies and Associations (BCCA) provides for an alarm bell procedure:

- In the SA/NV, the procedure must be activated when the net assets are reduced to less than half the share capital (Articles 7:228–7:229 BCCA).
- In the SRL/BV or SC/CV, the procedure must be activated when (i) the net assets are likely to become or have become negative (balance sheet test) *or* (ii) it is no longer certain that the company will be able to pay its debts as they fall due for at least the next 12 months (liquidity test) (Articles 5:153 and 6:119 BCCA).

The articles of association may provide for stricter conditions.

When one (or more) of those conditions is met, the directors must convene a general meeting of shareholders (within two months) to dissolve the company or ensure its continuity. If the directors propose to ensure the continuity, the agenda must also contain proposals for measures to be taken to ensure the continuity of the company. The proposals are set out in a special report. If the directors do not activate the procedure (or make mistakes so that the decision of the general meeting is null and void), the damage suffered by third parties is presumed to result from this failure to convene (which may lead to directors' liability).

In line with the alarm bell procedure, is the obligation of the directors to deliberate on the measures to be taken to safeguard the continuity of the economic activity of the company for a minimum period of 12 months when there are weighty and concurring facts that may jeopardise the continuity of the business (Article 2:52 BCCA).

Furthermore, statutory auditors who, in the performance of their duties, establish weighty and concurring facts that may jeopardise the continuity of the company's economic activity must inform the directors thereof in writing and in a comprehensive manner (Article 3:69 BCCA).

For completeness, it should be mentioned that Belgian law also contains a provision on directors' liability for wrongful trading (Article XX.227 CEL).

Question 11: Are there any other rules in the context of which the terms addressed in Questions 3, 5, and 8 are used?

In Book XX CEL, the term "cessation of payment" appears a number of times (e.g. bringing forward the date of cessation of payments, which is relevant for the bankruptcy trustee to have a lower burden of proof under fraudulent conveyance law).

We can also find this term in Article 489*bis* of the Criminal Law Code (insolvency-related crimes).

Question 12: Is the definition of (the subspecies of) insolvency identical in all legal fields or are there different definitions (e.g. different in insolvency law than in criminal law)?

It is identical.

II. INABILITY TO PAY DEBTS

Question 13: In your jurisdiction, is the term "inability to pay debts" defined in statute? If so, please give the wording in English translation. Is this definition (if any) specified in case law? If so, how?

The term "inability to pay debts" is not used autonomously in Belgian law. It is part of the criteria "cessation of payments in a persistent manner" and "impaired credit" (Article XX.99 CEL).

Question 14: Does your law refer to all debts or only to mature debts?

In principle, only mature debts.

Question 15: Which assets are taken into account when assessing the inability to pay debts: all (financial) assets or only those that are liquid, i.e. available on short notice?

All debtor's assets are taken into account to assess the debtor's inability to pay debts. Evidently, insolvency may derive from the fact that the assets are not sufficiently liquid to match the debts as they fall due.

Question 16: Is any liquidity gap (deficit between relevant financial means and relevant debts) relevant or does your law neglect minor gaps? If the latter, how is "minor" defined?

There is no statutory provision on this. Since the criteria are "cessation of payments in a persistent manner" and "impaired credit", it will usually not be a minor liquidity gap. However, the existence of one unpaid creditor may suffice to open a bankruptcy procedure.

Question 17: As far as the time aspect is concerned, does it matter whether the liquidity gap can be closed again in the short term? If so, how long is the grace period?

Yes, the criteria are "cessation of payments in a persistent manner" and "impaired credit". A temporary cessation of payments is not sufficient. The court assesses the grace period on a case-by-case basis.

Question 18: As far as the time aspect is concerned, is a debtor considered insolvent if the liquidity gap is not yet present but will occur soon? If so, how long is the prognosis period? (Note: this may also concern the difference between actual and likely/imminent inability to pay debts; cf. below Question 34).

No, if the liquidity gap is not yet present, there is no "cessation of payments".

Question 19: How is inability to pay debts established? Please communicate if there is a difference between a creditor and a debtor application or between different legal contexts.

a) Is a formal liquidity status (liquidity balance sheet) required?
There is no requirement of a "formal liquidity balance sheet". However, the *debtor* filing for bankruptcy must produce a number of financial documents, including the most recently published annual accounts, a recent balance sheet prepared in accordance with normal accounting rules (drafted in discontinuity), and a list of receivables and payables (with indication of the amount to be received or paid, as well as the due date) (Article XX.103 CEL). This information (in addition to the information collected in the context of the chambers for enterprises in difficulties) enables company courts to properly assess the company's liquidity position.

b) Is a sample of daily liquidity data (which do not amount to a proper liquidity status but show insufficient funds on different days within a certain period of time) sufficient?

In the context of bankruptcy proceedings, courts do not take into consideration daily liquidity data but do take into account the size and nature of overdue debts as well as any indications as to whether the cessation of payment is permanent.

c) Does the law provide for a rebuttable presumption? If so, under which conditions?

No.

d) Does the law provide for any technical circumstances (e.g. undisputed statutory demand, non-compliance with monetary judgments, unsuccessful enforcement proceedings, non-performance of a previous composition agreement in insolvency proceedings) the occurrence of which suffices to establish the debtor's insolvency?

No.

e) Other means?

No.

Question 20: Is insolvency (inability to pay debts, overindebtedness, etc.) subject to party autonomy in the proceedings or must the court clarify them *ex officio*?

Ex officio.

Question 21: In an overall view, does your law distinguish "inability to pay debts" from "financial difficulties"? If so, how?

"Inability to pay debts" will normally lead to cessation of payments and thus the obligation to file for bankruptcy (although this does not prevent the debtor from applying for restructuring proceedings; the obligation to file for bankruptcy is suspended as soon as a restructuring procedure is opened). "Financial difficulties" is a very broad term that applies in both liquidation and restructuring proceedings as well as in the truly preventive phase (detection, warning and guidance of companies in financial difficulties).

Question 22: In an overall view, does it matter under your law whether the debtor's inability to pay debts is present or future and reversible or irreversible?

Yes, if the debtor's inability to pay its debts is only future, then there is no cessation of payment. If the debtor's inability to pay its debts is reversible, then its credit is probably not impaired and/or the cessation of payments is not persistent. In those cases, the bankruptcy conditions are not met.

Question 23: Would you like to add any further aspects not covered by the above questions?

No.

III. CESSATION OF PAYMENTS

Question 24: In your jurisdiction, is "cessation of payments" a legal term used either in statute or in case law? (If the answer is "no", please continue with Question 31.)

Yes (Article XX.99 CEL).

Question 25: Is "cessation of payments" an autonomous ground to commence proceedings (triggering circumstance)? You may refer to Questions 6/7 or add additional information here.

A debtor (i) who is in cessation of payments in a persistent manner, and (ii) whose credit is impaired, meets the criteria to be declared bankrupt (Article XX.99 CEL). Both criteria must be met (although those criteria essentially mean the same thing, see answer to Question 8).

Question 26: Is "cessation of payments" a means to establish inability to pay debts? If so, by which mechanism (e.g. rebuttable presumption for inability to pay debts, cf. above Question 19(c))?

No, cessation of payment is the criterion and therefore not a means to establish inability to pay debts.

Question 27: How is "cessation of payments" defined? If it is defined in statute, please provide us here with an English translation of the relevant rule. Is this definition (if any) specified in case law? If so, how?

The term "cessation of payment" is not defined in statute. However, statute does clarify that the debtor must be in cessation of payments in a persistent manner (Article XX.99 CEL).

A definition that can be found in case law is the following (free translation): "the impossibility of meeting, within a reasonably short time, and with normal resources, [company] commitments that have become due" (Mons, 16 November 1988, JT 1989, 459).

Question 28: How is "cessation of payments" established?

Courts must assess all relevant circumstances which can serve as circumstantial evidence of the debtor's cessation of payments. The assessment of whether this criterion is met must be made by the court at the time of declaring the company bankrupt.

Question 29: Are there typical circumstances which provide circumstantial evidence that the debtor has ceased payments? If so, please list as many as possible.

Typical circumstances include non-payment of a substantial part of due liabilities (even if it is only one single but substantial claim); (several months of) non-payment of taxes and/or social security contributions; failure to pay or slow payment of wages and salaries; the debtor can only survive by fraudulent means (e.g. VAT fraud).

Question 30: Would you like to add any further aspects not covered by the above questions?

No.

IV. LIKELY/IMMINENT INABILITY TO PAY DEBTS

Question 31: Are the following terms available in your jurisdiction, either in statute or in case law? (If the answer is "no", please continue with Question 42.)

a) likely inability to pay debts
No (but see answer to Question 1 about the provisional administrator).

b) imminent inability to pay debts
No.

c) other (similar) terms
According to Article XX.45 CEL, restructuring proceedings and the transfer under judicial authority can be opened if the continuity of the debtor's activities is threatened either immediately or over time. This is also referred to as "*dreigende insolventie*" (Dutch-language version of Article I.23, 29° CEL, which can be translated as "imminent insolvency") or "*probabilité d'insolvabilité*" (French-language version of Article I.23, 29° CEL, which can be translated as "likelihood of insolvency"). For more details, see answer to Question 8.

Question 32: Is "likely/imminent inability to pay debts" an autonomous ground to commence proceedings (triggering circumstance)? You may refer to Questions 6/7 or add additional information here.

See answer to Question 31.

Question 33: If the answer to the previous Question is "yes", who may base filing for insolvency proceedings on it: only the debtor or also creditors?

Public reorganisation proceedings: only the debtor.

Private reorganisation proceedings: the debtor, creditors and equity holders (e.g. shareholders).

Transfer under judicial authority (a public proceeding): in principle, only the debtor. However, exceptions do exist. Such a transfer can be initiated by the public prosecutor, a creditor or anyone who has an interest in acquiring all or part of the company (even a competitor) if (i) the debtor meets the bankruptcy conditions and has not applied for a procedure of judicial reorganisation; (ii) the court rejects the application to open the reorganisation procedure, orders its early termination or cancels the reorganisation plan; (iii) the creditors do not approve the reorganisation plan; or (iv) the court refuses to approve the reorganisation plan (Article XX.84, §2 CEL).

Question 34: How are these terms defined? If they are defined in statute, please provide us here with an English translation of the relevant rules. Is this definition (if any) specified in case law? If so, how?

a) likely inability to pay debts

n.a.

b) imminent inability to pay debts

n.a.

Question 35: Do the terms "likely" and "imminent" require a prognosis regarding the point in time when actual inability to pay debts will occur? If so, how long is the time period for this prognosis?

The term "imminent insolvency" (Dutch-language version) or "likelihood of insolvency" (French-language version) (both meaning the immediate or imminent threat to the continuity of the debtor's activities) requires no such prognosis. See answer to Question 40.

Question 36: Does your law require a specific grade of certainty that inability to pay debts will eventually occur? If so, is 50.1% ("more likely than not") enough or are there alleviated or aggravated prerequisites?

No.

Question 37: Regarding "debts" and "financial means", are they defined in the same way as in the context of inability to pay debts (cf. above Questions 14/15)? If not, what are the differences?

No differences.

Question 38: Further to Question 37: Are "debts" considered which do currently not exist or are not yet due but will foreseeably come into existence and become due during the prognosis period?

Yes (although this will only be looked at very superficially, see answer to Question 40).

Question 39: Also further to Question 37: Are "financial means" considered which do currently not exist but will foreseeably become available during the prognosis period?

Yes (although this will only be looked at very superficially, see answer to Question 40).

Question 40: How are the terms "likely/imminent inability to pay debts" established?

If the request to open the restructuring proceedings or transfer under judicial authority emanates from the debtor, he shall attach to his petition an account of the events on which his request is based, showing that, in his opinion, the continuity of his activities is threatened immediately or over time (Article XX.41, §2, 1° CEL).

Courts have only marginal discretion (it is sufficient that the aforementioned condition appears to be satisfied, Article XX.46, §2 CEL) and can only refuse the opening of the proceedings in cases of abuse.

Question 41: Would you like to add any further aspects not covered by the above questions?

No.

V. OVERINDEBTEDNESS

Question 42: In your jurisdiction, is "overindebtedness", or "balance sheet insolvency" respectively, a legal term used either in statute or in case law? (If the answer is "no", please continue with Question 56.)

Overindebtedness or balance sheet insolvency is not used in Book XX CEL (insolvency code), nor is it a trigger to open insolvency proceedings. However, see answer to Question 10(c) about the alarm bell procedure.

Question 43: Is "overindebtedness" an autonomous ground to commence proceedings (triggering circumstance)? You may refer to Questions 6/7 or add additional information here.

n.a.

Question 44: If the answer to the previous Question is "yes", is this applicable to corporate insolvencies of legal persons only or also to personal bankruptcies of natural persons?

n.a.

Question 45: Is the term "overindebtedness" defined in statute? If so, please give the wording in English translation. Is this definition (if any) specified in case law? If so, how?

n.a.

Question 46: Does your law refer to all existing debts or only to mature debts?

n.a.

Question 47: Does the rank of certain debts play a role when establishing overindebtedness? In particular, is there any possibility to conclude agreements according to which certain debts shall not be taken into account (e.g. agreements on subsidiarity)?

n.a.

Question 48: Which assets are taken into account when overindebtedness is established: the complete set of assets or only a selection of them?

n.a.

Question 49: How are the debtor's assets valued: by referring to the liquidation value, the book value, the going concern value or in another way?

n.a.

Question 50: Is there any prognostic element, e.g. regarding the debtor's chances to continue the business?

n.a.

Question 51: If the answer to the previous Question is "yes", what exactly is the topic of the prognosis and how is it established?

n.a.

Question 52: If the answer to Question 50 is "yes", how long is the prognosis period?

n.a.

Question 53: How is overindebtedness established?

a) Is a formal balance sheet required?
n.a.

b) Does the yearly regular commercial balance sheet have any meaning (given that it is normally based on technical values and does not display undisclosed reserves)?
n.a.

c) Does the law provide for a presumption? If so, under which conditions?
n.a.

d) Other means?
n.a.

Question 54: Is the legal link to overindebtedness undisputed in literature or are there efforts to abolish it?

n.a.

Question 55: Would you like to add any further aspects not covered by the above questions?

No.

VI. REMAINING ISSUES

Question 56: Is there anything else you would like to share in the present context and that we should take into account?

In the context of chambers for enterprises in difficulties, the following information and data are collected for the purpose of identifying, warning and guiding companies in financial difficulties (Articles XX.21/1–XX.23 CEL):

- attachment notices,
- arrears in taxes and social security contributions,
- the financial health indicator calculated by the National Bank of Belgium,
- changes in the number of employees,
- changes in the registered office, and
- judgments in absentia, uncontested convictions and dissolution of commercial leases.

This information may indicate a debtor's imminent insolvency and the need to act quickly (Article XX.21 CEL).

BULGARIA

Hristina KIRILOVA

I. GENERAL

Question 1: How is insolvency (both in the context of liquidation and restructuring/reorganisation) regulated in your jurisdiction? Please give a brief overview, at least enumerating the relevant statutes.

The insolvency in Bulgaria is regulated by the commercial law – i.e. the Commerce Act (CA), Chapter IV "Insolvency".[1] In accordance with Article 607a CA, insolvency proceedings are initiated for a merchant/trader who is *unable to pay debts*, and/or a limited liability company, a joint stock company or a partnership limited by shares that is *unable to pay debts* and/or is *overindebted*.[2]

Namely, a merchant is insolvent if he/she is *unable to meet any due*:

1. monetary obligation arising out of, or related to a commercial transaction, including the validity, performance, non-performance, termination, invalidation or cancellation of that transaction, or the consequences from its termination; or
2. public-law obligation to the state or municipalities related to the merchant's business; or
3. obligation under a private state receivable; or
4. obligation for wages to at least one-third of his/her workers and employees, which has not been discharged for more than two months.[3]

The law introduced a rebuttable presumption of insolvency when the debtor has stopped paying (cessation of payments). The said presumption is applicable also

---

1 Published in the State Gazette (SG) 48/1991. Chapter IV "Insolvency", adopted in 1994, SG 63/1994, with last amendments published in the State Gazette (SG) No. 66/01.08.2023, effective 05.08.2023 – Art. 608, paras. 1 and 3 CA, Art. 631 CA, and Art. 760d CA.

2 Pursuant to Art. 612, para. 2 CA, insolvency proceedings for a bank and an insurer follow a different procedure, specified in a separate law. The provisions of CA apply, unless otherwise provided for in that separate law. The particularities in the special law which are relevant for banks and insurers are not included in the present answers.

3 Art. 608, para. 1 CA.

in cases when the debtor has paid, in part or in full, separate liabilities of some creditors. Insolvency is also presumed, if, under an individual enforcement proceeding (initiated by the creditor, who has filed an application for the opening of insolvency proceedings for enforcement of his/her final and effective claim), the claim remained partially or fully unpaid within six months after the debtor was served with a voluntary payment notice.

With the most recent amendments of the CA (SG 66/2023), the legislator also introduced insolvency for entrepreneurs. Pursuant to Article 760d, paragraph 1 CA, in addition to the grounds under Article 608, paragraph 1 CA, an entrepreneur is insolvent if he/she is unable to meet a due monetary obligation arising from or relating to his/her business/economic activity, craft or freelance operation.

The debtor shall not be insolvent when his/her difficulties are temporary or when he/she has sufficient assets to cover his/her debts without endangering the interests of his/her creditors. According to judicial practice (case law), the inability to pay must be permanent and objective (based on economic criteria), but not a consequence of legal obstacles or legitimate objections of the debtor (e.g. alleged invalidity of a particular transaction). It is accepted that the property relevant for determining the debtor's economic condition is that property which may quickly be sold, and not the property in general.

Bulgarian law also provides the possibility for initiation of insolvency proceedings against legal entities with registered capital – a limited liability company, a joint stock company or a partnership limited by shares – which is overindebted. A company is overindebted if its assets are not sufficient to cover its liabilities.[4]

The legal framework provides for uniform insolvency proceedings, which after the opening of the proceedings can end with restructuring, with an agreement between the debtor and all those creditors with accepted claims, or with liquidation (sale of assets).[5]

Alongside the arrangement of the insolvency/overindebtedness, the CA provides possibilities for pre-insolvency proceedings – stabilisation proceedings or merchant restructuring proceedings. Merchant restructuring proceedings (otherwise known as stabilisation proceedings) aim to avoid opening of insolvency proceedings by reaching an agreement between the merchant and

4 Art. 742, para. 1 CA.

5 The Bulgarian commercial law uses the term "liquidation" for a voluntary termination of a company which is not insolvent/overindebted. For the purposes of the insolvency, instead of "liquidation" the legislator uses the term "sale of assets". For the purposes of the national report, the term "liquidation" will be used with the meaning "sale of assets". The term "restructuring" will be used with the meaning of "rehabilitation" – namely, termination of the insolvency proceedings with adoption of a rehabilitation plan.

his/her creditors for the restructuring of his/her business, allowing the continuation of the business.[6] Stabilisation proceedings are initiated for a merchant who is not insolvent but is in imminent danger of insolvency and has possibility to continue his/her business.[7]

Question 2: Related to paragraph 10 above of the Introduction: seen from a principle-based perspective, what justifies the opening of insolvency proceedings in your jurisdiction?

The opening of insolvency proceedings is justified by the principles of equal treatment of creditors and universality, since individual enforcement proceedings are no longer acceptable when the debtor is substantively insolvent. At this stage of the debtor's financial status, collective proceedings are appropriate in the interest of equal treatment of all creditors. Other principles may also come into play, e.g. the principle of possible rehabilitation of the debtor's enterprise, or the principle of best possible satisfaction of the creditors' claims where creditors would be worse off without insolvency proceedings.

In accordance with Article 607 CA, insolvency proceedings aim to ensure fair satisfaction of creditors and an opportunity for rehabilitation of the debtor's enterprise, taking into consideration the interests of the debtor and the interest of his/her creditors and employees.

Question 3: Does your national law in the context of liquidation proceedings use one or more of the following terms (be it as a noun, be it as an adjective or adjunct) in whatever context:

a) inability to pay debts
Yes.

b) cessation of payments
Yes.

c) likely inability to pay debts
No.

d) imminent inability to pay debts
No.

e) overindebtedness?
Yes.

---

6 Art. 761, para. 1 CA.
7 Art. 762, para. 1 CA.

Question 4: Are the same terms (and with the same meaning) used in the rules on preliminary/interim insolvency proceedings (e.g. concerning the application stage of the proceedings)?

Yes.

Question 5: Does your national law in the context of restructuring proceedings (as referred to above at paragraph 8 of the Introduction, i.e. both pre-insolvency and within formal insolvency proceedings) use one or more of the following terms (be it as a noun, be it as an adjective or adjunct) in whatever context:

a) inability to pay debts
Yes, within formal insolvency proceedings.

b) cessation of payments
Yes, within formal insolvency proceedings.

c) likely inability to pay debts
No.

d) imminent inability to pay debts
Yes, but not in formal insolvency proceedings, only in stabilisation (merchant restructuring) proceedings.[8]

e) overindebtedness?
Yes, within formal insolvency proceedings.

Question 6: Which of the terms mentioned in Questions 3 and 5 are used for defining grounds to commence proceedings (triggering circumstances)?

a) insolvency proceedings
"Inability to pay debts" and "overindebtedness".

b) restructuring proceedings
"Inability to pay debts" and "overindebtedness" when restructuring is a stage of the formal insolvency proceedings following the decision for opening of the insolvency proceedings.

"Imminent inability to pay debts" when restructuring is used as a possibility to avoid the opening of insolvency proceedings (stabilisation proceedings or merchant restructuring proceedings).

Question 7: Does the answer to Question 6 include personal bankruptcies of natural persons or only corporate insolvencies of legal entities?

The answer to Question 6 *supra* includes only insolvency of legal entities (corporate insolvency) and insolvency of entrepreneurs. The Bulgarian legal

---

8 Art. 762, para. 1 CA.

framework still does not regulate insolvency for natural persons (e.g. consumers). However there is a pending project for regulation and implementation of the personal bankruptcies of natural persons.

Question 8: In your law, are there any other circumstances which trigger insolvency or restructuring proceedings?

No.

Question 9: Which of the terms mentioned in Questions 3, 5, and 8 are used in the context of transactions avoidance law?

"Inability to pay debts" and "overindebtedness".

Question 10: Which of the terms addressed in Questions 3, 5, and 8 are used in the context of directors' duties?

a) shift of duties (from shareholders to creditors)
In Bulgaria, the shift of duties is neither regulated nor defined in case law.

b) duties to commence insolvency proceedings
"Inability to pay debts" and "overindebtedness". In accordance with Article 626, paragraph 1 CA, a debtor who becomes insolvent or overindebted must request the opening of insolvency proceedings within 30 days. The same duty is assigned to the debtor's heir, the management body or his/her representatives, the liquidator of a commercial company[9] or a partner with unlimited liability, as the case may be. The authorised officer (business manager) is obliged to notify the merchant in writing of the insolvency within seven days.

Opening of insolvency proceedings due to overindebtedness can also be requested by a member of the management body of the commercial company or a liquidator.[10]

c) other duties (please describe)
Article 138, paragraph 3 CA – the managing director of a limited liability company must convene the General Meeting immediately should the losses exceed one-quarter of the capital, as well as when the net worth of the company under Article 247a, paragraph 2 CA falls below the amount of the registered capital.

---

9 This is the case when the company has started proceedings for voluntary termination (such proceedings are possible when the assets are sufficient to cover the liabilities of the company) but the liquidator has found that there are grounds to request opening of insolvency proceedings.

10 See the clarification *supra*.

Article 222, paragraph 3 CA – if the losses exceed one-half of the capital, a General Meeting of a joint stock company must be held not later than three months after establishing the losses.

Article 620a CA – in the presence of an imminent risk of insolvency and taking into account the interests of creditors, partners, shareholders and the sole owner of the trader's capital, as well as the workers and employees, the management of the trader is obliged to take all necessary actions to avoid the trader's insolvency and/or overindebtedness, as well as not to endanger the viability of the enterprise intentionally or with gross negligence.

Question 11: Are there any other rules in the context of which the terms addressed in Questions 3, 5, and 8 are used?

Yes, there are relevant provisions in the criminal and the tax law, in particular:

- Rules of the criminal law – Criminal Code, Article 227b–227f – "Crimes against creditors";
- Rules of the tax law – Tax and Social Insurance Procedure Code (TSIPC), "Responsibility of a third party" – Article 19, paragraphs 5, 6, 7 and 8 TSIPC.

Thus, the majority owners of the capital, including majority partners and shareholders, having that capacity on the day of occurrence of the obligations, who transfer in bad faith holdings or shares held by them so that they cease to be partners or shareholders, are liable for outstanding obligations for taxes and compulsory social security contributions. The liability is proportionate to their participation in the alienated part of the capital. Bad faith is presumed where the partner or shareholder was aware that the company was overindebted or unable to pay debts and the disposition was carried out before the earlier of the following two dates (the registration in the Commercial Register of the debtor's application for institution of insolvency proceedings, and the registration of the ruling of the insolvency court regarding the institution of bankruptcy proceedings with respect to the debtor). Individuals, possessing minority holdings in the capital, bear the same liability where they transfer in bad faith simultaneously or successively for a period not exceeding three months holdings or shares whose total amount constitutes a majority in the capital. This does not apply to companies whose shares are subject to public offering.

The liability above ceases when the insolvency court terminates the insolvency proceedings due to the approval of a rehabilitation plan or signing of an agreement between the debtor and those of his/her creditors with accepted claims in the insolvency proceedings.[11]

[11] An agreement under Art. 740 CA.

The individuals who have acted in hidden complicity are jointly liable with the insolvent company for the outstanding obligations for taxes and compulsory social security contributions.

The terms characterising the debtor's insolvency are always used and defined in the same sense and uniformly interpreted by the courts, no matter whether they are relevant in the context of insolvency/commercial law (and whether as a prerequisite for opening insolvency proceedings or transactions avoidance law) or in the context of criminal and tax law.

Question 12: Is the definition of (the subspecies of) insolvency identical in all legal fields or are there different definitions (e.g. different in insolvency law than in criminal law)?

There are no differences.

II. INABILITY TO PAY DEBTS

Question 13: In your jurisdiction, is the term "inability to pay debts" defined in statute? If so, please give the wording in English translation. Is this definition (if any) specified in case law? If so, how?

Inability to pay debts for merchants is defined in Article 608, paragraph 1 CA.

A merchant is insolvent is if he/she is *unable to meet any due*:

1. monetary obligation arising out of, or related to a commercial transaction, including the validity, performance, non-performance, termination, invalidation or cancellation of that transaction, or the consequences from its termination; or
2. public-law obligation to the State or municipalities related to the merchant's business; or
3. obligation under a private State receivable; or
4. obligation for wages to at least one-third of his/her workers and employees, which has not been discharged for more than two months.

Inability to pay debts for entrepreneurs is defined in Article 760d, paragraph 1 CA (introduced with the last amendments of the CA (SG 66/01.08.2023, effective 05.08.2023). Pursuant to Article 760d, paragraph 1 CA, in addition to the grounds under Article 608, paragraph 1 CA, an entrepreneur is insolvent if *unable to meet due* monetary obligation arising from or relating to his/her business/economic activity, craft or freelance operation.

Question 14: Does your law refer to all debts or only to mature debts?

"Inability to pay debts" is generally recognised as an objective financial status of the debtor at the relevant point in time. It compares the debtor's ability to pay his/her short-term liabilities (both mature debts and debts which will become due within one year) with his/her short-term assets on the balance sheet. It should be clarified that when assessing the financial status of the debtor, his/her obligations to all creditors are taken into consideration, not just obligations to the creditors who may request the opening of the insolvency proceedings. Inability to pay is assessed based on economic analysis, prepared by an expert, nominated by the court (most important are the liquidity ratios). The liquidity ratios evaluate whether, at a given date, short-term assets (current and those which will be acquired in the next 12 months) are sufficient to cover maturing liabilities and those due within the next 12 months. Usually, the relevant point in time is the date of the annual balance sheet (annual financial statement) (31 December of the relevant year) but in some cases the court may require an interim balance sheet to be prepared (Article 628, paragraph 1, item 1 CA).

Question 15: Which assets are taken into account when assessing the inability to pay debts: all (financial) assets or only those that are liquid, i.e. available on short notice?

When assessing the inability to pay debts, the expert (appointed by the court) takes into account only the liquid assets (assets that can usually be sold quickly). That includes primarily cash, money in regular bank accounts, shareholdings, receivables with a maturity of up to one year and inventories. However, the judge is not obliged to accept the records in the balance sheet, but he/she should consider the particularities of the case. For example, some receivables may be listed in the balance sheet, but they may be fictitious or uncertain. Inventory, on the other hand, may be stagnant and difficult to sell.

Question 16: Is any liquidity gap (deficit between relevant financial means and relevant debts) relevant or does your law neglect minor gaps? If the latter, how is "minor" defined?

No. Bulgarian law does not establish a liquidity gap. It takes a more general approach, for example requiring the illiquidity to be permanent or persistent (not being temporary or short-term, respectively). Pursuant to Article 631 CA, the court rejects the application when it finds that the debtor's difficulties are temporary or that she/he has assets sufficient to cover the obligations without jeopardising the interests of his/her creditors.

Question 17: As far as the time aspect is concerned, does it matter whether the liquidity gap can be closed again in the short term? If so, how long is the grace period?

n.a.

Question 18: As far as the time aspect is concerned, is a debtor considered insolvent if the liquidity gap is not yet present but will occur soon? If so, how long is the prognosis period? (Note: this may also concern the difference between actual and likely/imminent inability to pay debts; cf. below Question 34).

n.a.

Question 19: How is inability to pay debts established? Please communicate if there is a difference between a creditor and a debtor application or between different legal contexts.

All possibilities referred to *infra* can be used by debtors, creditors under commercial transactions, the National Revenue Agency for undischarged public-law obligations to the State or municipalities related to the merchant's business or obligations under a private State receivable and the Executive Agency "General Labour Inspectorate"[12] and creditors with undischarged monetary obligations arising from or relating to debtor's business/economic activity, craft or freelance operation.[13] However, creditors and third parties will typically not be able to draw up a liquidity balance sheet or to present daily liquidity data, since they do not have the necessary information. Hence, they will normally refer to the balance sheet published in the Commercial Register and register of non-profit legal entities which indicates debtor's inability to pay mature debts and/or his/her cessation of payments or request the insolvency court to collect the relevant data *ex officio*.

a) Is a formal liquidity status (liquidity balance sheet) required?
The debtor/third parties may request the insolvency court to collect such balance sheets *ex officio* or may refer to the balance sheets announced by the debtor in the Commercial Register and register of non-profit legal entities.

The debtor is also obliged to present, together with his/her application for opening of the insolvency proceedings:

1. a copy of the last annual financial report certified by a registered auditor together with the auditor's report and balance sheet as of the date of submission of the application, if the law provides for their preparation;
2. an inventory and assessment of assets and liabilities as of the date of submission of the application;

---

12 Art. 625 CA together with Art. 608, para. 1 CA.
13 Art. 760d, para. 1 CA.

3. lists of his or her creditors and debtors, indicating the addresses, type, amount, maturity and security of the claims;
4. an inventory of personal property and the property of the marital property community – if the debtor is a sole trader and an unlimitedly liable partner.[14]

b) Is a sample of daily liquidity data (which do not amount to a proper liquidity status but show insufficient funds on different days within a certain period of time) sufficient?
No.

c) Does the law provide for a rebuttable presumption? If so, under which conditions?
Yes. According to Article 608, paragraph 3 CA, inability to pay debts is rebuttably presumed where the debtor has ceased payments. This is applicable also in cases when the debtor has paid, in part or in full, some receivables of certain creditors.

d) Does the law provide for any technical circumstances (e.g. undisputed statutory demand, non-compliance with monetary judgments, unsuccessful enforcement proceedings, non-performance of a previous composition agreement in insolvency proceedings) the occurrence of which suffices to establish the debtor's insolvency?
Yes. In accordance with Article 608, paragraph 2 CA, the trader is assumed unable to fulfil an obligation under paragraph 1 if he/she has not presented for publication in the Commercial Register and register of non-profit legal entities his/her annual financial statements for the last three years prior to the submission of the application for the opening of insolvency proceedings.[15]

In accordance with Article 608, paragraph 4 CA, insolvency is also presumed, if, under an individual enforcement proceeding (initiated by the petitioning creditor) for enforcement of his/her final and effective court's order, the debt has remained partially or fully unpaid within six months after receiving a voluntary payment notice.

e) Other means?
None.

Question 20: Is insolvency (inability to pay debts, overindebtedness, etc.) subject to party autonomy in the proceedings or must the court clarify them *ex officio*?

The inability to pay debts/overindebted status of the debtor must be indicated with the application for opening of the insolvency proceedings. According to

[14] Art. 628, para. 1 CA.
[15] This presumption is not applicable for entrepreneurs – Art. 760d, para. 3 CA.

Article 628, paragraph 2 CA, a creditor or the Executive Agency "General Labour Inspectorate" presents, along with the application, written evidence and indicates other proof of the debtor's insolvency. According to Article 628, paragraph 4 CA, with his/her application, the debtor indicates the initial date of insolvency, or the initial date of overindebtedness, respectively. However, the court may request and collect evidence for inability to pay debts/overindebtedness of the debtor, and define the initial date of that statement *ex officio*.[16]

Question 21: In an overall view, does your law distinguish "inability to pay debts" from "financial difficulties"? If so, how?

"Inability to pay debts" is used by the legislator as a prerequisite for the opening of insolvency proceedings.[17] However, "difficulties, meaning financial difficulties" is used as a reason to refuse opening of the proceedings.[18]

Question 22: In an overall view, does it matter under your law whether the debtor's inability to pay debts is present or future and reversible or irreversible?

The debtor's inability to pay debts must be present. The law does not provide for the court to assess future insolvency. The legislator does not use the terms "reversible" and "irreversible". However, the inability to pay debts will be reversible if the court concludes that the debtor's difficulties in paying his/her debts are temporary (see answer to Question 21 *supra*).

Question 23: Would you like to add any further aspects not covered by the above questions?

No.

III. CESSATION OF PAYMENTS

Question 24: In your jurisdiction, is "cessation of payments" a legal term used either in statute or in case law? (If the answer is "no", please continue with Question 31.)

Yes (Article 608, paragraph 3 CA).

---

16 Art. 621a, para. 1, item 1 CA – "the court may, of its own motion, establish facts and collect evidence relevant to its decisions and determinations".
Interpretative Decision 1/2017, Supreme Court of Cassation of the Republic of Bulgaria, General Assembly of Chamber of Commerce – "the bankruptcy court may at any time *ex officio* collect evidence regarding the solvency of the debtor".

17 Art. 608, para. 1 CA, Art. 760d, para. 1 CA.

18 Art. 631 CA – the debtor is not insolvent when his/her difficulties are temporary or when he/she has sufficient assets to cover his/her debts without endangering the interests of his/her creditors.

Question 25: Is "cessation of payments" an autonomous ground to commence proceedings (triggering circumstance)? You may refer to Questions 6/7 or add additional information here.

No (see answer to next question).

Question 26: Is "cessation of payments" a means to establish inability to pay debts? If so, by which mechanism (e.g. rebuttable presumption for inability to pay debts, cf. above Question 19(c))?

According to Article 608, paragraph 3 CA, cessation of payments creates a statutory rebuttable presumption of the debtor's inability to pay debts (see *supra* at Question 19(c)).

Question 27: How is "cessation of payments" defined? If it is defined in statute, please provide us here with an English translation of the relevant rule. Is this definition (if any) specified in case law? If so, how?

There is no statutory definition of cessation of payments. Whether this is the case depends on a comprehensive evaluation of all relevant circumstances (see answers to Questions 28, 29 *infra*).

Question 28: How is "cessation of payments" established?

It is not established in statute. Due to judicial practice the insolvency court must assess all relevant circumstances in that regard.

Question 29: Are there typical circumstances which provide circumstantial evidence that the debtor has ceased payments? If so, please list as many as possible.

According to case law, typical circumstances may include:

- pressure by creditors through individual enforcement;
- non-payment of a substantial part of due liabilities even if it consists of only one single but substantial claim);
- putting off payment of a substantial amount of arrears for as long as possible (not: merely delaying payments);
- strategic partial payments (to the most pressing creditors only);
- slow payment/non-payment of wages and salaries;
- subsequent conclusion of instalment payment agreements that are not customary for the business and/or non-compliance with such instalment payment agreements;
- (several months of) non-payment of tax and social security contributions.

Question 30: Would you like to add any further aspects not covered by the above questions?

No.

IV. LIKELY/IMMINENT INABILITY TO PAY DEBTS

Question 31: Are the following terms available in your jurisdiction, either in statute or in case law? (If the answer is "no", please continue with Question 42.)

a) likely inability to pay debts
No.

b) imminent inability to pay debts
Yes, Bulgarian law recognises such term (Article 762, paragraph 1 CA). However, it is not a ground for the opening of insolvency proceedings but only for the opening of merchant restructuring proceedings (stabilisation proceedings).

c) other (similar) terms
No.

Question 32: Is "likely/imminent inability to pay debts" an autonomous ground to commence proceedings (triggering circumstance)? You may refer to Questions 6/7 or add additional information here.

The imminent inability to pay debts is an autonomous ground to request stabilisation proceedings.[19] It is not a ground to commence insolvency proceedings.

Question 33: If the answer to the previous Question is "yes", who may base filing for insolvency proceedings on it: only the debtor or also creditors?

Unlike the opening of insolvency proceedings, the opening of stabilisation proceedings can only be requested by the trader (the debtor) (Article 769, paragraph 1 CA).

Question 34: How are these terms defined? If they are defined in statute, please provide us here with an English translation of the relevant rules. Is this definition (if any) specified in case law? If so, how?

a) likely inability to pay debts
n.a.

19 Art. 762, para. 2 CA together with Art. 761, para. 1 CA.

b) imminent inability to pay debts

An immediate risk of insolvency (inability to pay debts) is present when the merchant, in view of the upcoming maturities of his/her monetary obligations in the next 12 months from the submission of the application for stabilisation, will find himself/herself unable to fulfil due monetary obligations or will cease payments (Article 762, paragraph 2 CA).

Question 35: Do the terms "likely" and "imminent" require a prognosis regarding the point in time when actual inability to pay debts will occur? If so, how long is the time period for this prognosis?

Yes. The relevant period is 12 months following the submission of the application for opening of stabilisation proceedings (see answer to Question 34 *supra*).

Question 36: Does your law require a specific grade of certainty that inability to pay debts will eventually occur? If so, is 50.1% ("more likely than not") enough or are there alleviated or aggravated prerequisites?

No.

Question 37: Regarding "debts" and "financial means", are they defined in the same way as in the context of inability to pay debts (cf. above Questions 14/15)? If not, what are the differences?

No differences.

Question 38: Further to Question 37: Are "debts" considered which do currently not exist or are not yet due but will foreseeably come into existence and become due during the prognosis period?

"Debts" means monetary obligations which will become due in the next 12 months from the submission of the application for stabilisation.

Question 39: Also further to Question 37: Are "financial means" considered which do currently not exist but will foreseeably become available during the prognosis period?

This is not an issue specifically addressed in statute for stabilisation proceedings.

Question 40: How are the terms "likely/imminent inability to pay debts" established?

There are no specific methods for establishing imminent inability to pay debts.

Pursuant to Article 770, paragraph 1 CA, when filing for the opening of stabilisation proceedings on this ground the debtor is obliged to present a stabilisation plan and to disclose the relevant information thereto.

The court may request additional evidence,[20] appoint an auditor,[21] and/or appoint an expert to clarify circumstances relevant to the proposed stabilisation plan for which special knowledge is required.[22]

Question 41: Would you like to add any further aspects not covered by the above questions?

No.

V. OVERINDEBTEDNESS

Question 42: In your jurisdiction, is "overindebtedness", or "balance sheet insolvency" respectively, a legal term used either in statute or in case law? (If the answer is "no", please continue with Question 56.)

Yes (Article 742, paragraph 1 CA together with Article 607a, paragraph 2 CA). It is a ground for the opening of insolvency proceedings, applicable only for legal entities with registered capital – a limited liability company, a joint stock company or a partnership limited by shares.

Question 43: Is "overindebtedness" an autonomous ground to commence proceedings (triggering circumstance)? You may refer to Questions 6/7 or add additional information here.

Yes (see answer to Question 42 *supra*).

Question 44: If the answer to the previous Question is "yes", is this applicable to corporate insolvencies of legal persons only or also to personal bankruptcies of natural persons?

It is applicable only to legal entities with registered capital (see answer to Question 42 *supra*).

Question 45: Is the term "overindebtedness" defined in statute? If so, please give the wording in English translation. Is this definition (if any) specified in case law? If so, how?

The term "overindebtedness" is defined in statute (Article 742, paragraph 1 CA) – a company is overindebted if its assets are not sufficient to cover its liabilities.

---

20 Art. 771, para. 4 CA.
21 Art. 784, para. 1 CA.
22 Art. 785, para. 1 CA.

Question 46: Does your law refer to all existing debts or only to mature debts?

To all existing debts.

Question 47: Does the rank of certain debts play a role when establishing overindebtedness? In particular, is there any possibility to conclude agreements according to which certain debts shall not be taken into account (e.g. agreements on subsidiarity)?

No.

Question 48: Which assets are taken into account when overindebtedness is established: the complete set of assets or only a selection of them?

The complete set of assets.

Question 49: How are the debtor's assets valued: by referring to the liquidation value, the book value, the going concern value or in another way?

Actually it is not clarified by law but in most cases the overindebtedness is established by a formal balance sheet. However, it has been argued in theory and in some cases that evaluation should refer to the real rather than the book value of the assets. The real value is mostly identified with the liquidation value – the value at which the assets will be sold when the business is wound up. The purpose is to determine whether, in the event of liquidation, the entire estate will be sufficient to satisfy creditors. The downside of this theory is that when bankruptcy proceedings are opened due to overindebtedness, liquidation does not necessarily have to take place because the proceedings can alternatively end up with the adoption of a recovery plan or an agreement between all those creditors with accepted claims and the debtor.

Question 50: Is there any prognostic element, e.g. regarding the debtor's chances to continue the business?

No. The formal approach adopted by the Bulgarian legislator (excess of liabilities over assets) does not take into consideration the potential viability of the company.

Question 51: If the answer to the previous Question is "yes", what exactly is the topic of the prognosis and how is it established?

n.a.

Question 52: If the answer to Question 50 is "yes", how long is the prognosis period?

n.a.

Question 53: How is overindebtedness established?

a) Is a formal balance sheet required?
Yes, a formal balance sheet is required. Such formal balance sheet is prepared by an expert nominated by the insolvency court at the stage of considering the application for the opening of insolvency proceedings. A formal balance sheet may also be drafted and presented by the debtor, but it should be checked and verified by a court expert.

b) Does the yearly regular commercial balance sheet have any meaning (given that it is normally based on technical values and does not display undisclosed reserves)?
Yes, the regular commercial balance sheet is the starting point, but the judge is not bound to accept the records in the balance sheet. The records in the balance sheet should be examined and verified by a court expert. The judge may also request preparation of a special overindebtedness balance sheet. In particular, this will be the case when the overindebtedness has occurred in the middle rather than the end of the calendar year.

c) Does the law provide for a presumption? If so, under which conditions?
No.

d) Other means?
No.

Question 54: Is the legal link to overindebtedness undisputed in literature or are there efforts to abolish it?

Overindebtedness is not disputable as a ground for opening of the insolvency proceedings. However, it is disputable what the content of overindebtedness should be. Prior to the recent legislative amendments,[23] overindebtedness was present if the company's assets were not sufficient to cover its monetary obligations. With the latest amendments, all the obligations of the company are now relevant. Despite the amendments some weakness remains, namely, it does not address the method to be used to evaluate the debtor's assets and the formal approach adopted by the Bulgarian legislator (excess of liabilities over assets) does not take into consideration the potential viability of the company.

[23] SG 66/01.08.2023, effective 05.08.2023.

Question 55: Would you like to add any further aspects not covered by the above questions?

No.

VI. REMAINING ISSUES

Question 56: Is there anything else you would like to share in the present context and that we should take into account?

No.

CROATIA

Jasnica GARAŠIĆ

I. GENERAL

Question 1: How is insolvency (both in the context of liquidation and restructuring/reorganisation) regulated in your jurisdiction? Please give a brief overview, at least enumerating the relevant statutes.

The basic legal source of insolvency law in Croatia is the Bankruptcy Act (Stečajni zakon, SZ).[1] It regulates pre-bankruptcy proceedings (Articles 1–20, 21–74a SZ) as well as uniform bankruptcy proceedings (Articles 1–20, 75–446 SZ). Pre-bankruptcy proceedings are restructuring proceedings, within which the rules of the EU Directive on restructuring and insolvency are implemented. Uniform bankruptcy proceedings can be liquidation proceedings or restructuring proceedings (including a transferring restructuring of the company – in German a so-called *übertragende Sanierung*) depending on the circumstances of the concrete case. Pre-bankruptcy proceedings are debtor-in-possession proceedings. Bankruptcy proceedings can be debtor-in-possession proceedings, especially if the bankruptcy proceedings in the case at hand are restructuring proceedings. Creditors at the creditors' meeting decide whether the specific bankruptcy proceeding will be liquidation or restructuring proceedings. In essence, Croatian bankruptcy proceedings are insolvency proceedings, but the Croatian legislator did not want to change the name of these proceedings for no reason other than established tradition. An official English translation of the Croatian Bankruptcy Act is not available.

The Consumer Bankruptcy Act (Zakon o stečaju potrošača, ZSP)[2] contains special rules for bankruptcy proceedings against the insolvent consumer's assets. Unfortunately, an official English translation of this Act is also not available.

The Act on Procedure of Extraordinary Management in Companies of Systemic Importance for the Republic of Croatia (Zakon o postupku izvanredne

---

1 Stečajni zakon, Official Gazette "*Narodne novine*" nos. 2015/71, 2017/104, 2022/36, 2024/27, hereinafter referred to as SZ.

2 Zakon o stečaju potrošača, Official Gazette "*Narodne novine*" nos. 2015/100, 2018/67, 2022/36, hereinafter referred to as SZP.

uprave u trgovačkim društvima od sistemskog značaja za Republiku Hrvatsku, ZPIUTD)[3] provides for special proceedings in the case of insolvency of companies that impact the entire economic, social, and financial stability of the Republic of Croatia. This Act has been applied only once, in the case of the Agrokor group of companies. An official English translation of this Act does not exist.

There are also special statutes that regulate proceedings in the case of insolvency of credit institutions, credit unions, financial institutions, insurance and reinsurance companies, etc.

Question 2: Related to paragraph 10 above of the Introduction: seen from a principle-based perspective, what justifies the opening of insolvency proceedings in your jurisdiction?

In the case of the inability of the debtor to pay its obligations as they become due, it is important to protect the equal treatment of all the debtor's creditors, which can only be achieved by the opening of bankruptcy proceedings. Sudden unforeseen events in the market may cause insolvency or imminent insolvency of the debtor. The opening of bankruptcy proceedings in such a case may help the debtor preserve and continue the business using a restructuring plan and it may help the debtor's creditors settle for a higher amount than would be obtained without the restructuring procedure. By means of a restructuring plan workplaces may be preserved, so that restructuring proceedings may have also a social component – protection of the workers/employees.

Question 3: Does your national law in the context of liquidation proceedings use one or more of the following terms (be it as a noun, be it as an adjective or adjunct) in whatever context:

a) inability to pay debts
Yes, in Article 5(2) and Article 6 SZ.

b) cessation of payments
Not directly in the definition of the inability to pay debts. But see the explanation of the presumption of inability to pay debts in the answer to Question 13. We can also mention the following rules. According to Article 126(1) the court will not appoint an expert to examine the debtor's economic and financial position if it establishes that the requirements for the opening of bankruptcy proceedings have been met without a prior examination of the debtor's ability to pay debts or overindebtedness, particularly when the debtor's inability to pay

[3] Zakon o postupku izvanredne uprave u trgovačkim društvima od sistemskog značaja za Republiku Hrvatsku, Official Gazette "*Narodne novine*" no. 2017/32, hereinafter referred to as ZPIUTD.

debts can be established beyond doubt from the circumstance that the debtor has ceased payments. In particular, the circumstance that the debtor has ceased its payments can be established from the report from legal entities performing the payment operations for the debtor (Article 126(2) SZ).

c) likely inability to pay debts
No.

d) imminent inability to pay debts
Yes, in Article 5(3)–(4) in connection with Article 4 SZ. The literal translation of this ground for the opening of bankruptcy and pre-bankruptcy proceedings in Croatian law is "threatening inability to pay" debts.

e) overindebtedness?
Yes, in Article 5(2) and Article 7 SZ.

Question 4: Are the same terms (and with the same meaning) used in the rules on preliminary/interim insolvency proceedings (e.g. concerning the application stage of the proceedings)?

Yes.

Question 5: Does your national law in the context of restructuring proceedings (as referred to above at paragraph 8 of the Introduction, i.e. both pre-insolvency and within formal insolvency proceedings) use one or more of the following terms (be it as a noun, be it as an adjective or adjunct) in whatever context:

a) inability to pay debts
Yes, in Article 5(2) and Article 6 SZ for restructuring within bankruptcy proceedings. Also in Article 5 SZP for consumer bankruptcy as well as in Article 4(1) ZPIUTD in connection with Article 5(2) and Article 6 SZ for companies of systemic importance for the Republic of Croatia.

b) cessation of payments
See the answer to Question 3(b) for restructuring within bankruptcy proceedings.

c) likely inability to pay debts
According to Article 20.a SZ the company's directors or management are required to take into account, where there is a likelihood of inability to pay:

1. the interests of creditors, equity-holders and other persons with a special interest in accordance with Article 232 SZ;
2. the need to take measures to avoid inability to pay;
3. the need to avoid deliberate or grossly negligent conduct that threatens the viability of the business.

d) imminent inability to pay debts
Yes, in Article 5(3)–(4) in connection with Article 4 SZ for restructuring within bankruptcy proceedings and in Article 4 SZ for restructuring within pre-bankruptcy proceedings, as well as in Article 4(1) ZPIUTD in connection with Article 5(3)–(4) SZ for companies of systemic importance for the Republic of Croatia.

Imminent inability to pay debts is not a bankruptcy ground for the opening of consumer bankruptcy proceedings.

e) overindebtedness?
Yes, in Article 5(2) and Article 7 SZ for restructuring within bankruptcy proceedings as well as in Article 4(1) ZPIUTD in connection with Article 5(2) and Article 7 SZ for companies of systemic importance for the Republic of Croatia.

Overindebtedness is not a bankruptcy ground for the opening of consumer bankruptcy proceedings.

Question 6: Which of the terms mentioned in Questions 3 and 5 are used for defining grounds to commence proceedings (triggering circumstances)?

a) insolvency proceedings

- "inability to pay debts" (Article 5(2) and Article 6 SZ);
- "imminent inability to pay debts" (Article 5(3)–(4) in connection with Article 4 SZ);
- "overindebtedness" (Article 5(2) and Article 7 SZ).

b) restructuring proceedings
Restructuring within bankruptcy proceedings:

- "inability to pay debts" (Article 5(2) and Article 6 SZ);
- "imminent inability to pay debts" (Article 5(3–4) in connection with Article 4 SZ);
- "overindebtedness" (Article 5(2) and Article 7 SZ).

Restructuring within pre-bankruptcy proceedings:

- "imminent inability to pay debts" (Article 4 SZ).

Restructuring within proceedings of extraordinary management in companies of systemic importance for the Republic of Croatia:

- "inability to pay debts" (Article 4(1) ZPIUTD in connection with Article 5(2) and Article 6 SZ);

- "imminent inability to pay debts" (Article 4(1) in connection with Article 5(3)–(4) in connection with Article 4 SZ);
- "overindebtedness" (Article 4(1) ZPIUTD in connection with Article 5(2) and Article 7 SZ).

Consumer bankruptcy proceedings:

- "inability to pay debts" (Article 5 ZSP).

Question 7: Does the answer to Question 6 include personal bankruptcies of natural persons or only corporate insolvencies of legal entities?

Both. However, imminent inability to pay debts and overindebtedness are not grounds on which to open consumer bankruptcy proceedings. The only ground for the opening of consumer bankruptcy proceedings is inability to pay debts (Article 5 ZSP).

Question 8: In your law, are there any other circumstances which trigger insolvency or restructuring proceedings?

No.

Question 9: Which of the terms mentioned in Questions 3, 5, and 8 are used in the context of transactions avoidance law?

Inability to pay debts (Articles 199–202 SZ).

Question 10: Which of the terms addressed in Questions 3, 5, and 8 are used in the context of directors' duties?

a) shift of duties (from shareholders to creditors)
According to Article 20.a(1) SZ, the company's directors or management are required to take into account the interests of creditors, equity-holders and other stakeholders, where there is a likelihood of inability to pay.

b) duties to commence insolvency proceedings
Article 110(2) SZ regulates the directors' duty to initiate bankruptcy proceedings without delay, at the latest 21 days from the date of "occurrence of a bankruptcy ground". Such imprecise wording of this rule would theoretically include inability to pay debts, imminent inability to pay debts and overindebtedness. However, considering that the debtor, according to Article 5(3) SZ in the case of its imminent inability to pay its debts, only "may" apply for bankruptcy proceedings and does not have to do it, we should conclude that the directors' duty to initiate bankruptcy proceedings does not exist in the case of the debtor's imminent inability to pay its debts.

c) other duties (please describe)
According to Article 20.a(2) SZ the company's directors or management are required to take into account, where there is a likelihood of inability to pay, the need to take measures to avoid inability to pay. They are also required to take into account, where there is a likelihood of inability to pay, the need to avoid deliberate or grossly negligent conduct that threatens the viability of the business (Article 20.a(3) SZ).

Question 11: Are there any other rules in the context of which the terms addressed in Questions 3, 5, and 8 are used?

The Croatian Company Act (Zakon o trgovačkim društvima, ZTD)[4] foresees in Article 626 the criminal liability of the directors of a company and some other persons if they have breached their duty to initiate bankruptcy proceedings, in the case of losses, inability to pay debts, and overindebtedness of a company.

Also, some of these terms are relevant in criminal law, regulated by the Croatian Criminal Act (Kazneni zakon, KZ):[5]

- the criminal offence of causing bankruptcy (Article 249 KZ): "inability to pay debts", "overindebtedness";
- the criminal offence of favouring a creditor (Article 250 KZ): "inability to pay debts".

There is also a criminal offence of receiving and giving bribes in the course of bankruptcy proceedings (Article 251 KZ), which does not address these terms, because bankruptcy proceedings have already been opened at the moment of the committing this felony.

The above-mentioned terms should be interpreted uniformly by the courts in all kinds of proceedings.

Question 12: Is the definition of (the subspecies of) insolvency identical in all legal fields or are there different definitions (e.g. different in insolvency law than in criminal law)?

Insolvency should be interpreted uniformly by the courts in all legal fields, i.e. in all kinds of proceedings.

4 Zakon o trgovačkim društvima, Official Gazette "*Narodne novine*" no. 1993/111, last amendment "*Narodne novine*" no. 2023/130, hereinafter referred to as ZTD.

5 Kazneni zakon, Official Gazette "*Narodne novine*" no. 2011/125, last amendment "*Narodne novine*" no. 2024/36, hereinafter referred to as KZ.

II. INABILITY TO PAY DEBTS

Question 13: In your jurisdiction, is the term "inability to pay debts" defined in statute? If so, please give the wording in English translation. Is this definition (if any) specified in case law? If so, how?

Yes, it is defined in statute. According to Article 6(1) sentence 1 SZ, an inability to pay debts exists if the debtor is not able to pay its mature monetary obligations on a more permanent basis. The same statute in Article 6(1) sentence 2 also explicitly states that the fact that the debtor has paid or can satisfy the claims of some creditors, in full or partly, does not in itself mean that the debtor is solvent. Thus, the debtor has to be able to satisfy the claims of *all* its creditors as these claims become due.

Croatian law contains a legal presumption of inability to pay debts. According to Article 6(2) SZ, the debtor shall be considered unable to pay:

- if in the Registry of the order of grounds for payment kept by the Financial Agency, the debtor has one or more registered non-executed grounds for payment in the period exceeding 60 days, on the basis of which payment should have been collected from any of the debtor's accounts, without any further consent of the debtor;
- if the debtor failed to pay three consecutive months' salary that the employee is entitled to according to a contract of employment, the ordinance on employment, a collective bargaining contract, or a special regulation, or according to any other act regulating the obligations of the employer towards the employee.

Here are some explanations of Croatian enforcement law to understand this legal presumption in two forms contained in the Croatian Bankruptcy Act.

The Financial Agency (FINA) is the leading Croatian provider of financial and electronic services. Although it is state-owned, FINA operates on free market principles. Its position and competencies are primarily regulated by the Law on Financial Agency (Zakon o Financijskoj agenciji, ZFA),[6] but also by some other legislative acts, which entrust FINA with certain authorities. According to the Act on Execution of Enforcement on Monetary Assets/Funds (Zakon o provedbi ovrhe na novčanim sredstvima, ZPONS)[7] the Financial Agency is entitled to execute enforcement against all bank accounts of a debtor (see Articles 2 and 4 ZPONS).

---

6 Zakon o Financijskoj agenciji, Official Gazette "*Narodne novine*" nos. 117/01, 60/04, 42/05.

7 Zakon o provedbi ovrhe na novčanim sredstvima, Official Gazette "*Narodne novine*" no. 2018/68, last amendment "*Narodne novine*" no. 2020/47, hereinafter referred to as ZPONS.

According to Article 204(1) sentence 1 of the Croatian Enforcement Act (Ovršni zakon, OZ)[8] the court shall order, by its ruling on enforcement on the monetary claim on the account, that the Financial Agency must issue an order to the bank to transfer the amount for which the enforcement has been determined from all accounts of the enforcement debtor which are kept under its/his/her personal identification number, to the account of the enforcement creditor. Such a ruling has the effect of an enforcement ruling that determines the seizure of the monetary claim and its transfer for collection (Article 204(1) sentence 2 OZ). The enforcement ruling shall be delivered to the Financial Agency, the enforcement creditor, and the enforcement debtor (Article 204(3) OZ). After receiving the enforcement ruling under Article 204(1) OZ, the Financial Agency shall order banks that maintain the debtor's accounts to seize the amount of funds from the debtor's accounts that they maintain which corresponds to the amount of the claim for collection determined by that ruling (Article 205(1) OZ). The Financial Agency shall start with the bank that maintains the earliest opened account or fixed-term funds (Article 8 ZPONS). By delivering the order referred to in Article 205(1) OZ to the bank, the enforcement creditor establishes a lien on the enforcement debtor's claim against the bank for the payment of funds in the account up to the amount of the seized claim (Article 205(2) OZ). If, upon delivery of the Financial Agency's order under Article 205(1) OZ, there are no funds in the enforcement debtor's account in the amount necessary for full collection (payment) of the claim, the bank shall, according to the Financial Agency's order, prohibit the disposal of the funds in the accounts and fixed-term funds of the enforcement debtor up to the amount specified in the Financial Agency's order, all until a new order from the Financial Agency (so-called account blockage – Article 205(3) OZ). The bank shall transfer the seized/confiscated funds when it receives an order from the Financial Agency (Article 206(1) OZ). The enforcement debtor may, after receiving the enforcement ruling, propose a postponement of enforcement for the reasons specified in Article 65 OZ (Article 206(2) sentence 1 OZ). The court shall decide on a proposal for postponement of enforcement, submitted within the deadline for appeal against the enforcement ruling, within eight days, and if it accepts the proposal, the ruling on postponement shall be immediately delivered to the Financial Agency in a written dispatch, and if necessary, communicated by fax, e-mail or in another convenient way (Article 206(2) sentence 2 OZ). If the Financial Agency does not receive a ruling on the postponement of the enforcement or a ruling on the cancellation of the enforcement ruling or a ruling on termination of the enforcement within 60 days from the day when the enforcement ruling was delivered to it, it will order the transfer of the seized/confiscated amount to

---

8 Ovršni zakon, Official Gazette "*Narodne novine*" no. 2012/12, last amendment "*Narodne novine*" no. 2024/06, hereinafter referred to as OZ.

the account specified in the enforcement ruling (Article 206(3) sentence 1 OZ). The Financial Agency will order the transfer even before the expiration of the 60 days if the enforcement debtor gives written consent to the Financial Agency expressly allowing the transfer of seized funds before the expiration of that period (Article 206(3) sentence 2 OZ).

There is also a possibility of a direct collection of the claims based on a valid ground for payment. Thus, the enforcement creditor is entitled to directly require the Financial Agency, without involving the court, to collect the claim based on a valid ground for payment by transferring funds from the enforcement debtor's bank account to the enforcement creditor's account specified in the request for direct collection, in which case the Financial Agency shall proceed as in the context of an enforcement ruling delivered by the court. According to Article 209(1) OZ and Article 5(7) ZPONS, a valid ground for payment can be: an enforceable decision of a domestic court or administrative body that has a certificate of enforceability, enforceable settlements concluded before a domestic court or administrative body, enforceable settlements reached in the process of peaceful settlement of disputes with the Republic of Croatia based on Article 186a of the Civil Procedure Act (Zakon o parničnom postupku, ZPP),[9] a debenture (*zadužnica*), a blank debenture, an order for payment of Croatian Radio-Television with a certificate of enforceability, a European enforcement order, a European payment order, and which all refer to the payment of a specific monetary claim, as well as the employer's calculation of non-payment of the due amount of salary, salary compensation or severance pay. The Financial Agency shall send a copy of the request for a direct collection of a claim with all information about a document based on which the direct collection of a claim is made, to the enforcement debtor, to the address specified in Article (1)–(5) OZ, immediately after entering the ground for payment in the Register of the order of grounds for payment (Article 209(5) OZ). The bank ordered by the Financial Agency to seize the enforcement debtor's account is obliged to notify the enforcement debtor without delay, in the usual way of notifying the account holder of changes in the account, that certain funds in its account have been seized and that the enforcement debtor can obtain the relevant information from the Financial Agency (certain branches of the Financial Agency – Article 209(6) OZ). After the enforcement debtor receives notification that a direct collection of a claim has been requested against it/him/her based on the document under Article 209(1) OZ, according to the provisions of Article 209(5) OZ, or after it/he/she learns in another way that such a collection has been requested against it/him/her, the enforcement debtor may propose to the court that it make a ruling ordering the Financial Agency to postpone the issuance of an order to

---

9 Zakon o parničnom postupku, Official Gazette "*Narodne novine*" no. 1991/53, last amendment "*Narodne novine*" no. 2022/80.

the banks for the transfer of seized funds, or a ruling declaring the seizure and transfer inadmissible (Article 210 OZ). If the Financial Agency, within 60 days from the day on which the document referred to in Article 209(1) OZ (a ground for payment) is delivered to it, does not receive a court ruling on postponing the issuance of an order to banks for the transfer of seized funds or a court ruling declaring the seizure and transfer inadmissible on the basis of on the enforcement document which was the ground of a request for the direct collection of a claim, it shall issue an order to the bank(s) to transfer the funds from the enforcement debtor's account to the enforcement creditor's account (Article 209(7) OZ).

Additionally, according to Article 3 no. 1 ZPONS, the ground for payment is also: an enforcement ruling, a security ruling, an order of the Ministry of Finance for collection under an activated state guarantee, an order for seizure in the case of the forced execution of an imposed final fine (*res iudicata*) in criminal and misdemeanour proceedings, an order for forced collection of a fine imposed by an executive ruling of the Croatian National Bank, an order for the execution of the decision of the Single Resolution Board on the imposition of fines and periodic penalties, as well as any other decision of the competent body accepting in whole or in part the proposal for enforcement.

The Register of the order of grounds for payments, which is kept and administered by the Financial Agency, is a unique database of all received grounds for payment of an individual enforcement debtor, of the state of their execution, and actions taken upon the execution of enforcement based on these grounds for payment (Article 6(1) ZPONS). The Financial Agency issues orders for the execution of the grounds for payment in the order in which they were entered in this Register if no other law stipulates otherwise (Article 7 ZPONS).

If any of the above-mentioned grounds for payment that are registered in the Register of the order of grounds for payments cannot be executed in the period exceeding 60 days from any of the debtor's accounts, without any further consent of the debtor, the debtor shall be considered unable to pay (Article 6(2) no. 1 SZ). The existence of these circumstances, on which the legal presumption is based, shall be proven by a certificate issued by the Financial Agency, which shall issue such a certificate upon request of the debtor or creditor without delay (Article 6(4) sentences 1–2 SZ). Otherwise, the Financial Agency shall be liable for any damage that the applicant may suffer as a result of the Agency's non-performance (Article 6(4) sentence 3 SZ).

The debtor shall be considered unable to pay also in a case when it/he/she fails to pay three consecutive months' salary that the employee is entitled to according to a contract of employment, the ordinance on employment, a collective bargaining contract, or a special regulation or according to any other act regulating the obligations of the employer towards the employee (Article 6(2) no. 2 SZ). The existence of these circumstances shall be proven by the calculation of unpaid salary performed in accordance with regulations (Article 6(5) sentence 1 SZ). In addition to the aforementioned calculation, the submitter of the proposal for the opening of bankruptcy proceedings shall submit a certificate of the Tax Administration of the Ministry of Finance, confirming that the submitted calculation of unpaid salary was performed in accordance with regulations (Article 6(5) sentence 2 SZ).

However, the legal presumption contained in its two forms in Article 6(2) nos. 1–2 SZ shall not be applied if, in the course of preliminary proceedings, the debtor satisfies all claims which should have been paid from all its/his/her accounts based on valid grounds for payment or in case of assumption of debt/access to debt (Article 6(3) sentence 1 SZ). The debtor can prove the satisfaction of claims only by a public or notarised document or a certificate issued by the Financial Agency (Article 6(3) sentence 2 SZ).

The existing legal presumption contained in Article 6(2) nos. 1–2 SZ in its two forms makes it extremely easy for the courts to establish the existence of a ground for the opening of bankruptcy proceedings. Most of the bankruptcy proceedings in the Republic of Croatia are opened based on this legal presumption, especially based on the circumstances contained in Article 6(2) no. 1 SZ. In very rare cases, where neither the circumstances necessary for the application of the legal presumption contained in Article 6(2) no. 1 nor those contained in Article 6(2) no. 2 SZ exist, the court might appoint one or more experts to examine, together with the court and the preliminary bankruptcy administrator, whether the debtor is insolvent, imminently insolvent or overindebted (Article 125 SZ).

The Bankruptcy Act itself does not explicitly determine whether the stated legal presumption is rebuttable or irrebuttable. In order to protect the rights of a potential bankruptcy debtor and prevent abuse by creditors, one should opt for the interpretation according to which it is a rebuttable presumption.

There is also a specific presumption of inability to pay debts in the event of the opening and immediate closing of so-called summary bankruptcy proceedings against a legal person.[10] Thus, if the debtor's legal representatives fail to submit a list of the debtor's assets and liabilities within 15 days in such summary bankruptcy proceedings, or if it arises from the list that the debtor has assets which are not sufficient to settle the foreseeable costs of the bankruptcy proceedings, and if, within 45 days, none of the creditors file a proposal to open bankruptcy proceedings and they fail to pay an advance for settling the costs of such proceedings, it shall be considered that the debtor is not able to pay its debts (Article 431 SZ).

---

10 "The court shall conduct summary bankruptcy proceedings against a legal entity if the following requirements are cumulatively met: 1) this legal person has no employees; 2) it has registered no executed grounds for payment in the Registry of the order of grounds for payment for an uninterrupted period of 120 days; 3) the requirements for the opening of other proceedings for deletion from the court register are not met" (Article 428 SZ).

In the Consumer Bankruptcy Act, the inability to pay is defined as the inability to fulfil mature monetary obligations (Article 5(2) ZSP). The consumer shall be considered unable to pay if he/she cannot fulfil one or more mature monetary obligations in the total amount of more than HRK 20,000 (EUR 2,656) for at least 90 consecutive days (Article 5(3) ZSP).

The Consumer Bankruptcy Act itself also does not explicitly determine whether the stated legal presumption is rebuttable or not. It should be interpreted as a rebuttable presumption for the same reasons already stated in the case of the Bankruptcy Act.

Question 14: Does your law refer to all debts or only to mature debts?

Croatian law refers only to existing mature debts, which the debtor cannot fulfil on a more permanent basis (Article 6(1) SZ). The Consumer Bankruptcy Act also mentions only mature monetary obligations (Article 5(2) ZSP).

The unpaid debts that are mature on the day of the opening of bankruptcy proceedings are decisive, but only if they are not a result of a short-term stagnation of payments.

Question 15: Which assets are taken into account when assessing the inability to pay debts: all (financial) assets or only those that are liquid, i.e. available on short notice?

The legal presumption of inability to pay debts, contained in Article 6(2) no. 1 SZ, which is applied in most of cases of the opening of bankruptcy proceedings, is based on the lack of funds in the debtor's accounts in its bank(s). The same is true for the legal presumption contained in Article 5(3) ZSP. In very rare cases when this legal presumption would not apply, the statute does not give an explicit answer as to which assets are taken into account when assessing the inability to pay debts. There is no published case law on this.

Question 16: Is any liquidity gap (deficit between relevant financial means and relevant debts) relevant or does your law neglect minor gaps? If the latter, how is "minor" defined?

Neither Croatian statute law nor the published case law mentions explicitly the possibility of ignoring minor liquidity gaps. But see a legal presumption of the existence of "inability to pay debts" in Article 6(2) SZ (answer to Question 13).

Question 17: As far as the time aspect is concerned, does it matter whether the liquidity gap can be closed again in the short term? If so, how long is the grace period?

If, at the time of deciding to open bankruptcy proceedings, the conditions for the application of the legal presumption under Article 6(2) no. 1 or no 2. SZ or under Article 5(3) ZSP are fulfilled, the court is obliged to open bankruptcy proceedings, regardless of how quickly the liquidity gap can be closed.

According to the logic of the things, if the inability to pay debts ceases to exist after the opening of bankruptcy proceedings, the court should at the request of the debtor discontinue bankruptcy proceedings, if it is assured that the debtor after such discontinuation will no longer be insolvent. The statute does not have an explicit rule on that.

Question 18: As far as the time aspect is concerned, is a debtor considered insolvent if the liquidity gap is not yet present but will occur soon? If so, how long is the prognosis period? (Note: this may also concern the difference between actual and likely/imminent inability to pay debts; cf. below Question 34).

If, at the time of making the decision to open bankruptcy proceedings, the liquidity gap is not yet present, the debtor will not be considered insolvent, even if the liquidity gap will occur soon.

But in such a situation, the debtor can be imminently insolvent in the sense described in the answer to Question 34.

Question 19: How is inability to pay debts established? Please communicate if there is a difference between a creditor and a debtor application or between different legal contexts.

Regardless of who is the submitter of the proposal to open bankruptcy proceedings – the debtor, a creditor or some third person or body (for example, the Financial Agency) – the methods of establishing the existence or non-existence of the debtor's inability to pay its/his/her mature debts will be the same.

a) Is a formal liquidity status (liquidity balance sheet) required?

The statute does not require a formal liquidity status (liquidity balance sheet).

In the majority of cases in which bankruptcy proceedings are opened based on the legal presumption contained in Article 6(2) no. 1 or no. 2 SZ or in Article 5(3) ZSP, a formal liquidity status will not matter.

In rare cases in which the legal presumption under Article 6(2) no. 1 and no. 2 SZ will not be applied and in which the court will establish insolvency with the help of a preliminary bankruptcy administrator and one or more experts (Article 125 SZ), this method could be used in practice.

b) Is a sample of daily liquidity data (which do not amount to a proper liquidity status but show insufficient funds on different days within a certain period of time) sufficient?

In the majority of cases in which bankruptcy proceedings are opened based on the legal presumption contained in Article 6(2) no. 1 or no. 2 SZ or in Article 5(3) ZSP, a sample of daily liquidity will not matter.

In rare cases in which the legal presumption under Article 6(2) no. 1 and no. 2 SZ will not be applied and in which the court will establish insolvency with the help of a preliminary bankruptcy administrator and one or more experts (Article 125 SZ), the preliminary bankruptcy administrator and expert(s) in their report, as well as the court in its decision on the opening of bankruptcy proceedings, may deduce the debtor's permanent inability to pay its mature monetary debts from an exemplary sample of daily liquidity data. There is no published case law on this.

c) Does the law provide for a rebuttable presumption? If so, under which conditions?
There is a legal presumption, see the comprehensive answer to Question 13.

d) Does the law provide for any technical circumstances (e.g. undisputed statutory demand, non-compliance with monetary judgments, unsuccessful enforcement proceedings, non-performance of a previous composition agreement in insolvency proceedings) the occurrence of which suffices to establish the debtor's insolvency?
See the answer to Question 13.

e) Other means?
See the answer to Question 26.

Question 20: Is insolvency (inability to pay debts, overindebtedness, etc.) subject to party autonomy in the proceedings or must the court clarify them *ex officio*?

As a rule, the court must clarify the insolvency, i.e. the existence of a bankruptcy ground, *ex officio* in so-called preliminary proceedings. The purpose of preliminary proceedings is to determine the prerequisites for the opening of bankruptcy proceedings, including the existence of a bankruptcy ground.

However, the court may render a decision (ruling) to open bankruptcy proceedings without preliminary proceedings, in the following cases:

1. if the existence of the ground for the opening of bankruptcy proceedings is established on the basis of a proposal/petition to open pre-bankruptcy proceedings;
2. if the Financial Agency files a proposal to open bankruptcy proceedings in accordance with Article 110(1) of the Bankruptcy Act;
3. if the debtor's legal representative or the individual debtor files a proposal to open bankruptcy proceedings;
4. if the creditor files a proposal to open bankruptcy proceedings and the debtor admits the existence of the bankruptcy ground;
5. if previously opened pre-bankruptcy proceedings were unsuccessful (Article 116 SZ).

But even in these cases, the court might open preliminary proceedings in order to establish the existence of a bankruptcy ground. In other words, the court is not bound by the bankruptcy debtor's proposal to open bankruptcy proceedings or by its admission/confession of the existence of a bankruptcy ground, especially if the court suspects abuse of the bankruptcy proceedings.

Question 21: In an overall view, does your law distinguish "inability to pay debts" from "financial difficulties"? If so, how?

No.

Question 22: In an overall view, does it matter under your law whether the debtor's inability to pay debts is present or future, and reversible or irreversible?

At the time of rendering of the decision to open bankruptcy proceedings, the inability to pay debts must be current, present. It does not matter whether this inability will exist in the future, or whether it is reversible or irreversible.

Imminent inability to pay debts, referring to the upcoming future inability to pay debts, is a separate ground for the opening of bankruptcy or pre-bankruptcy proceedings.

Question 23: Would you like to add any further aspects not covered by the above questions?

No.

III. CESSATION OF PAYMENTS

Question 24: In your jurisdiction, is "cessation of payments" a legal term used either in statute or in case law? (If the answer is "no", please continue with Question 31.)

Yes, in Article 126(2) SZ.

Question 25: Is "cessation of payments" an autonomous ground to commence proceedings (triggering circumstance)? You may refer to Questions 6/7 or add additional information here.

No. See the answer to Question 26.

Question 26: Is "cessation of payments" a means to establish inability to pay debts? If so, by which mechanism (e.g. rebuttable presumption for inability to pay debts, cf. above Question 19(c))?

Yes, it can be a means to establish inability to pay debts. According to Article 126(1) SZ, the court will not appoint an expert to examine the debtor's economic and financial condition if it establishes that the requirements for the opening of bankruptcy proceedings have been met without a prior examination of the debtor's ability to pay debts or overindebtedness, particularly when the debtor's inability to pay debts can be established beyond doubt from the circumstances which caused the debtor to cease payments. In particular, the fact that the debtor has ceased its payments can be established from the report of legal entities performing payment operations for the debtor (Article 126(2) SZ).

However, these rules will rarely be applied, because the conditions for the application of the legal presumption of inability to pay debts contained in Article 6(2) no. 1 or no. 2 SZ are in practice in most cases fulfilled.

Question 27: How is "cessation of payments" defined? If it is defined in statute, please provide us here with an English translation of the relevant rule. Is this definition (if any) specified in case law? If so, how?

There is no definition of "cessation of payments" in the statute nor in case law.

However, the conditions for the application of the legal presumption of inability to pay debts from Article 6(2) no. 1 SZ includes the fact that the execution of enforcement on the debtor's bank accounts has not been possible for more than 60 days. The conditions for the application of the legal presumption of inability to pay debts from Article 6(2) no. 2 SZ include the fact that the debtor did not pay three consecutive salaries that the employee is entitled to. See for more details the answer to Question 13.

Question 28: How is "cessation of payments" established?

See the answer to Question 27.

Question 29: Are there typical circumstances which provide circumstantial evidence that the debtor has ceased payments? If so, please list as many as possible.

Taking into consideration that the bankruptcy proceedings in the Republic of Croatia in most cases are opened by the application of the legal presumption of inability to pay debts contained in Article 6(2) no. 1 or no. 2 SZ, the courts have not determined typical circumstances which provide circumstantial evidence that the debtor has ceased payments.

Question 30: Would you like to add any further aspects not covered by the above questions?

No.

IV. LIKELY/IMMINENT INABILITY TO PAY DEBTS

Question 31: Are the following terms available in your jurisdiction, either in statute or in case law? (If the answer is "no", please continue with Question 42.)

a) likely inability to pay debts
No.

b) imminent inability to pay debts
Yes.

c) other (similar) terms
Yes, "likelihood of inability to pay debts", but only in the context of directors' duties (Article 20.a SZ). See the answers to Question 10(a)–(c).

Question 32: Is "likely/imminent inability to pay debts" an autonomous ground to commence proceedings (triggering circumstance)? You may refer to Questions 6/7 or add additional information here.

Yes. See the answers to Question 5 and Question 6.

Question 33: If the answer to the previous Question is "yes", who may base filing for insolvency proceedings on it: only the debtor or also creditors?

Only the debtor, according to Article 5(3) SZ.

Question 34: How are these terms defined? If they are defined in statute, please provide us here with an English translation of the relevant rules. Is this definition (if any) specified in case law? If so, how?

a) likely inability to pay debts
n.a.

b) imminent inability to pay debts
The imminent inability to pay debts exists if the submitter of the proposal to open proceedings makes it likely that the debtor will not be able to fulfil its/his/her existing obligations when they become due (Article 4(1) sentence 2 SZ for pre-bankruptcy proceedings and Article 5(4) SZ for bankruptcy proceedings). The definition of this ground is valid also for the procedure of extraordinary management in companies of systemic importance for the Republic of Croatia (Article 4(1) ZPIUTD). The imminent inability to pay debts is not a bankruptcy ground for the opening of consumer bankruptcy proceedings (Article 5(1) Consumer Bankruptcy Act).

It shall be considered that the imminent inability to pay debts exists if, at the time of submission of the proposal to open proceedings, circumstances have not arisen due to which it is considered that the debtor has become permanently unable to pay and if:

- in the Registry of order of grounds for payment kept by the Financial Agency, the debtor has one or more registered unexecuted grounds for payment, which should have been collected from any of the debtor's accounts, based on valid grounds for payment, without any further consent of the debtor (Article 4(2) no. 1 SZ); or
- if the debtor is more than 30 days overdue with the payment of salary that the employee is entitled to according to a contract of employment, the ordinance on employment, a collective bargaining contract or a special regulation, or according to any other act regulating the obligations of the employer towards the employee (Article 4(2) no. 2 SZ); or
- if the debtor has not paid the contributions and taxes related to the salary referred to in Article 4(2) no. 2 SZ within 30 days from the day the debtor was due to pay the salary to the employee (Article 4(2) no. 3 SZ).

The existence of the circumstances contained in Article 4(2) no. 1. SZ shall be proven by a certificate issued by the Financial Agency, which shall issue such a certificate upon request of the debtor or creditor without delay (Article 4(3) sentence 1 SZ). Otherwise, the Financial Agency shall be liable for damage that the applicant may suffer as a result of the Agency's non-performance (Article 4(3) sentence 2 SZ).

The existence of the circumstances contained in Article 4(2) nos. 2 and 3 SZ shall be proven by the calculation of unpaid salary, performed in accordance with regulations (Article 4(4) sentence 1 SZ). In addition to the aforementioned calculation, the submitter of the proposal for the opening of proceedings shall submit a certificate of the Tax Administration of the Ministry of Finance, confirming that the submitted calculation of unpaid salary was performed in accordance with regulations (Article 4(4) sentence 2 SZ).

The SZ contains the legal presumption in three forms in Article 4(2) nos. 1–3. Such a legal presumption in three possible forms makes it significantly easier for the courts to determine the existence of an imminent inability to pay debts. It applies not only in the case of the opening of pre-bankruptcy proceedings (Article 4(2) nos. 1–3), but also in the case of the opening of bankruptcy proceedings (Article 5(4) in connection with Article 4(2) nos. 1–3 SZ) as well as in the case of the opening of proceedings of extraordinary management in companies of systemic importance for the Republic of Croatia (Article 4(1) ZPIUTD).

The Bankruptcy Act itself does not explicitly determine whether the stated legal presumption is rebuttable or irrebuttable. In order to protect the rights of a potential bankruptcy debtor and prevent abuse by creditors, one should opt for the interpretation according to which it is a rebuttable presumption.

Question 35: Do the terms "likely" and "imminent" require a prognosis regarding the point in time when actual inability to pay debts will occur? If so, how long is the time period for this prognosis?

No, the statute does not explicitly say anything about a prognosis. However, see the timelines for the application of the legal presumption on the existence of the imminent inability to pay debts in three forms in Article 4(2) nos. 1–3 SZ, presented in the answer to Question 34.

Question 36: Does your law require a specific grade of certainty that inability to pay debts will eventually occur? If so, is 50.1% ("more likely than not") enough or are there alleviated or aggravated prerequisites?

No, it does not require any specific degree of certainty.

Question 37: Regarding "debts" and "financial means", are they defined in the same way as in the context of inability to pay debts (cf. above Questions 14/15)? If not, what are the differences?

No differences.

Question 38: Further to Question 37: Are "debts" considered which do currently not exist or are not yet due but will foreseeably come into existence and become due during the prognosis period?

The statute refers to the existing obligations (debts) that are not yet due, in respect of which the submitter of the proposal to open proceedings has shown it to be likely that the debtor will not be able to fulfil them when they become due (Article 4(1) sentence 2 SZ).

Question 39: Also further to Question 37: Are "financial means" considered which do currently not exist but will foreseeably become available during the prognosis period?

Usually, Croatian courts do not have to consider such "financial means", due to the fact that in most cases when pre-bankruptcy or bankruptcy proceedings are opened on the ground of imminent inability to pay debts, the legal presumption contained in Article 4(2) nos. 1–3 in connection with Article 5(4) SZ will be applied. See the answer to Question 34(b).

Question 40: How are the terms "likely/imminent inability to pay debts" established?

In most cases when pre-bankruptcy or bankruptcy proceedings are opened on the ground of imminent inability to pay debts, the legal presumption contained in Article 4(2) nos. 1–3 in connection with Article 5(4) SZ will be applied. See the answer to Question 34(b).

Question 41: Would you like to add any further aspects not covered by the above questions?

No.

V. OVERINDEBTEDNESS

Question 42: In your jurisdiction, is "overindebtedness", or "balance sheet insolvency" respectively, a legal term used either in statute or in case law? (If the answer is "no", please continue with Question 56.)

Yes, "overindebtedness" is a legal term used in statute (SZ).

Question 43: Is "overindebtedness" an autonomous ground to commence proceedings (triggering circumstance)? You may refer to Questions 6/7 or add additional information here.

Yes. It is provided for in Article 5(2) and defined in Article 7 SZ.

Question 44: If the answer to the previous Question is "yes", is this applicable to corporate insolvencies of legal persons only or also to personal bankruptcies of natural persons?

According to Article 7(1) SZ, overindebtedness as an autonomous ground to open proceedings is applicable to legal persons only.

Question 45: Is the term "overindebtedness" defined in statute? If so, please give the wording in English translation. Is this definition (if any) specified in case law? If so, how?

Yes, "overindebtedness" is defined in statute. According to Article 7(1) SZ "overindebtedness exists if the assets of debtor-legal entity does not cover its existing obligations".

However, Article 7(1) SZ shall not be applied:

- if, according to the circumstances of a case (development programme, available sources of funds, type of assets, obtained securities, etc.), it may be reasonably presumed that by continuing its business the debtor-legal entity will properly fulfil its obligations when they become due;
- if in respect of the obligations of the company that is a company of persons (*eine Personengesellschaft*) there exists joint and several liability of a shareholder of that company who is a natural person and whose assets are not subject to instituted or opened bankruptcy proceedings (Article 7(2) SZ).

According to Croatian law, the legal term "a company of persons" (*eine Personengesellschaft*) includes a public commercial company (*eine offene Handelsgesellschaft*), a general partnership (*eine Komanditgesellschaft*), an economic interest grouping (*eine wirtschaftliche Interessenvereinigung*), an association (*ein Verein*), a cooperative (*eine Genossenschaft*), and a union of cooperatives (*ein Genossenschaftsverband*).

We can say that actual overindebtedness is not relevant if, according to the circumstances of a case, there is no danger of a future inability of the debtor to fulfil its obligations when they become due.

Although the statute uses the broad term "existing obligations" in Article 7, it should be interpreted as "existing monetary obligations", i.e. an "existing obligation to pay" or "existing debts".

Cases where the opening of bankruptcy proceedings is based on the overindebtedness of the debtor are very, very rare in the practice of Croatian courts.

Question 46: Does your law refer to all existing debts or only to mature debts?

It refers to all existing debts.

Question 47: Does the rank of certain debts play a role when establishing overindebtedness? In particular, is there any possibility to conclude agreements according to which certain debts shall not be taken into account (e.g. agreements on subsidiarity)?

The statute does not mention such a possibility.

Question 48: Which assets are taken into account when overindebtedness is established: the complete set of assets or only a selection of them?

Given that the statute does not make any distinction, it should be concluded that all the debtor's assets should be taken into account when overindebtedness is established.

Question 49: How are the debtor's assets valued: by referring to the liquidation value, the book value, the going concern value or in another way?

The going concern value will be relevant if the circumstances of the case allow the reasonable prognosis that the debtor, by continuing its business, shall properly fulfil its obligations when they become due.

If the circumstances of the case do not give a basis for such a prognosis, then the liquidation value will be relevant.

Question 50: Is there any prognostic element, e.g. regarding the debtor's chances to continue the business?

Yes. See the answers to Questions 45 and 49.

Question 51: If the answer to the previous Question is "yes", what exactly is the topic of the prognosis and how is it established?

The exact topic of the prognosis is to establish whether it may be reasonably presumed that, by continuing its business the debtor will properly fulfil its existing monetary obligations when they become due.

The debtor should present some kind of its development programme, its business plan how to neutralise the overindebtedness in the sense that even if it exists, it will not exist in the future i.e. it will not jeopardise the fulfilment of its existing monetary obligations when they become due. In addition, the debtor must provide the court with information on its available sources of funds, on all its assets as well as on already obtained securities, that will enable the continuation of the debtor's business and proper fulfilment of its existing monetary obligations when they become due.

Question 52: If the answer to Question 50 is "yes", how long is the prognosis period?

The statute does not provide for a certain time period. The proper fulfilment of the existing debtor's obligations should not be in jeopardy when they become due.

Question 53: How is overindebtedness established?

a) Is a formal balance sheet required?

The statute does not require a formal balance sheet. However, in the very rare cases when the opening of bankruptcy proceedings is applied on the basis of overindebtedness as a bankruptcy ground, the formal balance sheet will be a starting point.

If necessary, the bankruptcy court shall appoint one or more experts who shall, within a period of 15 days, together with the bankruptcy judge and the interim bankruptcy administrator, if appointed, verify whether the debtor is overindebted (see Articles 125, 126 SZ).

Methods of determining the value of the debtor's assets in a case of its potential overindebtedness are not prescribed by statute.

b) Does the yearly regular commercial balance sheet have any meaning (given that it is normally based on technical values and does not display undisclosed reserves)?

No, because all debtor's assets must be taken into account.

c) Does the law provide for a presumption? If so, under which conditions?
No.

d) Other means?
No.

Question 54: Is the legal link to overindebtedness undisputed in literature or are there efforts to abolish it?

So far, the literature has not questioned "overindebtedness" as a ground for the opening of bankruptcy proceedings.

Question 55: Would you like to add any further aspects not covered by the above questions?

No.

VI. REMAINING ISSUES

Question 56: Is there anything else you would like to share in the present context and that we should take into account?

No.

CYPRUS

Andrie KYPRIDEMOU

I. GENERAL

Question 1: How is insolvency (both in the context of liquidation and restructuring/reorganisation) regulated in your jurisdiction? Please give a brief overview, at least enumerating the relevant statutes.

Under the Cypriot insolvency law framework, the insolvency of natural persons and of companies are regulated by separate legislation.

The liquidation of companies is provided for in Part V of the Companies Law, Chapter 113 of the Laws of Cyprus (CoLaw), which generally covers all proceedings for company incorporation, relocation, management, regulation, reorganisation and winding up. As concerns liquidation in particular, CoLaw outlines four proceedings that may be pursued for the winding up of companies, namely: liquidation by court order (CoLaw, Part V (II)), liquidation under Court supervision (CoLaw, Part V (IV)), voluntary liquidation by the members of the company and voluntary liquidation by its creditors (CoLaw, Part V (III)). Liquidation by court order is distinct from the other three proceedings, in that it may only commence by court order, following an application by the debtor-company itself or any of its creditors or members, the Official Receiver, the examiner of the company or any insolvency practitioner[1] acting under the European Insolvency Regulation.[2] All other insolvency proceedings commence with the adoption of a special resolution by the company's members to wind up the company.[3]

Accordingly, insolvent companies' restructuring is regulated by Part IVA of CoLaw, which provides for the appointment of an Examiner in the insolvent or likely insolvent company whose business is nevertheless viable partly or in whole as a going concern.[4] The Examiner will prepare a debt restructuring plan,

1 Companies Law Cap. 113 §213(1).
2 Regulation (EU) 2015/848 of the European Parliament and of the Council of 20 May 2015 on insolvency proceedings (recast).
3 Companies Law Cap. 113 §§203, 218.
4 Companies Law Cap. 113 §202A(1) and (2).

negotiate with the company's creditors and members and try to get the plan approved in order to restore the company's solvency. A company in examinership enjoys a four-month-long moratorium, which begins upon filing the Court petition for appointment of the Examiner in the company.[5]

As concerns insolvent individuals, the procedure for their bankruptcy is provided in Bankruptcy Law, Chapter 5 of the Laws of Cyprus (B.Law), while the "formal", court approved procedure for their debt restructuring was introduced in 2015 by the Law on the Insolvency of Natural Persons (Personal Repayment Plans and Debt Relief Orders) (PRP Law).

Unfortunately, there is no translation of any of these three laws in English updated post 2015 that core amendments were introduced by the new insolvency law framework. To this extent translation of all sections relating to the definition of insolvency and the related terms examined herein is being provided *infra*.

Question 2: Related to paragraph 10 above of the Introduction: seen from a principle-based perspective, what justifies the opening of insolvency proceedings in your jurisdiction?

The opening of insolvency proceedings, both for natural persons and companies alike, is undoubtedly justified by the debtors' inability to pay their debts, either as they fall due or because of overindebtedness, which triggers the requirement for the opening of collective proceedings, as the means to secure the equal treatment of creditors. At the same time commencement of insolvency proceedings ensures the debtors' protection from individual enforcement actions.

To this extent the definition of insolvency should be accurate at setting the point in time that debtors are unable to fulfil their obligations to the detriment of certain creditors that won't be able to recover a substantial part of the debts due unless such collective proceedings are triggered promptly and the insolvency estate is secured in this manner.

It is important to note at this point that under the Cypriot insolvency law, technically, neither the directors of an insolvent company, nor an insolvent individual has an *obligation* to file for the opening of insolvency proceedings when such conditions as are laid down in insolvency legislation for the opening of insolvency proceedings are present.[6] The effect of this is that insolvency

5 Companies Law Cap. 113 §202H(1).

6 There is no directors' disqualification law as such in Cyprus to lay down substantially deterrent rules for directors failing to identify and act promptly or with reasonable care in situations of an imminent insolvency. There is only §§307–313 of CoLaw, which provide for situations of fraudulent trading, alienation of company assets and other such criminal offences by fraudulent directors and §169Z of CoLaw, which is a direct translation of Article 19, Directive (EU) 2019/1023 on "Duties of directors where there is a likelihood of insolvency", still without laying down any specific penalty or other deterrent measures for those found liable under this section. To this extent this section cannot be enforced efficiently.

proceedings are most commonly opened by petition of the creditor due to debtors' immediate inability to pay debts, that is, cash-flow insolvency, while these debtors may have been overindebted, namely, balance sheet insolvent, for several years. As such, by the time that insolvency proceedings commence, the insolvency estate is usually inadequate for repayment of any portion of any unsecured debt anyhow, and the assets used as collateral for the secured debt of the debtor are depreciated to the extent that such debt is no longer secured by the value of the said asset in full.

To this extent, it can be argued that the conditions justifying the opening of insolvency proceedings fall short of securing efficiently some basic insolvency principles, such as protecting creditors' collective interests or securing the insolvency estate; a situation which inhibits the risk of creditors' domino insolvencies.

Question 3: Does your national law in the context of liquidation proceedings use one or more of the following terms (be it as a noun, be it as an adjective or adjunct) in whatever context:

a) inability to pay debts
Yes.

b) cessation of payments
No.

c) likely inability to pay debts
No.

d) imminent inability to pay debts
No.

e) overindebtedness?
Yes, it is in fact included in the interpretation of "inability to pay debts".

Question 4: Are the same terms (and with the same meaning) used in the rules on preliminary/interim insolvency proceedings (e.g. concerning the application stage of the proceedings)?

No – the requirements for the appointment of both Interim trustee in bankruptcy and Interim liquidator relate to the protection of the debtor's estate and they may only be appointed for a limited period pending hearing of the liquidation/bankruptcy petition, at which stage the insolvency of the debtor has not yet been examined by the Court.

Question 5: Does your national law in the context of restructuring proceedings (as referred to above at paragraph 8 of the Introduction, i.e. both pre-insolvency and within formal insolvency proceedings) use one or more of the following terms (be it as a noun, be it as an adjective or adjunct) in whatever context:

a) inability to pay debts
Yes.

b) cessation of payments
No.

c) likely inability to pay debts
Yes – "likelihood of insolvency".

d) imminent inability to pay debts
No.

e) overindebtedness?
Yes, it is included in the interpretation of "inability to pay debts".

Question 6: Which of the terms mentioned in Questions 3 and 5 are used for defining grounds to commence proceedings (triggering circumstances)?

a) insolvency proceedings
CoLaw §212 provides an interpretation of inability to pay debts for purposes of commencement of liquidation by court order, which includes, in fact, among other rebuttable presumptions, overindebtedness and reads as follows:

> a company is deemed unable to pay its debts –
>
> (a) …
> (b) … or
> (c) if it is proved to the satisfaction of the Court that the company is unable to pay its debts as they become due and, in its decision on whether the company is unable to pay its debts as they become due, the Court takes into account the company's contingent and future obligations; or
> (d) if it is proved to the satisfaction of the Court that the value of the company's assets is less than the amount of its liabilities, taking into account its contingent and future liabilities.

As concerns commencement of insolvency proceedings for natural persons, the requirement set out in B.Law is for the debtor to have committed an act of bankruptcy as provided in §3, which includes, among other rebuttable presumptions, "(d) if (the debtor) files with the Court a *declaration of his inability to pay his debts* or applies for voluntary bankruptcy".

b) restructuring proceedings

CoLaw, on the restructuring of companies through examinership, provides under §202A(1) that the Court may approve a petition for the appointment of an Examiner in the company when

> (a) the company *is insolvent* or there is *a likelihood of insolvency*, and
> (b) no resolution for the liquidation of the company has been approved and published in the Official Gazette of the Republic, and
> (c) no Court order for the liquidation of the company has been issued …[7]

The term "inability to pay debts" as such then comes into play through the definition of "insolvency", which means "the case in which a company is unable to pay its debts as per subsection (3) §202A",[8] which reads

> For the purposes of this section, a company is *unable to pay its debts* if –
>
> (a) [it] is unable to pay its debts at the time they become payable,
> (b) the value of its assets is less than the amount of its liabilities, taking into account its contingent and future liabilities, or
> (c) the provisions of section 212 apply in this regard.[9]

In that regard, the interpretation of "inability to pay debts" in restructuring proceedings also embeds overindebtedness.

Then §202N also provides the definition of "likelihood of insolvency", as this is referred in §202A *supra*, as being "the case where, in the opinion of the company's directors or the Court, it is reasonably likely that the company will become insolvent within twelve (12) months".

As concerns the restructuring of the debts of natural persons, PRP Law provides that such repayment plans are available to insolvent individuals, which, through their participation in such a repayment plan for five years, have a reasonable prospect to become solvent again. Then §2 PRP Law provides the interpretation of "insolvent", in relation to a debtor, as being "a debtor that is unable to pay his/her debts as they fall due".

Question 7: Does the answer to Question 6 include personal bankruptcies of natural persons or only corporate insolvencies of legal entities?

The answer to Question 6 includes both.

---

7 Companies Law Cap. 113 §202A(1).
8 Companies Law Cap. 113 §202N.
9 Companies Law Cap. 113 §202A(3).

Question 8: In your law, are there any other circumstances which trigger insolvency or restructuring proceedings?

Yes, there are several other circumstances which may trigger insolvency proceedings, for companies and natural persons alike.

Insolvency proceedings for companies

In particular, the liquidation of a company may commence voluntarily by special resolution of its members, which requires a majority of 75%, on any of the following grounds: (i) the period for duration of the company expires, if there is any such date set in the company's memorandum, or any event set out therein that shall trigger its dissolution has taken place; (ii) it is advisable to wind up the company due to its liabilities; (iii) the company is solvent, yet for any reason it wishes to be wound up.[10]

Also, a liquidation by court order may be pursued

(a) by application of a creditor who has process served the company with a demand letter for an amount in excess of five thousand euro, and the company has neglected for the following three weeks to pay the amount or secure or settle it to the reasonable satisfaction of the creditor; or
(b) if enforcement measures related to any judgment, ruling or order of the Court to the benefit of the creditor of the company, is returned in part or in whole unsatisfied;[11] or
(c) the company has not called its annual meeting or filed the annual report on this to the Registrar of Companies, or
(d) the company has not been operating for a period exceeding a calendar year, or
(e) in the case of a public company, its members decrease to less than 7 in number at any given time and the company fails to increase them, or
(f) the Court rules that it is *just and equitable* to dissolve the company (emphasis added).[12]

This last ground on which a company may be dissolved (i.e. that it is just and equitable to do so) is commonly examined by the Courts in petitions involving suppression of minority shareholder,[13] abuse of power by the company's directors, or an overall insolvent company, whose liquidation petition may have otherwise failed on procedural grounds relating, for example, to the petitioner's status. A most notable example of this is the case of *Re Agricultural and Livestock Farm G. Ch. G. Lytra Bros Ltd.*, in which the petitioners were minority shareholders and creditors of the company, but neither the grounds for a minority/sole

10 Companies Law Cap. 113 §261.
11 Companies Law Cap. 113 §212.
12 Companies Law Cap. 113 §211.
13 Companies Law Cap. 113 §202.

shareholder's liquidation petition, nor the grounds for a sole creditor's petition were proved to the satisfaction of the Court; yet, from the evidence submitted, it was apparent to the Court that the company was indeed insolvent.[14]

Insolvency proceedings for natural persons

Likewise, B.Law §3 provides that

> (1) The debtor commits an act of bankruptcy …
>
> (a) if … he fraudulently transfers, donates, delivers or transfers his property or any part thereof;
>
> (b) if … he makes any concession or transfer of his property or any part thereof, or creates a charge on it, which according to this Law or any other Law would be void as a fraudulent preference if the debtor were declared bankrupt;·
>
> (c) if execution by seizure of his goods has been effected against him, by suit in any Court, and the goods seized have either been sold or are held by the bailiff for twenty-one days …;
>
> (d) if he files with the Court a *declaration of his inability to pay his debts* or applies for voluntary bankruptcy;
>
> (e) if a creditor secures against him a final judgment or final court order for any sum, and, while the execution of the judgment or court order has not been stayed, the creditor serves process on the debtor, in Cyprus or elsewhere with the permission of the Court, a notice of bankruptcy under this Law and within seven days from the service of the notice on him, [the debt is not settled];
>
> (f) If, while he owes to a creditor a debt which may be proved in bankruptcy, he fails to pay, or to secure or settle such debt, within such time as shall be allowed by a court order issued by the Court at the petition of the creditor, provided always that no such application shall be entertained by the Court, unless the debtor has previously been served with a notice of bankruptcy requiring the payment of the debt and has been given notice of such application and called upon to show cause against it;
>
> (g) if a Personal Repayment Plan is deemed to have failed or terminated in accordance with the provisions of the [PRP Law].[15]

Question 9: Which of the terms mentioned in Questions 3, 5, and 8 are used in the context of transactions avoidance law?

In general, the main prerequisite that triggers transactions avoidance provisions in CoLaw, B.Law and PRP Law is the commencement of liquidation or bankruptcy proceedings, on any ground.

---

[14] Επί της αφορώσι την Γεοργοκτηνοτροφική Εταιρεία Α/φοι Γ.Χ.Γ. Λύτρα Λιμιτεδ, HE136386, Γενική Αίτηση 42/2017, 26.01.2018.

[15] Bankruptcy Law Cap. 5 §3(1).

However, "*inability to pay debts*" at the time the said transaction was concluded is still explicitly mentioned as an additional condition required to prove preference,[16] to declare a floating charge void,[17] and to cancel transactions at an undervalue concluded up to 10 years prior to the commencement of bankruptcy proceedings.[18]

Question 10: Which of the terms addressed in Questions 3, 5, and 8 are used in the context of directors' duties?

a) shift of duties (from shareholders to creditors)

n.a.

The newly adopted §169Z of CoLaw, which is a direct translation of Article 19, Directive (EU) 2019/1023 on "*Duties of directors where there is a likelihood of insolvency*", provides that where there is likelihood of insolvency (likely inability to pay debts[19]) the directors shall have regard to the interests of all creditors, members and other interested parties alike. This, however, does not amount to a shift of duties, especially considering that this section is inefficient in that it does not provide for any deterrent measures for any directors found liable under these provisions.

b) duties to commence insolvency proceedings

n.a.

c) other duties (please describe)

When there is likelihood of insolvency (likely inability to pay debts) the directors of a company also have duties to take steps to avoid insolvency and to avoid deliberate or grossly negligent conduct that threatens the viability of the business.[20]

Question 11: Are there any other rules in the context of which the terms addressed in Questions 3, 5, and 8 are used?

Inability to pay debts is also a prerequisite for a debtor to get a debt relief order.[21] Debt Relief Orders are provided for in PRP Law, yet as a different mechanism from PRPs, and they are available to insolvent individuals that are likely to remain insolvent for a period of one year following their application for a debt relief order.[22]

---

16 Bankruptcy Law Cap. 5 §47 and Companies Law Cap. 113 §301.

17 Companies Law Cap. 113 §303.

18 Bankruptcy Law Cap. 5 §46.

19 See answer to Question 6 *supra* on the restructuring of companies and relevant §§202A and 202N of Companies Law Cap. 113.

20 Companies Law Cap. 113 §169Z.

21 Insolvency of Natural Persons (Personal Repayment Plans and Debt Relief Orders) Law of 2015 §11(2).

22 Ibid.

The term "*insolvent*" is thereby ascribed to a debtor that is unable to pay his/her debts as they fall due.[23]

Question 12: Is the definition of (the subspecies of) insolvency identical in all legal fields or are there different definitions (e.g. different in insolvency law than in criminal law)?

n.a.

II. INABILITY TO PAY DEBTS

Question 13: In your jurisdiction, is the term "inability to pay debts" defined in statute? If so, please give the wording in English translation. Is this definition (if any) specified in case law? If so, how?

Corporate restructuring by appointment of an Examiner

CoLaw §202A (3) (interpreting inability to pay debts for purposes of appointing an Examiner in the company for its restructuring) reads:

> For the purposes of this section, a company is *unable to pay its debts* if –
>
> (a) [it] is unable to pay its debts at the time they become payable,
> (b) the value of its assets is less than the amount of its liabilities, taking into account its contingent and future liabilities, or
> (c) the provisions of article 212 apply in this regard.

Liquidation of companies

CoLaw §212 (interpreting inability to pay debts for purposes of commencement of liquidation by court order) reads:

> a company is deemed *unable to pay its debts* –
>
> (a) if a creditor, by assignment or otherwise, to whom the company owes an amount in excess of five thousand euro (€5.000), has served process on the company by delivering to its registered office a demand letter requiring the company to pay the amount due as such, and the company has neglected for the following three weeks to pay the amount or secure or settle it to the reasonable satisfaction of the creditor; or

---

23 Insolvency of Natural Persons (Personal Repayment Plans and Debt Relief Orders) Law of 2015 §2. This definition of "insolvent" debtor is common for both debt relief orders and PRPs (see answer to Question 6(b) *supra*).

(b) if enforcement or other proceedings adopted by judgment, ruling or order of the Court to the benefit of the creditor of the company, is returned in part or in whole unsatisfied; or
(c) if it is proved to the satisfaction of the Court that the company is unable to pay its debts as they become due and, in its decision on whether the company is unable to pay its debts as they become due, the Court takes into account the company's contingent and future obligation; or
(d) if it is proved to the satisfaction of the Court that the value of the company's assets is less than the amount of its liabilities, taking into account its contingent and future liabilities.

In *GIP Constructions Ltd v. Director of Social Insurances*,[24] which is a leading case in liquidations, the Court of Appeal clarified that the requirement for service of the demand letter to the debtor as per §212(a) *supra* is absolute and shall not be interpreted to include also registered mail. In this respect, the liquidation petition of GIP would have been doomed to fail, as the demand letter was delivered to the registered office of the company by registered mail. However, the Court of Appeal found that the court of first instance had rightfully issued a liquidation order for GIP on the grounds that it was just and equitable for GIP to be liquidated, since the overall evidence submitted to the Court proved that four writs of possession had been issued by the Courts against GIP and all four had been returned without being satisfied, hence, even though the liquidation petition did not include any reference to §212(b) *supra*, the Court could still use this evidence to issue the liquidation petition on grounds of being just and equitable to do so, as provided in §211(f).[25]

Question 14: Does your law refer to all debts or only to mature debts?

Corporate restructuring by appointment of an Examiner

All debts; the CoLaw provisions on examinership provide that any petitions for the appointment of an Examiner in the company should be accompanied by a Statement of Affairs of the company, which shall include a statement of all assets and liabilities, including any contingent and future liabilities.[26]

Liquidation of companies

§212(a) of CoLaw indeed refers to a "*creditor*" of the company, a term which has been interpreted numerous times by the British Courts, whose case law on this has been applied thereafter by the Cypriot Courts, as someone who is

---

24 *GIP Constructions Ltd v. Διευθυντή Τμήματος Κοινωνικών Ασφαλίσεων* (1991) 1 ΑΑΔ 14.
25 See answer to Question 8 *supra* on §211, Companies Law Cap. 113.
26 Companies Law Cap. 113 §202B(2)(c) and (4)(c).

owed an amount from a stated account, thus excluding "*a person whose debt is substantially disputed even if the company is in fact insolvent*".[27]

On the other hand, the requirements laid down in §212(c) and (d) explicitly provide that the Courts, in deciding on the overall inability of the company to pay its debts, should consider also any "*contingent or future liabilities*"; that is, substantially all debts of the company.

Further, in considering the overall requirements to commence liquidation proceedings, that is §211 in combination with §212, which specifies in fact the conditions of §211(e), the Courts have been eager to give a wide interpretation to the inability to pay debts. In particular, in *GIP*,[28] which has henceforth been applied in several other cases,[29] the Court of Appeal clarified that:

> The specificity of the circumstances in section 212 does not limit the generality of section 211 in relation to a company's inability to pay its debts. That is, the special reasons constitute certain circumstances that raise a statutory presumption of the existence of the inability to pay debts but do not exhaust the scope for admitting any other testimony that could tend to the same result. In English case law one also finds the following example. Evidence from the creditor that the debt owed to him has not been paid by the company within a reasonable period of time is prima facie evidence that the company is insolvent.[30]

Question 15: Which assets are taken into account when assessing the inability to pay debts: all (financial) assets or only those that are liquid, i.e. available on short notice?

Corporate restructuring by appointment of an Examiner

See answer to Question 14 *supra*.

Liquidation of companies

All assets as at the date the liquidation petition is filed, as per the Court procedural rules.

Question 16: Is any liquidity gap (deficit between relevant financial means and relevant debts) relevant or does your law neglect minor gaps? If the latter, how is "minor" defined?

Corporate restructuring by appointment of an Examiner

Yes, it is relevant. In fact the statement of affairs required for filing a petition for the appointment of an Examiner in the company shall include a statement of all

27 *Mann v. Golastein* [1968] 1 WLR 1091, *Re Lympne Investments* [1972] 1 WLR 523, as quoted in *Χατζηγιάννης Ανδρέας v. C. & J. Kyprianou Promotions Ltd.* (2010) 1 ΑΑΔ 991.

28 *GIP Constructions Ltd v. Διευθυντή Τμήματος Κοινωνικών Ασφαλίσεων* (1991) 1 ΑΑΔ 14.

29 See *Moulettaris M. Machinery Co Ltd v. Μιχάλη Ζήνωνος* (2001) 1 ΑΑΔ 1649.

30 *GIP Constructions Ltd v. Διευθυντή Τμήματος Κοινωνικών Ασφαλίσεων* (1991) 1 ΑΑΔ 14.

assets and liabilities, including contingent and future ones, as it is an absolute requirement in order to establish that the company is insolvent or in likelihood of insolvency through this statement,[31] for the independent expert to state that he/she is of this opinion in his/her relevant report.[32]

Liquidation of companies

The law ignores minor gaps. There is no case law defining "*minor gaps*", probably because in most cases there is no need to examine the total value of debts against its total liabilities, since "*[i]f the company is found unable to meet each of its financial obligations separately, this renders it unable to repay its debts*".[33]

Question 17: As far as the time aspect is concerned, does it matter whether the liquidity gap can be closed again in the short term? If so, how long is the grace period?

Corporate restructuring by appointment of an Examiner

Yes, certainly. Upon filing the petition for the appointment of an Examiner in the company (i) a moratorium of four months preventing all creditor actions against the company begins,[34] and (ii) a stay of all payments on historic debts of the company for the duration of the moratorium[35] is effected. During these four months that the moratorium is in place, the Examiner appointed in the company will promote measures for the business, or any part of it to return to profitability, so as to prove its viability through the adoption of a restructuring plan covering all historic debts. Therefore, any liquidity gap on commencement of the examinership proceedings shall be covered within the moratorium period.

Liquidation of companies

No. See answer to Question 16 *supra*.

---

31 Companies Law Cap. 113 §§202B(2)(c) and 202A(1)(a).

32 Companies Law Cap. 113 §202B(4). Either together with the petition for appointment of an Examiner or right after, an independent expert shall file a report stating his/her opinion on the insolvency or likelihood of insolvency of the company, its potential to become viable, either in whole or any part of it, as a going concern, on any deficit found, etc., reasoning these opinions in a statement of affairs, list of all creditors and cash flow projections.

33 *Re A Company N. 0012209 of 1991* reported in [1992] 1 WLR 351 as this is referenced in *Αίτηση των εταιρειών ETOURIST DEVELOPMENTS LTD και CHRIMA DEVELOPMENTS v. αναφορικά με την εταιρεία MAGIA OLD PEOPLE's HOME*, Αίτηση Αρ. 250/2016, 20.03.2018.

34 Companies Law Cap. 113 §202H(1).

35 Companies Law Cap. 113 §202Θ(1).

Question 18: As far as the time aspect is concerned, is a debtor considered insolvent if the liquidity gap is not yet present but will occur soon? If so, how long is the prognosis period? (Note: this may also concern the difference between actual and likely/imminent inability to pay debts; cf. below Question 34).

Corporate restructuring by appointment of an Examiner

Yes, considering that the purpose of examinership proceedings is to assist an insolvent company to become viable again. According to provisions introduced recently in examinership legislation, for purposes of harmonisation with Directive (EU) 2019/1023, likelihood of insolvency is enough to commence examinership proceedings[36] and such likelihood of insolvency, is defined as the case in which, "it is reasonably likely that the company will become insolvent within twelve (12) months".[37]

Liquidation of companies

No.

Question 19: How is inability to pay debts established? Please communicate if there is a difference between a creditor and a debtor application or between different legal contexts.

a) Is a formal liquidity status (liquidity balance sheet) required?
Yes, for corporate restructuring, as the independent expert's report will rely on the statement of affairs. See answer to Question 16 *supra*.

No, for liquidation of companies. Even though balance sheet insolvency is listed as one of the grounds establishing inability to pay debts,[38] it is hardly ever used, as explained in Question 16 *supra*.

b) Is a sample of daily liquidity data (which do not amount to a proper liquidity status but show insufficient funds on different days within a certain period of time) sufficient?
No.

c) Does the law provide for a rebuttable presumption? If so, under which conditions?
No.

d) Does the law provide for any technical circumstances (e.g. undisputed statutory demand, non-compliance with monetary judgments, unsuccessful

36 Companies Law Cap. 113 §202A(1).
37 Companies Law Cap. 113 §202N.
38 Companies Law Cap. 113 §212(d).

enforcement proceedings, non-performance of a previous composition agreement in insolvency proceedings) the occurrence of which suffices to establish the debtor's insolvency?

Yes, see CoLaw §212 in answer to Question 13 *supra* and B.Law §3 in answer to Question 8 *supra*.

e) Other means?

n.a.

Question 20: Is insolvency (inability to pay debts, overindebtedness, etc.) subject to party autonomy in the proceedings or must the court clarify them *ex officio*?

The Court must clarify them *ex officio*, except in the case of voluntary liquidations.

Question 21: In an overall view, does your law distinguish "inability to pay debts" from "financial difficulties"? If so, how?

Not really, in the sense that it determines "inability to pay debts" through several examples identifying financial difficulties.

Question 22: In an overall view, does it matter under your law whether the debtor's inability to pay debts is present or future and reversible or irreversible?

Yes, in relation to PRPs for the restructuring of debts of individuals and to Examinership for corporate restructuring.

Not really, though, since in relation to bankruptcy and liquidation, contingent and future debts are included in the test and, in any case, being unable to meet each of its financial obligations separately is enough to commence liquidation proceedings (see answer to Question 16 *supra* under "Liquidation of companies").

Question 23: Would you like to add any further aspects not covered by the above questions?

n.a.

III. CESSATION OF PAYMENTS

Question 24: In your jurisdiction, is "cessation of payments" a legal term used either in statute or in case law? (If the answer is "no", please continue with Question 31.)

No.

Question 25: Is "cessation of payments" an autonomous ground to commence proceedings (triggering circumstance)? You may refer to Questions 6/7 or add additional information here.

n.a.

Question 26: Is "cessation of payments" a means to establish inability to pay debts? If so, by which mechanism (e.g. rebuttable presumption for inability to pay debts, cf. above Question 19(c))?

n.a.

Question 27: How is "cessation of payments" defined? If it is defined in statute, please provide us here with an English translation of the relevant rule. Is this definition (if any) specified in case law? If so, how?

n.a.

Question 28: How is "cessation of payments" established?

n.a.

Question 29: Are there typical circumstances which provide circumstantial evidence that the debtor has ceased payments? If so, please list as many as possible.

n.a.

Question 30: Would you like to add any further aspects not covered by the above questions?

n.a.

IV. LIKELY/IMMINENT INABILITY TO PAY DEBTS

Question 31: Are the following terms available in your jurisdiction, either in statute or in case law? (If the answer is "no", please continue with Question 42.)

a) likely inability to pay debts
Yes, in fact it is "likelihood of insolvency" (see translation of §202N in answer to Question 6 *supra*).

b) imminent inability to pay debts
No.

c) other (similar) terms
No.

Question 32: Is "likely/imminent inability to pay debts" an autonomous ground to commence proceedings (triggering circumstance)? You may refer to Questions 6/7 or add additional information here.

Yes, it is in commencing corporate restructuring proceedings (see answer to Question 6 *supra*, translation of relevant legislation on corporate restructuring).

Question 33: If the answer to the previous Question is "yes", who may base filing for insolvency proceedings on it: only the debtor or also creditors?

The debtor – company, a creditor, a contingent or future creditor (including an employee), members of the company, a guarantor, any of these together or separately.[39]

Question 34: How are these terms defined? If they are defined in statute, please provide us here with an English translation of the relevant rules. Is this definition (if any) specified in case law? If so, how?

a) likely inability to pay debts
Yes, "likelihood of insolvency" (see translation of §202N in answer to Question 6 *supra*).

b) imminent inability to pay debts
n.a.

Question 35: Do the terms "likely" and "imminent" require a prognosis regarding the point in time when actual inability to pay debts will occur? If so, how long is the time period for this prognosis?

Within the next 12 months (see translation of §202N in Question 6 *supra*).

Question 36: Does your law require a specific grade of certainty that inability to pay debts will eventually occur? If so, is 50.1% ("more likely than not") enough or are there alleviated or aggravated prerequisites?

No, none of these. Just the opinion of the company's directors or the Court.

Question 37: Regarding "debts" and "financial means", are they defined in the same way as in the context of inability to pay debts (cf. above Questions 14/15)? If not, what are the differences?

"Debts": yes, they are defined in the same way as in the context of inability to pay debts, yet are also indirectly defined in case law through the definition of a "creditor" (see answer to Question 14 *supra* under "Liquidation of companies").

"Financial means": n.a.

---

39 Companies Law Cap. 113 §202B(1).

Question 38: Further to Question 37: Are "debts" considered which do currently not exist or are not yet due but will foreseeably come into existence and become due during the prognosis period?

n.a.

Question 39: Also further to Question 37: Are "financial means" considered which do currently not exist but will foreseeably become available during the prognosis period?

n.a.

Question 40: How are the terms "likely/imminent inability to pay debts" established?

See translation of §202N in answer to Question 6 *supra*.

Question 41: Would you like to add any further aspects not covered by the above questions?

n.a.

V. OVERINDEBTEDNESS

Question 42: In your jurisdiction, is "overindebtedness", or "balance sheet insolvency" respectively, a legal term used either in statute or in case law? (If the answer is "no", please continue with Question 56.)

Not these terms as such, yet balance sheet insolvency is set out as one of the circumstances which constitute "inability to pay debts" in corporate liquidation as set out in answer to Question 6 *supra* (see translation of §212(d) therein).

Question 43: Is "overindebtedness" an autonomous ground to commence proceedings (triggering circumstance)? You may refer to Questions 6/7 or add additional information here.

Yes. See answers to Questions 42 and 6 *supra*.

Question 44: If the answer to the previous Question is "yes", is this applicable to corporate insolvencies of legal persons only or also to personal bankruptcies of natural persons?

Corporate insolvencies only (see answers to Questions 42 and 6 *supra*).

Question 45: Is the term "overindebtedness" defined in statute? If so, please give the wording in English translation. Is this definition (if any) specified in case law? If so, how?

No. See answers to Question 42 *supra.*

Question 46: Does your law refer to all existing debts or only to mature debts?

All existing debts including "*contingent and future*" ones. See answers to Questions 42 and 6 *supra.*

Question 47: Does the rank of certain debts play a role when establishing overindebtedness? In particular, is there any possibility to conclude agreements according to which certain debts shall not be taken into account (e.g. agreements on subsidiarity)?

No.

Question 48: Which assets are taken into account when overindebtedness is established: the complete set of assets or only a selection of them?

See answer to Question 15 *supra.*

Question 49: How are the debtor's assets valued: by referring to the liquidation value, the book value, the going concern value or in another way?

Book value.

Question 50: Is there any prognostic element, e.g. regarding the debtor's chances to continue the business?

No.

Question 51: If the answer to the previous Question is "yes", what exactly is the topic of the prognosis and how is it established?

n.a.

Question 52: If the answer to the Question 50 is "yes", how long is the prognosis period?

n.a.

Question 53: How is overindebtedness established?

a) Is a formal balance sheet required?
n.a.

b) Does the yearly regular commercial balance sheet have any meaning (given that it is normally based on technical values and does not display undisclosed reserves)?
n.a.

c) Does the law provide for a presumption? If so, under which conditions?
No.

d) Other means?
n.a.

Question 54: Is the legal link to overindebtedness undisputed in literature or are there efforts to abolish it?

None of these, as it is not commonly used. It is kind of redundant as all other tests to establish "inability to pay debts" are easier to prove (see answer to Question 16 *supra* under "Liquidation of companies"). This is probably so also due to the fact that the directors of the company do not have an obligation to commence insolvency proceedings once they are aware of it (see relevant comment in answer to Question 2 *supra*).

Question 55: Would you like to add any further aspects not covered by the above questions?

n.a.

VI. REMAINING ISSUES

Question 56: Is there anything else you would like to share in the present context and that we should take into account?

n.a.

CZECH REPUBLIC

Tomáš Richter

I. GENERAL

Question 1: How is insolvency (both in the context of liquidation and restructuring/reorganisation) regulated in your jurisdiction? Please give a brief overview, at least enumerating the relevant statutes.

There is one insolvency code, Act 162/2006 Coll., as amended, referred to in Czech as *insolvenční zákon*. It will be abbreviated as the "IA" in this questionnaire.

Question 2: Related to paragraph 10 above of the Introduction: seen from a principle-based perspective, what justifies the opening of insolvency proceedings in your jurisdiction?

The insolvency (or threatening insolvency) of a debtor is a state of affairs in which the debtor is no longer able to pay all of its debts in full, whereby the policy goal is to settle the debtor's proprietary relationships with parties affected by the debtor's insolvency (or threatening insolvency) with the goal of achieving the highest possible, and in principle rateable, satisfaction of the debtor's creditors. This at least is the aim with respect to business debtors as codified in Section 1(a) of the IA. With respect to consumers, the aim stated in Section 1(b) of the IA is a discharge of debts (*oddlužení*).

Question 3: Does your national law in the context of liquidation proceedings use one or more of the following terms (be it as a noun, be it as an adjective or adjunct) in whatever context:

a) inability to pay debts
Yes, the Czech term is *platební neschopnost* (Section 3(1) of the IA). The term is used to denote one of the two grounds of insolvency – the cash-flow test.

b) cessation of payments
Yes, the Czech term is *zastavení plateb* (Section 3(2)(a) of the IA).

c) likely inability to pay debts
Not exactly, but the IA uses the term *hrozící úpadek*, i.e. threatening insolvency (Section 3(5) of the IA).

d) imminent inability to pay debts
No.

e) overindebtedness?
Yes, the Czech term is *předlužení*. The term is used to denote the second of the two grounds of insolvency – the balance sheet test.

Question 4: Are the same terms (and with the same meaning) used in the rules on preliminary/interim insolvency proceedings (e.g. concerning the application stage of the proceedings)?

Partly yes, esp. where the relevant legislation cross-refers to insolvency via the inability to pay debts as a bar to the use of the preventive restructuring framework. (Section 4(2) of the Preventive Restructuring Act 284/2023 which entered into effect in the Czech Republic on 23 September 2023).

Question 5: Does your national law in the context of restructuring proceedings (as referred to above at paragraph 8 of the Introduction, i.e. both pre-insolvency and within formal insolvency proceedings) use one or more of the following terms (be it as a noun, be it as an adjective or adjunct) in whatever context:

Note: The answers only apply to reorganisation (*reorganizace*) as one of the two procedural paths available to business debtors within the unitary insolvency proceedings under the IA, the other path being (insolvent) liquidation (*konkurs*). The preventive restructuring framework pursuant to the Preventive Restructuring Act mentioned in response to Question 4 is entirely different and it would be unhelpful to mix the two laws together.

Because the insolvency proceedings under the IA are unitary, commencing based on one and the same set of opening criteria and then branching into either liquidation or reorganisation, the answers here are exactly the same as to Question 3.

a) inability to pay debts
Yes, the Czech term is *platební neschopnost* (Section 3(1) of the IA). The term is used to denote one of the two grounds of insolvency – the cash-flow test.

b) cessation of payments
Yes, the Czech term is *zastavení plateb* (Section 3(2)(a) of the IA).

c) likely inability to pay debts
Not exactly, but the IA uses the term *hrozící úpadek*, i.e. threatening insolvency (Section 3(5) of the IA).

d) imminent inability to pay debts
No.

e) overindebtedness?
Yes, the Czech term is *předlužení* (Section 3(4) of the IA). The term is used to denote the other of the two grounds of insolvency – the balance sheet test.

Question 6: Which of the terms mentioned in Question 3 and 5 are used for defining grounds to commence proceedings (triggering circumstances)?

a) insolvency proceedings
Questions 3/5(a), (c) and (e). The term as per Questions 3/5(b) is a mere subspecies of Questions 3/5(a). Please note the overall comments in response to Question 5 – Czech insolvency proceedings are unitary, and this answer therefore applies to reorganisation (conducted within their framework) as well as to liquidation.

b) restructuring proceedings
None, but the existence of the state of insolvency for the inability to pay debts (i.e. cash-flow insolvency) operates as a bar preventing the use of the preventive restructuring framework (Section 4(2) of the Preventive Restructuring Act).

Question 7: Does the answer to Question 6 include personal bankruptcies of natural persons or only corporate insolvencies of legal entities?

Overindebtedness (Questions 3/5(e)) only applies as a triggering circumstance with respect to corporate debtors and to sole proprietors, i.e. to business debtors.

Question 8: In your law, are there any other circumstances which trigger insolvency or restructuring proceedings?

No.

Question 9: Which of the terms mentioned in Questions 3, 5, and 8 are used in the context of transactions avoidance law?

None – those provisions use the general term *úpadek*, i.e. insolvency, irrespective of whether occurring on the cash-flow or the balance sheet grounds.

Question 10: Which of the terms addressed in Questions 3, 5, and 8 are used in the context of directors' duties?

a) shift of duties (from shareholders to creditors)
n.a.

b) duties to commence insolvency proceedings

Those provisions use the general term *úpadek*, i.e. insolvency, irrespective of whether occurring on the cash-flow or the balance sheet grounds.

c) other duties (please describe)

n.a.

Question 11: Are there any other rules in the context of which the terms addressed in Question 3, 5, and 8 are used?

The general term insolvency (*úpadek*) is of course used throughout the IA and also in numerous other laws which relate or cross-refer to the IA.

Question 12: Is the definition of (the subspecies of) insolvency identical in all legal fields or are there different definitions (e.g. different in insolvency law than in criminal law)?

Identical, or rather, other laws are unlikely to have their own definition but are much more likely to cross-refer to the definitions given in the IA.

II. INABILITY TO PAY DEBTS

Question 13: In your jurisdiction, is the term "inability to pay debts" defined in statute? If so, please give the wording in English translation. Is this definition (if any) specified in case law? If so, how?

Section 3 of the IA defines cash-flow insolvency as follows:

> (1) The debtor is insolvent if it (a) has multiple creditors, (b) has due and payable monetary debts more than 30 days overdue, and (c) is not able to pay those debts (hereafter the "inability to pay debts").
>
> (2) The debtor shall be presumed to be unable to pay its monetary debts if (a) it has ceased to pay a substantial part of its monetary debts, or (b) it has been more than 3 months overdue with the payment of its monetary debts, or (c) it has not been possible to collect any of its due and payable monetary debts via execution proceedings, or (d) it has not performed a court-imposed obligation to submit the lists as per Section 104(1). [These are lists of assets, liabilities, and employees.]
>
> (3) A business debtor who keeps financial accounts shall be presumed to be able to pay its monetary debts if the difference between the amount of its due and payable monetary debts and the amount of its available liquidity means (hereafter the "liquidity gap") evidenced in a liquidity statement drawn up in accordance with the relevant sub-statutory regulations, amounts to less than one-tenth of its due and payable monetary debts, or if a future liquidity model drawn up in accordance with

> the relevant sub-statutory regulations evidences that the liquidity gap will fall below one-tenth of its due and payable monetary debts within the period for which the future liquidity model is drawn up. The liquidity statement or the future liquidity model must be drawn up in accordance with the relevant sub-statutory regulations by an auditor, a court-sworn expert or a party specialising in economic advice in the fields of insolvency and restructuring who meets the criteria set out in the relevant sub-statutory regulations.
>
> …
>
> (6) Sub-statutory regulations shall set out the contents, extent and the methods of drawing up liquidity statements and future liquidity models, as well as the lay-out, naming and contents of individual items of assets, liabilities, costs, earnings, incomes and expenses to be reported in liquidity statements and future liquidity models, the length of the periods for which the future liquidity models shall be drawn up, and the requirements to be met by persons authorised to draw up liquidity statements and future liquidity models.

Question 14: Does your law refer to all debts or only to mature debts?

To due and payable (i.e. mature) monetary debts – see response to Question 13 above.

Question 15: Which assets are taken into account when assessing the inability to pay debts: all (financial) assets or only those that are liquid, i.e. available on short notice?

Liquid assets only, although there has been controversial case law on this point, potentially including assets which would not generally be considered liquid or short-term.

Question 16: Is any liquidity gap (deficit between relevant financial means and relevant debts) relevant or does your law neglect minor gaps? If the latter, how is "minor" defined?

Yes. See response to Question 13 *supra*, Section 3(3) and (6) of the IA.

Question 17: As far as the time aspect is concerned, does it matter whether the liquidity gap can be closed again in the short term? If so, how long is the grace period?

Under Section 15 of the relevant sub-statutory regulation, Regulation 190/2017 Coll., the future liquidity model is short-term and must generally be drawn up for the period of the next eight weeks, although slight extensions are possible.

Question 18: As far as the time aspect is concerned, is a debtor considered insolvent if the liquidity gap is not yet present but will occur soon? If so, how long is the prognosis period? (Note: this may also concern the difference between actual and likely/imminent inability to pay debts; cf. below Question 34).

Please see response to Question 13 *supra*, Section 3(3) of the IA – the concept of the liquidity gap, as reported either in the liquidity statement or the future liquidity model submitted to the insolvency court by the debtor, can be used to trigger the presumption that the debtor is not cash-flow insolvent if the size of the gap is shown to be within the prescribed bounds. But the absence of these documents does not in itself operate as a negative procedural presumption.

Procedurally, the insolvency court will only consider the liquidity statement or the future liquidity model as a defence against a creditor's insolvency petition if such statements are filed by the debtor within 14 days of the notification of the commencement of insolvency proceedings in the insolvency register; the insolvency court may reasonably extend this time limit but only based on the debtor's application filed on particularly deserving grounds (Section 131(2) of the IA).

Question 19: How is inability to pay debts established? Please communicate if there is a difference between a creditor and a debtor application or between different legal contexts.

There is no difference between debtor- and creditor-filed petitions in this regard.

a) Is a formal liquidity status (liquidity balance sheet) required?
No.

b) Is a sample of daily liquidity data (which do not amount to a proper liquidity status but show insufficient funds on different days within a certain period of time) sufficient?
No, unless such data show that the statutory definition – and in particular the number of creditors and the length of time for which the debtor has been in arrears – has been met.

c) Does the law provide for a rebuttable presumption? If so, under which conditions?
Yes, please see response to Question 13 *supra*, Section 3(2) of the IA.

d) Does the law provide for any technical circumstances (e.g. undisputed statutory demand, non-compliance with monetary judgments, unsuccessful enforcement proceedings, non-performance of a previous composition agreement in insolvency proceedings) the occurrence of which suffices to establish the debtor's insolvency?
Yes, please see response to Question 13 *supra*, Section 3(2) of the IA.

e) Other means?
n.a.

Question 20: Is insolvency (inability to pay debts, overindebtedness, etc.) subject to party autonomy in the proceedings or must the court clarify them *ex officio*?

Ex officio.

Question 21: In an overall view, does your law distinguish "inability to pay debts" from "financial difficulties"? If so, how?

No, except in the context of the liquidity gap – see response to Question 13 *supra*, Section 3(3) of the IA.

Question 22: In an overall view, does it matter under your law whether the debtor's inability to pay debts is present or future and reversible or irreversible?

The inability to pay must be present. Within the bounds for the use of the concept of the liquidity gap (see response to Question 13 *supra*, Section 3(3) of the IA), one can say that it is "reversible."

Question 23: Would you like to add any further aspects not covered by the above questions?

No.

III. CESSATION OF PAYMENTS

Question 24: In your jurisdiction, is "cessation of payments" a legal term used either in statute or in case law? (If the answer is "no", please continue with Question 31.)

Yes, please see responses to Questions 5(b) and 6(a).

Question 25: Is "cessation of payments" an autonomous ground to commence proceedings (triggering circumstance)? You may refer to Questions 6/7 or add additional information here.

No.

Question 26: Is "cessation of payments" a means to establish inability to pay debts? If so, by which mechanism (e.g. rebuttable presumption for inability to pay debts, cf. above Question 19(c))?

Yes, as a rebuttable presumption – see response to Question 6(a).

Question 27: How is "cessation of payments" defined? If it is defined in statute, please provide us here with an English translation of the relevant rule. Is this definition (if any) specified in case law? If so, how?

There is no statutory definition. The Supreme Court's case law has defined the "cessation of payments" as

> the debtor's intentional action, its decision, to no longer pay its monetary obligations, usually accompanied by a declaration that the debtor will not pay. It shall suffice if the debtor does this with at least a substantial part of its obligations. (*In re Oleo Chemical*, case no. 29 NSČR 24/2013 of 30 April 2015).

Question 28: How is "cessation of payments" established?

See response to Question 27 – the court would have to be satisfied that the debtor has intentionally discontinued the payment of at least a substantial part of its obligations. If the debtor made a declaration to this effect in a recorded or otherwise provable manner, this will not be very difficult, barring perhaps questions as to what proportion of the obligations is to be considered as "substantial". If no such declaration has been made (or can be proven) and moreover, if the debtor denies that it would have intentionally stopped paying, establishing the cessation will be very difficult, as follows from the facts of the case reported in response to Question 27.

Question 29: Are there typical circumstances which provide circumstantial evidence that the debtor has ceased payments? If so, please list as many as possible.

See responses to Questions 27 and 28.

Question 30: Would you like to add any further aspects not covered by the above questions?

No.

IV. LIKELY/IMMINENT INABILITY TO PAY DEBTS

Question 31: Are the following terms available in your jurisdiction, either in statute or in case law? (If the answer is "no", please continue with Question 42.)

a) likely inability to pay debts

No. But the IA uses the term *hrozící úpadek*, i.e. threatening insolvency (Section 3(5) of the IA).

b) imminent inability to pay debts
No.

c) other (similar) terms
No.

Question 32: Is "likely/imminent inability to pay debts" an autonomous ground to commence proceedings (triggering circumstance)? You may refer to Questions 6/7 or add additional information here.

Threatening insolvency pursuant to Section 3(5) of the IA is an autonomous triggering circumstance; however, it is only available as a ground for the commencement of insolvency proceedings by the debtor (Section 97(7) of the IA), not by creditors.

Question 33: If the answer to the previous Question is "yes", who may base filing for insolvency proceedings on it: only the debtor or also creditors?

See response to Question 32 – only the debtor.

Question 34: How are these terms defined? If they are defined in statute, please provide us here with an English translation of the relevant rules. Is this definition (if any) specified in case law? If so, how?

a) likely inability to pay debts
Section 3(5) of the IA defines threatening insolvency as follows:

> (5) Insolvency is threatening if, upon consideration of all relevant circumstances, the debtor may be reasonably expected not to be able to pay a substantial part of its monetary debts as and when they fall due.

b) imminent inability to pay debts
n.a.

Question 35: Do the terms "likely" and "imminent" require a prognosis regarding the point in time when actual inability to pay debts will occur? If so, how long is the time period for this prognosis?

The law does not set out any specific prognosis period for the purposes of the concept of threatening insolvency under Section 3(5) of the IA.

Question 36: Does your law require a specific grade of certainty that inability to pay debts will eventually occur? If so, is 50.1% ("more likely than not") enough or are there alleviated or aggravated prerequisites?

No.

Question 37: Regarding "debts" and "financial means", are they defined in the same way as in the context of inability to pay debts (cf. above Questions 14/15)? If not, what are the differences?

n.a.

Question 38: Further to Question 37: Are "debts" considered which do currently not exist or are not yet due but will foreseeably come into existence and become due during the prognosis period?

Most likely yes, but there is no clarity on this. Section 3(5) of the IA has been used very infrequently, if at all.

Question 39: Also further to Question 37: Are "financial means" considered which do currently not exist but will foreseeably become available during the prognosis period?

Most likely yes, but there is no clarity on this. Section 3(5) of the IA has been used very infrequently, if at all.

Question 40: How are the terms "likely/imminent inability to pay debts" established?

n.a.

Question 41: Would you like to add any further aspects not covered by the above questions?

No.

V. OVERINDEBTEDNESS

Question 42: In your jurisdiction, is "overindebtedness", or "balance sheet insolvency" respectively, a legal term used either in statute or in case law? (If the answer is "no", please continue with Question 56.)

Yes, the Czech term is *předlužení*.

Question 43: Is "overindebtedness" an autonomous ground to commence proceedings (triggering circumstance)? You may refer to Questions 6/7 or add additional information here.

Yes.

Question 44: If the answer to the previous Question is "yes", is this applicable to corporate insolvencies of legal persons only or also to personal bankruptcies of natural persons?

This triggering circumstance only applies to corporate debtors and to sole proprietors (Section 3(4) of the IA).

Question 45: Is the term "overindebtedness" defined in statute? If so, please give the wording in English translation. Is this definition (if any) specified in case law? If so, how?

Section 3(4) of the IA defines overindebtedness as follows:

> (4) A debtor who is a legal entity or an individual business person is also insolvent if it is overindebted. Overindebtedness obtains if the debtor has multiple creditors and the sum of its liabilities exceeds the value of its assets. When determining the value of the debtor's assets, the further management thereof or the further operation of the debtor's business shall be taken into account if it can be reasonably assumed, upon the consideration of all the relevant circumstances, that the debtor will be able to continue with the management of its assets or the operation of its business.

Question 46: Does your law refer to all existing debts or only to mature debts?

Most likely all, although there has been uncertainty about this in the past. The issue seems to have been clarified in Supreme Court judgment *In re BONUS obchodní agentura* (case no. 29 NSČR 206/2017 of 31 July 2019).

Question 47: Does the rank of certain debts play a role when establishing overindebtedness? In particular, is there any possibility to conclude agreements according to which certain debts shall not be taken into account (e.g. agreements on subsidiarity)?

This is unclear. The law of overindebtedness is very undeveloped and many questions, including this one, are simply unanswered. My personal argument would be that, at the very least, universally subordinated debts should not be considered for the purposes of testing overindebtedness, but there is no tangible basis for this conclusion in the present law.

Question 48: Which assets are taken into account when overindebtedness is established: the complete set of assets or only a selection of them?

All assets.

Question 49: How are the debtor's assets valued: by referring to the liquidation value, the book value, the going concern value or in another way?

This is very unclear. But it follows from Section 3(4) of the IA that where a continued going concern can reasonably be expected, a going concern valuation should be applied.

Question 50: Is there any prognostic element, e.g. regarding the debtor's chances to continue the business?

Yes, see the language of Section 3(4) of the IA as translated in response to Question 45. But there is no meaningful guidance on how this prognosis should be conducted.

Question 51: If the answer to the previous Question is "yes", what exactly is the topic of the prognosis and how is it established?

See response to Question 50.

Question 52: If the answer to Question 50 is "yes", how long is the prognosis period?

See response to Question 50.

Question 53: How is overindebtedness established?

a) Is a formal balance sheet required?
No. Although this is very likely to be the first approximation.

b) Does the yearly regular commercial balance sheet have any meaning (given that it is normally based on technical values and does not display undisclosed reserves)?
Most likely not.

c) Does the law provide for a presumption? If so, under which conditions?
No.

d) Other means?
n.a.

Question 54: Is the legal link to overindebtedness undisputed in literature or are there efforts to abolish it?

I, for one, have argued that the implementation of the EU Restructuring Directive should be used as an opportunity to conduct a thorough review of the IA in as far as it relates to corporate debtors. I have proposed that, among other issues, such review takes up the question whether the IA should retain the "overindebtedness" test for corporate debtors, and also the threatening insolvency triggering ground, since these two grounds largely overlap with the ambit of the Preventive Restructuring Act, resulting in untrammelled arbitrage between the two legal regimes. However, those proposal gained no traction with the Czech Ministry of Justice and the Preventive Restructuring Act came into force without any review of the IA having been conducted, let alone adopted.

Question 55: Would you like to add any further aspects not covered by the above questions?

n.a.

VI. REMAINING ISSUES

Question 56: Is there anything else you would like to share in the present context and that we should take into account?

No.

ESTONIA

Anto Kasak

I. GENERAL

Question 1: How is insolvency (both in the context of liquidation and restructuring/reorganisation) regulated in your jurisdiction? Please give a brief overview, at least enumerating the relevant statutes.

Estonian insolvency laws and proceedings are divided by subject: legal persons or natural persons. Liquidation insolvency proceedings for legal persons are regulated under Pankrotiseadus (Bankruptcy Act, PankrS – https://www.riigiteataja.ee/en/eli/503052023007/consolide). Reorganisation insolvency proceedings for legal persons are governed by Saneerimisseadus (Reorganisation Act, SanS – https://www.riigiteataja.ee/en/eli/523032023005/consolide). Liquidation insolvency proceedings for natural persons are regulated under PankrS, unless otherwise provided Füüsilise isiku maksejõuetuse seadus (Natural Person Insolvency Act, FIMS – https://www.riigiteataja.ee/en/eli/511012023002/consolide). Restructuring of debts of natural persons is regulated only by FIMS. Furthermore, there is one unique reorganisation proceeding Compromise (*Kompromiss*) for both natural persons and legal persons under PankrS §§178–192 (Chapter 12).

Question 2: Related to paragraph 10 above of the Introduction: seen from a principle-based perspective, what justifies the opening of insolvency proceedings in your jurisdiction?

The opening of insolvency proceedings is justified by the so-called "Common Pool" effect, the situation where the debtor's funds are insufficient for satisfaction of all creditors' claims. The trigger for enforcement of collective proceedings might be different under an application by the debtor or by the creditor, and the estimation of the insolvency may be different under the "cash-flow" or "balance sheet" test, but the consequences are the same, collective insolvency proceedings (liquidation or reorganisation) shall be enforced. In such case the principle of collectivity and principle of equal treatment of creditors shall apply. Individual enforcement proceedings are not allowed anymore, and the estate of the debtor and the claims of the creditors are clarified in collective insolvency proceedings.

Question 3: Does your national law in the context of liquidation proceedings use one or more of the following terms (be it as a noun, be it as an adjective or adjunct) in whatever context:

a) inability to pay debts
Yes.

b) cessation of payments
No.

c) likely inability to pay debts
Yes.

d) imminent inability to pay debts
Yes.

e) overindebtedness?
Yes.

Question 4: Are the same terms (and with the same meaning) used in the rules on preliminary/interim insolvency proceedings (e.g. concerning the application stage of the proceedings)?

In case of appointment of the interim trustee (opening the preliminary bankruptcy proceedings) substantive insolvency is not necessary. The creditor shall prove the existence of the clear claim and substantiate (a lower standard of proof) the insolvency of the debtor by relying, *inter alia*, on at least one of the following circumstances:

(i) the debtor has failed to perform an obligation within 30 days after the obligation has fallen due and the creditor has cautioned the debtor in writing of the creditor's intention to file a bankruptcy petition (bankruptcy caution) and the debtor has thereafter failed to perform the obligation within 10 days;
(ii) it has not been possible within a period of three months to satisfy a claim in execution proceedings conducted with respect to the debtor due to lack of assets, or it has become evident in the execution proceedings that the assets of the debtor are insufficient for performing all the obligations thereof;
(iii) the debtor has destroyed, hidden or squandered the debtor's property or made grave errors in management as a result of which the debtor has become insolvent, or has intentionally caused the insolvency of the debtor in any other manner;
(iv) the debtor has notified the creditor, the court or the public of the inability of the debtor to perform the obligations thereof;
(v) the debtor has left Estonia in order to evade performance of the obligations thereof or is hiding with the same purpose.

Question 5: Does your national law in the context of restructuring proceedings (as referred to above at paragraph 8 of the Introduction, i.e. both pre-insolvency and within formal insolvency proceedings) use one or more of the following terms (be it as a noun, be it as an adjective or adjunct) in whatever context:

a) inability to pay debts
Yes.

b) cessation of payments
No.

c) likely inability to pay debts
Yes.

d) imminent inability to pay debts
Yes.

e) overindebtedness?
Yes.

Question 6: Which of the terms mentioned in Questions 3 and 5 are used for defining grounds to commence proceedings (triggering circumstances)?

a) insolvency proceedings

(i) "inability to pay debts" (PankrS §1 lg 2);
(ii) "overindebtedness" (PankrS §1 lg 3);
(iii) "likely inability to pay debts" (PankrS §31 lg 3);
(iv) "imminent inability to pay debts" (PankrS §31 lg 3).

b) restructuring proceedings

(i) "likely inability to pay debts" (SanS §7 lg 2 p 1 and §8 lg 1 p 1);
(ii) "imminent inability to pay debts" (SanS §7 lg 2 p 1 and §8 lg 1 p 1).

Question 7: Does the answer to Question 6 include personal bankruptcies of natural persons or only corporate insolvencies of legal entities?

Liquidation insolvency proceedings for natural person are regulated under FIMS and PankrS (see answer to Question 2). FIMS does not have any additional terms regarding liquidation insolvency proceedings (see answer to Question 6). Nevertheless, FIMS has some additional terms for restructuring proceedings for natural persons as follows:

(i) "likely inability to pay debts" (FIMS §19 lg 1);
(ii) "imminent inability to pay debts" (FIMS §19 lg 1).

Question 8: In your law, are there any other circumstances which trigger insolvency or restructuring proceedings?

No.

Question 9: Which of the terms mentioned in Questions 3, 5, and 8 are used in the context of transactions avoidance law?

Substantive insolvency is one of the prerequisites for certain grounds of transaction avoidance (PankrS §111 lg 1 p 2, §112 p 2, §113 lg 1 p 2 and 3, §114 lg 1 p 2 and §116^1 lg 1 p 2 and 3). In such cases the substantive insolvency is ascertained by combined interpretation of "inability to pay debts" and "overindebtedness".

Question 10: Which of the terms addressed in Questions 3, 5, and 8 are used in the context of directors' duties?

a) shift of duties (from shareholders to creditors)
Estonian law does not recognise the concept of the shift of duties from shareholders to creditors.

b) duties to commence insolvency proceedings
According to the §180 lg 5^1 and §306 lg 3^1 of the Äriseadustik (Commercial Code, ÄS – https://www.riigiteataja.ee/en/eli/509012023001/consolide), in the event of the likely inability to pay debts and imminent inability to pay debts the members of the management board of the limited liability company must take steps to overcome the economic difficulties, restore its liquidity, improve its profitability and ensure its sustainable management, including consider the filing of a reorganisation application.

ÄS §180 lg 5^1 and §306 lg 3^1 also set out that in the event of substantive insolvency the members of the management board of the limited liability company shall promptly, but not later than within 20 days after the date on which the insolvency became evident, file the bankruptcy application. In such cases the substantive insolvency is ascertained by the combined interpretation of "inability to pay debts" and "overindebtedness".

c) other duties (please describe)
ÄS §180 lg 5^1 and §306 lg 3^1 stipulates that the members of the management board of the limited liability company may no longer make payments on behalf of the limited liability company, unless making the payments in the situation of insolvency conforms to the due diligence requirements. The members of the management board must jointly and severally compensate the limited liability company for any payments made by the limited liability company, after the insolvency of the company became evident, which, under the given

circumstances, were not made with due diligence. In such cases the substantive insolvency is ascertained by the combined interpretation of "inability to pay debts" and "overindebtedness".

Question 11: Are there any other rules in the context of which the terms addressed in Questions 3, 5, and 8 are used?

Yes. Criminal responsibility may depend on inability to pay debts and overindebtedness.

Karistusseadustik (Criminal Code, KarS – https://www.riigiteataja.ee/en/eli/520032023010/consolide) §384 (Causing of Insolvency) stipulates that

> Knowing damaging of the financial situation of a debtor with respect to liabilities by a debtor who is a natural person, his or her legal representative, or by a member of the management body or a body substituting therefor of a debtor who is a legal person, if material decline in the solvency or insolvency of the debtor is caused thereby, is punishable by a pecuniary punishment or up to three years' imprisonment.

KarS §384[1] (Unequal Treatment of Creditors) stipulates that

> Preferring of one creditor to another in a manner knowingly prejudicial to such creditor by a member of a management body of a debtor who is a legal person or a body substituting therefor upon performance of the obligations of the debtor, if the ability of the debtor to satisfy the claims of injured creditors is decreased thereby by an amount corresponding to or exceeding major damage, is punishable by a pecuniary punishment or up to two years' imprisonment.

Insolvency is ascertained under KarS §384 and §384[1] by the combined interpretation of inability to pay debts and overindebtedness.

Question 12: Is the definition of (the subspecies of) insolvency identical in all legal fields or are there different definitions (e.g. different in insolvency law than in criminal law)?

The Supreme Court found that a situation of unequal treatment of creditors shall be determined in criminal proceeding by PankrS (3-1-1-49-11 as of 28 October 2011, p 34). Therefore, Supreme Court gives a guideline that the PankrS term "unequal treatment of creditors" shall be determined in criminal proceedings also under PankrS. Unfortunately, this guideline is not yet generalised to cover other terms of PankrS, which means that in another situation the Supreme Court may interpret substantive insolvency differently from the definition set out in PankrS. Anyhow, this Supreme Court decision supports the idea of unified insolvency terms, defined by PankrS.

II. INABILITY TO PAY DEBTS

Question 13: In your jurisdiction, is the term "inability to pay debts" defined in statute? If so, please give the wording in English translation. Is this definition (if any) specified in case law? If so, how?

The term "inability to pay debts" is set out in PankrS §1 lg 2. According to this paragraph, "a debtor is insolvent if the debtor is unable to satisfy the claim of a creditor that has fallen due and such inability, due to the debtor's financial situation, is not temporary".

The Supreme Court has specified that the mere fact that debts have fallen due does not indicate the permanent insolvency of the debtor. The Supreme Court added that the debtor is not permanently insolvent, if the assets of the debtor considerably exceed the debts of the debtor (3-2-1-120-12 as of 11 December 2002, p 7).

In the case of a bankruptcy application by the creditor only the debts already fallen due shall be taken into account in the estimation of the permanent insolvency (3-2-1-163-16 as of 22 February 2017, p 16).

The complicated detail regarding the interpretation of the inability to pay debts in Estonia is to give an estimation, if the debtor's inability to pay debts fallen due is not temporary. Neither the law nor the Supreme Court practice gives any unified guideline on when a debtor is permanently insolvent. Therefore, it is a matter of estimation in each individual case. For example, if the debtor is not capable of paying debts that have already fallen due straight away, but the debtor is capable of solving the issue in the near future, for example from forecasted future profit, the debtor is not permanently insolvent. Therefore, an important detail for estimation of the permanent insolvency of the debtor is profitable continuance of the activity of the debtor or so-called positive future expectation.

The Supreme Court supported the argument by stating that the debtor has the right to decline the permanent insolvency and rely on the positive future expectation, if such circumstances occur which give an objective third person reliable cause to believe that the debtor will possible be in a solvent financial situation in the future, taking into consideration all the possible future scenarios (3-2-1-74-13 as of 19 June 2013, p 22).

Another important perspective on the matter is whether the debtor is able to convert assets to liquid funds and, in future, pay off the debts without being permanently insolvent by the balance sheet test. Here is a link between inability to pay debts and overindebtedness. Even if the debtor is not capable of instantly paying debts already fallen due, but the debtor is able to solve the issue by realisation of assets or in any other way, without being insolvent by the balance sheet test, the debtor is not permanently insolvent.

In conclusion, inability to pay debts means, in Estonia, that the debtor does not have liquid funds to satisfy straight away the debts that have fallen due, and this situation is not temporary, which means that the debtor is unable to solve the issue in another way in the future, without being permanently insolvent by the balance sheet test too.

Question 14: Does your law refer to all debts or only to mature debts?

Estonian insolvency law does not distinguish between all debts and mature debts. Only in case of the creditor's bankruptcy application PankrS §15 lg 3 p 3 sets out a minimum debt amount that must have fallen due for a declaration of bankruptcy, which ranges from 1,000 euros to 12,500.

Question 15: Which assets are taken into account when assessing the inability to pay debts: all (financial) assets or only those that are liquid, i.e. available on short notice?

See answer to Question 13.

Question 16: Is any liquidity gap (deficit between relevant financial means and relevant debts) relevant or does your law neglect minor gaps? If the latter, how is "minor" defined?

PankrS does not emphasise the concept of liquidity gap. Nor has the Supreme Court given any specific guidelines on estimating the liquidity gap. Anyhow, estimation of the liquidity gap is essential in interpretation of the debtor's ability to satisfy the debts fallen due without any substantial delays (see answer to Question 13).

Question 17: As far as the time aspect is concerned, does it matter whether the liquidity gap can be closed again in the short term? If so, how long is the grace period?

Neither PankrS nor the Supreme Court practice indicates any specific time period for closing the liquidity gap.

Question 18: As far as the time aspect is concerned, is a debtor considered insolvent if the liquidity gap is not yet present but will occur soon? If so, how long is the prognosis period? (Note: this may also concern the difference between actual and likely/imminent inability to pay debts; cf. below Question 34).

Neither PankrS nor the Supreme Court practice indicates any specific time period for a future occurring liquidity gap.

Question 19: How is inability to pay debts established? Please communicate if there is a difference between a creditor and a debtor application or between different legal contexts.

a) Is a formal liquidity status (liquidity balance sheet) required?
Yes. In the case of a bankruptcy application by the debtor under PankrS §13 lg 2, the application shall substantiate the insolvency thereof by annexing to the bankruptcy application an explanation concerning the cause of the insolvency and a list of the debts and assets.

According to the PankrS §10 lg 1 a bankruptcy application by the creditor shall include the substantiation of the debtor's insolvency and prove the existence of a claim (also see answer to Question 4).

b) Is a sample of daily liquidity data (which do not amount to a proper liquidity status but show insufficient funds on different days within a certain period of time) sufficient?
No. See answer to Question 19(a).

c) Does the law provide for a rebuttable presumption? If so, under which conditions?
PankrS §31 lg 3 and 4 provide a presumption in the case of a legal person debtor's bankruptcy application. If a bankruptcy application is filed by a debtor who is a legal person, the debtor is presumed to be insolvent and the court shall also declare bankruptcy if insolvency is likely to occur in the future.

d) Does the law provide for any technical circumstances (e.g. undisputed statutory demand, non-compliance with monetary judgments, unsuccessful enforcement proceedings, non-performance of a previous composition agreement in insolvency proceedings) the occurrence of which suffices to establish the debtor's insolvency?
See answer to Question 19(c).

e) Other means?
None.

Question 20: Is insolvency (inability to pay debts, overindebtedness, etc.) subject to party autonomy in the proceedings or must the court clarify them *ex officio*?

According to PankrS §3 lg 3 a court shall in a bankruptcy matter, on its own initiative, from the filing of the bankruptcy petition until the end of the bankruptcy proceedings, take measures to ascertain the facts relevant to the bankruptcy proceedings and organise collection of the evidence necessary for the ascertainment of the facts unless otherwise provided by law.

Question 21: In an overall view, does your law distinguish "inability to pay debts" from "financial difficulties"? If so, how?

PankrS does not distinguish the term "inability to pay debts" from "financial difficulties". SanS §2 stipulates that

> The reorganisation of a debtor means the application of a set of measures on the basis of a reorganisation plan in order for a debtor to overcome economic difficulties, to restore its liquidity, improve its profitability and ensure its sustainable management.

Also according to SanS §7 lg 2 a reorganisation application shall include the reasons for the economic difficulties of the debtor.

Regarding natural persons, FIMS §2 lg 1 stipulates that "[t]he purpose of this Act is to enable debt restructuring or release from obligations for a natural person who is in payment difficulties through an insolvency petition, ensuring also the protection of creditors." Pursuant to FIMS §11 lg 2 the insolvency application of the natural person shall include "explanation about the payment difficulties and their causes".

Therefore, in the sense of defining insolvency for the purpose of commencement of bankruptcy, the term "financial difficulties" does not matter, but in the context of opening reorganisation proceedings, the term financial difficulties does have an effect.

Question 22: In an overall view, does it matter under your law whether the debtor's inability to pay debts is present or future and reversible or irreversible?

See answer to Question 19(c).

Question 23: Would you like to add any further aspects not covered by the above questions?

No.

III. CESSATION OF PAYMENTS

Question 24: In your jurisdiction, is "cessation of payments" a legal term used either in statute or in case law? (If the answer is "no", please continue with Question 31.)

No.

Question 25: Is "cessation of payments" an autonomous ground to commence proceedings (triggering circumstance)? You may refer to Questions 6/7 or add additional information here.

n.a.

Question 26: Is "cessation of payments" a means to establish inability to pay debts? If so, by which mechanism (e.g. rebuttable presumption for inability to pay debts, cf. above Question 19(c))?

n.a.

Question 27: How is "cessation of payments" defined? If it is defined in statute, please provide us here with an English translation of the relevant rule. Is this definition (if any) specified in case law? If so, how?

n.a.

Question 28: How is "cessation of payments" established?

n.a.

Question 29: Are there typical circumstances which provide circumstantial evidence that the debtor has ceased payments? If so, please list as many as possible.

n.a.

Question 30: Would you like to add any further aspects not covered by the above questions?

n.a.

IV. LIKELY/IMMINENT INABILITY TO PAY DEBTS

Question 31: Are the following terms available in your jurisdiction, either in statute or in case law? (If the answer is "no", please continue with Question 42.)

a) likely inability to pay debts
Yes.

b) imminent inability to pay debts
Yes.

c) other (similar) terms
No.

Question 32: Is "likely/imminent inability to pay debts" an autonomous ground to commence proceedings (triggering circumstance)? You may refer to Questions 6/7 or add additional information here.

Under PankrS §31 lg 3, the court shall declare the bankruptcy of the debtor according to the application of the legal person debtor, if insolvency is likely to occur in the future.

According to SanS §8 lg 1 a court opens reorganisation proceedings if the debtor has substantiated that:

(i) the debtor is not permanently insolvent, but is likely to become insolvent in the future;
(ii) the debtor requires reorganisation;
(iii) sustainable management of the undertaking is likely after the reorganisation.

In case of the application of a natural person a court will initiate debt restructuring proceedings under FIMS §19 lg 1 if the debtor has payment difficulties but is not permanently insolvent yet, especially where the payment difficulties of the debtor cannot obviously be overcome without the conduct of debt restructuring proceedings, among others, by realising the assets of the debtor to the extent that can be reasonably expected of the debtor.

Therefore, the term "likely/imminent inability to pay debts" is an autonomous ground to commence several proceedings.

Question 33: If the answer to the previous Question is "yes", who may base filing for insolvency proceedings on it: only the debtor or also creditors?

See answer to Question 32.

Question 34: How are these terms defined? If they are defined in statute, please provide us here with an English translation of the relevant rules. Is this definition (if any) specified in case law? If so, how?

a) likely inability to pay debts
See answer to Question 32.

b) imminent inability to pay debts
See answer to Question 32.

Question 35: Do the terms "likely" and "imminent" require a prognosis regarding the point in time when actual inability to pay debts will occur? If so, how long is the time period for this prognosis?

No.

Question 36: Does your law require a specific grade of certainty that inability to pay debts will eventually occur? If so, is 50.1% ("more likely than not") enough or are there alleviated or aggravated prerequisites?

No.

Question 37: Regarding "debts" and "financial means", are they defined in the same way as in the context of inability to pay debts (cf. above Questions 14/15)? If not, what are the differences?

Yes.

Question 38: Further to Question 37: Are "debts" considered which do currently not exist or are not yet due but will foreseeably come into existence and become due during the prognosis period?

Yes.

Question 39: Also further to Question 37: Are "financial means" considered which do currently not exist but will foreseeably become available during the prognosis period?

Yes.

Question 40: How are the terms "likely/imminent inability to pay debts" established?

See answer to Question 32.

Question 41: Would you like to add any further aspects not covered by the above questions?

No.

V. OVERINDEBTEDNESS

Question 42: In your jurisdiction, is "overindebtedness", or "balance sheet insolvency" respectively, a legal term used either in statute or in case law? (If the answer is "no", please continue with Question 56.)

PankrS §1 lg 3 stipulates that

> A debtor who is a legal person is insolvent also if the assets of the debtor are insufficient for covering the obligations thereof and, due to the debtor's financial situation, such insufficiency is not temporary. Claims that have not fallen due are also regarded as obligations.

The Supreme Court has explained that for the permanent insolvency of the debtor the cash-flow test and balance sheet test shall not be performed together. According to the particular case, it might be sufficient to declare the debtor in bankruptcy if either of the aforementioned tests is accomplished (3-2-1-188-12 of 25 February 2013, p 14).

In the case of the balance sheet test all debts shall be taken into account, the Supreme Court specified, including the debts which have not yet fallen due (3-2-1-163-16 of 22 February 2017, p 16).

An important detail is that Estonian balance sheet test includes the phrase "such insufficiency is not temporary". It means that even if the debtor is insolvent under the balance sheet test, but still has a positive option for the future to settle the debts, the debtor is not permanently insolvent. Regarding a "positive option for the future" see answer to Question 13.

The aforementioned means that "cash-flow" and "balance sheet" tests are linked in Estonian law by the phrase "if such insolvency is not temporary". Application of either of these tests needs an estimation of future perspectives which eventually links these two tests together under PankrS §1 lg 2 and 3.

In conclusion, the debtor is permanently insolvent if either of the aforementioned tests is positive and the debtor has no future perspective.

Question 43: Is "overindebtedness" an autonomous ground to commence proceedings (triggering circumstance)? You may refer to Questions 6/7 or add additional information here.

See answers to Questions 13 and 42.

Question 44: If the answer to the previous Question is "yes", is this applicable to corporate insolvencies of legal persons only or also to personal bankruptcies of natural persons?

The answers to Questions 13 and 42 are also applicable to the bankruptcy of a natural person.

Question 45: Is the term "overindebtedness" defined in statute? If so, please give the wording in English translation. Is this definition (if any) specified in case law? If so, how?

See answer to Question 42.

Question 46: Does your law refer to all existing debts or only to mature debts?

See answer to Question 14.

Question 47: Does the rank of certain debts play a role when establishing overindebtedness? In particular, is there any possibility to conclude agreements according to which certain debts shall not be taken into account (e.g. agreements on subsidiarity)?

No.

Question 48: Which assets are taken into account when overindebtedness is established: the complete set of assets or only a selection of them?

All the possible assets. Another question is the estimation of their value.

Question 49: How are the debtor's assets valued: by referring to the liquidation value, the book value, the going concern value or in another way?

The estimation of the value depends on many details. Even if it is not obligatory, the court believes usually the estimation of the interim trustee. Ordinarily the value is calculated on the basis of the liquidation value. If the insolvent debtor continues its activity and assets are sold as a going concern, the value shall be calculated according to this standard. In some specific cases, if it is complicated to estimate the value of the assets, the value might be calculated by other standards, for example Intellectual Property, knowhow, customer base, etc.

Question 50: Is there any prognostic element, e.g. regarding the debtor's chances to continue the business?

Neither Estonian insolvency law nor the Supreme Court practice provides any specific regulation for such kind of valuation. Such kind of valuation depends directly on the specific case.

Question 51: If the answer to the previous Question is "yes", what exactly is the topic of the prognosis and how is it established?

Neither Estonian insolvency law nor the Supreme Court practice provides any specific regulation for such kind of valuation. Such kind of valuation depends directly on the specific case.

Question 52: If the answer to Question 50 is "yes", how long is the prognosis period?

Neither Estonian insolvency law nor the Supreme Court practice provides any specific regulation for such kind of valuation. Such kind of valuation depends directly on the specific case.

Question 53: How is overindebtedness established?

a) Is a formal balance sheet required?
Yes. In case of a bankruptcy application by the debtor under PankrS §13 lg 2, the application shall substantiate the debtor's insolvency by annexing to the bankruptcy application an explanation concerning the cause of the insolvency and a list of the debts and assets (balance sheet).

According to the PankrS §10 lg 1 a bankruptcy application by the creditor shall include substantiation of the debtor's insolvency and prove the existence of a claim (also see answer to Question 4).

b) Does the yearly regular commercial balance sheet have any meaning (given that it is normally based on technical values and does not display undisclosed reserves)?
The yearly regular balance sheet submitted to the Commercial Register is just one piece documentary evidence used to estimate the insolvency of the debtor. The Annual Report to the register does not create civil rights or obligations, but only reflects the information from the debtor.

c) Does the law provide for a presumption? If so, under which conditions?
No.

d) Other means?
None.

Question 54: Is the legal link to overindebtedness undisputed in literature or are there efforts to abolish it?

Rational and productive discussion will always add some essential knowledge to society. In our humble opinion, there are still some issues left to explore regarding the definition and/or meaning and/or application of the term and the content of overindebtedness (for example the principles of valuation of assets and obligations). We certainly do not support abolishing the link to overindebtedness.

Question 55: Would you like to add any further aspects not covered by the above questions?

No.

VI. REMAINING ISSUES

Question 56: Is there anything else you would like to share in the present context and that we should take into account?

No.

FINLAND

Tuomas HUPLI

I. GENERAL

Question 1: How is insolvency (both in the context of liquidation and restructuring/reorganisation) regulated in your jurisdiction? Please give a brief overview, at least enumerating the relevant statutes.

The statutory definition of insolvency is established in the Bankruptcy Act (120/2004, hereinafter BA), the Restructuring of Enterprises Act (47/1993, hereinafter ResEntAct), the Act on the Adjustment of the Debts of a Private Individual (57/1993) and in the Act on the Recovery of Assets to Bankruptcy Estates (758/1991). In these statutes, the content of the definition is identical, with only minor divergences in the wordings. The substantive core is the same: insolvency means that the debtor is

- "unable, other than temporarily, to pay his or her debts when they fall due" – Section 4 of the Act on the Recovery of Assets to Bankruptcy Estates;
- "otherwise than temporarily unable to repay his or her debts as they fall due" – Chapter 2, Section 1(2) BA.

According to the wording of Section 3(1)(3) ResEntAct, insolvency means "the other than temporary inability of the debtor to repay its debts when they become due".

As mentioned *supra*, the differences in wordings are meaningless in substance. The decisive "message" of the Finnish legislator is that the statutory definition of insolvency refers to the cash-flow insolvency and, thus, not to the mere analysis of the debtor's balance sheet, or in any other way to the financial state of the debtor at a certain point of time. In short, considering the insolvency/solvency of the debtor requires a kind of prognosis.

The legal significance of insolvency is that it works as a general prerequisite for the opening of bankruptcy proceedings but also for the opening of proceedings aiming at the rehabilitation of the debtor (i.e. corporate restructuring and debt adjustment proceedings of a private individual). It is also established that certain transactions can only be avoided if the debtor was insolvent when the transaction was completed, or that the transaction was the cause, or among the causes, that finally constituted ("created") the insolvency of the debtor. Furthermore, a total reform of the Limited Liability Companies Act was enacted in 2006 (by the Act of 21.07.2006/624). Among the various aims of this reform was to increase the means of control over the distribution of the limited liability company's assets. So, according to Chapter 13, Section 2 of the Limited Liability Companies Act:

> Assets shall not be distributed, if it is known or should be known at the time of the distribution decision that the company is insolvent or that the distribution will cause the insolvency of the company.

Saying that the resolution – such as the court decision approving or dismissing the petition to open the bankruptcy proceedings, or any other statement on insolvency/solvency – is always based on a prognosis (prediction) holds true, but only when the law requires a look to the future. Regarding cases of transactions avoidance, distribution of assets of the limited liability company and certain criminal charges, these concern the past, not the future. In these contexts, there is no element of prognosis but instead an element of evaluating the circumstances afterwards.

Question 2: Related to paragraph 10 above of the Introduction: seen from a principle-based perspective, what justifies the opening of insolvency proceedings in your jurisdiction?

The primary answer to this question is that the insolvency of the debtor, as defined *supra*, justifies the opening of insolvency proceedings. Regarding especially the definition of insolvency, it is – or should be – required that in order to avoid the opening of insolvency proceedings, the debtor must be able to meet all of its liabilities. From this it follows that the very legitimacy of opening insolvency proceedings is based on the equal treatment of creditors. In principle, at least, the debtor is not entitled to avoid the opening of insolvency proceedings simply by paying the claim(s) of the creditor who has filed for the opening, if the other claims would be left unpaid as they fall due. Nevertheless, in the discussion concerning the Finnish law, the "right" of the debtor to avoid traditional bankruptcy by paying the claimant's receivables has become somewhat unclear. It has been held, even in the preambles of the Bankruptcy Act (Government Bill 26/2003, pp. 45–46), that the creditor who has filed for the opening of the bankruptcy proceedings would be forced to accept the payment offered by the debtor, even in cases where it is likely that some of the other creditors will shortly file their own applications and where the payment of the debtor is manifestly at risk of avoidance. This has been criticised in the legal literature precisely on the basis of insolvency: provided that the bankruptcy is clearly inevitable in the near future, the creditor should be entitled to reject the payment offered by the debtor. In that way, the creditors would be able to avoid unnecessary delay in the commencement of the bankruptcy and, perhaps, the detrimental effects of the debtor's behaviour during the delay.

Regarding the context of corporate restructuring, the Finnish law allows restructuring proceedings to be opened on the basis that "the debtor faces imminent insolvency" (Restructuring of Enterprises Act, Section 6(1)(2)). This was the content of Finnish law even before Directive (EU) 2019/1023 on preventive restructuring. Due to the said Directive, Finland, along with all the other Member States of the EU, was bound to adopt a "model" of restructuring proceedings which is only accessible for solvent debtors. Although the equal treatment of creditors is undoubtedly one of the aims of the new proceedings as well, the primary justification for the introduction of it is to prevent insolvency and by that way to protect employment, to promote cross-border movement of capital within the EU and, of course, to support various other goals with wider effects than those that have traditionally been considered as the scope of insolvency law. As a result of the implementation of the Directive, a new Chapter (Chapter 1 a) was amended to the ResEnt Act (promulgated by the Act of 25.05.2022/386), governing the proceeding under the title of "early restructuring". According to Section 4 b, the sole requirement for the opening of the early restructuring proceedings is that the debtor is under the threat of becoming insolvent.

It should be noted that under Finnish law, the concept of "imminent insolvency" is more or less identical to other similar terms, such as "likelihood of insolvency", "risk of insolvency" and "vicinity of insolvency".

Question 3: Does your national law in the context of liquidation proceedings use one or more of the following terms (be it as a noun, be it as an adjective or adjunct) in whatever context:

a) inability to pay debts
Yes.

b) cessation of payments
Yes.

c) likely inability to pay debts
No.

d) imminent inability to pay debts
No.

e) overindebtedness?
Yes.

Question 4: Are the same terms (and with the same meaning) used in the rules on preliminary/interim insolvency proceedings (e.g. concerning the application stage of the proceedings)?

Under the Finnish law, there is no preliminary/interim insolvency proceedings other than the application stage of the proceedings.

Question 5: Does your national law in the context of restructuring proceedings (as referred to above at paragraph 8 of the Introduction, i.e. both pre-insolvency and within formal insolvency proceedings) use one or more of the following terms (be it as a noun, be it as an adjective or adjunct) in whatever context:

a) inability to pay debts
Yes.

b) cessation of payments
No.

c) likely inability to pay debts
Yes (see the note in the answer to Question 2 *in fine*).

d) imminent inability to pay debts
Yes (see the note in the answer to Question 2 *in fine*).

e) overindebtedness?
No.

Question 6: Which of the terms mentioned in Questions 3 and 5 are used for defining grounds to commence proceedings (triggering circumstances)?

a) insolvency proceedings
Inablity to pay debts (as they fall due, provided that the inability is not merely temporary; Chapter 2, Section 1(2) BA and Section 6(2) ResEntAct).

Cessation of payments (cessation is established as a presumption of insolvency in Chapter 2, Section 3(2)(1) BA).

Overindebtedness ("A debtor in liquidation, a decedent's estate and a bankruptcy estate may be declared bankrupt also if its assets are not adequate for meeting its liabilities"; Chapter 2, Section 5 BA).

b) restructuring proceedings
Inability to pay debts (as they fall due, provided that the inability is not merely temporary, Section 6(2) ResEntAct).

Likely inability to pay debts (as they fall due, provided that the likely inability is not going to be merely temporary, Section 4 b ResEntAct).

Imminent inability to pay debts (as they fall due, provided that the imminent inability is not going to be merely temporary, Section 4 b ResEntAct).

NB: see also the answer to Question 2 *supra* concerning the common core of the concepts of "imminent insolvency" and "likelihood of insolvency".

Question 7: Does the answer to Question 6 include personal bankruptcies of natural persons or only corporate insolvencies of legal entities?

ResEntAct is not applicable to personal insolvency but may be applied to private entrepreneurs. Otherwise, the answer to Question 6 includes both personal bankruptcies and corporate insolvencies of legal entities.

Question 8: In your law, are there any other circumstances which trigger insolvency or restructuring proceedings?

Yes, there are. The "traditional" (the "original") model of corporate restructuring proceedings may be commenced if at least two creditors whose total claims represent at least one-fifth of the debtor's known debts, and who are not closely related to the debtor (as referred to in Section 3 of the Act on the Recovery of Assets to Bankruptcy Estates), file a joint application with the debtor or declare that they support the debtor's application. This provision, established in Section 6(1) ResEntAct, allows for the opening of traditional (i.e. not preventive) restructuring proceedings, provided that the debtor has gained a sufficient amount of support by the creditors. If this is the case, the court shall not investigate whether the debtor is insolvent or not, but the obstacles for opening proceedings, laid down in Section 7 ResEntAct, may still be applied if any dissenting creditor so requires (and provides evidence showing the existence of a specified obstacle). Overall, Section 6(1) of ResEntAct expresses the power of the (required percentage of) creditors to support the process of restructuring and, in that way, to avoid time-consuming investigations of the debtor's economic situation. Due to the fears of abuse, this opportunity was not adopted in the early, i.e. preventive, restructuring proceedings. As the harmonisation of insolvency laws proceeds to the next level in the EU, this choice of the Finnish law-makers can – and should – be reconsidered.

Question 9: Which of the terms mentioned in Questions 3, 5, and 8 are used in the context of transactions avoidance law?

- Inability to pay debts (Sections 4, 5, 10, 12 and 14 of the Act on the Recovery of Assets to Bankruptcy Estates);
- Overindebtedness (Sections 5, 6, 9 and 9 a of the Act on the Recovery of Assets to Bankruptcy Estates).

Question 10: Which of the terms addressed in Questions 3, 5, and 8 are used in the context of directors' duties?

a) shift of duties (from shareholders to creditors)
n.a.

b) duties to commence insolvency proceedings
n.a.

c) other duties (please describe)
Inability to pay debts (see also the answer to Question 1 *supra*):

According to Chapter 13, Section 2 of the Limited Liability Companies Act: "Assets shall not be distributed, if it is known or should be known at the time of the distribution decision that the company is insolvent or that the distribution will cause the insolvency of the company."

Question 11: Are there any other rules in the context of which the terms addressed in Questions 3, 5, and 8 are used?

Yes there are; certain provisions in the Criminal Code (Rikoslaki 39/1889 with amendments), Chapter 39, are based on the state of insolvency and/or insolvency proceedings:

> Section 1: Dishonesty by a debtor:
>
> A debtor who
>
> 1) destroys his or her property,
> 2) gives away or otherwise surrenders his or her property without an acceptable reason,
> 3) transfers his or her property abroad in order to place it beyond the reach of his or her creditors, or
> 4) increases his or her liabilities without basis,
>
> and thus causes himself or herself to become insolvent or essentially worsens his or her state of insolvency, shall be sentenced for *dishonesty by a debtor* to a fine or to imprisonment for at most two years.
>
> Section 6: Favouring a creditor:
>
> If a debtor, knowing that he or she is unable to meet his or her liabilities, in order to favour a certain creditor at the expense of the other creditors,
>
> 1) repays a debt before its maturity in circumstances where the repayment is irregular,
> 2) gives, for receivables of a creditor, collateral that had not been agreed upon or that the debtor had not promised at the time the debt arose,

3) uses an unusual means of payment to meet a liability in circumstances under which the payment cannot be deemed regular, or
4) undertakes another similar arrangement that improves the position of the creditor,

he or she shall be sentenced for *favouring a creditor* to a fine or to imprisonment for at most two years.

In addition, the concept of insolvency is used in Chapter 29, Section 4 as follows:

Tax violation:

A person who, to obtain economic benefit for himself or herself or for another person and for a reason other than insolvency or a stay on payments imposed by a court, fails to pay within the set time limit

1) a withholding tax, a tax-at-source or an asset transfer tax,
2) a turnover tax calculated per calendar month or a comparable tax on certain insurance premiums,
3) a value-added tax, or
4) an employer's social security contribution

shall, unless the act is punishable as tax fraud, be sentenced for a *tax violation* to a fine or to imprisonment for at most six months.

Question 12: Is the definition of (the subspecies of) insolvency identical in all legal fields or are there different definitions (e.g. different in insolvency law than in criminal law)?

It has been discussed, both in the Finnish legal literature and in court practice, whether insolvency should be defined identically when used (i) as a precondition for criminal responsibility (e.g. dishonesty by a debtor), for the opening of insolvency proceedings and for transactions avoidance, or (conversely) (ii) as a precondition for releasing the perpetrator (the accused person) from the criminal charge of tax violation. The Supreme Court of Finland has held that, although it would be desirable to define legal terms in various statutes in an identical manner, insolvency can be interpreted differently in the context of Tax violation (see, e.g., the Supreme Court ruling with the case identifier of KKO 2004:46, where the charge of tax violation was approved despite the fact that the economic situation of the debtor could have been described as insolvent on the basis of the traditional terms, i.e. the debtor was unable to pay its debts as they fell due, and this was not merely a temporary circumstance).

II. INABILITY TO PAY DEBTS

Question 13: In your jurisdiction, is the term "inability to pay debts" defined in statute? If so, please give the wording in English translation. Is this definition (if any) specified in case law? If so, how?

Under the law of Finland, inability to pay debts means the same as insolvency, as described *supra*.

Question 14: Does your law refer to all debts or only to mature debts?

All debts (provided that they can reasonably be expected to fall due in the future; that is, hypothetical liabilities fall outside of the court's consideration).

Question 15: Which assets are taken into account when assessing the inability to pay debts: all (financial) assets or only those that are liquid, i.e. available on short notice?

In principle, all assets with economic value – i.e. value that can be defined in monetary terms – are taken into account. The degree of liquidity is involved in the sense that although the book value of the debtor's assets may be very high, the inability to pay debts might exist if the asset(s) cannot be used for the payment of debts due to the cumbersome process of realisation, lack of buyers, or for some other similar reason.

Question 16: Is any liquidity gap (deficit between relevant financial means and relevant debts) relevant or does your law neglect minor gaps? If the latter, how is "minor" defined?

There is no exact answer to this question in Finnish law. As mentioned *supra*, inability to pay debts must remain longer than temporarily; that is, a temporary inability does not suffice for the opening of insolvency proceedings. A liquidity gap is among the circumstances that must be taken into account but the significance of the gap depends on the circumstances as a whole.

Question 17: As far as the time aspect is concerned, does it matter whether the liquidity gap can be closed again in the short term? If so, how long is the grace period?

The prevailing Finnish law does not provide an exact grace period. This question has also been left to be considered within the free evaluation of evidence.

Question 18: As far as the time aspect is concerned, is a debtor considered insolvent if the liquidity gap is not yet present but will occur soon? If so, how long is the prognosis period? (Note: this may also concern the

difference between actual and likely/imminent inability to pay debts; cf. below Question 34).

This question can – actually, must – be answered both yes and no. First, a debtor may be considered insolvent even if the liquidity gap is not present yet, provided that the evidence in the relevant case shows that it (i.e. the gap) will occur in the future. As to the length of the prognosis, no precise period is provided by Finnish law. Second, the sole fact that the liquidity gap takes place in the future does not necessarily lead to the conclusion that the debtor is insolvent; rather, it is – again – a question of the comprehensive evaluation of the present situation and the foreseeable circumstances.

Question 19: How is inability to pay debts established? Please communicate if there is a difference between a creditor and a debtor application or between different legal contexts.

"Establishing" the inability to pay debts may take place by any means of evidence, i.e. by written/electronic documents or oral testimony, such as hearing the accountants/auditors, book-keepers, directors or employees, contracting parties, etc., of the debtor company. There is a natural difference between the evidentiary "devices" available, on the one hand, to the debtor and, on the other, to creditors. For example, the creditors do not have access to the debtor's internal material that would be necessary for drawing up a liquidity balance sheet between the official accounting periods. Access for the creditors is limited to the previous financial statements, published by the Finnish Patent and Registration Office.

a) Is a formal liquidity status (liquidity balance sheet) required?
Not required.

b) Is a sample of daily liquidity data (which do not amount to a proper liquidity status but show insufficient funds on different days within a certain period of time) sufficient?
It depends on the particular case.

c) Does the law provide for a rebuttable presumption? If so, under which conditions?
Chapter 2, Section 3 BA, titled "Insolvency assumption", reads:

> (1) The debtor shall be deemed insolvent, if the debtor declares that he or she is insolvent and there are no special reasons for not accepting that declaration.
> (2) Unless it is otherwise proven, the debtor shall also be deemed insolvent especially if:
>   (1) the debtor has discontinued payments;
>   (2) it has been determined in enforcement proceedings during the six months preceding the filing of the petition for bankruptcy that the debtor cannot repay the claim in full; or

(3) a debtor, who is, or who during the year preceding the filing of the petition for bankruptcy has been, under the obligation to keep accounts, has not repaid the clear and due claim of the creditor within a week of the receipt of a reminder.

(3) The debtor may be declared bankrupt under paragraph (2)(3) only if the creditor files the relevant petition within three months of the time limit referred to in that provision and the claim still remains unpaid. The creditor shall serve the reminder referred to in that provision on the debtor by verifiable means or, if the criteria in chapter 11, section 7, of the Code of Judicial Procedure (*oikeudenkäymiskaari*) are met, in accordance with the procedure provided in that section. The reminder shall indicate the basis and the amount of the claim. In addition, it shall indicate that the creditor may petition for the bankruptcy of the debtor, unless the debt is repaid within a set time after the receipt of the reminder.

d) Does the law provide for any technical circumstances (e.g. undisputed statutory demand, non-compliance with monetary judgments, unsuccessful enforcement proceedings, non-performance of a previous composition agreement in insolvency proceedings) the occurrence of which suffices to establish the debtor's insolvency?

No other presumptions than explained *supra* in (c). Any other "technical circumstances" fall within the free evaluation of evidence.

e) Other means?

Any other (legal) means are available and fall within the free evaluation of evidence.

Question 20: Is insolvency (inability to pay debts, overindebtedness, etc.) subject to party autonomy in the proceedings or must the court clarify them *ex officio*?

This is quite a contradictory issue in Finnish law, especially when it comes to the differences between (i) bankruptcy liquidation and (ii) proceedings aiming at the rehabilitation of the debtor (both natural and legal persons). Regarding bankruptcy liquidation, the starting point seems to be clear, since Chapter 7, Section 11 BA establishes that "[t]he court shall inquire whether the prerequisites for bankruptcy are met." Moreover, according to Chapter 7, Section 5(4) BA, "[t]he court may require other evidence on the financial situation of the debtor, if this for some special reason is necessary for a decision on the matter." The principle of official inquiry, as a counterpart to the principle of party autonomy, is also expressed in Chapter 2, Section 3(1) BA as it allows the court to dismiss the debtor's own declaration of insolvency, provided that there are "special reasons for not accepting that declaration." A traditional example of special reasons is the case where it seems that the representatives of the debtor disagree on the financial situation, or when the sole purpose of the bankruptcy petition is to resolve the disputes inside the debtor organisation.

Regarding corporate restructuring and debt adjustment proceedings for private individuals, it is clear that the debtor is not able to enjoy the benefits of those proceedings simply by declaring itself insolvent. Thus, the court must investigate the insolvency or, in case of early restructuring, the likelihood of it.

Overall, as far as the alleged insolvency/likelihood of it is concerned, the principle of party autonomy is a lot weaker as compared to the majority of civil disputes. A creditor who files bankruptcy proceedings against the debtor must either be able to invoke the assumption of insolvency or to present some other evidence in order to prove the allegation of insolvency. As mentioned *supra*, the court is also allowed to require evidence other than that which the parties have presented whenever it is necessary for a proper decision to be made.

The analysis *supra* concerns the opening of insolvency proceedings. Since the concept of insolvency plays an important role in transactions avoidance law as well, and it may have significance in disputes over the distribution of assets of a limited liability company, it must be noted that the parties to these cases are free to settle them. In these contexts, the principle of party autonomy prevails. It follows that the court is not allowed to require any additional evidence on the financial situation of the debtor, or to consider circumstances or any particular "facts" which are not pleaded (alleged) in the case. So, the party who claims that the debtor was insolvent at the time of the transaction, or became insolvent because of it, bears the ordinary burden of proof concerning the insolvency. Likewise, the party who claims that the debtor was solvent, and did not become insolvent due to the transaction, also bears the ordinary burden of proof.

Question 21: In an overall view, does your law distinguish "inability to pay debts" from "financial difficulties"? If so, how?

In an overall view, yes. "Inability to pay debts" refers to serious, long-standing problems, while "financial difficulties" may exist even when the debtor is still able to pay its debts. It might be said – although generally – that financial difficulties are something that can be solved outside of insolvency proceedings, while the inability to pay debts gives access to those proceedings. Early, i.e. preventive, corporate restructuring "mitigates" the significance of this distinction (as preventive proceedings can only be opened when the debtor is on the verge of insolvency), but, at least in principle, the difference still exists.

Question 22: In an overall view, does it matter under your law whether the debtor's inability to pay debts is present or future and reversible or irreversible?

Yes, it matters very much. Based on the Preventive Restructuring Directive, the very idea of early restructuring is that the inability to pay debts does not yet exist but is likely to become real. If the inability is present at the time of the filing, the only available proceedings are traditional (not preventive) corporate restructuring or bankruptcy liquidation. The choice between the two is made precisely on the basis of whether the inability to pay, i.e. insolvency, is reversible or irreversible.

Question 23: Would you like to add any further aspects not covered by the above questions?

It would be useful to add that, although the Finnish law still rests on the separation between (i) liquidation bankruptcy and (ii) proceedings aiming at the rehabilitation of the debtor, bankruptcy proceedings can also be used for the purpose of reviving the solvency of the debtor. This may happen through the composition governed by Chapter 21 BA. There's nothing in the prevailing law that would prevent the content of the composition from being similar to the reorganisation plan under the ResEntAct. The precondition for the opening of bankruptcy with the aim of composition is the debtor's insolvency, just as it is in the "ordinary" type of bankruptcy. To confirm the composition in bankruptcy, the following requirements have to be met (Chapter 21, Section 1 BA):

> (1) … The prerequisites for s composition are that:
>   (1) the composition is supported by the debtor and by creditors whose voting strengths amount to no less than 70 per cent of the total votes of the creditors, as well as by every creditor whose voting strength is at least 10 per cent of the total votes of the creditors [Note by TH: the required support was reduced from 80/5 to 70/10 by the Act of 23.03.2023/481 based on the law drafting inspired by the Preventive Restructuring Directive];
>   (2) the creditors who have not consented to the composition receive, by virtue of the composition, a disbursement at least equal to that they would have received had the bankruptcy proceedings continued; and
>   (3) the liabilities of the bankruptcy estate have been paid or sufficient security has been posted for them.
>
> (2) A composition shall not restrict the rights of a creditor protected by collateral who objects to it.
>
> (3) The composition document shall contain an assessment of the estate administrator of the disbursements referred to in paragraph (1)(2).

The legal effects of the bankruptcy composition are governed in Chapter 21, Section 4 BA simply as follows:

> The certification of a composition shall conclude the bankruptcy proceedings.
>
> The appointment of the estate administrator and the authority of the creditors in bankruptcy shall cease.

As a result of the certified (i.e. confirmed) composition, the authority over the assets of the estate, as well as the authority to decide on the business and any other operations of the debtor, returns to the debtor. After that, the debtor is expected to fulfil the duties of the composition in the same manner as the debtor who executes the restructuring plan confirmed under the ResEntAct.

The purpose of "allowing" the bankruptcy composition is to provide an alternative to corporate restructuring proceedings since they are, in the general discussion at least, considered expensive and time-consuming. Unfortunately, this alternative has not gained any wider success in the Finnish insolvency practice (this was one of the reasons for reducing the required support for the composition in the law reform of 2023).

III. CESSATION OF PAYMENTS

Question 24: In your jurisdiction, is "cessation of payments" a legal term used either in statute or in case law? (If the answer is "no", please continue with Question 31.)

Yes, according to Chapter 2, Section 3(2)(1) BA, cessation of payments works as a rebuttable presumption that the debtor is insolvent (Chapter 2, Section 3(2)(1) BA), see also the answer to Question 19(c) *supra*; the translation in FINLEX uses the words "discontinued payments".

Question 25: Is "cessation of payments" an autonomous ground to commence proceedings (triggering circumstance)? You may refer to Question 6/7 or add additional information here.

No.

Question 26: Is "cessation of payments" a means to establish inability to pay debts? If so, by which mechanism (e.g. rebuttable presumption for inability to pay debts, cf. above Question 19(c))?

Yes, it is a rebuttable presumption that the debtor is insolvent.

Question 27: How is "cessation of payments" defined? If it is defined in statute, please provide us here with an English translation of the relevant rule. Is this definition (if any) specified in case law? If so, how?

Not defined in statute, but explained in the preambles (Government Bill 26/2003, p. 42) so that the cessation must indicate the general suspension of payments, not only the payments to one creditor or a couple of them. It is also stated that when the cessation is based on the dispute over the creditor's claims, there is no assumption of insolvency (provided of course that the reason for the dispute is not manifestly false).

Question 28: How is "cessation of payments" established?

There are no specific rules on that. Any (legal) evidence is available. The ideal situation is the debtor's own declaration to the creditors.

Question 29: Are there typical circumstances which provide circumstantial evidence that the debtor has ceased payments? If so, please list as many as possible.

Only one example is given in the Government Bill 26/2003, p. 42: the debtor has closed down its sales store (this must apply to any other business premises, at least when no other premises are still used in the ordinary course of business).

Question 30: Would you like to add any further aspects not covered by the above questions?

No.

IV. LIKELY/IMMINENT INABILITY TO PAY DEBTS

Question 31: Are the following terms available in your jurisdiction, either in statute or in case law? (If the answer is "no", please continue with Question 42.)

a) likely inability to pay debts
Not explicitly, but the precondition for the opening of early restructuring proceedings, namely that the debtor is under the threat of insolvency, inevitably requires certain degree (level) of likelihood.

b) imminent inability to pay debts
See (a) *supra*, and it can be added that the degree of likelihood varies from case to case. The texts of the statutes do not distinguish "likely" from "imminent", but this distinction is an "inherent" element of the system. See also the note in the answer to Question 2 *in fine*.

c) other (similar) terms
No.

Question 32: Is "likely/imminent inability to pay debts" an autonomous ground to commence proceedings (triggering circumstance)? You may refer to Questions 6/7 or add additional information here.

Yes, see the answers to Questions 2 and 6(b) *supra*.

Question 33: If the answer to the previous Question is "yes", who may base filing for insolvency proceedings on it: only the debtor or also creditors?

For early (i.e. preventive) restructuring and for debt adjustment proceedings for private persons, the debtor only. For bankruptcy liquidation and "traditional" (i.e. not preventive) restructuring, both.

Question 34: How are these terms defined? If they are defined in statute, please provide us here with an English translation of the relevant rules. Is this definition (if any) specified in case law? If so, how?

a) likely inability to pay debts
Defined in Section 3(1)(4) ResEntAct simply by stating that the threat of insolvency means the danger of the debtor becoming insolvent.

b) imminent inability to pay debts
Not defined. The "danger" in the state of imminent insolvency can be considered as "more dangerous" than it is in the mere "likelihood" of insolvency.

Question 35: Do the terms "likely" and "imminent" require a prognosis regarding the point in time when actual inability to pay debts will occur? If so, how long is the time period for this prognosis?

Yes, some kind of prognosis is required but is not defined in the law.

Question 36: Does your law require a specific grade of certainty that inability to pay debts will eventually occur? If so, is 50.1% ("more likely than not") enough or are there alleviated or aggravated prerequisites?

No specific degree of certainty is either defined or required. The question has been left to the free evaluation of evidence. It should be mentioned here that the general standard of evidence (the required degree of certainty) in civil disputes is defined in the Code of Judicial Procedure, Chapter 17, Section 2(2): "A circumstance may be taken as grounds for the judgment only on condition that a party has presented credible evidence regarding it." As a general principle, "more likely than not" is usually applied in Finnish court practice.

Question 37: Regarding "debts" and "financial means", are they defined in the same way as in the context of inability to pay debts (cf. above Questions 14/15)? If not, what are the differences?

No definition in Finnish law.

Question 38: Further to Question 37: Are "debts" considered which do currently not exist or are not yet due but will foreseeably come into existence and become due during the prognosis period?

Yes.

Question 39: Also further to Question 37: Are "financial means" considered which do currently not exist but will foreseeably become available during the prognosis period?

Yes.

Question 40: How are the terms "likely/imminent inability to pay debts" established?

There is no case law on this question. It is meant to be decided as a part of the free evaluation of evidence. See also the note in the answer to Question 2 *in fine*.

Question 41: Would you like to add any further aspects not covered by the above questions?

No.

V. OVERINDEBTEDNESS

Question 42: In your jurisdiction, is "overindebtedness", or "balance sheet insolvency" respectively, a legal term used either in statute or in case law? (If the answer is "no", please continue with Question 56.)

The term "overindebtedness" ("overindebted") is used in the Act on the Recovery of Assets to Bankruptcy Estates (758/1991): certain transactions, such as gifts and gift-like agreements, separation of marital estate (and the separation of assets in similar relationships), can only be avoided provided that the debtor was, or due to the transaction became, overindebted.

See also Chapter 2, Section 5 BA: "A debtor in liquidation, a decedent's estate and a bankruptcy estate may be declared bankrupt also if its assets are not adequate for meeting its liabilities." This precondition means the same as overindebtedness and balance sheet insolvency.

Question 43: Is "overindebtedness" an autonomous ground to commence proceedings (triggering circumstance)? You may refer to Question 6/7 or add additional information here.

See the answer to Question 42 *supra*.

Question 44: If the answer to the previous Question is "yes", is this applicable to corporate insolvencies of legal persons only or also to personal bankruptcies of natural persons?

Both (except that "a debtor in liquidation" only applies to limited liability companies).

Question 45: Is the term "overindebtedness" defined in statute? If so, please give the wording in English translation. Is this definition (if any) specified in case law? If so, how?

See the answer to Question 42 *supra* and also the Act on the Recovery of Assets to Bankruptcy Estates, Section 4 (sentence 2): "In this Act … Over-indebtedness means that the debtor's liabilities are greater than his or her assets."

Question 46: Does your law refer to all existing debts or only to mature debts?

All existing debts. See also the ruling of the Finnish Supreme Court, case identifier KKO 2001:29 where it was held that even a debt based on a guarantee must be considered a debt of the guarantor since the court had already ordered the guarantor to pay the main debt, the main debtor was in bankruptcy, the main debt was ordered to be paid out of the assets of the bankruptcy estate, and there were no other securities for the main debt.

Question 47: Does the rank of certain debts play a role when establishing overindebtedness? In particular, is there any possibility to conclude agreements according to which certain debts shall not be taken into account (e.g. agreements on subsidiarity)?

To my knowledge, there is no case law concerning this question. As a general principle, even the subordinated debts are considered as debts (not equity) and therefore must be taken into account when deciding whether the debtor is overindebted or not. But this may depend on the circumstances of the particular case.

Question 48: Which assets are taken into account when overindebtedness is established: the complete set of assets or only a selection of them?

As a main rule, the complete set.

Question 49: How are the debtor's assets valued: by referring to the liquidation value, the book value, the going concern value or in another way?

There is no specific rule concerning this question in Finnish law. Again, as the free evaluation of evidence prevails, any means and techniques of valuing the assets are available. They may even be applied concurrently. The minimum standard is that the principles of valuation are generally acceptable, i.e. not arbitrary/random.

Question 50: Is there any prognostic element, e.g. regarding the debtor's chances to continue the business?

It follows from the very nature of comparing the assets and liabilities against each other that some kind of prognostic element exists, concerning, e.g. the market situation, the maturity period of the debts, etc.

Question 51: If the answer to the previous Question is "yes", what exactly is the topic of the prognosis and how is it established?

There is no exact subject-matter of the prognosis. Regarding the elements of the prognosis, see the answer to Question 50 *supra*.

Question 52: If the answer to Question 50 is "yes", how long is the prognosis period?

It depends on the case, i.e. there's no general length of the period.

Question 53: How is overindebtedness established?

a) Is a formal balance sheet required?
Not required, but useful of course. A formal balance sheet is usually not available for natural persons.

b) Does the yearly regular commercial balance sheet have any meaning (given that it is normally based on technical values and does not display undisclosed reserves)?
Yes, it has, but it can hardly be the sole or decisive evidence precisely because it doesn't "tell the whole story".

c) Does the law provide for a presumption? If so, under which conditions?
No.

d) Other means?
Free evaluation of evidence.

Question 54: Is the legal link to overindebtedness undisputed in literature or are there efforts to abolish it?

No serious criticism has been made against the concept of overindebtedness.

Question 55: Would you like to add any further aspects not covered by the above questions?

n.a.

VI. REMAINING ISSUES

Question 56: Is there anything else you would like to share in the present context and that we should take into account?

No.

FRANCE

Reinhard DAMMANN

I. GENERAL

Question 1: How is insolvency (both in the context of liquidation and restructuring) regulated in your jurisdiction? Please give a brief overview, at least enumerating the relevant statutes.

French insolvency law was reformed in 2005, introducing a pre-insolvency "safeguard proceeding" (*procedure de sauvegarde*). The French Commercial Code (C. com.) construes safeguard proceedings as the "common law" proceedings which are provided for in Article L. 620-1 et seq. C. com. The aim of the procedure is to establish a debt restructuring plan. Accelerated safeguard proceedings is a subcategory of "normal" safeguard proceedings.

Regular insolvency proceedings, i.e. rehabilitation proceedings (*redressement judiciaire*), where the debtor is insolvent, are governed by Article L. 631-1 et seq. C. com. These provisions refer to Articles L. 620-1 et seq., save as otherwise provided. The objective of rehabilitation proceedings is to provide for a debt restructuring (like in safeguard proceedings) or the sale of the ongoing business, which is regulated in liquidation proceedings.

Liquidation proceedings are governed by Article L. 640-1 et seq. These provisions apply where the rehabilitation of the debtor is manifestly impossible. These proceedings regulate the sale of the ongoing business as a going concern and piecemeal liquidation.

Pursuant to Article L. 620-1 C. com., safeguard proceedings are available to debtors which are not in a situation of cessation of payment (*cessation des paiements*) but face difficulties that they are unable to overcome. The opening of safeguard proceedings is conditional upon a negative cash-flow insolvency test.

The definition of the concept of cash-flow insolvency (*cessation des paiements*) is set forth in Article L. 631-1, sentence 1 C. com. A debtor is considered to be insolvent when it is unable to meet its due and payable debts with its immediately available assets.

Hence in French law, the insolvency test is exclusively based on an assessment of cash flow. The debts which are subject to moratoria are excluded. The test also takes into consideration available credit lines (credit reserves). On the asset side, cash is defined as cash in a bank account plus assets that can be immediately turned into cash and credit reserves.

Overindebtedness (balance sheet insolvency) is disregarded in French law.

This cash-flow oriented approach facilitates pre-insolvency debt restructuring, since cash-flow insolvency can be rather easily cured by a standstill or a moratorium.

Insolvency proceedings in the sense of Annex A of the European Insolvency Regulation are safeguard (including accelerated safeguard), rehabilitation and liquidation proceedings.

Question 2: Seen from a principle-based perspective, what justifies the opening of insolvency proceedings in your jurisdiction?

A debtor *must* file and a creditor *may* file for the opening of rehabilitation proceedings when the debtor is cash-flow insolvent, i.e. when it is unable to meet its due and payable debts with its immediately available assets.

A debtor *may* file for the opening of safeguard proceedings provided it is not cash-flow insolvent but faces difficulties that it is unable to overcome.

Liquidation proceedings are opened where the rehabilitation of the debtor is manifestly impossible. This definition implies that the debtor is cash-flow insolvent and there is no reasonable prospect of presenting a debt restructuring plan or selling the business as a going concern.

Hence, safeguard and rehabilitation proceedings are justified by the rescue of the debtor/the business of the debtor as a going concern. The protection of the debtor and the preservation of jobs are the main justifications for the opening of these proceedings.

The equal treatment of creditors, as well as the principle of the best satisfaction of creditors, are subordinated to the rescue of the business as a going concern.

The best interest of creditors test has been recently introduced in debt restructuring proceedings (safeguard, rehabilitation proceedings) in September 2021 when France transposed the EU Restructuring and Insolvency Directive 2019/1023, provided that thresholds are met.

Question 3: Does your national law in the context of liquidation proceedings use one or more of the following terms (be it as a noun, be it as an adjective or adjunct) in whatever context:

a) inability to pay debts

No, but implied.

b) cessation of payments

No, but implied.

c) likely inability to pay debts

No.

d) imminent inability to pay debts
No.

e) overindebtedness?
No.

Question 4: Does your national law in the context of restructuring proceedings use one or more of the following terms (be it as a noun, be it as an adjective or adjunct) in whatever context:

a) inability to pay debts
No.

b) cessation of payments
Yes, as a negative condition.

c) likely inability to pay debts
No.

d) imminent inability to pay debts
No.

e) overindebtedness?
No.

Question 5: Which of the terms mentioned in Questions 3 and 4 are used for defining grounds to commence proceedings (triggering circumstances)?

a) insolvency proceedings
Cessation of payments, i.e. where the debtor is unable to meet its due and payable debts with its immediately available assets.

b) restructuring proceedings
Not in a situation of cessation of payment but facing difficulties that they are unable to overcome.

Question 6: Does the answer to Question 5 include natural persons or only legal entities?

No distinction is made between natural and legal persons.

Question 7: In your law, are there any other circumstances which trigger insolvency or restructuring proceedings?

Yes, but only in liquidation proceedings, where the court must be satisfied that the rehabilitation of the debtor is manifestly impossible.

Question 8: Which of the terms mentioned in Questions 3, 4, and 7 are used in the context of transactions avoidance law?

A legal action to void a transaction can only be started by the insolvency practitioner (IP) in the framework of judicial rehabilitation or judicial liquidation proceedings, where the voidable transaction occurred during the so-called suspect period.

The court determines the date on which the debtor is deemed to have become insolvent. It can be any date within the 18 months preceding the date of the judgment opening the proceedings. Hence, the suspect period starts on the date where the debtor has been found in *cessation of payment* by the court (Articles 632-1, 632-2, L. 632-3 C. com.)

Question 9: Which of the terms addressed in Questions 3, 4, and 7 are used in the context of directors' duties?

a) shift of duties (from shareholders to creditors)
In France, the shift of duties is neither regulated nor defined in case law.

b) duties to commence insolvency proceedings
There is a duty for the directors to file for the opening of rehabilitation proceedings in the event of cessation of payments (Article L. 631-4 C. com.)

There is a duty for the directors to file for the opening of liquidation proceedings in the event of cessation of payments (Article L. 640-4 C. com.)

c) other duties (please describe)
n.a.

Question 10: Are there any other rules in the context of which the terms addressed in Questions 3, 4, and 7 are used?

Article L. 653-3, 1° (L. 653-4, 4°) C. com. Personal bankruptcy in case of wrongful trading (with a personal interest) after the occurrence of cessation of payments.

Article L. 654-2, 1° C. com. Criminal bankruptcy in case of wilful deferral of the opening of rehabilitation or liquidation proceedings in view of fraudulent disposal of assets or fraudulent borrowing.

II. INABILITY TO PAY DEBTS

Question 11: In your jurisdiction, is the term "inability to pay debts" defined in statute? If so, please give the wording in English translation. Is this definition (if any) specified in case law? If so, how?

Pursuant to Art. L. 631-1 C. com. "a debtor which is unable to meet its due and payable debts with its immediately available assets is in cessation of payment."

Question 12: Does your law refer to all debts or only to mature debts?

Mature debts (due and payable).

Question 13: Which assets are taken into account when assessing the inability to pay debts: all (financial) assets or only those that are liquid, i.e. available on short notice?

Liquid assets, i.e. cash in a bank account plus assets that can be immediately turned into cash and credit reserves.

Question 14: Is any liquidity gap (deficit between relevant financial means and relevant debts) relevant or does your law neglect minor gaps? If the latter, how is "minor" defined?

No.

Question 15: As far as the time aspect is concerned, does it matter whether the liquidity gap can be closed again in the short term? If so, how long is the grace period?

There is no grace period.

Question 16: As far as the time aspect is concerned, is a debtor considered insolvent if the liquidity gap is not yet present but will occur soon? If so, how long is the prognosis period? (Note: this may also concern the difference between actual and likely/imminent inability to pay debts; cf. below Question 29).

No, there is no prognosis period nor a concept of future cash-flow insolvency.

There is, however, an exception for banks (see Article L. 613-26 of the French financial and monetary code: instant cessation of payment or in the near future).

Question 17: How is inability to pay debts established? Please communicate if there is a difference between a creditor and a debtor application or between different legal contexts.

a) Is a formal liquidity status (liquidity balance sheet) required?
No.

b) Is a sample of daily liquidity data sufficient?
Yes.

c) Does the law provide for a presumption? If so, under which conditions?
No.

d) Other means?
No.

Question 18: Would you like to add any further aspects not covered by the above questions?

Fraudulent loans and artificial or fraudulent cash procurement are disregarded.

In practice, courts are taking into consideration unpaid bills, tax and social security charges; accounting experts are often appointed to ascertain *ex post* the situation of the debtor in order to fix the beginning of the suspect period.

III. CESSATION OF PAYMENTS

Question 19: In your jurisdiction, is "cessation of payments" a legal term used either in statute or in case law? (If the answer is "no", please continue with Question 26.)

Yes.

Question 20: Is "cessation of payments" an autonomous ground to commence proceedings (triggering circumstance)? You may refer to Questions 5/6 or add additional information here.

Yes, for rehabilitation proceedings.

In liquidation proceedings there is an additional factor: the rehabilitation of the debtor is manifestly impossible.

Question 21: Is "cessation of payments" a means to establish inability to pay debts? If so, by which mechanism (e.g. rebuttable presumption for inability to pay debts, cf. above Question 17(c))?

Yes, the objective accounting test, based on the (contractual) maturity of the debts; it is not required that the creditor has requested payment.

Fraudulent loans and artificial or fraudulent cash procurement are disregarded.

Question 22: How is "cessation of payments" defined? If it is defined in statute, please provide us here with an English translation of the relevant rule. Is this definition (if any) specified in case law? If so, how?

Pursuant to Article L. 631-1 C. com. "a debtor which is unable to meet its due and payable debts with its immediately available assets is in cessation of payment."

Question 23: How is "cessation of payments" established?

The court relies in practice on the analysis by the IP and/or experts' opinions.

The IP conducts an objective review of the accounts and the (contractual) maturity of the debts; it is irrelevant whether the creditor has requested payment.

Moratoria and standstill agreements and grace periods are taken into consideration.

On the asset side, the IP conducts an objective review of the cash position, including cash equivalent items like liquid financial instruments.

Fraudulent loans and artificial or fraudulent cash procurements are disregarded.

Question 24: Are there typical circumstances which provide circumstantial evidence that the debtor has ceased payments? If so, please list as many as possible.

n.a.

Question 25: Would you like to add any further aspects not covered by the above questions?

No.

IV. LIKELY/IMMINENT INABILITY TO PAY DEBTS

Question 26: Are the following terms available in your jurisdiction, either in statute or in case law? (If the answer is "no", please continue with Question 37.)

a) likely inability to pay debts
No.

b) imminent inability to pay debts
No.

c) other (similar) terms
Article L. 620-1 C. com. refers to the concept of a situation where the debtor faces difficulties that it is unable to overcome.

Question 27: Is "likely/imminent inability to pay debts" an autonomous ground to commence proceedings (triggering circumstance)? You may refer to Questions 5/6 or add additional information here.

n.a.

Question 28: If the answer to the previous Question is "yes", who may base filing for insolvency proceedings on it: only the debtor or also creditors?

n.a.

Question 29: How are these terms defined? If they are defined in statute, please provide us here with an English translation of the relevant rules. Is this definition (if any) specified in case law? If so, how?

a) likely inability to pay debts

n.a.

b) imminent inability to pay debts

n.a.

Question 30: Do the terms "likely" and "imminent" require a prognosis regarding the point in time when actual inability to pay debts will occur? If so, how long is the time period for this prognosis?

n.a.

Question 31: Does your law require a specific grade of certainty that inability to pay debts will eventually occur? If so, is 50.1% ("more likely than not") enough or are there alleviated or aggravated prerequisites?

n.a.

Question 32: Regarding "debts" and "financial means", are they defined in the same way as in the context of inability to pay debts (cf. above Questions 12/13)? If not, what are the differences?

n.a.

Question 33: Further to Question 32: Are "debts" considered which do currently not exist or are not yet due but will foreseeably come into existence and become due during the prognosis period?

n.a.

Question 34: Also further to Question 32: Are "financial means" considered which do currently not exist but will foreseeably become available during the prognosis period?

n.a.

Question 35: How are the terms "likely/imminent inability to pay debts" established?

n.a.

Question 36: Would you like to add any further aspects not covered by the above questions?

French case law is rather liberal with respect to the interpretation of the concept of difficulties that the debtor is unable to overcome.

Initially, the law of 26 July 2005 provided for an additional test factor. The debtor had to demonstrate that the difficulties were of such nature that they would lead to cessation of payments. This condition of "treating insolvency" was abrogated by an ordonnance of 18 December 2008.

According to doctrine, only if the debtor artificially creates (financial) difficulties should the courts reject the application for the opening of safeguard proceedings.

V. OVERINDEBTEDNESS

Question 37: In your jurisdiction, is "overindebtedness", or "balance sheet insolvency" respectively, a legal term used either in statute or in case law? (If the answer is "no", please continue with Question 49.)

No.

Question 38: Is "overindebtedness" an autonomous ground to commence proceedings (triggering circumstance)? You may refer to Questions 5/6 or add additional information here.

n.a.

Question 39: Is the answer to the previous Question is "yes", is this applicable to legal persons only or also to natural persons?

n.a.

Question 40: Is the term "overindebtedness" defined in statute? If so, please give the wording in English translation. Is this definition (if any) specified in case law? If so, how?

n.a.

Question 41: Does your law refer to all existing debts or only to mature debts?

n.a.

Question 42: Which assets are taken into account when overindebtedness is established: the complete set of assets or only a selection of them?

n.a.

Question 43: How are the debtor's assets valued: by referring to the liquidation value, the book value, the going concern value or in another way?

n.a.

Question 44: Is there any prognostic element, e.g. regarding the debtor's chances to continue the business?

n.a.

Question 45: If the answer to the previous Question is "yes", what exactly is the topic of the prognosis and how is it established?

n.a.

Question 46: If the answer to the Question 44 is "yes", how long is the prognosis period?

n.a.

Question 47: How is overindebtedness established?

a) Is a formal balance sheet required?
n.a.

b) Does the yearly regular commercial balance sheet have any meaning (given that it is normally based on technical values and does not display undisclosed reserves)?
n.a.

c) Does the law provide for a presumption? If so, under which conditions?
n.a.

d) Other means?
n.a.

Question 48: Would you like to add any further aspects not covered by the above questions?

n.a.

VI. REMAINING ISSUES

Question 49: Is there anything else you would like to share in the present context and that we should take into account?

In my practice of French/German cross-border restructuring cases, the difference in the triggering events to file for the opening of insolvency proceedings has a huge impact.

Overindebtedness as an autonomous mandatory ground to commence insolvency proceedings creates an additional hurdle to restructuring the indebtedness of the debtor in out-of-court proceedings.

The "cessation of payment" triggering event can be cured rather easily in French law by entering into a standstill or moratorium whereas the situation is much more complex in Germany with the requirement of a positive continuation prognosis.

GERMANY

Reinhard Bork

I. GENERAL

Question 1: How is insolvency (both in the context of liquidation and restructuring) regulated in your jurisdiction? Please give a brief overview, at least enumerating the relevant statutes.

Germany has only one single insolvency statute, the Insolvenzordnung (InsO, Insolvency Regulation). It provides for uniform proceedings which can aim at liquidation as well as restructuring, depending on the case at hand. Both outcomes are regularly in the hands of an Insolvency Practitioner (*Insolvenzverwalter*) who can get instructions from the creditors' meeting. However, both variants are also available as debtor-in-possession proceedings. An English translation of the InsO is available at: http://www.gesetze-im-internet.de/englisch_inso/index.html.

Alongside the Insolvenzordnung, pre-insolvency proceedings are provided for in the Gesetz über den Stabilisierungs- und Restrukturierungsrahmen für Unternehmen (StaRUG, Act on the Stabilisation and Restructuring Framework for Enterprises), which is the transposition of the EU Directive on restructuring and insolvency into German law. The StaRUG offers a toolbox from which the debtor can pick what he or she needs (e.g. stay of enforcement, complete restructuring plan proceedings, plan confirmation only, etc.). StaRUG proceedings are debtor-in-possession proceedings. They aim at restructuring and are not available where the debtor is already unable to pay its mature debts. Unfortunately, no official English translation of the StaRUG is available.

In my answers below, I will highlight where the answers for restructuring proceedings under the InsO differ from those under the StaRUG.

Question 2: Related to paragraph 10 above of the Introduction: seen from a principle-based perspective, what justifies the opening of insolvency proceedings in your jurisdiction?

The opening of insolvency proceedings is first and foremost justified by the principles of equal treatment of creditors and collectivity, since individual enforcement proceedings are no longer acceptable where the debtor is substantively insolvent or substantive insolvency is imminent. At this stage of the debtor's financial crisis, collective proceedings are due in the interest of equal treatment of all creditors. Other principles may also come into play, e.g. the principle of debtor protection, where the substantively insolvent debtor needs help against single creditors with hold-out positions, or the principle of best possible satisfaction of the creditors' claims, where creditors would be worse off without insolvency proceedings.

Question 3: Does your national law in the context of liquidation proceedings use one or more of the following terms (be it as a noun, be it as an adjective or adjunct) in whatever context:

a) inability to pay debts
Yes.

b) cessation of payments
Yes.

c) likely inability to pay debts
No.

d) imminent inability to pay debts
Yes.

e) overindebtedness?
Yes.

Question 4: Are the same terms (and with the same meaning) used in the rules on preliminary/interim insolvency proceedings (e.g. concerning the application stage of the proceedings)?

Yes.

Question 5: Does your national law in the context of restructuring proceedings (as referred to above at paragraph 8 of the Introduction, i.e. both pre-insolvency and within formal insolvency proceedings) use one or more of the following terms (be it as a noun, be it as an adjective or adjunct) in whatever context:

a) inability to pay debts
Yes.

b) cessation of payments
Yes (but only under the InsO, not the StaRUG).

c) likely inability to pay debts
No.

d) imminent inability to pay debts
Yes.

e) overindebtedness?
Yes.

Question 6: Which of the terms mentioned in Questions 3 and 4 are used for defining grounds to commence proceedings (triggering circumstances)?

a) insolvency proceedings
"Inability to pay debts" (§17 InsO), "imminent inability to pay debts" (§18 InsO), "overindebtedness" (§19 InsO).

b) restructuring proceedings
Under the InsO: "inability to pay debts" (§17 InsO), "imminent inability to pay debts" (§18 InsO), "overindebtedness" (§19 InsO).

Under the StaRUG: "imminent inability to pay debts" (§29(1) StaRUG).

Question 7: Does the answer to Question 6 include natural persons or only legal entities?

Both.

Question 8: In your law, are there any other circumstances which trigger insolvency or restructuring proceedings?

No.

Question 9: Which of the terms mentioned in Questions 3, 5, and 8 are used in the context of transactions avoidance law?

"Inability to pay debts" (§§130–132 InsO).

Question 10: Which of the terms addressed in Questions 3, 5, and 8 are used in the context of directors' duties?

a) shift of duties (from shareholders to creditors)
In Germany, the shift of duties is neither regulated nor defined in case law. It is controversially discussed in literature but no clear picture can be drawn.

b) duties to commence insolvency proceedings
"Inability to pay debts" and "overindebtedness" (§15a InsO).

c) other duties (please describe)
n.a.

Question 11: Are there any other rules in the context of which the terms addressed in Questions 3, 5, and 8 are used?

Yes, they are relevant in some rules of criminal law:

- §283 Strafgesetzbuch (StGB, Criminal Code: fraudulent insolvency): "inability to pay debts", "imminent inability to pay debts", "overindebtedness";
- §283c StGB (preferential treatment of creditors): "inability to pay debts";
- §283d StGB (preferential treatment of debtors): "imminent inability to pay debts", "cessation of payments".

Further, they are used in some insolvency-related rules. Examples are §§1, 2, 4–6 Gesetz zur Abmilderung der Folgen der COVID-19-Pandemie im Zivil-, Insolvenz- und Strafverfahrensrecht (COVInsAG, Act to Temporarily Suspend the Obligation to File for Insolvency and to Limit Directors' Liability in the Case of Insolvency Caused by the COVID-19 Pandemic), now §§1, 2, 4–6 Gesetz zur vorübergehenden Anpassung sanierungs- und insolvenzrechtlicher Vorschriften zur Abmilderung von Krisenfolgen (SanInsKG, Act to Temporarily Adjust Restructuring and Insolvency Law Provisions for the Mitigation of Consequences of a Crisis): "inability to pay debts", "overindebtedness".

Note that the terms characterising the debtor's insolvency are always used and defined in the same sense and uniformly interpreted by the courts, no matter whether they are relevant in the context of insolvency law (and whether as a prerequisite for opening insolvency proceedings or for transactions avoidance law) or in the context of company or criminal law.

Question 12: Is the definition of (the subspecies of) insolvency identical in all legal fields or are there different definitions (e.g. different in insolvency law than in criminal law)?

They are identical.

II. INABILITY TO PAY DEBTS

Question 13: In your jurisdiction, is the term "inability to pay debts" defined in statute? If so, please give the wording in English translation. Is this definition (if any) specified in case law? If so, how?

Inability to pay debts is defined in §17(2) sentence 1 InsO which provides: "Debtors are deemed illiquid if they are unable to meet their mature obligations." However, this definition has been significantly specified by the German Bundesgerichtshof (BGH, Federal Supreme Court). According to the BGH (the leading case is the decision of 24.04.2005 – IX ZR 123/04, BGHZ 163, 134), it must be established that the debtor lacks the necessary means of payment and is therefore *permanently*, not only temporarily, unable to pay *a not insignificant part* of his or her due and seriously claimed[1] monetary liabilities. A short-term stagnation of payments does not lead to insolvency as long as it does not last for a "grace period" of more than three weeks, because it is then not a case of a permanent inability to pay. Further, very minor liquidity gaps are not taken into consideration; they are considered to constitute an insignificant inability to pay debts. According to the case law of the BGH, the liquidity gap is usually only significant if at least 10% of the due liabilities cannot be met; in this event, inability to pay debts is rebuttably presumed. If the liquidity gap is less than 10%, it is (rebuttably) presumed that the debtor is able to pay its mature debts, unless it is foreseeable that the liquidity gap will soon be higher than 10% (in which case the inability to pay debts is rebuttably presumed). Hence, for the BGH (as cited above), the 10% hurdle is more decisive for the burden of proof than for the substantive prerequisites of the debtor's insolvency.

Question 14: Does your law refer to all debts or only to mature debts?

Under German law, inability to pay debts must be established for a specific day. Which day is relevant depends on the rule which is applied (e.g. the day the court decides on the opening of insolvency proceedings, the day a director pays a creditor in breach of his or her insolvency-related duties, or the day a voidable preference has been performed). Hence, only the mature debts, i.e. those which are or become mature on this very day, can be taken into account. However, debts which are not mature on the day in question but will fall due within the next three weeks, also have to be taken account of when forecasting the development in the near future (see *supra* answer to Question 11 and *infra* answer to Question 16).

Question 15: Which assets are taken into account when assessing the inability to pay debts: all (financial) assets or only those that are liquid, i.e. available on short notice?

Since inability to pay debts must be established for a specific day, only the "quick assets", i.e. those which can be converted into money on this very day, can be taken into account. That includes primarily cash, money in regular bank

---

1 This additional feature is neither in the statute nor in accordance with section 271 of the German Civil Code (Bürgerliches Gesetzbuch – BGB), but is in line with settled case law; see, for example, BGH, 19.07.2007 – IX ZB 36/07, BGHZ 173, 286 para. 18; BGH, 24.02.2022 – IX ZR 250/20, ZRI 2022, 280, para. 23; BGH, 18.07.2019 – IX ZR 259/18, ZInsO 2019, 1790, para. 20. Admittedly, this case law only intends to cover such legal claims that have been deferred purely in fact – i.e. without any legally binding intention or recognisable declarations – and is content with any (express or implied) conduct of the creditor from which it can be concluded that he really wants satisfaction of his or her claim.

accounts, overdraft facilities, stock-exchange listed shares, receivables (but only if payment by the third party on this very day is certain), etc. However, assets which are not available on this day but can be realised within the three weeks after this day (see answer to Question 11) must also be taken into account within this prognosis.

Question 16: Is any liquidity gap (deficit between relevant financial means and relevant debts) relevant or does your law neglect minor gaps? If the latter, how is "minor" defined?

Minor gaps are ignored; "minor" is defined as up to 10% of all debts (see *supra* answer to Question 11).

Question 17: As far as the time aspect is concerned, does it matter whether the liquidity gap can be closed again in the short term? If so, how long is the grace period?

Yes, that matters. The grace period is three weeks (see *supra* answer to Question 11).

Question 18: As far as the time aspect is concerned, is a debtor considered insolvent if the liquidity gap is not yet present but will occur soon? If so, how long is the prognosis period? (Note: this may also concern the difference between actual and likely/imminent inability to pay debts; cf. below Question 34).

Under the circumstances described in this question, the debtor is not unable to pay debts on the relevant day, but he or she is imminently insolvent in the sense described below (see answer to Question 29).

Note, that the grace period described in answer to Question 11 refers to the irrelevance of the inability to pay the mature debts on the relevant day where the liquidity gap existing on this particular day can be closed within the next three weeks. It does not refer to a future inability to pay debts. Example: On 1 February, the debtor does not have the financial means to pay the mature debts on this day. Nevertheless, he or she is not insolvent (within the meaning of §17 InsO) if this liquidity gap will be closed within the next three weeks (before 21 February). Even if it is foreseeable that there will be a second liquidity gap in four weeks (1 March), this time not closable within another three weeks after this day (i.e. before 21 March), the debtor is not unable to pay his or her mature debts on 1 February but only on 1 March.

Question 19: How is inability to pay debts established? Please communicate if there is a difference between a creditor and a debtor application or between different legal contexts.

As a preliminary remark, all methods described below can be used by debtors, creditors, Insolvency Practitioners, and third parties in all relevant legal situations.

However, creditors and third parties will typically not be able to draw up a liquidity balance sheet or to present daily liquidity data, since they do not have the necessary information. Hence, they will normally refer to the debtor's cessation of payments.

a) Is a formal liquidity status (liquidity balance sheet) required?
This is one of various possibilities, used in all legal contexts. We call this optional way to establish inability to pay debts the "economic method" (see BGH, 19.07.2007 – IX ZB 36/07, BGHZ 173, 286 paragraph 30).

b) Is a sample of daily liquidity data (which do not amount to a proper liquidity status but show insufficient funds on different days within a certain period of time) sufficient?
Yes. According to latest case law of the BGH, courts may derive the debtor's permanent illiquidity to pay debts from an exemplary sample of daily liquidity data too. The leading case is the decision of 28.06.2022 – II ZR 112/21, NZI 2022, 787.

c) Does the law provide for a presumption? If so, under which conditions?
According to §17(2) sentence 2 InsO, inability to pay debts is rebuttably presumed where the debtor has ceased payments. This refers to cessation of payments as described below in answer to Question 22. We call this the "economic crime method".

d) Does the law provide for any technical circumstances (e.g. undisputed statutory demand, non-compliance with monetary judgments, unsuccessful enforcement proceedings, non-performance of a previous composition agreement in insolvency proceedings) the occurrence of which suffices to establish the debtor's insolvency?
No. These circumstances should be taken into account when establishing the debtor's cessation of payments but they are not means to establish directly inability to pay debts.

e) Other means?
None.

Question 20: Is insolvency (inability to pay debts, overindebtedness, etc.) subject to party autonomy in the proceedings or must the court clarify them *ex officio*?

The latter (*iura novit curia*).

Question 21: In an overall view, does your law distinguish "inability to pay debts" from "financial difficulties"? If so, how?

Yes. "Inability to pay debts" is a special stadium of financial difficulties.

Question 22: In an overall view, does it matter under your law whether the debtor's inability to pay debts is present or future and reversible or irreversible?

Yes, future inability to pay is not sufficient and reversibility is only relevant if the debtor will be able to pay all debts within the next three months.

Question 23: Would you like to add any further aspects not covered by the above questions?

No.

III. CESSATION OF PAYMENTS

Question 24: In your jurisdiction, is "cessation of payments" a legal term used either in statute or in case law? (If the answer is "no", please continue with Question 31.)

Yes (§17(2) sentence 2 InsO).

Question 25: Is "cessation of payments" an autonomous ground to commence proceedings (triggering circumstance)? You may refer to Questions 6/7 or add additional information here.

No (see answer to next question).

Question 26: Is "cessation of payments" a means to establish inability to pay debts? If so, by which mechanism (e.g. rebuttable presumption for inability to pay debts, cf. above Question 19(c))?

According to §17(2) sentence 2 InsO, cessation of payments creates a statutory rebuttable presumption of the debtor's inability to pay debts (see *supra* answer to Question 17(c)).

Question 27: How is "cessation of payments" defined? If it is defined in statute, please provide us here with an English translation of the relevant rule. Is this definition (if any) specified in case law? If so, how?

There is no statutory definition of cessation of payments. According to case law of the BGH (cf BGH, 06.05.2021 – IX ZR 72/20, BGHZ 230, 28 paragraph 15), cessation of payments is the external behaviour of the debtor through which an inability to pay is typically expressed. The relevant public must have the justified impression that the debtor is not in a position to fulfil his or her due payment obligations. Whether this is the case depends on a comprehensive evaluation of all relevant circumstances (see answers to Questions 23, 24).

Question 28: How is "cessation of payments" established?

Courts must assess all relevant circumstances which can serve as circumstantial evidence for the debtor's cessation of payments (see answer to Question 24).

Question 29: Are there typical circumstances which provide circumstantial evidence that the debtor has ceased payments? If so, please list as many as possible.

According to case law of the BGH (cf. BGH, 06.05.2021 – IX ZR 72/20, BGHZ 230, 28 paragraph 41), the most important and relevant circumstance is a confession or declaration by the debtor him- or herself (e.g. in a letter to his or her bank, asking for an extension of the credit line with the remark that without such an extension, due debts cannot be satisfied). All other circumstances are only relevant if they – individually or taken together as a whole – amount to such a declaration by the debtor. According to case law, typical circumstances include:

- pressure by creditors through dunning and/or enforcement
- sluggish payments to existentially important creditors
- non-payment of a substantial part of due liabilities even if it consists of only one single but substantial claim)
- (several months of) non-payment of social security contributions
- putting off payment of a substantial amount of arrears for as long as possible (not merely delaying payments)
- silence on invoices and reminders
- informing a major creditor of the liquidity issues
- closing the business premises
- escape from creditors (e.g. by fleeing the country)
- recovery by suppliers of goods subject to retention of title
- bouncing of cheques
- refusal of the bank to accept direct debits
- strategic partial payments (to the most pressing creditors only)
- slow payment of wages and salaries
- subsequent conclusion of instalment payment agreements that are not customary for the business
- non-compliance with such instalment payment agreements

It is not required that these circumstances concern more than one creditor or that there even are several unpaid creditors. If there is only one creditor and his or her demands for payment remain unsuccessful, this may give sufficient circumstantial evidence of the debtor's cessation of payments.

Question 30: Would you like to add any further aspects not covered by the above questions?

No.

IV. LIKELY/IMMINENT INABILITY TO PAY DEBTS

Question 31: Are the following terms available in your jurisdiction, either in statute or in case law? (If the answer is "no", please continue with Question 42.)

a) likely inability to pay debts
No (but see *infra* answer to Question 29).

b) imminent inability to pay debts
Yes (§18 InsO, §29 StaRUG).

c) other (similar) terms
No.

Question 32: Is "likely/imminent inability to pay debts" an autonomous ground to commence proceedings (triggering circumstance)? You may refer to Questions 6/7 or add additional information here.

According to §18(1) InsO, imminent inability to pay debts is a ground on which to commence proceedings.

Question 33: If the answer to the previous Question is "yes", who may base filing for insolvency proceedings on it: only the debtor or also creditors?

The debtor only (§18(1) InsO).

Question 34: How are these terms defined? If they are defined in statute, please provide us here with an English translation of the relevant rules. Is this definition (if any) specified in case law? If so, how?

a) likely inability to pay debts
n.a.

b) imminent inability to pay debts
According to §18(2) InsO, "a debtor is deemed to be faced with imminent inability to pay debts if it is likely that the debtor will be unable to meet existing obligations to pay on the date of their maturity". The forecasting period is generally to be 24 months. According to case law of the BGH (see BGH, 10.02.2022 – IX ZR 148/19, NZI 2022, 397), imminent insolvency requires a predominant probability (more than 50%) that the debtor will become unable to pay his or her mature debts within the next two years. Given this rather long prognosis period, "imminent" is more or less synonymous with "likely". So far, German jurisprudence has not realised the difference between probability and urgency when dealing with the term "imminent inability to pay debts", since "imminent" is equated with "likely" as a term of probability, not with any term of urgency. This is not only consistent but also consequential, since if an inability to pay debts will occur in (e.g.) 23 months, the problem is likely but not urgent.

Question 35: Do the terms "likely" and "imminent" require a prognosis regarding the point in time when actual inability to pay debts will occur? If so, how long is the time period for this prognosis?

Yes. The relevant time period is two years (see *supra* answer to Question 29).

Question 36: Does your law require a specific grade of certainty that inability to pay debts will eventually occur? If so, is 50.1% ("more likely than not") enough or are there alleviated or aggravated prerequisites?

Yes, 50.1% (see *supra* answer to Question 29, for establishment *infra* answer to Question 35).

Question 37: Regarding "debts" and "financial means", are they defined in the same way as in the context of inability to pay debts (cf. above Questions 14/15)? If not, what are the differences?

No differences.

Question 38: Further to Question 37: Are "debts" considered which do currently not exist or are not yet due but will foreseeably come into existence and become due during the prognosis period?

Yes.

Question 39: Also further to Question 37: Are "financial means" considered which do currently not exist but will foreseeably become available during the prognosis period?

Yes. All financial means (not only "quick assets" as referred to in the answer to Question 13) which are or will become available during the prognosis period are considered.

Question 40: How are the terms "likely/imminent inability to pay debts" established?

The normal (but not legally required) way is to draft a financial plan for the next two years, listing all debts and financial means to be expected for the prognosis period. However, depending on the case at hand, it may also suffice to demonstrate that a significant debt (e.g. a major loan or debenture) will become due in (e.g.) eight months and that the current turnover is under no circumstances sufficient to pay this debt. As regards establishing the probability of more than 50%, all means of evidence are permissible to convince the court that inability to pay debts is likely (as defined *supra* in answer to Question 31).

Question 41: Would you like to add any further aspects not covered by the above questions?

No.

V. OVERINDEBTEDNESS

Question 42: In your jurisdiction, is "overindebtedness", or "balance sheet insolvency" respectively, a legal term used either in statute or in case law? (If the answer is "no", please continue with Question 56.)

Yes.

Question 43: Is "overindebtedness" an autonomous ground to commence proceedings (triggering circumstance)? You may refer to Questions 6/7 or add additional information here.

Yes (§19 InsO).

Question 44: If the answer to the previous Question is "yes", is this applicable to legal persons only or also to natural persons?

To legal persons only. The reason is that the most important assets of a natural person – his or her personal skills – cannot be capitalised in a balance sheet.

Question 45: Is the term "overindebtedness" defined in statute? If so, please give the wording in English translation. Is this definition (if any) specified in case law? If so, how?

Yes. According to §19(2) InsO,

> overindebtedness exists if the debtor's assets no longer cover existing obligations to pay, unless it is predominant likely, considering the circumstances, that the enterprise will continue to exist for the next 12 months.

Specifications by case law are covered by the following questions.

Question 46: Does your law refer to all existing debts or only to mature debts?

To all existing debts.

Question 47: Does the rank of certain debts play a role when establishing overindebtedness? In particular, is there any possibility to conclude

agreements according to which certain debts shall not be taken into account (e.g. agreements on subsidiarity)?

In principle, all debts have to be taken into account. An exception is provided for in §19(2) sentence 2 InsO, according to which debts from shareholder loans to which a (simple) subsidiarity agreement applies must be left aside. The same holds true for claims of all kinds to which a (qualified) subsidiarity agreement, combined with an enforcement barrier, applies.

Question 48: Which assets are taken into account when overindebtedness is established: the complete set of assets or only a selection of them?

All assets.

Question 49: How are the debtor's assets valued: by referring to the liquidation value, the book value, the going concern value or in another way?

That depends on the prognosis (see *infra* answers to Questions 44 et seq.). If the prognosis is negative, the liquidation value is decisive; otherwise the going concern value is relevant. Hence, in the end, everything depends on the prognosis.

Question 50: Is there any prognostic element, e.g. regarding the debtor's chances to continue the business?

Yes.

Question 51: If the answer to Question 50 is "yes", what exactly is the topic of the prognosis and how is it established?

The prognosis relates to the debtor's chances to continue operating the business for the next 12 months. This requires the debtor's will to continue the business, a business plan for the next 12 months (which may include necessary restructuring and reorganisation steps), and a financial overview of the expected debts and available financial means. In the end, it is a prognosis concerning the debtor's medium-term ability to pay debts.

Question 52: If the answer to Question 50 is "yes", how long is the prognosis period?

12 months (temporarily reduced to four months for the financial years 2021–2023, §4 SanInsKG).

Question 53: How is overindebtedness established?

a) Is a formal balance sheet required?
Yes. However, it is not necessary (although possible) to include an auditor or accountant in the validation of the balance sheet. Typically, it is drafted by either the debtor (who is assisted by an accountant etc.) or a preliminary Insolvency Practitioner where overindebtedness is established at the application stage before the opening of the proceedings. When it comes to establishing overindebtedness in the context of directors' duties (claims for damages based on infringement of such duties), it is the Insolvency Practitioner (who may avail him- or herself of the assistance of an auditor).

b) Does the yearly regular commercial balance sheet have any meaning (given that it is normally based on technical values and does not display undisclosed reserves)?
No. The regular commercial balance sheet is only a starting point, since all assets (including non-displayed values) must be taken into account. A special overindebtedness balance sheet is required which displays all assets, including undisclosed reserves and otherwise not displayable assets (e.g. intangible assets), with their liquidation values.

c) Does the law provide for a presumption? If so, under which conditions?
No.

d) Other means?
No.

Question 54: is the legal link to overindebtedness undisputed in literature or are there efforts to abolish it?

It is heavily disputed in the literature but the legislator shows no intention of abolishing it.

Question 55: Would you like to add any further aspects not covered by the above questions?

No.

VI. REMAINING ISSUES

Question 56: Is there anything else you would like to share in the present context and that we should take into account?

No.

GREECE

Stathis Potamitis

I. GENERAL

Question 1: How is insolvency (both in the context of liquidation and restructuring/reorganisation) regulated in your jurisdiction? Please give a brief overview, at least enumerating the relevant statutes.

Greece has a uniform framework for insolvency and pre-insolvency procedures, Law 4738/2020 (the Insolvency Law) that includes a preventive restructuring proceeding transposing the EU Directive on Preventive Restructuring to Greek law. There are separate statutes dealing with business failure for financial institutions and insurance undertakings that are not dealt with in the response provided below.

Question 2: Related to paragraph 10 above of the Introduction: seen from a principle-based perspective, what justifies the opening of insolvency proceedings in your jurisdiction?

The opening of insolvency proceedings is justified by the need to permit the best possible satisfaction of all creditors in circumstances when resort to individual enforcement could lead to unfair allocation of recoveries or to loss of value for the debtor's estate that could be preserved by resort to collective proceedings. There are also additional considerations that should be noted, such as the preservation of the going concern of the debtor's enterprise in order to avoid disruption within its sphere of economic activity and to preserve employment positions. Last but not least, the opening of insolvency proceedings may serve as a route to debt discharge for individuals.

Question 3: Does your national law in the context of liquidation proceedings use one or more of the following terms (be it as a noun, be it as an adjective or adjunct) in whatever context:

a) inability to pay debts
Yes.

b) cessation of payments
Yes.

c) likely inability to pay debts
No.

d) imminent inability to pay debts
Yes.

e) overindebtedness?
No.

Question 4: Are the same terms (and with the same meaning) used in the rules on preliminary/interim insolvency proceedings (e.g. concerning the application stage of the proceedings)?

Yes.

Question 5: Does your national law in the context of restructuring proceedings (as referred to above at paragraph 8 of the Introduction, i.e. both pre-insolvency and within formal insolvency proceedings) use one or more of the following terms (be it as a noun, be it as an adjective or adjunct) in whatever context:

a) inability to pay debts
Yes.

b) cessation of payments
Yes.

c) likely inability to pay debts
Yes.

d) imminent inability to pay debts
Yes.

e) overindebtedness?
No.

Question 6: Which of the terms mentioned in Questions 3 and 5 are used for defining grounds to commence proceedings (triggering circumstances)?

a) insolvency proceedings
"Cessation of payments" (Article 77 Insolvency Law), "inability to pay debts" and "imminent inability to pay debts" (Article 77 Insolvency Law)

b) restructuring proceedings
"Inability to pay debts" and "imminent inability to pay debts" (Article 32 Insolvency Law)

Please note that "possibility of insolvency" is also a triggering event under Article 32 paragraph 2 of the Insolvency Law, while "cessation of payments" is a condition that would permit the ratification of a restructuring agreement without the debtor's consent (Article 34).

Question 7: Does the answer to Question 6 include personal bankruptcies of natural persons or only corporate insolvencies of legal entities?

Both.

Question 8: In your law, are there any other circumstances which trigger insolvency or restructuring proceedings?

A showing of likelihood (possibility) of insolvency would permit a court to ratify a restructuring agreement that would in other respects also satisfy the ratification requirements (please see response to Question 5)

Question 9: Which of the terms mentioned in Questions 3, 5, and 8 are used in the context of transactions avoidance law?

Cessation of payments (Article 116 Insolvency Law).

Question 10: Which of the terms addressed in Questions 3, 5, and 8 are used in the context of directors' duties?

a) shift of duties (from shareholders to creditors)
n.a. [There is no express provision in relation to the shift of duties. However, the provisions of Article 127 of the Insolvency Law regarding (i) the liability to creditors for trading while insolvent, (ii) the exclusion from such liability if the delay in filing for insolvency proceedings is caused by negotiations to avert insolvency for the benefit, *inter alia*, of creditors, and (iii) the liability to creditors for causing insolvency through willful misconduct or gross negligence, indicate that such a shift takes place as insolvency becomes more likely and in any event upon cessation of payments.]

b) duties to commence insolvency proceedings
"Cessation of payments" (Article 127 Insolvency Law).

c) other duties (please describe)
n.a.

Question 11: Are there any other rules in the context of which the terms addressed in Questions 3, 5, and 8 are used?

Preferential treatment of creditor (Article 198 Insolvency Law): "cessation of payments", "imminent inability to pay debts".

Asset dissipation (Article 199 Insolvency Law): "cessation of payments", "imminent inability to pay debts".

Question 12: Is the definition of (the subspecies of) insolvency identical in all legal fields or are there different definitions (e.g. different in insolvency law than in criminal law)?

The same.

II. INABILITY TO PAY DEBTS

Question 13: In your jurisdiction, is the term "inability to pay debts" defined in statute? If so, please give the wording in English translation. Is this definition (if any) specified in case law? If so, how?

"Inability to pay debts" is part of the definition of "cessation of payments". In particular, "cessation of payments" is defined as "inability to satisfy its due and payable monetary obligations generally and permanently" (Article 77 Insolvency Law). The same provision also introduces the following rebuttable presumption of cessation of payments:

> [the non-payment of] due and payable obligations to the State, Social Security Institutions or credit and financing institutions in an amount that is at least 40% of its total due and payable obligations for a period of at least 6 months, provided that its unpaid liabilities exceed the amount of Euro 30,000.

Question 14: Does your law refer to all debts or only to mature debts?

Debts that are considered are those that are due and payable, i.e. mature.

Question 15: Which assets are taken into account when assessing the inability to pay debts: all (financial) assets or only those that are liquid, i.e. available on short notice?

There is no specific provision in the law, possibly because cessation of payments is a finding of actual non-payment over a period of time (see the rebuttable presumption in our response to Question 13); as to whether that inability is permanent, assets that are hard to monetarise would probably not be considered.

Question 16: Is any liquidity gap (deficit between relevant financial means and relevant debts) relevant or does your law neglect minor gaps? If the latter, how is "minor" defined?

Our law does not provide for a liquidity test other than the concept of cessation of payments discussed above under Question 13.

Question 17: As far as the time aspect is concerned, does it matter whether the liquidity gap can be closed again in the short term? If so, how long is the grace period?

n.a. – see our response to Question 16.

Question 18: As far as the time aspect is concerned, is a debtor considered insolvent if the liquidity gap is not yet present but will occur soon? If so, how long is the prognosis period? (Note: this may also concern the difference between actual and likely/imminent inability to pay debts; cf. below Question 34).

n.a. – see our response to Question 14.

Question 19: How is inability to pay debts established? Please communicate if there is a difference between a creditor and a debtor application or between different legal contexts.

a) Is a formal liquidity status (liquidity balance sheet) required?
No.

b) Is a sample of daily liquidity data (which do not amount to a proper liquidity status but show insufficient funds on different days within a certain period of time) sufficient?
Case law does not appear to take into consideration daily liquidity data but takes into account the size and nature of overdue debts as well as any indications as to whether the inability to pay is permanent or temporary.

c) Does the law provide for a rebuttable presumption? If so, under which conditions?
Yes, please see our response to Question 13.

d) Does the law provide for any technical circumstances (e.g. undisputed statutory demand, non-compliance with monetary judgments, unsuccessful enforcement proceedings, non-performance of a previous composition agreement in insolvency proceedings) the occurrence of which suffices to establish the debtor's insolvency?
No.

e) Other means?
None.

Question 20: Is insolvency (inability to pay debts, overindebtedness, etc.) subject to party autonomy in the proceedings or must the court clarify them *ex officio*?

The court must clarify them.

Question 21: In an overall view, does your law distinguish "inability to pay debts" from "financial difficulties"? If so, how?

Yes, inability to pay debts as they fall due should be of a permanent nature ("cessation of payments") in order for a debtor to be declared bankrupt.

Question 22: In an overall view, does it matter under your law whether the debtor's inability to pay debts is present or future and reversible or irreversible?

Yes. For cessation of payments, the debtor's inability to pay debts should be present and irreversible.

Question 23: Would you like to add any further aspects not covered by the above questions?

No.

III. CESSATION OF PAYMENTS

Question 24: In your jurisdiction, is "cessation of payments" a legal term used either in statute or in case law? (If the answer is "no", please continue with Question 31.)

Yes – please see responses to Questions 6, 9, 10, 11 and 13.

Question 25: Is "cessation of payments" an autonomous ground to commence proceedings (triggering circumstance)? You may refer to Questions 6/7 or add additional information here.

Yes.

Question 26: Is "cessation of payments" a means to establish inability to pay debts? If so, by which mechanism (e.g. rebuttable presumption for inability to pay debts, cf. above Question 19(c))?

As noted in our response to Question 11, "cessation of payments" is defined by reference to "inability to pay debts".

Question 27: How is "cessation of payments" defined? If it is defined in statute, please provide us here with an English translation of the relevant rule. Is this definition (if any) specified in case law? If so, how?

Please see our response to Question 13.

Question 28: How is "cessation of payments" established?

Courts must assess all relevant circumstances which can serve as circumstantial evidence of the debtor's cessation of payments.

Question 29: Are there typical circumstances which provide circumstantial evidence that the debtor has ceased payments? If so, please list as many as possible.

According to case law, typical circumstances include:

- non-payment of a substantial part of due liabilities (even if it is only one single but substantial claim);
- (several months of) non-payment of taxes and/or social security contributions;
- non-payment of (postdated) cheques;
- failure to pay slow payment of wages and salaries.

Article 77 Insolvency Law expressly provides that the selective satisfaction of due and payable monetary obligations does not exclude cessation of payments, which may consist in the inability to satisfy even just one material monetary liability.

Question 30: Would you like to add any further aspects not covered by the above questions?

No.

IV. LIKELY/IMMINENT INABILITY TO PAY DEBTS

Question 31: Are the following terms available in your jurisdiction, either in statute or in case law? (If the answer is "no", please continue with Question 42.)

a) likely inability to pay debts
Yes, Article 32 paragraph 2 of the Insolvency Law provides that a restructuring agreement may be entered into and ratified if there is a possibility of insolvency of the debtor that can be lifted by the implementation of the restructuring agreement (I believe that the expressions "possibility of insolvency" and "likely inability to pay debts" are equivalent).

b) imminent inability to pay debts
Yes, Article 32 Insolvency Law (for preventive restructuring) and Article 77 Insolvency Law (for insolvency).

c) other (similar) terms
No.

Question 32: Is "likely/imminent inability to pay debts" an autonomous ground to commence proceedings (triggering circumstance)? You may refer to Questions 6/7 or add additional information here.

According to Article 32 and Article 77 Insolvency Law, imminent inability to pay debts is a ground on which to commence restructuring and insolvency proceedings respectively.

According to Article 32 Insolvency Law, possibility of insolvency is a ground to commence restructuring proceedings.

Question 33: If the answer to the previous Question is "yes", who may base filing for insolvency proceedings on it: only the debtor or also creditors?

The debtor only (Article 77 Insolvency Law).

Question 34: How are these terms defined? If they are defined in statute, please provide us here with an English translation of the relevant rules. Is this definition (if any) specified in case law? If so, how?

a) likely inability to pay debts
As noted, the expression in the statute is "possibility of insolvency"; as this a recent enactment, we do not yet have any case law.

b) imminent inability to pay debts
Not defined.

Question 35: Do the terms "likely" and "imminent" require a prognosis regarding the point in time when actual inability to pay debts will occur? If so, how long is the time period for this prognosis?

The law does not specify a period of time for the prognosis.

Question 36: Does your law require a specific grade of certainty that inability to pay debts will eventually occur? If so, is 50.1% ("more likely than not") enough or are there alleviated or aggravated prerequisites?

No.

Question 37: Regarding "debts" and "financial means", are they defined in the same way as in the context of inability to pay debts (cf. above Questions 14/15)? If not, what are the differences?

No differences.

Question 38: Further to Question 37: Are "debts" considered which do currently not exist or are not yet due but will foreseeably come into existence and become due during the prognosis period?

Yes. While the law does not specifically refer to this point, the nature of the prognosis necessitates taking projected future debts into account (e.g. future wages of employees, future purchases of raw materials, etc.).

Question 39: Also further to Question 37: Are "financial means" considered which do currently not exist but will foreseeably become available during the prognosis period?

Yes. While the law does not specifically refer to this point, the nature of the prognosis necessitates taking projected financial means into account.

Question 40: How are the terms "likely/imminent inability to pay debts" established?

The law does not specify how the test is satisfied. Depending on the circumstances, a finding that one or more significant debts will soon become due and that there is no expectation to refinance or pay such debts from projected cash flow should be sufficient.

Question 41: Would you like to add any further aspects not covered by the above questions?

No.

V. OVERINDEBTEDNESS

Question 42: In your jurisdiction, is "overindebtedness", or "balance sheet insolvency" respectively, a legal term used either in statute or in case law? (If the answer is "no", please continue with Question 56.)

No.

Question 43: Is "overindebtedness" an autonomous ground to commence proceedings (triggering circumstance)? You may refer to Questions 6/7 or add additional information here.

n.a.

Question 44: If the answer to the previous Question is "yes", is this applicable to corporate insolvencies of legal persons only or also to personal bankruptcies of natural persons?

n.a.

Question 45: Is the term "overindebtedness" defined in statute? If so, please give the wording in English translation. Is this definition (if any) specified in case law? If so, how?

n.a.

Question 46: Does your law refer to all existing debts or only to mature debts?

n.a.

Question 47: Does the rank of certain debts play a role when establishing overindebtedness? In particular, is there any possibility to conclude agreements according to which certain debts shall not be taken into account (e.g. agreements on subsidiarity)?

n.a.

Question 48: Which assets are taken into account when overindebtedness is established: the complete set of assets or only a selection of them?

n.a.

Question 49: How are the debtor's assets valued: by referring to the liquidation value, the book value, the going concern value or in another way?

n.a.

Question 50: Is there any prognostic element, e.g. regarding the debtor's chances to continue the business?

n.a.

Question 51: If the answer to the previous Question is "yes", what exactly is the topic of the prognosis and how is it established?

n.a.

Question 52: If the answer to Question 50 is "yes", how long is the prognosis period?

n.a.

Question 53: How is overindebtedness established?

a) Is a formal balance sheet required?
n.a.

b) Does the yearly regular commercial balance sheet have any meaning (given that it is normally based on technical values and does not display undisclosed reserves)?
n.a.

c) Does the law provide for a presumption? If so, under which conditions?
n.a.

d) Other means?
n.a.

Question 54: Is the legal link to overindebtedness undisputed in literature or are there efforts to abolish it?

n.a.

Question 55: Would you like to add any further aspects not covered by the above questions?

n.a.

VI. REMAINING ISSUES

Question 56: Is there anything else you would like to share in the present context and that we should take into account?

No.

HUNGARY

Zoltan FABOK

I. GENERAL

Question 1: How is insolvency (both in the context of liquidation and restructuring/reorganisation) regulated in your jurisdiction? Please give a brief overview, at least enumerating the relevant statutes.

The Hungarian corporate insolvency law distinguishes between liquidation and reorganisation types of (pre-)insolvency proceedings.

Liquidation proceedings are aimed at the dissolution of the insolvent indebted business organisation, without preservation of the corporate entity, by partial or total satisfaction of creditors' claims through the sale of the debtor's assets, either in whole or in part. This type of procedure is *liquidation proceedings* (*felszámolási eljárás*), which is regulated by Act XLIX of 1991 on Bankruptcy and Liquidation Proceedings ("Insolvency Act"). No official translation of the Insolvency Act is available. For the purposes of this research project, I have used (with some modifications) the unofficial translation available in the database of Wolters Kluwer (Jogtár®).

The reorganisation types of corporate insolvency proceedings, on the other hand, are aimed at rescuing the debtor company by granting a moratorium on payments and making an attempt at collective arrangement with creditors and a possible reorganisation. This type of procedure includes corporate *bankruptcy proceedings* (*csődeljárás*), also regulated by the Insolvency Act; *restructuring proceedings* (*szerkezetátalakítási eljárás*), introduced by Act LXIV of 2021 on Restructuring and Amending Certain Acts for Harmonisation Purposes, implementing the Restructuring Directive[1] ("Restructuring Act"); and reorganisation proceedings (*vállalkozások reorganizációja*) introduced as part of the COVID-19 exceptional legislation.[2] No official translation of

[1] EU Directive 2019/1023 on preventive restructuring frameworks, on discharge of debt and disqualifications, and on measures to increase the efficiency of procedures concerning restructuring, insolvency and discharge of debt, and amending Directive (EU) 2017/1132.

[2] Articles 48–73 of Act XCIX of 2021 on the Transitional Provisions related to the State of Emergency ("Transitional Act"). Under the current rules, companies can initiate

the Restructuring Act is available. For the purposes of this research project, I have used (with some modifications) the unofficial translation available in the database of Wolters Kluwer (Jogtár®).

Both corporate bankruptcy and restructuring proceedings may be initiated by the debtor only.

The concept of "debtor" in the Insolvency Act (and, somewhat differently, in the Restructuring Act) is rather broadly defined. Special rules apply to certain business organisations, such as insurance companies, credit institutions, private pension funds, associations and foundations (beyond the scope of this report).

For natural persons, (judicial) debt settlement proceedings of natural persons (*természetes személyek adósságrendezési eljárása*) are available which were implemented in a separate piece of legislation in 2015[3] and the principles of which are substantially different from those of corporate insolvency proceedings.

For the purposes of this questionnaire, I have focused on the provisions of the Insolvency Act, and those of the Restructuring Act.

Regarding directors' liability and duties, Act V of 2013 on the Civil Code ("Civil Code") includes some relevant provisions. The English version of the Civil Code is available at: https://njt.hu/jogszabaly/en/2013-5-00-00.

Question 2: Related to paragraph 10 above of the Introduction: seen from a principle-based perspective, what justifies the opening of insolvency proceedings in your jurisdiction?

In the context of *liquidation proceedings*,

(i) the interest of (singular) creditors dominates in:
   - liquidation following a "statutory demand" (undisputed creditors' claims) (§27(2)(a) Insolvency Act);
   - liquidation due to non-compliance with a final judgment (§27(2)(b) Insolvency Act);
   - liquidation following an unsuccessful individual enforcement process (§27(2)(c) Insolvency Act);

(ii) the idea of collectivity prevails in:
   - liquidation due to non-performance of the composition/reorganisation plan/restructuring plan adopted in previous corporate bankruptcy, liquidation proceedings, reorganisation or restructuring proceedings (§27(2)(d) Insolvency Act);

reorganisation proceedings until 31 December 2024, with the possibility to continue ongoing proceedings following this deadline.

3 Act CV of 2015 on Debt Settlement of Natural Persons.

- liquidation due to failed corporate bankruptcy proceedings (no composition) (§27(2)(e) Insolvency Act);
- liquidation proceedings opened *ex officio* (initiated by the company registration court or the criminal court) (§22(1)(c)–(d) Insolvency Act);

(iii) the principle of the interests of the general body of creditors and collectivity dominates (but also elements of the protection of the shareholders/directors of the debtor appear) in:
- liquidation initiated by the insolvent debtor (§27(2)(f) Insolvency Act).

In the context of corporate *bankruptcy proceedings*, the protection of the debtor and the idea of collectivity dominate.

In the context of *restructuring proceedings*, the protection of the debtor dominates but also the idea of collectivity is present (however, limited in the non-public version of the restructuring proceedings).

Question 3: Does your national law in the context of liquidation proceedings use one or more of the following terms (be it as a noun, be it as an adjective or adjunct) in whatever context:

a) inability to pay debts
Yes.

b) cessation of payments
Yes (only in relation to directors' duties, see answer to Question 10(b) *infra*).

c) likely inability to pay debts
No.

d) imminent inability to pay debts
Yes (imminent insolvency).

e) overindebtedness?
Yes.

Question 4: Are the same terms (and with the same meaning) used in the rules on preliminary/interim insolvency proceedings (e.g. concerning the application stage of the proceedings)?

In principle, there are no preliminary/interim insolvency proceedings in Hungary. Nevertheless, the appointment of a temporary administrator (as an interim measure) may be requested prior to the opening of liquidation proceedings if, *inter alia*, the creditor is able to show that the satisfaction of its claim is likely to be jeopardised (§24/A(2) Insolvency Act). Note that different rules apply in the insolvency proceedings of strategically important companies (see §65 et seq. Insolvency Act).

Question 5: Does your national law in the context of restructuring proceedings (as referred to above at paragraph 8 of the Introduction, i.e. both pre-insolvency and within formal insolvency proceedings) use one or more of the following terms (be it as a noun, be it as an adjective or adjunct) in whatever context:

I am answering the above questions with a focus on corporate *bankruptcy* and *restructuring* proceedings.

a) inability to pay debts
Yes – corporate bankruptcy proceedings.

b) cessation of payments
No.

c) likely inability to pay debts
Yes – restructuring proceedings (likelihood of insolvency).

d) imminent inability to pay debts
Yes – corporate bankruptcy proceedings.

e) overindebtedness?
No.

Question 6: Which of the terms mentioned in Questions 3 and 5 are used for defining grounds to commence proceedings (triggering circumstances)?

a) insolvency proceedings

- Inability to pay debts:
  - for corporate bankruptcy proceedings (§3(1)(b) Insolvency Act – no in-depth examination by the court);
  - for liquidation proceedings initiated by the debtor/receiver (§27(2)(f) Insolvency Act – no in-depth examination by the court).
- Imminent inability to pay debts (imminent insolvency):
  - for corporate bankruptcy proceedings (§3(1)(b) Insolvency Act – no in-depth examination by the court);
  - for liquidation proceedings initiated by the debtor/receiver (§27(2)(f) Insolvency Act – no in-depth examination by the court).
- Overindebtedness:
  - for liquidation proceedings initiated by the debtor/receiver (§27(2)(f) Insolvency Act – no in-depth examination by court).

b) restructuring proceedings

- Likely inability to pay debts (likelihood of insolvency):
  - for restructuring proceedings (§3(1) point 8, §6(1) Restructuring Act).

Although the COVID-related reorganisation proceedings are considered out-of-scope, please note that "imminent inability to pay debts" (imminent insolvency) is a ground on which to commence reorganisation proceedings (§§49–50 Transitional Act).

Question 7: Does the answer to Question 6 include personal bankruptcies of natural persons or only corporate insolvencies of legal entities?

Only corporate insolvencies.

Note that opening debt settlement proceedings of natural persons requires a combination of several grounds, including *inter alia* overindebtedness.

Question 8: In your law, are there any other circumstances which trigger insolvency or restructuring proceedings?

Liquidation proceedings:

- The debtor's failure to settle or contest his previously uncontested or acknowledged contractual debts within 20 days of the due date, and failure to satisfy such debt upon receipt of the creditor's written payment notice ("statutory demand") (§27(2)(a) Insolvency Act);
- Non-compliance with a final judgment (§27(2)(b) Insolvency Act);
- Unsuccessful individual enforcement process against the debtor (§28(2)(c) Insolvency Act);
- Non-performance of the composition/reorganisation plan/restructuring plan adopted in previous corporate bankruptcy, liquidation proceedings, reorganisation or restructuring proceedings (§28(2)(d) Insolvency Act);
- Failed corporate bankruptcy proceedings (no composition adopted/ approved) (§28(2)(e) Insolvency Act);
- *Ex officio* opening grounds (for liquidation proceedings initiated by the company registration court or the criminal court) (§22(1)(c)–(d) Insolvency Act)

Note that the triggering circumstances listed in answer to Question 6(a) *supra* concern only those proceedings initiated by the debtor. However, the vast majority of liquidations are initiated either at the request of creditors or automatically – see the list in that section *supra*. In those proceedings, the substantial insolvency or its elements (inability to pay debts, cessation of payment, likely inability to pay debts, imminent inability to pay debts, overindebtedness) are either not examined (statutory demand) or only an indirect conclusion can be drawn about the debtor's insolvency or its elements (e.g. unsuccessful enforcement process).

As for one of the *ex officio* opening grounds, it should be noted that the irregularities in the company's operation may lead to forced deregistration proceedings (*kényszertörlési eljárás*), which often turn into liquidation proceedings (see §22(1)(c) of the Insolvency Act). Such irregularities may include the irretrievability of the lawful operation of the company, the unknown location of the company, the failure to file annual accounts, the failure to complete solvent liquidation proceedings within the statutory period, etc. – see Act V of 2006 on Public Company Information, Company Registration and Winding-up Proceedings ("Company Registration Act"). In such cases, however, the initiation of forced deregistration and liquidation proceedings should be seen as a deterrent rather than a sign of actual insolvency.

Question 9: Which of the terms mentioned in Questions 3, 5, and 8 are used in the context of transactions avoidance law?

None. The "suspect period" is calculated backwards from the filing date of the liquidation petition (§40 Insolvency Act).

Question 10: Which of the terms addressed in Questions 3, 5, and 8 are used in the context of directors' duties?

a) shift of duties (from shareholders to creditors)

- *imminent* inability to pay debts (imminent insolvency) – once the debtor is in a state of imminent insolvency the directors are required to consider the interests of the creditors (§33/A Insolvency Act; §3:118 Civil Code).

b) duties to commence insolvency proceedings

- imminent inability to pay debts (imminent insolvency),
- cessation of payments,
- overindebtedness.

Note: In Hungary, the director has no implicit obligation to file for insolvency. However, the director is obliged to convene the shareholders' meeting of a limited liability company or a company limited by shares once (*inter alia*) at least one of the above circumstances has occurred. Ultimately, the shareholders' meeting may be obliged to decide about the termination of the debtor (§3:189, 3:270 Civil Code).

c) other duties (please describe)

n.a.

Question 11: Are there any other rules in the context of which the terms addressed in Questions 3, 5, and 8 are used?

- Imminent inability to pay debts (imminent insolvency) – imminent insolvency is the ground for opening reorganisation proceedings under the umbrella of the COVID-related Transitional Act (§§49–50 Transitional Act); the definition used by the Transitional Act is virtually identical to the one included in §33/A (3) Insolvency Act.

- Imminent inability to pay debts (imminent insolvency) – §404 Act C of 2012 on the Criminal Code ("Criminal Code"); the Criminal Code uses the term in the same sense as the Insolvency Act.
- "Insolvency" – §404 Criminal Code; interestingly, the Criminal Code uses the term "insolvency" without providing for or referring to any definition of insolvency. A commentary[4] emphasises that the "economic" and "legal" concepts of insolvency are to be distinguished. However, no explanation is offered as to the concept of "economic" insolvency.

Question 12: Is the definition of (the subspecies of) insolvency identical in all legal fields or are there different definitions (e.g. different in insolvency law than in criminal law)?

- See my answers to Question 11 *supra*.
- §167(1) of Act CCXXXVII of 2013 on Credit Institutions and Financial Enterprises (Banking Act) uses the term "imminent danger of financial failure (illiquidity)". This means that the credit institution is in a liquidity crisis, which may result in the institution being unable to meet its liabilities as they fall due in the short term.[5]
- §167(2) Banking Act uses the term "insolvency". According to the commentary,[6] insolvency means that the institution is unable to meet its own funds requirements, or the value of its liabilities exceeds the value of its assets and liabilities.
- Act XXXVII of 2014 on the further development of the institutional system to strengthen the safety of certain actors in the financial intermediary system ("Resolution Act") uses the terms "insolvent" or "likely to become insolvent" and defines the terms as follows:

  §17(2) An institution is insolvent or is likely to become insolvent if

  (a) it is in breach of the requirements for maintaining its licence to operate or, on the basis of available quantifiable data (capital adequacy, profitability and portfolio quality), will be in breach of those requirements in the near future, but no later than 12 months, is likely to be in breach of those requirements to an extent that would lead to the withdrawal of its licence, in particular because it has incurred or is likely to incur losses resulting in the loss of all or a significant part of its own funds as set out in Regulation (EU) No. 575/2013;

4 *Karsai (ed.)*, Nagykommentár a Büntető Törvénykönyvről szóló 2012. évi C. törvényhez (Comprehensive Commentary to the Act C of 2012 on the Criminal Code), electronic edition, §404.

5 *Gálfalvi/Kovács/Palasikné/Seregdi*, Nagykommentár a hitelintézetekről és a pénzügyi vállalkozásokról szóló 2013. évi CCXXXVII. törvényhez (Comprehensive Commentary on Act CCXXXVII of 2013 on Credit Institutions and Financial Enterprises), electronic edition, §167.

6 ibid.

(b) its asset(s) would not cover the claims of known creditors or, on the basis of available quantifiable data (capital adequacy, profitability and portfolio quality), would be unlikely to do so in the near future or within 12 months at the latest, which would lead to the withdrawal of its licence;
(c) the institution is not in default of its obligations relating to its financial services, ancillary financial services, investment services business or ancillary investment services business or, on the basis of available quantifiable data (deposit coverage ratio, balance sheet coverage ratio, foreign exchange funding ratio for a credit institution), is likely to default in the near future or within 12 months at the latest; or
(d) the institution is seeking or receiving exceptional public financial assistance, unless such public assistance is intended to address serious disturbances in the economy of the country and to safeguard financial stability and is granted in one of the following forms:
    (da) a state guarantee or equivalent support to facilitate access to the MNB's [National Bank of Hungary] monetary policy instruments,
    (db) a state guarantee or equivalent support for newly created liabilities,
    (dc) an increase in equity or the purchase of an equity item by the state on the basis of the private market investor principle, where neither paragraphs (a) to (c) nor the circumstances requiring the write-off or restructuring of the equity item exist at the time the aid is granted.

- Act CLXXV of 2011 on the right of association, public benefit status and the operation and support of non-governmental organisations ("Civil Act") basically refers to the formal grounds for opening liquidation proceedings as provided for in the Insolvency Act, with some amendments (§10 Civil Act).

II. INABILITY TO PAY DEBTS

Question 13: In your jurisdiction, is the term "inability to pay debts" defined in statute? If so, please give the wording in English translation. Is this definition (if any) specified in case law? If so, how?

§3(1)(b) Insolvency Act (definition of debtor) provides that "'insolvent debtor' shall mean any economic operator that *was not able to settle its debt (debts) … on the date when they are due*" (emphasis added).

Likewise, §27(2)(f) Insolvency Act provides:

> The court shall declare the debtor insolvent
>
> …
>
> (f) [in proceedings initiated by the debtor or receiver] if … the debtor *was unable … to settle its debt (debts) on the date when they are due …* (emphasis added).

Question 14: Does your law refer to all debts or only to mature debts?

Only mature (overdue) debts.

Question 15: Which assets are taken into account when assessing the inability to pay debts: all (financial) assets or only those that are liquid, i.e. available on short notice?

I am not aware of any case law dealing with this issue, probably because, in practice, the courts do not examine inability to pay on the merits, but usually rely on the debtor's declaration, assuming that the required annexes (e.g. a balance sheet) are attached. Since "inability to pay" is a ground for opening corporate bankruptcy proceedings (which can only be initiated by the debtor) and liquidation proceedings initiated by the debtor/receiver (see answer to Question 6(a) *supra*), the court typically accepts the debtor's declaration.

Question 16: Is any liquidity gap (deficit between relevant financial means and relevant debts) relevant or does your law neglect minor gaps? If the latter, how is "minor" defined?

n.a.

Question 17: As far as the time aspect is concerned, does it matter whether the liquidity gap can be closed again in the short term? If so, how long is the grace period?

It does not matter, but the question is of limited relevance due to the circumstances described above in the answer to Question 15.

Question 18: As far as the time aspect is concerned, is a debtor considered insolvent if the liquidity gap is not yet present but will occur soon? If so, how long is the prognosis period? (Note: this may also concern the difference between actual and likely/imminent inability to pay debts; cf. below Question 34).

As far as the term "inability to pay debts" is concerned, the future liquidity gap is not relevant. Concerning "imminent inability to pay debts", please refer to the answer to Question 35 *infra*).

Question 19: How is inability to pay debts established? Please communicate if there is a difference between a creditor and a debtor application or between different legal contexts.

"Inability to pay debts" qualifies only as a ground for insolvency proceedings applied for by the debtor (such as corporate bankruptcy proceedings or liquidation proceedings initiated by the debtor/receiver).

a) Is a formal liquidity status (liquidity balance sheet) required?
Yes.

b) Is a sample of daily liquidity data (which do not amount to a proper liquidity status but show insufficient funds on different days within a certain period of time) sufficient?
No.

c) Does the law provide for a rebuttable presumption? If so, under which conditions?
In liquidation proceedings initiated by the creditor the debtor is required by law to respond to the petition within a short time-frame (eight days). If the debtor fails to respond, its insolvency shall be presumed (§24(3) Insolvency Act).

d) Does the law provide for any technical circumstances (e.g. undisputed statutory demand, non-compliance with monetary judgments, unsuccessful enforcement proceedings, non-performance of a previous composition agreement in insolvency proceedings) the occurrence of which suffices to establish the debtor's insolvency?
Yes, those circumstances and some others listed in answer to Question 8 qualify as stand-alone grounds for opening liquidation proceedings.

e) Other means?
None.

Question 20: Is insolvency (inability to pay debts, overindebtedness, etc.) subject to party autonomy in the proceedings or must the court clarify them *ex officio*?

The "inability to pay debts" must be proven by the debtor filing for insolvency proceedings, but in practice the court normally does not carry out an in-depth investigation.

Question 21: In an overall view, does your law distinguish "inability to pay debts" from "financial difficulties"? If so, how?

The term "financial difficulties" is used by the Restructuring Act. It is not a defined term but the Explanatory Report to the Restructuring Act seems to suggest that "financial difficulties" occur ahead of insolvency in time.

Question 22: In an overall view, does it matter under your law whether the debtor's inability to pay debts is present or future and reversible or irreversible?

The term "inability to pay debts" refers to the present/past. Reversibility/irreversibility is irrelevant.

Question 23: Would you like to add any further aspects not covered by the above questions?

Regarding Question 15 it should be noted that corporate bankruptcy proceedings, if unsuccessful, turn automatically into liquidation proceedings. This is one of the reasons why bankruptcy proceedings are so unpopular in Hungary. Courts usually accept that companies filing for bankruptcy are indeed in serious financial difficulties and usually do not conduct a detailed investigation into the occurrence of inability to pay debts or imminent insolvency but simply accept the debtor's declaration if it is supported by the annexes (e.g. a balance sheet).

III. CESSATION OF PAYMENTS

Question 24: In your jurisdiction, is "cessation of payments" a legal term used either in statute or in case law? (If the answer is "no", please continue with Question 31.)

The term is used by the Civil Code.

Question 25: Is "cessation of payments" an autonomous ground to commence proceedings (triggering circumstance)? You may refer to Questions 6/7 or add additional information here.

It is not an autonomous ground for opening proceedings; it is relevant in the context of directors' duties – see Question 10(b) *supra*.

Question 26: Is "cessation of payments" a means to establish inability to pay debts? If so, by which mechanism (e.g. rebuttable presumption for inability to pay debts, cf. above Question 19(c))?

No.

Question 27: How is "cessation of payments" defined? If it is defined in statute, please provide us here with an English translation of the relevant rule. Is this definition (if any) specified in case law? If so, how?

I am not aware of any definition or relevant case law. Perhaps the case law relating to "stoppage of payment" in Article 43 of the Convention Providing a Uniform Law for Bills of Exchange and Promissory Notes (Geneva, 7 June 1930), which is part of Hungarian law, may be instructive.

In the Civil Code, the relevant provision reads as follows:

§3:189 Civil Code

[Mandatory convocation of the members' meeting]

(1) The managing director shall without delay convene the members' meeting, or initiate its decision-making process without having to hold a meeting in order to provide for the necessary measures whenever it comes to his attention that:

...

c) the company is on the brink of insolvency or *has stopped making payments* (emphasis added)

Note that §3:189 concerns private limited-liability companies while §3:270 contains an identical provision in relation to limited companies.

Question 28: How is "cessation of payments" established?

See answer to Question 27 *supra*. Courts must assess all relevant circumstances which can serve as circumstantial evidence for the debtor's cessation of payments.

Question 29: Are there typical circumstances which provide circumstantial evidence that the debtor has ceased payments? If so, please list as many as possible.

I am not aware of any relevant case law based on the current legislation. In the pre-WW2 Hungarian insolvency law, the case law identified several circumstances indicating probable "cessation of payment"[7] which may potentially be instructive in the current legal environment, as well:

- the merchant's "absconding";
- the repayment of debts with goods to creditors who "run" on the merchant;
- the transfer of the warehouse to a management committee chosen by the creditors for the purpose of selling;
- execution (enforcement) proceedings against the debtor;
- the debtor has not paid his creditors when their claims are due, but pays for a whole year only to the person who executes enforcement measures against him;
- the debtor he has bargained with his creditors and in the meantime has declared his insolvency or has asked them for a moratorium;
- a company which obtains credit by pledging its own claims has ceased to pay.

Question 30: Would you like to add any further aspects not covered by the above questions?

No.

---

[7] *Fónagy*, A gazdasági társaság tulajdonosainak és vezető tisztségviselőinek felelőssége a fizetésképtelenségért (Liability of the Shareholders and Directors of the Company for Insolvency), PhD dissertation, 2011, p. 35.

IV. LIKELY/IMMINENT INABILITY TO PAY DEBTS

Question 31: Are the following terms available in your jurisdiction, either in statute or in case law? (If the answer is "no", please continue with Question 42.)

a) likely inability to pay debts
Yes – §3(1) point 8 Restructuring Act.

b) imminent inability to pay debts
Yes – §33/A(3), §3(1)(b), §27(2)(f) Insolvency Act, §49 Transitional Act.

c) other (similar) terms
No.

Question 32: Is "likely/imminent inability to pay debts" an autonomous ground to commence proceedings (triggering circumstance)? You may refer to Questions 6/7 or add additional information here.

Please refer to the answer to Question 6.

Question 33: If the answer to the previous Question is "yes", who may base filing for insolvency proceedings on it: only the debtor or also creditors?

Only the debtor (in case of liquidation proceedings also the receiver).

Question 34: How are these terms defined? If they are defined in statute, please provide us here with an English translation of the relevant rules. Is this definition (if any) specified in case law? If so, how?

a) likely inability to pay debts
§3(1) point 8 Restructuring Act:

> Likelihood of insolvency [literally: Likelihood of becoming insolvent]: a situation in which there are reasonable grounds for assuming that the debtor will be unable to meet its outstanding payment obligations when they fall due, unless further measures are taken.

b) imminent inability to pay debts
§33/A(3) Insolvency Act reads:

> The occurrence of imminent insolvency [literally: a situation constituting a threat of insolvency] is the date from which the directors of the business organisation foresaw, or ought reasonably (as is expected from persons in such positions) to have foreseen, that the business organisation would be unable to meet its debts as they fall due.

§49 Transitional Act virtually mirrors §33/A(3) Insolvency Act.

§3(1)(b) and §27(2)(f) Insolvency Act arguably refer to §33/A(3) Insolvency Act.

Question 35: Do the terms "likely" and "imminent" require a prognosis regarding the point in time when actual inability to pay debts will occur? If so, how long is the time period for this prognosis?

No prognosis is required by law.

Regarding "imminent insolvency", in several cases, Hungarian courts have applied the current ratio test or the quick ratio test to determine the cash-flow situation of the company. The current ratio is a basic indicator calculated by dividing total current assets by total current liabilities (including intercompany liabilities); the quick ratio, by contrast, takes into account the most liquid current assets: it is calculated by adding cash and equivalents, marketable investments, and accounts receivable, and dividing that sum by current liabilities. This approach suggests that the time-frame should be no longer than one year. However, this is not the only indicator taken into consideration by the courts.

With regard to the "likelihood of insolvency", which is a fairly new concept, no further support can be found either in the statute or in case law.

Question 36: Does your law require a specific grade of certainty that inability to pay debts will eventually occur? If so, is 50.1% ("more likely than not") enough or are there alleviated or aggravated prerequisites?

The concept of "imminent insolvency" focuses on the cash-flow situation of the debtor. The Kúria (Highest Court of Hungary) found that regarding the occurrence of imminent insolvency, the relevant question is whether the debtor is able to settle its debts when they fall due. If the debtor is unable to do so because it has neither liquid assets nor credit to settle its debts and it is unable to agree with its creditors on a different kind of performance or adjustment of the due date, then imminent insolvency occurs even if the other assets of the debtor exceeds the amount of debts.[8]

As the concept of imminent insolvency developed in Hungary in the context of directors' liability (wrongful trading), the courts generally examined the occurrence of imminent insolvency retrospectively, i.e. from the perspective of the actual insolvency. That is why the courts do not normally need to guess the probability of an eventual actual insolvency (whatever it means) because necessarily the latter has already occurred at the time of the examination, given that wrongful trading litigation can only be initiated during the liquidation proceedings.

8 BH2014. 188. (Kúria Gfv. VII. 30.247/2013.).

Question 37: Regarding "debts" and "financial means", are they defined in the same way as in the context of inability to pay debts (cf. above Questions 14/15)? If not, what are the differences?

Please refer to answer to Question 35.

Question 38: Further to Question 37: Are "debts" considered which do currently not exist or are not yet due but will foreseeably come into existence and become due during the prognosis period?

Please refer to answer to Question 35.

Question 39: Also further to Question 37: Are "financial means" considered which do currently not exist but will foreseeably become available during the prognosis period?

Please refer to answer to Question 35.

Question 40: How are the terms "likely/imminent inability to pay debts" established?

- Likely inability to pay debts (likelihood of insolvency) is a ground for opening restructuring proceedings (Question 6(b) *supra*). The debtor filing for restructuring proceedings is required to present the reasons supporting the likelihood of insolvency and the creditors have the right to object. The court makes its decision summarily.
- Imminent inability to pay debts (imminent insolvency) is mainly established in wrongful trading litigation, retrospectively. In this context, the courts may apply the current ratio or quick ratio tests (Questions 35 and 36 *supra*). In other cases, (also) further circumstances have been taken into consideration: overdue tax debts, an ongoing enforcement process, liquidation proceedings initiated by a creditor (not yet opened – see statutory demand in answer to Question 8 *supra*), overdue loan or rental fees or procedural or administrative costs, redundancies of workers, commencement of corporate bankruptcy proceedings (!).[9]

The above tests may be instructive regarding the opening of reorganisation proceedings but no case law is available – most probably the threshold is low because courts tend to accept the declarations of debtors in proceedings initiated by them.

---

9 *A Kúria Polgári Kollégiuma Joggyakorlat-elemző Csoportjának összefoglaló véleménye a vezető tisztségviselők hitelezőkkel szembeni felelőssége" tárgykörben* (Summary Opinion of the Jurisprudence Analysis Group of the Civil Chamber of the Kúria on the "Liability of Directors towards Creditors"), p. 21, available at: https://kuria-birosag.hu/sites/default/files/joggyak/osszefoglalo_velemeny_6.pdf.

Question 41: Would you like to add any further aspects not covered by the above questions?

The concept of likelihood of insolvency was created with a view to distinguishing it from imminent insolvency: the likelihood of insolvency occurs, typically, earlier in time.[10]

V. OVERINDEBTEDNESS

Question 42: In your jurisdiction, is "overindebtedness", or "balance sheet insolvency" respectively, a legal term used either in statute or in case law? (If the answer is "no", please continue with Question 56.)

Yes.

Question 43: Is "overindebtedness" an autonomous ground to commence proceedings (triggering circumstance)? You may refer to Questions 6/7 or add additional information here.

Yes (§27(2)(f) Insolvency Act), please refer to the answer to Question 6(a).

Question 44: If the answer to the previous Question is "yes", is this applicable to corporate insolvencies of legal persons only or also to personal bankruptcies of natural persons?

Only corporate insolvencies.

Note that opening debt settlement proceedings of natural persons requires a combination of several grounds including, *inter alia*, overindebtedness.

Please refer to the answer to Question 7.

Question 45: Is the term "overindebtedness" defined in statute? If so, please give the wording in English translation. Is this definition (if any) specified in case law? If so, how?

Yes, §27(2)(f) Insolvency Act reads as follows:

> §27(2) The court shall declare the debtor insolvent
>
> ...
>
> (f) [in proceedings initiated by the debtor or receiver] if *the debtor's liabilities exceed the debtor's assets*, or the debtor was unable or presumably will not be able to settle its debt (debts) on the date when they are due ... (emphasis added).

As for the sectorial legislation please refer to answer to Question 12.

---

10 See Explanatory Report to Restructuring Act, §3.

Question 46: Does your law refer to all existing debts or only to mature debts?

To all existing debts.

Question 47: Does the rank of certain debts play a role when establishing overindebtedness? In particular, is there any possibility to conclude agreements according to which certain debts shall not be taken into account (e.g. agreements on subsidiarity)?

Agreement on subordination of creditors' claims is, in principle, allowed, but it has no role when establishing overindebtedness.

Question 48: Which assets are taken into account when overindebtedness is established: the complete set of assets or only a selection of them?

All fixed assets and current assets of the debtor.

Question 49: How are the debtor's assets valued: by referring to the liquidation value, the book value, the going concern value or in another way?

The court would have a look at the book value as it appears from the balance sheet.

Question 50: Is there any prognostic element, e.g. regarding the debtor's chances to continue the business?

No.

Question 51: If the answer to the previous Question is "yes", what exactly is the topic of the prognosis and how is it established?

n.a.

Question 52: If the answer to the Question 50 is "yes", how long is the prognosis period?

n.a.

Question 53: How is overindebtedness established?

a) Is a formal balance sheet required?
Yes, but typically no audit is required.

b) Does the yearly regular commercial balance sheet have any meaning (given that it is normally based on technical values and does not display undisclosed reserves)?
Yes, if it is no older than three months.

c) Does the law provide for a presumption? If so, under which conditions?
No.

d) Other means?
n.a.

Question 54: Is the legal link to overindebtedness undisputed in literature or are there efforts to abolish it?

Its significance is limited for the time being, so I am not aware of any ongoing discussion. However, the long-awaited new insolvency act may bring some changes.

Question 55: Would you like to add any further aspects not covered by the above questions?

The concept of overindebtedness is of little significance under the current (general) insolvency legislation, since it is only one of the grounds for opening liquidation proceedings initiated by the debtor/receiver. Courts tend to accept the debtor's declarations in such proceedings, and therefore usually no detailed evidence is required.

VI. REMAINING ISSUES

Question 56: Is there anything else you would like to share in the present context and that we should take into account?

Regarding the "statutory demand" according to §27(2)(a) Insolvency Act, let me add some explanation.

Liquidation proceedings aimed at debt collection have become widespread in Hungary in the last few decades. The main characteristic of those proceedings is that a creditor, in order to exert pressure, initiates liquidation proceedings against the (not necessarily substantially insolvent) debtor. The commencement of the liquidation proceedings presupposes a formal notice sent to the debtor, a minimum of 20 days after the uncontested and acknowledged contractual debt is due. If the debtor has failed to dispute its debt in writing prior to the service of the formal notice to the debtor then insolvency is presumed and the debtor, if it wants to avoid being liquidated, has very limited options except for paying off the creditor who sent the notice or settling the case. In effect, liquidation proceedings aimed at debt collection have become a relatively cheap, simple and relatively quick alternative to "ordinary" civil proceedings in the area of uncontested claims.

Although liquidation proceedings aimed at debt collection as described above are time-efficient and simple, they have significant downsides, as well:

- The court de facto obliges the debtor to pay without investigating the merits of the case.
- Paradoxically, this type of "liquidation" proceedings can only be successful from the perspective of the creditor if the debtor is not substantially insolvent therefore it can perform the payment obligation vis-à-vis the creditor.
- This type of "liquidation" proceedings attaches a disproportionally strict legal sanction (opening of liquidation) to the "negligence" of the debtor (i.e. in failing to dispute the creditor's claim in time).

Based on the above considerations, the legislator is considering fine-tuning the concept of liquidation proceedings aimed at debt collection in the prospective new insolvency act.

IRELAND

Simon Murphy

I. GENERAL

Question 1: How is insolvency (both in the context of liquidation and restructuring/reorganisation) regulated in your jurisdiction? Please give a brief overview, at least enumerating the relevant statutes.

The Companies Act 2014 is the key piece of legislation with respect to insolvency as it is the legislation that governs the processes relating to insolvency, restructuring and winding up. The key restructuring processes such as Examinership, at Section 508, and the various types of liquidation, starting at Section 559, and are all contained within the Companies Act 2014.

Question 2: Related to paragraph 10 above of the Introduction: seen from a principle-based perspective, what justifies the opening of insolvency proceedings in your jurisdiction?

The general requirement for the opening of restructuring proceedings is that a company is, or is likely to be, unable to pay its debts. With respect to winding-up proceedings the general requirement is that (i) a company is unable to pay its debts, (ii) it is just and equitable that the company should be wound up, (iii) it is in the public interest that a company should be wound up, or (iv)a restructuring proceeding has failed.

Question 3: Does your national law in the context of liquidation proceedings use one or more of the following terms (be it as a noun, be it as an adjective or adjunct) in whatever context:

a) inability to pay debts
Yes.

b) cessation of payments
No.

c) likely inability to pay debts
No.

d) imminent inability to pay debts
No.

e) overindebtedness?
No.

Question 4: Are the same terms (and with the same meaning) used in the rules on preliminary/interim insolvency proceedings (e.g. concerning the application stage of the proceedings)?

The same requirements are applied for the appointment of an insolvency practitioner on an interim basis once the court is satisfied that an interim appointment is required.

Question 5: Does your national law in the context of restructuring proceedings (as referred to above at paragraph 8 of the Introduction, i.e. both pre-insolvency and within formal insolvency proceedings) use one or more of the following terms (be it as a noun, be it as an adjective or adjunct) in whatever context:

a) inability to pay debts
Yes.

b) cessation of payments
No.

c) likely inability to pay debts
Yes – stated as "a company is, or is likely to be, unable to pay its debts …".

d) imminent inability to pay debts
No.

e) overindebtedness?
No.

Question 6: Which of the terms mentioned in Questions 3 and 5 are used for defining grounds to commence proceedings (triggering circumstances)?

a) insolvency proceedings
"Inability to pay debts".

b) restructuring proceedings
"Unable to pay its debts" and "likely inability to pay debts".

Question 7: Does the answer to Question 6 include personal bankruptcies of natural persons or only corporate insolvencies of legal entities?

Only corporate insolvencies of legal entities.

Question 8: In your law, are there any other circumstances which trigger insolvency or restructuring proceedings?

Yes, pursuant to Section 569 of the Companies Act 2014, insolvency proceedings may be triggered by a court for reasons including;

(a) if the company has by special resolution resolved that the company be wound up by the court,
(b) if the company does not commence its business within a year after the date of its incorporation or suspends its business for a continuous period of 12 months,
(c) if the members of the company are all deceased or no longer exist,
(d) if the company is unable to pay its debts,
(e) if the court is of the opinion that it is just and equitable that the company should be wound up,
(f) if the court is satisfied that the company's affairs are being conducted, or the powers of the directors are being exercised, in a manner oppressive to any member or in disregard of his or her interests as a member and that, despite the existence of an alternative remedy, winding up would be justified in the general circumstances of the case but this paragraph is subject to subsection (2), or
(g) if the court is satisfied, on a petition of the Director, that it is in the public interest that the company should be wound up.

Question 9: Which of the terms mentioned in Questions 3, 5, and 8 are used in the context of transactions avoidance law?

Pursuant to Section 604 of the Companies Act 2014 in transaction avoidance proceedings in the context of a liquidation the relevant term is "a company which is unable to pay its debts as they become due".

Question 10: Which of the terms addressed in Questions 3, 5, and 8 are used in the context of directors' duties?

a) shift of duties (from shareholders to creditors)

The European Union (Preventive Restructuring) Regulations 2022 add additional provisions to the Companies Act 2014. A new provision, Section 224A of the Companies Act 2014, cites the inability of a company to pay its debts as a relevant matter where the duties of a director shift to have regard to the interests of the creditors.

b) duties to commence insolvency proceedings

Section 586 of the Companies Act 2014 requires that a voluntary liquidation be initiated where the company "cannot by reason of its liabilities continue its business".

c) other duties (please describe)
The new Section 224A of the Companies Act 2014 also includes a duty for directors where they believe, or have reasonable cause to believe, that the company is, or is likely to be, unable to pay its debts, to (i) take steps to avoid insolvency, and (ii) avoid deliberate or grossly negligent conduct that threatens the viability of the business of the company.

Question 11: Are there any other rules in the context of which the terms addressed in Questions 3, 5, and 8 are used?

Yes, the following instances arise in relation to a company that is unable to pay its debts:

(i) Pursuant to Section 584 of the Companies Act 2014, where a company commenced a liquidation as a solvent entity, if the liquidator of the company forms the view that the company is unable to pay its debts, there is a duty upon the liquidator to change to following the procedure for an insolvent liquidation of the company.
(ii) In insolvency proceedings it is a requirement that a company in liquidation is unable to pay its debts for a court to impose personal liability on any individual for the debts of that company. This is pursuant to Section 247 of the Companies Act 2014.
(iii) Sections 509 and 570 of the Companies Act 2014 specifically set out the basis upon which a company will be deemed unable to pay its debts, namely:
   (a) it is unable to pay its debts as they fall due,
   (b) the value of its assets is less than the amount of its liabilities, taking into account its contingent and prospective liabilities, or
   (c) it fails to discharge a demand for payment from a creditor within 21 days – with specific monetary requirements for the level of the debt demanded.
(iv) With respect to action to be taken against directors of insolvent companies, Section 818 of the Companies Act 2014 defines an insolvent company as "a company that is unable to pay its debts".

Question 12: Is the definition of (the subspecies of) insolvency identical in all legal fields or are there different definitions (e.g. different in insolvency law than in criminal law)?

Yes.

II. INABILITY TO PAY DEBTS

Question 13: In your jurisdiction, is the term "inability to pay debts" defined in statute? If so, please give the wording in English translation. Is this definition (if any) specified in case law? If so, how?

It is stated in the Companies Act 2014, Section 569(d) that "[a] company may be wound up by the court if … the company is unable to pay its debts" and Section 570(a) states:

> A company shall be deemed to be unable to pay its debts … if a creditor … indebted in a sum exceeding €10,000 then due, has served on the company … a demand in writing requiring the company to pay the sum so due, and … the company has for 21 days after the date of the service neglected to pay the sum.

Question 14: Does your law refer to all debts or only to mature debts?

All debts; there is no definition of mature debts.

Question 15: Which assets are taken into account when assessing the inability to pay debts: all (financial) assets or only those that are liquid, i.e. available on short notice?

The assets of the company are not necessarily considered in whether the company has an ability to pay its debts; rather whether the company has paid those debts when they have been demanded.

Question 16: Is any liquidity gap (deficit between relevant financial means and relevant debts) relevant or does your law neglect minor gaps? If the latter, how is "minor" defined?

In determining inability to pay debts, a court will look at the financial position of the company in relation to both the "balance sheet" and "cash flow" tests. A failure of either tests can lead to an inability to pay debts. The High Court of Ireland in *Club Tivoli Ltd. v. Companies Act* [2005] IEHC 468 set out the basis on whether a company is "commercially insolvent":

> either where such company is unable to pay its debts as they fall due (the cash flow test) or where its liabilities (including the value, in practical terms of its contingent and perspective liabilities) exceed the realisable value of its assets (the "balance sheet" test). The two tests are interrelated. The company which is commercially insolvent in the cash flow sense only is generally heading towards insolvency in the balance sheet sense also. This is because the adverse cash flow is eating into its capital base. Conversely a company which is commercially insolvent in the balance sheet sense

only is generally heading towards insolvency in the cash flow sense also because the cash flow will need to be used sooner or later to meet the balance sheet deficiency.

The courts have a discretion as to ordering the immediate insolvency of a company or whether the company should be afforded further time. For example, where a borrower has defaulted on repayment of a loan, a lender must demand repayment and provide a reasonable period for repayment to be made prior to the appointment of a receiver to the security for the loan. The reasonable period is fact-specific but usually very short, around 24–48 hours.

Question 17: As far as the time aspect is concerned, does it matter whether the liquidity gap can be closed again in the short term? If so, how long is the grace period?

No grace period is defined, and it is at the discretion of the court.

Question 18: As far as the time aspect is concerned, is a debtor considered insolvent if the liquidity gap is not yet present but will occur soon? If so, how long is the prognosis period? (Note: this may also concern the difference between actual and likely/imminent inability to pay debts; cf. below Question 34).

The prognosis period is not defined.

Question 19: How is inability to pay debts established? Please communicate if there is a difference between a creditor and a debtor application or between different legal contexts.

a) Is a formal liquidity status (liquidity balance sheet) required?
No.

b) Is a sample of daily liquidity data (which do not amount to a proper liquidity status but show insufficient funds on different days within a certain period of time) sufficient?
No.

c) Does the law provide for a rebuttable presumption? If so, under which conditions?
No.

d) Does the law provide for any technical circumstances (e.g. undisputed statutory demand, non-compliance with monetary judgments, unsuccessful enforcement proceedings, non-performance of a previous composition agreement in insolvency proceedings) the occurrence of which suffices to establish the debtor's insolvency?
Yes, Section 570(a) of the Companies Act 2014 states that:

> A company shall be deemed to be unable to pay its debts … if a creditor … indebted in a sum exceeding €10,000 then due, has served on the company … a demand in writing requiring the company to pay the sum so due, and … the company has for 21 days after the date of the service neglected to pay the sum.

e) Other means?

Yes, Section 570 of the Companies Act 2014 goes on to state:

> "For the purposes of this Act, a company shall be deemed to be unable to pay its debts—
>
> (a) if—
> (i) a creditor, by assignment or otherwise, to whom the company is indebted in a sum exceeding €10,000 then due, has served on the company (by leaving it at the registered office of the company) a demand in writing requiring the company to pay the sum so due, and
> (ii) the company has, for 21 days after the date of the service of that demand, neglected to pay the sum or to secure or compound for it to the reasonable satisfaction of the creditor,
>
> or
>
> (b) if—
> (i) 2 or more creditors, by assignment or otherwise, to whom, in aggregate, the company is indebted in a sum exceeding €20,000 then due, have served on the company (by leaving it at the registered office of the company) a demand in writing requiring the company to pay the sum so due, and
> (ii) the company has, for 21 days after the date of the service of that demand, neglected to pay the sum or to secure or compound for it to the reasonable satisfaction of each of the creditors,
>
> or
>
> (c) if execution or other process issued on a judgment, decree or order of any court in favour of a creditor of the company is returned unsatisfied in whole or in part, or
> (d) if it is proved to the satisfaction of the court that the company is unable to pay its debts, and in determining whether a company is unable to pay its debts, the court shall take into account the contingent and prospective liabilities of the company."

Question 20: Is insolvency (inability to pay debts, overindebtedness, etc.) subject to party autonomy in the proceedings or must the court clarify them *ex officio*?

It is subject to party autonomy.

Question 21: In an overall view, does your law distinguish "inability to pay debts" from "financial difficulties"? If so, how?

Yes, an inability to pay debts is required for a creditor winding up and can be proven by the failure of the debtor to discharge sums due and owing following a demand. "Financial difficulties" is not a feature of the law.

Question 22: In an overall view, does it matter under your law whether the debtor's inability to pay debts is present or future and reversible or irreversible?

While not set out in the legislation, the wide discretion provided to the court means that in a practical sense that if a debtor's inability to pay debts was temporary or reversable, the debtor would most likely be afforded an opportunity to put in place the necessary steps to rectify its solvency position.

Question 23: Would you like to add any further aspects not covered by the above questions?

n.a.

III. CESSATION OF PAYMENTS

Question 24: In your jurisdiction, is "cessation of payments" a legal term used either in statute or in case law? (If the answer is "no", please continue with Question 31.)

No.

Question 25: Is "cessation of payments" an autonomous ground to commence proceedings (triggering circumstance)? You may refer to Questions 6/7 or add additional information here.

n.a.

Question 26: Is "cessation of payments" a means to establish inability to pay debts? If so, by which mechanism (e.g. rebuttable presumption for inability to pay debts, cf. above Question 19(c))?

n.a.

Question 27: How is "cessation of payments" defined? If it is defined in statute, please provide us here with an English translation of the relevant rule. Is this definition (if any) specified in case law? If so, how?

n.a.

Question 28: How is "cessation of payments" established?

n.a.

Question 29: Are there typical circumstances which provide circumstantial evidence that the debtor has ceased payments? If so, please list as many as possible.

n.a.

Question 30: Would you like to add any further aspects not covered by the above questions?

n.a.

IV. LIKELY/IMMINENT INABILITY TO PAY DEBTS

Question 31: Are the following terms available in your jurisdiction, either in statute or in case law? (If the answer is "no", please continue with Question 42.)

a) likely inability to pay debts
Yes.

b) imminent inability to pay debts
No.

c) other (similar) terms
No.

Question 32: Is "likely/imminent inability to pay debts" an autonomous ground to commence proceedings (triggering circumstance)? You may refer to Questions 6/7 or add additional information here.

Yes, in seeking to enter into a court restructuring process under Section 509 of the Companies Act 2014 one of the grounds for entry is that "a company is, or is likely to be, unable to pay its debts".

Question 33: If the answer to the previous Question is "yes", who may base filing for insolvency proceedings on it: only the debtor or also creditors?

It is possible for both the debtor and a creditor to seek to invoke the court restructuring process under Section 509 of the Companies Act 2014; however, where the ground sought for entry is that the company is likely to be unable to pay its debts, it would only the debtor that would invoke this provision.

Question 34: How are these terms defined? If they are defined in statute, please provide us here with an English translation of the relevant rules. Is this definition (if any) specified in case law? If so, how?

a) likely inability to pay debts
The term is not defined but case law suggests that the consideration for the court is whether the insolvency of the company is imminent, if it has not already come about.

b) imminent inability to pay debts
n.a.

Question 35: Do the terms "likely" and "imminent" require a prognosis regarding the point in time when actual inability to pay debts will occur? If so, how long is the time period for this prognosis?

No.

Question 36: Does your law require a specific grade of certainty that inability to pay debts will eventually occur? If so, is 50.1% ("more likely than not") enough or are there alleviated or aggravated prerequisites?

No.

Question 37: Regarding "debts" and "financial means", are they defined in the same way as in the context of inability to pay debts (cf. above Questions 14/15)? If not, what are the differences?

See answer to Question 15.

Question 38: Further to Question 37: Are "debts" considered which do currently not exist or are not yet due but will foreseeably come into existence and become due during the prognosis period?

See answer to Question 15.

Question 39: Also further to Question 37: Are "financial means" considered which do currently not exist but will foreseeably become available during the prognosis period?

See answer to Question 15.

Question 40: How are the terms "likely/imminent inability to pay debts" established?

The likely inability to pay debts is usually proffered by the debtor company when seeking a restructuring process, so it is not estimated by a creditor.

Question 41: Would you like to add any further aspects not covered by the above questions?

n.a.

V. OVERINDEBTEDNESS

Question 42: In your jurisdiction, is "overindebtedness", or "balance sheet insolvency" respectively, a legal term used either in statute or in case law? (If the answer is "no", please continue with Question 56.)

The term "balance sheet insolvency" is used in case law.

Question 43: Is "overindebtedness" an autonomous ground to commence proceedings (triggering circumstance)? You may refer to Questions 6/7 or add additional information here.

No, only a likely inability to pay debts.

Question 44: If the answer to the previous Question is "yes", is this applicable to corporate insolvencies of legal persons only or also to personal bankruptcies of natural persons?

n.a.

Question 45: Is the term "overindebtedness" defined in statute? If so, please give the wording in English translation. Is this definition (if any) specified in case law? If so, how?

No.

Question 46: Does your law refer to all existing debts or only to mature debts?

There is no concept of mature debts.

Question 47: Does the rank of certain debts play a role when establishing overindebtedness? In particular, is there any possibility to conclude agreements according to which certain debts shall not be taken into account (e.g. agreements on subsidiarity)?

No, there is no distinction between the ranking of creditors when considering if a company is "balance sheet insolvent".

Question 48: Which assets are taken into account when overindebtedness is established: the complete set of assets or only a selection of them?

The complete set of assets.

Question 49: How are the debtor's assets valued: by referring to the liquidation value, the book value, the going concern value or in another way?

A comparison is provided of the likely return to creditors of realisation of the assets of the debtor on a liquidation basis, against the return to creditors on a restructuring of the debtor.

Question 50: Is there any prognostic element, e.g. regarding the debtor's chances to continue the business?

No.

Question 51: If the answer to the previous Question is "yes", what exactly is the topic of the prognosis and how is it established?

n.a.

Question 52: If the answer to Question 50 is "yes", how long is the prognosis period?

n.a.

Question 53: How is overindebtedness established?

a) Is a formal balance sheet required?
Yes.

b) Does the yearly regular commercial balance sheet have any meaning (given that it is normally based on technical values and does not display undisclosed reserves)?
No – a simple balance sheet is used to demonstrate an insolvent position when taking into account liabilities, to include contingent liabilities.

c) Does the law provide for a presumption? If so, under which conditions?
No.

d) Other means?
n.a.

Question 54: Is the legal link to overindebtedness undisputed in literature or are there efforts to abolish it?

There have been no efforts to abolish it.

Question 55: Would you like to add any further aspects not covered by the above questions?

n.a.

VI. REMAINING ISSUES

Question 56: Is there anything else you would like to share in the present context and that we should take into account?

n.a.

ITALY

Renato MANGANO

I. GENERAL

Question 1: How is insolvency (both in the context of liquidation and restructuring/reorganisation) regulated in your jurisdiction? Please give a brief overview, at least enumerating the relevant statutes.

In the field of insolvency law, insolvency and other similar concepts are regulated by Legislative Decree 12 January 2019, No. 14, containing the Code of Business Crisis and Insolvency (Codice della crisi d'impresa e dell'insolvenza, hereinafter CCII; www.normattiva.it). This Code entered into force on 15 July 2022.

Question 2: Related to paragraph 10 above of the Introduction: seen from a principle-based perspective, what justifies the opening of insolvency proceedings in your jurisdiction?

The principles of unity, universality, efficiency, transparency and predictability.

Question 3: Does your national law in the context of liquidation proceedings use one or more of the following terms (be it as a noun, be it as an adjective or adjunct) in whatever context:

a) inability to pay debts
Yes.

b) cessation of payments
No.

c) likely inability to pay debts
No.

d) imminent inability to pay debts
No.

e) overindebtedness?
Yes, albeit to a limited extent.

Question 4: Are the same terms (and with the same meaning) used in the rules on preliminary/interim insolvency proceedings (e.g. concerning the application stage of the proceedings)?

n.a.

Question 5: Does your national law in the context of restructuring proceedings (as referred to above at paragraph 8 of the Introduction, i.e. both pre-insolvency and within formal insolvency proceedings) use one or more of the following terms (be it as a noun, be it as an adjective or adjunct) in whatever context:

a) inability to pay debts
Yes.

b) cessation of payments
No.

c) likely inability to pay debts
Yes.

d) imminent inability to pay debts
No.

e) overindebtedness?
Yes, albeit to a limited extent.

Question 6: Which of the terms mentioned in Questions 3 and 5 are used for defining grounds to commence proceedings (triggering circumstances)?

a) insolvency proceedings
Insolvency (*insolvenza*); overindebtedness (*sovraindebitamento*).

b) restructuring proceedings
Insolvency (*insolvenza*); overindebtedness (*sovraindebitamento*); likely inability to pay debts (*crisi*); likelihood of likely inability to pay debts (*crisi probabile*).

Question 7: Does the answer to Question 6 include personal bankruptcies of natural persons or only corporate insolvencies of legal entities?

Yes, the answer to Question 6 *does* include personal bankruptcies of natural persons.

Question 8: In your law, are there any other circumstances which trigger insolvency or restructuring proceedings?

Yes, there are. Depending on the specific type of the company in question and the specific statute under which that company is run, Italian administrative law lays down that public regulators may request the opening of "compulsory administrative liquidation proceedings" (*liquidazione coatta amministrativa*) either because a "situation of severe mismanagement" has been ascertained or because it is in the public interest to liquidate the company. As regards the regulation of "compulsory administrative liquidation proceedings", see Articles 293 to 321 CCII; and as regards the fact that "compulsory administrative liquidation proceedings" may be opened independently of the existence of a situation of distress, see Article 298 CCII.

Question 9: Which of the terms mentioned in Questions 3, 5, and 8 are used in the context of transactions avoidance law?

Only insolvency.

Question 10: Which of the terms addressed in Questions 3, 5, and 8 are used in the context of directors' duties?

a) shift of duties (from shareholders to creditors)
Overindebtedness, although the Italian law-maker employs in this field a (linguistically) different expression which reads: "insufficiency of the company's assets for the satisfaction of creditors' claims" (*insufficienza del patrimonio sociale al soddisfacimento dei crediti*).

b) duties to commence insolvency proceedings
n.a.

c) other duties (please describe)
n.a.

Question 11: Are there any other rules in the context of which the terms addressed in Questions 3, 5, and 8 are used?

Article 1186 of the Civil Code also employs the term "insolvency". However, this term is commonly accepted as a synonym of non-fulfilment of obligations.

Question 12: Is the definition of (the subspecies of) insolvency identical in all legal fields or are there different definitions (e.g. different in insolvency law than in criminal law)?

Basically, there are no concurrent definitions of insolvency or other similar concepts. Under the previous insolvency law statute, Royal Decree 16 March 1942, No. 267 (usually known as "Legge fallimentare"; www.normattiva.it), one scholar maintained that, while the concept of insolvency as a trigger event to open insolvency law proceedings implied a prospective evaluation of the firm (prognosis), the concept of insolvency in transaction avoidance law did not imply any prospective evaluation but referred rather to a specific point in time (diagnosis). In this respect, see *Terranova*, Insolvenza. Stato di crisi.

Sovraindebitamento, Giappichelli, Torino 2013, p. 57 et seq., and, as regards insolvency in transaction avoidance law, p. 90 et seq. However, it is controversial whether that doctrinal distinction, which was also accepted by the courts, is still applicable to the current legal framework. Although the current definition of insolvency is textually the same as in the past (compare the text of Article 2.1.(b) CCII with Article 5.2 Regio Decreto 267/1942), the introduction of the concept of "crisis" (*crisi*) in the terms that are specified in Article 2.1.(a) CCII, seems to have reduced to a diagnosis the concept of insolvency as a trigger event in the opening of insolvency law proceedings. However, since the CCII entered into force on 15 July 2022 there are not yet any academic papers or legal judgments that can prove this impression.

II. INABILITY TO PAY DEBTS

Question 13: In your jurisdiction, is the term "inability to pay debts" defined in statute? If so, please give the wording in English translation. Is this definition (if any) specified in case law? If so, how?

Italian law defines "inability to pay debts" within the definition of insolvency. Indeed, the "inability to pay debts" is the most important symptom of insolvency. Article 2.1.(b) CCII lays down that:

> "Insolvency" is the debtor's state that is displayed either by the debtor's non-fulfilment of obligations or by other symptoms proving that the debtor is no longer able to satisfy his or her obligations regularly.
>
> (*«insolvenza»: lo stato del debitore che si manifesta con inadempimenti od altri fatti esteriori, i quali dimostrino che il debitore non è più in grado di soddisfare regolarmente le proprie obbligazioni*).

Question 14: Does your law refer to all debts or only to mature debts?

Traditionally, Italian law refers to all debts.

Question 15: Which assets are taken into account when assessing the inability to pay debts: all (financial) assets or only those that are liquid, i.e. available on short notice?

Traditionally, Italian law does not make any distinction.

Question 16: Is any liquidity gap (deficit between relevant financial means and relevant debts) relevant or does your law neglect minor gaps? If the latter, how is "minor" defined?

Traditionally, Italian law does not make any distinction.

Question 17: As far as the time aspect is concerned, does it matter whether the liquidity gap can be closed again in the short term? If so, how long is the grace period?

Traditionally, Italian law does not make any distinction.

Question 18: As far as the time aspect is concerned, is a debtor considered insolvent if the liquidity gap is not yet present but will occur soon? If so, how long is the prognosis period? (Note: this may also concern the difference between actual and likely/imminent inability to pay debts; cf. below Question 34).

Since the entry into force of CCII, Italian law seems no longer to consider the debtor as insolvent only because a liquidity gap, which is not yet present, is expected to occur soon. By contrast, this situation of potential distress is certainly required by the prerequisite of crisis (*crisi*), which *corresponds to* a situation of "likely inability to pay". In this case the prognosis period is 12 months (see Article 2.1.a CCII).

Question 19: How is inability to pay debts established? Please communicate if there is a difference between a creditor and a debtor application or between different legal contexts.

a) Is a formal liquidity status (liquidity balance sheet) required?
No.

b) Is a sample of daily liquidity data (which do not amount to a proper liquidity status but show insufficient funds on different days within a certain period of time) sufficient?
No.

c) Does the law provide for a rebuttable presumption? If so, under which conditions?
Within the definition of insolvency, "the inability to pay" itself is considered as the basis of a rebuttable presumption. In effect, this is capable of proving that the debtor is insolvent, unless the opposite has been demonstrated. Traditionally, other bases of the presumption (symptoms) of insolvency have been the debtor's escape and the debtor's suicide.

d) Does the law provide for any technical circumstances (e.g. undisputed statutory demand, non-compliance with monetary judgments, unsuccessful enforcement proceedings, non-performance of a previous composition agreement in insolvency proceedings) the occurrence of which suffices to establish the debtor's insolvency?
No.

e) Other means?
See the answer to Question 13.

Question 20: Is insolvency (inability to pay debts, overindebtedness, etc.) subject to party autonomy in the proceedings or must the court clarify them *ex officio*?

In principle, party autonomy is irrelevant. However, a *pactum de non petendo* concluded between the debtor and the most significant of his or her creditors may be relevant.

Question 21: In an overall view, does your law distinguish "inability to pay debts" from "financial difficulties"? If so, how?

No.

Question 22: In an overall view, does it matter under your law whether the debtor's inability to pay debts is present or future and reversible or irreversible?

Yes, albeit at an interpretative level only.

Question 23: Would you like to add any further aspects not covered by the above questions?

No.

III. CESSATION OF PAYMENTS

Question 24: In your jurisdiction, is "cessation of payments" a legal term used either in statute or in case law? (If the answer is "no", please continue with Question 31.)

No.

Question 25: Is "cessation of payments" an autonomous ground to commence proceedings (triggering circumstance)? You may refer to Questions 6/7 or add additional information here.

n.a.

Question 26: Is "cessation of payments" a means to establish inability to pay debts? If so, by which mechanism (e.g. rebuttable presumption for inability to pay debts, cf. above Question 19(c))?

n.a.

Question 27: How is "cessation of payments" defined? If it is defined in statute, please provide us here with an English translation of the relevant rule. Is this definition (if any) specified in case law? If so, how?

n.a.

Question 28: How is "cessation of payments" established?

n.a.

Question 29: Are there typical circumstances which provide circumstantial evidence that the debtor has ceased payments? If so, please list as many as possible.

n.a.

Question 30: Would you like to add any further aspects not covered by the above questions?

n.a.

IV. LIKELY/IMMINENT INABILITY TO PAY DEBTS

Question 31: Are the following terms available in your jurisdiction, either in statute or in case law? (If the answer is "no", please continue with Question 42.)

a) likely inability to pay debts
Yes.

b) imminent inability to pay debts
No.

c) other (similar) terms
Likelihood of likely inability to pay debts (*crisi probabile*).

Question 32: Is "likely/imminent inability to pay debts" an autonomous ground to commence proceedings (triggering circumstance)? You may refer to Questions 6/7 or add additional information here.

Yes, likely inability to pay debts is a triggering event only of restructuring proceedings.

Question 33: If the answer to the previous Question is "yes", who may base filing for insolvency proceedings on it: only the debtor or also creditors?

Basically, only the debtor. However, under certain conditions the debtor's creditors may propose competing plans (Article 90 CCII).

Question 34: How are these terms defined? If they are defined in statute, please provide us here with an English translation of the relevant rules. Is this definition (if any) specified in case law? If so, how?

a) likely inability to pay debts
According to Article 2.1.(a) CCII, "likely inability to pay debts" (*crisi*) is "a financial state that can evolve into insolvency and that occurs when the prospective cash flows are not capable of covering the firm's debts in the next twelve months" (this is a free translation of "*lo stato del debitore che rende probabile l'insolvenza e che si manifesta con l'inadeguatezza dei flussi di cassa prospettici a far fronte alle obbligazioni nei successivi dodici mesi*").

b) imminent inability to pay debts
n.a.

Question 35: Do the terms "likely" and "imminent" require a prognosis regarding the point in time when actual inability to pay debts will occur? If so, how long is the time period for this prognosis?

The term "likely" refers to a prognosis of 12 months.

Question 36: Does your law require a specific grade of certainty that inability to pay debts will eventually occur? If so, is 50.1% ("more likely than not") enough or are there alleviated or aggravated prerequisites?

n.a.

Question 37: Regarding "debts" and "financial means", are they defined in the same way as in the context of inability to pay debts (cf. above Questions 14/15)? If not, what are the differences?

n.a.

Question 38: Further to Question 37: Are "debts" considered which do currently not exist or are not yet due but will foreseeably come into existence and become due during the prognosis period?

n.a.

Question 39: Also further to Question 37: Are "financial means" considered which do currently not exist but will foreseeably become available during the prognosis period?

n.a.

Question 40: How are the terms "likely/imminent inability to pay debts" established?

"Likely inability to pay debts" is established by reference to a prognosis according to which the prospective cash flows seem incapable of covering the firm's debts in the next 12 months.

Question 41: Would you like to add any further aspects not covered by the above questions?

No.

V. OVERINDEBTEDNESS

Question 42: In your jurisdiction, is "overindebtedness", or "balance sheet insolvency" respectively, a legal term used either in statute or in case law? (If the answer is "no", please continue with Question 56.)

Yes.

Question 43: Is "overindebtedness" an autonomous ground to commence proceedings (triggering circumstance)? You may refer to Questions 6/7 or add additional information here.

Yes. This is the trigger event that is required to open insolvency proceedings, whether they be for liquidation or rescue, for both non-traders and small traders.

Question 44: If the answer to the previous Question is "yes", is this applicable to corporate insolvencies of legal persons only or also to personal bankruptcies of natural persons?

Overindebtedness is applicable to both corporate and personal insolvency proceedings.

Question 45: Is the term "overindebtedness" defined in statute? If so, please give the wording in English translation. Is this definition (if any) specified in case law? If so, how?

Yes, Article 2.1.(c) lays down:

> "over-indebtedness" means any situation of either pre-insolvency or insolvency referring to consumers, small traders, farmers, professionals, innovative start-ups under Law Decree 18 October 2012 No. 179 converted, with amendments, by Law No 221 of 17 December 2012, and of any other debtor who is not subject to judicial liquidation or compulsory administrative liquidation or other liquidation procedures provided for by the Civil Code or special laws in the event of crisis or insolvency.

(*«sovraindebitamento»: lo stato di crisi o di insolvenza del consumatore, del professionista, dell'imprenditore minore, dell'imprenditore agricolo, delle start-up innovative di cui al decreto-legge 18 ottobre 2012, n. 179, convertito, con modificazioni, dalla legge 17 dicembre 2012, n. 221, e di ogni altro debitore non assoggettabile alla liquidazione giudiziale ovvero a liquidazione coatta amministrativa o ad altre procedure liquidatorie previste dal codice civile o da leggi speciali per il caso di crisi o insolvenza*).

As a result, under Italian law the term "overindebtedness", which now clashes with the traditional definition of "overindebtedness", has become an umbrella term including both "likely inability to pay debts" and "inability to pay debts". Arguably, this policy has been chosen in order to adopt collective law measures typical of insolvency law to deal with the distress of all persons and entities that are not included in the definition of "non-small traders" without removing the traditional dogma according to which, in Italy, insolvency law refers to non-small traders only.

Question 46: Does your law refer to all existing debts or only to mature debts?

Italian law refers to both.

Question 47: Does the rank of certain debts play a role when establishing overindebtedness? In particular, is there any possibility to conclude agreements according to which certain debts shall not be taken into account (e.g. agreements on subsidiarity)?

n.a.

Question 48: Which assets are taken into account when overindebtedness is established: the complete set of assets or only a selection of them?

n.a.

Question 49: How are the debtor's assets valued: by referring to the liquidation value, the book value, the going concern value or in another way?

n.a.

Question 50: Is there any prognostic element, e.g. regarding the debtor's chances to continue the business?

Yes. See the answer to Question 45.

Question 51: If the answer to the previous Question is "yes", what exactly is the topic of the prognosis and how is it established?

See the answers to Question 12.

Question 52: If the answer to the Question 50 is "yes", how long is the prognosis period?

See the answers to Questions 18, 34 and 35.

Question 53: How is overindebtedness established?

a) Is a formal balance sheet required?
No.

b) Does the yearly regular commercial balance sheet have any meaning (given that it is normally based on technical values and does not display undisclosed reserves)?
No.

c) Does the law provide for a presumption? If so, under which conditions?
See the answer to Question 19.

d) Other means?
n.a.

Question 54: Is the legal link to overindebtedness undisputed in literature or are there efforts to abolish it?

This concept of overindebtedness is new, but for a critical appraisal see *Mangano*, The New Italian Regulation on Over-indebtedness – A Snapshot, in *Carballo Fidalgo (ed.)*, Sobreendeudamiento de consumidores: Estrategias para garantizar una segunda oportunidad, Bosch Editor, Barcelona 2019.

Question 55: Would you like to add any further aspects not covered by the above questions?

No.

VI. REMAINING ISSUES

Question 56: Is there anything else you would like to share in the present context and that we should take into account?

No, there is not.

LATVIA

Madara STURITE

I. GENERAL

Question 1: How is insolvency (both in the context of liquidation and restructuring/reorganisation) regulated in your jurisdiction? Please give a brief overview, at least enumerating the relevant statutes.

Insolvency in the Republic of Latvia is regulated by the Insolvency Law. This law applies to all, except credit institutions. Insolvency of credit institutions is regulated by the Credit Institutions Law.

Question 2: Related to paragraph 10 above of the Introduction: seen from a principle-based perspective, what justifies the opening of insolvency proceedings in your jurisdiction?

The Latvian Insolvency Law sets out the principles to be followed in the process. These are defined in Article 6 of the Law.

They are:

1) principle of the preservation of rights – the rights of creditors acquired prior to proceedings are respected during the proceedings. The restriction of rights of creditors specified within the scope of the proceedings may not be greater than is necessary for achieving the objective of the respective proceedings;
2) principle of creditor equality – creditors are given equal opportunities to participate in proceedings and receive satisfaction of their claims, in accordance with the obligations which they have established with the debtor prior to the commencement of proceedings;
3) the principle of prohibition against arbitrariness – a creditor and debtor may not perform individual activities which cause harm to the interests of the creditors in general;
4) principle of honouring of obligations – measures which allow the obligations undertaken by a debtor to be honoured in a greater amount shall be applicable within the scope of proceedings;
5) principle of effectiveness of proceedings – such measures which allow the objective of the proceedings to be achieved in the most complete manner with the least resources shall be applicable within the scope of proceedings;

6) principle of quick turnover – the task of the proceedings is to maintain a commercially lawful quick turnover. The sale of the property of a debtor shall be performed in order to ensure the return thereof to commercially lawful circulation as quickly as possible;
7) principle of transparency – in order to ensure credibility, information on proceedings must be accessible to all persons involved in the proceedings, thereby promoting the observation of the interests of these persons and the achievement of the objectives of the proceedings. An exception is information the unrestricted disclosure of which might harm the lawful interests of a debtor or a creditor;
8) principle of good faith – persons involved in proceedings shall use their rights and fulfil their duties in good faith. A debtor and creditor may not use the proceedings in order to make a living unfairly.

Question 3: Does your national law in the context of liquidation proceedings use one or more of the following terms (be it as a noun, be it as an adjective or adjunct) in whatever context:

a) inability to pay debts
Yes.

b) cessation of payments
No.

c) likely inability to pay debts
Yes.

d) imminent inability to pay debts
No.

e) overindebtedness?
No.

Question 4: Are the same terms (and with the same meaning) used in the rules on preliminary/interim insolvency proceedings (e.g. concerning the application stage of the proceedings)?

Yes.

Question 5: Does your national law in the context of restructuring proceedings (as referred to above at paragraph 8 of the Introduction, i.e. both pre-insolvency and within formal insolvency proceedings) use one or more of the following terms (be it as a noun, be it as an adjective or adjunct) in whatever context:

a) inability to pay debts
Yes.

b) cessation of payments
No.

c) likely inability to pay debts
Yes.

d) imminent inability to pay debts
No.

e) overindebtedness?
No.

Question 6: Which of the terms mentioned in Questions 3 and 5 are used for defining grounds to commence proceedings (triggering circumstances)?

a) insolvency proceedings
"Inability to pay debts".

b) restructuring proceedings
"Likely inability to pay debts".

Question 7: Does the answer to Question 6 include personal bankruptcies of natural persons or only corporate insolvencies of legal entities?

It includes both.

Question 8: In your law, are there any other circumstances which trigger insolvency or restructuring proceedings?

The Latvian Insolvency Law doesn't provide for a so-called "balance sheet test", which means that a court can declare insolvency even in circumstances where a person's (legal or private) assets exceed its liabilities.

The Law sets out the signs of insolvency. It is sufficient for the court to find one of the signs in order to declare insolvency.

For *legal persons* those signs are:

According to Insolvency Law Article 57(1):

> Insolvency proceedings of a legal person shall be applied to a debtor if any of the following features of insolvency proceedings of a legal person exists:
>
> 1) when applying compulsory execution means it has not been possible to execute the court ruling regarding the recovery of debt from the debtor;
> 2) the debtor – a limited liability company or a joint stock company – has not honoured one or more debt obligations from which the principal debt amount separately or in total exceeds EUR 4268 and which are past due, and the creditor or creditors have issued or sent a warning at the sender's own expense to the legal address of the debtor regarding the intention to submit an application for insolvency proceedings of a legal person, and the debtor has not settled the debt

or raised justified objections to the claim within three weeks after handing over of the warning to the postal operator;

3) the debtor – another subject referred to in Section 56 of this Law – has not honoured one or more debt obligations from which the principal debt amount separately or in total exceeds EUR 2134 and which are past due, and the creditor or creditors have issued or sent a warning at the sender's own expense to the legal address of the debtor regarding the intention to submit an application for insolvency proceedings of a legal person, and the debtor has not settled the debt or raised justified objections to the claim within three weeks after handing over of the warning to the postal operator;
4) the debtor has not paid an employee their work remuneration in full, compensation for damages in connection with an accident at work or an occupational disease or has not made the mandatory social insurance payments within two months after the day specified for payment. Unless the day of payment of work remuneration is specified in the employment contract, this day shall be considered to be the first working day of the following month;
5) the debtor has not honoured its obligations which are past due for more than two months;
6) according to the initial financial report of liquidation the debtor has insufficient assets to satisfy all the justified claims of creditors, or this condition is discovered during the course of liquidation.

For *private persons* under Insolvency Law Article 129:

(i) this person does not have the possibility of settling debt obligations for which the due date has been set, and the debt obligations exceed EUR 5,000 in total;
(ii) in connection with provable circumstances, it will not be possible for this person to settle his debt obligations which will be due within a year and the debt obligations exceed EUR 10,000 in total;
(iii) this person does not have a possibility to settle debt obligations out of which at least one debt obligation is based on an unsettled ancillary obligation or joint obligation between the debtor and the interested person if the debt exceeds EUR 5,000.

Question 9: Which of the terms mentioned in Questions 3, 5, and 8 are used in the context of transactions avoidance law?

None of them.

Question 10: Which of the terms addressed in Questions 3, 5, and 8 are used in the context of directors' duties?

a) shift of duties (from shareholders to creditors)

In Latvia, the shift of duties is neither regulated nor defined in case law.

b) duties to commence insolvency proceedings
Inability to pay debts.

c) other duties (please describe)
There are no others.

Question 11: Are there any other rules in the context of which the terms addressed in Questions 3, 5, and 8 are used?

No.

Question 12: Is the definition of (the subspecies of) insolvency identical in all legal fields or are there different definitions (e.g. different in insolvency law than in criminal law)?

The definition of insolvency is identical in all legal fields in Latvia.

II. INABILITY TO PAY DEBTS

Question 13: In your jurisdiction, is the term "inability to pay debts" defined in statute? If so, please give the wording in English translation. Is this definition (if any) specified in case law? If so, how?

As indicated in the answer to Question 8 – Latvian Insolvency Law sets out specific signs, which are considered to be signs of insolvency. Neither the Law nor the case law defines the term "inability to pay debts", because the definition of it is linked to the presence or absence of these signs. If any of the signs of insolvency is established, it is presumed that the person (legal or private) is unable to pay their debts.

Question 14: Does your law refer to all debts or only to mature debts?

Latvian law refers to all debts.

Question 15: Which assets are taken into account when assessing the inability to pay debts: all (financial) assets or only those that are liquid, i.e. available on short notice?

All assets.

Question 16: Is any liquidity gap (deficit between relevant financial means and relevant debts) relevant or does your law neglect minor gaps? If the latter, how is "minor" defined?

It is not defined.

Question 17: As far as the time aspect is concerned, does it matter whether the liquidity gap can be closed again in the short term? If so, how long is the grace period?

n.a.

Question 18: As far as the time aspect is concerned, is a debtor considered insolvent if the liquidity gap is not yet present but will occur soon? If so, how long is the prognosis period? (Note: this may also concern the difference between actual and likely/imminent inability to pay debts; cf. below Question 34).

n.a.

Question 19: How is inability to pay debts established? Please communicate if there is a difference between a creditor and a debtor application or between different legal contexts.

Inability to pay debts is established by a court decision declaring insolvency proceedings. This procedural document presumes that the person is unable to pay debts. The court declares insolvency if it finds any of the signs of insolvency (please see answer to Question 8).

a) Is a formal liquidity status (liquidity balance sheet) required?
No.

b) Is a sample of daily liquidity data (which do not amount to a proper liquidity status but show insufficient funds on different days within a certain period of time) sufficient?
n.a.

c) Does the law provide for a rebuttable presumption? If so, under which conditions?
If a legal person is found to have any of the signs specified in Article 57 of the Latvian Insolvency Law which are related to inability/unwillingness to repay a debt (in particular those specified in paragraphs 2–5, please see the answer to Question 8), the person has the option to repay the debt until the application is considered by the court. In such a case, insolvency is not declared.

> 2) the debtor – a limited liability company or a joint stock company – has not honoured one or more debt obligations from which the principal debt amount separately or in total exceeds EUR 4268 and which are past due, and the creditor or creditors have issued or sent a warning at the sender's own expense to the legal address of the debtor regarding the intention to submit an application for insolvency proceedings of a legal person, and the debtor has not settled the debt or raised justified objections to the claim within three weeks after handing over of the warning to the postal operator;

3) the debtor – another subject referred to in Section 56 of this Law – has not honoured one or more debt obligations from which the principal debt amount separately or in total exceeds EUR 2134 and which are past due, and the creditor or creditors have issued or sent a warning at the sender's own expense to the legal address of the debtor regarding the intention to submit an application for insolvency proceedings of a legal person, and the debtor has not settled the debt or raised justified objections to the claim within three weeks after handing over of the warning to the postal operator;

4) the debtor has not paid an employee their work remuneration in full, compensation for damages in connection with an accident at work or an occupational disease or has not made the mandatory social insurance payments within two months after the day specified for payment. Unless the day of payment of work remuneration is specified in the employment contract, this day shall be considered to be the first working day of the following month;

5) the debtor has not honoured its obligations which are past due for more than two months[.]

d) Does the law provide for any technical circumstances (e.g. undisputed statutory demand, non-compliance with monetary judgments, unsuccessful enforcement proceedings, non-performance of a previous composition agreement in insolvency proceedings) the occurrence of which suffices to establish the debtor's insolvency?
Following the wording of the question, all the signs of insolvency that I referred to in Question 8 should be considered as technical circumstances.

e) Other means?
No.

Question 20: Is insolvency (inability to pay debts, overindebtedness, etc.) subject to party autonomy in the proceedings or must the court clarify them *ex officio*?

It is subject to party autonomy.

Question 21: In an overall view, does your law distinguish "inability to pay debts" from "financial difficulties"? If so, how?

No.

Question 22: In an overall view, does it matter under your law whether the debtor's inability to pay debts is present or future and reversible or irreversible?

It does not matter.

Question 23: Would you like to add any further aspects not covered by the above questions?

n.a.

III. CESSATION OF PAYMENTS

Question 24: In your jurisdiction, is "cessation of payments" a legal term used either in statute or in case law? (If the answer is "no", please continue with Question 31.)

No.

Question 25: Is "cessation of payments" an autonomous ground to commence proceedings (triggering circumstance)? You may refer to Questions 6/7 or add additional information here.

n.a.

Question 26: Is "cessation of payments" a means to establish inability to pay debts? If so, by which mechanism (e.g. rebuttable presumption for inability to pay debts, cf. above Question 19(c))?

n.a.

Question 27: How is "cessation of payments" defined? If it is defined in statute, please provide us here with an English translation of the relevant rule. Is this definition (if any) specified in case law? If so, how?

n.a.

Question 28: How is "cessation of payments" established?

n.a.

Question 29: Are there typical circumstances which provide circumstantial evidence that the debtor has ceased payments? If so, please list as many as possible.

n.a.

Question 30: Would you like to add any further aspects not covered by the above questions?

n.a.

IV. LIKELY/IMMINENT INABILITY TO PAY DEBTS

Question 31: Are the following terms available in your jurisdiction, either in statute or in case law? (If the answer is "no", please continue with Question 42.)

a) likely inability to pay debts
Yes.

b) imminent inability to pay debts
No.

c) other (similar) terms
No.

Question 32: Is "likely/imminent inability to pay debts" an autonomous ground to commence proceedings (triggering circumstance)? You may refer to Questions 6/7 or add additional information here.

Yes, this is directly related to the answer to Question 8 on the signs of insolvency, which are defined by the Latvian Insolvency Law. In the event that a creditor establishes any of the specified signs:

> 2) the debtor – a limited liability company or a joint stock company – has not honoured one or more debt obligations from which the principal debt amount separately or in total exceeds EUR 4268 and which are past due, and the creditor or creditors have issued or sent a warning at the sender's own expense to the legal address of the debtor regarding the intention to submit an application for insolvency proceedings of a legal person, and the debtor has not settled the debt or raised justified objections to the claim within three weeks after handing over of the warning to the postal operator;
>
> 3) the debtor – another subject referred to in Section 56 of this Law – has not honoured one or more debt obligations from which the principal debt amount separately or in total exceeds EUR 2134 and which are past due, and the creditor or creditors have issued or sent a warning at the sender's own expense to the legal address of the debtor regarding the intention to submit an application for insolvency proceedings of a legal person, and the debtor has not settled the debt or raised justified objections to the claim within three weeks after handing over of the warning to the postal operator;
>
> 4) the debtor has not paid an employee their work remuneration in full, compensation for damages in connection with an accident at work or an occupational disease or has not made the mandatory social insurance payments within two months after

the day specified for payment. Unless the day of payment of work remuneration is specified in the employment contract, this day shall be considered to be the first working day of the following month;

5) the debtor has not honoured its obligations which are past due for more than two months;

it is presumed that the person is likely/imminently unable to pay debts.

Question 33: If the answer to the previous Question is "yes", who may base filing for insolvency proceedings on it: only the debtor or also creditors?

Only creditors.

Question 34: How are these terms defined? If they are defined in statute, please provide us here with an English translation of the relevant rules. Is this definition (if any) specified in case law? If so, how?

a) likely inability to pay debts
The term is not defined.

b) imminent inability to pay debts
The term is not defined.

Question 35: Do the terms "likely" and "imminent" require a prognosis regarding the point in time when actual inability to pay debts will occur? If so, how long is the time period for this prognosis?

n.a.

Question 36: Does your law require a specific grade of certainty that inability to pay debts will eventually occur? If so, is 50.1% ("more likely than not") enough or are there alleviated or aggravated prerequisites?

No.

Question 37: Regarding "debts" and "financial means", are they defined in the same way as in the context of inability to pay debts (cf. above Questions 14/15)? If not, what are the differences?

Yes.

Question 38: Further to Question 37: Are "debts" considered which do currently not exist or are not yet due but will foreseeably come into existence and become due during the prognosis period?

Yes.

Question 39: Also further to Question 37: Are "financial means" considered which do currently not exist but will foreseeably become available during the prognosis period?

Yes.

Question 40: How are the terms "likely/imminent inability to pay debts" established?

Please see the answer to Question 32.

Question 41: Would you like to add any further aspects not covered by the above questions?

n.a.

V. OVERINDEBTEDNESS

Question 42: In your jurisdiction, is "overindebtedness", or "balance sheet insolvency" respectively, a legal term used either in statute or in case law? (If the answer is "no", please continue with Question 56.)

No.

Question 43: Is "overindebtedness" an autonomous ground to commence proceedings (triggering circumstance)? You may refer to Questions 6/7 or add additional information here.

n.a.

Question 44: If the answer to the previous Question is "yes", is this applicable to corporate insolvencies of legal persons only or also to personal bankruptcies of natural persons?

n.a.

Question 45: Is the term "overindebtedness" defined in statute? If so, please give the wording in English translation. Is this definition (if any) specified in case law? If so, how?

n.a.

Question 46: Does your law refer to all existing debts or only to mature debts?

n.a.

Question 47: Does the rank of certain debts play a role when establishing overindebtedness? In particular, is there any possibility to conclude agreements according to which certain debts shall not be taken into account (e.g. agreements on subsidiarity)?

n.a.

Question 48: Which assets are taken into account when overindebtedness is established: the complete set of assets or only a selection of them?

n.a.

Question 49: How are the debtor's assets valued: by referring to the liquidation value, the book value, the going concern value or in another way?

n.a.

Question 50: Is there any prognostic element, e.g. regarding the debtor's chances to continue the business?

n.a.

Question 51: If the answer to the previous Question is "yes", what exactly is the topic of the prognosis and how is it established?

n.a.

Question 52: If the answer to Question 50 is "yes", how long is the prognosis period?

n.a.

Question 53: How is overindebtedness established?

a) Is a formal balance sheet required?
n.a.

b) Does the yearly regular commercial balance sheet have any meaning (given that it is normally based on technical values and does not display undisclosed reserves)?
n.a.

c) Does the law provide for a presumption? If so, under which conditions?
n.a.

d) Other means?
n.a.

Question 54: Is the legal link to overindebtedness undisputed in literature or are there efforts to abolish it?

n.a.

Question 55: Would you like to add any further aspects not covered by the above questions?

n.a.

VI. REMAINING ISSUES

Question 56: Is there anything else you would like to share in the present context and that we should take into account?

n.a.

LITHUANIA

Frank Heemann

I. GENERAL

Question 1: How is insolvency (both in the context of liquidation and restructuring/reorganisation) regulated in your jurisdiction? Please give a brief overview, at least enumerating the relevant statutes.

Insolvency is regulated in two statutes, namely in the Law on Insolvency of Legal Entities (JANI), which governs restructuring and bankruptcy proceedings of legal persons,[1] and in the Law on Bankruptcy of Natural Persons (FABI),[2] which regulates bankruptcy proceedings for individuals.

JANI provides for two types of proceedings for legal entities: bankruptcy and restructuring proceedings. Bankruptcy proceedings aim at the liquidation of the debtor (composition agreements between the debtor and the creditors are, however, possible but rarely used). These bankruptcy proceedings can be conducted as in-court proceedings but also as out-of-court (extrajudicial) proceedings. JANI also provides for restructuring proceedings, the goal of which is the rescue of the debtor by way of a creditor-approved restructuring plan. JANI is rather young, having come into effect on 1 January 2020 with amendments in mid-2021 aimed at transposing the Preventive Restructuring Directive 2019/1023. One of the major changes introduced by JANI concerns the definition of insolvency as explained in more detail in the questions below.

FABI provides for one type of proceedings: bankruptcy proceedings for individuals. It foresees partial satisfaction of creditor claims based on a

---

1 Law on Insolvency of Legal Entities of the Republic of Lithuania (Lietuvos Respublikos juridinių asmenų nemokumo įstatymas) 13 June 2019, No. XIII-2221 (as amended) JANI entered into effect on 1 January 2020 and replaced two separate statutes which previously regulated bankruptcy and restructuring proceedings for legal entities: the Enterprise Bankruptcy Law (EBL) and the Enterprise Restructuring Law (ERL). Enterprise Bankruptcy Law of Republic of Lithuania (Lietuvos Respublikos įmonių bankroto įstatymas) 20 March 2001, No. IX-216. Enterprise Restructuring Law of Republic of Lithuania (Lietuvos Respublikos įmonių restruktūrizavimo įstatymas) 20 March 2001, No. IX-218.

2 Law on Bankruptcy of Natural Persons of the Republic of Lithuania (Lietuvos Respublikos fizinių asmenų bankroto įstatymas) 22 December 2015, No. XII-2235.

creditor-approved plan. FABI offers debt write-off for the debtor if the statutory requirements are met.

The appointment of an insolvency practitioner is mandatory in bankruptcy proceedings under JANI and FABI. The appointment of an insolvency practitioner in restructuring proceedings is not mandatory but is common practice. Restructuring proceedings are debtor-in-possession proceedings, so that the insolvency practitioner – if appointed – fulfils a supervisory function.

Question 2: Related to paragraph 10 above of the Introduction: seen from a principle-based perspective, what justifies the opening of insolvency proceedings in your jurisdiction?

JANI names in its Article 3 the following five principles of insolvency proceedings:

1) the principle of *efficiency*, meaning that in the course of insolvency process a balance must be maintained between the interests of a legal person in financial difficulties and the interests of creditors with a view to maximising satisfaction of the creditors' claims within a reasonable minimum period of time;
2) the principle of *equality of creditors*, meaning that creditors with similar claims shall be given equal opportunities to participate in the insolvency proceedings in order to satisfy their claims and to protect their other rights and legitimate interests;
3) the principle of *transparency*, meaning that information on the insolvency process shall be made available in a timely manner to all persons involved in the insolvency proceedings in order to ensure the safeguarding of the rights and legitimate interests of these persons, except for the cases when it is necessary to protect personal data protected by legal acts or information comprising a commercial/industrial secret;
4) the principle of *judicial leading* in the proceedings, meaning that the court may, of its own motion, obligate participants in the insolvency process to conduct procedural actions, collect evidence and control the actions of the parties to the insolvency proceedings in order to ensure the effective course of the in-court insolvency process and the public interest;
5) the principle of *professionalism*, meaning that the persons administering insolvency proceedings must perform their duties professionally, ensuring a high level of their professional knowledge and ability and acting in such a way as to ensure the good repute of a representative of the profession (emphasis added).

The opening of insolvency proceedings is justified to ensure the implementation of these principles, particularly the principle of collective and equal treatment of creditors.

In the context of bankruptcy proceedings, courts have repeatedly stated that the goal of bankruptcy proceedings is not only to remove insolvent companies from the market and thus ensure market stability and stimulate economic growth, but also to protect the interests of the debtor's creditors and the debtor itself (see Lithuanian Court of Appeal, 13 October 2022, Civil case no. e2-1048-933/2022, paragraph 26).

Question 3: Does your national law in the context of liquidation proceedings use one or more of the following terms (be it as a noun, be it as an adjective or adjunct) in whatever context:

a) inability to pay debts
Yes, albeit with a slightly different wording: in JANI "cannot meet its property obligations in due time" ("*laiku negali vydyti turtinių prievolių*", Article 2 paragraph 7 JANI), and in FABI "is unable to discharge his liabilities, as they mature" ("*negali vykdyti skolinių įsipareigojimų*", Article 2 no. 2 FABI).

b) cessation of payments
No.

c) likely inability to pay debts
No.

d) imminent inability to pay debts
No.

e) overindebtedness?
Yes, albeit expressed by "the state, where the legal person's liabilities exceed the value of its assets" (Article 2 paragraph 7 JANI).

Question 4: Are the same terms (and with the same meaning) used in the rules on preliminary/interim insolvency proceedings (e.g. concerning the application stage of the proceedings)?

In Lithuania, there are not preliminary/interim insolvency proceedings equivalent to the German *vorläufiges Insolvenzverfahren*. However, the terms discussed in Question 3 apply also in the application stage, i.e. the stage between filing/acceptance of a request for opening of insolvency proceedings and the actual opening of the proceedings.

Question 5: Does your national law in the context of restructuring proceedings (as referred to above at paragraph 8 of the Introduction, i.e. both pre-insolvency and within formal insolvency proceedings) use one or more of the following terms (be it as a noun, be it as an adjective or adjunct) in whatever context:

a) inability to pay debts
Yes (see answer to Question 3(a)).

b) cessation of payments
No.

c) likely inability to pay debts

Yes, but expressed more broadly by "likelihood of insolvency of the legal person – a situation in which there is a substantial likelihood of the legal person's becoming insolvent within the next three months" (Article 2 paragraph 7^1 JANI); see also *infra* answer to Question 31.

d) imminent inability to pay debts

Yes, but expressed more broadly by "likelihood of insolvency of the legal person – a situation in which there is a substantial likelihood of the legal person's becoming insolvent within the next three months" (Article 2 paragraph 7^1 JANI); see also *infra* answer to Question 31.

e) overindebtedness?

Yes, albeit expressed by "state, where the legal person's liabilities exceed the value of its assets" (Article 2 paragraph 7 JANI).

Question 6: Which of the terms mentioned in Questions 3 and 5 are used for defining grounds to commence proceedings (triggering circumstances)?

a) insolvency proceedings

"Insolvency" is the ground for commencing insolvency proceedings for legal persons (Article 21 paragraph 2 JANI); "insolvency" exists in case of inability to pay debts and/or overindebtedness (see answers to Question 3(a) and (e)).

"Insolvency" is also the ground for commencing insolvency proceedings for individuals (Article 6 paragraph 1 FABI); "insolvency" exists in case of inability to pay debts if certain additional conditions are met (see answers to Question 3(a) and Question 13).

b) restructuring proceedings

None of the terms is used directly in the law for defining grounds to commence restructuring proceedings for legal persons (NB: there are no restructuring proceedings for individuals), however, indirectly the law refers to inability to pay debts, overindebtedness and likely/imminent inability to pay debts.

For legal persons, JANI defines the opening grounds in Article 21 paragraph 1 as follows:

> Restructuring proceedings are opened if all the following conditions are met:
>
> 1) the legal person is in financial difficulties;
> 2) the legal person is viable;
> 3) the legal person is not being wound up as a result of bankruptcy.

The legal person is in financial difficulties if it is "insolvent or there is a likelihood of the legal person's becoming insolvent" (Article 2 paragraph 5 JANI).

The legal person is insolvent "when it cannot meet its property obligations in due time or when the legal person's liabilities exceed the value of its assets" (Article 2 paragraph 7 JANI).

Likelihood of insolvency of the legal person refers to a "situation in which it there is a substantial likelihood of the legal person's becoming insolvent within the next three months" (Article 2 paragraph 7^1 JANI).

Viability of a legal person means "the state of a legal person when the legal person carries out economic and commercial activities that will enable it to discharge its obligations in the future" (Article 2 paragraph 6 JANI).

Question 7: Does the answer to Question 6 include personal bankruptcies of natural persons or only corporate insolvencies of legal entities?

Yes, see answer to Question 6 with reference to Question 3(a) for explanations concerning bankruptcies of natural persons.

Question 8: In your law, are there any other circumstances which trigger insolvency or restructuring proceedings?

No, but see Question 19(e) for additional circumstances to be taken into account according to court practice.

Question 9: Which of the terms mentioned in Questions 3, 5, and 8 are used in the context of transactions avoidance law?

Inability to pay debts is used in the form of a reference to certain transaction avoidance scenarios "for the invalidation of transactions which are contrary to the purposes of activities of the legal person and which could have affected the legal person's inability to settle with creditors ..." (Article 64 paragraph 1 no. 1 and Article 72 paragraph 1 no. 1 JANI), and similarly, in Article 12 paragraph 3 FABI, "the invalidation of transactions that could have had an effect on the natural person's ability to meet liabilities in respect of his creditors").

Question 10: Which of the terms addressed in Questions 3, 5, and 8 are used in the context of directors' duties?

a) shift of duties (from shareholders to creditors)

Likely/imminent inability to pay debts (Article 6 paragraph 1 JANI); however, the law speaks of likelihood of insolvency, which then encompasses likely/imminent inability to pay debts (see answers to Question 6(b) and Question 31 for relevant definitions).

(NB: this duty applies to the head of the legal entity (*vadovas*) not to board members in the sense of the board of directors.)

b) duties to commence insolvency proceedings
Inability to pay debts and overindebtedness (Article 6 paragraph 2 JANI, see also answers to Question 3(a) and (e)).

(NB: this duty applies to the head of the legal entity (*vadovas*) not to board members in the sense of the board of directors.)

c) other duties (please describe)
The law establishes a duty for the head of the legal person to immediately inform the members of the legal person of the likelihood of insolvency/the insolvency, and to propose

- to resolve the question of financial difficulty (Article 6 paragraph 1 no. 1 JANI) if the legal person faces a likelihood of insolvency.
- to resolve the question of restoring the legal person's solvency (Article 6 paragraph 2 no. 1 JANI) if the legal person is insolvent.

(NB: this duty applies to the head of the legal entity (*vadovas*) not to board members in the sense of the board of directors.)

Question 11: Are there any other rules in the context of which the terms addressed in Questions 3, 5, and 8 are used?

The Criminal Code refers to inability to pay debts in Article 208 (Dishonesty of a Debtor) by stating:

> 1. A person who, owing to a difficult economic situation or insolvency, when facing obvious bankruptcy and *being unable to meet all creditors' claims*, meets claims of only one or several of them or secures claims of one or several creditors and thereby incurs property damage to the remaining creditors shall be punished …
>
> 4. A legal entity shall also be held liable for the acts provided for in this Article.

Question 12: Is the definition of (the subspecies of) insolvency identical in all legal fields or are there different definitions (e.g. different in insolvency law than in criminal law)?

Courts in criminal proceedings apply the definition of insolvency the same way as civil courts (including insolvency courts), as recently confirmed by the Lithuanian Supreme Court in a ruling the criminal offence according to Article 208 of the Criminal Code (Dishonesty of a Debtor, see Lithuanian Supreme Court, 13 June 2023, case no. 2K-157-788/2023, paragraph 7).

II. INABILITY TO PAY DEBTS

Question 13: In your jurisdiction, is the term "inability to pay debts" defined in statute? If so, please give the wording in English translation. Is this definition (if any) specified in case law? If so, how?

Legal persons: There is no definition of "inability to pay debts" in statute.

Individuals: Article 2 paragraph 2 FABI states: "Insolvency of a natural person – the condition of a natural person, where he is unable to discharge his liabilities, as they mature, exceeding 25 minimum monthly wages … approved by the Government of the Republic of Lithuania."

The minimum monthly salary is EUR 924 (2024), so that the overdue debt must amount to more than EUR 23,100 (2024).

Question 14: Does your law refer to all debts or only to mature debts?

Legal persons: the statute JANI is silent on this question.

Based on most recent case law, inability to pay debts refers to the mature debts. In addition, the inability to pay debts must be systematic, i.e. not be merely temporary (see Lithuanian Court of Appeal, 27 July 2023, Civil case no. e2-747-910/2023, paragraph 25.)

Individuals: the law refers to mature debts which must exceed a defined threshold (see answer to Question 13).

Question 15: Which assets are taken into account when assessing the inability to pay debts: all (financial) assets or only those that are liquid, i.e. available on short notice?

Statute: silent.

Court practice: Only liquid assets, including those whose true value can be realised on short notice (see Lithuanian Court of Appeal, 13 October 2022, Civil case no. e2-1048-933/2022, paragraphs 29, 33; Lithuanian Court of Appeal, 27 July 2023, Civil case no. e2-747-910/2023, paragraph 25 et seq.)

Question 16: Is any liquidity gap (deficit between relevant financial means and relevant debts) relevant or does your law neglect minor gaps? If the latter, how is "minor" defined?

Statute: silent.

Court practice is not specific, either, on this point but seems to indicate that minor liquidity gaps may be ignored, provided that the debtor can show that in the case at hand, and taking into account the history and the dynamics of its financial indicators, the company is only in temporary financial difficulties that can be resolved by preserving the company as a functioning market participant (a going concern).

(See Lithuanian Court of Appeal, 13 October 2022, Civil case no. e2-1048-933/2022, paragraphs 25, 26; Lithuanian Court of Appeal, 27 July 2023, Civil case no. e2-747-910/2023, paragraph 25.)

Question 17: As far as the time aspect is concerned, does it matter whether the liquidity gap can be closed again in the short term? If so, how long is the grace period?

Statute: the law does not provide clear guidance.

Court practice: Court practice is not specific either on this point, but indicates that short-term liquidity gaps may be ignored, provided that the debtor can show that in the case at hand, and taking into account the history and tendency of the development of its financial situation, the company is only in temporary, non-systematic financial difficulties that can be resolved by preserving the company as a functioning market participant.

(See Lithuanian Court of Appeal, 13 October 2022, Civil case no. e2-1048-933/2022, paragraphs 25, 26; Lithuanian Court of Appeal, 27 July 2023, Civil case no. e2-747-910/2023, paragraph 25.)

Question 18: As far as the time aspect is concerned, is a debtor considered insolvent if the liquidity gap is not yet present but will occur soon? If so, how long is the prognosis period? (Note: this may also concern the difference between actual and likely/imminent inability to pay debts; cf. below Question 34).

In the situation described the debtor is not considered insolvent.

Future inability to pay debts might fulfil the criteria of a likelihood of insolvency (see Question 6(b)).

Question 19: How is inability to pay debts established? Please communicate if there is a difference between a creditor and a debtor application or between different legal contexts.

The responses and comments *infra* apply in principle irrespective of whether a creditor or a debtor files an application. However, differences come into play from a civil procedural perspective (burden of proof, see answer to Question 20).

a) Is a formal liquidity status (liquidity balance sheet) required?
No (see *infra* (e)).

b) Is a sample of daily liquidity data (which do not amount to a proper liquidity status but show insufficient funds on different days within a certain period of time) sufficient?
No, not by itself (see *infra* (e)).

c) Does the law provide for a rebuttable presumption? If so, under which conditions?
No (see *infra* (e)).

d) Does the law provide for any technical circumstances (e.g. undisputed statutory demand, non-compliance with monetary judgments, unsuccessful enforcement proceedings, non-performance of a previous composition agreement in insolvency proceedings) the occurrence of which suffices to establish the debtor's insolvency?
No, not by itself, but these criteria might be deemed important facts when assessing the debtor's solvency/insolvency (see *infra* (e)).

e) Other means?
According to the Lithuanian Supreme Court (Court of Cassation) the insolvency of a legal person is associated also with other serious financial difficulties, which are reflected by the following signs:

(i) the legal person no longer carries out the activities defined in its articles of association or the activities carried out in the long term generate only losses and there are no prospects for restoring the normal performance of activities and stabilisation of the situation;
(ii) the legal person systematically fails to fulfil its obligations to creditors;
(iii) the legal person does not have sufficient assets for the satisfaction of the financial claims of creditors (Supreme Court of Lithuania, 20 May 2019, Civil case no. e3K-3-105-684/2019, paragraph 50).

(NB: this decision was rendered based on the definition of insolvency in the previous Enterprise Bankruptcy Law, in which "insolvency" was defined differently than the new JANI; the Lithuanian Court of Appeal and lower courts, however, have in multiple decisions rather uncritically reiterated this practice and signs when assessing "insolvency" under the new JANI: e.g. Lithuanian Court of Appeal, 13 October 2022, Civil case no. e2-1048-933/2022, paragraph 25; Lithuanian Court of Appeal, 27 July 2023, Civil case no. e2-747-910/2023, paragraph 14.).

Court practice holds that when deciding on the issue of opening of bankruptcy proceedings, it is important to thoroughly ascertain in each case whether the company is actually insolvent and will no longer be able to carry out its activities, or whether the company is in only temporary financial difficulties that can be resolved by preserving the company as a functioning market participant (Lithuanian Court of Appeal, 13 October 2022, paragraph 26; 27 July 2023, paragraph 15; see also Lithuanian Court of Appeal, 18 June 2024, Civil case no. e2-443-577/2024, paragraphs 22, 31).

This assessment of the debtor's insolvency must not be performed in a formalistic manner. According to court practice, in cases in which the formal criteria of insolvency are met, it is necessary to assess additionally the factual circumstances related to the legal person under assessment (from a solvency point of view) and in this regard to assess:

> the nature of the activities (inter alia, the extent to which the activities carried out are characterised by fluctuations and the trend of the markets in which the activities in question are being carried out),
>
> retrospective aspects (past results of the activities carried out, the way in which they have changed and the like),
>
> results (whether the activity has recently generated benefits or losses),
>
> prospects (whether the legal entity, even if it is in financial difficulties, can, in a short term, resume normal operations, stabilize its situation and eventually start generating economic or other benefits), etc.
>
> In addition, not only the legal person's own liabilities to creditors (payment rankings, structure, change, etc.), but also the trade receivables of the legal person being assessed, i.e. the trade receivable's size, structure, relationship to overdue liabilities to creditors, the prospect of getting satisfaction on these trade receivables, etc.

(See Supreme Court of Lithuania, 20 May 2019, Civil case no. e3K-3-105-684/2019, paragraph 49, Lithuanian Court of Appeal, 21 December 2023, Civil case no. e2-1176-933-2023, paragraph 31.)

Similarly, in the context of an individual's bankruptcy proceedings under FABI, the Lithuanian Supreme Court, interpreting the concept of insolvency of an individual, has noted the need to examine the debtor's prospect of settling the debt in the future

> according to Art. 2(2) of FABI, when deciding whether a natural person is able to meet his/her obligations, the court, inter alia, must assess the prospect of the development of the debt obligations, taking into account the person's assets and the person's incomes, i.e. the court must determine not only that the amount of debts maturing exceeds 25 MMA, but also whether the person objectively does not have the possibility to settle these debts either at the moment or within a reasonable period of time.

(See Kaunas Regional Court (Appellate Court), 28 September 2021, Civil case no. e2S-1526-924/2021, paragraphs 29 and 44 with references to Supreme Court decisions.)

Question 20: Is insolvency (inability to pay debts, overindebtedness, etc.) subject to party autonomy in the proceedings or must the court clarify them *ex officio*?

Insolvency is subject to party autonomy in the proceedings (Article 15 paragraph 2 JANI; Articles 12, 178 Civil Procedural Code). In the context of a corporate debtor opening proceedings (i.e. between the formal acceptance of an opening request and the decision to (not) open proceedings), there is an increased obligation on the court to be "active" which, however, does not amount to *ex officio* assessment. The defendant (debtor/company) bears the burden of proving that it is not insolvent (cf. Lithuanian Court of Appeal, 13 October 2022, Civil case no. e2-1048-933/2022, paragraphs 28, 37; Lithuanian Court of Appeal, 27 July 2023, Civil case no. e2-747-910/2023, paragraph 20).

Insolvency in the context of an individual's opening proceedings is in principle established following the same rules as explained above in the context of corporate insolvency proceedings. Insolvency is subject to party autonomy in individuals' bankruptcy proceedings (Article 5 paragraph 1 FABI; Article 178 Civil Procedural Code) and there is an increased obligation, in opening proceedings, for the court to be active (see Lithuanian Supreme Court, 19 November 2014, Civil case no. 3K-3-516/2014, p. 8), however this does not – as a rule – amount to *ex officio* assessment. In practice, insolvency courts tend to be more active in individuals' bankruptcy cases, e.g. by obliging the individual debtor to provide additional documents and information (based on Article 5 paragraph 3 FABI). One reason for this might be that the court examines the filing request in oral proceedings (whereas filing requests in corporate insolvencies are usually examined and decided in written proceedings). However, at the end of the day, also in individuals' bankruptcy cases, the individual must prove that it fulfils the requirements for opening proceedings, including his/her bankruptcy and honesty (*sąžiningumas*).

In the context of insolvency-related civil liability litigation for damages against the head of the company or other responsible persons (e.g. late filing, unlawful trading) the burden of proof usually follows the rules applied in standard civil disputes. According to Lithuanian legal doctrine and court practice, the liability of the head of the company and other responsible persons is based on tort (delict) and usually requires:

(i) unlawful conduct,
(ii) loss/damage,
(iii) causal link between the unlawful conduct and the loss/damages and
(iv) fault, i.e. negligent or deliberated behaviour

(Article 13 paragraph 1 JANI; Articles 6.246–6.249 Civil Code).

The claimant (e.g. bankruptcy administrator) must prove conditions (i), (ii) and (iii). Upon proof of these facts, the fault of the defendant is presumed and consequently he/she must prove that they did not act negligently or deliberately (Articles 178 and 182 paragraph 4 Civil Procedural Code (see e.g. Lithuanian Supreme Court, 16 October 2017, Civil case no. 3K-7-177-701/2017, paragraph 41)).

Different rules apply once the insolvency court has formally established so-called bankruptcy fraud (*tyčinis bankrotas*) in the sense of Article 70 paragraph 1 JANI:

> A court shall establish bankruptcy fraud where it determines that the insolvency of a legal person was due to deliberately poor management of the legal person (act and/or omission) and/or transactions entered into on behalf of the legal person, where it became known or should have been known that the entry into the transactions violates the rights and/or legitimate interests of creditors.

Once bankruptcy fraud is established, the above-mentioned conditions (i) unlawful act and (iii) causal link between unlawful conduct and damage are deemed to be established prejudicial facts, the other two conditions (ii) loss/damage and (iv) fault are presumed, so that the burden of proving a lack of loss/damage and fault lies with the defendant (see Lithuanian Supreme Court, 23 November 2018, Civil case no. 3K-456-378/2018).

Question 21: In an overall view, does your law distinguish "inability to pay debts" from "financial difficulties"? If so, how?

Yes, these terms are defined and used differently. See also answers to Questions 3, 5 and 6.

The term "financial difficulties" encompasses the inability to pay debts and the likelihood of insolvency.

Likelihood of insolvency means the state of a legal person in which there is a substantial likelihood of the legal person's becoming insolvent within the next three months.

Question 22: In an overall view, does it matter under your law whether the debtor's inability to pay debts is present or future and reversible or irreversible?

Yes, these aspects matter.

Question 23: Would you like to add any further aspects not covered by the above questions?

n.a.

III. CESSATION OF PAYMENTS

Question 24: In your jurisdiction, is "cessation of payments" a legal term used either in statute or in case law? (If the answer is "no", please continue with Question 31.)

No.

Question 25: Is "cessation of payments" an autonomous ground to commence proceedings (triggering circumstance)? You may refer to Questions 6/7 or add additional information here.

n.a.

Question 26: Is "cessation of payments" a means to establish inability to pay debts? If so, by which mechanism (e.g. rebuttable presumption for inability to pay debts, cf. above Question 19(c))?

n.a.

Question 27: How is "cessation of payments" defined? If it is defined in statute, please provide us here with an English translation of the relevant rule. Is this definition (if any) specified in case law? If so, how?

n.a.

Question 28: How is "cessation of payments" established?

n.a.

Question 29: Are there typical circumstances which provide circumstantial evidence that the debtor has ceased payments? If so, please list as many as possible.

n.a.

Question 30: Would you like to add any further aspects not covered by the above questions?

n.a.

IV. LIKELY/IMMINENT INABILITY TO PAY DEBTS

Question 31: Are the following terms available in your jurisdiction, either in statute or in case law? (If the answer is "no", please continue with Question 42.)

a) likely inability to pay debts
Yes (as part of the definition of likelihood of insolvency in Article 2 paragraph 7^1 JANI, see also answer to Question 5(c)).

b) imminent inability to pay debts
Yes (as part of the definition of likelihood of insolvency in Article 2 paragraph 7^1 JANI, see also answer to Question 5(c)).

c) other (similar) terms
"Likelihood of insolvency of a legal person" is defined in Article 2 paragraph 7^{1} JANI as "a situation in which there is a substantial likelihood of the legal person's becoming insolvent within the next three months."

Question 32: Is "likely/imminent inability to pay debts" an autonomous ground to commence proceedings (triggering circumstance)? You may refer to Questions 6/7 or add additional information here.

Yes; if other conditions are met then likely/imminent inability to pay debts (as part of the definition of "likelihood of insolvency") constitutes a ground upon which to commence restructuring proceedings (see answers to Questions 31, 5, 6(b)).

Question 33: If the answer to the previous Question is "yes", who may base filing for insolvency proceedings on it: only the debtor or also creditors?

Both (see Articles 4, 17, 21 in connection with Article 2 paragraphs 5 and 6 JANI). However, a creditor may file only if it has an overdue claim against the debtor exceeding 10 minimum monthly salaries (Article 4 paragraph 2 JANI; for the year 2024 this means that the claim must exceed EUR 9,240 (10 × EUR 924, see answer to Question 13)).

Question 34: How are these terms defined? If they are defined in statute, please provide us here with an English translation of the relevant rules. Is this definition (if any) specified in case law? If so, how?

a) likely inability to pay debts
See answers to Questions 5 and 31.

b) imminent inability to pay debts
See answers to Questions 5 and 31.

Question 35: Do the terms "likely" and "imminent" require a prognosis regarding the point in time when actual inability to pay debts will occur? If so, how long is the time period for this prognosis?

The term is three months. See answer to Question 31.

Question 36: Does your law require a specific grade of certainty that inability to pay debts will eventually occur? If so, is 50.1% ("more likely than not") enough or are there alleviated or aggravated prerequisites?

Statutory material law does not define a specific degree of certainty that inability to pay debts will eventually occur. Reliable court practice has not developed yet, since this concept of "likelihood of insolvency" – and with this the concepts of likely/imminent inability to pay debt – were introduced only recently.

Notwithstanding the above, the Lithuanian Court of Appeal recently heard a case in which the debtor requested the opening of restructuring proceedings while a third party objected, arguing *inter alia* that the debtor was solvent. The Court of Appeal upheld the first instance court's opening decision concluding:

> Given that there is no single model for determining the likelihood of insolvency when a company is solvent, but in the event of a dispute as to the point in time at which insolvency is likely to arise, if factors (such as the loss of a significant transaction, the emergence of a large tort claim, the emergence of a pandemic, etc.) are identified that could threaten the company's insolvency, priority should be given to the restructuring procedures.

(See Lithuanian Court of Appeal, 6 April 2023, Civil case no. e2-413-407/2023, paragraph 41; Lithuanian Court of Appeal, 18 June 2024, Civil case no. e2-443-577/2024.)

Question 37: Regarding "debts" and "financial means", are they defined in the same way as in the context of inability to pay debts (cf. above Questions 14/15)? If not, what are the differences?

Statutory law does not provide guidance. Reliable court practice has not developed yet, since this concept of "likelihood of insolvency" – and with this the concepts of likely/imminent inability to pay debt – were introduced only recently. However, I would expect that court practice will assess inability to pay debts by using the same developed principles and criteria as in the context of "debts" and "financial means". For more details see answer to Question 19.

Question 38: Further to Question 37: Are "debts" considered which do currently not exist or are not yet due but will foreseeably come into existence and become due during the prognosis period?

Statutory law does not provide clear guidance. Reliable court practice has not developed yet, since this concept of "*likelihood of insolvency*" – and with this the concepts of likely/imminent inability to pay debt – were introduced only recently. However, I would expect debts to be considered that will foreseeably come into existence and become due during the prognosis period.

Question 39: Also further to Question 37: Are "financial means" considered which do currently not exist but will foreseeably become available during the prognosis period?

Statutory law does not provide clear guidance. Reliable court practice has not developed yet, since this concept of "likelihood of insolvency" – and with this the concepts of likely/imminent inability to pay debts – were introduced only recently. However, I would expect financial means to be considered that will foreseeably come into existence and become due during the prognosis period.

Question 40: How are the terms "likely/imminent inability to pay debts" established?

Statutory law does not provide guidance. Reliable court practice has not developed yet, since this concept of "likelihood of insolvency" – and with this the concepts of likely/imminent inability to pay debt – were introduced only recently (see Lithuanian Court of Appeal, 18 June 2024, Civil case no. e2-443-577/2024, paragraph 21 et seq.). However, I would expect that court practice will assess inability to pay debts by using the same developed principles and criteria as in the context of debts and financial means (for more details see answer to Question 19). Furthermore, developing court practice in the context of likelihood of insolvency seems to confirm two things: firstly, the standard civil procedural rules apply concerning burden of proof of the parties and the examination of evidence by the court (see Lithuanian Court of Appeal, 4 April 2023, Civil case no. e2-413-407/2023, paragraph 30 et seq.). This is in line with established court practice for the determination of insolvency/solvency. Secondly, in cases of dispute and doubt, preference should be given to an affirmation of a likelihood of insolvency allowing the opening of restructuring proceedings (see Lithuanian Court of Appeal, 4 April 2023, Civil case no. e2-413-407/2023, paragraph 41 et seq.). This is also in line with recent court practice concerning the question, whether bankruptcy (liquidation) or restructuring proceedings should be opened. In case of doubt, preference should be given to the opening of restructuring proceedings (Lithuanian Court of Appeal, 18 June 2024, Civil case no. e2-443-577/2024, paragraphs 22, 31).

Question 41: Would you like to add any further aspects not covered by the above questions?

n.a.

V. OVERINDEBTEDNESS

Question 42: In your jurisdiction, is "overindebtedness", or "balance sheet insolvency" respectively, a legal term used either in statute or in case law? (If the answer is "no", please continue with Question 56.)

Yes (see answer to Question 3).

Question 43: Is "overindebtedness" an autonomous ground to commence proceedings (triggering circumstance)? You may refer to Questions 6/7 or add additional information here.

Yes, for legal persons (see answers to Questions 6 and 7).

Question 44: If the answer to the previous Question is "yes", is this applicable to corporate insolvencies of legal persons only or also to personal bankruptcies of natural persons?

To corporate insolvencies only (see answers to Questions 6 and 7).

Question 45: Is the term "overindebtedness" defined in statute? If so, please give the wording in English translation. Is this definition (if any) specified in case law? If so, how?

The law speaks of "overindebtedness" as the "state of the legal person … when liabilities of the legal person exceed the value of its assets" (see Article 2 paragraph 7 JANI). There is no further definition in the law itself.

Court practice does not further specify this definition. However, see *infra* answer to Question 46.

Question 46: Does your law refer to all existing debts or only to mature debts?

Current statutory law does not distinguish between debts and mature debts. As a starting point, all debts are to be taken into account. However, applying additional principles developed in case law (see answer to Question 19(e)), the court will assess facts and evidence, including the maturity of debts, to determine whether they support the insolvency (e.g. formal overindebtedness) or whether they are rather of a non-systematic and temporary nature that do not prevent the debtor from continuing or recommencing successful business or other activities.

Question 47: Does the rank of certain debts play a role when establishing overindebtedness? In particular, is there any possibility to conclude agreements according to which certain debts shall not be taken into account (e.g. agreements on subsidiarity)?

Current statutory law does not distinguish between ranking of debts. As a starting points, all debts are to be taken into account. Lithuanian law does not recognise *de jure* recategorisation of certain debt into subordinate debt, as, for example, German law previously did (*eigenkapitalsersetzende Darlehen*). Neither would local accounting standards in the context of normal corporations (as compared to financial institutions) allow shareholder debt to be recategorised for balance sheet purposes as subordinate debt based on agreements between shareholder and company. However, applying additional principles developed in case law (see answer to Question 19), the court will assess facts and evidence to determine whether they support the insolvency (e.g. formal overindebtedness) or whether they are rather of a non-systematic and temporary nature that does not prevent the debtor from continuing or recommencing successful business or other activities. In this context courts would probably take into consideration subordination of shareholder debt, as it shows that the shareholder is not enforcing its claim.

Question 48: Which assets are taken into account when overindebtedness is established: the complete set of assets or only a selection of them?

The complete set of assets is taken into consideration, including assets that are not included in the balance sheet. The real value of the assets is to be determined based on financial statements, accounting data and other evidence presented to the court by the parties or collected on the initiative of the court. As explained *supra* in answer to Question 19(e), the court will also assess additional criteria, including trends of the financial indicators, to determine whether in the case at hand the financial difficulties are systematic and not merely temporary.

Question 49: How are the debtor's assets valued: by referring to the liquidation value, the book value, the going concern value or in another way?

Neither statutory law nor case law define exactly how the debtor's assets are to be valued. Overindebtness has to be established by determining the real value of the assets. See answers to Question 48 and Question 19(e) for more details. Unlike e.g. Germany, in Lithuanian opening proceedings courts usually do not appoint experts to determine overindebtedness, inability to pay debts or similar. Rather, the court relies on the facts and evidence presented by the parties in the case at hand and, less often, on additional evidence requested by the court on its own initiative (e.g. by questioning the general manager or accountant of the debtor).

Question 50: Is there any prognostic element, e.g. regarding the debtor's chances to continue the business?

Yes, there is a prognostic element. However, this is not stated in the law and not applied in a formalised way. Rather, the prospects of the debtor continuing or recommencing its business activities is one of the criteria assessed by courts when assessing "insolvency" (see answer to Question 19(e)).

Question 51: If the answer to the previous Question is "yes", what exactly is the topic of the prognosis and how is it established?

The prospect of a debtor continuing or recommencing its economic or other activity is one important aspect of establishing whether the financial difficulties are of a systematic or a merely temporary nature. If there is a positive prognosis, then based on current court practice and the case at hand, the court will either be unlikely to deem the company insolvent at all even if a formal approach would confirm illiquidity or overindebtedness, or in situations, in which the court must decide whether bankruptcy (liquidation) or restructuring proceedings should be opened, in case of doubt, preference would be given to the opening of restructuring proceedings (see answer to Question 40).

Question 52: If the answer to Question 50 is "yes", how long is the prognosis period?

Not defined in law or court practice.

Question 53: How is overindebtedness established?

a) Is a formal balance sheet required?
No formal balance sheet like the German *Überschuldungsstatus* is required for the assessment of overindebtedness.

b) Does the yearly regular commercial balance sheet have any meaning (given that it is normally based on technical values and does not display undisclosed reserves)?
Yes, but it is (only) one of the relevant documents for the assessment of "insolvency", including overindebtedness.

c) Does the law provide for a presumption? If so, under which conditions?
No.

d) Other means?
See answer to Question 19(e).

Question 54: Is the legal link to overindebtedness undisputed in literature or are there efforts to abolish it?

Overindebtness, as a stand-alone trigger and insolvency ground, was established only recently. Shortly before and after the introduction of this new concept, there were discussions and criticism levelled at it. Currently, there are no serious discussions or even efforts to abolish it.

Question 55: Would you like to add any further aspects not covered by the above questions?

n.a.

VI. REMAINING ISSUES

Question 56: Is there anything else you would like to share in the present context and that we should take into account?

n.a.

LUXEMBOURG

Pier Mario LUPINU

I. GENERAL

Question 1: How is insolvency (both in the context of liquidation and restructuring/reorganisation) regulated in your jurisdiction? Please give a brief overview, at least enumerating the relevant statutes.

The general insolvency regime for Luxembourg is governed by:

- Law of 14 April 1886 on composition with creditors, as amended;
- Grand Ducal Regulation of 24 May 1935 on controlled management;
- Luxembourg Commercial Code (hereinafter, the "Commercial Code"), which deals more specifically with stays of payments and bankruptcy proceedings;
- Council Regulation (EC) No. 848/2015 of 20 May 2015 on insolvency proceedings;[1]
- Law of 7 August 2023 on business preservation and modernisation of the bankruptcy law.[2]

The Luxembourg legal framework for insolvency distinguishes between bankruptcy proceedings, in which the procedure foresees the wind up of

1 Regulation (EU) 2015/848 of the European Parliament and of the Council of 20 May 2015 on insolvency proceedings (recast) OJ of 5 June 2015, L141/19.

2 Loi du 7 août 2023 relative à la préservation des entreprises et portant modernisation du droit de la faillite, modifiant : 1° le livre III du Code de commerce ; 2° le livre II, titre IX, chapitre II, section I du Code pénal ; 3° les articles 257 et 555 du Nouveau Code de Procédure civile ; 4° la loi modifiée du 10 août 1915 concernant les sociétés commerciales ; 5° la loi uniforme modifiée sur les lettres de change et billets à ordre, telle qu'elle a été introduite dans la législation nationale par la loi du 8 janvier 1962 ; 6° la loi modifiée du 7 juillet 1971 portant, en matière répressive et administrative, institution d'experts, de traducteurs et d'interprètes, de conciliateurs d'entreprise et mandataires de justice assermentés et complétant les dispositions légales relatives à l'assermentation des experts, traducteurs et interprètes ; 7° la loi modifiée du 23 juillet 1991 ayant pour objet de réglementer les activités de sous-traitance ; 8° la loi modifiée du 8 juin 1999 sur le budget, la comptabilité et la trésorerie de l'État ; 9° la loi modifiée du 19 décembre 2002 concernant le registre de commerce et des sociétés ainsi que la comptabilité et les comptes annuels des entreprises ; 10° la loi modifiée du 5 août 2005 sur les contrats de garantie financière. Dossier n° 6539A.

the debtor (Articles 437 et seq. of the Commercial Code) and three types of proceedings in which the objective is that of the reorganisation of the debtor, namely (i) controlled management (Grand Ducal Decree of 24 May 1935 on controlled management), (ii) composition with creditors to avoid bankruptcy (Law of 14 April 1886 on composition with creditors, as amended) and (iii) stay of payments (Articles 593 et seq. of the Commercial Code).

The above list should include other proceedings which specifically target credit institutions, insurance undertakings and investment funds. However, those proceedings do not fall within the scope of the present work.

The available reorganisation measures were not used in practice and a significant reform of this regime was foreseen and has been ongoing for several years. In this context, Directive 2019/1023 on preventive restructuring frameworks[3] gave the push to the Luxembourg legislator to undertake a significant overhaul and modernisation of its reorganisation regime by introducing the above-mentioned Law of 7 August 2023 (see more in the answer to Question 56 *infra*).

Question 2: Related to paragraph 10 above of the Introduction: seen from a principle-based perspective, what justifies the opening of insolvency proceedings in your jurisdiction?

In Luxembourg, insolvency proceedings target debtors that are engaged in commercial activities, meaning that those activities are their profession. Those debtors can be subject to insolvency proceedings when two conditions are met *cumulatively*, namely, they cannot pay debts as they fall due (i.e. cessation of payments) and they do not have access to credit (Article 437 of the Commercial Code).

Question 3: Does your national law in the context of liquidation proceedings use one or more of the following terms (be it as a noun, be it as an adjective or adjunct) in whatever context:

a) inability to pay debts

No. According to Luxembourg law, cash-flow insolvency shall be regarded as the inability to raise credit.

b) cessation of payments

Yes, in the context of the opening of insolvency proceedings.

3 Directive (EU) 2019/1023 of the European Parliament and of the Council of 20 June 2019 on preventive restructuring frameworks, on discharge of debt and disqualifications, and on measures to increase the efficiency of procedures concerning restructuring, insolvency and discharge of debt, and amending Directive (EU) 2017/1132 (Directive on restructuring and insolvency), OJ of 26 June 2019, L172/18.

c) likely inability to pay debts
No.

d) imminent inability to pay debts
No.

e) overindebtedness?
No. The Luxembourg regime for overindebtedness applies to natural persons only.

Question 4: Are the same terms (and with the same meaning) used in the rules on preliminary/interim insolvency proceedings (e.g. concerning the application stage of the proceedings)?

Yes.

Question 5: Does your national law in the context of restructuring proceedings (as referred to above at paragraph 8 of the Introduction, i.e. both pre-insolvency and within formal insolvency proceedings) use one or more of the following terms (be it as a noun, be it as an adjective or adjunct) in whatever context:

a) inability to pay debts
No. See answer to Question 3(a) *supra.*

b) cessation of payments
Yes. The Law of 7 August 2023 on reorganisation procedures modifies Article 442 of the Commercial Code which refers to the cessation of payments.

c) likely inability to pay debts
No. In theory, such inability is mentioned in the context of the suspension of payments, but it must not be interpreted in connection to the element of time. Instead, it refers to the event that triggers the circumstances leading to the request for the suspension of payments.[4]

d) imminent inability to pay debts
No. See answer to Question 5(c) *supra.*

e) overindebtedness?
No. See answer to Question 3(e) *supra.*

Question 6: Which of the terms mentioned in Questions 3 and 5 are used for defining grounds to commence proceedings (triggering circumstances)?

a) insolvency proceedings
"Cessation of payments", which should not be confused with the concept of insolvency. While insolvency presumes a "balance sheet test", according to

4 See *Winandy*, Manuel de droit des sociétés, Legitech, Luxembourg 2019, p. 1015.

Luxembourg law the cessation of payments does not have statutory elements that characterise it. Hence, it is largely at the discretion of the judge to declare that the debtor has ceased payments.[5]

b) restructuring proceedings
"Cessation of payments". If, in this respect, natural persons are considered too, then overindebtedness should be included.

Question 7: Does the answer to Question 6 include personal bankruptcies of natural persons or only corporate insolvencies of legal entities?

Since in Luxembourg there is an overindebtedness procedure (*surendettement*) applicable to individuals, the answer to Question 6 includes both personal bankruptcies of natural persons and corporate insolvencies of legal entities.

Question 8: In your law, are there any other circumstances which trigger insolvency or restructuring proceedings?

Next to the inability to pay debts or the cessation of payments, the circumstance of the impossibility for the debtor to raise credit from banks, suppliers or creditors (*ébranlement du crédit*, a sort of credit crunch) is one of the circumstances that trigger insolvency.

Question 9: Which of the terms mentioned in Questions 3, 5, and 8 are used in the context of transactions avoidance law?

The cessation of payments is used in the context of transactions avoidance law, since the court has to determine the occurrence of such cessation together with the duration of the "hardening period" following the transaction.

Question 10: Which of the terms addressed in Questions 3, 5, and 8 are used in the context of directors' duties?

a) shift of duties (from shareholders to creditors)
n.a.

b) duties to commence insolvency proceedings
There is a statutory obligation for directors to file for bankruptcy within one month of the cessation of payments. Should directors breach their filing obligations, they can be held liable under Luxembourg law. Therefore, cessation of payments is the only term used among those addressed.

c) other duties (please describe)
n.a.

---

5 Ibid., pp. 929–930.

Question 11: Are there any other rules in the context of which the terms addressed in Questions 3, 5, and 8 are used?

No.

Question 12: Is the definition of (the subspecies of) insolvency identical in all legal fields or are there different definitions (e.g. different in insolvency law than in criminal law)?

Luxembourg law does not encompass a definition of insolvency. The legislation mentioned in Question 1 *supra* makes use of the French term *faillite* (i.e. bankruptcy) for identifying what is generally understood as insolvency. For example, the term bankruptcy (*faillite*) is used in Article 438 of the Commercial Code also for those circumstances in which it becomes a criminal offence ("*La faillite ... est qualifiée banqueroute frauduleuse et punie criminellement*").

II. INABILITY TO PAY DEBTS

Question 13: In your jurisdiction, is the term "inability to pay debts" defined in statute? If so, please give the wording in English translation. Is this definition (if any) specified in case law? If so, how?

No, it is not defined. The criteria for insolvency under Luxembourg law are the cessation of payments and the inability to raise credit.

Question 14: Does your law refer to all debts or only to mature debts?

Luxembourg law refers to mature debts. In fact, one of the key criteria for identifying a debt under Luxembourg insolvency law is its enforceability (or, better, collectability), meaning that the debt is due.

Question 15: Which assets are taken into account when assessing the inability to pay debts: all (financial) assets or only those that are liquid, i.e. available on short notice?

According to the Commercial Code, debts need to be certain, liquid, due and payable.

Question 16: Is any liquidity gap (deficit between relevant financial means and relevant debts) relevant or does your law neglect minor gaps? If the latter, how is "minor" defined?

In Luxembourg, next to the debts that have not been paid there is the need to ascertain the impossibility for the debtor to obtain credit. See Question 6(a) *supra*. The financial means as such have to be considered in a broader sense. This means that the judge will consider also the ability of the debtor to raise additional credit or to expect forthcoming payments.

Question 17: As far as the time aspect is concerned, does it matter whether the liquidity gap can be closed again in the short term? If so, how long is the grace period?

Luxembourg law focuses on the certainty of the debt. It should be permanent, because if it is temporary it cannot be sufficient to declare the cessation of payments. Therefore, temporary financial difficulties cannot be considered in this respect. Nevertheless, there can be a temporary cessation of payments in the context of the suspension of payments when the debtor is not insolvent (Article 593 of the Commercial Code).[6] The debtor is also allowed to suspend its obligations unilaterally in the context of a reorganisation procedure under the Law of 7 August 2023.

Question 18: As far as the time aspect is concerned, is a debtor considered insolvent if the liquidity gap is not yet present but will occur soon? If so, how long is the prognosis period? (Note: this may also concern the difference between actual and likely/imminent inability to pay debts; cf. below Question 34).

The certainty of the debt is the relevant element when talking about time. The debtor is considered insolvent when the debt has fallen due on the day that the bankruptcy judgment takes place or before if it falls within the hardening period. A debt that will occur soon cannot be considered certain or permanent under Luxembourg law. Therefore, it cannot be considered for bankruptcy purposes but only for the suspension of payments or reorganisation procedures (see answer to Question 17 *supra*). It is important to highlight that, in case of reorganisation procedures, the debtor cannot be considered as insolvent already from the moment in which such debtor files a request for reorganisation (Article 18(1) of the Law of 7 August 2023).

Question 19: How is inability to pay debts established? Please communicate if there is a difference between a creditor and a debtor application or between different legal contexts.

a) Is a formal liquidity status (liquidity balance sheet) required?
While the balance sheet test is not relevant under Luxembourg law, the liquidity of the debt is one of the key elements that the judge has to evaluate when the two

6 *Winandy*, ibid., p. 1015.

conditions of the cessation of payments and the inability to raise credit occur simultaneously.

b) Is a sample of daily liquidity data (which do not amount to a proper liquidity status but show insufficient funds on different days within a certain period of time) sufficient?
No. Liquidity and certainty of the debt are conditions that the judge should be able to verify when the bankruptcy judgment occurs. An element linked to the sample of daily liquidity data can be presumed in the case in which the debtor files for bankruptcy, as such debtor is required to present a balance sheet of his business (Article 441 of the Commercial Code).[7]

c) Does the law provide for a rebuttable presumption? If so, under which conditions?
No. Certainty is one of the pillars that help the judge in establishing the characteristics of a debt. The case in which a rebuttable presumption is relevant is in the event of the requirement to demonstrate the centre of main interests (COMI). Such COMI should correspond to the registered office of a Luxembourg company.

d) Does the law provide for any technical circumstances (e.g. undisputed statutory demand, non-compliance with monetary judgments, unsuccessful enforcement proceedings, non-performance of a previous composition agreement in insolvency proceedings) the occurrence of which suffices to establish the debtor's insolvency?
Yes, for example, in the case of fraudulent bankruptcy. As concerns a composition agreement (*concordat*), the creditors can request its annulment and the judge can examine such agreement on his/her own initiative every three months. As a result, the judge can declare bankruptcy or annul the composition agreement (Article 26 of the Law of 14 April 1886 on composition with creditors to prevent bankruptcy: https://legilux.public.lu/eli/etat/leg/loi/1886/04/14/n1/jo).[8]

e) Other means?
n.a.

Question 20: Is insolvency (inability to pay debts, overindebtedness, etc.) subject to party autonomy in the proceedings or must the court clarify them *ex officio*?

Discretion over bankruptcy proceedings lies with the court, including the decision on whether the conditions are met. Commonly creditors or shareholders cannot

7 *Winandy*, ibid., pp. 938–939.
8 Ibid., pp. 934–936.

exercise any form of control or influence over the process or the decisions to be made by the judge. However, the receiver (*curateur*) has the option to involve them by exercising the receiver's own discretion.

Question 21: In an overall view, does your law distinguish "inability to pay debts" from "financial difficulties"? If so, how?

Yes. It could be interpreted that Luxembourg law makes this distinction. The inability to pay debts stems from the cessation of payments (voluntary or involuntary) but, at the same time, the debtor should have problems with its creditworthiness or inability to raise credit from banks, suppliers or creditors. This circumstance could be interpreted as a financial difficulty.

Question 22: In an overall view, does it matter under your law whether the debtor's inability to pay debts is present or future and reversible or irreversible?

Yes, it matters. While the refusal or impossibility to pay a single debt (regardless of the amount) which is certain, liquid and payable should, in theory, suffice to establish the cessation of payments, a simple temporary problem of cash flow does not imply insolvency, provided that the debtor succeeds in obtaining the necessary credit to continue operations and honour commitments. In this way, it can be considered that the inability to pay, linked to the ability to obtain credit, could be reversible. This also applies in the case of the suspension of payments and the reorganisation of businesses (see answer to Question 17 *supra*).

Question 23: Would you like to add any further aspects not covered by the above questions?

No.

III. CESSATION OF PAYMENTS

Question 24: In your jurisdiction, is "cessation of payments" a legal term used either in statute or in case law? (If the answer is "no", please continue with Question 31.)

Yes, in Articles 437, 440, 445, 446, 447, 449, 466, 472 and 473 of the Commercial Code and Articles 75 and 77 of the Law of 7 August 2023, which introduce the term of the cessation of payments in Articles 442 and 490 of the Commercial Code.

Question 25: Is "cessation of payments" an autonomous ground to commence proceedings (triggering circumstance)? You may refer to Questions 6/7 or add additional information here.

Cessation of payments can be definitely considered as a triggering circumstance. However, it is not an autonomous ground since it should be accompanied by the inability or impossibility for the debtor to raise credit (*ébranlement du crédit*).

Question 26: Is "cessation of payments" a means to establish inability to pay debts? If so, by which mechanism (e.g. rebuttable presumption for inability to pay debts, cf. above Question 19(c))?

Yes. It is important that the debt is certain, liquid and payable (i.e. due). These are the criteria on which the judge would need to base the judgment.

Question 27: How is "cessation of payments" defined? If it is defined in statute, please provide us here with an English translation of the relevant rule. Is this definition (if any) specified in case law? If so, how?

The cessation of payments is not defined in the Commercial Code. However, it can be presupposed through the non-payment of certain, liquid and payable debts as, for example, social security payments or salaries, term or conditional debts and simply natural obligations are not sufficient.

Question 28: How is "cessation of payments" established?

The cessation of payments, if established cumulatively with the condition of the inability to raise credit, prompts the debtor/merchant/company to file for bankruptcy within one month, to be counted from the day of the cessation of payments (Article 440 of the Commercial Code). The cessation can be assumed from the basic rules concerning debts, which have to be certain, liquid and mature on the day of the court's decision to open the bankruptcy proceedings or within the hardening period. Hence non-mature debts are considered null and void.

Question 29: Are there typical circumstances which provide circumstantial evidence that the debtor has ceased payments? If so, please list as many as possible.

No, because the determination of whether the debtor has ceased payments is a matter for the discretion of the judge.[9]

---

9 *Winandy*, ibid., p. 928.

Question 30: Would you like to add any further aspects not covered by the above questions?

No.

IV. LIKELY/IMMINENT INABILITY TO PAY DEBTS

Question 31: Are the following terms available in your jurisdiction, either in statute or in case law? (If the answer is "no", please continue with Question 42.)

a) likely inability to pay debts
No.

b) imminent inability to pay debts
No.

c) other (similar) terms
No.

Question 32: Is "likely/imminent inability to pay debts" an autonomous ground to commence proceedings (triggering circumstance)? You may refer to Questions 6/7 or add additional information here.

No.

Question 33: If the answer to the previous Question is "yes", who may base filing for insolvency proceedings on it: only the debtor or also creditors?

n.a.

Question 34: How are these terms defined? If they are defined in statute, please provide us here with an English translation of the relevant rules. Is this definition (if any) specified in case law? If so, how?

a) likely inability to pay debts
n.a.

b) imminent inability to pay debts
n.a.

Question 35: Do the terms "likely" and "imminent" require a prognosis regarding the point in time when actual inability to pay debts will occur? If so, how long is the time period for this prognosis?

n.a.

Question 36: Does your law require a specific grade of certainty that inability to pay debts will eventually occur? If so, is 50.1% ("more likely than not") enough or are there alleviated or aggravated prerequisites?

n.a.

Question 37: Regarding "debts" and "financial means", are they defined in the same way as in the context of inability to pay debts (cf. above Questions 14/15)? If not, what are the differences?

n.a.

Question 38: Further to Question 37: Are "debts" considered which do currently not exist or are not yet due but will foreseeably come into existence and become due during the prognosis period?

n.a.

Question 39: Also further to Question 37: Are "financial means" considered which do currently not exist but will foreseeably become available during the prognosis period?

n.a.

Question 40: How are the terms "likely/imminent inability to pay debts" established?

n.a.

Question 41: Would you like to add any further aspects not covered by the above questions?

No.

V. OVERINDEBTEDNESS

Question 42: In your jurisdiction, is "overindebtedness", or "balance sheet insolvency" respectively, a legal term used either in statute or in case law? (If the answer is "no", please continue with Question 56.)

Yes. Overindebtedness (*surendettement*) is a term used in the Law of 8 January 2013 concerning overindebtedness[10] and the Grand-Ducal Regulation

[10] Loi du 8 janvier 2013 concernant le surendettement, in force from 1 February 2014: https://legilux.public.lu/eli/etat/leg/loi/2013/01/08/n1/jo.

of 17 January 2014 implementing the law of 8 January 2013 concerning overindebtedness,[11] which is the most recent law on overindebtedness, having modified Article 536 of the Commercial Code and replaced the previous Law of 8 December 2000 on the same topic.[12] The recent Law of 7 August 2023 (see answer to Questions 1 *supra* and 56 *infra*) also brings novelties concerning the regime of overindebtedness.

The previous law included a conventional settlement phase (*phase de règlement conventionnel*) before the Mediation Commission and then a judicial settlement phase (*phase de règlement judiciaire*) before the Justice of the Peace. The Law of 8 January 2013 is supplemented by the introduction of a third phase in the form of a civil bankruptcy procedure known as a personal recovery procedure (*procédure de rétablissement personnel*). This third phase is characterised by subsidiarity with respect to the previous two other phases. If the measures adopted in those two phases fail, meaning that the overindebted debtor is in an "irremediably compromised situation", the personal recovery procedure can be activated.

Question 43: Is "overindebtedness" an autonomous ground to commence proceedings (triggering circumstance)? You may refer to Questions 6/7 or add additional information here.

Yes, even though in Luxembourg is considered as an autonomous ground with reference to natural persons.

Question 44: If the answer to the previous Question is "yes", is this applicable to corporate insolvencies of legal persons only or also to personal bankruptcies of natural persons?

It is exclusively applicable to personal bankruptcies of natural persons resident in the Grand Duchy of Luxembourg.

Question 45: Is the term "overindebtedness" defined in statute? If so, please give the wording in English translation. Is this definition (if any) specified in case law? If so, how?

Yes. Article 2 of the Law concerning overindebtedness (see answer to Question 42 *supra*) states that the situation of overindebtedness of natural persons is characterised by the manifest impossibility for the debtor domiciled in the Grand Duchy of Luxembourg to meet all of his non-professional debts due and

[11] Règlement grand-ducal du 17 janvier 2014 portant exécution de la loi du 8 janvier 2013 concernant le surendettement: https://data.legilux.public.lu/filestore/eli/etat/leg/rgd/2014/01/17/n1/jo/fr/html/eli-etat-leg-rgd-2014-01-17-n1-jo-fr-html.html.

[12] See: https://legilux.public.lu/eli/etat/leg/loi/2000/12/08/n1/jo.

falling due as well as the commitment that the debtor has given to guarantee or to pay jointly and severally the debt of an individual entrepreneur or a company if the debtor has not been, in fact or in law, a manager of the latter company.[13]

Question 46: Does your law refer to all existing debts or only to mature debts?

In light of the explanation provided in Question 44 *supra*, the debts that are eligible for this process are all those considered "non-professional". Those debts include bank debts, such as real estate loans, consumer loans, account overdrafts; debts for current charges, such as unpaid energy, water, telephone and tax bills; debts resulting from a guarantee given in favour of an entrepreneur or a company; and, under certain specific conditions, maintenance debts (i.e. alimony to children or spouse), rent arrears and fines linked to a criminal conviction, or even reparations to victims. The nature of these debts leads to the assumption that all existing debts falling within the above categories can be considered eligible.

Question 47: Does the rank of certain debts play a role when establishing overindebtedness? In particular, is there any possibility to conclude agreements according to which certain debts shall not be taken into account (e.g. agreements on subsidiarity)?

Following the judicial liquidation, if the judge terminates the personal recovery procedure for insufficient assets (*insuffisance d'actif*), this will result in the cancellation of all non-professional debts. However, the cancellation does not apply to debts that the guarantor has paid in place of the debtor. The same applies to alimony debts and monetary reparations awarded to victims of acts of wilful violence for the damage suffered. For this last category, cancellation can take place if there is an agreement for the forgiveness, rescheduling or cancellation of the debts.

Question 48: Which assets are taken into account when overindebtedness is established: the complete set of assets or only a selection of them?

Please see the answer to Question 46 *supra*.

Question 49: How are the debtor's assets valued: by referring to the liquidation value, the book value, the going concern value or in another way?

See answer to Question 48 *supra*.

---

13 See Chambre des Salaries Luxembourg, "Le surendettement et la procédure de règlement collectif", *Dialogue thematique no. 2* (2014), 7, available at: https://www.csl.lu/app/uploads/2020/08/201405_csl_lesurendettementetlaproceduredereglementcollectif.pdf.

Question 50: Is there any prognostic element, e.g. regarding the debtor's chances to continue the business?

In principle, the overindebted debtor is subject to the obligation of good conduct and such obligation applies to the three phases of the collective debt settlement procedure explained in Question 42 *supra*. Moreover, the debtor shall not favour any of his creditors. Concerning the chances to continue the business, this is not foreseen in Luxembourg because overindebtedness is strictly linked to the non-professional nature of the debts.

Question 51: If the answer to the previous Question is "yes", what exactly is the topic of the prognosis and how is it established?

See answer to Question 50 *supra*.

Question 52: If the answer to Question 50 is "yes", how long is the prognosis period?

n.a.

Question 53: How is overindebtedness established?

a) Is a formal balance sheet required?
No.

b) Does the yearly regular commercial balance sheet have any meaning (given that it is normally based on technical values and does not display undisclosed reserves)?
No.

c) Does the law provide for a presumption? If so, under which conditions?
The only presumption can be the good conduct of the debtor which, however, refers to the period of the various phases listed in Question 42 *supra* and not the period preceding the submission of the dossier to the Overindebtedness Information and Advice Service (*Service d'information et de conseil en matière de surendettement*, SICS).

d) Other means?
According to the provisions contained in the Law of 8 December 2000, an overindebted debtor has to submit his request for conventional debt settlement to the SICS, which examines the file and, in consultation with the debtor, his creditors and, where applicable, other organisations providing services for the benefit of the debtor, draws up a draft recovery plan which the debtor submits to the Mediation Commission. The Law of 8 January 2013 made the Mediation Commission the main actor deciding on the admission of the debtor's request and subsequently entrusting the SICS with examining such request. See also answer to Question 45 *supra*.

Question 54: Is the legal link to overindebtedness undisputed in literature or are there efforts to abolish it?

While the legal link is undisputed, the recent Law of 7 August 2023 provides modifications affecting overindebtedness. These, however, do not go in the direction of abolishing but rather broadening the types of proceedings to settle the procedure.

Question 55: Would you like to add any further aspects not covered by the above questions?

No, but please refer to Questions 42 and 56 *supra* for the "novelties" in Luxembourg with reference to the regime of overindebtedness.

VI. REMAINING ISSUES

Question 56: Is there anything else you would like to share in the present context and that we should take into account?

Luxembourg's Parliament recently approved the Law of 7 August 2023 mentioned in Question 1 *supra* which, apart from introducing a new regime for the reorganisation of businesses, modifies certain articles of the third "book" of the Commercial Code, the one concerning insolvency. The Law came into force on 1 November 2023.

This has been a long-awaited law, not only because it follows the delayed transposition of Directive 2019/1023, but also because such law sees the light after more than a decade since the presentation of the Draft Bill (n° 6539).[14]

The new law contains four aspects: preventive, restorative, repressive and social.

- The preventive aspect aims at collecting data concerning companies in financial difficulties in order to channel them into reorganisation procedures at a stage when those procedures can be still efficient and will avoid bankruptcy.
- The restorative aspect targets natural persons in the position of entrepreneurs that have already experienced a failure of their business and therefore are given a sort of "second chance" under the new Law. In this respect, the good faith of the entrepreneur is an essential element.

[14] Following the entry into force of the Directive 2019/1023, Draft Bill no. 6539 was split in two (i.e. 6539A and 6539B). Draft Bill no. 6539A is the one that was then approved, becoming the Law of 7 August 2023. Draft Bill no. 6539B concerns modifications to the compulsory liquidation regime and it is still under discussion in the Parliament.

- The repressive aspect has the objective of eradicating or limiting the phenomenon of abandoning a business and then starting a new one without experiencing any consequences from such behaviour. This phenomenon leaves a number of so-called "empty shells", and Luxembourg aims to eliminate those abandoned businesses in a convenient and efficient manner, while avoiding bankruptcy proceedings. Unlike the restorative aspect, the key element in this respect is the bad faith of the entrepreneur.
- The social aspect has as its main objective the protection of the workers of failing or distressed companies. In fact, this aspect states that all the rights and obligations that are included in the relevant employment contracts will be transferred to the purchaser, although the latter still retains the possibility (to be duly supported by technical, economic and organisational reasons) to choose the employees that it wants to retain.

MALTA

Arthur GALEA SALOMONE

I. GENERAL

Question 1: How is insolvency (both in the context of liquidation and restructuring/reorganisation) regulated in your jurisdiction? Please give a brief overview, at least enumerating the relevant statutes.

Pre-insolvency and restructuring are regulated by the Pre-Insolvency Act (Act No. XXIV of 2022). The Pre-Insolvency Act partially transposes EU Directive 2019/1023 on preventive restructuring frameworks, on discharge of debt and disqualifications, and on measures to increase the efficiency of procedures concerning restructuring, insolvency and discharge of debt. The law provides for early warning signs of insolvency and restructuring procedures directed at avoiding insolvency.

There is no separate Insolvency Act in Malta. Liquidation and insolvency are extensively regulated in terms of the Companies Act (Chapter 368 of the Laws of Malta) (hereinafter the "Companies Act") which provides for members voluntary winding up, creditors voluntary winding up and court winding up.

Insolvency practitioners are regulated by the Insolvency Practitioners Act (Act XXV of 2022). The Act partially transposes EU Directive 2019/1023 and introduces comprehensive regulation for insolvency practitioners. Such practitioners need to be authorised to act as an insolvency practitioner. The Act also introduces the Insolvency and Receivership Service within the Malta Business Registry to act as the Competent Authority, which will regulate the conduct of insolvency practitioners.

Question 2: Related to paragraph 10 above of the Introduction: seen from a principle-based perspective, what justifies the opening of insolvency proceedings in your jurisdiction?

There are various principle-based justifications for the opening of insolvency proceedings. One justification is the suspension of the pursuit of rights and remedies by individual creditors and its replacement by collective proceedings, providing for a regulated and orderly realisation of assets and distribution of proceeds. Collective proceedings are also a means of upholding the *par condicio creditorum* principle, by which creditors are treated equally, saving lawful preferences which allow for distribution of proceeds and settlement of debts in accordance with established ranking rules. Insolvency proceedings cater for the avoidance and reversal of transactions which unfairly prejudice the general body of creditors, such as is the case with transaction avoidance provisions. Insolvency proceedings also provide the means to divest directors of the management and administration of the company they run, enabling an examination of their conduct and the imposition of liability for culpable management and/or the meting out of disqualification orders, thereby protecting the public against future improper trading by delinquent directors.

Question 3: Does your national law in the context of liquidation proceedings use one or more of the following terms (be it as a noun, be it as an adjective or adjunct) in whatever context:

a) inability to pay debts
Yes.

b) cessation of payments
No.

c) likely inability to pay debts
No.

d) imminent inability to pay debts
No.

e) overindebtedness?
No.

Question 4: Are the same terms (and with the same meaning) used in the rules on preliminary/interim insolvency proceedings (e.g. concerning the application stage of the proceedings)?

At application stage for insolvent winding up reference is still made to inability to pay debts.

Question 5: Does your national law in the context of restructuring proceedings (as referred to above at paragraph 8 of the Introduction, i.e. both pre-insolvency and within formal insolvency proceedings) use one or more of the following terms (be it as a noun, be it as an adjective or adjunct) in whatever context:

a) inability to pay debts
No.

b) cessation of payments
No.

c) likely inability to pay debts
No.

d) imminent inability to pay debts
No.

e) overindebtedness?
No.

Question 6: Which of the terms mentioned in Questions 3 and 5 are used for defining grounds to commence proceedings (triggering circumstances)?

a) insolvency proceedings
Inability to pay debts may trigger insolvent liquidation.

b) restructuring proceedings
Likelihood of insolvency may trigger restructuring proceedings.

Question 7: Does the answer to Question 6 include personal bankruptcies of natural persons or only corporate insolvencies of legal entities?

Personal bankruptcy is regulated separately under the Commercial Code (Chapter 13 of the Laws of Malta). All of the answers in this questionnaire relate to insolvency of limited liability companies. The term insolvency is only used in relation to limited liability companies, whereas the term bankruptcy is used in relation to personal traders, partnerships *en commandite* and partnerships *en nom collectif*. This dichotomy in terminology is also attributable to the different sources of law. Whereas the drafting of the insolvency provisions relating to limited liability companies in the Companies Act was influenced by English statutory law applicable at the time, the provisions relating to bankruptcy of partnerships *en commandite* and partnerships *en nom collectif* were influenced principally by Continental European law, particularly Italian law. This dichotomous influence is typical of a mixed system of law and manifests itself in other areas of Maltese law.

Question 8: In your law, are there any other circumstances which trigger insolvency or restructuring proceedings?

There are no express provisions at law which mandatorily require directors to file for restructuring.

Under the Pre-Insolvency Act directors shall, by reference to early warning tools and any other information reasonably available to them, continuously monitor developments that may expose the debtor to a *likelihood of insolvency* and, where such developments are identified, take appropriate countermeasures with a view to preventing insolvency and ensuring business viability. In practice this obligation may lead to filing for restructuring, but it need not necessarily do so.

There are no express provisions at law which mandatorily require directors to place a company into insolvent liquidation, though there may be consequences for directors who continue to trade in circumstances where director(s) knew, or ought to have known prior to the dissolution of the company that there was no reasonable prospect that the company would avoid being dissolved due to its insolvency (e.g. liability for wrongful trading under Section 316 of the Companies Act).

Under Section 316 of the Companies Act, the court may declare a director liable to make such payment towards the company's assets as the court thinks fit where a company has been dissolved and is insolvent and it appears that the director knew, or ought to have known prior to the dissolution of the company that there was no reasonable prospect that the company would avoid being dissolved due to its insolvency. It is a defence for a director to show that, in the circumstances, he took every step he ought to have taken with a view to minimising the potential loss to the company's creditors. In practice this duty to mitigate loss may lead a director to consider taking action to put the company into insolvent liquidation.

Question 9: Which of the terms mentioned in Questions 3, 5, and 8 are used in the context of transactions avoidance law?

None of the terms are expressly used. Section 303(1) of the Companies Act on *Fraudulent Preference* provides as follows:

> Every privilege, hypothec or other charge, or transfer or other disposal of property or rights, and any payment, execution or other act relating to property or rights made or done by or against a company, and any obligation incurred by the company within six months before the dissolution of the company shall be deemed to be a fraudulent preference against its creditors whether it is of a gratuitous nature or an onerous nature if it constitutes a transaction at an undervalue or if a preference is given, unless the person in whose favour it is made, done or incurred, proves that he did not know and did not have reason to believe that the company was likely to be dissolved by reason of insolvency, and in the event of the company being so dissolved every such fraudulent preference shall be void.

Question 10: Which of the terms addressed in Questions 3, 5, and 8 are used in the context of directors' duties?

a) shift of duties (from shareholders to creditors)

In recent years, judgments of the Maltese courts increasingly make reference to the duty of directors to take into account the interests of creditors when the company is in serious financial difficulties. From a review of court judgments on the matter, one cannot conclude that any one particular term of the ones referred to in Questions 3, 5, and 8 is invariably used by the courts to mark the time when directors are expected to displace shareholders' interests in favour of creditors' interests. In a 2014 judgment (*All Invest Company Limited v. X and Others*) the Civil Court recognised a duty owed by the directors to the creditors when the company is on the "threshold" of insolvency.[1]

b) duties to commence insolvency proceedings

See answer to Question 8.

c) other duties (please describe)

Imminent likelihood of inability to pay one's debts also triggers formal obligations upon directors to convene a general meeting of the company.

Section 329A of the Companies Act provides as follows:

> Where the directors of a company become aware that the company is *unable to pay its debts or is imminently likely to become unable to pay its debts*, they shall forthwith, not later than thirty days from when the fact became known to them, duly convene a general meeting of the company by means of a notice to that effect for a date not later than forty days from the date of the notice for the purpose of reviewing the company's position and of determining what steps should be taken to deal with the situation, including consideration as to whether the company should be dissolved or, where applicable, whether the company should make a company recovery application (emphasis added).

The wording used by the Companies Act for public companies (as opposed to private companies) is different. In the case of public companies, no reference is made to inability to pay debts or imminent likelihood of inability to pay debts. Reference in the side note is made to "serious loss of capital", and the test under Section 104(1) of the Companies Act is as follows:

> Where the net assets of a public company are half or less of its called-up issued share capital, the directors shall, not later than thirty days from the earliest day on which that fact is known to any director of the company, duly convene a general meeting of the company by means of a notice to that effect for a date not later than forty days from the date of the notice for the purpose of considering whether any, and if so, what steps should be taken to deal with the situation, including consideration as to whether the company should be dissolved.

"Net assets" for this purpose are defined as the aggregate of the company's assets less the aggregate of its liabilities. The term "liabilities" in this context expressly includes any amount retained as reasonably necessary for the purpose of

1 *All Invest Company Limited v. X and Others*, First Hall, Civil Court, 17 March 2014.

providing for any liability or loss which is either likely to be incurred or certain to be incurred but uncertain as to its amount or as to the date on which it will arise.

Question 11: Are there any other rules in the context of which the terms addressed in Questions 3, 5, and 8 are used?

The term *likelihood of insolvency* is used within the context of duties of officials of the debtor to monitor early warning signs of insolvency as well as to initiate preventive restructuring applications.

The terminology *imminently likely to become unable to pay its debts* is used within the context of company recovery procedures.

Question 12: Is the definition of (the subspecies of) insolvency identical in all legal fields or are there different definitions (e.g. different in insolvency law than in criminal law)?

Personal bankruptcy is regulated separately, under the Commercial Code. The operative trigger is *suspension of payments*.

II. INABILITY TO PAY DEBTS

Question 13: In your jurisdiction, is the term "inability to pay debts" defined in statute? If so, please give the wording in English translation. Is this definition (if any) specified in case law? If so, how?

Inability to pay debts is defined in terms of Section 214(5) of the Companies Act, which specifies that a

> company shall be deemed to be unable to pay its debts
>
> (a) if a debt due by the company has remained unsatisfied in whole or in part after twenty-four weeks from the enforcement of an executive title against the company by any of the executive acts specified in article 273 of the Code of Organization and Civil Procedure; or
>
> (b) if it is proved to the satisfaction of the court that the company is unable to pay its debts, account being taken also of contingent and prospective liabilities of the company.

As is evident from the above, the test for inability to pay one's debts is alternative. The alternative tests have been applied in a number of cases, though in the Maltese system principles judicially enunciated do not make law and thus we do not have *case law* in the strict sense of the term. Having said that, judgments have authoritative value for the purposes of interpretation and application of law.

It is also relevant to point out that inability to pay one's debts is one of the causes of dissolution in respect of which the court has a discretion. In fact, Section 214(2) of the Companies Act provides that:

> a company *may* be dissolved and wound up by the court in the following cases –
>
> (i) if the business of the company is suspended for an uninterrupted period of twenty-four months;
> (ii) the company is unable to pay its debts.

Question 14: Does your law refer to all debts or only to mature debts?

The term "debts" is not expressly defined, though all debts are considered, account being taken also of the contingent and prospective liabilities of the company.

Question 15: Which assets are taken into account when assessing the inability to pay debts: all (financial) assets or only those that are liquid, i.e. available on short notice?

All assets on the company's balance sheet are taken into consideration, though there are judgements which have made it clear that "it is not sufficient for the company to be able to meet its obligations if its total liabilities can ultimately be met only by the realisation of its assets over a lengthy period" (*International AB v. Aluminium Extrusions Limited*).[2]

Question 16: Is any liquidity gap (deficit between relevant financial means and relevant debts) relevant or does your law neglect minor gaps? If the latter, how is "minor" defined?

As stated above the court has a discretion to dissolve and wind up a company for inability to pay debts. Admittedly there is less room for discretion in applying the test under Section 214(5)(a) of the Companies Act. This is based on an objective ascertainment of facts, that is, has a debt owed by the company remained unsatisfied in whole or in part after 24 weeks from the enforcement of an executive title against the company by any of the executive acts specified in Article 273 of the Code of Organization and Civil Procedure? The prospect of payment and liquidity after the lapse of the above period will not necessarily eradicate the inability to pay one's debt.

The courts may be expected to be more tolerant and exercise their discretion in the face of temporary liquidity shortages in applying the test under Section 214(5)(b) of the Companies Act, which requires proof to the satisfaction

2 *International AB v. Aluminium Extrusions Ltd*, First Hall, Civil Court, May 2003.

of the court that the company is unable to pay its debts, account being taken also of contingent and prospective liabilities of the company.

Within the strict context of the definition of inability to pay debts under Section 214(5) of the Companies Act, there are, however, no specific or clear rules as to what constitutes a "minor" liquidity gap.

Question 17: As far as the time aspect is concerned, does it matter whether the liquidity gap can be closed again in the short term? If so, how long is the grace period?

The reply to Question 16 applies *mutates mutandes* to Question 17 dealing with the time aspect. Within the context of the insolvency tests under Section 214(5)(a) of the Companies Act, there are, however, no specific or clear rules as to the duration of the grace period for closure of a liquidity gap.

On a separate note, reference is expressly made to a time period in the context of the declaration of solvency which is required to be filed by directors if a winding up is to proceed as a solvent members' voluntary winding up. In this case, under Section 268 of the Companies Act, in the declaration of solvency the directors are required to declare that

> they have made a full inquiry into the affairs of the company, and that, having so done, they have formed the opinion that the company will be able to pay its debts in full within such period not exceeding twelve months from the date of dissolution as may be specified in the declaration.

Question 18: As far as the time aspect is concerned, is a debtor considered insolvent if the liquidity gap is not yet present but will occur soon? If so, how long is the prognosis period? (Note: this may also concern the difference between actual and likely/imminent inability to pay debts; cf. below Question 34).

Account is taken also of contingent and prospective liabilities of the company.

Question 19: How is inability to pay debts established? Please communicate if there is a difference between a creditor and a debtor application or between different legal contexts.

See answer to Question 13 as to what constitutes inability to pay one's debts. The alternative tests under Section 214(5) of the Companies Act apply equally to debtor or creditor applications.

a) Is a formal liquidity status (liquidity balance sheet) required?
Within court proceedings relating to insolvency on the basis of Section 214(5) of the Companies Act, inability to pay one's debts is proven by evidence which includes submission of the financial statements of the company, including balance sheets and cash-flow statements.

b) Is a sample of daily liquidity data (which do not amount to a proper liquidity status but show insufficient funds on different days within a certain period of time) sufficient?
No.

c) Does the law provide for a rebuttable presumption? If so, under which conditions?
n.a.

d) Does the law provide for any technical circumstances (e.g. undisputed statutory demand, non-compliance with monetary judgments, unsuccessful enforcement proceedings, non-performance of a previous composition agreement in insolvency proceedings) the occurrence of which suffices to establish the debtor's insolvency?
Yes. As explained in answer to Question 13, insolvency may be established by a court

> if a debt due by the company remains unsatisfied in whole or in part after twenty-four weeks from the enforcement of an executive title against the company by any of the executive acts specified in article 273 of the Code of Organization and Civil Procedure.

e) Other means?
n.a.

Question 20: Is insolvency (inability to pay debts, overindebtedness, etc.) subject to party autonomy in the proceedings or must the court clarify them *ex officio*?

There is ascertainment of inability to pay debts by the courts. The courts ascertain inability to pay debts. Not only is there court ascertainment of inability to pay debts, but, as explained above in answer to Question 13, the court has a discretion whether to place a company into court winding up on the grounds of inability to pay debts.

Question 21: In an overall view, does your law distinguish "inability to pay debts" from "financial difficulties"? If so, how?

Inability to pay one's debts and financial difficulties are certainly not coterminous. Inability to pay one's debts implies financial difficulties, but the converse is not necessarily so. Financial difficulties may be temporary and do not necessarily constitute inability to pay debts, which is a term defined at law. (See answer to Question 13.)

Question 22: In an overall view, does it matter under your law whether the debtor's inability to pay debts is present or future and reversible or irreversible?

For the purposes of applying the test under Section 214(5)(b) of the Companies Act, current or prospective inability to pay debts and reversibility or non-reversibility may be considerations a court takes into consideration in exercising its discretion under Section 214(2).

Question 23: Would you like to add any further aspects not covered by the above questions?

No.

III. CESSATION OF PAYMENTS

Question 24: In your jurisdiction, is "cessation of payments" a legal term used either in statute or in case law? (If the answer is "no", please continue with Question 31.)

Cessation of payments is not a legal term ordinarily used in statute or case law.

Question 25: Is "cessation of payments" an autonomous ground to commence proceedings (triggering circumstance)? You may refer to Questions 6/7 or add additional information here.

n.a.

Question 26: Is "cessation of payments" a means to establish inability to pay debts? If so, by which mechanism (e.g. rebuttable presumption for inability to pay debts, cf. above Question 19(c))?

n.a.

Question 27: How is "cessation of payments" defined? If it is defined in statute, please provide us here with an English translation of the relevant rule. Is this definition (if any) specified in case law? If so, how?

n.a.

Question 28: How is "cessation of payments" established?

n.a.

Question 29: Are there typical circumstances which provide circumstantial evidence that the debtor has ceased payments? If so, please list as many as possible.

n.a.

Question 30: Would you like to add any further aspects not covered by the above questions?

Not necessary.

IV. LIKELY/IMMINENT INABILITY TO PAY DEBTS

Question 31: Are the following terms available in your jurisdiction, either in statute or in case law? (If the answer is "no", please continue with Question 42.)

a) likely inability to pay debts
No.

b) imminent inability to pay debts
No.

c) other (similar) terms
The terminology *imminently likely to become unable to pay its debts* is used within the context of company recovery procedures.

The same term (*imminently likely to become unable to pay its debts*) is also used within the context of Section 329A of the Companies Act (see answer to Question 10(c)), triggering a duty on the directors to convene a general meeting of the company for the purpose of reviewing the company's position and of determining what steps should be taken to deal with the situation, including consideration of whether the company should be dissolved or, where applicable, whether the company should make a company recovery application.

Question 32: Is "likely/imminent inability to pay debts" an autonomous ground to commence proceedings (triggering circumstance)? You may refer to Questions 6/7 or add additional information here.

No.

Question 33: If the answer to the previous Question is "yes", who may base filing for insolvency proceedings on it: only the debtor or also creditors?

n.a.

Question 34: How are these terms defined? If they are defined in statute, please provide us here with an English translation of the relevant rules. Is this definition (if any) specified in case law? If so, how?

a) likely inability to pay debts
No express definition.

b) imminent inability to pay debts
No express definition.

Question 35: Do the terms "likely" and "imminent" require a prognosis regarding the point in time when actual inability to pay debts will occur? If so, how long is the time period for this prognosis?

No specific or express rule on time period.

Question 36: Does your law require a specific grade of certainty that inability to pay debts will eventually occur? If so, is 50.1% ("more likely than not") enough or are there alleviated or aggravated prerequisites?

No.

Question 37: Regarding "debts" and "financial means", are they defined in the same way as in the context of inability to pay debts (cf. above Questions 14/15)? If not, what are the differences?

Though "debts" is not a defined term, all debts are considered, account being taken also of contingent and prospective liabilities of the company. "Financial means" is not a defined term.

Question 38: Further to Question 37: Are "debts" considered which do currently not exist or are not yet due but will foreseeably come into existence and become due during the prognosis period?

Account is taken also of contingent and prospective liabilities of the company.

Question 39: Also further to Question 37: Are "financial means" considered which do currently not exist but will foreseeably become available during the prognosis period?

"Financial means" is not a defined term.

Question 40: How are the terms "likely/imminent inability to pay debts" established?

There is no clearly defined test for "likely/imminent inability to pay debts" as in the case of inability to pay debts. The term "likely" is ordinarily regarded as a term of probability and the term "imminent" imports a sense of urgency or quasi-immediacy.

Question 41: Would you like to add any further aspects not covered by the above questions?

n.a.

V. OVERINDEBTEDNESS

Question 42: In your jurisdiction, is "overindebtedness", or "balance sheet insolvency" respectively, a legal term used either in statute or in case law? (If the answer is "no", please continue with Question 56.)

"Overindebtedness" is not a strict legal term, nor is the term "balance sheet insolvency". The test under Section 214(5)(b) of the Companies Act is sometimes loosely referred to as balance sheet insolvency. The reason for this is that English statute law was one of sources of the insolvency provisions in the Companies Act. English judgments and British academic authors are authoritatively quoted by Maltese judges in support of their interpretations. However, there are differences between the balance sheet insolvency under English law and the test under Section 214(5)(b) of the Companies Act sometimes loosely referred to as balance sheet insolvency.

Question 43: Is "overindebtedness" an autonomous ground to commence proceedings (triggering circumstance)? You may refer to Questions 6/7 or add additional information here.

"Overindebtedness" is not a strict legal term.

Question 44: If the answer to the previous Question is "yes", is this applicable to corporate insolvencies of legal persons only or also to personal bankruptcies of natural persons?

n.a.

Question 45: Is the term "overindebtedness" defined in statute? If so, please give the wording in English translation. Is this definition (if any) specified in case law? If so, how?

n.a.

Question 46: Does your law refer to all existing debts or only to mature debts?

n.a.

Question 47: Does the rank of certain debts play a role when establishing overindebtedness? In particular, is there any possibility to conclude agreements according to which certain debts shall not be taken into account (e.g. agreements on subsidiarity)?

n.a.

Question 48: Which assets are taken into account when overindebtedness is established: the complete set of assets or only a selection of them?

n.a.

Question 49: How are the debtor's assets valued: by referring to the liquidation value, the book value, the going concern value or in another way?

n.a.

Question 50: Is there any prognostic element, e.g. regarding the debtor's chances to continue the business?

n.a.

Question 51: If the answer to the previous Question is "yes", what exactly is the topic of the prognosis and how is it established?

n.a.

Question 52: If the answer to Question 50 is "yes", how long is the prognosis period?

n.a.

Question 53: How is overindebtedness established?

n.a.

a) Is a formal balance sheet required?
n.a.

b) Does the yearly regular commercial balance sheet have any meaning (given that it is normally based on technical values and does not display undisclosed reserves)?
n.a.

c) Does the law provide for a presumption? If so, under which conditions?
n.a.

d) Other means?
n.a.

Question 54: Is the legal link to overindebtedness undisputed in literature or are there efforts to abolish it?

n.a.

Question 55: Would you like to add any further aspects not covered by the above questions?

n.a.

VI. REMAINING ISSUES

Question 56: Is there anything else you would like to share in the present context and that we should take into account?

No.

THE NETHERLANDS

Ben SCHUIJLING and Michael VEDER*

I. GENERAL

Question 1: How is insolvency (both in the context of liquidation and restructuring/reorganisation) regulated in your jurisdiction? Please give a brief overview, at least enumerating the relevant statutes.

Introduction

The Dutch Bankruptcy Act ("Faillissementswet", hereafter also "Fw") regulates both liquidation as well as restructuring proceedings. It currently provides for four types of proceedings:

1. bankruptcy (*faillissement*);
2. suspension of payments (*surseance van betaling*);
3. natural persons' debt relief arrangement (*schuldsaneringsregeling natuurlijke personen*); and
4. preventive restructuring scheme (*homologatie van een onderhands akkoord*, also referred to by its acronym "WHOA").[1]

Title I (Articles 1–213rr Fw) governs bankruptcy proceedings (*faillissement*). The opening of bankruptcy proceedings is commonly described as implementing a general attachment on the debtor's assets for the collective benefit of its creditors. The objective of bankruptcy proceedings is the liquidation of the debtor's assets and the distribution of the proceeds thereof to its creditors. A debtor can be declared bankrupt if it has ceased to pay its debts. If a debtor is declared bankrupt, an Insolvency Practitioner ("curator") is appointed. The

* We are grateful for assistance in preparing this report from Matthijs van Essen of Beaufort Transformations and transactions and external PhD candidate at the Radboud Business Law Institute and the Nijmegen School of Management.

1 An (unofficial) English translation of the Dutch Bankruptcy Act can be found in *Warendorf et al. (eds.)*, Warendorf Dutch Civil and Commercial Law Legislation, Deventer, Wolters Kluwer 2022. Translations of statutory texts in this report are generally taken from this publication.

Insolvency Practitioner's primary task is to liquidate the debtor's estate and to use the proceeds to pay the debtor's creditors. In practice, bankruptcy proceedings serve as an important instrument for the reorganisation and continuation of businesses in financial distress (through a sale (i.e. liquidation of assets) of (part of) the debtor's business as a going concern).

Title II (Articles 214–283 Fw) governs suspension of payments proceedings (*surseance van betaling*). An entrepreneur who expects not to be able to continue to discharge its liabilities as and when they fall due may apply for suspension of payments (see Article 214(1) Fw). Suspension of payments is automatically and immediately granted by the court following the filing of a petition by the debtor (see Article 215(1) Fw). Suspension of payments is initially granted on a provisional basis. The decision to grant definitive suspension of payments may be blocked by creditors (see Article 218(2) Fw). The suspension of payments proceedings can be described as implementing a general deferment of payment of ordinary unsecured and non-preferential claims against the debtor. During the period for which the suspension of payments has been granted, creditors with unsecured and non-preferential claims cannot seek redress against the debtor's assets. The objective of the proceedings is to provide an instrument for the reorganisation and continuation of (partially) viable businesses in financial distress. In practice, it does not serve as a satisfactory instrument for the reorganisation of debtors in financial distress; generally, it is nothing more than a first step towards the debtor's bankruptcy.

Title III (Articles 284–362 Fw) governs the natural persons' debt relief arrangement (*schuldsaneringsregeling natuurlijke personen*). A natural person may apply for an order for the application of debt relief, if it is reasonably foreseeable that he or she will not be able to continue payment of his or her debts as they fall due or if he or she finds him- or herself in a position of no longer being able to pay his or her debts. This debt relief is a liquidation procedure, although it may also result in the adoption of a composition plan (*akkoord*). The objective of the natural persons' debt relief arrangement is to provide overindebted natural persons – whether they conduct a business or an independent profession or not – with the possibility of a "fresh start". During the proceedings, the debtor's assets are liquidated for the benefit of his or her creditors and the debtor must make maximum efforts to generate funds to repay his or her creditors. The proceedings in principle result in a discharge of the debtor for any remaining unpaid debts.

Title IV (Articles 369–387 Fw) governs preventive restructuring proceedings (*homologatie van een onderhands akkoord*, commonly referred to by its acronym "WHOA"). The WHOA, which entered into force on 1 January 2021, is intended to facilitate the financial restructuring of debtors in financial distress and to prevent such debtors from entering bankruptcy proceedings. This "Dutch scheme" is available to debtors that find themselves in a position where it is

reasonably likely that they will be unable to continue to pay their debts. The proceedings serve as implementation of the EU Directive on restructuring and insolvency.[2]

Question 2: Related to paragraph 10 above of the Introduction: seen from a principle-based perspective, what justifies the opening of insolvency proceedings in your jurisdiction?

The opening of liquidation proceedings (bankruptcy) is justified by the principle of collectivity and the principle of equal treatment of creditors. Unless otherwise provided, a creditor can have recourse for his claim against all the debtor's assets and creditors have, amongst themselves, an equal right to be paid from the net proceeds of the property of their debtor in proportion to their claims.

As a starting point, when a debtor is solvent and able to pay its debts, a creditor is free to collect and enforce its claims as it sees fit, without taking into account the interests of the other creditors. From the debtor's perspective, the debtor is free to decide on the order in which it satisfies its obligations. The debtor is not required to pay its creditors at the same time or *pro rata*, nor is the debtor required to pay preferential creditors before ordinary creditors.

However, when the debtor is no longer solvent and/or is unable to meet its debts, a common pool problem is likely to occur with uncoordinated enforcement actions by individual creditors. The factual and legal chaos that may occur jeopardises the equal treatment of creditors. The collective proceedings of bankruptcy overcome (aspects of) this common pool problem and safeguard the principle of equal treatment of creditors.

So, ultimately the very concurrence of enforcement by creditors, their pushing and chasing to demand payment, their race to get hold of something of the debtor's assets, the conflicts that result from this, the danger that the less persecutory creditors will miss out on payment completely, are the circumstances that necessitate and motivate the opening of a bankruptcy, with an impartial seizure and distribution of the proceeds of the debtor's assets among its creditors. It is not in the state of the debtor's assets, but in the state of creditors not being paid, that bankruptcy finds its reason for existence.

For the (preventive) restructuring proceedings, a different rationale applies. These proceedings are justified at an earlier stage of financial difficulties where

---

2 Directive (EU) 2019/1023 of the European Parliament and of the Council of 20 June 2019 on preventive restructuring frameworks, on discharge of debt and disqualifications, and on measures to increase the efficiency of procedures concerning restructuring, insolvency and discharge of debt, and amending Directive (EU) 2017/1132 (Directive on restructuring and insolvency).

the opening of a bankruptcy may still be averted in a way that serves the interests of the debtor, its creditors and other stakeholders, e.g. by means of a (short) stay of individual enforcement actions or a composition plan.

Question 3: Does your national law in the context of liquidation proceedings use one or more of the following terms (be it as a noun, be it as an adjective or adjunct) in whatever context:

a) inability to pay debts
No.

b) cessation of payments
Yes, see Article 1(1) Fw for the opening of bankruptcy: "ceased to pay his debts as they fall due".

Cessation of payment is also one (of two) grounds for applying for a natural persons' debt relief arrangement. See Article 284(l) Fw: "if he finds himself in a position of no longer being able to pay his debts."

c) likely inability to pay debts
Such term is used as one (of two) grounds for applying for a natural persons' debt relief scheme. See Article 284(l) Fw: "if it is reasonably foreseeable that the debtor will not be able to continue payment of his debts".

d) imminent inability to pay debts
No.

e) overindebtedness?
No.

Question 4: Are the same terms (and with the same meaning) used in the rules on preliminary/interim insolvency proceedings (e.g. concerning the application stage of the proceedings)?

No. Dutch law does not distinguish a preliminary/interim phase in insolvency proceedings from the main proceedings, in the sense that an application phase with distinct features precedes the actual opening of insolvency proceedings.

With respect to preventive restructuring proceedings (WHOA), it must be noted that the court may not be involved until the end of the restructuring process when it is seized with a request to sanction a restructuring plan. However, the court may already be involved at the early stages of the proceedings, for example when a request for the appointment of a restructuring expert is filed, or access to certain supportive measures (such as a stay) is requested. Sanctioning of a restructuring plan or access to supportive measures requires that the court has determined that the debtor finds itself in a position where it is reasonably likely that it will be unable to continue to pay its debts.

Question 5: Does your national law in the context of restructuring proceedings (as referred to above at paragraph 8 of the Introduction, i.e. both pre-insolvency and within formal insolvency proceedings) use one or more of the following terms (be it as a noun, be it as an adjective or adjunct) in whatever context:

a) inability to pay debts
No.

b) cessation of payments
No.

c) likely inability to pay debts
Yes, this term is used as a requirement for the provisional granting of suspension of payments. See Article 214(1) Fw: "A debtor who expects not to be able to continue to pay his debts as they fall due".

Also, the likelihood of an inability to pay debts is required for access to preventive restructuring proceedings (WHOA). See Article 370(1) Fw: "If a debtor finds itself in a position where it is reasonably likely that it will not be able to continue to pay its debts".

d) imminent inability to pay debts
No.

e) overindebtedness?
No.

Question 6: Which of the terms mentioned in Questions 3 and 5 are used for defining grounds to commence proceedings (triggering circumstances)?

a) insolvency proceedings
Note: We understand "insolvency proceedings" in this question to refer to liquidation proceedings.

Bankruptcy: A debtor can be declared bankrupt if it has ceased to pay its debts (cessation of payments), cf. Article 1(1) Fw.

Natural persons' debt relief arrangement: A natural person may apply for an order for the application of a debt relief arrangement, if it is reasonably foreseeable that he or she will not be able to continue payment of his or her debts as they fall due (likely inability to pay debts) or if he or she finds him- or herself in a position of no longer being able to pay his or her debts (cessation of payments), see Article 284 Fw.

b) restructuring proceedings
Suspension of payments: A debtor that expects not to be able to continue to discharge its liabilities as and when they fall due may apply for suspension of payments (likely inability to pay debts), see Article 214(1) Fw.

Preventive restructuring procedure (WHOA): The "Dutch scheme" is available to debtors that find themselves in a position where it is reasonably likely that they will not be able to continue to pay their debts (likely inability to pay debts), see Article 370(1) Fw.

Question 7: Does the answer to Question 6 include personal bankruptcies of natural persons or only corporate insolvencies of legal entities?

Yes, it includes personal bankruptcies. Natural persons that do not carry on an independent profession or business (consumers) do not have access to suspension of payments proceedings (see Article 214(4) Fw) or preventive restructuring proceedings (WHOA) (see Article 369(1) Fw).

Question 8: In your law, are there any other circumstances which trigger insolvency or restructuring proceedings?

No.

Question 9: Which of the terms mentioned in Questions 3, 5, and 8 are used in the context of transactions avoidance law?

None of these terms are used in the context of transactions avoidance law.

Avoidance rules in bankruptcy are governed by Articles 42 and 47 Fw. Article 42 governs the avoidance of voluntary legal acts while Article 47 governs the avoidance of performances that were due.

In short, the avoidance of voluntary transactions requires (actual or constructive) knowledge of prejudice to creditors. With regard to this requirement, case law has clarified that the test is whether at the time of the performance of the legal act, the opening of bankruptcy proceedings and a deficit therein was foreseeable with a reasonable degree of probability for both the debtor and its counterparty.[3] The foreseeability of the future opening of the debtor's bankruptcy obviously includes the foreseeability of the existence of the relevant triggering circumstances.

Question 10: Which of the terms addressed in Questions 3, 5, and 8 are used in the context of directors' duties?

a) shift of duties (from shareholders to creditors)

Dutch law *does* regulate a shift in the duties of directors from shareholders to creditors in the face of insolvency. This shift is, however, not codified, but rather follows from case law and can be considered gradual. The shift is not triggered, as such, by one of the terms addressed in the questions above.

---

3 Hoge Raad 22 December 2009, ECLI:NL:HR:2009:BI8493 (*ABN AMRO v. Van Dooren q.q. III*).

Directors have a statutory duty to act in the interests of the company and its affiliated enterprise. From this it follows that, as a rule, they should promote the continued success of that enterprise. In a situation of imminent insolvency, this means they will have to consider whether there is a need to take steps to prevent insolvency.

This does not mean that directors must continue the business under all circumstances or avoid insolvency at all costs. Directors are liable to a creditor if they entered into legal acts on behalf of the company when they knew, or ought to have known, that the company would not be able to meet its obligations, and would not provide a remedy for the damage to be suffered by the creditor as a result of that default.[4] If the interests of those involved are ultimately better served by declaring the company bankrupt and dissolving it, directors will have to decide to do so.

So, directors are not obliged to avert bankruptcy under all circumstances, and they are not permitted to close their eyes to the situation of impending insolvency. They must consider in a timely manner what measures ought to be taken in the given circumstances. Directors have some discretion as to whether measures should be taken, and if so, which ones.

b) duties to commence insolvency proceedings

See *supra* under (a). The director's duty might entail an obligation to apply for the opening of insolvency proceedings. However, this obligation is not codified and is not triggered by a prescribed event or situation.

c) other duties (please describe)

"Inability to pay" is used in special legislation that regulates directors' duties towards the tax authorities and compulsory sectoral pension funds.

Directors are obligated to immediately inform the tax authorities or the relevant pension fund if the company is unable to pay certain of its taxes (including taxes on wages, and VAT) or its contributions to the pension fund respectively. If a director fails to do so, it is assumed that any non-payment of these taxes or pension contributions is the result of the director's mismanagement. As a result, the director will be held jointly liable for the unpaid tax and pension contribution debts.[5] Here the term "inability to pay" is only directed at the inability to pay tax or pension contributions debts at the time these debts mature. The concept does not consider the ability to pay other creditors. So, rather than an inability to pay debts in general, it relates to the inability to pay the tax man or pension fund on the due date.

---

4 E.g. Hoge Raad 6 October 1989, ECLI:NL:HR:1989:AB9521 (*Beklamel*).

5 See Article 36 Invorderingswet 1990 and Article 23 Wet verplichte deelneming in een bedrijfstakpensioenfonds 2000.

Question 11: Are there any other rules in the context of which the terms addressed in Questions 3, 5, and 8 are used?

Yes, rules regarding directors' duties (and liability) use terms that most resemble the term "likely inability to pay debts" as referred to in this document.

Article 2:216 of the Dutch Civil Code ("DCC") – in short – states that directors must approve a distribution to shareholders. A solvency test must be carried out. Directors may not approve a distribution when they know or ought to know that, after the distribution, the company will not be able to pay its debts as they fall due.

Based on tort (Article 6:162 of the DCC), directors may be held liable for damage inflicted on the insolvency estate and/or on individual creditors when the director played a role in incurring new debts on behalf of the company or when the director caused or allowed the company to breach existing contractual or statutory obligations. In both cases the standard of "serious reproach" must be met. The standard of serious reproach is met if the director knew or should have known that the company would not be able to meet its debts and would not offer a remedy for the loss.

Question 12: Is the definition of (the subspecies of) insolvency identical in all legal fields or are there different definitions (e.g. different in insolvency law than in criminal law)?

To our knowledge the definitions of insolvency are identical across legal fields.

II. INABILITY TO PAY DEBTS

Question 13: In your jurisdiction, is the term "inability to pay debts" defined in statute? If so, please give the wording in English translation. Is this definition (if any) specified in case law? If so, how?

No, see also answers to Questions 34 and 40. Inability to pay debts is considered a subcategory of "cessation of payments" but is not defined in statute.

Question 14: Does your law refer to all debts or only to mature debts?

All debts. However, only existing claims that can be admitted in the insolvency proceedings are relevant and at least one of the claims should be mature. See answer to Question 28.

Question 15: Which assets are taken into account when assessing the inability to pay debts: all (financial) assets or only those that are liquid, i.e. available on short notice?

All assets.

Question 16: Is any liquidity gap (deficit between relevant financial means and relevant debts) relevant or does your law ignore minor gaps? If the latter, how is "minor" defined?

Minor gaps may be ignored and this is left to the discretion of the court.

Question 17: As far as the time aspect is concerned, does it matter whether the liquidity gap can be closed again in the short term? If so, how long is the grace period?

This may be a relevant factor, but no explicit terms or grace periods are provided for in the Dutch Bankruptcy Act.

Question 18: As far as the time aspect is concerned, is a debtor considered insolvent if the liquidity gap is not yet present but will occur soon? If so, how long is the prognosis period? (Note: this may also concern the difference between actual and likely/imminent inability to pay debts; cf. below Question 34).

No. Future debts are not taken into consideration when determining whether a debtor has ceased to pay its debts.[6]

Question 19: How is inability to pay debts established? Please communicate if there is a difference between a creditor and a debtor application or between different legal contexts.

a) Is a formal liquidity status (liquidity balance sheet) required?
n.a.

b) Is a sample of daily liquidity data (which do not amount to a proper liquidity status but show insufficient funds on different days within a certain period of time) sufficient?
n.a.

c) Does the law provide for a rebuttable presumption? If so, under which conditions?
n.a.

d) Does the law provide for any technical circumstances (e.g. undisputed statutory demand, non-compliance with monetary judgments, unsuccessful enforcement proceedings, non-performance of a previous composition agreement in insolvency proceedings) the occurrence of which suffices to establish the debtor's insolvency?
n.a.

e) Other means?
n.a.

6 See Hoge Raad 11 July 2014, ECLI:NL:HR:2014:1681 (*Berzona*).

Question 20: Is insolvency (inability to pay debts, overindebtedness, etc.) subject to party autonomy in the proceedings or must the court clarify them *ex officio*?

No, it is not subject to party autonomy. The court must establish that the conditions for opening insolvency proceedings have been met, with the exception of suspension of payments which is provisionally granted at the mere request of the debtor (see Introduction in answer to Question 1).

Question 21: In an overall view, does your law distinguish "inability to pay debts" from "financial difficulties"? If so, how?

Not as such, but where financial difficulties lead to a situation where it is reasonably likely that a debtor will not be able to continue to pay its debts, insolvency law comes into the picture.

Question 22: In an overall view, does it matter under your law whether the debtor's inability to pay debts is present or future and reversible or irreversible?

As stated earlier, inability to pay is considered as a subcategory of cessation of payments (see also answer to Question 26). If the debtor has ceased to pay its debts (which, of course, does not include future debts) it can be declared bankrupt. Future inability to pay debts is relevant in relation to suspension of payments proceedings and preventive restructuring proceedings (WHOA).

Question 23: Would you like to add any further aspects not covered by the above questions?

n.a.

III. CESSATION OF PAYMENTS

Question 24: In your jurisdiction, is "cessation of payments" a legal term used either in statute or in case law? (If the answer is "no", please continue with Question 31.)

Yes.

Question 25: Is "cessation of payments" an autonomous ground to commence proceedings (triggering circumstance)? You may refer to Questions 6/7 or add additional information here.

Yes, see answer to Question 6.

Question 26: Is "cessation of payments" a means to establish inability to pay debts? If so, by which mechanism (e.g. rebuttable presumption for inability to pay debts, cf. above Question 19(c))?

No. For the opening of bankruptcy proceedings (Article 1(1) Fw), only the cessation of payments needs to be present. Moreover, the (in)ability of the debtor to pay its debts is not necessary to establish this condition. Rather it is the other way around: an inability to pay debts is a means to establish that the debtor has ceased to pay its debts. Under Dutch law, a debtor that might be able to pay its debts, but does not, may also be declared bankrupt (see also answer to Question 28). Consequently, in practice, a bankruptcy petition may be – and often is – used as a debt collection tool by creditors that may thereby "convince" the debtor to pay.

It is helpful to know that the Dutch legislator explicitly deviated from other insolvency codes that prescribed inability to pay as the relevant trigger for bankruptcy, in particular the former German "Konkursordnung". Rather than the financial state of the debtor, the situation in which the creditors find themselves (being unpaid) was chosen as the relevant trigger for bankruptcy, in particular since the financial state of the debtor is an internal matter that is very hard for outsiders to establish.

Question 27: How is "cessation of payments" defined? If it is defined in statute, please provide us here with an English translation of the relevant rule. Is this definition (if any) specified in case law? If so, how?

Cessation of payments is defined in Article 1(1) of the Fw as follows:

> A debtor in a situation where he has ceased to pay his debts as they fall due, shall be declared bankrupt by a court order, either on his own application or on the petition of one or more of his creditors.

With respect to the interpretation given to this term in case law, see below at Question 28.

Question 28: How is "cessation of payments" established?

The criteria to establish a cessation of payment within the meaning of Article 1(1) Fw that justifies the opening of bankruptcy proceedings, have been developed in case law.

There are two requirements:[7]

1. the debtor has more than one creditor (requirement of plurality); and
2. the debtor is in the situation of having ceased to pay its debts.

---

7 See (with further references) *Wessels*, Faillietverklaring (Wessels Insolventierecht nr. I), 5th ed., Deventer, Wolters Kluwer 2018, pp. 105–138.

Requirement 1: Plurality of creditors

This is a necessary prerequisite for the establishment of cessation of payment. This requirement follows from the collective nature of the insolvency proceedings. If there is only one creditor awaiting payment, then individual enforcement actions are appropriate instead of the opening of bankruptcy proceedings. This means that an applicant creditor not only needs to prove that he has a claim against the debtor, but also that there is at least one claim by another creditor. This other claim is also referred to as a supporting claim (*steunvordering*). This supporting claim cannot be a future debt soon to arise from an existing contract.[8]

The claims on which a bankruptcy petition is based must be able to be admitted in the bankruptcy proceedings. This means that claims that cannot be enforced against the debtor's assets in bankruptcy proceedings (inadmissible claims, *niet verifieerbare vorderingen*) cannot serve to establish a plurality of creditors. Examples are penalty payments forfeited prior to the opening of the procedure, which are by law not enforceable in bankruptcy.

At least one of the creditors needs to have a claim that is already due and payable.[9] This may be the applicant's claim or the supporting claim. The *other* claim does not have to be mature, its amount does not have to be settled, and it does not have to be a monetary claim. It is sufficient that the claim exists at the time the bankruptcy is opened. The supporting claim may stem from the same legal relationship as the applicant's claim and the creditors may be related parties, as long as each creditor has an independent claim against the debtor. In this respect the claims of various bodies and parts of the state are all considered claims of the same creditor.[10] It is not required that the creditor of the supporting claim actually supports the request for the opening of the bankruptcy proceedings.[11]

Requirement 2: Condition of having ceased to pay

Even if the plurality requirement is met, it still needs to be established that the debtor is in the situation of having ceased to pay its debts. Paying in this sense has the broad meaning of the fulfilment of legal obligations. It has to be established that the debtor is actually not paying its mature debts. It is irrelevant whether the debtor has ceased to pay because he was *unable* or *unwilling* to do so. It is explicitly not required that the debtor's assets fall short of covering its (mature) debts.[12] The court has great discretion in determining whether the debtor has ceased to pay.

---

8 Hoge Raad 11 July 2014, ECLI:NL:HR:2014:1681 (*Berzona*).
9 Hoge Raad 18 March 1983, NJ 1983/568.
10 Hoge Raad 26 October 2018, ECLI:NL:HR:2018:1988.
11 Hoge Raad 7 May 1993, NJ 1993/403.
12 Hoge Raad 22 March 1946, NJ 1946/233 and Hoge Raad 7 February 1958, NJ 1958/202.

It does not necessarily follow from the existence of any debts and the failure to pay them that the debtor is in the situation of having ceased to pay its debts. Practically everybody has some unpaid debts at some point in time. That, in itself, does not justify the declaration of bankruptcy. There can be good reasons why the debtor is not paying a certain creditor, for example if the claim is (not unfoundedly) disputed. Another example can be (deeply) subordinated claims that are only payable upon liquidation. The non-payment of such subordinated claims cannot support the conclusion that the debtor has ceased to pay.[13]

It can be noted that case law provides negative factors in establishing the cessation of payments, i.e. circumstances that cannot contribute to that conclusion. Positive factors, including more technical criteria, to establish the required condition are basically lacking in Dutch law. This finds its origin in Dutch procedural law. The establishment of the required condition is considered a highly factual assessment that cannot be (fully) reviewed in an appeal before the Supreme Court.

For the establishment of cessation of payments it suffices that the facts or circumstances which show that the debtor is in a situation where he has ceased to pay his debts as and when they fall due, are summarily established (Article 6(3) Fw). This means that the cessation of payments is established by means of a brief, simple examination. The legislator's main intention was to ease the burden of proof on the applicant creditor when the debtor denies his situation and employs all kinds of defences and chicanery. Nevertheless, the court must give a reasoned judgment and may not declare bankruptcy with the mere finding that it was summarily established that the debtor has ceased to pay the relevant debts.

Question 29: Are there typical circumstances which provide circumstantial evidence that the debtor has ceased payments? If so, please list as many as possible.

In general, the actual non-payment of mature debts is the only relevant circumstance that can evidence the cessation of payments.

Question 30: Would you like to add any further aspects not covered by the above questions?

n.a.

---

13 Hoge Raad 24 October 1997, NJ 1998/68 and Hoge Raad 27 June 2008, JOR 2008/248 (*Dairex*).

IV. LIKELY/IMMINENT INABILITY TO PAY DEBTS

Question 31: Are the following terms available in your jurisdiction, either in statute or in case law? (If the answer is "no", please continue with Question 42.)

a) likely inability to pay debts
Yes.

b) imminent inability to pay debts
No.

c) other (similar) terms
n.a.

Question 32: Is "likely/imminent inability to pay debts" an autonomous ground to commence proceedings (triggering circumstance)? You may refer to Questions 6/7 or add additional information here.

Yes, in relation to suspension of payments proceedings, natural persons' debt relief arrangements, and preventive restructuring proceedings (WHOA); see answers to Questions 6/7.

Question 33: If the answer to the previous Question is "yes", who may base filing for insolvency proceedings on it: only the debtor or also creditors?

Preventive restructuring proceedings (WHOA) can be initiated by the debtor, see Article 370(1) Fw.

Each creditor, shareholder, works council or personnel representative body established under statutory provisions by the undertaking carried on by the debtor can initiate preventive restructuring proceedings (WHOA) by filing an application with the district court for the appointment of a restructuring expert, who then may propose a restructuring plan to the debtor's creditors and shareholders (see Article 371(1) Fw).

Only the debtor may file for suspension of payments proceedings (see Article 214(1) Fw).

Only the debtor may file an application for natural persons' debt relief arrangements (see Article 284(1) Fw).

Question 34: How are these terms defined? If they are defined in statute, please provide us here with an English translation of the relevant rules. Is this definition (if any) specified in case law? If so, how?

a) likely inability to pay debts
In relation to preventive restructuring proceedings, Article 370(1) Fw provides (unofficially translated) as follows:

> If a debtor finds itself in a position where it is reasonably likely that it will not be able to continue to pay its debts, it can offer its creditors and its shareholders, or some of them, an arrangement which provides for a variation of their rights and which can be ratified by the court in accordance with Article 384.

The provision does not provide any further guidance as to how it must be determined (by the court) that the debtor is reasonably unlikely to be able to continue to pay its debts. See further below at Question 40.

In relation to suspension of payments proceedings, Article 214(1) Fw provides (unofficially translated) as follows: A debtor who expects not to be able to continue to discharge his liabilities as and when they fall due may apply for suspension of payments. Since suspension of payments is (provisionally) granted automatically at the debtor's request and without the court assessing whether the debtor's expectations are justified (see also above in answer to Question 1 (Introduction)), the term does not require any further clarification (in statute or case law).

In relation to natural persons' debt relief arrangements, Article 284(1) Fw provides (unofficially translated) as follows:

> A natural person may apply for an order for the application of a debt relief arrangement, if it is reasonably foreseeable that he will not be able to continue payment of his debts as they fall due or if he finds himself in a position of no longer being able to pay his debts.

b) imminent inability to pay debts

n.a.

Question 35: Do the terms "likely" and "imminent" require a prognosis regarding the point in time when actual inability to pay debts will occur? If so, how long is the time period for this prognosis?

No, although it must be established that it is reasonably likely that the debtor will not be able to continue to pay its debts (see also answer to Question 40).

Question 36: Does your law require a specific grade of certainty that inability to pay debts will eventually occur? If so, is 50.1% ("more likely than not") enough or are there alleviated or aggravated prerequisites?

No.

Question 37: Regarding "debts" and "financial means", are they defined in the same way as in the context of inability to pay debts (cf. above Questions 14/15)? If not, what are the differences?

Yes.

Question 38: Further to Question 37: Are "debts" considered which do currently not exist or are not yet due but will foreseeably come into existence and become due during the prognosis period?

n.a.

Question 39: Also further to Question 37: Are "financial means" considered which do currently not exist but will foreseeably become available during the prognosis period?

n.a.

Question 40: How are the terms "likely/imminent inability to pay debts" established?

Based on the explanatory memorandum to Article 370(1) Fw, the term "likely inability to pay debts" – in relation to preventive restructuring proceedings (WHOA) – requires that the debtor is able to meet its current obligations, yet foresees that there is no realistic prospect of averting future insolvency without a restructuring of its debts.[14] The memorandum further indicates that there can be "some time" in between the current state of being able to pay its debts and the expected (future) moment of insolvency. An example is mentioned in which a debtor foresees that it will not be able to repay a loan that matures in a year and that it thus will become insolvent on that future date.[15] In that case the debtor is able to initiate preventive restructuring proceedings (WHOA), based on Article 370(1) Fw.

Case law with respect to the initiation of preventive restructuring proceedings has thus far not provided much guidance as to how the courts should establish whether it is reasonably likely that the debtor will be unable to continue to pay its debts. In most instances, the case law merely mentions that the conditions have been met without providing further explanation.

Question 41: Would you like to add any further aspects not covered by the above questions?

n.a.

V. OVERINDEBTEDNESS

Question 42: In your jurisdiction, is "overindebtedness", or "balance sheet insolvency" respectively, a legal term used either in statute or in case law? (If the answer is "no", please continue with Question 56.)

No.

---

[14] *Kamerstukken II* 2018/19, 35 249, nr. 3, pp. 33–34.

[15] *Kamerstukken II* 2018/19, 35 249, nr. 3, p. 34.

Question 43: Is "overindebtedness" an autonomous ground to commence proceedings (triggering circumstance)? You may refer to Questions 6/7 or add additional information here.

No.

Question 44: If the answer to the previous Question is "yes", is this applicable to corporate insolvencies of legal persons only or also to personal bankruptcies of natural persons?

n.a.

Question 45: Is the term "overindebtedness" defined in statute? If so, please give the wording in English translation. Is this definition (if any) specified in case law? If so, how?

n.a.

Question 46: Does your law refer to all existing debts or only to mature debts?

n.a.

Question 47: Does the rank of certain debts play a role when establishing overindebtedness? In particular, is there any possibility to conclude agreements according to which certain debts shall not be taken into account (e.g. agreements on subsidiarity)?

n.a.

Question 48: Which assets are taken into account when overindebtedness is established: the complete set of assets or only a selection of them?

n.a.

Question 49: How are the debtor's assets valued: by referring to the liquidation value, the book value, the going concern value or in another way?

n.a.

Question 50: Is there any prognostic element, e.g. regarding the debtor's chances to continue the business?

n.a.

Question 51: If the answer to the previous Question is "yes", what exactly is the topic of the prognosis and how is it established?

n.a.

Question 52: If the answer to Question 50 is "yes", how long is the prognosis period?

n.a.

Question 53: How is overindebtedness established?

a) Is a formal balance sheet required?
n.a.

b) Does the yearly regular commercial balance sheet have any meaning (given that it is normally based on technical values and does not display undisclosed reserves)?
n.a.

c) Does the law provide for a presumption? If so, under which conditions?
n.a.

d) Other means?
n.a.

Question 54: Is the legal link to overindebtedness undisputed in literature or are there efforts to abolish it?

n.a.

Question 55: Would you like to add any further aspects not covered by the above questions?

n.a.

VI. REMAINING ISSUES

Question 56: Is there anything else you would like to share in the present context and that we should take into account?

n.a.

POLAND

Marek Porzycki and Anna Rachwał

I. GENERAL

Question 1: How is insolvency (both in the context of liquidation and restructuring/reorganisation) regulated in your jurisdiction? Please give a brief overview, at least enumerating the relevant statutes.

Polish insolvency legislation consists of two laws:

- Law of 28 February 2003 on Bankruptcy (BL) (Prawo upadłościowe) (originally "Law on Bankruptcy and Rehabilitation" (Prawo upadłościowe i naprawcze), title changed with effect from 01.01.2016);
- Law of 15 May 2015 on Restructuring (RL) (Prawo restrukturyzacyjne), in force since 01.01.2016.

Both laws provide for several types of insolvency proceedings, as listed below:

1. A single type of *bankruptcy proceedings* (*postępowanie upadłościowe*) (provided for by the BL, applicable only in case of actual insolvency) – usually involving winding-up of the debtor's assets, but conclusion of an arrangement is allowed if possible.

   A specific form of bankruptcy proceedings is applicable to natural persons – non-entrepreneurs: consumer bankruptcy (so-called *upadłość konsumencka*) (Articles 491^{1}–491^{24} BL).
2. Four types of *restructuring proceedings* (*postępowania restrukturyzacyjne*) are provided for by the RL, applicable both in case of actual insolvency and threat of insolvency:
   - arrangement approval proceedings (*postępowanie o zatwierdzenie układu*) (Articles 210–226h RL) – approval of an out-of-court arrangement by a subsequent court decision;
   - fast arrangement proceedings (*przyspieszone postępowanie układowe*) (Articles 227–264 RL) – conclusion of an arrangement within traditional proceedings (including the opening, course and closure), applicable if

the total sum of contentious claims does not exceed 15% of the total amount of all claims; includes debtor-in-possession under supervision of a court supervisor;
- arrangement proceedings (*postępowanie układowe*) (Articles 265–282 RL) – conclusion of an arrangement within traditional proceedings (including the opening, course and closure), applicable if the total sum of contentious claims exceeds 15% of the total sum of all claims; includes debtor-in-possession under supervision of a court supervisor;
- reorganisation proceedings (*postępowanie sanacyjne*) (Articles 283–323 RL) – comprehensive restructuring of the debtor's enterprise by a professional administrator, including (in principle) divestment of the debtor, ending by conclusion of an arrangement;

3. Arrangement approval proceedings for natural persons not carrying out any business activity (*postępowanie o zatwierdzenie układu na zgromadzeniu wierzycieli przez osobę fizyczną nieprowadzącą działalności gospodarczej*) (Articles 491^{25}–491^{38} BL) – specific, rarely used proceedings intended as an alternative to consumer bankruptcy, introduced in 2020.

Question 2: Related to paragraph 10 above of the Introduction: seen from a principle-based perspective, what justifies the opening of insolvency proceedings in your jurisdiction?

The opening of *bankruptcy proceedings* under the BL is mainly justified by the need to ensure a collective enforcement of claims against an insolvent debtor (see Article 1(1) and (2) BL) leading to an equitable distribution of proceeds among creditors in orderly proceedings, with loss-sharing according to the provisions on creditor ranking. Furthermore, in case of natural persons, the principle of debtor protection comes into play, as the law aims to reintegrate insolvent debtors into the economy by discharging their remaining unsatisfied debts.

In case of *restructuring proceedings*, the law distinguishes between the situation of actual insolvency and threat of insolvency as well as between legal persons[1] and natural persons and other entities, with corresponding differences as to the right to request the opening of restructuring proceedings. As long as the debtor is threatened by insolvency but not yet insolvent, the decision on initiating the restructuring rests solely in his or her hands, as the proceedings can in principle be opened only *on request of the debtor* (Article 7 RL). The possibility of the opening of restructuring proceedings (only one of the four types described in answer to Question 1 *supra* – reorganisation proceedings)

[1] Includes corporations but not partnerships, which do not have full legal personality under Polish law.

on request of a creditor, giving the creditors much more influence over the outcome for the debtor, including the possibility of forcing a takeover or winding-up, is limited only to cases of actual insolvency and only to debtors being legal persons (excluding natural persons and partnerships) (Article 283(2) RL). Although the provisions on the purposes of proceedings (Article 3 RL) do not differentiate between those two situations, it is clear from this distinction that in those cases where the proceedings can be opened on request of the debtor only, the principle of debtor protection and the willingness to provide him or her with a "second chance" is the main justification for the opening of restructuring proceedings. For proceedings against insolvent legal persons which can be opened on request of a creditor, realisation of creditor rights gains more importance, as, in such situations, creditors may opt for requesting the opening of reorganisation proceedings simply as an alternative to lodging a request for bankruptcy.

Question 3: Does your national law in the context of liquidation proceedings use one or more of the following terms (be it as a noun, be it as an adjective or adjunct) in whatever context:

a) inability to pay debts
Yes. In Article 11(1) BL insolvency is defined as loss of ability to meet mature monetary obligations.

b) cessation of payments
This term is not directly used in the BL; however a payment delay exceeding three months triggers a statutory presumption of inability to pay (Article 11(1a) BL).

c) likely inability to pay debts
No.

d) imminent inability to pay debts
No.

e) overindebtedness?
Yes, it is provided for as an additional form of insolvency for legal persons and entities (Article 11(2) BL).

Question 4: Are the same terms (and with the same meaning) used in the rules on preliminary/interim insolvency proceedings (e.g. concerning the application stage of the proceedings)?

There are no specific definitions different from those above applicable in preliminary proceedings (Polish: *postępowanie w przedmiocie ogłoszenia upadłości* – literally: proceedings on the declaration of bankruptcy). The role of such proceedings is the examination of grounds for the opening of actual bankruptcy proceedings, including the insolvency of the debtor.

Question 5: Does your national law in the context of restructuring proceedings (as referred to above at paragraph 8 of the Introduction, i.e. both pre-insolvency and within formal insolvency proceedings) use one or more of the following terms (be it as a noun, be it as an adjective or adjunct) in whatever context:

a) inability to pay debts
Yes, by reference to the definitions of the BL (Article 6(2) RL). The RL does not include its own definition of insolvency and refers to the definitions of the BL.

b) cessation of payments
Yes, indirectly, by reference to the definitions of the BL (Article 6(2) RL).

c) likely inability to pay debts
Indirectly, in Article 6(1) and (3) RL, referring to the debtor being threatened by insolvency. A threat of insolvency exists if "the economic situation of the debtor indicates that he may become insolvent in a short time" and justifies the opening of restructuring proceedings under the RL.

d) imminent inability to pay debts
There is no distinction between "likely" or "imminent" insolvency in the RL, as a threat of insolvency is used as grounds for the opening of restructuring proceedings.

e) overindebtedness?
Yes, by reference to the definitions of the BL (Article 6(2) RL).

Question 6: Which of the terms mentioned in Questions 3 and 5 are used for defining grounds to commence proceedings (triggering circumstances)?

a) insolvency proceedings
Insolvency, defined as (i) inability to pay mature monetary debts (Article 11(1) BL), with a statutory presumption of inability to pay debts applying in case of delay in payment exceeding three months (Article 11(1a) BL), or (ii) overindebtedness persisting for more than 24 months (Article 11(2) BL).

b) restructuring proceedings
Insolvency, defined by reference to the BL (Article 6(2) RL).

Threat of insolvency, existing if "the economic situation of the debtor suggests that he may become insolvent in a short time" (Article 6(3) RL).

Question 7: Does the answer to Question 6 include personal bankruptcies of natural persons or only corporate insolvencies of legal entities?

For natural persons (both entrepreneurs and non-entrepreneurs) and partnerships with at least one natural person as a fully liable partner, insolvency is defined only as inability to pay due monetary debts (Article 11(1) and (7) BL).

For legal persons and partnerships with no natural persons as fully liable partners, both definitions of insolvency apply, including both inability to pay due monetary debts (Article 11(1) BL) and overindebtedness (Article 11(2) BL).

Question 8: In your law, are there any other circumstances which trigger insolvency or restructuring proceedings?

No.

Question 9: Which of the terms mentioned in Questions 3, 5, and 8 are used in the context of transactions avoidance law?

None.

The definition of insolvency is not repeated in transactions avoidance provisions of the insolvency law, as their application is triggered by the opening of insolvency proceedings, not by substantive insolvency of the debtor.

"Insolvency", without a specific definition, is used to define a detrimental act for the purpose of applying the general transactions avoidance provisions of the civil law (*actio Pauliana*, Article 527 et seq. Civil Code).

Question 10: Which of the terms addressed in Questions 3, 5, and 8 are used in the context of directors' duties?

a) shift of duties (from shareholders to creditors)
There is no specific regulation nor any definition of the shift of duties exists.

b) duties to commence insolvency proceedings
The existence of a "ground for the opening of bankruptcy proceedings" (Article 21(1) BL), which includes both inability to pay debts and overindebtedness as referred to above (see answers to Questions 3, 6 and 7), triggers a director's duty to file a request for the opening of insolvency proceedings.

c) other duties (please describe)
n.a.

Question 11: Are there any other rules in the context of which the terms addressed in Questions 3, 5, and 8 are used?

Specific terms addressed in Questions 3, 5 and 8 are used only in the insolvency law (BL and RL).

There are some provisions of other branches of law (in particular civil law, criminal law and company law) where the general term "insolvency" (*niewypłacalność*) is used. The most important of those provisions include the following.

Civil law:

- Article 33^1(2) of the Civil Code, a general provision on entities with legal capacity but without full legal personality. This provision states a general rule of subsidiary liability of members for the debts of such entities, materialising once the entity becomes insolvent;
- Article 458 of the Civil Code, a general rule of the law of obligations providing for accelerated maturity of a claim in case of insolvency of the debtor;
- Article 527 et seq. of the Civil Code, general (non-insolvency) provisions on the *actio Pauliana*. An act of a debtor is defined as detrimental when it leads to insolvency of the debtor or increases the degree of his or her insolvency.

Criminal law:

- Article 300(1) of the Criminal Code, introducing the crime of obstructing creditor satisfaction by fraudulent acts in circumstances where there is a threat of insolvency (*niewypłacalność*) or bankruptcy (*upadłość*);
- Article 301 of the Criminal Code, providing for the crime of fraudulent insolvency or bankruptcy;
- Article 302(1) of the Criminal Code, providing for the crime of selective satisfaction of creditors in case of a threat of insolvency or bankruptcy.

Company law:

- Article 21^4(1) and Article 21^{12}(2) of the Code of Commercial Companies, regulating grounds for refusing to follow instructions issued by holding companies to subsidiaries in groups of companies, as well as liability for damages caused by such instructions. Both provisions were introduced in 2022 as part of a controversial regulation of groups of companies.

Question 12: Is the definition of (the subspecies of) insolvency identical in all legal fields or are there different definitions (e.g. different in insolvency law than in criminal law)?

In the provisions of the Civil Code listed *supra* (answer to Question 11) the term "insolvency" is used in the sense of substantive insolvency but without any reference to the definitions of the BL. Such solution is considered to give the courts a certain margin of discretion in the interpretation of this term. In general, literal interpretation is supported by legal commentators with a rather vague explanation of "insolvency" as a situation where the assets of the debtor do not allow for full satisfaction of debts, and enforcement of claims according to general rules cannot lead to the satisfaction of creditors.[2] Only a minority of more recent commentators advocate an interpretation of the term "insolvency" used in the Civil Code by reference to the definition used in the Bankruptcy Law.[3]

In the provisions of the Criminal Code listed under Question 11 there is equally little precision regarding the interpretation of the term "insolvency" as under the Civil Code. In general, as both the terms "insolvency" (*niewypłacalność*) and "bankruptcy" (*upadłość*) are used, it is understood that the former refers to the situation of the debtor (substantive insolvency) while the latter refers to specific proceedings (bankruptcy proceedings being one of the types of insolvency proceedings under Polish law).

As regards the term "insolvency" used in the provisions of the Code of Commercial Companies mentioned under Question 11, it is generally accepted by the commentators that it refers to insolvency as defined by the BL.[4]

II. INABILITY TO PAY DEBTS

Question 13: In your jurisdiction, is the term "inability to pay debts" defined in statute? If so, please give the wording in English translation. Is this definition (if any) specified in case law? If so, how?

Inability to pay debts is used to define insolvency in Article 11(1) BL which provides: "The debtor is insolvent if he has lost the ability to meet his mature monetary obligations."

This definition is applied together with a statutory presumption of Article 11(1a) BL providing that the debtor is presumed to have lost the ability to meet his mature monetary obligations if the delay in payment exceeds three months (see also answers to Questions 19(c) and 24–29).

Most case law regarding the definition of insolvency dates from the time before the insolvency law reform of 2015 (which entered into force on 1 January 2016), when an earlier version of Article 11(1) BL[5] defined insolvency in a way more similar to the cessation of payments, as a situation when the debtor does not

---

2 Most recent commentators quote in this context a fundamental work on the *actio Pauliana* by *Pyziak-Szafnicka*, Ochrona wierzyciela w razie niewypłacalności dłużnika, Warszawa 1995, p. 89 et seq. It is to be noted that the use of the term "insolvency" in the Civil Code pre-dates the more widespread application of insolvency law, which was out of use until 1989 and still only rarely in use in the mid-1990s. That created conditions favourable for disregarding the definitions of insolvency law when interpreting the term "insolvency" used in the Civil Code.

3 *Zoll*, in *Olejniczak (ed.)*, Prawo zobowiązań – część ogólna, System Prawa Prywatnego, vol. 6, 3rd ed., Warszawa 2018, pp. 1138–1139.

4 *Szumański* in Kodeks spółek handlowych. Komentarz do zmian (tzw. prawo holdingowe), Warszawa 2022, paras. 34–42 to Art. 21^4.

5 At the time, the law was titled the Bankruptcy and Rehabilitation Law (Prawo upadłościowe i naprawcze).

fulfil his mature obligations. Under this earlier wording a discrepancy developed between the general practice of bankruptcy courts and the (rarely issued) case law of the Supreme Court. While the bankruptcy courts mostly applied a simplified literal interpretation of the provision that resulted in regarding any delay in paying at least two debts as amounting to insolvency (the so-called "two invoices rule"), the Supreme Court tried to apply a systemic interpretation and interpret insolvency as a durable failure to meet all or a significant part of the obligations of the debtor, resulting from the lack of sufficient means.[6] The current wording of Article 11 BL results from the decision of the legislator to put an end to this discrepancy in favour of the interpretation proposed by the Supreme Court and to curb the abusive practices of some creditors who used the "two invoices rule" in order to file bankruptcy requests intended as debt collection measures instead of initiating enforcement proceedings.[7]

As a result, under the current wording of Article 11(1) BL, it is generally accepted that the inability to pay debts must result from economic causes, in particular from the lack of means to meet the obligations of the debtor. Furthermore, in order to constitute insolvency this situation should be lasting and definitive (which is also reinforced by the use of the wording "loss of ability" instead of simple "inability"), and at the time of assessment, the debtor should not be expected to regain the ability to pay in the future.[8]

Question 14: Does your law refer to all debts or only to mature debts?

Article 11(1) BL refers only to mature monetary debts.

Question 15: Which assets are taken into account when assessing the inability to pay debts: all (financial) assets or only those that are liquid, i.e. available on short notice?

All assets of the debtor are taken into account when assessing the inability to pay, as the inability must be lasting in order to amount to insolvency (see *supra*, answer to Question 13).

Question 16: Is any liquidity gap (deficit between relevant financial means and relevant debts) relevant or does your law neglect minor gaps? If the latter, how is "minor" defined?

Minor liquidity gaps are not considered to amount to insolvency. First, that results from the generally accepted interpretation that the loss of the ability to

6 Supreme Court judgments of 19 January 2011, V CSK 211/10; and 13 May 2011, V CSK 352/10.

7 See explanatory memorandum to the draft Restructuring Law in Parliamentary print (*Druk sejmowy*) no. 2824 of 09.10.2014, pp. 65–66.

8 See *Filipiak* in *Hrycaj/Jakubecki/Witosz (eds.),* Prawo restrukturyzacyjne i upadłościowe. System Prawa Handlowego, vol. 6, 2nd ed., Warszawa, 2020, pp. 725–728.

pay needs to be lasting (see answer to Question 13). Second, minor liquidity gaps usually involve payment delays not exceeding three months, which do not trigger the application of the presumption under Article 11(1a) BL.

Question 17: As far as the time aspect is concerned, does it matter whether the liquidity gap can be closed again in the short term? If so, how long is the grace period?

Yes, that results from the presumption of Article 11(1a) BL, which applies only in case of payment delays exceeding three months.

Question 18: As far as the time aspect is concerned, is a debtor considered insolvent if the liquidity gap is not yet present but will occur soon? If so, how long is the prognosis period? (Note: this may also concern the difference between actual and likely/imminent inability to pay debts; cf. below Question 34).

No. While the loss of the ability to pay debts may occur before the three months of delay provided in the (rebuttable) presumption of Article 11(1a) BL, there must be an already existing payment delay regarding at least two obligations to two different creditors in order to consider a debtor to be insolvent. A likely or imminent liquidity gap may only constitute a *threat* of insolvency within the meaning of Article 6(3) RL[9] (see answers to Questions 31–40).

Question 19: How is inability to pay debts established? Please communicate if there is a difference between a creditor and a debtor application or between different legal contexts.

There is no difference in the criteria for establishing the insolvency of a debtor between cases initiated on request of a creditor and of the debtor. However, there are differences between the content of the respective applications, with the creditor being only required to provide prima facie evidence of the grounds for his or her application, including insolvency of the debtor (Article 22(1)(3) BL), while the debtor is required to provide detailed information on his or her assets, liabilities and economic situation, including a balance sheet (a list provided in Article 23(1) BL).

a) Is a formal liquidity status (liquidity balance sheet) required?
No.

b) Is a sample of daily liquidity data (which do not amount to a proper liquidity status but show insufficient funds on different days within a certain period of time) sufficient?
Not required.

---

9 *Filipiak*, ibid., p. 727.

It has been suggested by a commentator that an assessment against the International Standards on Auditing, as well as an indicator analysis based on selected items of the debtor's balance sheet should be used as ancillary tools to establish the loss of the debtor's ability to meet his mature monetary obligations. However, they should be used in a flexible way only to facilitate the court's assessment and should under no circumstances constitute stand-alone criteria.[10]

c) Does the law provide for a rebuttable presumption? If so, under which conditions?

Yes, Article 11(1a) BL provides for a rebuttable presumption that the debtor has lost the ability to meet his mature monetary obligations if the delay in payment exceeds three months.

d) Does the law provide for any technical circumstances (e.g. undisputed statutory demand, non-compliance with monetary judgments, unsuccessful enforcement proceedings, non-performance of a previous composition agreement in insolvency proceedings) the occurrence of which suffices to establish the debtor's insolvency?

No.

However, any such circumstances clearly demonstrate a delay in payment of a mature monetary obligation; so they can be used for the purposes of applying the presumption in Article 11(1a) BL.

e) Other means?

n.a.

Question 20: Is insolvency (inability to pay debts, overindebtedness, etc.) subject to party autonomy in the proceedings or must the court clarify them *ex officio*?

In principle the court has to clarify the insolvency of the debtor *ex officio*. There is no requirement for the parties to provide material proof of insolvency. However, there is a requirement to provide prima facie evidence for the grounds of the insolvency application and in the case of the debtor's application there are further requirements to provide detailed information on the debtor's economic situation[11] (see answer to Question 19 above).

---

10 *Filipiak*, ibid., pp. 728–730.

11 In procedural law a requirement to provide prima facie evidence excludes any requirement to provide full material proof (Art. 243 of the Civil Procedure Code in conjunction with Art. 35 BL). See *Adamus*, Prawo upadłościowe. Komentarz, 3rd ed. Warszawa 2021, para. 7 to Art. 22.

Question 21: In an overall view, does your law distinguish "inability to pay debts" from "financial difficulties"? If so, how?

The term "financial difficulties" does not appear in Polish law in the context of the definition of insolvency. A reference to the economic situation of the debtor indicating possible insolvency in near future is an element in the definition of the "threat of insolvency" in Article 6(3) RL (see answers to Questions 31 et seq.).

Question 22: In an overall view, does it matter under your law whether the debtor's inability to pay debts is present or future and reversible or irreversible?

Yes. Only a *present* inability to pay debts qualifies as insolvency under Article 11(1) BL. *Future* (expected) inability may constitute a threat of insolvency under Article 6(3) RL.

Although there is no specific mention of this issue in the wording of the law, according to the generally agreed opinion, inability to pay debts should be lasting to constitute insolvency. "Lasting" is less than irreversible but clearly excludes cases where it is easily reversible. At the time of assessment, the debtor should not be expected to regain the ability to pay in the future (see answer to Question 13).

Question 23: Would you like to add any further aspects not covered by the above questions?

n.a.

III. CESSATION OF PAYMENTS

Question 24: In your jurisdiction, is "cessation of payments" a legal term used either in statute or in case law? (If the answer is "no", please continue with Question 31.)

Cessation of payments (strictly: delay in meeting monetary obligations exceeding three months) is only used as part of the statutory presumption of inability to pay debts in Article 11(1a) BL.

Previously, before the insolvency law reform of 2015 (which entered into force on 1 January 2016), insolvency was defined as a situation when the debtor does not meet his mature obligations. This wording was changed to the current one based on inability to pay. See answer to Question 13.

Question 25: Is "cessation of payments" an autonomous ground to commence proceedings (triggering circumstance)? You may refer to Questions 6/7 or add additional information here.

No.

Question 26: Is "cessation of payments" a means to establish inability to pay debts? If so, by which mechanism (e.g. rebuttable presumption for inability to pay debts, cf. above Question 19(c))?

Yes. A delay in meeting monetary obligations exceeding three months triggers a rebuttable presumption of inability to pay debts under Article 11(1a) BL.

Question 27: How is "cessation of payments" defined? If it is defined in statute, please provide us here with an English translation of the relevant rule. Is this definition (if any) specified in case law? If so, how?

The wording of the current presumption of inability to pay debts in Article 11(1a) is: "It is presumed that the debtor has lost the ability to meet his mature monetary obligations if the delay in meeting monetary obligations exceeds three months".

Until 2015 the wording of Article 11(1) BRL was: "The debtor is insolvent if he does not meet his mature obligations."

Question 28: How is "cessation of payments" established?

By a payment delay exceeding three months.

Question 29: Are there typical circumstances which provide circumstantial evidence that the debtor has ceased payments? If so, please list as many as possible.

Typical circumstances include unpaid invoices, in particular following repeated payment requests, non-compliance with court judgments, and unsuccessful enforcement proceedings.

Question 30: Would you like to add any further aspects not covered by the above questions?

n.a.

IV. LIKELY/IMMINENT INABILITY TO PAY DEBTS

Question 31: Are the following terms available in your jurisdiction, either in statute or in case law? (If the answer is "no", please continue with Question 42.)

a) likely inability to pay debts
No.

b) imminent inability to pay debts
No.

c) other (similar) terms
Article 6(3) RL provides that restructuring proceedings can be open against a debtor "*threatened by insolvency*" i.e. a debtor whose economic situation indicates a likelihood of insolvency in a short time ("the economic situation of the debtor indicates that he may become insolvent in a short time"). In our view, the term is closer to "likely" than to "imminent" but also includes a time factor. The term "threatened by insolvency" relates to both forms of insolvency – inability to pay debts (Article 11(1) BL) as well as to balance sheet insolvency (Article 11(2) BL)[12] (see also answer to Question 45).

Question 32: Is "likely/imminent inability to pay debts" an autonomous ground to commence proceedings (triggering circumstance)? You may refer to Questions 6/7 or add additional information here.

Yes, a threat of insolvency is an autonomous triggering circumstance but only for restructuring proceedings opened upon a request by the debtor (Article 6(3) RL).

Question 33: If the answer to the previous Question is "yes", who may base filing for insolvency proceedings on it: only the debtor or also creditors?

Only the debtor can file a request to open restructuring proceedings based on a threat of insolvency (Article 7(1) RL in conjunction with Article 283(2) RL).

The creditor is entitled to request solely the opening of reorganisation proceedings based on actual insolvency of the debtor, the latter being a legal person (Article 283(2) RL) (see answers to Questions 1 and 2).

Question 34: How are these terms defined? If they are defined in statute, please provide us here with an English translation of the relevant rules. Is this definition (if any) specified in case law? If so, how?

a) likely inability to pay debts
Article 6 RL reads:

> (1) Restructuring proceedings may be conducted against an insolvent debtor or a debtor threatened by insolvency.
>
> ....
>
> (3) A debtor threatened by insolvency shall mean a debtor whose economic situation indicates that in a short time he may become insolvent.

12 *Filipiak*, fn. 8 *supra*, pp. 78, 80.

It is to be noted that the threat of insolvency under Article 6(3) RL refers to both forms of insolvency, i.e. cash-flow and balance sheet insolvency as defined in Article 11 BL (see answer to Question 31).

To our knowledge no published case law refers specifically to the threat of insolvency as referred to in Article 6(3) RL.

b) imminent inability to pay debts
n.a. (see answer to Question 31).

Question 35: Do the terms "likely" and "imminent" require a prognosis regarding the point in time when actual inability to pay debts will occur? If so, how long is the time period for this prognosis?

Yes, such prognosis is required, as indicated by the need to evaluate the economic situation of the debtor. Neither the statute nor case law provides for a specific time-frame; whether the debtor is likely to become insolvent in "a short time" depends on the circumstances of the particular case and the specifics of the business concerned. It has been specified by a commentator that "a short time" does not necessarily need to be "short" in the common sense of the word, but rather "short" from the business perspective of the debtor, and may amount even to six months.[13] There is no need to indicate a specific moment when actual insolvency is expected to occur.

Question 36: Does your law require a specific grade of certainty that inability to pay debts will eventually occur? If so, is 50.1% ("more likely than not") enough or are there alleviated or aggravated prerequisites?

There is no specific degree of certainty required. According to some commentators even a low degree of probability could be sufficient for the opening of restructuring proceedings.[14]

Question 37: Regarding "debts" and "financial means", are they defined in the same way as in the context of inability to pay debts (cf. above Questions 14/15)? If not, what are the differences?

Yes, as "insolvency" is defined in Article 6(2) RL by reference to the definition of the BL, so a "threat of insolvency" refers to the same definition. It needs to be noted that the "threat of insolvency" refers also to overindebtedness (see answer to Question 31).

---

13 *Filipiak*, fn. 8 *supra*, p. 79.

14 *Zimmerman*, Prawo upadłościowe. Prawo restrukturyzacyjne. Komentarz, 7th ed., 2022, para. 1 to Art. 6 RL.

Question 38: Further to Question 37: Are "debts" considered which do currently not exist or are not yet due but will foreseeably come into existence and become due during the prognosis period?

There is no specific exclusion in this regard. Debts *not yet due* are to be taken into account with a view to deciding whether the debtor would be able to pay them as they become mature (within "a short time", see answer to Question 35) while the debts *not yet existing* might only be considered if there is a high probability of their coming into existence and a subsequent default of the debtor (both within the "short time" frame as provided in Article 6(3) RL).

Question 39: Also further to Question 37: Are "financial means" considered which do currently not exist but will foreseeably become available during the prognosis period?

Yes.

Question 40: How are the terms "likely/imminent inability to pay debts" established?

There are no specific rules as to the way the prognosis is to be established. The debtor has to provide the court with complex financial documentation and draft a preliminary restructuring plan including, *inter alia*, the analysis of the debtor's financial situation and an assessment of reasons for the crisis (Articles 9, 10 RL). The court examines the documents provided and assesses the situation according to general rules at its own discretion.

Question 41: Would you like to add any further aspects not covered by the above questions?

n.a.

V. OVERINDEBTEDNESS

Question 42: In your jurisdiction, is "overindebtedness", or "balance sheet insolvency" respectively, a legal term used either in statute or in case law? (If the answer is "no", please continue with Question 56.)

Yes, Article 11(2) BL.

Question 43: Is "overindebtedness" an autonomous ground to commence proceedings (triggering circumstance)? You may refer to Questions 6/7 or add additional information here.

Yes, Article 11(2) BL.

The existence of overindebtedness alone, even without the inability to pay debts, justifies the opening of bankruptcy proceedings. However, at the same time the insolvency law reform of 2015 has confirmed that overindebtedness has less importance as a form of insolvency under Polish law and can be considered ancillary to the inability to pay, which is the main ground upon which to open proceedings.[15] This is reflected in the requirement that overindebtedness has to persist for at least 24 months in order to constitute insolvency in the meaning of Article 11(2) BL (see answer to Question 45 below).

Question 44: If the answer to the previous Question is "yes", is this applicable to corporate insolvencies of legal persons only or also to personal bankruptcies of natural persons?

Overindebtedness is only applicable to corporate insolvencies – of all legal persons and commercial partnerships, as long as no natural person is fully liable for the partnership's debts (Article 11(2) and (7) BL). The latter include registered partnership (Polish: *spółka jawna*, comparable to German *offene Handelsgesellschaft*), professional partnership (Polish: *spółka partnerska*; comparable to German *Partnerschaftsgesellschaft*), limited partnership (Polish: *spółka komandytowa*, comparable to German *Kommanditgesellschaft*) and limited joint-stock partnership (Polish: *spółka komandytowo-akcyjna*, comparable to German: *Kommanditgesellschaft auf Aktien*).

Question 45: Is the term "overindebtedness" defined in statute? If so, please give the wording in English translation. Is this definition (if any) specified in case law? If so, how?

Article 11 BL reads:

> ...
>
> (2) A debtor being a legal person or an entity without legal personality which is granted legal capacity under a separate law [includes partnerships] is also insolvent when his monetary obligations exceed the value of his assets and this situation persists for a period exceeding twenty-four months.
>
> (3) Assets referred to in paragraph 2 do not include assets which are to be excluded from the bankruptcy estate.
>
> (4) Monetary obligations referred to in paragraph 2 do not include future obligations, including obligations subject to a suspensive condition, as well as obligations to a shareholder resulting from a loan or another transaction with similar effect, as referred to in Article 342(1)(4) [shareholder claims resulting from loans or similar transactions are subordinated claims].

15 Explanatory memorandum to the draft Restructuring Law in Parliamentary print (*Druk sejmowy*) no. 2824 of 09.10.2014, p. 66.

(5) Monetary obligations of the debtor are presumed to exceed the value of his assets if his obligations included in the balance sheet, excluding reserves for liabilities and liabilities to related entities, exceed the value of his assets and this situation persists for a period exceeding twenty-four months
(6) The court may dismiss the request for the opening of bankruptcy proceedings if the debtor is not under threat of losing the ability to meet his mature monetary obligations in a short time.
(7) Paragraphs 2–6 shall not apply to partnerships under the Law of 15 September 2000 – Code of Commercial Companies when at least one of the partners fully liable with all his estate for the liabilities of the partnership is a natural person.

The reason for including only overindebtedness persisting for more than 24 months as amounting to insolvency triggering the opening of bankruptcy or restructuring proceedings[16] is the intention to avoid premature opening of bankruptcy proceedings in cases where the debtor is able to pay his debts as they fall due and the overindebtedness is not expected to last, especially in initial phases of the business activity when newly established companies have not yet started to generate profits. Overindebtedness is in principle only then considered as problematic for the market situation if it leads to disturbances in the debtor's ability to pay.[17] The length of this period has been set at 24 months in order to include in any case a full reporting year and two yearly balance sheets.[18]

Question 46: Does your law refer to all existing debts or only to mature debts?

All existing monetary debts are taken into consideration, subject to Article 11(4) BL. Only monetary debts are to be taken into account, which thus excludes non-monetary obligations. The law also explicitly excludes future obligations, conditional obligations (included in the balance sheet reserves, Article 11(5) BL), as well as obligations to shareholders (see answer to Question 47).

Moreover, as overindebtedness is defined as a long-term situation persisting for at least 24 months (see answer to Question 45), it should be noted that the scope and type of obligations taken into consideration when establishing insolvency may vary over time (some obligations may be extinguished while some new ones may arise during the relevant 24-month period).

Question 47: Does the rank of certain debts play a role when establishing overindebtedness? In particular, is there any possibility to conclude

16 Although overindebtedness persisting for a shorter period may constitute a threat of insolvency under Art. 6(3) RL, see Questions 31–40.
17 Explanatory memorandum to the draft RL, p. 66.
18 *Filipiak*, fn. 8 *supra*, p. 741.

agreements according to which certain debts shall not be taken into account (e.g. agreements on subsidiarity)?

The ranking of creditors under Article 342 BL is mandatory and non-negotiable. Similar effects cannot either be achieved under general civil law, as a *pactum de non petendo* agreement has no effect in civil proceedings.[19]

Debts to the main shareholders of a company, which are subordinated under Article 342(1)(4) BL, are excluded by law from being taken into account when establishing overindebtedness (Article 11(4) BL). This category includes debts to shareholders having not less than 10% of the votes at the general shareholders' meeting (this threshold does not apply if they hold a managerial position at the company) or debts to shareholders exercising direct or indirect control over the company, arising under a loan or similar transaction concluded within five years before the filing for bankruptcy (Article 342(5) and (6) BL).

Question 48: Which assets are taken into account when overindebtedness is established: the complete set of assets or only a selection of them?

All assets, with the exception of assets excluded from the (future) bankruptcy estate, are taken into account (Article 11(3) BL).

Question 49: How are the debtor's assets valued: by referring to the liquidation value, the book value, the going concern value or in another way?

The book value has initial relevance for the presumption of Article 11(5) (see answer to Question 53(c) below), as the debtor's balance sheets available to the creditors via the National Court Register enable them to establish whether the presumption of overindebtedness applies.[20]

However, for actually establishing the value of assets for the purposes of assessing overindebtedness, the actual market value should be used. Whether liquidation value or going concern value is ultimately used should depend on the prognosed outcome, with going concern value being applied if the debtor is expected to continue his or her business.[21]

Question 50: Is there any prognostic element, e.g. regarding the debtor's chances to continue the business?

Yes. Under Article 11(6) BL even if the overindebtedness has persisted for more than 24 months, the court may still dismiss the request for the opening of

---

[19] *Porzycki/Rachwał*, National Report for Poland, in *Faber/Vermunt/Kilborn/Richter/Tirado*, Ranking and Priority of Creditors, OUP, Oxford 2016, p. 401, para. 13.74.

[20] *Zimmerman*, fn. 14 *supra*, para. 14 to Art. 11 RL.

[21] See explanatory memorandum to the draft RL, p. 66; see *Zimmerman*, fn. 14 *supra*, para. 15 to Art. 11 RL; *Filipiak*, fn. 8 *supra*, p. 742.

bankruptcy proceedings if the debtor is not under threat of losing the ability to meet his mature monetary obligations within a short time.

Moreover, overindebtedness is defined as a situation persisting for at least 24 months, which in itself is intended to filter out most cases with a positive prognosis.

Question 51: If the answer to the previous Question is "yes", what exactly is the topic of the prognosis and how is it established?

A request for the opening of bankruptcy proceedings based on overindebtedness of the debtor may be dismissed by the court if there is no risk of the debtor losing the ability to pay his mature monetary debts in a short time (Article 11(6) BL).

Question 52: If the answer to Question 50 is "yes", how long is the prognosis period?

There is no specific time-frame provided for the prognosis period, as Article 11(6) BL provides for perspective of "a short time". The length of the period depends on the particularities of the case and overall financial situation of the debtor.

It should be also noted that the same wording ("a short time") is used to define the threat of insolvency as a ground for the opening of restructuring proceedings (Article 6(3) RL) (see answer to Question 35 above).

Question 53: How is overindebtedness established?

a) Is a formal balance sheet required?
Yes.

First, a balance sheet is needed to apply the presumption of Article 11(5) BL. Second, in the case of a debtor's request to open bankruptcy proceedings, a separate balance sheet, drafted for the specific purpose of filing for bankruptcy no later than 30 days before lodging the request, should be attached by the debtor (Article 22(1)(2) BL). This requirement applies irrespective of whether the bankruptcy request is based on overindebtedness or on inability to pay.

b) Does the yearly regular commercial balance sheet have any meaning (given that it is normally based on technical values and does not display undisclosed reserves)?
Yes, the required period of 24 months is specifically intended to include in any case two yearly balance sheets. They are relevant for the presumption of Article 11(5) BL as well as having informative value for the debtor, indicating the need to assess the market value of assets in order to confirm or exclude overindebtedness within the meaning of the BL.[22]

---

22 *Filipiak*, fn. 8 *supra*, p. 740.

c) Does the law provide for a presumption? If so, under which conditions?

Yes, according to Article 11(5) BL, monetary obligations of the debtor are presumed to exceed the value of his assets if his obligations included in the balance sheet, excluding reserves for liabilities and liabilities to related entities, exceed the value of his assets and this situation persists for a period exceeding 24 months.

As the presumption refers to the balance sheet, it is based on the book value of the assets of the debtor, not their market value as applied for the purposes of establishing overindebtedness (see answer to Question 49). Another discrepancy exists between the exclusion of liabilities to related entities for the purposes of the presumption, in line with balance sheet items specified in accounting rules, and the exclusion of debts to shareholders for the purposes of establishing overindebtedness (Article 11(4) BL, see answer to Question 47). As a result of those discrepancies, the role of the presumption is not to establish overindebtedness, as it varies from its actual definition, but rather to serve as a warning sign to the debtor or to creditors having access to its balance sheet, signalling that overindebtedness is likely and needs to be assessed against the criteria of Article 11(2)–(4) BL.[23]

d) Other means?

n.a.

Question 54: Is the legal link to overindebtedness undisputed in literature or are there efforts to abolish it?

There are no efforts to abolish the criterion of overindebtedness, although it is widely considered secondary and less important than the inability to pay. Such assessment of its role led to its relative weakening by the insolvency law reform of 2015, which introduced the 24-month period referred to in Article 11(2) BL.

Question 55: Would you like to add any further aspects not covered by the above questions?

n.a.

VI. REMAINING ISSUES

Question 56: Is there anything else you would like to share in the present context and that we should take into account?

No.

---

[23] See *Zimmerman*, fn. 14 *supra*, para. 14 to Art. 11 RL.

PORTUGAL

Catarina SERRA

I. GENERAL

Question 1: How is insolvency (both in the context of liquidation and restructuring/reorganisation) regulated in your jurisdiction? Please give a brief overview, at least enumerating the relevant statutes.

Portugal has only one insolvency statute, the Código da Insolvência e Recuperação de Empresas[1] (CIRE). It provides for uniform insolvency proceedings which can be aimed at liquidation as well as restructuring, depending on the case at hand. Both outcomes are regularly in the hands of an Insolvency Practitioner (*administrador da insolvência*) who can get instructions from the creditors' meeting. Unfortunately, no official English translation of the CIRE is available.

The CIRE also provides for pre-insolvency instruments. The first consists of hybrid proceedings and may take two forms depending on the nature of the debtor: *Processo Especial de Revitalização*[2] (PER), applicable to businesses (single traders and companies), and *Processso Especial para Acordo de Pagamento*[3] (PEAP), applicable to non-traders (natural and legal persons). The second is an out-of-court instrument called *Regime Extrajudicial de Recuperação de Empresas*[4] (RERE), which is applicable exclusively to businesses. Both pre-insolvency instruments are aimed at restructuring and are not available where the debtor is in actual insolvency (inability to pay debts or overindebtedness). The RERE is regulated in a separate statute – Law No. 8/2018, of 2 March. Unfortunately, no official English translation of Law No. 8/2018 is available.

In the context of the "COVID-19 emergency legislation", the Portuguese legislator created transitory[5] proceedings: *Processo Extraordinário de Viabilização de Empresas* (PEVE),[6] which was applicable to insolvent and pre-insolvent businesses.

---

1 Translation: Insolvency and Restructuring Law Act.
2 Translation: Special Revitalisation Proceedings.
3 Translation: Special Proceedings aimed at a Payment Agreement.
4 Translation: Out-of-Court Regime for Business Restructuring.
5 Initially in effect until 31 December 2021. The deadline was later extended until 30 June 2023.
6 Translation: Extraordinary Proceedings for Business Viability.

The PEVE was regulated in a separate statute – Law No. 75/2020, of 27 November. Given the fact that the PEVE is no longer in force, it will not be considered for the purpose of the following questions/answers.

Please take note that, under Portuguese insolvency law:

1. The term "inability to pay mature debts" or "to fulfil overdue obligations" (corresponding to the German *Zahlungunsfähigkeit*) is definitory rather than defined; it is the core element of the definition of "insolvency" (corresponding to the German *Insolvenz*).
2. The key term is, in fact, "insolvency", which comprehends, primarily, "inability to pay (mature) debts", and, by force of an equivalence made by law, also "overindebtedness" (corresponding to the German *Überschuldung*).
3. The term "insolvency" is used, indiscriminately, with the meaning of inability to pay debts and with the meaning of overindebtedness, except for the purpose of the duty to file for insolvency, as clarified below (see *infra* – answer to Question 9(b)).

Therefore, I will consider that whenever law refers, generally, to "insolvency" both terms/situations are referred/covered.

Question 2: Related to paragraph 10 above of the Introduction: seen from a principle-based perspective, what justifies the opening of insolvency proceedings in your jurisdiction?

The opening of insolvency proceedings is primarily justified by the principle of equal treatment of creditors (*par conditio creditorum*), given the fact that individual enforcement proceedings are no longer acceptable where the debtor is substantively insolvent or substantive insolvency is imminent. Other principles may also come into play, e.g. the principle of debtor protection where the insolvent debtor needs help against single creditors with hold-out positions, or the principle of best possible satisfaction of the creditors' claims where creditors would be worse off without insolvency proceedings.

Question 3: Does your national law in the context of liquidation proceedings use one or more of the following terms (be it as a noun, be it as an adjective or adjunct) in whatever context:

a) inability to pay debts

Yes, taken as synonymous with inability to fulfil obligations (as the core term of the definition of insolvency).

b) cessation of payments

Yes, though under the formula: "general suspension of payment of mature debts".

c) likely inability to pay debts
No.

d) imminent inability to pay debts
Yes, though under the formula: "imminent insolvency".

e) overindebtedness?
Yes, though under the formula: "manifest superiority of liabilities over assets".

Question 4: Are the same terms (and with the same meaning) used in the rules on preliminary/interim insolvency proceedings (e.g. concerning the application stage of the proceedings)?

In the rules of preliminary/interim insolvency proceedings the only (common) terms used are "inability to pay debts" and "imminent insolvency", with the same meaning.

The other (exclusive) term used is "difficult economic situation".

Question 5: Does your national law in the context of restructuring proceedings (as referred to above at paragraph 8 of the Introduction, i.e. both pre-insolvency and within formal insolvency proceedings) use one or more of the following terms (be it as a noun, be it as an adjective or adjunct) in whatever context:

a) inability to pay debts
Yes (as the core term of the definition of insolvency).

b) cessation of payments
Yes, but only in the context of insolvency (i.e. and not of pre-insolvency) proceedings.

Also the formula is slightly different: "general suspension of payment of mature debts".

c) likely inability to pay debts
No.

d) imminent inability to pay debts
Yes, though under the formula: "imminent insolvency".

e) overindebtedness?
Yes, but only in the context of insolvency (i.e. and not of pre-insolvency) proceedings.

Also the formula is slightly different: "manifest superiority of liabilities over assets".

Question 6: Which of the terms mentioned in Questions 3 and 5 are used for defining grounds to commence proceedings (triggering circumstances)?

a) insolvency proceedings

The terms used to designate the grounds to commence insolvency proceedings aimed at liquidation are:

- inability to pay debts (Article 3(1) CIRE),
- imminent inability to pay debts (Article 3(4) CIRE),
- overindebtedness (Article 3(2) CIRE),
- cessation of payments (Article 20(1)(a) CIRE).

b) restructuring proceedings

The terms used to designate the grounds to commence insolvency proceedings aimed at restructuring are:

- inability to pay debts (Article 3(1) CIRE),
- imminent inability to pay debts (Article 3(4) CIRE),
- overindebtedness (Article 3(2) CIRE),
- cessation of payments (Article 20(1)(a) CIRE).

The terms used to designate the grounds to commence pre-insolvency restructuring proceedings provided in CIRE (PER and PEAP) are:

- imminent inability to pay debts (Article 17-A(1) CIRE).

The terms used to designate the circumstances that trigger pre-insolvency restructuring instruments provided in Law No. 8/2018 (RERE) are:

- imminent inability to pay debts (Article 3(1)(b) of Law No. 8/2018).

Question 7: Does the answer to Question 6 include personal bankruptcies of natural persons or only corporate insolvencies of legal entities?

Both.

It should be noted, however, that not all of the above-mentioned proceedings apply to natural persons.

Question 8: In your law, are there any other circumstances which trigger insolvency or restructuring proceedings?

Yes: difficult economic situation (Article 17-A(1) CIRE and Article 3(1)(b) of Law No. 8/2018); it triggers PER/PEAP and RERE (alternatively to imminent insolvency).

It is defined as the situation where the debtor faces serious difficulty in fulfilling its obligations on time, namely because it has a lack of liquidity or because it is unable to obtain credit (Article 17-B CIRE).

Question 9: Which of the terms mentioned in Questions 3, 5, and 8 are used in the context of transactions avoidance law?

Insolvency (with the meaning of "inability to pay debts" and "overindebtedness") (Article 120(5)(a) CIRE) and imminent insolvency (Article 120(5)(b) CIRE).

Question 10: Which of the terms addressed in Questions 3, 5, and 8 are used in the context of directors' duties?

a) shift of duties (from shareholders to creditors)
In Portugal, the shift of duties is neither regulated nor defined in case law. It is controversially discussed in literature, but no clear picture can be drawn.

b) duties to commence insolvency proceedings
Insolvency (exclusively with the meaning of "inability to pay debts") (Article 18(1) CIRE).

c) other duties (please describe)
No.

Question 11: Are there any other rules in the context of which the terms addressed in Questions 3, 5, and 8 are used?

Yes, they are relevant in some rules of criminal law:

- Article 227 Código Penal[7] (entitled "Fraudulent insolvency"): the term "insolvency", with the meaning of inability to pay debts and overindebtedness, is used in paragraph (1) of the norm.
- Article 228 Código Penal (entitled "Negligent insolvency"): the term "insolvency", with the meaning of inability to pay debts and overindebtedness, is used in paragraph (1) of the norm.
- Article 229 Código Penal (entitled "Favouring creditors"): the term "insolvency", with the meaning of inability to pay debts and overindebtedness, and the term "imminent insolvency" are used in paragraph (1) of the norm.
- Article 229-A Código Penal (entitled "Aggravation"): the term "insolvency", with the meaning of inability to pay debts and overindebtedness, is used in the norm.

---

7 Translation: Penal Code.

Besides, they are used in many norms of the Civil Code, in particular:

- Article 429 Código Civil (insolvency of the debtor as grounds for the *exceptio non adimpleti contractus*);
- Article 780 Código Civil (insolvency of the debtor as grounds for the creditor demanding performance before the term agreed).

Question 12: Is the definition of (the subspecies of) insolvency identical in all legal fields or are there different definitions (e.g. different in insolvency law than in criminal law)?

The definition of insolvency (and of its subspecies) is identical or, to put it rigorously, it is commonly understood that all rules of other laws refer to insolvency (and its subspecies) as defined in insolvency law.

II. INABILITY TO PAY DEBTS

Question 13: In your jurisdiction, is the term "inability to pay debts" defined in statute? If so, please give the wording in English translation. Is this definition (if any) specified in case law? If so, how?

The term "inability to pay debts" (*Zahlungunsfähigkeit*) is definitory rather than defined; it is the core element of the definition of "insolvency" (*Insolvenz*). The key term is, in fact, "insolvency", which comprehends, primarily, "inability to pay (mature) debts", and, by force of an equivalence made by law, also "overindebtedness" (*Überschuldung*).

According to Article 3(1) CIRE, insolvency is the situation where the debtor is unable to pay its (mature) debts.

Question 14: Does your law refer to all debts or only to mature debts?

Only to mature debts.

Question 15: Which assets are taken into account when assessing the inability to pay debts: all (financial) assets or only those that are liquid, i.e. available on short notice?

All assets are taken into account.

Evidently, insolvency may derive from the fact that the assets are not sufficiently liquid to match the debts as they fall due.

Question 16: Is any liquidity gap (deficit between relevant financial means and relevant debts) relevant or does your law neglect minor gaps? If the latter, how is "minor" defined?

In earlier statutes and in legal literature, insolvency with the meaning of inability to pay debts was/is usually associated with a liquidity gap, due to there being assets that cannot be swiftly liquidated and to the unavailability of credit to the debtor.

Nowadays, Portuguese law makes only two references to a (an undiscriminated) liquidity gap: firstly, in Article 17-B CIRE, in the definition of difficult economic situation (the situation where the debtor faces serious difficulty in fulfilling its obligations on time, namely because it has a lack of liquidity or because it is unable to obtain credit), which is one of the two circumstances that may trigger PER and PEAP; secondly, in Article 3(1)(b) of Law No. 8/2018, which is one of the two circumstances that may trigger RERE.

Question 17: As far as the time aspect is concerned, does it matter whether the liquidity gap can be closed again in the short term? If so, how long is the grace period?

Portuguese law contains no express references to a temporal delimitation of the liquidity gap, although the possibility of the gap being closed in the short term may be/is frequently taken into account by the parties (debtor, creditors) and the court for the purpose of drawing the line between insolvency and pre-insolvency on a case-by-case basis.

Question 18: As far as the time aspect is concerned, is a debtor considered insolvent if the liquidity gap is not yet present but will occur soon? If so, how long is the prognosis period? (Note: this may also concern the difference between actual and likely/imminent inability to pay debts; cf. below Question 34).

No: when the liquidity gap is expected to occur soon but is not yet present, the debtor is generally considered to be in imminent insolvency (not in actual insolvency).

Question 19: How is inability to pay debts established? Please communicate if there is a difference between a creditor and a debtor application or between different legal contexts.

As a preliminary remark, there are no specific methods for establishing inability to pay debts in the case of a debtor's application. Portuguese law provides specific methods only for the case of applications by creditors and individuals other than the debtor.

a) Is a formal liquidity status (liquidity balance sheet) required?

Formal liquidity status (liquidity balance sheet) is not required but it is a possible method for establishing inability to pay debts.

b) Is a sample of daily liquidity data (which do not amount to a proper liquidity status but show insufficient funds on different days within a certain period of time) sufficient?
A sample of daily liquidity data may be sufficient, depending on the case.

c) Does the law provide for a rebuttable presumption? If so, under which conditions?
Yes, in Article 20 CIRE.

Actually, the (rebuttable) presumptions contemplate the only methods for establishing inability to pay debts in the case of applications by creditors and other individuals. This is to say the list of circumstances is exhaustive.

There are eight circumstances that lead to the (rebuttable) presumption of insolvency of the debtor. The person filing for insolvency has to claim and prove, at least, one of them for its application to be formally accepted (i.e. for him/her to be recognised as a person entitled to file for insolvency).

- Paragraph (a) refers to the general suspension/cessation of payment of mature debts;
- Paragraph (b) refers to the non-fulfilment of one or more obligations which, due to their amount or the circumstances of their non-fulfilment, reveal the inability of the debtor to punctually meet most of its obligations;
- Paragraph (c) refers to the disappearance of the owner of the company or of the debtor's managers/directors or the abandonment of the place where the company has its headquarters or carries out its main activity, related to the debtor's lack of solvency and without appointment of a suitable substitute;
- Paragraph (d) refers to the dissipation, abandonment, hasty or ruinous liquidation of assets and fictitious creation of credits;
- Paragraph (e) refers to the insufficiency of seizable assets to pay the creditor's claim verified in an enforcement proceeding against the debtor;
- Paragraph (f) refers to the non-compliance of obligations provided for in the insolvency plan or in the payment plan, under the conditions set out in subparagraph (a) of paragraph 1 and paragraph 2 of Article 218;
- Paragraph (g) refers to the general default, in the last six months, of debts of any of the following types:
  - tax debts;
  - social security contributions;
  - debts arising from an employment contract, or from the breach or termination of this contract;
  - rent from any type of lease, including finance, installments of the purchase price or loan secured by the respective mortgage, relative to the place where the debtor carries out his activity or has his headquarters or residence;

- Paragraph (h) refers to the manifest superiority of liabilities over assets according to the last approved balance sheet, or a delay of more than nine months in approving and depositing the accounts, when there is such a duty (this paragraph is applicable only if the debtor is one of the entities referred to in paragraph 2 of Article 3, that is, is a legal person or a separate patrimony with limited liability).

d) Does the law provide for any technical circumstances (e.g. undisputed statutory demand, non-compliance with monetary judgments, unsuccessful enforcement proceedings, non-performance of a previous composition agreement in insolvency proceedings) the occurrence of which suffices to establish the debtor's insolvency?

Yes (see *infra* answer to Question 19(c)).

e) Other means?

No.

Question 20: Is insolvency (inability to pay debts, overindebtedness, etc.) subject to party autonomy in the proceedings or must the court clarify them *ex officio*?

The court should clarify them, although, in practice, it does not.

Question 21: In an overall view, does your law distinguish "inability to pay debts" from "financial difficulties"? If so, how?

No.

The only reference to "difficulties" is in the concept of difficult economic situation, defined in Article 17-B CIRE as the situation where the debtor faces serious difficulty in fulfilling its obligations on time, namely because it has a lack of liquidity or because it is unable to obtain credit (Article 17-A(1) CIRE and Article 3(1)(b) of Law No. 8/2018).

Question 22: In an overall view, does it matter under your law whether the debtor's inability to pay debts is present or future and reversible or irreversible?

The debtor's inability to pay debts must be present; a future inability to pay debts will be relevant only for the purpose of the opening of preventive restructuring proceedings, as it matches imminent insolvency.

The reversible character of the debtor's inability to pay debts may be relevant only for the purpose of stimulating creditors to agree on an insolvency plan aimed at rescue.

Question 23: Would you like to add any further aspects not covered by the above questions?

No.

III. CESSATION OF PAYMENTS

Question 24: In your jurisdiction, is "cessation of payments" a legal term used either in statute or in case law? (If the answer is "no", please continue with Question 31.)

Yes, though under the formula: "general suspension of payment of mature debts".

Question 25: Is "cessation of payments" an autonomous ground to commence proceedings (triggering circumstance)? You may refer to Questions 6/7 or add additional information here.

The cessation of payments is not exactly an autonomous ground to commence proceedings or a triggering circumstance.

It is rather the circumstance that leads to the (rebuttable) presumption of insolvency (Article 20(1)(a) CIRE).

In order to facilitate the proof that the debtor is insolvent/unable to pay its (mature) debts, the legislator established (rebuttable) presumptions on the basis of certain situations in Article 20(1) CIRE, one being cessation of payments or, to be precise, the general suspension of payment of mature debts (see *supra* answer to Question 19(c)).

Question 26: Is "cessation of payments" a means to establish inability to pay debts? If so, by which mechanism (e.g. rebuttable presumption for inability to pay debts, cf. above Question 19(c))?

Yes. By means of a rebuttable presumption (see *supra* answer to Question 19(c)).

Question 27: How is "cessation of payments" defined? If it is defined in statute, please provide us here with an English translation of the relevant rule. Is this definition (if any) specified in case law? If so, how?

Cessation of payments (*rectius*: general suspension of payment of mature debts) is not defined in statute nor does doctrine provide a definition. It is considered fairly clear.

Question 28: How is "cessation of payments" established?

There are no specific methods for establishing cessation of payments.

The person filing for insolvency who claims cessation of payments is allowed to produce evidence using all the means of proof which are admissible under general procedural law.

Question 29: Are there typical circumstances which provide circumstantial evidence that the debtor has ceased payments? If so, please list as many as possible.

No.

Question 30: Would you like to add any further aspects not covered by the above questions?

No.

IV. LIKELY/IMMINENT INABILITY TO PAY DEBTS

Question 31: Are the following terms available in your jurisdiction, either in statute or in case law? (If the answer is "no", please continue with Question 42.)

a) likely inability to pay debts
No.

b) imminent inability to pay debts
Yes.

c) other (similar) terms
Difficult economic situation.

Question 32: Is "likely/imminent inability to pay debts" an autonomous ground to commence proceedings (triggering circumstance)? You may refer to Questions 6/7 or add additional information here.

Yes, though under the formula: "imminent insolvency".

Question 33: If the answer to the previous Question is "yes", who may base filing for insolvency proceedings on it: only the debtor or also creditors?

Imminent inability to pay debts/imminent insolvency is an autonomous ground to commence insolvency proceedings/a triggering circumstance, but only when the person filing for insolvency is the debtor (Article 3(4) CIRE).

This is so for, mainly, two reasons:

1. it is generally believed that individuals other than the debtor are not in a position to assess such an undefined, imprecise situation;

2. if individuals other than the debtor were entitled to claim imminent inability to pay debts/imminent insolvency and it were false, the damage to the debtor would be significant.

Question 34: How are these terms defined? If they are defined in statute, please provide us here with an English translation of the relevant rules. Is this definition (if any) specified in case law? If so, how?

a) likely inability to pay debts
n.a.

b) imminent inability to pay debts
The term is not defined in statute but is generally defined in case law (and legal literature) as the situation where it is foreseeable that the debtor will become unable to pay its debts when they are due/mature.

Question 35: Do the terms "likely" and "imminent" require a prognosis regarding the point in time when actual inability to pay debts will occur? If so, how long is the time period for this prognosis?

Imminent insolvency/imminent inability to pay debts requires a prognosis which may only be assessed on a case-by-case basis. The relevant point in time is when the debts are due/mature.

Question 36: Does your law require a specific grade of certainty that inability to pay debts will eventually occur? If so, is 50.1% ("more likely than not") enough or are there alleviated or aggravated prerequisites?

No.

Question 37: Regarding "debts" and "financial means", are they defined in the same way as in the context of inability to pay debts (cf. above Questions 14/15)? If not, what are the differences?

They are not defined in statute but they are understood in case law (and in legal literature) in the same way in both situations.

Question 38: Further to Question 37: Are "debts" considered which do currently not exist or are not yet due but will foreseeably come into existence and become due during the prognosis period?

Yes (see *supra* answers to Questions 34(b) and 35).

Question 39: Also further to Question 37: Are "financial means" considered which do currently not exist but will foreseeably become available during the prognosis period?

Yes, though this is not an issue specifically addressed in statute.

Question 40: How are the terms "likely/imminent inability to pay debts" established?

There are no specific methods for establishing imminent insolvency/imminent inability to pay debts.

When filing for insolvency on this ground the debtor is allowed to produce evidence using all the means of proof which are admissible under general procedural law.

Question 41: Would you like to add any further aspects not covered by the above questions?

To clarify, in answer to Question 28 I covered only imminent insolvency/imminent inability to pay debts as a ground to commence insolvency proceedings. It should be stressed that imminent insolvency/imminent inability to pay debts is also a ground to commence pre-insolvency proceedings (PER/PEAP/RERE) and in the same terms described *supra*.

V. OVERINDEBTEDNESS

Question 42: In your jurisdiction, is "overindebtedness", or "balance sheet insolvency" respectively, a legal term used either in statute or in case law? (If the answer is "no", please continue with Question 56.)

Yes, though under the formula: "manifest superiority of liabilities over assets".

Question 43: Is "overindebtedness" an autonomous ground to commence proceedings (triggering circumstance)? You may refer to Questions 6/7 or add additional information here.

Yes.

Under Portuguese law, overindebtedness (*rectius*: manifest superiority of liabilities over assets) equals insolvency as inability to pay debts, except for the purpose of the duty to file for insolvency (see *supra* answers to Question 1 and Question 9(b)).

The equivalence is a rule that was preserved from earlier statutes.

The reasoning under the rule is that, when the assets of the legal person or separate patrimony are the only assets available for the satisfaction of the creditors, the manifest superiority of liabilities necessarily means inability to pay.

Question 44: If the answer to the previous Question is "yes", is this applicable to corporate insolvencies of legal persons only or also to personal bankruptcies of natural persons?

It is applicable only to legal persons and separate patrimonies provided they have limited liability (i.e. the firm's owners are not personally liable to the firm's creditors) (Article 3(2) CIRE).

Question 45: Is the term "overindebtedness" defined in statute? If so, please give the wording in English translation. Is this definition (if any) specified in case law? If so, how?

Overindebtedness (*rectius*: manifest superiority of liabilities over assets) is not defined in statute, nor does doctrine provide a definition. It is considered fairly clear.

Question 46: Does your law refer to all existing debts or only to mature debts?

As a rule, all existing debts.

The law contemplates the possibility of considering identifiable elements even if not included in the balance sheet, in which case they are to be taken at their fair value (Article 3(3)(a) CIRE).

The law also contemplates the possibility excluding the debts that only have to be paid at the expense of distributable funds or the remaining assets after the rights of the debtor's other creditors have been satisfied or safeguarded (Article 3(3)(c) CIRE).

Question 47: Does the rank of certain debts play a role when establishing overindebtedness? In particular, is there any possibility to conclude agreements according to which certain debts shall not be taken into account (e.g. agreements on subsidiarity)?

No to both questions.

Question 48: Which assets are taken into account when overindebtedness is established: the complete set of assets or only a selection of them?

The law provides no exception, so it is assumed that the complete set of assets is to be considered.

Question 49: How are the debtor's assets valued: by referring to the liquidation value, the book value, the going concern value or in another way?

Like assets, debts are, as a rule, valued according to the applicable accounting rules (Article 3(2) *in fine*, CIRE), which means their book value.

The law contemplates the possibility of considering identifiable elements as assets and liabilities even if not included in the balance sheet, in which case they are to be taken at their fair value (Article 3(3)(a) CIRE).

Furthermore, when the debtor is the owner of a company, the assessment is based on a perspective of continuity or liquidation, depending on which appears more likely, but in any case excluding the goodwill item (Article 3(3)(b) CIRE).

Question 50: Is there any prognostic element, e.g. regarding the debtor's chances to continue the business?

Yes (see *supra* answer to Question 49).

Question 51: If the answer to the previous Question is "yes", what exactly is the topic of the prognosis and how is it established?

There are no elements apart from those pursuant to Article 3(3)(b) and already mentioned (see *supra* answer to Question 49).

Question 52: If the answer to Question 50 is "yes", how long is the prognosis period?

There are no elements apart from those pursuant to Article 3(3)(b) and already mentioned (see *supra* answer to Question 49).

Question 53: How is overindebtedness established?

a) Is a formal balance sheet required?
A formal balance sheet is not required but it is a possible, and fairly efficient, method for establishing overindebtedness.

b) Does the yearly regular commercial balance sheet have any meaning (given that it is normally based on technical values and does not display undisclosed reserves)?
A yearly regular commercial balance sheet is not excluded as a relevant means of establishing or contributing to the establishment of overindebtedness.

c) Does the law provide for a presumption? If so, under which conditions?
No.

d) Other means?
No.

Question 54: Is the legal link to overindebtedness undisputed in literature or are there efforts to abolish it?

There is no relevant dispute on the legal reference to overindebtedness.

Question 55: Would you like to add any further aspects not covered by the above questions?

No.

VI. REMAINING ISSUES

Question 56: Is there anything else you would like to share in the present context and that we should take into account?

I would like to clarify that:

1. In my answers to the questionnaire, "inability to pay (mature) debts" equals "inability to fulfil (overdue) obligations".
2. In Portuguese insolvency law, the key concept/term is "insolvency" and it designates, primarily, inability to pay debts/inability to fulfil obligations, but it also covers overindebtedness. As the two terms are treated autonomously in the questionnaire, I have chosen to take legal references to "insolvency" as being to "inability to pay debts/to fulfil obligations". Hopefully, the point is clear in my answers to the questionnaire.

ANNEX: TRANSLATION OF THE RELEVANT PROVISIONS OF CIRE

Article 3
Situation of insolvency

1 – A debtor who is unable to fulfil its overdue obligations shall be considered insolvent.
2 – Legal persons and separate patrimonies for whose debts no natural person is personally and unlimitedly liable, directly or indirectly, are also considered insolvent when their liabilities manifestly exceed their assets, assessed in accordance with the applicable accounting standards.
3 – The previous provision ceases to be applicable when assets exceed liabilities, assessed in accordance with the following rules:
   a) Identifiable elements, even if not included in the balance sheet, are considered as assets and liabilities at their fair value;

   b) When the debtor is the owner of a company, the assessment is based on a perspective of continuity or liquidation, depending on which appears more likely, but in any case excluding the goodwill item;
   c) Liabilities do not include debts that only have to be paid at the expense of distributable funds or the remaining assets after the rights of the debtor's other creditors have been satisfied or safeguarded.

4 – Merely imminent insolvency is equivalent to actual insolvency, in the case where it is the debtor who files for insolvency.

Article 17-B CIRE
Notion of difficult economic situation

For the purposes of this Code, a company is in a difficult economic situation if it faces serious difficulty in fulfilling its obligations on time, namely because it has a lack of liquidity or because it is unable to obtain credit.

Article 20 CIRE
Other subjects entitled to file for insolvency

1 – The declaration of insolvency of a debtor may be requested by whoever is legally responsible for his debts, by any creditor, even if conditional and whatever the nature of his credit, or by the Attorney General, on behalf of the entities whose interests are legally entrusted to him, if one of the following facts occurs:
   a) General suspension of payment of overdue obligations;
   b) non-fulfilment of one or more obligations which, due to their amount or the circumstances of their non-fulfilment, reveal the inability of the debtor to punctually meet most of its obligations;
   c) Disappearance of the owner of the company or of the debtor's managers/directors or abandonment of the place where the company has its headquarters or carries out its main activity, related to the debtor's lack of solvency and without appointment of a suitable substitute;
   d) Dissipation, abandonment, hasty or ruinous liquidation of assets or fictitious creation of credits;
   e) Insufficiency of seizable assets to pay the creditor's claim verified in an enforcement proceeding against the debtor;
   f) Non-fulfilment of obligations provided for in the insolvency plan or in the payment plan, under the conditions set out in subparagraph a) of paragraph 1 and paragraph 2 of Article 218;
   g) General default, in the last six months, of debts of any of the following types:
      i) Tax debts;
      ii) Social security contributions;

- iii) Debts arising from an employment contract, or from the breach or termination of this contract;
- iv) Rent from any type of lease, including finance, installments of the purchase price or loan secured by the respective mortgage, relative to the place where the debtor carries out his activity or has his headquarters or residence;

h) If the debtor is one of the entities referred to in paragraph 2 of Article 3, manifest superiority of liabilities over assets according to the last approved balance sheet, or a delay of more than nine months in approving and depositing the accounts, when there is such a duty.

ROMANIA

Flavius-Iancu Moțu and Andreea Deli-Diaconescu

I. GENERAL

Question 1: How is insolvency (both in the context of liquidation and restructuring/reorganisation) regulated in your jurisdiction? Please give a brief overview, at least enumerating the relevant statutes.

Insolvency, as a notion of substantive law, is regulated in Romania by three acts:

1. Law no. 85/2014 on the prevention of insolvency proceedings and on the insolvency proceedings (applicable to commercial insolvencies)

According to Law no. 85/2014, Article 5(29), "insolvency" is

> The specific state of the debtor's estate when the debtor's available cash resources are insufficient to pay the debtor's ascertained (uncontested), liquidated and due debts. The debtor is presumed to be insolvent/in insolvency when it has not paid such a debt at least 60 days after its maturity; the presumption is rebuttable.

Article 5, pt. 72 sets a threshold value (*de minimis*) for a debt/several debts aggregated necessary to trigger the opening of the insolvency proceedings: RON 50,000 (approx. EUR 10,000);

By way of exception:

- Law no. 85/2014, Article 5(30) defines the "insolvency of a credit institution" as any of the following situations a credit institution may find itself in:
  - (a) its manifest inability to pay its mature debts using its available cash resources;
  - (b) the credit institution's solvency indicator drops below 2%;
  - (c) the withdrawal of its authorisation, pursuant to the law, due to its financial recovery being unattainable.
- Law no. 85/2014, Article 5(30) defines the "insolvency of an insurance firm" as any of the following situations an insurance firm may find itself in:
  - (a) its manifest inability to pay its mature debts using its available cash resources;

(b) the withdrawal of its authorisation due to the insurance firm not complying with the solvency legal requirements;
(c) the withdrawal of the authorisation granted to a residual insurance firm created in the resolution proceedings.

For credit institutions and for insurance firms, the only insolvency proceedings available under Law no. 85/2014 are liquidation proceedings. They do have restructuring proceedings available under other statutory instruments.

A couple of extra mentions:

First:

When drafting its own commercial insolvency legislation, Romania decided to follow the American model (US Code Title 11) and placed the reorganisation proceedings with the ambit of the insolvency proceedings.

Therefore, in order to access the reorganisation proceedings, a debtor must, in the first place, have its insolvency proceedings opened. Only at a later moment (i.e. after all the creditors have lodged their claims and a final list of creditors is drafted by the judicial administrator), the debtor may propose a reorganisation plan to the creditors in the list, seeking, usually, a moratorium on the payment of its debts, a haircut of the said debts or a combination of them. Hence, the debtor must "persuade" its creditors that its (substantive) insolvency is reversible, i.e. it is able to pay the pre-commencement debts (as accepted by the creditors that have voted the reorganisation plan or had the plan "crammed-down" on them) and the post/commencement debts.

Should the creditor not persuade the creditors to accept the reorganisation plan or should the reorganisation fail, the debtor's (substantive) insolvency will be deemed to be irreversible and the debtor is subject to liquidation proceedings, within the same wide framework of the insolvency proceedings.

The debtor's reorganisation failure necessarily entails the opening of the liquidation proceedings, and there is no going back (i.e. should the debtor pay all its debts during the liquidation proceedings, it still cannot save himself from being struck off).

Second:

The (rather) new act amending the Law no. 85/2014[1] that has transposed Directive (EU) 2019/1023 lays down a definition of "difficulty" (distress), in Article 5(26²):

> the condition caused by any circumstance resulting in a temporary impairment of business giving rise to a real and serious threat to the debtor's future ability to pay its

1 Law no. 216/2022, which came into force on 20 July 2022.

> debts as they fall due, unless appropriate measures are taken; the distressed debtor is able to meet its obligations as they fall due.

Moreover, it has brought a new proviso: "Preventive restructuring proceedings … shall be applicable only to debtors in difficulty that *are not in insolvency*."

Presently, a debtor's access to pre-insolvency proceedings is conditional upon the debtor bringing proof that he is not insolvent; this situation has led the divergent case law.[2]

The act amending Law no. 85/2014 that has transposed the Directive (EU) 2019/1023 has also eliminated from Law no. 85/2014 the definition of "imminent insolvency", in an attempt to avoid the risk of creating confusion between the statutory definition of "difficulty" and the statutory definition of "imminent insolvency".

In conclusion: "difficulty" and "insolvency" describe successive degrees of intensity of the same concept: the debtor's (in)ability to pay its debts.

- "Difficulty" (the lower step) would describe the debtor's reversible future inability to pay its debts (*in toto* or partially).
- "Insolvency" (the upper step) would describe the debtor's present inability to pay its debts (*in toto* or partially). While "reorganisation" would point to the debtor's present, but reversible inability to pay its debts (*in toto* or partially), "liquidation" would describe the debtor's present, but irreversible inability to pay its debts.

2. Law (Act) no. 151/2015 on the insolvency proceedings applicable to the natural persons (applicable to non-commercial, consumer insolvencies).

According to Law no. 151/2015, Article 3(12): "insolvency" is

> The specific state of the debtor's estate when the debtor's available cash resources are insufficient to pay his debts, as they become due. The debtor is presumed to be insolvent/in insolvency when he has not paid his debt(s) towards one or more creditors at least 90 days after it has/they have become due; the presumption is rebuttable.

Article 3(24) sets a threshold value (*de minimis*) for a debt to trigger the opening of the insolvency proceedings: 15 x the national guaranteed minimum salary in 2023, i.e. RON 28,470 (approximately EUR 5,700).

---

2 The survey published in the insolvency review publication "Phoenix" No. 84/2023, *Moțu/Deli*, "Noul concordat preventiv la 6 luni de la intrarea in vigoare a Legii nr. 216/2022", addressed the issue of the divergent case law, analysing the reasons employed by the Romanian courts in order to grant or dismiss the petitions to open pre-insolvency proceedings. Some of the most interesting points in the courts' reasoning were the judicial attempts to make a distinction between "difficulty" and "insolvency"; yet, such distinctions remain inconsistent in the judicial practice.

3. Government Emergency Ordinance (GEO) no. 46/2013 on the insolvencies of the self-governing territorial units (municipalities)

According to GEO no. 46/2013, Article 3(r): "insolvency" is:

> The specific state of territorial unit's estate when it experiences financial difficulties and/or a severe lack of cash resources, entailing its non-payment of its liquidated and due debts for a specific period of time. The territorial unit is presumed to be insolvent/in insolvency in any of the following situations:
>
> r1) when it has not paid its non-contentious liquidated debts that exceed 50% of the expenditures laid down in its general budget at least 120 days after they have matured;
>
> r2) when it has not paid the outstanding remuneration (wages) laid down in its budget at least 120 days after they have matured;

There is no threshold value (*de minimis*) in GEO no. 46/2013.

4. Apart from these *leges speciales*, the Romanian Civil Code, Article 1417(2) defines "insolvability"[3] as follows:

> The state of insolvability is the situation when the estate's assets against which enforcement can be sought are inferior, as to their monetary value, to the estate's due debts. Unless otherwise provided for in the law, the state of insolvability is to be declared by a court of law, which, to this end, may take into consideration various circumstances, such as: the debtor's sudden disappearance, the non-payment of the debts as they become due, the debtor's estate being subject to enforcement proceedings or other similar circumstances.

Question 2: Related to paragraph 10 above of the Introduction: seen from a principle-based perspective, what justifies the opening of insolvency proceedings in your jurisdiction?

In a nutshell: the debtor's inability to pay his/its ascertained (uncontested), liquidated and due debts using his/its cash resources justifies the opening of insolvency proceedings under the Romanian law.

---

[3] For historic reasons, the Romanian legislation makes a distinction between "insolvency" and "insolvability". In the middle of the 19th century, Romania had no civil code or commercial code. It "imported" the French Napoleon Code and made it the Romanian Civil Code in 1856, and it "imported" the Italian Commercial Code and made it the Romanian Commercial Code in 1887. As early as 1887, the civil jurisdiction and the commercial jurisdiction were separate. The term "insolvability" was specific to the Civil Code of 1856, and it survived in the new Romanian Civil Code of 2009. The Commercial Code of 1887 only recognised the concept of liquidation (*faliment*). Until 2004, the term "insolvability" was used for both traders (natural persons that are professional traders and companies) and non-traders (persons not involved in trading). In 2004, Law no. 64/1995, inspired by the US Code Chapter 11, introduced the term "insolvency", strictly related to insolvency proceedings. From 2004 onwards, the legal literature and case law have strived to make a clear-cut distinction between the two terms.

Elaborating on the justification above:

The Romanian insolvency statutes address the debtor's inability to pay the above-mentioned debts using two wordings:

1. one describing the status or condition of the debtor's estate: "when the debtor's available cash resources are insufficient to pay the debtor's ascertained (uncontested), liquidated and due debts";
2. one related to the debtor himself: "[the debtor's] manifest inability to pay his/its mature debts using its available cash resources".

Both wordings point to the same concept: the debtor's estate lacks, at a specific moment, the cash needed to pay the ascertained (uncontested), liquidated and due debts.

We have used the term "cash resources", as the Romanian statutes do not count assets that are easy to liquidate (bonds, stock etc.) as resources when assessing the debtor's insolvency.

As indicated *supra* in our answer to Question 1, the insolvency judge, when assessing whether the debtor is insolvent or not, ascertains:

1. that the debtor's estate does not possess enough cash to pay the ascertained (uncontested), liquidated and due debts;
2. that this situation is highly imminent (only when petitioned by the debtor) or present (when petitioned either by the creditor or by the debtor).

Should the situation be future and ascertainable, the debtor may only access the pre-insolvency, preventive proceedings.

In conclusion, the Romanian legislation relies on a rather restrictive balance sheet test (the test would be more appropriately named "cash resources test", as it does not consider any other assets that are easy to turn into cash).

When the debtor petitions the court seeking the opening of insolvency proceedings, the debtor needs to submit, as evidence, the annual financial statement drafted for the previous year and the balance sheet drafted for the month previous to the month the petition is lodged with the court. Obviously, that financial statement and that balance sheet only offer a static "snap-shot" of the debtor's assets and liabilities, with no relevant information as to the cash flow in and out of the debtor's estate.

Although these two terms have roughly the same meaning, their separate usage: "insolvability" outside insolvency proceedings and "insolvency" strictly within insolvency proceedings, respectively, has led to the present situation, where Romanian statutes regulate these two notions separately. The members of the legal community in Romania still use these terms distinctly, according to the context: "insolvency" strictly within the ambit of insolvency proceedings, and "insolvability" outside of insolvency proceedings.

Question 3: Does your national law in the context of liquidation proceedings use one or more of the following terms (be it as a noun, be it as an adjective or adjunct) in whatever context:

a) inability to pay debts

Yes. The term "inability to pay debts" is employed *verbatim* by Law no. 85/2014 on the prevention of insolvency proceedings and on insolvency proceedings (applicable to commercial insolvencies), Article 5(30) and (31), when defining the "insolvency of the credit institution" and the "insolvency of the insurance firm".

The "inability to pay debts", as a term, seems to be related to the debtor as a person.

Apart from the definitions of the "insolvency of the credit institution" and of the "insolvency of the insurance firm" in the Law no. 85/2014, the Romanian statutes on insolvency, when regulating insolvency, contain references not to the debtor as a person, but to the debtor's estate. Thus, their wording is less related to "the (in)ability to pay debts" and more related to the relationship between the due debts and the cash resources available to cover those debts.

In insolvency practice, the term *faliment* (the liquidation insolvency proceedings) points to a debtor that is irreversibly unable to pay its debts.

b) cessation of payments

n.a. (Yes, but not defining the moment when a debtor becomes insolvent).

Law no. 85/2014, Article 169 regulates directors' liability.

According to Law no. 85/2014, Article 169(1), the judicial administrator/ the judicial liquidator of a debtor (legal person) may bring a claim against the debtor's director(s) or against any other person that have/has caused the debtor's insolvency, by any of the following actions:

> c) carrying on the debtor's business, for the director's benefit, while the continuation of the debtor's activities would manifestly result in the debtor going into cessation of payments;
>
> ...
>
> f) using ruinous means to obtain liquidities for the debtor, in order to delay the debtor from going into cessation of payments;
>
> g) having made preferential payments in the month previous to the moment the debtor went into cessation of payments[.]

In our opinion, these references to the "cessation of payments" are a vestigial matter, due to the use of this notion by the previous statutory provisions governing insolvency.[4]

4 Law no. 64/1995 on reorganisation proceedings and bankruptcy addressed the "insolvency" by reference to the cessation of payments: "Any creditor who holds an undisputed, liquidated

However, it should be stressed that in the legal literature[5] and in the case law, the cessation of payments (of due debts) is considered as the observable element of a debtor's insolvency.

c) likely inability to pay debts
n.a.

d) imminent inability to pay debts
n.a.

As pointed out in our answer to Question 1, the act amending Law no. 85/2014 that has transposed Directive (EU) 2019/1023 has eliminated from Law no. 85/2014 the definition of "imminent insolvency", in an attempt to avoid confusion between the statutory definition of "difficulty" and the statutory definition of "imminent insolvency".

The term "imminent insolvency" survived, though. According to Law no. 85/2014, Article 66(4), a debtor whose insolvency is imminent may submit a petition seeking the opening of insolvency proceedings. The debtor is not under any obligation to submit such a petition before its insolvency is actual. The creditors do not enjoy this prerogative.

e) overindebtedness?
n.a.

Question 4: Are the same terms (and with the same meaning) used in the rules on preliminary/interim insolvency proceedings (e.g. concerning the application stage of the proceedings)?

The debtor's petition seeking the opening of insolvency proceedings is to be decided upon within a 10-day term, in *ex parte* (non-contradictory) proceedings. The terms mentioned in Question 3, if applicable, are used in the said proceedings and they have the same meaning.

The creditor/creditor's application seeking the opening of insolvency proceedings against a debtor is heard in adversarial proceedings. The terms mentioned in Question 3, if applicable, are used in the said proceedings and they have the same meaning.

When drafting the act amending Law no. 85/2014 which has transposed the Directive (EU) 2019/1023, the legislator was rather keen on avoiding any overlapping between the situation of "insolvency" a debtor may find himself in, on one hand, and the situation of "difficulty" a debtor may experience, on the

---

and due claims against a debtor may file with the tribunal a petition against that debtor; the debtor is presumed to be insolvent when he had ceased to make payments to that creditor for at least thirty (30) days". Law no. 64/1995 was repealed by Law no. 85/2006, which contained a *statutory definition* of the insolvency.

5 *Bufan (ed.),* Tratat practic de insolventa, 2nd ed., Cap. VII – Deschiderea procedurii de insolventa, Hamangiu publishing house, 2022, p. 297, para. 62.

other. Therefore, the terms (a) inability to pay debts, (b) cessation of payments, (c) likely inability to pay debts, and (d) imminent inability to pay debts are not used in the context of the pre-insolvency preventive proceedings.

Starting from the premises discussed under Question 1, the technical concept introduced in the pre-insolvency preventive proceedings is that of "future reversible inability to pay debts".

There are three tools by which pre-insolvency proceedings are "tested" for eligibility: (i) the absence of insolvency; (ii) the *temporary* impairment of the debtor's *future ability* to pay debts as they fall due; and (iii) the *current ability* to pay existing debts as they fall due.

The assessment of non-existence of insolvency of a debtor for such proceedings is a regulatory requirement to avoid collision with *current* inability to pay debts already due.

In conclusion, the term "*likely inability to pay future debts*" defines the pre-insolvency proceedings, provided that *the debtor is able to pay current debts.*

Question 5: Does your national law in the context of restructuring proceedings (as referred to above at paragraph 8 of the Introduction, i.e. both pre-insolvency and within formal insolvency proceedings) use one or more of the following terms (be it as a noun, be it as an adjective or adjunct) in whatever context:

Preliminary comment:

1. For the pre-insolvency, preventive proceedings ("restructuring agreement" and *concordat preventiv* – they are both "restructuring"), the Romanian statutes use the concept of "difficulty" (= distress), i.e.

> the condition caused by any circumstance resulting in a temporary impairment of business giving rise to a real and serious threat to the debtor's future ability to pay its debts as they fall due, unless appropriate measures are taken; the distressed debtor is able to meet its obligations as they fall due.

The court tests whether the debtor is in a state of "difficulty" in order to open the pre-insolvency, preventive proceedings.

The terms (a) inability to pay debts, (b) cessation of payments, (c) likely inability to pay debts and (d) imminent inability to pay debts are not likely to be used in the context of pre-insolvency, preventive proceedings.

The debtor's "inability to pay the debts", as the debts have been the subject of a moratorium and/or of a haircut via the "restructuring agreement" or via the "restructuring plan",[6] is good grounds on which to seek the judicial ending of

[6] The *concordat preventiv* proceedings employ a "restructuring plan" (*plan de restructurare*) in order to restructure the debtor or its activity. The Romanian legislator has kept the name *concordat preventiv* for these proceedings as they are listed in the Annex A of the European Insolvency Regulation.

the "restructuring agreement"/"*concordat preventiv*" and the opening of "general insolvency proceedings". Yet, when seeking such an order, the applicant rather brings into question the debtor's ability to perform under the restructuring agreement/restructuring plan and to pay the ongoing activity costs and debts than the debtor's ability to pay the pre-commencement debts.

Another term used in this context is "non-performance under the restructuring agreement/restructuring plan".

2. In the Romanian statutes, the "insolvency proceedings" are an "umbrella concept", covering three stages. A debtor in insolvency has three options:

(a) When the debtor's insolvency is present and irreversible, the debtor may choose the "simplified liquidation proceedings". No restructuring is available during such proceedings.
(b) When the debtor's insolvency is present and reversible and the debtor already envisages accessing restructuring proceedings, the debtor may apply for the opening of "general insolvency proceedings", mentioning in the application that he intends to submit a reorganisation plan. After the list of creditors is finalised, the debtor then proposes a reorganisation plan to the creditors. If voted by the creditors or "crammed down" on the creditors, the "judicial reorganisation proceedings" commence.
(c) When either a creditor brings/several creditors bring an application seeking the opening of insolvency proceedings or the debtor is unsure whether a reorganisation plan would be successful, the creditor(s) or the debtor may apply for the opening of "general insolvency proceedings". After the list of creditors is finalised, the debtor/the judicial administrator/a creditor may propose a reorganisation plan to the creditors. If voted by the creditors or crammed down on the creditors, the "judicial reorganisation proceedings" commence. If not voted by the creditors or not crammed down on the creditors, the debtor goes into "general liquidation proceedings".

The insolvency judge tests whether the debtor is in a state of "insolvency" in order to open either the "simplified liquidation proceedings" or the "general insolvency proceedings".

The opening of "judicial reorganisation proceedings" is a later stage of the "general insolvency proceedings", therefore the insolvency judge does not assess (for a second time) whether the debtor is insolvent, because the debtor's insolvency has already been assessed when the "general insolvency proceedings" were commenced. Subsequently, there is little chance (if any) that the terms: (a) inability to pay debts, (b) cessation of payments, (c) likely inability to pay debts and (d) imminent inability to pay debts will be used in the context of the "judicial reorganisation proceedings".

The debtor's inability to pay the debts, as they have been the subject of a moratorium and/or of a haircut, is good grounds on which to seek the judicial ending of the "judicial reorganisation proceedings" and the opening of the "general liquidation proceedings". Yet, when seeking such an order, the applicant rather brings into question the debtor's ability to perform under the reorganisation plan and to pay the post-commencement debts than the debtor's ability to pay the pre-commencement debts.

Another term used in this context is "non-performance under the reorganisation plan".

a) inability to pay debts
Yes. Please see the preliminary comment above.

b) cessation of payments
n.a.

c) likely inability to pay debts
n.a.

d) imminent inability to pay debts
n.a.

e) overindebtedness?
n.a.

Question 6: Which of the terms mentioned in Questions 3 and 5 are used for defining grounds to commence proceedings (triggering circumstances)?

a) insolvency proceedings

- The term "inability to pay debts":

  It is either the term "inability to pay debts", when the statutes are referring to the debtor himself or "the specific state of the debtor's estate when the debtor's available cash resources are insufficient to pay the debtor's ascertained (uncontested), liquidated and due debts.", when the statutes point to the debtor's estate.
- The term "imminent inability to pay debts":

  According to Law no. 85/2014, Article 66(4), "the debtor whose state of insolvency is to occur imminently may file a petition with the court seeking the application of the provisions in this title." The said title in the Law no. 85/2014 regulates the insolvency procedures.

b) restructuring proceedings
Please see our answer to Question 5.

Pre-insolvency, preventive proceedings employ the concept of difficulty. Therefore, none of the terms mentioned in Question 3 and Question 5 are used for defining grounds to commence pre-insolvency, preventive proceedings.

In the context of formal insolvency proceedings, the terms "inability to pay debts" and "imminent inability to pay debts" are used to define triggering circumstances to commence "general insolvency proceedings". The "general insolvency proceedings" are a compulsory procedural step prior to the opening of the "judicial reorganisation proceedings".

When, during "judicial reorganisation proceedings", the debtor fails to perform under the reorganisation plan, the debtor's inability to pay the debts, as they have been the subject of a moratorium and/or of a haircut, is good grounds on which to seek the judicial ending of the "judicial reorganisation proceedings" and the opening of "general liquidation proceedings". Yet, when seeking such an order, the applicant rather brings into question the debtor's ability to perform under the reorganisation plan and to pay the post-commencement debts than the debtor's ability to pay the pre-commencement debts.

Question 7: Does the answer to Question 6 include personal bankruptcies of natural persons or only corporate insolvencies of legal entities?

Yes, the consumer insolvency (bankruptcy of natural persons) and the insolvency of the municipalities rely on the same triggering circumstance: "the inability to pay debts".

The Romanian insolvency statutes regulating the consumer insolvency and the insolvency of the municipalities do not rely, as a triggering circumstance, on the "imminent inability to pay debts".

Please see our answer to Question 1.

Question 8: In your law, are there any other circumstances which trigger insolvency or restructuring proceedings?

For (formal) insolvency proceedings, no.

Following our answer to Question 1, a debtor is declared insolvent when his cash resources are insufficient to cover the debts that are (uncontested), liquidated and due. In order to facilitate the creditor's (claimant's) burden of proof, Law no. 85/2014 on the prevention of insolvency proceedings and on insolvency proceedings lays down a rebuttable legal presumption that the debtor is insolvent if it fails to pay a debt for more than 60 days after the said debt's due date.

The legal doctrine[7] agrees that it is rather difficult for creditors to come to know the exact reasons behind the debtor's inability to pay its debts. Thus, the legislator set out in Law no. 85/2014 the above-mentioned presumption of insolvency.

---

7 *Bufan*, ibid., p. 264.

The Romanian Constitutional Court gave a detailed reasoning on the functioning of this legal presumption of insolvency:

> Setting out of this presumption – in which case it falls on the debtor to produce the proof to the contrary – is justified by the need to expedite the insolvency proceedings, as a principle underlying the business law relations, as well as by the need to avoid the creditor's obligation to produce the proof of insolvency, which would be impossible as long as the creditor does not have access to the debtor's documents and data regarding the money available thereof.[8]

In the context of providing evidence during the hearing of the application by the creditor(s) to open insolvency proceedings, the existence of ordinary enforcement proceedings that *did not result in funds recovered, sufficient to satisfy the creditor(s)' claim(s)* is considered conclusive evidence as to the debtor being insolvent.

Other circumstances have also been considered relevant in the case law,[9] such as *the lack of liquidities/funds*:

> Insolvency is not characterised by the general poor state of affairs of the concerned trader or by the existence of liabilities greater than the debtor's assets, i.e. its insolvency, but by *a lack of funds necessary* to cover debts due and payable; insolvency is closely related to the inability to pay, seen as the *effective cessation of payments* (emphasis added).

On the contrary, should the debtor produce evidence as to his *solvency*, such pieces of evidence strongly support the dismissal of the application by the creditor(s) to open insolvency proceedings:

> As regards the liabilities, the debtor rebutted the presumption of its insolvency by producing evidence that it holds liquidities higher in value than the total amount of the previously listed debts. Specifically, the debtor proved that, at the time the appeal was under consideration, it had liquid assets the amount of which is much higher that its undisputed, liquidated and due debts. The debtor's solvency is thus proven by *its statement of account* (emphasis added).[10]

---

8 Decision no. 1586/19.11.2019, Constitutional Court of Romania, published in the Official Journal, Part I, No. 71 of 30 January 2010.

9 Timişoara Court of Appeal, II-a Civil Division, Decision no. 2225/2012, quoted in *Terzea*, Codul insolvenţei adnotat, cu doctrină şi jurisprudenţă, Universul Juridic publishing house, Bucharest 2022, p. 51.

10 Cluj Court of Appeal, II Civil Division, Decision no. 201/2018, quoted in *Terzea*, ibid., p. 267.

Question 9: Which of the terms mentioned in Questions 3, 5, and 8 are used in the context of transactions avoidance law?

In a nutshell: none.

Elaborating on our answer:

1. The legal provisions in Law no. 85/2014 on pre-insolvency, preventive proceedings do not lay down any rules on the avoidance of the debtor's transactions. The avoidance actions specific to insolvency proceedings may not be used in the context of pre-insolvency, preventive proceedings. In theory, the revocatory action (*actio pauliana*) regulated by the Civil Code is available during pre-insolvency, preventive proceedings as long as the debtor is also in "insolvability";[11] as the provisions regulating pre-insolvency, preventive proceedings were brought as amendments to Law no. 85/2014 in 2022, there is as yet no case law where a creditor has sought the avoidance of a transaction concluded by a debtor subject to pre-insolvency, preventive proceedings.

2. In the context of insolvency (be it a commercial insolvency, a natural person's insolvency or a municipality's insolvency), avoidance actions are only available after the insolvency proceedings are opened.

When laying down the conditions for a transaction to be avoided, all the insolvency statutes contain explicit references to the moment of the opening of the insolvency proceedings. There are no explicit references to the debtor's inability to pay, to the cessation of payments, to the debtor's likely inability to pay debts, to the debtor's imminent inability to pay debts or to the debtor's overindebtedness. As the "inability to pay debts" is the triggering circumstance for the opening of insolvency proceedings, one may infer that the provisions in the insolvency statutes regulating avoidance actions *indirectly* point to the debtor's *inability to pay*, but, again, the terms mentioned in Question 3, Question 5 and Question 8 are not used, as such, in the context of transactions avoidance law.

3. In the general Romanian civil law context, the provisions in the Romanian Civil Code laying down the rules of the revocatory action (*actio pauliana*) only contain an explicit reference to the debtor's 'insolvability'.

According to the Romanian Civil Code, Article 1562:

> (1) Should a creditor prove he has sustained some damage, he may seek that the debtor's acts concluded to defraud his interests, such as the acts that have created or enhanced his state of insolvability, may not be invoked against him.
> (2) A contract for consideration or a payment made under such a contract may only be declared non-invocable against such a creditor when the other contracting party or the recipient knew the fact that the debtor is thus creating or enhancing his state of insolvability.

[11] Please see our answer to Question 1, and fn. 26.

According to the Romanian Civil Code, Article 1417(2), the state of *insolvability* is defined as:

> the situation when the estate's assets against which enforcement can be sought are inferior, as to their monetary value, to the estate's due debts. Unless otherwise provided for in the law, the state of insolvability is to be declared by a court of law, which, to this end, may take into consideration various circumstances, such as: the debtor's sudden disappearance, the non-payment of the debts as they become due, the debtor's estate being subject to enforcement proceedings or other similar circumstances.

Again, there are no explicit references to the debtor's inability to pay, to the cessation of payments, to the debtor's likely inability to pay debts, to the debtor's imminent inability to pay debts or to the debtor's overindebtedness. As the "inability to pay [all] debts" is the consequence of the estate's assets against which enforcement can be sought being "inferior, as to their monetary value, to the estate's due debts", one may appreciate that the rules on the revocatory action (*actio pauliana*) in the Romanian Civil Code *indirectly* point to the debtor's *inability to pay*.

Question 10: Which of the terms addressed in Questions 3, 5, and 8 are used in the context of directors' duties?

a) shift of duties (from shareholders to creditors)

The relevant rule in Law no. 31/1990 on companies contains an explicit reference to the (moment of the) opening of insolvency proceedings, only. As mentioned above in our answer to Question 9, as the "inability to pay debts" is the triggering circumstance for the opening of insolvency proceedings, one may conclude that the provisions in the insolvency statutes regulating the avoidance actions *indirectly* point to the debtor's *inability to pay*.

b) duties to commence insolvency proceedings

The only Romanian statute on insolvency that lays down rules on the duties to commence insolvency proceedings is Law no. 85/2014 on the prevention of insolvency proceedings and on insolvency proceedings (applicable to commercial insolvencies).

According to Law no. 85/2014, Article 66(1): "A debtor in insolvency has the duty to lodge a petition seeking the opening of insolvency proceedings with the court no later than 30 days after the state of insolvency has occurred."

The circumstance triggering the opening of the insolvency proceedings is the debtor's "inability to pay his debts"; hence one may conclude that the provisions in the insolvency statute regulating the duty to commence insolvency proceedings *indirectly* point to the debtor's *inability to pay*.

c) other duties (please describe)

According to the Romanian corporate law regulations, it falls on the directors to act *prudently* and *diligently*.

The standard to be used when looking into this obligation is the *duty of care*.

Once the company becomes insolvent, it is incumbent on the director(s) to file a petition seeking the opening of the insolvency proceedings.

Correspondently, should the company go into the state of "difficulty" (please see our answer to Question 1) (= future inability to pay debts), the director's *duty of care* entails the obligation to take all the appropriate measures to avoid the company becoming unable to pay its debts.

Question 11: Are there any other rules in the context of which the terms addressed in Questions 3, 5, and 8 are used?

Yes, the "cessation of payments" in the context of directors' liability.

According to Law no. 85/2014, Article 169(1), the judicial administrator/ the judicial liquidator of a debtor (legal person) may bring a claim against the debtor's director(s) or against any other person that has caused the debtor's insolvency, by any of the following actions:

c) carrying on the debtor's business, for the director's benefit, while the continuation of the debtor's activities would manifestly result in the debtor going into cessation of payments;
f) using ruinous means to obtain liquidities for the debtor, in order to delay the debtor from going into cessation of payments;
g) having made preferential payments in the month previous to the moment the debtor went into cessation of payments.

Please see also our answer to Question 3.

Question 12: Is the definition of (the subspecies of) insolvency identical in all legal fields or are there different definitions (e.g. different in insolvency law than in criminal law)?

"Insolvency" is only defined in the three statutes we have mentioned in our answer to Question 1:

1. Law no. 85/2014 on the prevention of insolvency proceedings and on insolvency proceedings (applicable to commercial insolvencies)

According to Law no. 85/2014, Article 5(29), "insolvency" is:

> The specific state of the debtor's estate when the debtor's available cash resources are insufficient to pay the debtor's ascertained (uncontested), liquidated and due debts. The debtor is presumed to be insolvent/in insolvency when it has not paid such a debt at least 60 days after its maturity; the presumption is rebuttable.

Article 5, point 72 sets a threshold value (*de minimis*) for one or more debts aggregated necessary to trigger the opening of insolvency proceedings: RON 50,000 (approximately EUR 10,000).

By way of exception:

- Law no. 85/2014, Article 5(30) defines the "insolvency of a credit institution" as any of the following situations a credit institution may find itself in:
  (a) its manifest inability to pay its mature debts using its available cash resources;
  (b) the credit institution's solvency indicator drops below 2%;
  (c) the withdrawal of its licence, pursuant to the law, due to its financial recovery being unattainable.
- Law no. 85/2014, Article 5(30) defines the "insolvency of an insurance firm" as any of the following situations an insurance firm may find itself in:
  (a) its manifest inability to pay its mature debts using its available cash resources;
  (b) the withdrawal of its licence due to the insurance firm not complying with the solvency legal requirements;
  (c) the withdrawal of the licence granted to a residual insurance firm created in the resolution proceedings.

2. Law (Act) no. 151/2015 on the insolvency proceedings applicable to the natural persons (applicable to non-commercial, consumer insolvencies)

According to Law no. 151/2015, Article 3(12): "insolvency" is:

> The specific state of the debtor's estate when the debtor's available cash resources are insufficient to pay his debts, as they become due. The debtor is presumed to be insolvent/in insolvency when he has not paid his debt towards one or more creditors at least 90 days after it has/they have become due; the presumption is rebuttable.

Article 3(24) sets a threshold value (*de minimis*) for a debt to trigger the opening of the insolvency proceedings: 15 x the national guaranteed minimum salary.

3. Government Emergency Ordinance no. 46/2013 on insolvencies of the self-governing territorial units (municipalities)

According to GEO no. 46/2013, Article 3(r): "insolvency" is:

> The specific state of territorial unit's estate when it experiences financial difficulties and/or a severe lack of cash resources, entailing its non-payment of its liquidated and due debts for a specific period of time. The territorial unit is presumed to be insolvent/in insolvency in any of the following situations:
>
> r1) when it has not paid its non-contentious liquidated debts that exceed 50% of the expenditures laid down in its general budget at least 120 days after they have matured;
>
> r2) when it has not paid the outstanding remunerations (wages) laid down in its budget at least 120 days after they have matured;

No threshold value (*de minimis*) appears in GEO no. 46/2013.

4. The (rather) new act amending Law no. 85/2014 that has transposed Directive (EU) 2019/1023 lays down a definition of "difficulty" (distress), in Article 5(26²):

> the condition caused by any circumstance resulting in a temporary impairment of business giving rise to a real and serious threat to the debtor's future ability to pay its debts as they fall due, unless appropriate measures are taken; the distressed debtor is able to meet its obligations as they fall due.

Moreover, it has brought a new proviso: "The preventive restructuring proceedings … shall be applicable only to debtors in difficulty that *are not in insolvency*" (emphasis added).

"Difficulty" and "insolvency" describe successive degrees of intensity of the same concept: the debtor's (in)ability to pay its debts.

"Difficulty" (the lower step) would describe the debtor's reversible future inability to pay its debts (*in toto* or partially).

"Insolvency" (the upper step) would describe the debtor's present inability to pay its debts (*in toto* or partially). While "reorganisation" would point to the debtor's present, but reversible inability to pay its debts (*in toto* or partially), "liquidation" would describe the debtor's present, but irreversible inability to pay its debts.

5. Apart from these *leges speciales*, the Romanian Civil Code, Article 1417(2) defines "insolvability" as follows:

> The state of insolvability is the situation when the estate's assets against which enforcement can be sought are inferior, as to their monetary value, to the estate's due debts. Unless otherwise provided for in the law, the state of insolvability is to be declared by a court of law, which, to this end, may take into consideration various circumstances, such as: the debtor's sudden disappearance, the non-payment of the debts as they become due, the debtor's estate being subject to enforcement proceedings or other similar circumstances.

The Romanian legal commentators have termed the "insolvability" "accounting insolvency". Interestingly enough, the Romanian Civil Code, Article 1417(1) lays down the rule according to which a debtor that is either in a state of "insolvability" or in a state of "insolvency", duly declared by a court of law, is subject to the acceleration of the maturity of his debts, hence all his debts become immediately due and payable. This rule in the Romanian Civil Code is in direct contradiction to the rules in Law no. 85/2014 on executory contracts.

6. Another Romanian statute that employs the notion of "insolvability" (= accounting insolvency) is Law no. 227/2015 on the tax code.

According to the Romanian Tax Code, Article 176(1):

> For the purposes of this law, a debtor is insolvable if his income or his assets that enforcement may be sought against have a monetary value lower than his fiscal obligations. The same rule applies if the debtor has no income or no such assets.

II. INABILITY TO PAY DEBTS

Question 13: In your jurisdiction, is the term "inability to pay debts" defined in statute? If so, please give the wording in English translation. Is this definition (if any) specified in case law? If so, how?

In a nutshell: no.

Elaborating on our answer:

Law no. 85/2014, Article 5 (30) defines the "insolvency of a credit institution" as any of the following situations a credit institution may find itself in:

(a) its *manifest inability to pay* its mature *debts* using its available cash resources;
(b) the credit institution's solvency indicator drops below 2%;
(c) the withdrawal of its licence, pursuant to the law, due to its financial recovery being unattainable.

Law no. 85/2014, Article 5(30) defines the "insolvency of an insurance firm" as any of the following situations an insurance firm may find itself in:

(a) its *manifest inability to pay* its mature *debts* using its available cash resources;
(b) the withdrawal of its licence due to the insurance firm not complying with the solvency legal requirements;
(c) the withdrawal of the licence granted to a residual insurance firm created in the resolution proceedings.

Formally, the term "inability to pay" is used to define "insolvency". Apparently, the Romanian legislator deemed the term "inability to pay" explicit enough and did not feel the need to further define it.

The legal doctrine[12] considers that "insolvency *implies* that the debtor is unable to pay its debts as they fall due". The relationship between insolvency and inability to pay is traditional under Romanian law. The inability to pay is deemed

> to reflect the state of the debtor's assets, which makes it impossible to pay the debts due with the available money. Thus, insolvency equals the actual insufficiency of liquid

12 *Bufan*, fn. 6, p. 262 et seq.

> assets, the absence of funds necessary to pay the due obligations. When, irrespective of the reason, the debtor is unable to generate liquidity at a rate commensurate with his outstanding obligations (because, for example, the assets in its estate are not liquid or cannot be used to pay debts, because they are invested in long-term operations), we consider that the debtor is insolvent because of its inability to pay, i.e. to satisfy its creditors from the amounts it owes.

The case law[13] sees the "inability to pay debts" as *an effect of the absence of payments*:

> failure to pay debts when due must be the consequence of the debtor's inability to pay its outstanding liabilities out of the money available; the proof of such inability – which is an internal condition of the debtor – may consist in any element capable of demonstrating the existence of an external and objective event: the cessation of payments.

Please see also the correlations between "insolvency", "inability to pay debts" and "effective cessation of payments" in the case law quoted under Question 8.

Question 14: Does your law refer to all debts or only to mature debts?

When defining "insolvency" or referring to "insolvency", the reference is made to mature debts, only.

Moreover, when regulating the legal rebuttable presumption of insolvency, the debtor is deemed to be insolvent when he has failed to pay his ascertained (uncontested) and liquidated debts that matured at least 60 days before the creditor's application seeking the opening of insolvency proceedings has been submitted.

Question 15: Which assets are taken into account when assessing the inability to pay debts: all (financial) assets or only those that are liquid, i.e. available on short notice?

The letter of the Romanian law takes into account money only (not even other liquid assets such as money market instruments or marketable securities).

While rather controversial, the case law allows for some flexibility:[14] "the debtor who, having benefited from certain subsidies, does not make payments

---

13 Timişoara Court of Appeal, II Civil Division, Civil Decision of 12 July 2021, available at https://www.rejust.ro/juris/dde3g7g8.

14 *Bufan*, fn. 6 *supra*, p. 263, para. 33: "if the debtor has receivables to collect from its own debtors, insofar as the law-maker did not intend for such a situation to be likely to prevent the applicability of the rules on insolvency, there did exist some courts of law who disregarded this aspect and were not firm in applying the law – probably for social considerations."

to his suppliers on a regular basis, but at the time it collects those subsidies, is not in a state of insolvency".

The legal authors[15] have concluded that

> whenever a determination is made in respect of the debtor's available money, one should consider only the present, not the future amounts, because it is the financial standing of the debtor at the time a petition for insolvency is filed and determined upon, that is under scrutiny. This is why the courts of law shall not rely on future income of benefits of the debtor, because they cannot be considered at the time a determination is made on insolvency, but only on the current financial standing of the debtor's estate.

It has been pointed out that[16]

> it is not necessary to have an absolute cessation of payments but the cessation of payments must be real, result from the absence of money available for the payment of due and payable debts and outlines the financial imbalance of the debtor.

However, older case law[17] has set out some solutions taking into account future incomes, such as the financial benefits that would be achieved during the year, as reflected in the management report of the previous year.

Question 16: Is any liquidity gap (deficit between relevant financial means and relevant debts) relevant or does your law neglect minor gaps? If the latter, how is "minor" defined?

Considering "insolvency" from a substantive point of view:

The Romanian statutory instruments do not address this issue. The apparent conclusion would be that any liquidity gap, no matter how small, equates to insolvency. Adding the fact that, according to Romanian law, the test used to determine insolvency is the balance sheet test, insolvency is instantaneous.

However, from a procedural point of view:

According to the rules in Law no. 85/2014 on the prevention of insolvency proceedings and on insolvency proceedings (applicable to commercial insolvencies), neither the debtor nor any creditor may seek the opening of the insolvency proceedings unless the unpaid debt(s) that are uncontested

---

15 *Bufan*, fn. 6 *supra*, p. 265, para. 35.

16 *Comsa*, Inceperea procedurii reorganizarii judiciare si a falimentului la cererea creditorilor, *Phoenix*, 11/2005, p. 23.

17 Bucharest Tribunal, Commercial Division, Sentence no. 3372 of 24 September 1997, quoted in *Bufan*, fn. 6 *supra*, p. 265, n. 5.

(ascertained), liquidated and at least 60 days overdue have a value of at least RON 50,000 (approximately EUR 10,000).

According to the rules in Law no. 151/2015 on insolvency proceedings applicable to natural persons (applicable to non-commercial, consumer insolvencies), the threshold value (*de minimis*) for a debt to trigger the opening of insolvency proceedings is 15 x the national guaranteed minimum salary: in 2023, RON 28,470 (approximately EUR 5,700).

The Government Emergency Ordinance no. 46/2013 on insolvencies of the self-governing territorial units (municipalities) lays down no threshold value (*de minimis*).

Question 17: As far as the time aspect is concerned, does it matter whether the liquidity gap can be closed again in the short term? If so, how long is the grace period?

According to the rules in Law no. 85/2014 on the prevention of insolvency proceedings and on insolvency proceedings (applicable to commercial insolvencies), the grace period is 60 days.

According to the rules in Law no. 151/2015 on insolvency proceedings applicable to natural persons (applicable to non-commercial, consumer insolvencies), the grace period is 90 days.

The Government Emergency Ordinance no. 46/2013 on insolvencies of the self-governing territorial units (municipalities) lays down no grace period.

Question 18: As far as the time aspect is concerned, is a debtor considered insolvent if the liquidity gap is not yet present but will occur soon? If so, how long is the prognosis period? (Note: this may also concern the difference between actual and likely/imminent inability to pay debts; cf. below Question 34).

As the Romanian law stands, should the liquidity gap not be present yet, but it will occur in the future, the debtor is not in insolvency, but *in difficulty*. In this situation, pre-insolvency, preventive, restructuring proceedings are available to the debtor.

As pointed out *supra* (please see our answer to Question 1), the act amending Law no. 85/2014 that transposed Directive (EU) 2019/1023 has brought in the definition of "difficulty" and has eliminated the statutory definition of "imminent insolvency". "Imminent insolvency" was a subspecies of "insolvency" in the previous version of Law no. 85/2014, before the transposition of Directive (EU) 2019/1023 into the Romanian legislation. The purpose of the said amendment was to avoid the risk of the statutory definition of "difficulty" and the statutory definition of "imminent insolvency" overlapping.

The definition of "imminent insolvency" in the previous version of Law no. 85/2014 reads as follows: "[a debtor's insolvency is imminent] whenever the debtor is proven to be unable to pay his debts, as they fall due, with his cash resources available on the dates of their maturities".

As we have mentioned in our answer to Question 3, although the statutory definition of "imminent insolvency" has not survived into Law no. 85/2014, as amended by Law no. 216/2022, Article 66(4) still allows a debtor whose insolvency is imminent to submit a petition seeking the opening of insolvency proceedings. Unlike the situation where the debtor is actually insolvent, if his insolvency is only imminent, the debtor is not under the obligation to file for insolvency, but only has the possibility to do so.

Anyway, neither under the previous version of Law no. 85/2014 nor as the Romanian legislation stands now, was/is there a prognosis period provided for when assessing insolvency.[18]

Question 19: How is inability to pay debts established? Please communicate if there is a difference between a creditor and a debtor application or between different legal contexts.

Preliminary comment:

The debtor's petition is heard in *ex parte*, non-adversarial proceedings. The insolvency judge decides upon the debtor's application after hearing written evidence only. The debtor's petition is deemed to be an acknowledgment of the debts and an acknowledgment of his inability to pay them, hence of insolvency. In principle, the insolvency judge only makes a formal verification of the written evidence submitted by the debtor along his petition. *Inter alia*, the debtor must produce: the annual financial statement drawn up for the previous year (containing a statement of financial position, a statement of profit and loss, and a statement of cash flows), the balance sheet drawn up for the month prior to the moment the petition is filed with the court, and a list of his creditors, comprising all his liquidated debts, secured or not, contested or not, due or not yet mature. Thus, the insolvency judge is getting a rather comprehensive view of the debtor's (in)ability to pay his debts. Of course, should the written evidence prove that the debtor does not owe anything or his debts do not reach the *de minimis* threshold or the debtor has enough cash resources to pay his debts, the debtor's petition will be dismissed. The debtor's mere acknowledgment of the debts and of his inability to pay them is not sufficient evidence for the opening of insolvency proceedings.

Should the debtor submit inaccurate written evidence, the decision to open insolvency proceedings may be opposed by any creditor. The decision opening the insolvency proceedings is published in the (electronic) Romanian Bulletin

[18] Please see our answer to Question 35.

of Insolvency Proceedings, and all the creditors in the list submitted by the debtor along with his petition are notified about the opening of the insolvency proceedings, via registered post. The decision opening the insolvency proceedings sets out a specific time limit for the creditors to bring their applications opposing the decision.

The application by the creditor(s) seeking the opening of insolvency proceedings needs to be accompanied by evidence as to the debt(s). The procedural provisions do not limit the evidence to written evidence, yet, in practice, other types of evidence are rarely heard.

The creditor(s) must prove that the debt(s) is/are ascertained (and if contested by the debtor, also that there are no good grounds for the debtor to contest it/them), is/are liquidated and overdue at least 60 days in commercial insolvencies/90 days in consumer insolvencies.

Both Law no. 85/2014 and Law no. 151/2015 lay down rebuttable presumptions that a debtor who has not paid his ascertained (uncontested), liquidated and due debts for more than 60 days (commercial debts)/90 days (consumer debts) is insolvent.

As soon as the creditor(s) has/have proven the above-mentioned facts, the burden of proof shifts to the debtor. The debtor may contest the debt(s), by way of a simple response, and/or his inability to pay the debt(s), by way of a formal contestation. In most cases where the debtor's contestation is successful, he brings proof of having enough *cash* to cover the debt(s) the creditor(s) have relied upon. The case law shows that future income, immediately and ascertainably payable, is also accepted as proof of cash resources. Having enough *assets* that may be liquidated in order to pay the debts is not accepted as proof of solvency. The case law also emphasises that insolvency proceedings are not to be used to force a solvent debtor's hand to pay a contested debt.

a) Is a formal liquidity status (liquidity balance sheet) required?

- *According to Law no. 85/2014 (commercial insolvencies)*, Article 67(1)(a), *the debtor* must submit, along with his petition, *inter alia*, the balance sheet drawn up for the month prior to the moment the petition is filed with the court.

  The said balance sheet contains the debtor's assets, cash resources, liabilities, income and expenditure, listed in groups, for the month prior to the moment the petition is filed with the court.

  The application by the creditor(s) does not need to be accompanied by any such document. Neither is the debtor, as a defendant, under any obligation to disclose such a liquidity balance sheet during the pre-opening proceedings. (Should the application by the creditor(s) be successful, the debtor will need to submit, *inter alia*, such a document to the insolvency practitioner appointed by the insolvency judge as judicial administrator/judicial liquidator.)

- *According to Law no. 151/2015 (consumer insolvencies)*, Article 13(5), *the debtor* must submit, along with his petition, a list of his assets, income sources and cash resources, as well as a list of his debts and other obligations. There is no specific document containing this information, the debtor draws up these lists as he sees fit.

  The application by the creditor(s) (applicable only to the liquidation proceedings) does not need to be accompanied by any such document.

b) Is a sample of daily liquidity data (which do not amount to a proper liquidity status but show insufficient funds on different days within a certain period of time) sufficient?

No.

c) Does the law provide for a rebuttable presumption? If so, under which conditions?

Both Law no. 85/2014 and Law no. 151/2015 lay down rebuttable presumptions that a debtor who has not paid his ascertained (uncontested), liquidated and due debts for more than 60 days (commercial debts)/90 days (consumer debts) is insolvent.

d) Does the law provide for any technical circumstances (e.g. undisputed statutory demand, non-compliance with monetary judgments, unsuccessful enforcement proceedings, non-performance of a previous composition agreement in insolvency proceedings) the occurrence of which suffices to establish the debtor's insolvency?

Under Law no. 85/2014 (commercial insolvencies), the debtor's petition is deemed to be an acknowledgment of the debts and of its inability to pay them. Should the written evidence submitted along with the petition prove that the debtor does not owe anything or his debts do not reach the *de minimis* threshold or the debtor has enough cash resources to pay its debts, the debtor's petition will be dismissed. The debtor's mere acknowledgment of the debts and of its inability to pay them is not sufficient evidence for the opening of insolvency proceedings.

Should the debtor fraudulently file for insolvency (e.g. to obtain an automatic stay) and thus be granted the opening of insolvency proceedings, the decision opening the insolvency proceedings may be opposed by any creditor. The decision is published in the (electronic) Romanian Bulletin of Insolvency Proceedings, and all the creditors in the list submitted by the debtor along with his petition are notified about the opening of the insolvency proceedings, via registered post. The decision opening the insolvency proceedings sets out a specific time limit for the creditors to bring their applications opposing the decision.

The opposition is not an ordinary appeal. The decision opening the insolvency proceedings upon the debtor's petition is given in *ex parte* proceedings; hence the creditors have not been summoned to those proceedings and they cannot be bound by the findings of the insolvency judge in the said decision (even if not appealed, the said decision does not enjoy the status of *res judicata*, as it has not been given at the end of adversarial proceedings). Thus, the creditors may simply oppose the decision opening the insolvency proceedings upon the debtor's petition, bringing evidence as to the debtor not in fact being insolvent. The opposing application(s) is/are heard by the same insolvency judge that passed the decision opening the insolvency proceedings upon the debtor's petition. Should the opposition be well grounded, the insolvency judge will revoke the decision granting the opening of insolvency proceedings upon the debtor's petition, and the insolvency proceedings come to an end.

When the application to open insolvency proceedings is brought by one or more creditors and the debtor fails to lodge a contestation of his state of insolvency within the time limit laid down by Law no. 85/2014, Article 72(3) (i.e. 10 days after being duly served with the application), the debtor is presumed to be insolvent.

Monetary claims that have been upheld by final court decisions and are overdue at least 60 days are also good grounds upon which to establish the debtor's insolvency, as such claims are non-contestable.

In the past there was a trend in the judicial practice placing an obligation on the creditor to seek the judicial enforcement (via court officers, bailiffs) of his claim prior to bringing his application for the opening of debtor's insolvency proceedings.[19] This trend was, nonetheless, rather debatable, as the insolvency statutes never required the creditor to obtain an enforceable court decision (or other type of *titre executoire*) prior to bringing his application.

As the judicial practice stands now, a creditor's unsuccessful attempt to recover the debt in previous judicial enforcement proceedings is only *additional proof* to establish the debtor's insolvency. No writ of enforcement is required in order to open the insolvency proceedings.

A debtor who has failed either in out-of-court negotiations or in pre-insolvency proceedings is under a legal obligation to bring a petition for the commencement of insolvency proceedings, within the prescribed time-limit. Thus, such failures may be considered good grounds for the opening of insolvency proceedings.

We need to mention here that all the above-mentioned situations are grounds sufficient to *presume* that the debtor is insolvent. Still, they are all rebuttable presumptions.

e) Other means?

As the case law shows, a debtor's cessation of payments is an ostensible manifestation of insolvency.

Firstly, in order to consider the cessation of payments as an *indicium* of insolvency, it must be effective; the present situation of the debtor must reveal his inability to pay the accrued debts.

---

19 Piteşti Court of Appeal, Commercial Division, Decision no. 509/4.05.2007, quoted in Insolvenţă. Practică judiciară 2007. Legislaţie comercială 2006–2007. Recursul în interesul legii, Moroşan, Botoşani 2007, pp. 23–30.

Secondly, the debtor's cessation of payments must have *objective*, i.e. it must be the consequence of the debtor's actual inability to pay his debts, regardless of whether or not the debtor chooses to pay them or not.

Question 20: Is insolvency (inability to pay debts, overindebtedness, etc.) subject to party autonomy in the proceedings or must the court clarify them *ex officio*?

Before the insolvency proceedings have been opened, the debtor's insolvency is subject to party autonomy, only.

Moreover, the jurisdiction *ratione materiae* to open insolvency proceedings lies with specialised judges only.[20] Thus, should the matter of a party's insolvency be brought to the attention of a non-specialised court, incidentally, or as a counterclaim/crossclaim, the non-specialised court cannot assume jurisdiction to hear or determine whether a party is insolvent or not.

In conclusion, the only procedural way to invoke a party's insolvency *before the opening of the insolvency proceedings* is to lodge a petition or an application with the court. The petition/application is heard by a specialised insolvency judge.

After the insolvency proceedings have been opened, a party's insolvency can be invoked both by the other party or the court, *ex officio*.

Question 21: In an overall view, does your law distinguish "inability to pay debts" from "financial difficulties"? If so, how?

Please see our answer to Question 1.

"Difficulty" and "insolvency" describe successive degrees of intensity of the same concept: the debtor's (in)ability to pay its debts. "Financial difficulties" would be a subspecies of "difficulty".

"Difficulty" (the lower step) would describe the debtor's reversible future inability to pay its debts (*in toto* or partially). It allows the debtor to access the pre-insolvency, preventive procedures to achieve restructuring.

"Insolvency" (the upper step) would describe the debtor's present inability to pay its debts (*in toto* or partially). It allows the debtor to access the insolvency procedures.

---

20 Most second-level courts in Romania (*tribunale*) are not specialised courts, but they have a division that hears commercial cases (commercial litigation, company law cases, insolvency). Within the said division, only some judges (*judecători-sindici*) are specialised in insolvency matters. Those judges have exclusive jurisdiction to hear petitions/applications seeking the opening of insolvency proceedings. Once an insolvency judge has opened insolvency proceedings against a certain debtor, the same judge shall hear all the actions related to the insolvency of the said debtor (e.g. transactions avoidance actions, directors' liability actions). Exceptionally, there are four *tribunale specializate* that hear commercial cases only. It is customary that all the judges in the four *tribunale specializate* are also specialised *judecători-sindici*.

Question 22: In an overall view, does it matter under your law whether the debtor's inability to pay debts is present or future and reversible or irreversible?

Yes.

Please see our answers to Questions 1, 3(a), 4 and 21.

"Difficulty" (the lower step) would describe the debtor's reversible future inability to pay its debts (*in toto* or partially). It allows the debtor to access the pre-insolvency, preventive procedures to restructure.

"Insolvency" (the upper step) would describe the debtor's present inability to pay its debts (*in toto* or partially).

The debtor's present, but reversible inability to pay its debts (*in toto* or partially) allows the debtor to access the insolvency procedure of "judicial reorganisation" (a formal restructuring procedure). The debtor's inability to pay is limited to the pre-commencement debts. While enjoying the stay of individual enforcements of the pre-commencement debts, the debtor should not accumulate any new, post-commencement debts, but be able to pay them as they become due. If the debtor is unable to pay the post-commencement debts as they come due, its inability to pay becomes irreversible.

The debtor's present, but irreversible inability to pay its debts only allows it to access the liquidation procedure.

The debtor's inability to pay its debts may know different *intensities* over time and its *reversibility* is a useful criterion in marking the difference between restructuring (both in pre-insolvency or formal insolvency) procedures and the liquidation procedure.

Question 23: Would you like to add any further aspects not covered by the above questions?

Particularly in times of economic crisis, creditors have regarded insolvency as an effective means of *forcing the debtor's hand to pay his debts*. The establishment of the rebuttable presumption of a debtor's insolvency deriving from the non-payment of debts overdue for more than 60 days (commercial insolvencies), plus the relatively restrictive means to rebut it, have been the source of long-standing and ongoing doctrinal disputes.

It was thus considered that

> reality has shown that, although aware that the debtor was not insolvent, many creditors filed applications for the opening of insolvency proceedings, hoping that the defendant would pay the claim to avoid an unfavourable solution which would adversely impact it, even if the only thing that could be made was the temporarily appointed insolvency practitioner sending the legal notifications. This is why we believe that insolvency can still be used as a formidable weapon in the hands of an unscrupulous creditor who wants to intimidate a fearful debtor, although it cannot represent a means of enforcement available to an isolated creditor, in order to satisfy its claims, no matter how much damage they have suffered and how legitimate they may be.

Against the backdrop of the current economic crisis, the above remains valid.

Although it became effective recently (July 2022), the Romanian statute transposing Directive (EU) 2019/1023 has created a rather precarious distinction between "difficulty" and "insolvency", which favours the first. A better set of distinguishing criteria in the statutory provisions would be most welcome. The different functions of the procedures – be it restructuring or liquidation – may thus be achieved.[21]

III. CESSATION OF PAYMENTS

Question 24: In your jurisdiction, is "cessation of payments" a legal term used either in statute or in case law? (If the answer is "no", please continue with Question 31.)

Yes, but not defining the moment a debtor becomes insolvent.

For its statutory use, please see our answers to Questions 3(b) and 19(e).

It has no statutory definition.

The term "cessation of payments" is also used by the legal authors. According to some legal academic writers,[22] it consists of two layers: a visible part – the cessation of payments – and the invisible part – the insolvency as a "pathological" condition of the debtor's estate.

In the case law, the term is used as follows:[23]

> The failure to pay a debt when it falls due represents merely the presumed effect of the debtor's inability to pay its debts out of the available cash resources. The basic condition that needs to be considered at the time the petition is filed is whether or not the debtor is indeed in a state of *cessation of payments*. Insofar as the debtor makes payments on a regular basis to its suppliers as well as to its employees ... *there can be no cessation of payments* (emphasis added).

Question 25: Is "cessation of payments" an autonomous ground to commence proceedings (triggering circumstance)? You may refer to Questions 6/7 or add additional information here.

No. Please see our answers to Questions 6 and 7.

---

21 *Bufan (ed.),* Tratat practic de insolventa, 1st ed., Cap. VII – Deschiderea procedurii de insolventa, Hamangiu publishing house, 2014, p. 237, para. 37.

22 *Băcanu*, Patru cărţi despre procedura reorganizării şi lichidării judiciare, in *Revista de Drept Comercial* no. 5/1996, pp. 166–167.

23 Calarasi Tribunal, Civil Division, Decision no. 52/2022 of 19 April 2022, available at https://www.rejust.ro/juris/394636d3g.

Question 26: Is "cessation of payments" a means to establish inability to pay debts? If so, by which mechanism (e.g. rebuttable presumption for inability to pay debts, cf. above Question 19(c))?

The cessation of payments may be an *indicium* of the debtor's inability to pay his debts. Please see our answers to Questions 19(c) and 25.

The cessation of payments does not give rise to a legal presumption of the debtor's inability to pay his debts.

Still, according to the Romanian Code of Civil Procedure, Article 329, the insolvency judge may rely on judge-made presumptions in order to decide upon a creditor's application.

Practically, the cessation of payments, uncorroborated by other evidence, would itself be insufficient proof that the debtor is unable to pay his debts.

Question 27: How is "cessation of payments" defined? If it is defined in statute, please provide us here with an English translation of the relevant rule. Is this definition (if any) specified in case law? If so, how?

There is no statutory definition of the "cessation of payments" in the Romanian legislation. Please see our answer to Question 24.

Question 28: How is "cessation of payments" established?

Being a matter of fact (and not a deed), all types of evidence are admissible to prove the "cessation of payments".

Being a negative state of facts, the creditor has to prove that the debt is ascertained (uncontested), liquidated and due. Should the creditor prove the said features of the debt he relies upon in his application, the burden of proof shifts to the debtor, who needs to prove he has made the necessary payments to cover the debt. The debtor's inability to prove he has made such payments allows for a judge-made presumption that the cessation of payments occurred after the last payment made by the debtor.

Question 29: Are there typical circumstances which provide circumstantial evidence that the debtor has ceased payments? If so, please list as many as possible.

Although it may seem paradoxical, a partial payment may be proof that the debtor has ceased to make payments.

Law no. 85/2014 (commercial insolvencies) uses the term "insufficient cash resources" and not the term "absence of cash resources", which means that insolvency proceedings are applicable even if the debtor does have some cash resources and makes some payments, but the money is not enough to pay all outstanding debts.

To avoid the opening of insolvency proceedings, the debtor must prove he has enough cash resources available to cover all debts due and payable which the creditor(s) have relied upon in his/their application.

Other circumstantial pieces of evidence are:

- the absence of ongoing business activity, which is the source of income/liquidities necessary to cover the due debts (no trade);
- a creditor's failure to recover the debt in prior judicial enforcement proceedings;
- the debtor's failure to pay the sums of money laid down in court orders or other writs of enforcement, for a significant period of time;
- the debtor's failure to renew the appointment of its director(s);
- the debtor's failure to lodge his financial statements with the tax authorities;
- the debtor closing his business facilities (shops, factories, etc.).

Question 30: Would you like to add any further aspects not covered by the above questions?

In Romanian legislation, the term "cessation of payments" was replaced with the term "state of insolvency". Please see our answer to Question 3(b).

Some of the legal academic writers[24] still consider that the two terms basically describe the same state of facts: a complex state which consists, *inter alia*, in the debtor's inability to pay its debts when they fall due. Other legal authors[25] consider that the "cessation of payments" suggests an irreversible condition, incompatible with recovery, which is the reason why they have proposed replacing it with the term "stay of payments", in order to better suggest that the debtor's condition is temporary, the debtor being likely to resume payments once the collective insolvency proceedings are commenced.

IV. LIKELY/IMMINENT INABILITY TO PAY DEBTS

Question 31: Are the following terms available in your jurisdiction, either in statute or in case law? (If the answer is "no", please continue with Question 42.)

a) likely inability to pay debts

Yes, the term "likely inability to pay future debts" is used in the statutory definition of "difficulty". Please see our answer to Question 1. A debtor in "difficulty"

---

24 *Schiau*, Regimul juridic al insolventei comerciale, C.H. Beck, Bucuresti 2001, p. 106.

25 *Turcu*, Suspendarea plăţilor – testul insolvenţei – o posibilă soluţie de echilibru între deschiderea precoce şi deschiderea tardivă a procedurii, in *Revista de Drept Comercial* no. 10/2005, p. 17.

may access pre-insolvency, preventive procedures to restructure itself, provided he is able to pay his present debts and he is not in insolvency.

b) imminent inability to pay debts
Please see our answer to Question 3(d).

The statutory definition of "imminent insolvency" in the previous version of Law no. 85/2014, that referred to the debtor's "imminent inability to pay his debts", has been eliminated by the amending Law no. 216/2022.

The surviving reference in Law no. 85/2014, Article 66(4) to the debtor's "imminent insolvency" does not define it or use the term "imminent inability to pay debts". Still, its meaning is that a debtor that will certainly become unable to pay his debts in a very short time may (but is not under an obligation to) file a petition seeking the opening of insolvency proceedings.

c) other (similar) terms
n.a.

Question 32: Is "likely/imminent inability to pay debts" an autonomous ground to commence proceedings (triggering circumstance)? You may refer to Questions 6/7 or add additional information here.

Please see our answer to Question 31(a) with regard to the "likely inability to pay debts".

Please see our answers to Questions 6 and 7 with regard to the "imminent inability to pay debts".

Question 33: If the answer to the previous Question is "yes", who may base filing for insolvency proceedings on it: only the debtor or also creditors?

When seeking the opening of insolvency proceedings, relying on the imminent inability to pay, the debtor, only.

When seeking the opening of *concordat preventiv* proceedings (i.e. pre-insolvency, preventive proceedings), relying on the "likely inability to pay debts", the debtor. One or more creditors may initiate such proceedings, too; yet they must obtain the debtor's agreement to subject himself to such proceedings prior to the filing of the application.

Question 34: How are these terms defined? If they are defined in statute, please provide us here with an English translation of the relevant rules. Is this definition (if any) specified in case law? If so, how?

a) likely inability to pay debts
No. Please see our answer to Question 31(a).

In a recent judicial decision the insolvency judge held that the debtor's "likely inability to pay debts" was the following situation:

> the debtor does have some money available but, according to its allegations, using this money to pay the banking creditor before other creditors would obviously lead to an imbalance in its activity, which would indeed jeopardise its chances of recovery; the report on the debtor's state of difficulty reveals a downward trend in its turnover, with rising energy costs, the abrupt changes in the price of energy having a strong impact on the debtor's business, and generating the situation of difficulty which it has sought to overcome by filing of the present application.[26]

b) imminent inability to pay debts
No. Please see our answers to Questions 31(b) and 18.

Question 35: Do the terms "likely" and "imminent" require a prognosis regarding the point in time when actual inability to pay debts will occur? If so, how long is the time period for this prognosis?

In the context of the pre-insolvency, preventive procedure ("likely inability to pay"), Law no. 85/2014, Article 6(2)(c) reads as follows:

> The debtor proves he is in difficulty submitting a report drafted by the restructuring administrator or by the *concordat* administrator, which includes at least the following elements:
>
> …
>
> c) the financial indicators applicable to that debtor, which may point out the existence of a threat to the debtor's future ability to pay its debts when due, over a period of maximum 24 months from the occurrence of those circumstances.

Thus, the prognosis period for the pre-insolvency, preventive procedure is 24 months.

For insolvency proceedings ("imminent inability to pay"), the statutory instruments neither point to a moment in time, nor require the insolvency judge to consider such a moment.

Our opinion is that the prognosis period should definitely be shorter in the case of imminent insolvency.

Question 36: Does your law require a specific grade of certainty that inability to pay debts will eventually occur? If so, is 50.1% ("more likely than not") enough or are there alleviated or aggravated prerequisites?

No, the statutory instruments do not lay down any requirement in this respect.

---

26 Judgment no. 162/F/CC/2022, issued by Hunedoara Tribunal, not published.

Still, the "likely inability to pay" seems to be both:

1. conditional upon the debtor not initiating restructuring proceedings;
2. not imminent, but presumably occurring in the future.

In conclusion (at least) 50.1% certainty would describe quite accurately the likelihood of the debtor not being able to pay his debts in the future.

The imminent inability to pay seems to be much more certain. It would not be a matter of "if", but a matter of "when". The debtor could only save himself from becoming unable to pay his debts if something extraordinary were to happen (e.g. an investor buying the business).

Question 37: Regarding "debts" and "financial means", are they defined in the same way as in the context of inability to pay debts (cf. above Questions 14/15)? If not, what are the differences?

Yes.

Question 38: Further to Question 37: Are "debts" considered which do currently not exist or are not yet due but will foreseeably come into existence and become due during the prognosis period?

In the context of pre-insolvency, preventive proceedings, yes.

In the context of imminent insolvency, since the prognosis period should be shorter, debts not yet due but which will foreseeably come into existence and become due during the prognosis period should be considered, but the debts that do not exist yet.

Question 39: Also further to Question 37: Are "financial means" considered which do currently not exist but will foreseeably become available during the prognosis period?

Yes.

As the recent case law shows, the insolvency judge, while considering the debtor's state of difficulty, has accepted the predictability of such financial resources by reference to the delayed availability of some guarantees, based on the contractual terms, in relation to the future debts:

> In this matter, the court finds that the debtor's … financial distress was caused precisely by its *impossibility* to convert the non-performance collateral into resources available to the company, and that is the reason why it was unable to cover its short-term liabilities. The company's distress was caused by the *unfavourable ratio between the early maturities of its debts* to its current suppliers

> (short-term debts) and the late maturities of its contractual partners' obligations to proceed to the reception of the works … and to *release the collateral* (emphasis added).[27]

Question 40: How are the terms "likely/imminent inability to pay debts" established?

In theory, establishing "likely/imminent inability to pay debts" is about (i) the short-term low liquidity ratio, and (ii) the long-term unsustainable indebtedness.

In pre-insolvency, preventive proceedings ("likely inability to pay"), Law no. 85/2014, Article 6(2)(c) reads as follows:

> The debtor proves he is in difficulty submitting a report drafted by the restructuring administrator or by the *concordat* administrator, which includes at least the following elements:
>
> a) the nature of difficulty, *i.e.* a description of the circumstances that temporarily impair the business and the expected effects thereof;
> b) the internal and external factors giving rise to the debtor's difficulty;
> c) the financial indicators applicable to that debtor, which may point to the existence of a threat to the debtor's future ability to pay its debts when due, over a maximum period of 24 months from the occurrence of those circumstances;
> d) the reason why the difficulty cannot be regarded as naturally reversible even if the debtor continues to carry out its planned activity in the absence of proper recovery actions.

In insolvency proceedings ("imminent inability to pay"), Law no. 85/2014, Article 67(1) requires the debtor to submit, along with his petition, as evidence, the annual financial statement drafted for the previous year and the balance sheet drafted for the month prior to the month the petition is lodged with the court. Obviously, that financial statement and that balance sheet only offer a static, snap-shot of the debtor's assets and liabilities, with no relevant information as to the cash flow in and out of the debtor's estate. Therefore, the debtor should supplement the evidence with other pieces, in order to prove that the inflow of cash is certain to diminish or cease (proof of termination of contracts, deeds evidencing certain and large expenditure in the near future, etc.).

Question 41: Would you like to add any further aspects not covered by the above questions?

The term "likely inability to pay debts" is currently a typical feature of pre-insolvency, preventive proceedings (restructuring frameworks).

---

[27] Judgment issued by Dolj Tribunal, not published.

The case law has shown, after the transposition of Directive (EU) 2019/1023, that a debtor *cannot survive long enough* in pre-insolvency proceedings unless he can rely on money available to pay his debts as they become due.

V. OVERINDEBTEDNESS

Question 42: In your jurisdiction, is "overindebtedness", or "balance sheet insolvency" respectively, a legal term used either in statute or in case law? (If the answer is "no", please continue with Question 56.)

No.

Question 43: Is "overindebtedness" an autonomous ground to commence proceedings (triggering circumstance)? You may refer to Questions 6/7 or add additional information here.

n.a.

Question 44: If the answer to the previous Question is "yes", is this applicable to corporate insolvencies of legal persons only or also to personal bankruptcies of natural persons?

n.a.

Question 45: Is the term "overindebtedness" defined in statute? If so, please give the wording in English translation. Is this definition (if any) specified in case law? If so, how?

n.a.

Question 46: Does your law refer to all existing debts or only to mature debts?

n.a.

Question 47: Does the rank of certain debts play a role when establishing overindebtedness? In particular, is there any possibility to conclude agreements according to which certain debts shall not be taken into account (e.g. agreements on subsidiarity)?

n.a.

Question 48: Which assets are taken into account when overindebtedness is established: the complete set of assets or only a selection of them?

n.a.

Question 49: How are the debtor's assets valued: by referring to the liquidation value, the book value, the going concern value or in another way?

n.a.

Question 50: Is there any prognostic element, e.g. regarding the debtor's chances to continue the business?

n.a.

Question 51: If the answer to the previous Question is "yes", what exactly is the topic of the prognosis and how is it established?

n.a.

Question 52: If the answer to Question 50 is "yes", how long is the prognosis period?

n.a.

Question 53: How is overindebtedness established?

a) Is a formal balance sheet required?
n.a.

b) Does the yearly regular commercial balance sheet have any meaning (given that it is normally based on technical values and does not display undisclosed reserves)?
n.a.

c) Does the law provide for a presumption? If so, under which conditions?
n.a.

d) Other means?
n.a.

Question 54: Is the legal link to overindebtedness undisputed in literature or are there efforts to abolish it?

n.a.

Question 55: Would you like to add any further aspects not covered by the above questions?

n.a.

VI. REMAINING ISSUES

Question 56: Is there anything else you would like to share in the present context and that we should take into account?

While insolvency may be a complex situation where economics and law collide, its legal definition should remain simple.

It is a fact that most companies in the European common market are SMEs, and SMEs are not usually sophisticated enough to work with difficult legal definitions.

Moreover, insolvency is trying hard to lose its stigma and needs to appear simple to use, fair and friendly to its beneficiaries.

We believe that a short, principle-based definition would work just fine.

SLOVAKIA

Dávid Oršula

I. GENERAL

Question 1: How is insolvency (both in the context of liquidation and restructuring/reorganisation) regulated in your jurisdiction? Please give a brief overview, at least enumerating the relevant statutes.

In Slovakia, insolvency is regulated under the Act on Bankruptcy and Restructuring (act No. 7/2005 Coll.), which has covered both liquidation and restructuring since 2006. As a consequence of the EU Directive on "preventive restructurings", Slovakia has adopted a special code on this topic. Consequently, the act No. 111/2022 Coll. on the Resolution of Imminent Insolvency has regulated preventive restructuring proceedings in Slovakia since July 2022. Moreover, a few decrees and ordinances of the Ministry of Justice of Slovakia provide for further legislative framework.

Question 2: Related to paragraph 10 above of the Introduction: seen from a principle-based perspective, what justifies the opening of insolvency proceedings in your jurisdiction?

The opening of insolvency proceedings is justified by the principles of equal treatment of creditors and thus the collective satisfaction of creditors, since individual satisfaction in regular enforcement proceedings leads to unjustified positions of creditors. Collective proceedings are due in the interest of equal treatment of all creditors. Other principles, such as the principle of debtor protection against creditors, or the principle of best possible satisfaction of the creditors' claims, where creditors would be worse off without insolvency proceedings, apply accordingly.

Question 3: Does your national law in the context of liquidation proceedings use one or more of the following terms (be it as a noun, be it as an adjective or adjunct) in whatever context:

a) inability to pay debts
Yes.

b) cessation of payments
No.

c) likely inability to pay debts
No.

d) imminent inability to pay debts
Yes.

e) overindebtedness?
Yes.

Question 4: Are the same terms (and with the same meaning) used in the rules on preliminary/interim insolvency proceedings (e.g. concerning the application stage of the proceedings)?

Yes.

Question 5: Does your national law in the context of restructuring proceedings (as referred to above at paragraph 8 of the Introduction, i.e. both pre-insolvency and within formal insolvency proceedings) use one or more of the following terms (be it as a noun, be it as an adjective or adjunct) in whatever context:

a) inability to pay debts
Yes.

b) cessation of payments
No.

c) likely inability to pay debts
No.

d) imminent inability to pay debts
Yes.

e) overindebtedness?
Yes.

Question 6: Which of the terms mentioned in Questions 3 and 5 are used for defining grounds to commence proceedings (triggering circumstances)?

a) insolvency proceedings
The correct term is "insolvency", which is the universal definition for both inability to pay debts and overindebtedness.

b) restructuring proceedings
The correct term is "insolvency", which is the universal definition for both inability to pay debts and overindebtedness. In preventive restructuring proceedings, the proper term is "imminent insolvency", while the law further adds that the term covers mostly "imminent inability to pay debts".

Question 7: Does the answer to Question 6 include personal bankruptcies of natural persons or only corporate insolvencies of legal entities?

Yes.

Question 8: In your law, are there any other circumstances which trigger insolvency or restructuring proceedings?

No.

Question 9: Which of the terms mentioned in Questions 3, 5, and 8 are used in the context of transactions avoidance law?

None of them.

Question 10: Which of the terms addressed in Questions 3, 5, and 8 are used in the context of directors' duties?

a) shift of duties (from shareholders to creditors)
Imminent inability to pay debts.

b) duties to commence insolvency proceedings
The term "insolvency" is used, which is the universal definition for both inability to pay debts and overindebtedness.

c) other duties (please describe)
n.a.

Question 11: Are there any other rules in the context of which the terms addressed in Questions 3, 5, and 8 are used?

n.a.

Question 12: Is the definition of (the subspecies of) insolvency identical in all legal fields or are there different definitions (e.g. different in insolvency law than in criminal law)?

The definition of insolvency including any of its subspecies is covered exclusively in the insolvency law. There are no different definitions.

II. INABILITY TO PAY DEBTS

Question 13: In your jurisdiction, is the term "inability to pay debts" defined in statute? If so, please give the wording in English translation. Is this definition (if any) specified in case law? If so, how?

A legal person is insolvent if it is unable to meet within 90 days past their due date at least two monetary obligations to more than one creditor. For the purposes of assessing the debtor's solvency, all claims that originally belonged to only one creditor during the 90 days prior to the filing of the bankruptcy petition shall be considered as a single claim. A legal person shall be presumed to be solvent if, having regard to all the circumstances, it can reasonably be expected that the management of its assets or the operation of its business can be continued and the difference between the amount of its outstanding monetary liabilities and its monetary assets (hereinafter referred to as the "liquidity gap") is less than one-tenth of the amount of its outstanding monetary liabilities or, within a period of not more than 60 days, the liquidity gap falls below such a threshold.

A natural person is insolvent if they are unable to meet within 180 days past its due date at least one monetary obligation. If a monetary claim cannot be enforced against the debtor or if the debtor has failed to comply with an obligation imposed on it/him/her by a summons of the court for proving its solvency following a creditor's bankruptcy petition (Section 19(1)(a) of the Act), it/he/she shall be presumed to be insolvent.

There is no relevant case law.

Question 14: Does your law refer to all debts or only to mature debts?

n.a. The law refers to overdue debts, which is a term different from mature debts.

Question 15: Which assets are taken into account when assessing the inability to pay debts: all (financial) assets or only those that are liquid, i.e. available on short notice?

Liquid financial assets.

The full statutory definition (in Section 2 of the Decree No. 197/2022 of the Ministry of Justice of the Slovak Republic, which provides details on options how inability to pay debts, liquidation gap and imminent inability to pay debts are to be established) reads:

> For the purposes of determining insolvency, monetary assets are:
>
> a) cash,
> b) claims on an account, deposit or other form of deposit with a bank or branch of a foreign bank or with a foreign bank established in a Member State of the

Organisation for Economic Co-operation and Development with less than three months' notice,

c) monetary claims, securities and financial instruments maturing within 30 days, where it is reasonable to expect, with the exercise of professional diligence, that they will be duly and punctually discharged,

d) monetary claims, securities and financial instruments not more than 30 days overdue if, in the exercise of professional diligence, they can reasonably be expected to be duly settled within 30 days of their due date,

e) cash receivables, securities and financial instruments which are repayable on demand (sight) if it is reasonable in the exercise of professional diligence to expect that they would be duly and punctually discharged if they were called for repayment the following day.

Monetary assets shall not include cash, receivables or securities denominated in the currency of a State that is not a Member State of the Organisation for Economic Co-operation and Development.

Question 16: Is any liquidity gap (deficit between relevant financial means and relevant debts) relevant or does your law neglect minor gaps? If the latter, how is "minor" defined?

See answers to Questions 13 and 15.

There is no definition of a minor gap.

Question 17: As far as the time aspect is concerned, does it matter whether the liquidity gap can be closed again in the short term? If so, how long is the grace period?

See answer to Question 13: yes, the liquidity gap can be closed within 60 days. Applies only to legal persons.

Question 18: As far as the time aspect is concerned, is a debtor considered insolvent if the liquidity gap is not yet present but will occur soon? If so, how long is the prognosis period? (Note: this may also concern the difference between actual and likely/imminent inability to pay debts; cf. below Question 34).

No, a debtor is not considered to be insolvent. However, a debtor is considered to be *imminently* insolvent, if it will be imminently unable to pay debts. Imminent inability to pay debts occurs if within 12 months the liquidity gap occurs. (Comment: the statutory wording is not perfect here.)

Question 19: How is inability to pay debts established? Please communicate if there is a difference between a creditor and a debtor application or between different legal contexts.

Applies to legal persons:

a) Is a formal liquidity status (liquidity balance sheet) required?
No.

If the debtor files the bankruptcy petition, he is obliged to attach to the petition a list of his assets, a list of his liabilities and a list of his related parties. If the debtor keeps double-entry bookkeeping, he must also attach to the petition the latest regular individual financial statements together with the extraordinary individual financial statements, if they were drawn up later than the latest regular individual financial statements; if the individual financial statements have been audited, he must also attach to the petition the auditor's report.

In the case of a creditor's petition, they don't have to attach any document related to the liquidity status. Upon the court's summons, the debtor must prove his solvency by submitting:

- a list of all his monetary obligations with which he was 90 days in arrears at the date of the opening of the insolvency proceedings,
- a list of all its bank accounts with a summary of the balances at the date of the opening of the insolvency proceedings,
- a statement of cash balances at the date of the opening of the insolvency proceedings and at the date of submission of that information to the court,
- a list of the claims which can be expected, with professional diligence, to be settled within 90 days of the opening of the insolvency proceedings at the latest.

b) Is a sample of daily liquidity data (which do not amount to a proper liquidity status but show insufficient funds on different days within a certain period of time) sufficient?
No.

c) Does the law provide for a rebuttable presumption? If so, under which conditions?
Yes, see answer to Question 13.

d) Does the law provide for any technical circumstances (e.g. undisputed statutory demand, non-compliance with monetary judgments, unsuccessful enforcement proceedings, non-performance of a previous composition agreement in insolvency proceedings) the occurrence of which suffices to establish the debtor's insolvency?
No.

e) Other means?
n.a.

Question 20: Is insolvency (inability to pay debts, overindebtedness, etc.) subject to party autonomy in the proceedings or must the court clarify them *ex officio*?

The court reviews and clarifies; there is no party autonomy.

Question 21: In an overall view, does your law distinguish "inability to pay debts" from "financial difficulties"? If so, how?

The term "financial difficulties" does not exist. (It existed during COVID for temporary stay.)

Question 22: In an overall view, does it matter under your law whether the debtor's inability to pay debts is present or future and reversible or irreversible?

Absolutely. Present inability to pay debts (ITPD) triggers the debtor's insolvency and thus the obligation to file, while future ITPD triggers the shift of debtor's directors' duties towards creditors. A reversible ITPD gives the debtor a chance to prove his solvency.

Question 23: Would you like to add any further aspects not covered by the above questions?

n.a.

III. CESSATION OF PAYMENTS

Question 24: In your jurisdiction, is "cessation of payments" a legal term used either in statute or in case law? (If the answer is "no", please continue with Question 31.)

No.

Question 25: Is "cessation of payments" an autonomous ground to commence proceedings (triggering circumstance)? You may refer to Questions 6/7 or add additional information here.

n.a.

Question 26: Is "cessation of payments" a means to establish inability to pay debts? If so, by which mechanism (e.g. rebuttable presumption for inability to pay debts, cf. above Question 19(c))?

n.a.

Question 27: How is "cessation of payments" defined? If it is defined in statute, please provide us here with an English translation of the relevant rule. Is this definition (if any) specified in case law? If so, how?

n.a.

Question 28: How is "cessation of payments" established?

n.a.

Question 29: Are there typical circumstances which provide circumstantial evidence that the debtor has ceased payments? If so, please list as many as possible.

n.a.

Question 30: Would you like to add any further aspects not covered by the above questions?

n.a.

IV. LIKELY/IMMINENT INABILITY TO PAY DEBTS

Question 31: Are the following terms available in your jurisdiction, either in statute or in case law? (If the answer is "no", please continue with Question 42.)

a) likely inability to pay debts
Yes.

b) imminent inability to pay debts
No.

c) other (similar) terms
n.a.

Question 32: Is "likely/imminent inability to pay debts" an autonomous ground to commence proceedings (triggering circumstance)? You may refer to Questions 6/7 or add additional information here.

No. It is not a statutory trigger. Imminent inability to pay debts (iITPD) shifts the debtor's directors' duties towards creditors, and also allows for preventive restructuring measures.

Question 33: If the answer to the previous Question is "yes", who may base filing for insolvency proceedings on it: only the debtor or also creditors?

Not insolvency proceedings, just preventive restructuring and only the debtor may file.

Question 34: How are these terms defined? If they are defined in statute, please provide us here with an English translation of the relevant rules. Is this definition (if any) specified in case law? If so, how?

a) likely inability to pay debts
n.a.

b) imminent inability to pay debts
The debtor is in a state of imminent insolvency, in particular, if its inability to pay debts has become imminent. A debtor's inability to pay debts is imminent if, taking into account all the circumstances, it can reasonably be assumed that inability to pay debts will occur within 12 calendar months.

Question 35: Do the terms "likely" and "imminent" require a prognosis regarding the point in time when actual inability to pay debts will occur? If so, how long is the time period for this prognosis?

Regarding "imminent" see answer to Question 34.

Question 36: Does your law require a specific grade of certainty that inability to pay debts will eventually occur? If so, is 50.1% ("more likely than not") enough or are there alleviated or aggravated prerequisites?

There is no number in the statutes, and there is no case law. Mathematically and using legal logic and interpretation methods, 50+% certainty should be sufficient.

Question 37: Regarding "debts" and "financial means", are they defined in the same way as in the context of inability to pay debts (cf. above Questions 14/15)? If not, what are the differences?

Yes.

Question 38: Further to Question 37: Are "debts" considered which do currently not exist or are not yet due but will foreseeably come into existence and become due during the prognosis period?

Yes – any debts which will influence the iITPD within 12 months are relevant for this purpose.

Question 39: Also further to Question 37: Are "financial means" considered which do currently not exist but will foreseeably become available during the prognosis period?

See answer to Question 15.

Question 40: How are the terms "likely/imminent inability to pay debts" established?

The debtor or the debtor's directors must establish iITPD from their bookkeeping.

Question 41: Would you like to add any further aspects not covered by the above questions?

n.a.

V. OVERINDEBTEDNESS

Question 42: In your jurisdiction, is "overindebtedness", or "balance sheet insolvency" respectively, a legal term used either in statute or in case law? (If the answer is "no", please continue with Question 56.)

Yes, it is named "overindebtedness".

Question 43: Is "overindebtedness" an autonomous ground to commence proceedings (triggering circumstance)? You may refer to Questions 6/7 or add additional information here.

Yes. Overindebtness is a subcategory of insolvency and is a triggering circumstance for the debtor to file for bankruptcy.

Question 44: If the answer to the previous Question is "yes", is this applicable to corporate insolvencies of legal persons only or also to personal bankruptcies of natural persons?

Legal persons only.

Question 45: Is the term "overindebtedness" defined in statute? If so, please give the wording in English translation. Is this definition (if any) specified in case law? If so, how?

Yes.

An overindebted person is one who is required to keep accounts under a special regulation (double bookkeeping), has more than one creditor and the value of his liabilities exceeds the value of his assets. In determining the value of the liabilities and the value of the assets, the accounting records or the value determined by an expert's opinion shall be taken into account, which shall prevail over the accounting records, and the expected results of the further administration of the assets or the expected results of the further operations of the undertaking shall also be taken into account if, having regard to all the circumstances, it can reasonably be assumed that it will be possible to continue the administration of the assets or the operations of the undertaking. The value of the liabilities shall not include the value of liabilities which are linked to a subordination obligation or the value of liabilities which would be satisfied in the order of junior claims in insolvency.

Comment: junior claims are particularly those claims of affiliated creditors. The statutory definition of affiliated persons is extremely broad.

Question 46: Does your law refer to all existing debts or only to mature debts?

All debts.

Question 47: Does the rank of certain debts play a role when establishing overindebtedness? In particular, is there any possibility to conclude agreements according to which certain debts shall not be taken into account (e.g. agreements on subsidiarity)?

Yes, see answer to Question 45.

Question 48: Which assets are taken into account when overindebtedness is established: the complete set of assets or only a selection of them?

All assets, but see answer to Question 45.

Question 49: How are the debtor's assets valued: by referring to the liquidation value, the book value, the going concern value or in another way?

See answer to Question 45.

Question 50: Is there any prognostic element, e.g. regarding the debtor's chances to continue the business?

See answer to Question 45.

Question 51: If the answer to the previous Question is "yes", what exactly is the topic of the prognosis and how is it established?

The law does not provide anything further on this point. There is no case law.

Question 52: If the answer to Question 50 is "yes", how long is the prognosis period?

n.a. See answer to Question 45.

Question 53: How is overindebtedness established?

a) Is a formal balance sheet required?
Yes.

b) Does the yearly regular commercial balance sheet have any meaning (given that it is normally based on technical values and does not display undisclosed reserves)?

No judge will want to get into discussions on undisclosed reserves. The balance sheet is the Alpha and Omega. However, undisclosed reserves would normally be displayed if liabilities and assets were valuated by an expert's opinion (see answer to Question 45).

c) Does the law provide for a presumption? If so, under which conditions?

No.

d) Other means?

No.

Question 54: Is the legal link to overindebtedness undisputed in literature or are there efforts to abolish it?

There is little literature worth reading. Literature is basically rephrasing the laws, ending where your problem starts.

Question 55: Would you like to add any further aspects not covered by the above questions?

No.

VI. REMAINING ISSUES

Question 56: Is there anything else you would like to share in the present context and that we should take into account?

n.a.

SLOVENIA

Miodrag DORDEVIC

I. GENERAL

Question 1: How is insolvency (both in the context of liquidation and restructuring/reorganisation) regulated in your jurisdiction? Please give a brief overview, at least enumerating the relevant statutes.

In the Slovenian legal system insolvency is regulated by the Financial Operations, Insolvency Proceedings, and Compulsory Dissolution Act (in the Slovenian language: Zakon o finančnem poslovanju, postopkih zaradi insolventnosti in prisilnem prenehanju, ZFPPIPP).

> Insolvency is the situation that arises where the debtor:
>
> 1. is unable at the relevant point in time to pay his mature debts (continuous illiquidity), or
> 2. becomes long-term unable to pay their debts (Article 14(1) ZFPPIPP).

Insolvency is the reason for initiation of insolvency proceedings (compulsory settlement proceedings, simplified compulsory settlement proceedings and bankruptcy proceedings (Article 5 ZFPPIPP)).

Preventive restructuring proceedings shall be initiated if the debtor has not yet become insolvent, but it is likely that they will become insolvent within one year (Article 44d(1) ZFPPIPP).

Compulsory dissolution (forced termination) proceedings consist of cancellation from the court register without liquidation and compulsory liquidation (Article 6 ZFPPIPP). The aforementioned proceedings are not initiated by the insolvency of the debtor.

Question 2: Related to paragraph 10 above of the Introduction: seen from a principle-based perspective, what justifies the opening of insolvency proceedings in your jurisdiction?

Insolvency proceedings shall be initiated when a debtor becomes insolvent and when other conditions stipulated by the Act for each type of procedure are satisfied (Article 50 ZFPPIPP).

Question 3: Does your national law in the context of liquidation proceedings use one or more of the following terms (be it as a noun, be it as an adjective or adjunct) in whatever context:

a) inability to pay debts
Yes.

b) cessation of payments
No.

c) likely inability to pay debts
No (the preventive restructuring proceedings commence when there is a likelihood of insolvency, which means that ZFPPIPP does not explicitly use the term likely inability to pay debts).

d) imminent inability to pay debts
No.

e) overindebtedness?
Yes.

Question 4: Are the same terms (and with the same meaning) used in the rules on preliminary/interim insolvency proceedings (e.g. concerning the application stage of the proceedings)?

Yes.

Question 5: Does your national law in the context of restructuring proceedings (as referred to above at paragraph 8 of the Introduction, i.e. both pre-insolvency and within formal insolvency proceedings) use one or more of the following terms (be it as a noun, be it as an adjective or adjunct) in whatever context:

a) inability to pay debts
Yes.

b) cessation of payments
No.

c) likely inability to pay debts
No (same explanation as with the Question 3).

d) imminent inability to pay debts
No.

e) overindebtedness?
Yes.

Question 6: Which of the terms mentioned in Questions 3 and 5 are used for defining grounds to commence proceedings (triggering circumstances)?

a) insolvency proceedings
Inability to pay debts; overindebtedness (insolvency – see answer to Question 2 *supra*).

b) restructuring proceedings
None; the triggering circumstance for the commencement of the preventive restructuring proceeding is the likelihood of insolvency.

Question 7: Does the answer to Question 6 include personal bankruptcies of natural persons or only corporate insolvencies of legal entities?

Question 6(a) includes natural persons; Question 6(b) includes only legal entities.

Question 8: In your law, are there any other circumstances which trigger insolvency or restructuring proceedings?

No.

Question 9: Which of the terms mentioned in Questions 3, 5, and 8 are used in the context of transactions avoidance law?

Overindebtedness.

Question 10: Which of the terms addressed in Questions 3, 5, and 8 are used in the context of directors' duties?

a) shift of duties (from shareholders to creditors)
Inability to pay debts, overindebtedness.

b) duties to commence insolvency proceedings
Inability to pay debts, overindebtedness.

c) other duties (please describe)
Duty of equal treatment of creditors (on the occurrence of insolvency, the company must make no payments nor must it assume any new obligations, with the exception of those which are essential for the continuing operation of the company) (Article 34 ZFPPIPP).

Question 11: Are there any other rules in the context of which the terms addressed in Questions 3, 5, and 8 are used?

No.

Question 12: Is the definition of (the subspecies of) insolvency identical in all legal fields or are there different definitions (e.g. different in insolvency law than in criminal law)?

In general, it is the same definition.

II. INABILITY TO PAY DEBTS

Question 13: In your jurisdiction, is the term "inability to pay debts" defined in statute? If so, please give the wording in English translation. Is this definition (if any) specified in case law? If so, how?

Inability to pay debts is defined in Article 11 ZFPPIPP as a positive definition (when is the debtor able to pay debts):

- Liquidity *[in terms of short-term ability to pay debts: author's note]* is the capacity of a legal or natural person to, within a given period of time, settle all liabilities falling due within such a period of time (Article 11(1)ZFPPIPP).
- Solvency *[in terms of long-term ability to pay debts: author's note]* is the permanent capacity of a legal or natural person to perform all obligations when they fall due (Article 11, paragraph 2 ZFPPIPP).

Question 14: Does your law refer to all debts or only to mature debts?

Mature debts.

Question 15: Which assets are taken into account when assessing the inability to pay debts: all (financial) assets or only those that are liquid, i.e. available on short notice?

When speaking about short-term ability to pay debts (liquidity) only liquid financial assets (those available on short notice) are taken into account.

When speaking about long-term ability to pay debts (solvency) all assets are taken into account.

Question 16: Is any liquidity gap (deficit between relevant financial means and relevant debts) relevant or does your law neglect minor gaps? If the latter, how is "minor" defined?

The liquidity gap is 60 days/two months and it is defined within the rebutabble presumptions (Article 14(2) ZFPPIPP) that presume the existence of continuous illiquidity (Article 14(1)-1), which is one of the triggering circumstances for the existence of insolvency.

Question 17: As far as the time aspect is concerned, does it matter whether the liquidity gap can be closed again in the short term? If so, how long is the grace period?

No, it does not matter if the liquidity gap can be closed in the short term.

Question 18: As far as the time aspect is concerned, is a debtor considered insolvent if the liquidity gap is not yet present but will occur soon? If so, how long is the prognosis period? (Note: this may also concern the difference between actual and likely/imminent inability to pay debts; cf. below Question 34).

No, the debtor is not considered insolvent if the liquidity gap is not yet present but will occur soon.

Question 19: How is inability to pay debts established? Please communicate if there is a difference between a creditor and a debtor application or between different legal contexts.

a) Is a formal liquidity status (liquidity balance sheet) required?
The law provides presumptions in Article 14 ZFPPIPP (see below, (c)). In paragraphs 2 and 3 are rebuttable presumptions – i.e. presumed unless it is proven otherwise. In those cases, the debtor has the opportunity to prove that he is not insolvent. Free evaluation of evidence applies in those cases.

b) Is a sample of daily liquidity data (which do not amount to a proper liquidity status but show insufficient funds on different days within a certain period of time) sufficient?
See (a) (free evaluation of evidence).

c) Does the law provide for a rebuttable presumption? If so, under which conditions?
Yes, the law provides for presumptions in paragraphs 2–4 of Article 14 ZFPPIPP:

> (2) Unless it is proven otherwise, a debtor shall be considered continuously illiquid:
>
> 1. for a debtor who is a legal person, businessperson or a private person:
>   - if he/she is more than two months in arrears in meeting one or more obligations in a total amount exceeding 20 per cent of the amount of his/her liabilities shown in the last published annual report or
>   - if the funds in his/her accounts are insufficient for executing the enforcement order or realising the enforcement draft, and such situation continues without interruption for a period of 60 days or with interruptions for more than 60 days of the most recent 90-day period, and such situation continues on the date prior to filing the petition for the initiation of insolvency proceedings, or

   - if he/she does not have at least one bank account open with payment services provision in the Republic of Slovenia and if he/she has not settled his/her liabilities under the enforcement order within 60 days of the date when the enforcement order becomes final,
2. for a debtor for whom compulsory settlement has been initiated and ended by a final confirmation of compulsory settlement if he/she is more than two months in arrears with
   - payment of his/her liabilities under the confirmed compulsory settlement or
   - payment of his/her liabilities arising prior to the commencement of compulsory settlement to creditors with the right to a separate satisfaction, or
   - the scheduled implementation of other financial restructuring measures defined by the financial restructuring plan,
3. for a debtor who is a consumer:
   - if he/she is delayed for more than two months in meeting one or more obligations in the total amount exceeding the amount of three times the amount of his/her salary, compensation or other remunerations received in a regular manner in periods not longer than two months, or
   - if he/she is unemployed and does not receive any other regular remunerations and is delayed in meeting his/her obligations for more than two months, in an amount exceeding EUR 1,000.

(3) Unless it is proven otherwise, a debtor shall be considered long-term unable to pay its debts:

1. if the value of his/her assets is less than the sum of his/her liabilities (hereinafter: overindebtedness),
2. for a debtor who is a company: also if the loss for the current year together with the losses brought forward amounts to one half of the share capital, and such loss cannot be deducted from profit brought forward or from reserves.

(4) It shall be considered, and evidence to the contrary shall not be allowed, that a legal person, entrepreneur or private person becomes continuously illiquid if it is delayed for more than two months:

1. in paying wages to its employees up to the level of the minimum wage or
2. in paying taxes and contributions which the payer must calculate and pay together with the wages to its employees,

and such situation continues on the day prior to filing a petition in bankruptcy.

d) Does the law provide for any technical circumstances (e.g. undisputed statutory demand, non-compliance with monetary judgments, unsuccessful enforcement proceedings, non-performance of a previous composition agreement in insolvency proceedings) the occurrence of which suffices to establish the debtor's insolvency?

Within question (c), there have already been presented the rebuttable presumptions, and some of them are bound to i.e. unsuccessful enforcement proceedings (Article 14(2)-1) or a delay of payments agreed upon in the compulsory settlement agreement (Article 14(2)-2).

e) Other means?
No.

Question 20: Is insolvency (inability to pay debts, overindebtedness, etc.) subject to party autonomy in the proceedings or must the court clarify them *ex officio*?

It must be clarified by the court (insolvency proceedings are judicial proceedings).

Question 21: In an overall view, does your law distinguish "inability to pay debts" from "financial difficulties"? If so, how?

The term "financial difficulties" is not a legal term in Slovenian insolvency legislation.

Question 22: In an overall view, does it matter under your law whether the debtor's inability to pay debts is present or future and reversible or irreversible?

If the inability to pay debts is present, it is a reason to commence insolvency proceeding. If the inability to pay debts is likely (future), which is one of the triggering circumstances for the likelihood of insolvency, it is a reason to commence preventive restructuring proceeding. Our legislation does not distinguish between a reversible or irreversible inability to pay debts.

Question 23: Would you like to add any further aspects not covered by the above questions?

No.

III. CESSATION OF PAYMENTS

Question 24: In your jurisdiction, is "cessation of payments" a legal term used either in statute or in case law? (If the answer is "no", please continue with Question 31.)

No.

Question 25: Is "cessation of payments" an autonomous ground to commence proceedings (triggering circumstance)? You may refer to Questions 6/7 or add additional information here.

n.a.

Question 26: Is "cessation of payments" a means to establish inability to pay debts? If so, by which mechanism (e.g. rebuttable presumption for inability to pay debts, cf. above Question 19(c))?

n.a.

Question 27: How is "cessation of payments" defined? If it is defined in statute, please provide us here with an English translation of the relevant rule. Is this definition (if any) specified in case law? If so, how?

n.a.

Question 28: How is "cessation of payments" established?

n.a.

Question 29: Are there typical circumstances which provide circumstantial evidence that the debtor has ceased payments? If so, please list as many as possible.

n.a.

Question 30: Would you like to add any further aspects not covered by the above questions?

n.a.

IV. LIKELY/IMMINENT INABILITY TO PAY DEBTS

Question 31: Are the following terms available in your jurisdiction, either in statute or in case law? (If the answer is "no", please continue with Question 42.)

a) likely inability to pay debts
Not explicitly. Insolvency can be triggered by (among others) a debtor being long-term unable to pay their debts. Following this, the likelihood of a debtor being long-term unable to pay its debts can trigger the likelihood of insolvency although the term "likely inability to pay debts" is not explicitly mentioned in ZFPPIPP.

b) imminent inability to pay debts
No.

c) other (similar) terms
No.

Question 32: Is "likely/imminent inability to pay debts" an autonomous ground to commence proceedings (triggering circumstance)? You may refer to Questions 6/7 or add additional information here.

Refer to Question 6.

Question 33: If the answer to the previous Question is "yes", who may base filing for insolvency proceedings on it: only the debtor or also creditors?

The preventive restructuring proceeding is not an insolvency proceeding because the debtor is not yet insolvent. But only the debtor can file for a preventive restructuring proceeding (Article 44f ZFPPIPP).

Question 34: How are these terms defined? If they are defined in statute, please provide us here with an English translation of the relevant rules. Is this definition (if any) specified in case law? If so, how?

a) likely inability to pay debts
Refer to Question 31.

b) imminent inability to pay debts
No.

Question 35: Do the terms "likely" and "imminent" require a prognosis regarding the point in time when actual inability to pay debts will occur? If so, how long is the time period for this prognosis?

If there exists a likelihood of insolvency, because it is likely that the debtor will be unable to pay its debts, in this case the term likely refers to a one-year period.

Question 36: Does your law require a specific grade of certainty that inability to pay debts will eventually occur? If so, is 50.1% ("more likely than not") enough or are there alleviated or aggravated prerequisites?

The law does not require a specific degree of certainty other than "likely".

Question 37: Regarding "debts" and "financial means", are they defined in the same way as in the context of inability to pay debts (cf. above Questions 14/15)? If not, what are the differences?

Defined the same way, see *supra* Questions 14 and 15.

Question 38: Further to Question 37: Are "debts" considered which do currently not exist or are not yet due but will foreseeably come into existence and become due during the prognosis period?

No, only existing debts.

Question 39: Also further to Question 37: Are "financial means" considered which do currently not exist but will foreseeably become available during the prognosis period?

No, only existing financial means.

Question 40: How are the terms "likely/imminent inability to pay debts" established?

Free evaluation of evidence applies.

Question 41: Would you like to add any further aspects not covered by the above questions?

No.

V. OVERINDEBTEDNESS

Question 42: In your jurisdiction, is "overindebtedness", or "balance sheet insolvency" respectively, a legal term used either in statute or in case law? (If the answer is "no", please continue with Question 56.)

"Overindebtedness is one of the rebuttable presumptions upon which insolvency is based. Unless it is proven otherwise, a debtor shall be considered long-term unable to pay its debts if the value of his/her assets is less than the sum of his/her liabilities (hereinafter: overindebtedness)" (Article 14(3)-1 ZFPPIPP).

Question 43: Is "overindebtedness" an autonomous ground to commence proceedings (triggering circumstance)? You may refer to Questions 6/7 or add additional information here.

Yes, it is an autonomous ground to commence insolvency proceedings (see answer to Question 5 *supra*).

Question 44: If the answer to the previous Question is "yes", is this applicable to corporate insolvencies of legal persons only or also to personal bankruptcies of natural persons?

Applicable to legal persons and natural persons also.

Question 45: Is the term "overindebtedness" defined in statute? If so, please give the wording in English translation. Is this definition (if any) specified in case law? If so, how?

See answer to Question 42 *supra*.

Question 46: Does your law refer to all existing debts or only to mature debts?

All existing debts.

Question 47: Does the rank of certain debts play a role when establishing overindebtedness? In particular, is there any possibility to conclude agreements according to which certain debts shall not be taken into account (e.g. agreements on subsidiarity)?

No.

Question 48: Which assets are taken into account when overindebtedness is established: the complete set of assets or only a selection of them?

Complete set of assets.

Question 49: How are the debtor's assets valued: by referring to the liquidation value, the book value, the going concern value or in another way?

Before commencing the insolvency proceedings, the debtor's assets are valued by their book value (in accordance with Slovenian Accounting Standards (2016) – Standard 39.1: https://si-revizija.si/datoteke/standardi/3034/sas-2016-en.pdf).

Question 50: Is there any prognostic element, e.g. regarding the debtor's chances to continue the business?

If the chance to continue the business refers to the period after the end of insolvency proceeding, the answer is no. If the chance to continue the business refers to the period within insolvency proceedings, the answer is as follows, under Article 317 ZFPPIPP:

> (1) Upon the initiation of bankruptcy proceedings, the debtor in bankruptcy may resume the production or carrying out of other operations in relation to his/her activity (hereinafter: continuation of the operation of the debtor in bankruptcy), providing that the court permits continuation of the operation of the debtor in bankruptcy
>
> ...
>
> (6) The court shall permit the continuation of the operation of the debtor in bankruptcy:
>
> 1. with the consent from the creditors' committee upon application by the receiver,
> 2. if this results in more favourable conditions for the sale of assets of the debtor in bankruptcy which are used in such operations as a business unit, and
> 3. if the continuation of operations does not represent a breach of the principle of risk limitation referred to in Article 228 of this Act.

Question 51: If the answer to the previous Question is "yes", what exactly is the topic of the prognosis and how is it established?

The prognosis is based on more favourable conditions for the sale of assets of the debtor.

"The court shall decide on the continuation of the operation of the debtor in bankruptcy on the proposal by the receiver and on the basis of the consent of the creditors' committee" (Article 317, paragraph 2 ZFPPIPP). Free evaluation of evidence applies.

Question 52: If the answer to Question 50 is "yes", how long is the prognosis period?

Until the asset is sold.

Question 53: How is overindebtedness established?

a) Is a formal balance sheet required?
Free evaluation of evidence applies.

b) Does the yearly regular commercial balance sheet have any meaning (given that it is normally based on technical values and does not display undisclosed reserves)?
Free evaluation of evidence applies.

c) Does the law provide for a presumption? If so, under which conditions?
See Question 19(c) *supra* (Article 14(3)-1 ZFPPIPP).

d) Other means?
n.a.

Question 54: Is the legal link to overindebtedness undisputed in literature or are there efforts to abolish it?

Undisputed.

Question 55: Would you like to add any further aspects not covered by the above questions?

No.

VI. REMAINING ISSUES

Question 56: Is there anything else you would like to share in the present context and that we should take into account?

No.

SPAIN

Nuria BERMEJO*

I. GENERAL

Question 1: How is insolvency (both in the context of liquidation and restructuring/reorganisation) regulated in your jurisdiction? Please give a brief overview, at least enumerating the relevant statutes.

Under Spanish law, insolvency is regulated in the Consolidated Text of Insolvency Act ("Texto Refundido de la Ley Concursal", hereinafter TRLC).[1] This provision was adopted by Royal Law-Decree 1/2020, of 5 May,[2] and amended by Act 16/2022, of 5 September,[3] which implements into Spanish law Directive (EU) 1023/2019 of 20 June 2019 on restructuring and insolvency.

As provided for in Article 2(1) TRLC, insolvency (*insolvencia*) is the legal standard to be met to open insolvency proceedings (*concurso de acreedores*).[4] In accordance with well-established case law, insolvency does not correspond to aggravated losses or to liabilities exceeding assets.[5]

Article 2(3) TRLC makes a distinction between current or actual insolvency (*insolvencia actual*) and imminent insolvency (*insolvencia inminente*). A debtor is in a state of current insolvency when it is not able to regularly pay its due debts. In contrast, a debtor is in a state of imminent insolvency when it foresees that in the following three months it will not be able to pay its debts in a timely

* This contribution has been produced as part of the research project PID2022-138664NB-C22, funded by the Spanish Ministry of Science and Innovation (MCIN/AEI/10.13039/501100011033/FEDER, UE).

1 Between 2004 and 2015, Act 22/2003, of 9 July, Insolvency Act (Spanish Official Gazette No. 164, of 10 July) underwent a large number of amendments which were consolidated in the Consolidated Text of the Spanish Insolvency Act.

2 Spanish Official Gazette No. 7, of 7 May.

3 Spanish Official Gazette No. 214, of 6 September.

4 Article 2(1) TRLC: "The opening of insolvency proceedings will proceed in case of the debtor's insolvency".

5 In a situation of aggravated losses, the debtor is not insolvent if it can still meet its obligations because it is able to obtain funding. See Judgments of the Spanish Supreme Court No. 122/2014, of 1 April, legal ground 13; No. 275/2015, of 7 May, legal ground 7; and No. 269/2016, of 22 April, legal ground 5. See also Order of Madrid Provincial Court No. 136/2008, of 17 April, legal ground 5.

and regular manner. While current insolvency implies an actual default on the part of the debtor, imminent insolvency entails a debtor's prognosis about its future ability to fulfil its obligations. As a result, creditors and other legitimate persons aside than the debtor – partners being personally liable for the debtor's liabilities (Article 3(1) and (3) TRLC) – are not entitled to request the opening of insolvency proceedings on the basis of imminent insolvency. Moreover, the duty to file for insolvency only applies when the debtor is currently insolvent (Article 5(1) TRLC).

In order to establish (current) insolvency, creditors and other legitimate persons other than the debtor must rely on facts that constitute external indications of this situation. These facts are listed in Article 2(4) TRLC as follows:

(i) the existence of a previous administrative or judicial final decision declaring debtor's insolvency;
(ii) the lack of unencumbered assets in the debtor's estate to hold a lien and obtain payment;
(iii) the existence of liens encumbering the debtor's estate in a general manner;
(iv) the general cessation of regular payments;
(v) the general cessation of the payment of tax or social security claims during the three months preceding the filing, or of labour-related claims of the last three months; and
(vi) the asset stripping or hasty or ruinous liquidation of the debtor's assets.[6]

In contrast, the debtor can rely in any external circumstance to prove the inability to pay debts.

Together with likelihood of insolvency (*probabilidad de insolvencia*), "current insolvency" and "imminent insolvency" are also relevant legal standards for preventive restructuring frameworks. A debtor is likely to become insolvent when it is objectively foreseeable that it will not be able to regularly pay the debts that will become due in the next two years if a restructuring plan is not adopted (Article 584(2) TRLC).

Only a debtor being currently or imminently insolvent or likely to become insolvent is entitled to communicate to the court the commencement of negotiations with creditors to adopt a restructuring plan (Articles 584(1) TRLC).[7] Moreover, the debtor and creditors having signed the restructuring plan can

---

6 Article 2(4) TRLC: "The request for the opening of insolvency proceedings filed by a creditor must be founded on any of the following external facts revealing the state of insolvency".

7 Article 584(1) TRLC: "The communication of the commencement of negotiations or the confirmation of a restructuring plan shall proceed when the debtor is in a state of likelihood of insolvency, imminent insolvency or current insolvency".
Article 584(2) TRLC: "A probability of insolvency is considered to exist when it is objectively foreseeable that the debtor will not be able to regularly meet the obligations that will become due within the next two years if a restructuring plan is not concluded".

request the judicial confirmation of the plan when the debtor is currently or imminently insolvent or likely to become insolvent (Articles 584(1), 636 and 643(1) TRLC).[8]

Finally, current insolvency, imminent insolvency and likelihood of insolvency entitle a debtor to apply to the court to appoint an expert with a view to inviting bids for the acquisition of one or more productive units (pre-pack sale *ex* Article 224 ter TRLC).[9] These units will be sold afterwards within the corresponding insolvency proceedings (Article 224 sexies TRLC), or outside them. In order to open these proceedings general requirements must be fulfilled.

Question 2: Related to paragraph 10 above of the Introduction: seen from a principle-based perspective, what justifies the opening of insolvency proceedings in your jurisdiction?

Under Spanish law, the main principle underlying the opening of insolvency proceedings (*concurso de acreedores*) is the collective satisfaction of creditors.[10] These proceedings can be either reorganisation or liquidation proceedings. Thus, claims can be satisfied within these proceedings either through the adoption of a composition agreement between the debtor and its (unsecured) creditors (Articles 315 to 405 TRLC), or through the liquidation of the debtor's estate and the distribution of the proceeds among the creditors (Articles 406 to 440 TRLC).

The early opening of insolvency proceedings contributes to avoiding a loss of value of the debtor's assets that may complicate or even impede the adoption of the most appropriate solution for the satisfaction of claims.[11]

8 Article 636(1) TRLC: "The judicial confirmation of a restructuring plan adopted in accordance with the provisions of this title can be requested from the court when the debtor is in a state of likelihood of insolvency or imminent insolvency".
Article 636(2) TRLC: "When the debtor is in a state of current insolvency, the confirmation of the restructuring plan can be requested from the court provided that a request for the opening of insolvency proceedings has not been admitted".
Article 643(1) TRLC: "The debtor or any affected creditor who signed the restructuring plan is entitled to request the judicial confirmation of it. The application shall be signed by a barrister and a solicitor".

9 Article 224 ter TRLC: "In the event of likelihood of insolvency, imminent insolvency or current insolvency, the debtor, whether a natural or legal person, whatever the activity in which it is engaged, may request the court having jurisdiction for the opening of insolvency proceedings to appoint an expert with a view to inviting bids from third parties for the acquisition, with cash payment, of one or more productive units owned by the applicant, even if they have ceased their activity".

10 See Preamble of Act 22/2003.

11 See Preamble of Act 22/2003.

Question 3: Does your national law in the context of liquidation proceedings use one or more of the following terms (be it as a noun, be it as an adjective or adjunct) in whatever context:

Under Spanish insolvency law, some of these terms are used in the context of insolvency proceedings that may end up with the liquidation of the debtor's estate. Others are not used directly, but closely-related expressions are employed in this context.

a) inability to pay debts

This term is used in the Consolidated Text of the Spanish Insolvency Act to define "current insolvency" as the situation where the debtor is not able to regularly pay its due debts (Article 2(3) TRLC).[12]

This situation obliges the debtor to apply to the corresponding court for the opening of insolvency proceedings that may end up with the liquidation of its estate (Article 5(1) TRLC; see answer to Question 10). This also obliges it to request the court to open the liquidation phase of insolvency proceedings when the debtor knows that it is unable to meet the payments involved in the composition entered into with its creditors and the obligations incurred after the court's approval of the composition (Article 407 TRLC).[13]

The same situation also entitles a debtor to apply to the court to appoint an expert with a view to inviting bids for the acquisition of one or more productive units (Article 224 ter TRLC). Since the debtor is obliged to request the opening of insolvency proceedings in this situation, the units must be sold afterwards within the corresponding insolvency proceedings (Articles 224 quinquies and sexies TRLC). In order to open these proceedings general requirements must be fulfilled.

b) cessation of payments

This term is included in the list of external facts that creditors and other legitimate persons other than the debtor must invoke in order to establish the debtor's insolvency and obtain the opening of insolvency proceedings over the debtor's estate that may end in liquidation (see answer to Question 1). These facts include, among others, the general cessation of regular payments (Article 2(4)(4°) TRLC), and the general cessation of the payment of tax or

12 Article 2(3) TRLC: "Insolvency may be current or imminent. A debtor is currently insolvent when it is not able to regularly satisfy its due obligations. The debtor is imminently insolvent when it foresees that it will not be able to satisfy its obligations in a timely and regular manner in the following three months".

13 Article 407 TRLC: "During the validity of the composition, the debtor must request the liquidation as soon as it becomes aware of the impossibility of complying with the payments agreed to in it and the obligations entered into after the approval of this composition".

social security claims during the three months preceding the filing, or of labour-related claims of the last three months (Article 2(4)(5°) TRLC).[14]

When these situations of cessation of payments occur, it is presumed – subject to proof to the contrary – that the debtor was aware of the situation of current insolvency (Article 5(2) TRLC). It is then obliged to request the court for the opening of insolvency proceedings that may result in the liquidation of its estate (Article 5(1) TRLC) (see answer to Question 10).

c) likely inability to pay debts

The expression used in the Consolidated Text of Spanish Insolvency Act is "likelihood of insolvency". As explained above (see answer to Question 1), a debtor is likely to become insolvent when it is objectively foreseeable that it will not be able to regularly pay the debts that will become due in the next two years if a restructuring plan is not adopted (Article 584(2) TRLC).[15]

The likelihood of insolvency entitles a debtor to apply to the court to appoint an expert with a view to inviting bids for the acquisition of one or more productive units (Article 224 ter TRLC). These units can be sold afterwards within the corresponding insolvency proceedings (Article 224 sexies TRLC). In order to open these proceedings general requirements must be fulfilled.

d) imminent inability to pay debts

Similar expressions are used in the Consolidated Text of Spanish Insolvency Act when it refers to "imminent insolvency" and defines it as the situation where the debtor foresees that it will not be able to pay its debts in a timely and regular manner in the following three months (Article 2(3) TRLC).[16]

In this situation, the debtor can request to the court for the opening of insolvency proceedings that may end up with the liquidation of its estate (Article 2(2) TRLC).

The same situation also entitles a debtor to apply to the court to appoint an expert with a view to inviting bids for the acquisition of one or more productive units (Article 224 ter TRLC). These units can be sold afterwards within the

14 Article 2(4)(4°) and (5°) TRLC: "The request for the opening of insolvency proceedings filed by a creditor must be founded on any of the following external facts revealing the state of insolvency:

...

4°. General cessation of regular payment of the debtor's claims.

5°. General cessation of payment of due tax claims during the three months prior to the request for the opening of insolvency proceedings; social security contributions and other concepts of joint contribution during the same period of time, or salaries and other remuneration corresponding to labour relationships of the three last months".

15 See fn. 7.

16 See fn. 12.

corresponding insolvency proceedings (Article 224 sexies TRLC). In order to open these proceedings general requirements must be fulfilled.

e) overindebtedness
No.

Question 4: Are the same terms (and with the same meaning) used in the rules on preliminary/interim insolvency proceedings (e.g. concerning the application stage of the proceedings)?

Under Spanish insolvency law, some of these terms are used in preliminary insolvency proceedings. Others are not used directly, but closely-related expressions are employed in this context.

a) inability to pay debts
As mentioned above (see answers to Questions 1 and 3), "current insolvency" is defined as a situation where the debtor is not able to regularly pay its due debts (Article 2(3) TRLC).[17] This situation obliges the debtor to ask the court for the opening of insolvency proceedings (Article 5(1) TRLC; see answer to Question 10).

In accordance with Article 6(1) TRLC, the debtor must state in the request to open insolvency proceedings whether it is currently or imminently insolvent and prove either of these situations.

Current insolvency is also one of the three situations of financial distress that entitles a debtor to ask the court to appoint an expert before the opening of insolvency proceedings with a view to inviting bids for the acquisition of one or more productive units (Article 224 ter TRLC).[18] The debtor must therefore refer to one of these situations in the request addressed to the court. In order to open insolvency proceedings general requirements must be fulfilled.

Furthermore, in the context of preventive restructuring frameworks, when the breach of a restructuring plan is caused by insolvency, any entitled person – i.e. the debtor, its creditors, and the partners being personally liable for the debtor's liabilities (Article 3(1) and (3) TRLC) – may ask the court for the opening of insolvency proceedings (Article 671(2) TRLC). However, when the insolvency is current, the debtor must apply to the court to open these proceedings (Article 5(1) TRLC; see answer to Question 10).

b) cessation of payments
Pursuant to Article 13(1) TRLC, creditors and other legitimate persons aside than the debtor must state in the request to open insolvency proceedings any of the facts on which they must rely to establish the debtor's insolvency

---

[17] See fn. 12.
[18] See fn. 9.

(see answer to Question 1). These facts include, among others, the general cessation of regular payments (Article 2(4)(4º) TRLC), and the cessation of the payment of tax claims or social security claims during the three months before the filing, or of labour-related claims of the last three months (Article 2(4)(5º) TRLC).[19]

Moreover, when these situations of cessation of payments occur, it is presumed – subject to proof to the contrary – that the debtor was aware of the situation of current insolvency (Article 5(2) TRLC). It is then obliged to apply to the court to open insolvency proceedings (Article 5(1) TRLC) (see answer to Question 10).

c) likely inability to pay debts

As explained above (see answers to Questions 1 and 3), a debtor is likely to become insolvent when it is objectively foreseeable that it will not be able to regularly pay the debts that will become due in the next two years if a restructuring plan is not adopted (Article 584(2) TRLC).[20]

The likelihood of insolvency is one of the three situations of financial distress that entitle a debtor to apply to the court to appoint an expert before the opening of insolvency proceedings with a view to inviting bids for the acquisition of one or more productive units (Article 224 ter TRLC).[21] The debtor must therefore refer to one of those situations in the request addressed to the court. In order to open insolvency proceedings general requirements must be fulfilled.

d) imminent inability to pay debts

As mentioned above (see Questions 1 and 3), "imminent insolvency" is defined as the situation where the debtor foresees that it will not be able to pay its debts in a timely and regular manner in the following three months (Article 2(3) TRLC).[22]

In accordance with Article 6(1) TRLC, the debtor must state in the request for the opening of insolvency proceedings whether it is currently or imminently insolvent and prove any of these situations.

Moreover, imminent insolvency is one of the three situations of financial distress that entitle a debtor to ask the court to appoint an expert before the opening of insolvency proceedings with a view to inviting bids for the acquisition of one or more productive units (Article 224 ter TRLC).[23] The debtor must therefore refer to one of those situations in the request addressed to the court. In order to open insolvency proceedings general requirements must be fulfilled.

e) overindebtedness

No.

---

[19] See fn. 14.
[20] See fn. 7.
[21] See fn. 9.
[22] See fn. 12.
[23] See fn. 9.

Question 5: Does your national law in the context of restructuring proceedings (as referred to above at paragraph 8 of the Introduction, i.e. both pre-insolvency and within formal insolvency proceedings) use one or more of the following terms (be it as a noun, be it as an adjective or adjunct) in whatever context:

Under Spanish insolvency law, some of these terms are used in the context of restructuring proceedings – either in preventive frameworks or in formal insolvency proceedings that may end up with the reorganisation of the debtor's estate. Others are not used directly, but closely-related expressions are employed in this context.

a) inability to pay debts

The situation of "current insolvency" – which, as mentioned before, refers to the situation where the debtor is not able to pay its due debts (see answers to Questions 1 and 3) – obliges the debtor to request the opening of insolvency proceedings that may end up with the reorganisation of its estate (Article 5(1) TRLC) (see answer to Question 10).

In addition, "current insolvency" is one of the three situations of financial distress that constitute a relevant legal standard for preventive restructuring frameworks – i.e. current insolvency, imminent insolvency and likelihood of insolvency (Articles 584(1) and 636(2) TRLC).[24]

A debtor being currently insolvent is entitled to communicate to the court the commencement of negotiations with its creditors with a view to adopting a restructuring plan (Article 584(1) TRLC). Likewise, "current insolvency" permits the judicial confirmation of the plan to be requested (Article 584(1) TRLC). However, when the debtor is currently insolvent, the confirmation of the plan can only be requested if the court has not previously admitted a petition by creditors for the opening of insolvency proceedings (Article 636(2) TRLC). The effective existence of a situation of "current insolvency" is only verified by the court when the judicial confirmation of the plan is requested (Article 638(1°) TRLC). Consequently, the confirmation order can be contested by dissenting or non-voting creditors, *inter alia*, when the debtor is not currently or imminently insolvent or likely to be insolvent (Article 654(3°) TRLC), and by dissenting shareholders, *inter alia*, when it is not currently or imminently insolvent (Article 656(1)(3°) TRLC).

Moreover, in the context of the confirmation of a restructuring plan, when the debtor is currently insolvent, shareholders' pre-emptive rights are excluded (Article 631(4) TRLC), and the plan can be confirmed by the court against the vote of the majority of the shareholders (Article 640(2) TRLC).[25]

---

[24] See fns. 7 and 8.

[25] For an example, see Judgment No. 26/2023, of 4 September, of Barcelona Commercial Court No. 2.

b) cessation of payments

As mentioned above (see answers to Questions 1 and 3), the general cessation of regular payments and the general cessation of the payment of tax, or social security claims during the three months preceding the filing, or of labour-related claims of the last three months are some of the external facts revealing the debtor's insolvency. Creditors and other legitimate persons other than the debtor must refer to any of these facts to establish the debtor's current insolvency (Article 2(4)(4°) and (5°) TRLC), and to obtain the opening of insolvency proceedings over the debtor's estate that may end up in reorganisation.[26]

When these situations of cessation of payments occur, it is presumed – subject to proof to the contrary – that the debtor was aware of the situation of current insolvency (Article 5(2) TRLC). It is then obliged to request to the court to open insolvency proceedings (Article 5(1) TRLC) (cf. Question 10).

In addition, "current insolvency" is one of the three situations of financial distress that constitutes a relevant legal standard for preventive restructuring frameworks – i.e. current insolvency, imminent insolvency and likelihood of insolvency (Articles 584(1) TRLC 636(2) TRLC).[27]

A debtor being currently insolvent is entitled to communicate to the court the commencement of negotiations with its creditors to adopt a restructuring plan (Article 584(1) TRLC). Likewise, "current insolvency" permits the judicial confirmation of the plan to be requested (Article 584(1) TRLC). However, when the debtor is currently insolvent, the judicial confirmation of the plan can only be requested if the court has not previously admitted a petition by creditors for the opening of insolvency proceedings (Article 636(2) TRLC). The effective existence of a situation of "current insolvency" is only verified by the court when the judicial confirmation of the plan is requested (Article 638(1°) TRLC).[28] Consequently, the confirmation order can be contested by dissenting or non-voting creditors, *inter alia*, when the debtor is not currently or imminently insolvent or likely to be insolvent (Article 654(3°), and by dissenting shareholders, *inter alia*, when it is not currently or imminently insolvent (Article 656(1)(3°) TRLC).

In the context of the confirmation of a restructuring plan, when the debtor is currently insolvent, shareholders' pre-emptive rights are excluded (Article 631(4) TRLC), and the plan can be confirmed by the court against the vote of the majority of the shareholders (Article 640(2) TRLC).

---

26 See fn. 14.

27 See fns. 7 and 8.

28 See Order No. 218/2024, of 16 July, of Las Palmas de Gran Canaria Commercial Court No. 2, legal ground 4. The judge considered that the existence of a cessation of payments could not be inferred from the sole will or interpretation of the creditors. In this case, a change of control clause allowed the early maturity of several financial instruments. Following the acquisition by an investor of a majority stake in the company, the creditors enforced their claims against the debtor, who did not respond to the requests for payment.

c) likely inability to pay debts

The "likelihood of insolvency" is one of the three situations of financial distress that constitute a relevant legal standard for preventive restructuring frameworks – i.e. current insolvency, imminent insolvency and likelihood of insolvency (Articles 584(1) and 636 TRLC).[29] It was introduced into Spanish law as a result of the implementation of Directive (EU) 1023/2019 of 20 June 2019 on restructuring and insolvency. A debtor is likely to become insolvent when it is objectively foreseeable that it will not be able to regularly pay the debts that will become due in the next two years if a restructuring plan is not adopted (Article 584(2) TRLC).[30]

A debtor likely to become insolvent is entitled to communicate to the court the commencement of negotiations with its creditors to adopt a restructuring plan (Article 584(1) TRLC). Moreover, "likelihood of insolvency" permits the judicial confirmation of the plan to be requested (Article 584(1) TRLC). The effective existence of a situation of "likelihood of insolvency" is only verified by the court when the judicial confirmation of the plan is requested (Article 638(1º) TRLC). Consequently, the confirmation order can be contested by dissenting or non-voting creditors, *inter alia*, when the debtor is not likely to become insolvent, or currently or imminently insolvent (Article 654(3º) TRLC).

d) imminent inability to pay debts

As mentioned above (see answers to Questions 1 and 3), "imminent insolvency" refers to the situation where the debtor foresees that in the following three months it will not be able to pay its debts in a timely and regular manner (Article 2(3) TRLC).[31] This situation does not oblige the debtor to request the opening of insolvency proceedings. It only entitles the debtor to request it (Articles 2(2) and 5(1) TRLC).[32]

In addition, "imminent insolvency" is one of the three situations of financial distress that constitute a relevant legal standard for preventive restructuring frameworks – i.e. current insolvency, imminent insolvency and likelihood of insolvency (Articles 584(1) and 636(1) TRLC).[33]

A debtor being imminently insolvent is entitled to communicate to the court the commencement of negotiations with its creditors to adopt a restructuring plan (Article 584(1) TRLC). Likewise, "imminent insolvency" permits the judicial confirmation of the plan to be requested (Article 584(1) TRLC). The effective existence of a situation of "imminent insolvency" is only verified by the court

29 See fns. 7 and 8.

30 See fn. 7.

31 See fn. 12.

32 Judgment of Cádiz Provincial Court No. 289/2023, of 22 March, legal ground 5.

33 See fns. 7 and 8.

when the judicial confirmation of the plan is requested (Article 638(1°) TRLC). Consequently, the confirmation order can be contested by dissenting or non-voting creditors, *inter alia*, when the debtor is not currently or imminently insolvent or likely to become insolvent (Article 654(3°), and by dissenting shareholders, *inter alia*, when it is not currently or imminently insolvent (Article 656(1)(3°) TRLC).

In the context of the confirmation of a restructuring plan, when the debtor is imminently insolvent shareholders' pre-emptive rights are excluded (Article 631(4) TRLC), and the plan can be confirmed by the court against the vote of the majority of shareholders (Article 640(2) TRLC).

e) overindebtedness
No.

Question 6: Which of the terms mentioned in Questions 3 and 5 are used for defining grounds to commence proceedings (triggering circumstances)?

a) insolvency proceedings
Inability to pay debts; cessation of payments, and imminent inability to pay debts (as "imminent insolvency").

b) restructuring proceedings
Inability to pay debts (as "current insolvency"); cessation of payments (as "current insolvency"); imminent inability to pay debts (as "imminent insolvency"); and likely inability to pay debts (as "likelihood of insolvency").

Question 7: Does the answer to Question 6 include personal bankruptcies of natural persons or only corporate insolvencies of legal entities?

It includes natural persons and legal entities. Article 2 TRLC refers to the "debtor's insolvency" and debtors may be either natural persons or legal entities (Article 1(1) TRLC).

The Consolidated Text of Spanish Insolvency Act provides for special insolvency proceedings for microenterprises, that are also applicable to natural persons and legal entities (Article 685 TRLC; see answer to Question 11).

Question 8: In your law, are there any other circumstances which trigger insolvency or restructuring proceedings?

No.

Question 9: Which of the terms mentioned in Questions 3, 5, and 8 are used in the context of transactions avoidance law?

None of them.

Question 10: Which of the terms addressed in Questions 3, 5, and 8 are used in the context of directors' duties?

a) shift of duties (from shareholders to creditors)
n.a.

b) duties to commence insolvency proceedings
"Inability to pay debts" and "cessation of payments", but only in an indirect way (as "current insolvency").

Article 5(1) TRLC imposes a duty on the debtor to commence insolvency proceedings in the two months following the date it knew or should have known that it was in a state of current insolvency.[34] This duty applies to the directors of insolvent companies (Article 444 TRLC). As mentioned above (see answers to Questions 1 and 3), this situation is defined in the Spanish insolvency law as the debtor's inability to regularly pay its due debts (Article 2(3) TRLC).[35]

Pursuant to Article 5(2) TRLC, it is presumed, subject to proof to the contrary, that the debtor was aware of the state of current insolvency where one of the facts listed in Article 2(4) TRLC occurs.[36] The general cessation of regular payments (Article 2(4)(4°) TRLC), and the general cessation of the payment of tax or social security claims during the three months preceding the filing, or of labour-related claims of the last three months (Article 2(4)(5°) TRLC) are two of the six facts included in this provision (see answers to Question 1).

c) other duties (please describe)
n.a.

Question 11: Are there any other rules in the context of which the terms addressed in Questions 3, 5, and 8 are used?

These terms are also used in the rules applicable to the special insolvency proceedings for microenterprises set out in the Consolidated Text of the Spanish Insolvency Act (Articles 685 to 720 TRLC).

When the debtor is a microenterprise, the opening of these special insolvency proceedings can be requested from the court when the debtor is currently, imminently or likely to become insolvent (Article 686(1) TRLC). The debtor is obliged to request the opening of these proceedings when it is currently insolvent (Article 686(2) TRLC).

---

34 Article 5(1) TRLC: "The debtor must request the opening of insolvency proceedings within two months following the date when it knew or should have known the state of current insolvency".

35 See fn. 12.

36 Article 5(2) TRLC: "Unless proven otherwise, it shall be presumed that the debtor knew that it was in a state of insolvency when any of the external facts that may be invoked by other legitimate persons to open insolvency proceedings occurs".

Within the framework of these proceedings, a microenterprise is entitled to communicate to the court the commencement of negotiations with its creditors in order to adopt a continuation plan or to sell the business as a going concern in any of these situations of financial distress (Article 690(1) TRLC). Likewise, a microenterprise must be in one of these situations to request the judicial confirmation of the plan (Articles 698 bis (6)(1ª) TRLC).

The liquidation phase of these proceedings must be opened, *inter alia*, when the debtor is currently insolvent and no continuation plan has been adopted or confirmed by the court, or when the debtor has breached a previously adopted continuation plan (Article 705(1) TRLC).

Question 12: Is the definition of (the subspecies of) insolvency identical in all legal fields or are there different definitions (e.g. different in insolvency law than in criminal law)?

Since the amendment introduced by Organic Act 1/2015, of 30 March,[37] the Spanish Criminal Code uses the terms "current insolvency" and "imminent insolvency" to define different insolvency-related offences (i.e. Articles 259(1) and 260(1) Criminal Code).[38] These terms and their meaning are identical to those used in the Consolidated Text of the Spanish Insolvency Act.

In contrast, Spanish labour legislation refers to a particular concept of insolvency in the context of wage protection. In accordance with Article 33(1) of the Law on the Statute of Workers ("Ley del Estatuto de los Trabajadores", hereinafter ET),[39] the Wage Guarantee Fund (*Fondo de Garantía Salarial*) will satisfy outstanding wages when the employer is insolvent or insolvency proceedings are opened regarding its estate. For the purposes of this provision, "insolvency" is defined as the situation where labour-related claims cannot be satisfied after the judicial enforcement of these claims has been requested. In order to activate the guarantee provided by the Wage Guarantee Fund, after hearing the Fund, the labour court will adopt a decision declaring this situation (Article 33(6) ET).

---

37 Spanish Official Gazette No. 37, of 31 March.

38 Article 259(1) Criminal Code: "Whoever, in a situation of actual or imminent insolvency, engages in any of the following conducts, shall be punished with a prison sentence of one to four years and a fine of eight to twenty-four months: …". See https://www.mjusticia.gob.es/es/AreaTematica/DocumentacionPublicaciones/Documents/Criminal_Code_2016.pdf.
Article 260(1) Criminal Code: "The debtor who, in a situation of actual or imminent insolvency, favours any of the creditors by carrying out a deed of disposal of assets or of generation of obligations to pay for an unenforceable credit or to provide a guarantee that they are not entitled to, if the transaction cannot be justified from an economic or business perspective, shall be punished with a prison sentence of six months to three years or a fine of eight to twenty-four months. See https://www.mjusticia.gob.es/es/AreaTematica/DocumentacionPublicaciones/Documents/Criminal_Code_2016.pdf.

39 Royal Legislative Decree No. 2/2015, of 23 October (Spanish Official Gazette No. 255, of 24 October).

II. INABILITY TO PAY DEBTS

Question 13: In your jurisdiction, is the term "inability to pay debts" defined in statute? If so, please give the wording in English translation. Is this definition (if any) specified in case law? If so, how?

Under Spanish insolvency law, "inability to pay debts" corresponds to the definition of *insolvencia actual* or "current insolvency" (Article 2(3) TRLC).[40] However, the Consolidated Text of the Spanish Insolvency Act does not provide any specific definition of the term "inability to pay debts".

In accordance with the legal literature and case law, "inability to pay debts" is a functional concept that cannot be identified with illiquidity, aggravated losses, asset imbalance or overindebtedness.[41] Actually, the reasons for being unable to pay the due debts are irrelevant.[42]

"Inability to pay debts" refers to debtor's aptitude or capacity "to regularly satisfy its due debts" (Article 2(3) TRLC). Therefore, a debtor who is able to pay its due obligations, but in an irregular manner, is currently insolvent.[43] There are different views among the scholars about the meaning of "regular payment", but in accordance with the most accepted view and case law, a payment is regular when it is made by normal means and under market conditions. This excludes situations where, for example, the debtor has undertaken a hasty or ruinous liquidation of its assets with the purpose of satisfying all or part of its debts.[44] Moreover, "inability to pay debts" refers to a state – "the state of insolvency" – that endures in time. Therefore, temporary arrears in the payment of debts do not make the debtor unable to pay.[45] As explained below, the inability to pay refers to debts that are already due (see answer to Question 14).

---

40 See fn. 12.

41 *Rojo*, "Comentario del artículo 2 LC", in *Rojo/Beltrán (eds.)*, Comentario de la Ley concursal, t. I, Civitas, Madrid 2004, pp. 164–193, pp. 170–171. In the same vein, see also *Pulgar*, "Comentario del artículo 2 TRLC", in *Pulgar (ed.)*, Comentario a la Ley Concursal. Texto Refundido de la Ley Concursal, 2nd ed., t. I, Wolters Kluwer, Madrid 2020, pp. 167–198, pp. 170–172. In the case law, see Judgments of the Supreme Court No. 122/2014, legal ground 13; No. 275/2015, of 7 May, legal ground 7; and No. 269/2016, legal ground 5; Judgments of Barcelona Provincial Court No. 208/2013, of 21 May, legal ground 6; and No. 100/2016, of 29 April, legal ground 4; Order of Madrid Provincial Court No. 136/2008, legal ground 5; and Judgment No. 2/2023, of 9 January, of Barcelona Commercial Court No. 4, legal ground 4.

42 *Rojo*, Comentario LC, fn. 41, p. 170; *Pulgar*, Comentario TRLC, fn. 41, p. 170. In the case law, see Judgment of Madrid Provincial Court No. 279/2008, of 18 November, legal ground 3.

43 *Rojo*, Comentario LC, fn. 41, p. 172.

44 Ibid., p. 172. In the case law, see Judgment of the Supreme Court No. 122/2014, legal ground 13; Judgment of Madrid Provincial Court No. 279/2008, of 18 November, legal ground 3; Judgment of Barcelona Provincial Court No. 100/2016, of 21 April, legal ground 4; and Judgment No. 2/2023 of Barcelona Commercial Court No. 4, legal ground 4.

45 *Rojo*, Comentario LC, fn. 41, p. 172; *Pulgar*, Comentario TRLC, fn. 41, p. 171.

Question 14: Does your law refer to all debts or only to mature debts?

The legal definition of "current insolvency" does not refer to all debts, but only to due debts – "inability to regularly pay its due debts".[46] Under Spanish law, due obligations are those that can be judicially enforced against the debtor.[47] Obligations are not due when they are subject to a term, a condition, a *pactum de non petendo*, or when they are null and void.[48] Therefore, maturity is a relevant circumstance – but not the only one – for considering that the payment of the debt is due.

Question 15: Which assets are taken into account when assessing the inability to pay debts: all (financial) assets or only those that are liquid, i.e. available on short notice?

As a general rule, all the debtor's assets are taken into account to assess its inability to pay debts. The Consolidated Text of the Spanish Insolvency Act does not exclude illiquid assets. Likewise, no exclusion is foreseen in case law or in legal literature. However, the lack of liquidity of certain assets may have a negative impact on the debtor's ability to pay its debts and, consequently, on the debtor's solvency.[49]

Question 16: Is any liquidity gap (deficit between relevant financial means and relevant debts) relevant or does your law neglect minor gaps? If the latter, how is "minor" defined?

Under Spanish insolvency law, the amount of the deficit between financial means and debts is not relevant to establishing the debtor's inability to pay debts.[50]

Question 17: As far as the time aspect is concerned, does it matter whether the liquidity gap can be closed again in the short term? If so, how long is the grace period?

Yes, it does. As mentioned above (see answer to Question 13), according to a general view, a debtor who cannot temporarily pay its due debts is not insolvent. However, the Consolidated Text of the Spanish Insolvency Act does not provide for any specific grace period.

---

46 In the case law, see Judgment of Barcelona Provincial Court No. 100/2016, legal ground 4, and Judgment No. 2/2023 of Barcelona Commercial Court No. 4, legal ground 4.

47 *Díez Picazo*, Fundamentos de Derecho civil patrimonial, t. II, 4th ed., Civitas, Madrid 1993, p. 539.

48 *Pulgar*, Comentario TRLC, fn. 41, p. 184.

49 *Rojo*, Comentario LC, fn. 41, pp. 170–171.

50 Ibid., p. 171.

Question 18: As far as the time aspect is concerned, is a debtor considered insolvent if the liquidity gap is not yet present but will occur soon? If so, how long is the prognosis period? (Note: this may also concern the difference between actual and likely/imminent inability to pay debts; cf. below Question 34).

As explained above (see answer to Question 1), the debtor is imminently insolvent when it is not insolvent at the present time, but it foresees that in the next three months it will not be able to pay its debts in a timely and regular manner (Article 2(3) TRLC).

Originally, Spanish insolvency law did not specify the duration of the prognosis period. However, it was considered that the inability to pay debts should appear in the short term and, accordingly, it was suggested that this period could not be longer than six months.[51] After the amendment introduced by Act 16/2022, the prognosis period was limited to three months to distinguish "imminent insolvency" from "likelihood of insolvency".[52]

Question 19: How is inability to pay debts established? Please communicate if there is a difference between a creditor and a debtor application or between different legal contexts.

Creditors and other legitimate persons other than the debtor – partners being personally liable for the debtor's liabilities (Article 3(1) and (3) TRLC) – must only rely on external facts listed in Article 2(4) TRLC. These persons must state in their petition the fact or facts relied upon and provide evidence of them (Article 13(3) TRLC). In order to prove these facts, they can make use of any means of proof, including testimonial evidence, but this alone is not sufficient (Article 13(3) TRLC).

In contrast, the debtor can rely in any external circumstance to prove its inability to pay debts and must provide documental evidence of it – i.e. accounting records, expert opinions, etc. (Article 6(1) TRLC). It can also invoke the external facts listed in Article 2(4) TRLC, but it is not limited to them.[53] However, a debtor's application does not constitute by itself an indication of its inability to pay due debts.[54] The court must examine the documents provided by the debtor and if it considers that objective and subjective conditions for the opening of insolvency proceedings are met, it must open them on the next working day (Article 10(2) TRLC).

---

51 *Rojo*, Comentario LC, fn. 41, pp. 176–177.

52 *Garcimartín*, "El Derecho preconcursal: una visión general", Anuario de Derecho Concursal (ADCo), no. 57, 2022, V (electronic version).

53 *Rojo*, "Comentario del artículo 14 LC", in *Rojo/Beltrán (eds.)*, Comentario de la Ley concursal, t. I, Civitas, Madrid 2004, pp. 379–388, p. 384; *Pulgar*, Comentario TRLC, fn. 41, p. 188.

54 *Rojo*, Comentario LC, fn. 41, p. 384.

a) Is a formal liquidity status (liquidity balance sheet) required?
In the case of a debtor's application, debtors who are legally required to keep accounting records must provide the annual accounts for the last three financial years and, therefore, the corresponding balance sheets (Article 8(1)(1°) TRLC).

No formal liquidity status is required for a creditor's application and the application of other legitimate persons other than the debtor (see Article 13(1) TRLC). They must refer to any of the external facts listed in Article 2(4) TRLC that reveal the debtor's current insolvency (Article 13(1) and (3) TRLC), and they can provide any evidence to prove these facts (see *infra* answers to Questions (c) and 28).

b) Is a sample of daily liquidity data (which do not amount to a proper liquidity status but show insufficient funds on different days within a certain period of time) sufficient?
A sample of daily liquidity data showing insufficient funds may not be sufficient to establish inability to pay due debts if it only shows the debtor's temporarily difficulties in paying them or if the debtor is able to obtain the necessary funding to meet its obligations.

c) Does the law provide for a rebuttable presumption? If so, under which conditions?
As explained before (see answer Question 1), Article 2(4) of the Spanish Insolvency Act contains a comprehensive list of external indications of current insolvency (*numerus clausus*). They not only allow the court to presume the debtor's insolvency, but also indicate a particularly serious insolvency situation.[55] These facts are:

(i) the existence of a previous administrative or judicial final decision declaring the debtor's insolvency;
(ii) the lack of unencumbered assets in the debtor's estate to hold a lien and obtain payment;
(iii) the existence of liens encumbering the debtor's estate in a general manner;
(iv) the general cessation of regular payments;
(v) the general cessation of the payment of tax, social security, or labour-related claims during the three months preceding the filing, and
(vi) the asset stripping or hasty or ruinous liquidation of the debtor's assets.

Creditors and other legitimate persons other than the debtor – partners being personally liable for the debtor's liabilities (Article 3(1) and (3) TRLC) – must only rely on external facts listed in Article 2(4) TRLC. These persons must state in their petition the fact or facts relied upon, and provide evidence of them

55 *Rojo*, Comentario LC, fn. 41, p. 168.

(Article 13(3) TRLC). In order to prove these facts, they can make use of any means of proof, including testimonial evidence, but this alone is not sufficient (Article 13(3) TRLC).

When creditors invoke the facts mentioned under (i)–(iii), the court shall declare the opening of the insolvency proceedings on the next working day (Article 14(2)(1°) TRLC). In this case, these external indications of insolvency act are irrebuttable presumptions.

In contrast, when creditors invoke the facts mentioned under (iv)–(vi), and when other legitimate persons invoke any of the facts included in Article 2(4) TRLC, the debtor can object that they do not exist or that, despite them, it was not insolvent at that moment or it is no longer insolvent (Articles 14(2)(2°) and 20 TRLC). The external indications of insolvency thus act as rebuttable presumptions in these cases.

In the context of preventive restructuring frameworks, when the breach of a restructuring plan is caused by insolvency, any legitimate person – i.e. the debtor, its creditors, and the partners being personally liable for the debtor's liabilities (Article 3(1) and (3) TRLC) – may apply to the court for the opening of insolvency proceedings (Article 671(2) TRLC) (see answer to Question 4). However, the breach alone is not sufficient to establish the debtor's insolvency. Insolvency must be established in accordance with the general rules.

d) Does the law provide for any technical circumstances (e.g. undisputed statutory demand, non-compliance with monetary judgments, unsuccessful enforcement proceedings, non-performance of a previous composition agreement in insolvency proceedings) the occurrence of which suffices to establish the debtor's insolvency?

Apart from the external facts mentioned under (c) *supra* that act as irrebuttable presumptions, the debtor's acceptance of the petition to open insolvency proceedings is considered an acknowledgment of the state of insolvency and, thus, of the debtor's inability to pay debts.[56] The court must therefore declare the opening of the proceedings (Article 19 TRLC).

In addition, as mentioned above (see answer to Question 3), the debtor is obliged to apply to the court to open the liquidation phase of the insolvency proceedings when it knows that it is unable to meet the payments agreed in the composition entered into with its creditors, and the obligations it incurred after the court's approval of the composition (Article 407 TRLC). This circumstance is sufficient to open the liquidation phase of these proceedings. Following the request, the court must open this phase within 10 days (Article 406 TRLC).

e) Other means?

n.a.

---

56 *Rojo*, Comentario LC, fn. 41, p. 181.

Question 20: Is insolvency (inability to pay debts, overindebtedness, etc.) subject to party autonomy in the proceedings or must the court clarify them *ex officio*?

Insolvency is not subject to party autonomy. It is for the judge to decide whether insolvency exists, on the basis of the evidence provided by the parties (Articles 10(2) and 24 TRLC).

Question 21: In an overall view, does your law distinguish "inability to pay debts" from "financial difficulties"? If so, how?

No.

Question 22: In an overall view, does it matter under your law whether the debtor's inability to pay debts is present or future and reversible or irreversible?

It does not matter whether debtor's inability to pay debts is present or future. Indeed, in the case of imminent insolvency – which entails a forecast about its future inability to pay debts (see Question 1) – the debtor may also request that the court open insolvency proceedings (Article 2(3) TRLC), communicate to the court the commencement of negotiation with its creditors for the adoption of a restructuring plan (Article 584 TRLC), or request the judicial confirmation of the plan (Article 636 TRLC). Likewise, it can request that the court appoint an expert in order to invite bids for the acquisition of one or more productive units (Article 224 ter TRLC).

In contrast, the Consolidated Text of the Spanish Insolvency Act does not make any reference to the irreversible nature of the inability to pay debts. What is more, according to case law, it is not required that the inability to pay debts is definitive and irreversible.[57]

Question 23: Would you like to add any further aspects not covered by the above questions?

No.

III. CESSATION OF PAYMENTS

Question 24: In your jurisdiction, is "cessation of payments" a legal term used either in statute or in case law? (If the answer is "no", please continue with Question 31.)

Yes, it is used in the Consolidated Text of the Spanish Insolvency Act. The cessation of regular payments (*sobreseimiento generalizado en el pago corriente*

57 Judgments of the Barcelona Provincial Court No. 208/2013, legal ground 6; and No. 100/2016, legal ground 4.

de las obligaciones del deudor) is one of the external facts on which creditors or other legitimate persons other than the debtor must rely in order to establish the debtor's insolvency (Article 2(4)(4º) TRLC).[58]

Likewise, the occurrence of a cessation of payments constitutes a rebuttable presumption that the debtor knew that it was currently insolvent (Article 5(2) TRLC). This is relevant for establishing that it infringed its duty to file for insolvency. The duty is considered to be infringed when the debtor does not file for insolvency in the two months following the date it knew or should have known that it was currently insolvent (Article 5(1) TRLC) (see answer to Question 10 *supra*).

Question 25: Is "cessation of payments" an autonomous ground to commence proceedings (triggering circumstance)? You may refer to Questions 6/7 or add additional information here.

Under Spanish insolvency law, "cessation of payments" is not an autonomous ground for initiating insolvency proceedings or having access to preventive restructuring frameworks. It is one of the external facts that must be invoked by creditors and other legitimate persons other than the debtor to establish the debtor's current insolvency in their request to open insolvency proceedings (Article 2(4)(4º) TRLC).[59] The debtor can also invoke this fact to establish insolvency in its request for the opening of insolvency proceedings.

In contrast, under the former Spanish insolvency law "cessation of payments" was the triggering event of insolvency proceedings – *quiebra* – (Articles 874 and 876 II of the Spanish Commercial Code – now repealed).[60]

Question 26: Is "cessation of payments" a means to establish inability to pay debts? If so, by which mechanism (e.g. rebuttable presumption for inability to pay debts, cf. above Question 19(c))?

As mentioned before (see answer to Questions 1 and 19(c)), it constitutes an external indication that the debtor is not able to regularly pay its due debts and, therefore, it is in a state of current insolvency (Article 2(4) TRLC). Creditors and other legitimate persons must rely on any of the external facts listed in Article 2(4) TRLC – including cessation of payments – in order to request that the court open insolvency proceedings and they must provide evidence of them.

The debtor can oppose the request by providing evidence that it is up to date with its payments, or it is not insolvent despite having ceased them (Article 20 TRLC).

58 See fn. 14.

59 See fn. 14.

60 *Paz-Ares/Virgós/Bermejo*, "National Report for Spain", in *McBryde/Flessner/Kortmann (eds.)*, Principles of European Insolvency Law, Kluwer Legal Publishers, Deventer 2003, pp. 579–621, p. 583.

Question 27: How is "cessation of payments" defined? If it is defined in statute, please provide us here with an English translation of the relevant rule. Is this definition (if any) specified in case law? If so, how?

Cessation of payments is not defined in the Consolidated Text of the Spanish Insolvency Act. However, the case law relating to the former Article 876 of the Spanish Commercial Code – now repealed – remains applicable to define it.[61]

According to a general view, cessation of payments must show an absolute inability to pay debts. Therefore, it must be present and definitive. Temporary cash-flow difficulties that can be overcome within a short period of time are not considered cessation of payments.[62] Cessation of payments also implies that the debtor has failed to pay the generality of its claims – not just one important claim – to its creditors. In addition, these claims must be due and undisputed.[63] Likewise, unpaid claims should not represent a minimal amount of the debtor's claims.[64]

Question 28: How is "cessation of payments" established?

As mentioned above (see answer to Question 19), creditors and other legitimate persons other than the debtor can make use of any means of proof to establish this fact, including testimonial evidence, but this alone is not sufficient (Article 13(3) TRLC).

The debtor can only prove "cessation of payments" by providing documentary evidence – i.e. accounting records, expert opinions, etc. (Article 6(1) TRLC).

Question 29: Are there typical circumstances which provide circumstantial evidence that the debtor has ceased payments? If so, please list as many as possible.

According to the case law, the closure of the business or the absence of all economic activity may constitute circumstantial evidence that the debtor has ceased payments.[65]

---

61 *Pulgar*, Comentario TRLC, fn. 41, p. 191. In the case law, see Orders of Barcelona Provincial Court No. 38/2006, of 27 January, legal grounds 2 and 4; and No. 121/2006, of 24 March, legal ground 3; Order of Madrid Provincial Court No. 136/2008, of 17 April, legal ground 5.

62 See *Rojo*, Comentario LC, fn. 41, pp. 187–188; *Pulgar*, Comentario TRLC, fn. 41, pp. 170–171. In the case law, see Orders of Barcelona Provincial Court No. 38/2006, of 27 January, legal ground 4, and No. 121/2006, of 24 March, legal ground 3; Order of Madrid Provincial Court No. 136/2008, of 17 April, legal ground 5.

63 See *Pulgar*, Comentario TRLC, fn. 41, pp. 191–192. In the case law, see Orders of Barcelona Provincial Court No. 38/2006, of 27 January, legal ground 4; and No. 121/2006, of 24 March, legal ground 3; Order of Madrid Provincial Court No. 136/2008, of 17 April, legal ground 5; Order of Gran Canaria Provincial Court No. 56/2023, of 13 February, legal ground 3.

64 *Pulgar*, Comentario TRLC, fn. 41, p. 192.

65 Judgment of the Murcia Provincial Court of 31 May 2005. In the former regulation, the personal disappearance of the debtor was tantamount to the cessation of payments. See *Paz-Ares/Virgós/Bermejo*, Principles, fn. 60, p. 583.

Question 30: Would you like to add any further aspects not covered by the above questions?

As mentioned *supra* (see answers to Questions 1, 3(b) and 5(b)), a sectorial cessation of payments is also relevant for establishing the debtor's insolvency. This is so in the case of the general cessation of the payment of tax or social security claims during the three months preceding the filing, or of labour-related claims of the last three months. It constitutes an external indication that the debtor is not able to regularly pay its due debts and is therefore in a state of current insolvency (Article 2(4) TRLC).

IV. LIKELY/IMMINENT INABILITY TO PAY DEBTS

Question 31: Are the following terms available in your jurisdiction, either in statute or in case law? (If the answer is "no", please continue with Question 42.)

a) likely inability to pay debts
Not exactly, but the expression "likelihood of insolvency" is available in the Consolidated Text of the Spanish Insolvency Act.

As mentioned before – see answers to Questions 1, 3(c) and 5(c) – a debtor is likely to be insolvent when it is objectively foreseeable to an external observer that it will not be able to regularly pay the debts which will become due in the next two years if a restructuring plan is not adopted (Article 584(2) TRLC).[66]

The "likelihood of insolvency" is a legal standard for initiating preventive restructuring frameworks – communication of the commencement of negotiations with creditors (Article 584(1) TRLC), and judicial confirmation of a restructuring plan (Article 636(1) TRLC).[67]

In addition, in such a situation, the debtor can request that the court appoint an expert in order to invite bids for the acquisition of one or more productive units (Article 224 ter TRLC).[68]

b) imminent inability to pay debts
Not exactly, but the expression "imminent insolvency" is available in the Consolidated Text of the Spanish Insolvency Act.

As mentioned before – see answers to Questions 1, 3(d) and 5(d) – the debtor is imminently insolvent when it foresees that in the next three months it will not be able to pay its debts in a timely and regular manner (Article 2(3) TRLC).[69] Imminent insolvency thus entails a debtor's prognosis about its future ability

66 See fn. 7.
67 See fn. 8.
68 See fn. 9.
69 See fn. 12.

to fulfil its obligations that is closer in time to "inability to pay debts" than to "likelihood of insolvency".

However, in the case of preventive restructuring frameworks, this prognosis must be made from the point of view of an external observer, since creditors can also request the confirmation of restructuring plans (see answer to Question 33).[70]

Imminent insolvency is a legal standard for formal insolvency proceedings (Article 2(3) TRLC) and preventive restructuring frameworks – communication of the commencement of negotiations with creditors (Article 584(1) TRLC) and judicial confirmation of a restructuring plan (Article 636(1) TRLC). Moreover, in this situation debtor can request that the court appoint an expert in order to invite bids for the acquisition of one or more productive units (Article 224 ter TRLC).

c) other (similar) terms
No.

Question 32: Is "likely/imminent inability to pay debts" an autonomous ground to commence proceedings (triggering circumstance)? You may refer to Questions 6/7 or add additional information here.

Yes. See the information provided in answers to Questions 5(c) and (d), 6 and 31.

Question 33: If the answer to the previous Question is "yes", who may base filing for insolvency proceedings on it: only the debtor or also creditors?

Only the debtor may file for formal insolvency proceedings on the basis of imminent insolvency.

In the context of preventive restructuring frameworks, only the debtor can communicate to the court the commencement of negotiations for the adoption of a restructuring plan based on likelihood of insolvency or imminent insolvency (Article 585(1) TRLC). In contrast, the debtor or affected creditors who signed the restructuring plan can request that the court confirm the plan in any of these situations (Article 643(1) TRLC).

Question 34: How are these terms defined? If they are defined in statute, please provide us here with an English translation of the relevant rules. Is this definition (if any) specified in case law? If so, how?

a) likely inability to pay debts
See the information provided in answer to Question 31.

---

70 *Garcimartín*, "Sobre el nuevo régimen aplicable a los planes de reestructuración (y algunas novedades en el libro IV)", Revista General de Insolvencias & Reestructuraciones (I & R), no. 7, 2022, pp. 51–91, p. 57, and n. 4.

b) imminent inability to pay debts

See the information provided in answer to Question 31.

Question 35: Do the terms "likely" and "imminent" require a prognosis regarding the point in time when actual inability to pay debts will occur? If so, how long is the time period for this prognosis?

In accordance with the Consolidated Text of the Spanish Insolvency Act, both terms require a prognosis regarding a future moment when actual inability to pay debts will occur. "Imminent" refers to a period of three months (Article 2(3) TRLC), and "likely" refers to a period of two years (Article 584(2) TRLC). Thus, the likelihood of insolvency is a state prior to imminent insolvency that in turn precedes current insolvency.[71]

As explained above (see answer to Question 18), the Spanish Insolvency Act originally did not specify the duration of the prognosis period for imminent insolvency. After the amendment introduced by Act 16/2022, the prognosis period was limited to three months to distinguish "imminent insolvency" from "likelihood of insolvency".

Question 36: Does your law require a specific grade of certainty that inability to pay debts will eventually occur? If so, is 50.1% ("more likely than not") enough or are there alleviated or aggravated prerequisites?

Not explicitly. However, according to some views, the likelihood of insolvency requires that, from the point of view of an external observer, it is more likely than not – i.e. more than 50% certain – that the debtor will not be able to satisfy the debts which will become due in the next two years if a restructuring plan is not adopted.[72]

Question 37: Regarding "debts" and "financial means", are they defined in the same way as in the context of inability to pay debts (cf. above Questions 14/15)? If not, what are the differences?

Yes, in the case of financial means. In contrast, debts to be considered are those which *will become due* during the prognosis period.

Question 38: Further to Question 37: Are "debts" considered which do currently not exist or are not yet due but will foreseeably come into existence and become due during the prognosis period?

As explained above (see answer to Question 37), debts that are not yet due – i.e. because they are subject to a condition or a term – but will foreseeably become

71 *Garcimartín*, ADCo, No. 57 (2022), fn. 52, V.

72 *Garcimartín*, I&R, No. 7 (2022), fn. 70, p. 57.

due during the prognosis period must be considered in making the prognosis about the debtor's future ability to pay debts (Article 2(3) TRLC).[73]

In contrast, non-existing debts are not expressly mentioned in the Consolidated Text of the Spanish Insolvency Act. However, I do not see any difficulty in taking into account non-existing debts that will foreseeably come into existence and become due during the prognosis period. Indeed, under Spanish insolvency law, contingent and conditional claims may be affected by restructuring plans (Article 616(2) TRLC). Therefore, in my view, they can also be considered in making the prognosis about the debtor's future ability to pay debts.

Question 39: Also further to Question 37: Are "financial means" considered which do currently not exist but will foreseeably become available during the prognosis period?

Yes.

Question 40: How are the terms "likely/imminent inability to pay debts" established?

The debtor cannot establish "likelihood of insolvency" or "imminent insolvency" on the basis of an external fact. It must establish them on the basis of an objective reasoning of probability.[74] The same happens when creditors request from the court confirmation of a restructuring plan on the basis of any of these situations.[75]

In formal insolvency proceedings, it is for the corresponding court to determine whether this reasoning is sufficiently substantiated before deciding to open insolvency proceedings (Article 10(2) TRLC).[76] In contrast, in preventive restructuring frameworks the court does not verify these situations when it receives the debtor's communication of commencement of negotiation with creditors (Article 590 TRLC). It needs only verify them when the judicial confirmation of the restructuring plan is requested by the debtor or the relevant creditors (Article 638(1°) TRLC).[77] Thus, a restructuring plan cannot be confirmed by the court if the objective reasoning of probability is not sufficiently substantiated. Likewise, the confirmation order can be contested by dissenting or non-voting creditors (Article 654(3°) TRLC), and dissenting shareholders

73 *Pulgar*, Comentario TRLC, fn. 41, pp. 185–186.

74 With regard to "imminent insolvency" in insolvency proceedings, see *Rojo*, Comentario LC, fn. 41, p. 177.

75 *Garcimartín*, I&R, No. 7 2022, fn. 70, p. 57, and n. 4, and ADCo, No. 57 (2022), fn. 52, V.

76 *Rojo*, Comentario LC, fn. 41, pp. 177–178.

77 *Garcimartín*, ADCo, No. 57 (2022), fn. 52, V.

(Article 656(1)(3º) TRLC), *inter alia*, when the likelihood of insolvency or the imminent insolvency have not been established.

Question 41: Would you like to add any further aspects not covered by the above questions?

No.

V. OVERINDEBTEDNESS

Question 42: In your jurisdiction, is "overindebtedness", or "balance sheet insolvency" respectively, a legal term used either in statute or in case law? (If the answer is "no", please continue with Question 56.)

No.

Question 43: Is "overindebtedness" an autonomous ground to commence proceedings (triggering circumstance)? You may refer to Questions 6/7 or add additional information here.

n.a.

Question 44: If the answer to the previous Question is "yes", is this applicable to corporate insolvencies of legal persons only or also to personal bankruptcies of natural persons?

n.a.

Question 45: Is the term "overindebtedness" defined in statute? If so, please give the wording in English translation. Is this definition (if any) specified in case law? If so, how?

n.a.

Question 46: Does your law refer to all existing debts or only to mature debts?

n.a.

Question 47: Does the rank of certain debts play a role when establishing overindebtedness? In particular, is there any possibility to conclude agreements according to which certain debts shall not be taken into account (e.g. agreements on subsidiarity)?

n.a.

Question 48: Which assets are taken into account when overindebtedness is established: the complete set of assets or only a selection of them?

n.a.

Question 49: How are the debtor's assets valued: by referring to the liquidation value, the book value, the going concern value or in another way?

n.a.

Question 50: Is there any prognostic element, e.g. regarding the debtor's chances to continue the business?

n.a.

Question 51: If the answer to the previous Question is "yes", what exactly is the topic of the prognosis and how is it established?

n.a.

Question 52: If the answer to Question 50 is "yes", how long is the prognosis period?

n.a.

Question 53: How is overindebtedness established?

a) Is a formal balance sheet required?
n.a.

b) Does the yearly regular commercial balance sheet have any meaning (given that it is normally based on technical values and does not display undisclosed reserves)?
n.a.

c) Does the law provide for a presumption? If so, under which conditions?
n.a.

d) Other means?
n.a.

Question 54: Is the legal link to overindebtedness undisputed in literature or are there efforts to abolish it?

n.a.

Question 55: Would you like to add any further aspects not covered by the above questions?

n.a.

VI. REMAINING ISSUES

Question 56: Is there anything else you would like to share in the present context and that we should take into account?

No.

SWEDEN

Hans RENMAN

I. GENERAL

Question 1: How is insolvency (both in the context of liquidation and restructuring/reorganisation) regulated in your jurisdiction? Please give a brief overview, at least enumerating the relevant statutes.

There is only one statutory definition of insolvency in Swedish law. This definition can be found in chapter 1 section 2 sub-section 2 of the Bankruptcy Act (SFS 1987:672), which provides as follows: "Insolvency means that the debtor is unable to duly pay his debts and that this inability is not merely temporary."

It is prerequisite for the opening of bankruptcy (insolvent liquidation) proceedings that the debtor is insolvent.

The Company Restructuring Act does not include a definition of insolvency but one prerequisite for opening restructuring proceedings is "financial difficulties" which is defined as follows in chapter 2 section 10 sub-section 1 of the Company Restructuring Act:

> it can be presumed that the debtor cannot pay its due and payable debts or that such inability [Swedish: *illikviditet*, i.e. inability to pay even if the inability is only temporary] will exist within a short time or that the debtor, in some other respect, is having financial difficulties which entail a risk of insolvency.

Question 2: Related to paragraph 10 above of the Introduction: seen from a principle-based perspective, what justifies the opening of insolvency proceedings in your jurisdiction?

The opening of insolvency proceedings (bankruptcy or restructuring) is first and foremost justified by the principles of equal treatment of creditors and collectivity, since individual enforcement proceedings are no longer acceptable where the debtor is substantively insolvent or substantive insolvency is imminent. At this stage of the debtor's financial crisis, collective proceedings are appropriate in the interest of equal treatment of all creditors. Other principles may also come into play, e.g. the principle of debtor protection, where the substantively insolvent debtor needs help against single creditors with hold-out positions, or the principle of best possible satisfaction of the creditors' claims, where creditors would be worse off without insolvency proceedings.

Question 3: Does your national law in the context of liquidation proceedings use one or more of the following terms (be it as a noun, be it as an adjective or adjunct) in whatever context:

a) inability to pay debts
Yes.

b) cessation of payments
Yes.

c) likely inability to pay debts
No.

d) imminent inability to pay debts
No.

e) overindebtedness?
No (only as a safe harbour against claims for avoidance of a gift or other transactions in the nature of a gift, see answer to Question 9 *infra*).

Question 4: Are the same terms (and with the same meaning) used in the rules on preliminary/interim insolvency proceedings (e.g. concerning the application stage of the proceedings)?

n.a.

Question 5: Does your national law in the context of restructuring proceedings (as referred to above at paragraph 8 of the Introduction, i.e. both pre-insolvency and within formal insolvency proceedings) use one or more of the following terms (be it as a noun, be it as an adjective or adjunct) in whatever context:

a) inability to pay debts
Yes.

b) cessation of payments
No.

c) likely inability to pay debts
Yes.

d) imminent inability to pay debts
Yes.

e) overindebtedness?
No (only as a safe harbour against claims for avoidance of a gift or other transactions in the nature of a gift, see answer to Question 9 *infra*).

Question 6: Which of the terms mentioned in Questions 3 and 5 are used for defining grounds to commence proceedings (triggering circumstances)?

a) insolvency proceedings
Inability to duly pay debts if this inability is not merely temporary (chapter 1 section 2 sub-section 2 of the Bankruptcy Act), see answer to Question 1 *supra*.

b) restructuring proceedings
Likelihood that the debtor cannot pay its due and payable debts or that such inability will exist within a short time or that the debtor, in some other respect, is having financial difficulties which entail a risk of insolvency (chapter 2 section 10 sub-section 1 of the Company Restructuring Act), see answer to Question 1 *supra*.

Question 7: Does the answer to Question 6 include personal bankruptcies of natural persons or only corporate insolvencies of legal entities?

Both.

Question 8: In your law, are there any other circumstances which trigger insolvency or restructuring proceedings?

No.

Question 9: Which of the terms mentioned in Questions 3, 5, and 8 are used in the context of transactions avoidance law?

The scope of the term "insolvency" used in the context of transaction avoidance law is – according to case law and the legal literature – broad, and encompasses the following situations:

- *Inability to pay debts*: Existing inability to pay debts provided that the inability is not only temporary,
- *Likely inability to pay debt*: Forecasted inability to pay debts provided that the inability will occur with sufficient probability and is not only temporary, and
- *Imminent inability to pay debts*: Forecasted imminent inability to pay debts provided that the inability will occur with sufficient probability and is not only temporary.

"Overindebtedness": Under certain provisions on transaction avoidance (gifts, division of marital estate, payments of wages, fees, or pension; and transfers to pension funds). Proof that the debtor after the transaction retained executable property which clearly corresponded to the debts is a ground for dismissal of the claim for avoidance.

Question 10: Which of the terms addressed in Questions 3, 5, and 8 are used in the context of directors' duties?

a) shift of duties (from shareholders to creditors)
It has been argued that the duties shift from shareholders to creditors when the debtor becomes insolvent. The term insolvency in this context probably has a scope which corresponds with the scope in transaction avoidance proceedings, see answer to Question 9 *supra*.

b) duties to commence insolvency proceedings
No.

c) other duties (please describe)
n.a.

[The directors have a duty to prepare a balance sheet for liquidation purposes if the equity is less than half of the registered share capital, and take other prescribed actions in connection thereto described in the Companies Act.]

Question 11: Are there any other rules in the context of which the terms addressed in Questions 3, 5, and 8 are used?

Yes, they are relevant in some rules on criminal law:

- Chapter 11 section 1 brottsbalken (BrB, Criminal Code: dishonesty to creditors): "insolvent or manifest danger of becoming insolvent"
- Chapter 11 section 3 BrB (careless disregard for creditors): "insolvent or in manifest danger of becoming insolvent"
- Chapter 11 section 4 BrB (improper favouring of a creditor): "insolvent"

Note, that the term insolvency shall according to case law (Supreme Court of Sweden, 7 October 2013, NJA 2013 p. 822 paragraph 3) always be used and defined in the same sense and uniformly interpreted by the courts, no matter whether they are relevant in the context of insolvency law or in the context of company or criminal law. It has, however, been argued in the legal literature that the term "insolvency" in practice does not have the same meanings in all contexts. The definition of insolvency is sufficiently vague to accommodate a flexible application, taking into account what is considered appropriate in a given situation.[1]

---

[1] See *Lindskog*, Betalning, 3rd ed., Norstedts Juridik 2022, p. 874, n. 3050: "Insolvency is a normative concept, and the normative purpose of the applicable rule may have an impact on the definition of the concept."

Question 12: Is the definition of (the subspecies of) insolvency identical in all legal fields or are there different definitions (e.g. different in insolvency law than in criminal law)?

There is only one statutory definition of insolvency, see answer to Question 1 *supra*, but it has been argued that the application in practice differs depending on what is considered appropriate in a given situation, see answer to Question 11 *supra*.

II. INABILITY TO PAY DEBTS

Question 13: In your jurisdiction, is the term "inability to pay debts" defined in statute? If so, please give the wording in English translation. Is this definition (if any) specified in case law? If so, how?

As mentioned under Question 1 *supra* there is in Swedish law only one statutory definition of insolvency, and this definition can be found in chapter 1 section 2 sub-section 2 of the Bankruptcy Act.

There are several cases from the Swedish Supreme Court regarding the meaning of the insolvency definition. The leading case is the *Suderbagar* case (a criminal law case about a baker who paid a debt to himself shortly before the bakery was declared bankrupt) NJA 2013 p. 833 (paragraph 4) where the Supreme Court made the following statement:

> The insolvency assessment is forward looking and includes a forecast. That a debtor at a certain time is unable to duly pay his debts does not necessarily mean that he shall be considered insolvent. In the form of a forecast assessment, it must be examined whether it can be said with a sufficient degree of certainty that the debtor's finances can be expected to have, within an acceptable time, so improved that he will be able to pay his debts as they fall due. Only if this is not the case, is insolvency at hand.

Question 14: Does your law refer to all debts or only to mature debts?

The law refers to all debts, not only to mature debts. The inability to pay debts is established for a specific day. Which day is relevant depends on the rule which is applied (e.g. the day the court decides on the opening of insolvency proceedings, the day a director pays a creditor in breach of his or her insolvency-related duties, or the day when a voidable preference has been performed).

The debtor can, according to case law and the legal literature, be insolvent on the day in question even if the debtor has no mature debt, if it can be said with sufficient degree of certainty that the debtor will in the future become unable to pay its due debts, provided that this inability will not be only temporary.

Question 15: Which assets are taken into account when assessing the inability to pay debts: all (financial) assets or only those that are liquid, i.e. available on short notice?

All assets that can be made liquid on sufficiently short notice shall be taken into account. Since inability to pay debts must be established for a specific day, only assets that can be used quickly enough for paying debts can be taken into account. These include primarily cash, money in regular bank accounts, overdraft facilities, stock-exchange listed shares, receivables, etc. However, assets which are not available on this day but can be realised within a reasonable time must also be taken into account within this prognosis. It has been stated in the legal literature that, as a rule of thumb, a payment delay that is longer than six months after the due date of a debt is not acceptable.[2]

Question 16: Is any liquidity gap (deficit between relevant financial means and relevant debts) relevant or does your law neglect minor gaps? If the latter, how is "minor" defined?

Swedish law is not clear on this point. Swedish Supreme Court case NJA 2017 p. 882 can be interpreted as ruling that minor gaps are ignored.[3]

Question 17: As far as the time aspect is concerned, does it matter whether the liquidity gap can be closed again in the short term? If so, how long is the grace period?

Swedish law is not clear on this point. See the rule of thumb mentioned in answer to Question 15 *supra*.

Question 18: As far as the time aspect is concerned, is a debtor considered insolvent if the liquidity gap is not yet present but will occur soon? If so, how long is the prognosis period? (Note: this may also concern the difference between actual and likely/imminent inability to pay debts; cf. below Question 34).

A debtor can be considered insolvent even if the liquidity gap is not present yet but will occur in the future. The length of the prognosis period has not been clarified in case law. It has been mentioned in the legal literature that rarely is it possible to make a prognosis with sufficient certainty if the prognosis period is longer than one or two years. Exceptions are possible, for example if the debtor has a disputed debt of a very high amount and it will take several years before there is an enforceable judgment against the debtor (see answers to Questions 14

2 *Renman*, Återvinning enligt 4 kap. konkurslagen, 3rd ed. 2020, p. 159.
3 Ibid., p. 177.

and 15 *supra*).[4] The disputed debt is relevant when assessing whether the debtor is insolvent if there is sufficient probability that the court or arbitral tribunal will approve the creditor's claim. A future liquidity gap is relevant only if the future inability to pay is not only temporary (as a rule of thumb: the gap is longer than six months after the debt became due/matured but was not paid).

Question 19: How is inability to pay debts established? Please communicate if there is a difference between a creditor and a debtor application or between different legal contexts.

As a preliminary remark, all methods described below can be used by debtors, creditors, Insolvency Practitioners, and third parties in all relevant legal situations. However, creditors and third parties will typically not be able to draw up a liquidity balance sheet or to present daily liquidity data, since they do not have access to the necessary information. They will normally refer to the debtor's failure to pay after having received a formal payment demand under the insolvency presumption in chapter 2 section 9 of the Bankruptcy Act.

a) Is a formal liquidity status (liquidity balance sheet) required?
This is one of various possibilities, used in all legal contexts.

b) Is a sample of daily liquidity data (which do not amount to a proper liquidity status but show insufficient funds on different days within a certain period of time) sufficient?
This is one of various possibilities, used in all legal contexts.

c) Does the law provide for a rebuttable presumption? If so, under which conditions?
There are rebuttable presumptions in chapter 2 sections 8 and 9 of the Bankruptcy Act in the situation where a creditor has applied for the opening of bankruptcy (liquidation), whereby the debtor shall be presumed insolvent if:

(i) at the time of enforcement pursuant to chapter 4 of the Enforcement Code, it has been shown that within the six months immediately preceding the bankruptcy petition, the debtor lacked assets sufficient to pay the attachment claim in full;
(ii) the debtor has declared that the debtor is suspending his/her/its payments; or
(iii) the debtor, who not later than one year prior to the bankruptcy petition has been subject to an accounting obligation, has been reminded to pay an uncontested due and payable debt but has failed to do so within one week, and the creditor has petitioned, within three weeks after the reminder, that the debtor shall be declared bankrupt, and the debt remains unpaid when the court assesses the petition.

4 Ibid., p. 167.

The court can also presume that the debtor is insolvent if the debtor files for liquidation or consents to a creditor's application for bankruptcy (chapter 2 section 7 of the Bankruptcy Act).

d) Does the law provide for any technical circumstances (e.g. undisputed statutory demand, non-compliance with monetary judgments, unsuccessful enforcement proceedings, non-performance of a previous composition agreement in insolvency proceedings) the occurrence of which suffices to establish the debtor's insolvency?
Yes, see answer to Question 19(c) *supra*.

e) Other means?
None.

Question 20: Is insolvency (inability to pay debts, overindebtedness, etc.) subject to party autonomy in the proceedings or must the court clarify them *ex officio*?

That depends on the context. In a criminal process the court must be convinced that an insolvency requirement is met. Otherwise, the court will normally not question the parties' joint opinion regarding insolvency.

Question 21: In an overall view, does your law distinguish "inability to pay debts" from "financial difficulties"? If so, how?

Yes, "inability to pay debt" is an important component in the statutory definition of insolvency (see answer to Question 1 *supra*) and is a prerequisite in several situations. "Financial difficulties" is not used as a prerequisite. The term is used in chapter 1 section 1 of the Company Restructuring Act to describe the general purpose of the Act.

Question 22: In an overall view, does it matter under your law whether the debtor's inability to pay debts is present or future and reversible or irreversible?

No, not in principle. The debtor can, according to case law and the legal literature, be insolvent on the particular day even if the debtor has no mature claim, if it can be said with sufficient degree of certainty that the debtor will in the future become unable to pay its due debts provided that this inability will not be only temporary, see answer to Question 14 *supra*. Insolvency can be lifted if it can be assessed that the inability to pay is no longer of a permanent nature but only temporary.

Question 23: Would you like to add any further aspects not covered by the above questions?

No.

III. CESSATION OF PAYMENTS

Question 24: In your jurisdiction, is "cessation of payments" a legal term used either in statute or in case law? (If the answer is "no", please continue with Question 31.)

Yes, it is a rebuttable presumption that the debtor is insolvent (see Question 19(c) *supra*).

Question 25: Is "cessation of payments" an autonomous ground to commence proceedings (triggering circumstance)? You may refer to Questions 6/7 or add additional information here.

No.

Question 26: Is "cessation of payments" a means to establish inability to pay debts? If so, by which mechanism (e.g. rebuttable presumption for inability to pay debts, cf. above Question 19(c))?

Yes, it is a rebuttable presumption that the debtor is insolvent (see answer to Question 19(c) *supra*).

Question 27: How is "cessation of payments" defined? If it is defined in statute, please provide us here with an English translation of the relevant rule. Is this definition (if any) specified in case law? If so, how?

See Question 19(c) *supra.*

Question 28: How is "cessation of payments" established?

See Question 19(c) *supra.*

Question 29: Are there typical circumstances which provide circumstantial evidence that the debtor has ceased payments? If so, please list as many as possible.

n.a.

Question 30: Would you like to add any further aspects not covered by the above questions?

No.

IV. LIKELY/IMMINENT INABILITY TO PAY DEBTS

Question 31: Are the following terms available in your jurisdiction, either in statute or in case law? (If the answer is "no", please continue with Question 42.)

a) likely inability to pay debts
As mentioned under Question 9 *supra*, the scope of the term "insolvency" is – in the context of transaction avoidance law (and also in other contexts) – broad, and encompasses the following situations:

- *Inability to pay debts*: Existing inability to pay debts provided that the inability is not only temporary;
- *Likely inability to pay debt*: Forecasted inability to pay debts, provided that the inability will occur with sufficient probability and is not only temporary; and
- *Imminent inability to pay debts*: Forecasted imminent inability to pay debts, provided that the inability will occur with sufficient probability and is not only temporary.

b) imminent inability to pay debts
See (a) *supra*.

c) other (similar) terms
No.

Question 32: Is "likely/imminent inability to pay debts" an autonomous ground to commence proceedings (triggering circumstance)? You may refer to Questions 6/7 or add additional information here.

Yes, it is a ground for commencing restructuring (reorganisation) proceedings, see answer to Question 6(b). (It is not used an autonomous ground to commence bankruptcy (liquidation) proceedings, but the scope of the term "insolvency" is broad, see answers to Question 13 and 31(a) *supra*.)

Question 33: If the answer to the previous Question is "yes", who may base filing for insolvency proceedings on it: only the debtor or also creditors?

Both.

Question 34: How are these terms defined? If they are defined in statute, please provide us here with an English translation of the relevant rules. Is this definition (if any) specified in case law? If so, how?

a) likely inability to pay debts
No, it is not defined. According to case law and the legal literature the scope of the term "insolvency" is broad, see answers to Questions 13 and 31(a) *supra*.

It is stated in the preparatory works to the Company Restructuring Act that the difference between "risk of insolvency" and "insolvency" is the level of probability that the debtor is or will be unable to pay debts and that this inability will be only temporary.

b) imminent inability to pay debts
No, it is not defined. According to case law and the legal literature the scope of the term "insolvency" is broad, see answers to Questions 13 and 31(a) *supra*.

Question 35: Do the terms "likely" and "imminent" require a prognosis regarding the point in time when actual inability to pay debts will occur? If so, how long is the time period for this prognosis?

Yes, a prognosis is required. It is expressly mentioned chapter 2 section 10 sub-section 1 of the Company Restructuring Act that the time period for the prognosis regarding illiquidity (inability to pay debt, also including temporary inability) is "short" (see answer to Question 1 *supra*).

Question 36: Does your law require a specific grade of certainty that inability to pay debts will eventually occur? If so, is 50.1% ("more likely than not") enough or are there alleviated or aggravated prerequisites?

No, not as regards the term "inability to pay debts", but as regards the term "insolvency" (inability to pay debts that is not only temporary), the Supreme Court has described the degree of certainty as "sufficient" (see Question 13 *supra*).

Question 37: Regarding "debts" and "financial means", are they defined in the same way as in the context of inability to pay debts (cf. above Questions 14/15)? If not, what are the differences?

There is no definition.

Question 38: Further to Question 37: Are "debts" considered which do currently not exist or are not yet due but will foreseeably come into existence and become due during the prognosis period?

Yes.

Question 39: Also further to Question 37: Are "financial means" considered which do currently not exist but will foreseeably become available during the prognosis period?

Yes.

Question 40: How are the terms "likely/imminent inability to pay debts" established?

There is no case law on this. In practice the threshold is so low that, as far as is known, this prerequisite has always deemed to be met if it has been invoked by a debtor who has filed for restructuring proceedings.

Question 41: Would you like to add any further aspects not covered by the above questions?

No.

V. OVERINDEBTEDNESS

Question 42: In your jurisdiction, is "overindebtedness", or "balance sheet insolvency" respectively, a legal term used either in statute or in case law? (If the answer is "no", please continue with Question 56.)

No, but see answer to Question 9 regarding the relevance of overindeptedness under certain provisions on transaction avoidance (gifts, division of marital estate, payments of wages, fees, or pension; and transfers to pension funds). Proof that the debtor after the transaction retained executable property which clearly corresponded to the debts is a ground for dismissal of the claim for avoidance.

Question 43: Is "overindebtedness" an autonomous ground to commence proceedings (triggering circumstance)? You may refer to Questions 6/7 or add additional information here.

n.a.

Question 44: If the answer to the previous Question is "yes", is this applicable to corporate insolvencies of legal persons only or also to personal bankruptcies of natural persons?

n.a.

Question 45: Is the term "overindebtedness" defined in statute? If so, please give the wording in English translation. Is this definition (if any) specified in case law? If so, how?

n.a.

Question 46: Does your law refer to all existing debts or only to mature debts?

n.a.

Question 47: Does the rank of certain debts play a role when establishing overindebtedness? In particular, is there any possibility to conclude agreements according to which certain debts shall not be taken into account (e.g. agreements on subsidiarity)?

n.a.

Question 48: Which assets are taken into account when overindebtedness is established: the complete set of assets or only a selection of them?

n.a.

Question 49: How are the debtor's assets valued: by referring to the liquidation value, the book value, the going concern value or in another way?

n.a.

Question 50: Is there any prognostic element, e.g. regarding the debtor's chances to continue the business?

n.a.

Question 51: If the answer to the previous Question is "yes", what exactly is the topic of the prognosis and how is it established?

n.a.

Question 52: If the answer to Question 50 is "yes", how long is the prognosis period?

n.a.

Question 53: How is overindebtedness established?

a) Is a formal balance sheet required?
n.a.

b) Does the yearly regular commercial balance sheet have any meaning (given that it is normally based on technical values and does not display undisclosed reserves)?
n.a.

c) Does the law provide for a presumption? If so, under which conditions?
n.a.

d) Other means?
n.a.

Question 54: Is the legal link to overindebtedness undisputed in literature or are there efforts to abolish it?

n.a.

Question 55: Would you like to add any further aspects not covered by the above questions?

n.a.

VI. REMAINING ISSUES

Question 56: Is there anything else you would like to share in the present context and that we should take into account?

No.

UNITED KINGDOM

Sarah Paterson

I. GENERAL

Question 1: How is insolvency (both in the context of liquidation and restructuring/reorganisation) regulated in your jurisdiction? Please give a brief overview, at least enumerating the relevant statutes.

The Insolvency Act 1986 provides for administration, liquidation, and company voluntary arrangements.

Two important restructuring procedures are found in the Companies Act 2006: the scheme of arrangement and the Part 26A restructuring plan. Director disqualification is dealt with by the Company Directors Disqualification Act 1986.

Question 2: Related to paragraph 10 above of the Introduction: seen from a principle-based perspective, what justifies the opening of insolvency proceedings in your jurisdiction?

In order to place a company in administration, other than where the holder of a floating charge appoints an administrator, the company must be unable, or likely to become unable, to pay its debts. Where the holder of a floating charge appoints an administrator, the charge must have become enforceable. In either case, the administration order must be reasonably likely to achieve the purpose of the administration (set out in paragraph 3 of Schedule B1 to the Insolvency Act 1986).

Liquidation may be sought in several different circumstances of which the most important are that:

- the company is unable to pay its debts;
- the court is of the opinion that it is just and equitable that the company should be wound up; or
- the Secretary of State seeks a winding up in the public interest.

No financial condition applies to schemes of arrangement or company voluntary arrangements, although in practice financial condition will be important when the court determines whether to sanction a scheme of arrangement and in any challenge to a company voluntary arrangement. In order for a company to pursue a Part 26A restructuring plan it must meet two threshold financial condition tests:

- that the company has encountered, or is likely to encounter, financial difficulties that are affecting, or will or may affect, its ability to carry on business as a going concern; and
- that the purpose of the compromise or arrangement which is proposed is to eliminate, reduce or prevent, or mitigate the effect of, any of those financial difficulties (section 901A of the Companies Act 2006).

Question 3: Does your national law in the context of liquidation proceedings use one or more of the following terms (be it as a noun, be it as an adjective or adjunct) in whatever context:

a) inability to pay debts
Yes.

b) cessation of payments
No.

c) likely inability to pay debts
Likely to become unable to pay its debts

d) imminent inability to pay debts
No.

e) overindebtedness?
No.

Question 4: Are the same terms (and with the same meaning) used in the rules on preliminary/interim insolvency proceedings (e.g. concerning the application stage of the proceedings)?

I do not follow this question. Does it refer to other types of proceeding which may be available, for example where the assets are in jeopardy (e.g. provisional liquidation)? Or to something else?

Question 5: Does your national law in the context of restructuring proceedings (as referred to above at paragraph 8 of the Introduction, i.e. both pre-insolvency and within formal insolvency proceedings) use one or more of the following terms (be it as a noun, be it as an adjective or adjunct) in whatever context:

a) inability to pay debts
No.

b) cessation of payments
No.

c) likely inability to pay debts
No.

d) imminent inability to pay debts
No.

e) overindebtedness?
No.

Question 6: Which of the terms mentioned in Questions 3 and 5 are used for defining grounds to commence proceedings (triggering circumstances)?

a) insolvency proceedings
"Unable to pay its debts or likely to become unable to pay its debts" is used – but note that this is not a requirement when a floating charge holder seeks to appoint an administrator, and that a winding up can be sought on other grounds (see the answer to Question 1).

b) restructuring proceedings
There is no financial condition for company voluntary arrangements or schemes of arrangement. In order for a company to pursue a Part 26A restructuring plan it must meet two threshold financial condition tests:

- that the company has encountered, or is likely to encounter, financial difficulties that are affecting, or will or may affect, its ability to carry on business as a going concern; and
- that the purpose of the compromise or arrangement which is proposed is to eliminate, reduce or prevent, or mitigate the effect of, any of those financial difficulties.

Question 7: Does the answer to Question 6 include personal bankruptcies of natural persons or only corporate insolvencies of legal entities?

Legal entities. Personal bankruptcy is dealt with separately.

Question 8: In your law, are there any other circumstances which trigger insolvency or restructuring proceedings?

There are no provisions which explicitly require directors to file for insolvency or restructuring proceedings. Section 214 of the Insolvency Act 1986 (the "wrongful trading" provision) provides that directors may be liable to contribute to the company's net assets if, at the point at which they knew or should have known that there was no reasonable prospect of avoiding insolvent liquidation or administration, they failed to take every step with a view to minimising the potential loss to the company's creditors as they ought to have taken. In practice, this may cause directors to arrive at a point in time at which they conclude they must trigger insolvency proceedings to avoid potential personal liability. Fraudulent trading and the common law duty to have regard to creditor interests may also be relevant. However, there is no statutory provision explicitly mandating triggering of insolvency or restructuring proceedings.

Question 9: Which of the terms mentioned in Questions 3, 5, and 8 are used in the context of transactions avoidance law?

For transactions at an undervalue (section 238 Insolvency Act 1986); preferences (section 239 Insolvency Act 1986); and setting aside floating charges (section 245 Insolvency Act 1986), inability to pay debts is relevant – either at the time of the relevant transaction or as a result of it.

Question 10: Which of the terms addressed in Questions 3, 5, and 8 are used in the context of directors' duties?

a) shift of duties (from shareholders to creditors)

The majority in the Supreme Court in *BTI 2014 LLC v. Sequana SA* [2022] UKSC 25 ("*Sequana*") considered that the creditor-regarding duty is engaged when the directors know or ought to know that the company is insolvent or bordering on insolvency, or that an insolvent liquidation or administration is probable. This may not form part of the ratio of the case but given that it is Supreme Court authority, it is likely that lower courts will follow it. However, the justices did not arrive at a firm conclusion on the meaning of "insolvent" or "bordering on insolvency" in this context. Lord Reed was "inclined to think that the term can conveniently and aptly be understood in this context in accordance with the tests laid down in section 123(1)(e) and section 123(2) of the 1986 Act" (at paragraph [88]). However, for Lady Arden, "temporary commercial insolvency should be excluded" so that, when dealing with the trigger for creditors' interests to override those of shareholders, she preferred, "a test of irreversible insolvency, which makes insolvent liquidation irreversible". She also understood Lord Briggs to be adopting a similar approach, although he was not explicit on the point (at paragraphs [307]–[311]).

b) duties to commence insolvency proceedings

n.a.

c) other duties (please describe)

n.a.

Question 11: Are there any other rules in the context of which the terms addressed in Questions 3, 5, and 8 are used?

n.a.

Question 12: Is the definition of (the subspecies of) insolvency identical in all legal fields or are there different definitions (e.g. different in insolvency law than in criminal law)?

I cannot answer this question.

II. INABILITY TO PAY DEBTS

Question 13: In your jurisdiction, is the term "inability to pay debts" defined in statute? If so, please give the wording in English translation. Is this definition (if any) specified in case law? If so, how?

Yes: in section 123 of the Insolvency Act 1986:

> (1) A company is deemed unable to pay its debts—
> (a) if a creditor (by assignment or otherwise) to whom the company is indebted in a sum exceeding £750 then due has served on the company, by leaving it at the company's registered office, a written demand (in the prescribed form) requiring the company to pay the sum so due and the company has for 3 weeks thereafter neglected to pay the sum or to secure or compound for it to the reasonable satisfaction of the creditor, or
> (b) if, in England and Wales, execution or other process issued on a judgment, decree or order of any court in favour of a creditor of the company is returned unsatisfied in whole or in part, or
> (c) if, in Scotland, the inducide of a charge for payment on an extract decree, or an extract registered bond, or an extract registered protest, have expired without payment being made, or
> (d) if, in Northern Ireland, a certificate of unenforceability has been granted in respect of a judgment against the company, or
> (e) if it is proved to the satisfaction of the court that the company is unable to pay its debts as they fall due.
> (2) A company is also deemed unable to pay its debts if it is proved to the satisfaction of the court that the value of the company's assets is less than the amount of its liabilities, taking into account its contingent and prospective liabilities.
> (3) The money sum for the time being specified in subsection (1)(a) is subject to increase or reduction by order under section 416 in Part XV.

Question 14: Does your law refer to all debts or only to mature debts?

In the leading case of *BNY Corporate Services Ltd. v. Eurosail-UK-3BL plc and others* [2013] UKSC 28 ("*Eurosail*"), the Supreme Court held (at paragraph [37]):

> The "cash flow" test is concerned, not simply with the petitioner's own presently-due debt, nor only with the other presently-due debt owed by the company, but also with debts falling due in the reasonably near future …

This gives rise to difficult questions on the relationship between the cash flow test and section 123(2). In *Eurosail* the Supreme Court went on to say:

> The express reference to assets and liabilities is in my view a practical recognition that once the court has moved beyond the reasonably near future … any attempt to apply a cash-flow test will become completely speculative, and a comparison of present assets with present and future liabilities (discounted for contingencies and deferment) becomes the only sensible test.

As reflected in this passage, section 123(2) expressly refers to contingent and prospective liabilities, although note that these are "taken into account". No explicit guidance is offered on how to discount "for contingencies and deferment", although cases exist in other contexts on discounting future liabilities (for example, in the context of proving for debts), which the courts may look to for guidance in appropriate cases.

Question 15: Which assets are taken into account when assessing the inability to pay debts: all (financial) assets or only those that are liquid, i.e. available on short notice?

At first instance in *Eurosail*, Morrit C held that it was not possible to take contingent assets into account for the purposes of section 123(2). Lord Neuberger MR took the same approach in the Court of Appeal. The point was not expressly dealt with in the Supreme Court in *Eurosail*, but the Court of Appeal in *Re Rococo Developments Ltd; Evans v. Jones* [2016] EWCA Civ 660 inferred from this that the Supreme Court had been satisfied with this interpretation.

Question 16: Is any liquidity gap (deficit between relevant financial means and relevant debts) relevant or does your law neglect minor gaps? If the latter, how is "minor" defined?

The courts have emphasised the "flexible and fact-sensitive" nature of the cash-flow test and the element of judgement both in reaching a determination under section 123(2) and on the interaction between sections 123(1) and 123(2). It is worth noting that if lenders terminate a loan agreement and demand repayment, the borrower is given a "reasonable time" to repay, which does not extend to the length of time that would be required to refinance the loan – see *Bank of Baroda v. Panessar* [1987] Ch 395.

Question 17: As far as the time aspect is concerned, does it matter whether the liquidity gap can be closed again in the short term? If so, how long is the grace period?

See *supra* for the flexible and fact-sensitive nature of the approach. For example, in *Bucci v. Carman (Liquidator of Casa Estates (UK) Ltd)* [2014] EWCA Civ 383, the court said (at paragraph [29]),

> even when applying the cash-flow test it is not enough merely to ask … whether the company is for the time being able to pay its debts as they fall due … a realistic examination may reveal that a company is on any commercial view insolvent even though it may continue to pay its debts as they fall due.

Similarly, in *Evans and Jones* [2016] EWCA Civ 660, the Court of Appeal said (at paragraph [24]) that

> One of the lessons that emerges clearly from *Eurosail* is that the statutory test in section 123 must not be mechanistically applied, but must be applied in a way that has regard to commercial reality … even though a company may continue to pay its debts it may yet be "on any commercial view insolvent".

In *Myers v. Kestrel Acquisitions Ltd.* [2015] EWHC 916 (Ch) all parties agreed that the company was balance sheet insolvent but the defendants argued that the court should take into account the prospect of a restructuring. The court declined to do so because "the nature of any scheme of arrangement, if one is needed, is at best no more than an aspiration" (at paragraph [91]).

Question 18: As far as the time aspect is concerned, is a debtor considered insolvent if the liquidity gap is not yet present but will occur soon? If so, how long is the prognosis period? (Note: this may also concern the difference between actual and likely/imminent inability to pay debts; cf. below Question 34).

The relevant test for "likely to become unable to pay its debts" is the balance of probabilities (essentially, more than 50%). See also the answer to Question 15 *supra*.

Question 19: How is inability to pay debts established? Please communicate if there is a difference between a creditor and a debtor application or between different legal contexts.

There are no specific requirements, although note the "specific" tests in section 123(1)(a) and (b) set out in answer to Question 11 *supra*.

a) Is a formal liquidity status (liquidity balance sheet) required?
n.a.

b) Is a sample of daily liquidity data (which do not amount to a proper liquidity status but show insufficient funds on different days within a certain period of time) sufficient?
n.a.

c) Does the law provide for a rebuttable presumption? If so, under which conditions?
Rebuttable presumptions apply in some parts of the vulnerable transactions regime.

d) Does the law provide for any technical circumstances (e.g. undisputed statutory demand, non-compliance with monetary judgments, unsuccessful enforcement proceedings, non-performance of a previous composition agreement in insolvency proceedings) the occurrence of which suffices to establish the debtor's insolvency?
Yes: as set out in Question 13,

> (1) A company is deemed unable to pay its debts—
>
> (a) if a creditor (by assignment or otherwise) to whom the company is indebted in a sum exceeding £750 then due has served on the company, by leaving it at the company's registered office, a written demand (in the prescribed form) requiring the company to pay the sum so due and the company has for 3 weeks thereafter neglected to pay the sum or to secure or compound for it to the reasonable satisfaction of the creditor, or
> (b) if, in England and Wales, execution or other process issued on a judgment, decree or order of any court in favour of a creditor of the company is returned unsatisfied in whole or in part, or
> (c) if, in Scotland, the induciae of a charge for payment on an extract decree, or an extract registered bond, or an extract registered protest, have expired without payment being made, or
> (d) if, in Northern Ireland, a certificate of unenforceability has been granted in respect of a judgment against the company …

e) Other means?
n.a.

Question 20: Is insolvency (inability to pay debts, overindebtedness, etc.) subject to party autonomy in the proceedings or must the court clarify them *ex officio*?

Where an administration appointment is made out of court, the court will only test inability to pay debts in the event of a challenge. Difficult questions arise if the applicant is relying on section 123(2) because, as set out in Question 13, that provides that "[a] company is also deemed unable to pay its debts *if it is proved to the satisfaction of the court* that ..." (emphasis added).

Question 21: In an overall view, does your law distinguish "inability to pay debts" from "financial difficulties"? If so, how?

As set out in the answer to Question 6(b), in order for a company to pursue a Part 26A restructuring plan it must meet two threshold financial condition tests:

- that the company has encountered, or is likely to encounter, financial difficulties that are affecting, or will or may affect, its ability to carry on business as a going concern; and
- that the purpose of the compromise or arrangement which is proposed is to eliminate, reduce or prevent, or mitigate the effect of, any of those financial difficulties.

Thus far, the courts have suggested that there is a relatively low threshold for financial difficulties – see, for example, *Re Hurricane Energy Plc* [2021] EWHC 1418 (Ch) at paragraph [22]: "The threshold for Condition A is, however, relatively low. It is enough that the Company is likely to encounter financial difficulties that may affect its ability to carry on business as a going concern."

Question 22: In an overall view, does it matter under your law whether the debtor's inability to pay debts is present or future and reversible or irreversible?

See Questions 16 and 17, for the flexible and fact-sensitive nature of the approach. As noted in Question 17, in *Casa Estates* [2014] EWCA Civ 383, the court said (at paragraph [29]),

> even when applying the cash-flow test it is not enough merely to ask ... whether the company is for the time being able to pay its debts as they fall due ... a realistic examination may reveal that a company is on any commercial view insolvent even though it may continue to pay its debts as they fall due.

Similarly, in *Evans v. Jones* [2016] EWCA Civ 660, the Court of Appeal said (at paragraph [24]) that

> One of the lessons that emerges clearly from *Eurosail* is that the statutory test in section 123 must not be mechanistically applied, but must be applied in a way that

has regard to commercial reality … even though a company may continue to pay its debts it may yet be "on any commercial view insolvent".

In *Myers v. Kestrel Acquisitions* [2015] EWHC 916 (Ch) all parties agreed that the company was balance sheet insolvent but the defendants argued that the court should take into account the prospect of a restructuring. The court declined to do so because "the nature of any scheme of arrangement, if one is needed, is at best no more than an aspiration" (at paragraph [91]).

Question 23: Would you like to add any further aspects not covered by the above questions?

n.a.

III. CESSATION OF PAYMENTS

Question 24: In your jurisdiction, is "cessation of payments" a legal term used either in statute or in case law? (If the answer is "no", please continue with Question 31.)

No.

Question 25: Is "cessation of payments" an autonomous ground to commence proceedings (triggering circumstance)? You may refer to Questions 6/7 or add additional information here.

n.a.

Question 26: Is "cessation of payments" a means to establish inability to pay debts? If so, by which mechanism (e.g. rebuttable presumption for inability to pay debts, cf. above Question 19(c))?

n.a.

Question 27: How is "cessation of payments" defined? If it is defined in statute, please provide us here with an English translation of the relevant rule. Is this definition (if any) specified in case law? If so, how?

n.a.

Question 28: How is "cessation of payments" established?

n.a.

Question 29: Are there typical circumstances which provide circumstantial evidence that the debtor has ceased payments? If so, please list as many as possible.

n.a.

Question 30: Would you like to add any further aspects not covered by the above questions?

n.a.

IV. LIKELY/IMMINENT INABILITY TO PAY DEBTS

Question 31: Are the following terms available in your jurisdiction, either in statute or in case law? (If the answer is "no", please continue with Question 42.)

a) likely inability to pay debts
Likely to become unable to pay its debts.

b) imminent inability to pay debts
No.

c) other (similar) terms
n.a.

Question 32: Is "likely/imminent inability to pay debts" an autonomous ground to commence proceedings (triggering circumstance)? You may refer to Questions 6/7 or add additional information here.

This is a separate ground for the court to make an administration order (see Insolvency Act 1986, Schedule B1, paragraph 11) or for the company or its directors to appoint an administrator out of court.

Question 33: If the answer to the previous Question is "yes", who may base filing for insolvency proceedings on it: only the debtor or also creditors?

See *supra*.

Question 34: How are these terms defined? If they are defined in statute, please provide us here with an English translation of the relevant rules. Is this definition (if any) specified in case law? If so, how?

a) likely inability to pay debts
The burden of proof is the balance of probabilities (see *supra* in answer to Questions 14 and 15, *Eurosail* at paragraph [48]).

b) imminent inability to pay debts
n.a.

Question 35: Do the terms "likely" and "imminent" require a prognosis regarding the point in time when actual inability to pay debts will occur? If so, how long is the time period for this prognosis?

n.a.

Question 36: Does your law require a specific grade of certainty that inability to pay debts will eventually occur? If so, is 50.1% ("more likely than not") enough or are there alleviated or aggravated prerequisites?

See *supra*.

Question 37: Regarding "debts" and "financial means", are they defined in the same way as in the context of inability to pay debts (cf. above Questions 14/15)? If not, what are the differences?

n.a.

Question 38: Further to Question 37: Are "debts" considered which do currently not exist or are not yet due but will foreseeably come into existence and become due during the prognosis period?

See the answer to Question 14.

Question 39: Also further to Question 37: Are "financial means" considered which do currently not exist but will foreseeably become available during the prognosis period?

See the answer to Question 14.

Question 40: How are the terms "likely/imminent inability to pay debts" established?

This is a fact-sensitive question.

Question 41: Would you like to add any further aspects not covered by the above questions?

n.a.

V. OVERINDEBTEDNESS

Question 42: In your jurisdiction, is "overindebtedness", or "balance sheet insolvency" respectively, a legal term used either in statute or in case law? (If the answer is "no", please continue with Question 56.)

The test in section 123(2) of the Insolvency Act 1986 ("A company is also deemed unable to pay its debts if it is proved to the satisfaction of the court that the value of the company's assets is less than the amount of its liabilities, taking into account its contingent and prospective liabilities") is often referred to colloquially as the "balance sheet test". However, the Supreme Court in *Eurosail* was at pains to emphasise that this is not to be taken literally (see paragraph [1]).

Question 43: Is "overindebtedness" an autonomous ground to commence proceedings (triggering circumstance)? You may refer to Questions 6/7 or add additional information here.

Where the relevant ground is that the company is unable to pay its debts or likely to become unable to pay its debts, it would include section 123(2).

Question 44: If the answer to the previous Question is "yes", is this applicable to corporate insolvencies of legal persons only or also to personal bankruptcies of natural persons?

Legal persons. Personal bankruptcy is dealt with separately.

Question 45: Is the term "overindebtedness" defined in statute? If so, please give the wording in English translation. Is this definition (if any) specified in case law? If so, how?

See the answers to Question 14 and Question 42 *supra*.

Case law has been important in legislative interpretation, particularly the Supreme Court decision in *Eurosail*. See the answer to Question 12 *supra* for the relationship between section 123(1)(e) and section 123(2). Crucially, the Supreme Court in *Eurosail* also stated that the test of the "point of no return" should not "pass into common usage as a paraphrase of the effect of section 123(2)" (as suggested by Lord Neuberger MR in the Court of Appeal) – [2013] UKSC 28 at paragraphs [42] and [48].

Question 46: Does your law refer to all existing debts or only to mature debts?

The test provides that contingent and prospective liabilities are to be "taken into account".

Question 47: Does the rank of certain debts play a role when establishing overindebtedness? In particular, is there any possibility to conclude agreements according to which certain debts shall not be taken into account (e.g. agreements on subsidiarity)?

In *Eurosail*, the structured finance arrangement included a post-enforcement call option (PECO). Broadly, this was designed to ensure that the issuer of the notes was "bankruptcy remote", and provided that in the event of a shortfall an independent associate of the issuer had the right to call for the notes at a nominal price. The company with the benefit of the call option could then release claims against the issuer.

As Eurosail was not deemed insolvent under section 123(2), the question of the effect of this PECO was irrelevant. Nonetheless, *obiter dicta* remarks were made which are likely to be persuasive in subsequent cases. Very broadly, the PECO did not affect the liabilities of the issuer to the noteholders and therefore could not save Eurosail from being insolvent under section 123(2). The PECO might affect the ability of a party actually to wind up the issuer but that was a separate point.

Of course, it would be possible to expand the effect of this type of provision so that it *did* impact the liabilities owed by the issuer to the noteholders. In other words, it is possible to conceive of bankruptcy remote structures which would go beyond affecting winding up.

Question 48: Which assets are taken into account when overindebtedness is established: the complete set of assets or only a selection of them?

See the answer to Question 15.

Question 49: How are the debtor's assets valued: by referring to the liquidation value, the book value, the going concern value or in another way?

No explicit guidance is given. Once again, it is likely to be a fact-sensitive question.

Question 50: Is there any prognostic element, e.g. regarding the debtor's chances to continue the business?

See various answers already provided – likely to be a fact-sensitive question.

Question 51: If the answer to the previous Question is "yes", what exactly is the topic of the prognosis and how is it established?

n.a.

Question 52: If the answer to Question 50 is "yes", how long is the prognosis period?

n.a.

Question 53: How is overindebtedness established?

a) Is a formal balance sheet required?
The courts have described the company's accounts as "strong prima facie evidence" – *HLC Environmental Projects (in liquidation)* [2013] EWHC 2876 at paragraph [81]. However, the court in HLC went on to say that "the question of whether, under published accountancy standards, good or best practice would have required [a contingency's] inclusion in company accounts is not a central consideration" (ibid. at paragraph [83]). In other words, the accounts are not determinative.

b) Does the yearly regular commercial balance sheet have any meaning (given that it is normally based on technical values and does not display undisclosed reserves)?
n.a.

c) Does the law provide for a presumption? If so, under which conditions?
n.a.

d) Other means?
n.a.

Question 54: Is the legal link to overindebtedness undisputed in literature or are there efforts to abolish it?

n.a.

Question 55: Would you like to add any further aspects not covered by the above questions?

n.a.

VI. REMAINING ISSUES

Question 56: Is there anything else you would like to share in the present context and that we should take into account?

n.a.

The content of your monograph
of European law is referenced on
www.stradalex.eu
Strada lex Europe
The reference of European law
online
Access, anywhere and at anytime, the European
legal information that your profession needs,
thanks to the Strada lex Europe database.
If you have any questions, would like a price
quotation, a personalised presentation or free
training, contact us on:
+ 32 (0)2 548 07 13 ou info@
stradalex.eu www.stradalex.eu
strada lex
EUROPE
THE CERTAINTY OF
BEING PROPERLY AIDED

www.ingramcontent.com/pod-product-compliance
Ingram Content Group UK Ltd.
Pitfield, Milton Keynes, MK11 3LW, UK
UKHW051933150926
8656IPUK00005B/35

9 781839 705571